COMPLEX HUNTER-GATHERERS

The Anthropology of Pacific North America
Herbert D. G. Maschner and
Katherine L. Reedy-Maschner, series editors

THE ANTHROPOLOGY
OF PACIFIC
NORTH AMERICA

COMPLEX HUNTER-GATHERERS

Evolution and Organization of Prehistoric Communities on the Plateau of Northwestern North America

Edited by

William C. Prentiss and Ian Kuijt

The University of Utah Press
Salt Lake City

THE ANTHROPOLOGY OF PACIFIC NORTH AMERICA
Herbert D. G. Maschner and
Katherine L. Reedy-Maschner, series editors

The Defiance House Man colophon is a registered trademark of the University of Utah Press. It is based on a four-foot-tall, Ancient Puebloan pictograph (late PIII) near Glen Canyon, Utah.

09 08 07 06 05 04
5 4 3 2 1

Library of Congress Cataloging-in-Publication Data

Complex hunter-gatherers : evolution and organization of prehistoric communities on the plateau of northwestern North America / edited by William C. Prentiss and Ian Kuijt.
p. cm.—(The anthropology of Pacific North America)
Includes bibliographical references and index.
ISBN 0-87480-793-X (hardcover : alk. paper)
1. Paleo-Indians—Columbia Plateau—Hunting. 2. Paleo-Indians—Canada, Western—Hunting. 3. Hunting and gathering societies—Columbia Plateau. 4. Hunting and gathering societies—Canada, Western. 5. Columbia Plateau—Antiquities. 6. Canada, Western—Antiquities. I. Prentiss, William C., 1960– . II. Kuijt, Ian. III. Series.
E78.C63C66 2004
979.5'01—dc22 2004002520

CONTENTS

INTRODUCTION

THE ARCHAEOLOGY OF THE PLATEAU REGION OF NORTHWESTERN NORTH AMERICA—APPROACHES TO THE EVOLUTION OF COMPLEX HUNTER-GATHERERS

William C. Prentiss and Ian Kuijt

Today, as in the prehistoric past, the Plateau region of northwestern North America exists as a land of remarkable environmental and social contrasts of which many members of the general public are unaware. The Plateau is often conceptualized as two regions, the Northern or Canadian Plateau and the Southern or Columbia Plateau. From an archaeological, ethnographical, and prehistoric standpoint, this modern geopolitical separation is largely meaningless because the cultural context of First Nation lifeways often cross-cuts significant environmental zones. The Plateau environment, for example, stretches from the Coast and Cascade ranges to the Rocky Mountains and includes astounding variation in geophysical and vegetative conditions, including deserts, grasslands, parkland forests, and even rain forest environments. In some areas, the Plateau is etched by the deep valleys of the Columbia and Fraser river systems that served as major corridors of movement for fish species, habitats for terrestrial mammals, and locations for the founding of human communities in prehistory. With its great diversity in plant and animal resources, the Plateau favored an equally high variety of hunter-gatherer societies and social complexity that remains largely unrecognized by archaeologists and the general public. Hunter-gatherers on the eastern margins of the Plateau were traditionally more mobile, maintaining somewhat flexible band membership and relatively egalitarian social relations. In stark contrast, many on the western edges lived in densely packed winter villages, controlling access to optimal hunting and fishing locations, participating in elite trade networks, and maintaining ranked and stratified societies. The indigenous societies of many areas of the Plateau achieved a high degree of social complexity that in many ways is comparable to that of the much better known Northwest Coast groups, leaving behind a dramatic archaeological record featuring winter "pithouse" villages, fortifications, specialized food-collecting sites, meeting grounds, rock art sites, and cemeteries. Ethnographic research carried out in this region during the past 120 years has provided one of the most extensive sources of information on indigenous peoples in North America. The combined ethnographic and archaeological records make the Plateau, similar to the neighboring Northwest Coast, one of the most important regions in the world for study of the evolution and organization of complex hunter-gatherer cultures.

This book seeks to redirect attention to the Plateau region of western North America as a means of furthering our understanding of the nature of the prehistoric social organization, subsistence practices, and lifeways of those living on the Plateau, as well as to expand on this foundation to recognize the broader implications of this work in understanding the evolution and organization of complex hunter-gatherers in general. As a first step in this process, we aim to introduce and review the current state of the research in late period archaeology on the Plateau. By "late period" we mean the period associated with the emergence of semisedentary hunter-gatherer communities supported by subsistence intensification tactics particularly involving salmon and various root crops. This period began between 3,500 and 4,000 years ago and persisted into recent historic times, and it was periodically characterized by the presence of large aggregated communities within which we see material manifestations of emerging social inequality. In order to accomplish this, we have organized contributions to the book in four sections. The first section of the book introduces the cultural chronology of the Plateau defined as the Southern and

Northern subregions. The next section addresses evolutionary processes, household archaeology, and exchange. Here, authors explore reasons why the complex communities of the late prehistoric period emerged. The third section provides overviews and studies in the archaeology of Plateau communities, with an emphasis on the exploitation of plant resources. This section offers reviews of current research contributions but also provides new contributions to our understanding of the structure and organization of early Plateau societies. The final section features broad assessments of the current contribution of Plateau archaeology by a researcher known for her globally significant contributions to the archaeology of complex hunter-gatherers. This current chapter starts this process, seeking to introduce major strands of Plateau archaeological research and provide the reader with a short review of critical published resources in Plateau archaeology. To do this we establish the concept of complex hunter-gatherers and follow with an introduction to the hunter-gatherers of the Plateau and their environment. Then, we provide a broad introduction to major contributions and research issues in late period Plateau archaeology. Throughout these discussions, we provide a wide range of citations of formally published sources designed to aid the professional researcher, student, or interested layperson in the pursuit of Plateau archaeology.

COMPLEX HUNTER-GATHERERS

These days, the term *complex* has become an important word in archaeological circles. By describing societies in terms of variation in degree of complexity, we attempt to avoid neo-evolutionary concepts such as band–tribe–chiefdom–state and their inherent progressivist assumptions. When they are applied to hunter-gatherers, researchers establish a dichotomy between those considered complex versus others described as generalized (Hayden 1995), generic (Binford 2001), or simple (Burch and Ellana 1994). Generalized hunter-gatherers are often described as egalitarian with a high sharing ethic, residentially mobile, and organized in bands with flexible group membership. In contrast, complex hunter-gatherers are typically described as less residentially mobile (often relatively sedentary), with formal group membership in the form of lineages, sodalities, and so on and a distinct ability to acquire and use wealth for purposes of increasing status. Indeed, among some groups, wealth, power, and ability to command non-kin labor may be inherited. For some, such as Burch and Ellanna (1994), the dichotomy between simple and complex is misleading, and they alternatively argue that a wide range of intermediate variation exists.

Indeed, some archaeologists have suggested that perhaps all human societies are complex. Speth (1990) has argued that the concept of the egalitarian society should be dispensed with, thereby recognizing the inherent complexity of all human societies. He correctly notes that even among mobile, low-density hunter-gatherer societies, asymmetrical relationships may exist between individuals over access to basic subsistence items and other goods. This has the effect of producing some forms of incipient social ranking along lines of age, gender, physical power, and personal charisma. Speth asserts that inequality is recognizable in a variety of contexts, including prey- and part-distribution procedures, enforcement of food taboos, snacking associated with differential skill in the food quest, and variability in food-sharing practices. It is indeed abundantly clear that even among societies viewed by anthropologists as egalitarian, competitive social relationships do exist, as reflected, for example, in competition over mates, between individuals, and within households (see Berreman 1978; Flanagan 1989; Flanagan and Rayner 1988; Hawkes et al. 2001; Keene 1991). These competitive relationships may be played out through differential food-sharing practices, fights, or other strategies, and there appear to be good Darwinian reasons for their persistence in different forms in different societies (Hawkes 1993; Hawkes et al. 2001; Hill and Hurtado 1996) associated with issues of inclusive fitness.

Many researchers have attempted to define complex hunter-gatherers. In doing so, Arnold (2001) argues, we must not democratize the concept of complexity to the point that there is no way to partition sociocultural variability. She argues that significant differences in sociopolitical organization are recognizable and that we must reserve the term *complex* to those fitting a well-defined criterion. Definitions include those emphasizing "specific traits or developments" (Arnold 1996), sociopolitical integration, and subsistence security. Arnold (1996) notes that the trait-based approaches (e.g., Barnard and Woodburn 1988; Brown 1985; Price 1985; Woodburn 1980; Woodman 1985) seek to define specific characteristics, such as different forms of art, monuments, exchange, and storage strategies, as markers of complexity. In general these definitions look for delayed-return economies, markers of social hierarchy, and extensive exchange networks as indicators of complexity.

In contrast to the trait-based approach, several authors have offered organizational approaches to defining complex hunter-gatherers. Along these lines, Arnold (1996) argues that a more effective definition would be one that considers the sociopolitical means by which leaders develop and maintain control over labor. Specific traits are merely by-products of distinct variation in the means by which labor is organized and power is distributed within society. Thus, to Arnold (1993, 1996, 2001, this volume), *complex* refers to societies where leadership and status are inherited and those leaders have control over non-kin labor. Hayden (1995) offers a similar, though more inclusive, definition, emphasizing the capacity of groups to maintain exclusive control over food produced by themselves and to use food surpluses as a means (among others) of leveraging new levels of power. Hayden defines three types of "transegalitarian" societies, termed despots, reciprocators, and entrepreneurs. Complexity for Hayden does not necessarily require inheritance of status and leadership position.

A third approach to defining hunter-gatherer complexity comes from recent work by Lewis Binford (2001), termed here the subsistence security approach. Rather than partitioning variability in hunter-gatherer systems along lines of power and labor control, Binford is particularly concerned with the strategies employed by hunter-gatherer groups seeking to decrease subsistence uncertainty and to minimize risk. Relying on a massive cross-cultural survey of ethnographic hunter-gatherer groups, he argues that hunter-gatherers vary on the basis of degree of population packing. Nonpacked hunter-gatherers (typically generalized or generic) tend to have a relatively strong sharing ethos but still no guarantee of equal rights to every individual. Binford notes that what is most important in these societies is the maintenance of trust and respectability between members of interreliant groups. This, in turn, insures higher degrees of access to critical resources for all participating individuals across large geographic areas. In contrast, groups living under more packed conditions insure access to their resources through territorial defense, labor hierarchies for the production of food surplus, and the reciprocal exchange of nonfood goods for food from outside groups. Binford's break point between complex and generic hunter-gatherers therefore appears to come at the point where a landscape is packed with so many hunter-gatherers that mobility is constricted and subsistence intensification pressures occur (for an earlier application of this approach, see Binford 1968a). Consequently, hunter-gatherer groups alter their social and territorial arrangements favoring expanding intraregional distinctions in wealth and influence.

The advantages of the sociopolitical and security approaches to defining *complexity* are evident in their emphasis on organization. Clearly, a wide range of societies developed the organizational capacity to maintain subsistence security under territorial conditions through intensification tactics; to manipulate labor, often through the establishment of debt relations; and to develop economically based status hierarchies. In areas associated with agriculture, food production often emerged in contexts associated with the prior presence of complex hunter-gatherers. Examples include Jomon (Imamura 1996), Natufian and Neolithic (Bar-Yosef and Meadow 1995; Kuijt and Goring-Morris 2002), Mesolithic China (Chang 1981) and Southeast Asia (Higham 1995), the Archaic of eastern North America (Brown 1985; Smith 1995), and Mesolithic northern Europe (Price 1985; Rowly-Conwy 1983). Clearly, these societies featured many preconditions of complexity including sedentism, the production of subsistence surpluses, exchange networks featuring utilitarian and prestige goods, and indicators of differential wealth acquisition between different social units. In many cases, however, it remains unclear whether status was ascribed or achieved, yet these were clearly far more complex societies than had come earlier and in some cases were more complex than some later agricultural forms (see Kuijt 2000). Many contexts, particularly associated with the northern Pacific Rim and the western Arctic (Arnold 1996; Burch and Ellana 1994; Koyama and Thomas 1981; Price and Brown 1985), evolved similar societies—varying in subsistence emphases and in individual and corporate strategies for gaining and maintaining power—that never took the step toward agriculture. Some societies were characterized by hereditary status differences (e.g., Haida, Tlingit, Tsimshian, Koniag, Aleut, Lillooet, Chumash, Calusa), whereas others (e.g., Tareumiut, Mackenzie Eskimo, Norton and Kotzebue Sound Eskimo) depended on wealth acquisition but did not normally inherit leadership positions. As noted by Hayden (1995), many Plateau societies embodied these characteristics and are perhaps best described also as complex hunter-gatherers.

ETHNOGRAPHIC COMPLEX HUNTER-GATHERERS ON THE PLATEAU

It is well known that the impact of Euro-American and Canadian contact seriously affected the overall population levels, economic orientation, and social organization of indigenous societies throughout the continent. Nonetheless, we are still able to recognize a wide range of ethnographic societies from the Plateau. Generalized hunter-gatherers appear to have only existed on the eastern margins of the Plateau. There is little in the ethnographic record, for example, to suggest that the Kutenai, Flathead, or Pend d'Oreille had any form of ranking, individual or corporate resource patch ownership, or wealth-building strategies such as competitive feasting or potlatching (e.g., Hayden 1995). Rather, chiefs were elected for specific duties based primarily on abilities. Acquired resources were generally dispersed within bands, promoting a substantial degree of socioeconomic egalitarianism (Brunton 1998; Malouf 1998; Teit 1930).

Ethnographically, complex hunter-gatherers, when defined most broadly (e.g., Binford 2001; Hayden 1995), were found throughout much of the Plateau. Two major groupings are recognizable: those with ranking based primarily on wealth and those in which status was strictly inherited. Together these categories are synonymous with Feinman's (1998) network societies. In no case, however, are true chiefdoms (Arnold 2001; Hayden 1995) recognizable on the Plateau. Variability in sociopolitical organization appears to closely correspond to ecological context (Hayden 1992a, 1995) and degree of population packing (Binford 2001). Contexts favoring maximized access to migrating salmon tended to support the most densely packed and socially complex groups, such as the Wasco/Wishram of The Dalles, Oregon (French and French 1998; Spier and Sapir 1930), and the Lillooet and Canyon Division Shuswap of the Middle Fraser Canyon, British Columbia (Hayden 1992a; Teit 1906, 1909). These societies were stratified with distinctions between free people and slaves and further distinctions between elite and common people, marked prominently by corporate ownership of resource-harvesting locales (Hayden 1992a; Teit 1906), participation in wide-ranging elite exchange networks (Hayden and Schulting 1997), and displays of wealth (French and French 1998; Teit 1906).

In contrast, the Middle to Upper Columbia, the Lower Snake, the Upper Fraser, and the Thompson systems supported slightly less aggregated populations. Groups in these areas included the Thompson (Teit 1900), Eastern and Southern Shuswap (Teit 1909), and Okanagan and Sinixt (Lakes) (Teit 1930); various Mid-Columbia Salishan speakers such as the Wenatchie, Spokane, and Coeur d'Alene (Miller 1998; Teit 1930); and a number of Mid-Columbia and Lower Snake River Sahaptian speakers such as the Yakima, Tenino, and Umatilla (Hunn 1990; Hunn and French 1998). Although there is substantial variability, the latter societies tended to feature ranking based on wealth and various personality characteristics. Wealth building in these contexts required successful warfare, marriage arrangements, household goods production and exchange, and feasting practices (Hayden 1995). There is, however, little evidence for corporate ownership of foraging landscapes.

THE PLATEAU AS A CONTEXT FOR HUNTER-GATHERER ADAPTATIONS

Within the Plateau there is a remarkable variety of distinct environmental zones that facilitated the development of a wide range of hunter-gatherer lifeways (Chatters 1998). Geographically, the Plateau is flanked on the west by the Cascade and Coast ranges and on the east by the Rocky Mountains (Figure I.1). To the south, the Blue-Ochoco Mountains separate the Plateau from the basin and range physiographic province, while on the north the Plateau grades into the subarctic forests of central British Columbia. The interior Plateau itself was, and continues to be, a highly diverse physical landscape with remarkable variation in vegetation, precipitation, and seasonal temperatures. The arid Columbia Basin is an open landscape of grasslands and sagebrush steppe surrounded by transitional and xeric montane forests. Grasslands become highly patchy in the north as the Okanagan Highlands give way to the rolling Fraser and Thompson Plateaus, now dominated by mesic and subalpine forests. As noted by Chatters (1998), the climate of the Plateau is a consequence of maritime and continental influences. Moisture moves inland from the coast often as a consequence of storms associated with the Aleutian Low pressure system and occasionally during the summer when the Pacific High pressure system expands northward. However, much of the coastal moisture is deposited before reaching the Plateau because of the rain shadow effect of the Cascade and Coast ranges. This is particularly visible in the contrast between the arid Southern Plateau and the adjacent forested Cascade Range. From the north, arctic high-pressure systems can bring cold dry air, leading to very low winter temperatures and clear skies. In general, the Plateau is characterized by short, hot summers and long, cold winters. In some locations summer temperatures can reach over 100°F, and winter temperatures can drop below 0°F.

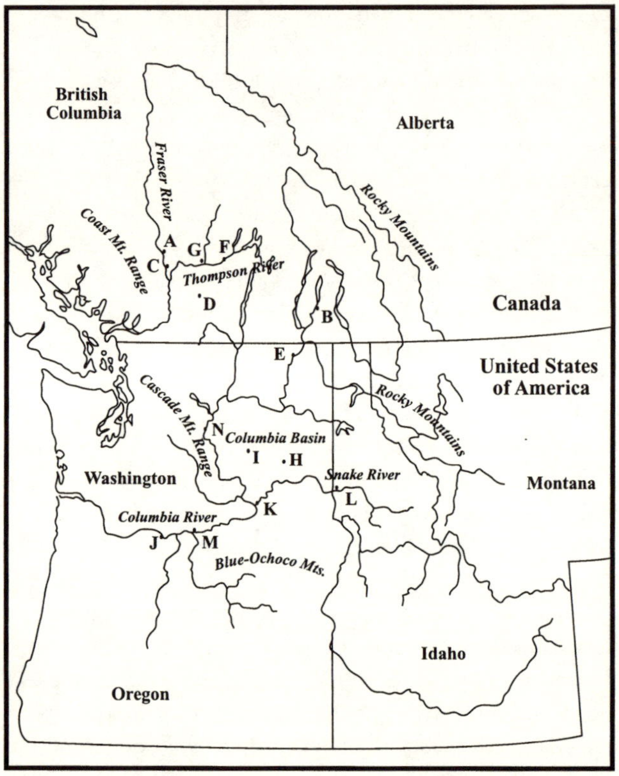

Figure I.1. The Plateau region of northwestern North America.

Hunter-gatherer peoples of the Plateau were dependent on a wide array of plant and animal resources (Chatters 1998; Lepofsky and Peacock, this volume). Prehistoric Plateau cultural diversity and complexity are strongly correlated with resource characteristics (Binford 2001;

Hayden 1992a, 1995). Probably most critical to Plateau populations, other than on the eastern margin, were the massive runs of anadromous fish, particularly salmon. Easy access to enormous concentrations of salmon favored dense population aggregations around specific river locations, such as The Dalles and the Lillooet area. Salmon provided an accessible, high-density, storable protein and fat source, critical for winter survival on the Plateau (Hunn 1990; Kennedy and Bouchard 1992; Kew 1992; Romanoff 1992). However, as noted by Hunn (1990), salmon only provided a portion of the caloric contribution to the diet because of its relatively narrow periods of availability, restricted access points, and problems with storage (Romanoff 1992). Chatters (1998) and Kew (1992) outline normal annual cycles of salmon availability in the Columbia and Fraser systems. Briefly, spring provides early chinook salmon *(Oncorhynchus tschawytscha)* and late steelhead trout *(O. mykiss)* runs. By midsummer through early fall, salmon are generally abundant, with significant chinook, sockeye *(O. nerka)*, pink *(O. gorbuscha)*, and coho *(O. kisutch)* runs. Fall to early winter runs include coho and steelhead. Kew (1992) points out that although salmon were a generally reliable resource, there could be significant interannual fluctuations in the size of the runs. Kew also notes that the numbers and quality of fish diminish significantly with distance from the sea. This had the effect of limiting aboriginal population sizes in contexts of poor salmon availability (Sneed 1971; for an example from the coast, see also Donald and Mitchell 1975).

Although a variety of other protein sources, such as resident fish, birds, and small mammals, was important to aboriginal populations, ungulate resources were nearly as important as, and in some contexts more important than, salmon (Chatters 1998; Romanoff 1985). Chatters (1998) lists nine species of ungulate indigenous to the Plateau, including elk *(Cervus elaphus)*, moose *(Alces alces)*, caribou *(Rangifer tarandus)*, mule deer *(Odocoileus hemionus)*, white-tailed deer *(Odocoileus virginianus)*, bison *(Bison bison)*, bighorn sheep *(Ovis canadensis)*, mountain goat *(Oreamnos americanus)*, and pronghorn *(Antilocapra americana)*. Some species, such as moose, mountain goat, and caribou, were available only in montane contexts or more northerly latitudes. Others, such as deer, elk, and sheep, tended to be common in the more open transitional and xeric forests as well as at higher elevations. A final group (bison and pronghorn) was limited to open grassland contexts, generally in the Columbia Basin. Ungulates formed a particularly critical resource in contexts where salmon either were not available or were limited in quality or accessibility. In contexts of greatest cultural complexity, such as the Mid-Fraser Canyon, deer-hunting locales could be owned by elite groups (Teit 1909). Deer and other ungulate products, in these contexts, not only were sources of basic food, clothing, and tools but also could be used as prestige markers (Hayden 1997; Teit 1906, 1909, 1912).

It is well known that excess consumption of protein under conditions of limited fat or carbohydrate consumption can lead to severe malnutrition and even starvation (Speth 1983). Because most animal resources on the Plateau provided little fat, particularly during the winter months, plant resources were fundamental as a source of carbohydrates in addition to other critical nutrients (Hunn 1990; Peacock 1998; Thoms 1989; Turner 1992, 1997; Turner et al. 1990; and see Kuijt and Prentiss, this volume; and Lepofsky and Peacock, this volume). Over 20 species of roots were used by Plateau peoples. Of particular importance were camas *(Camassia quamashe)* and several other members of the lily family; members of the purslane family, including spring beauty *(Claytonia lanceolata)* and bitterroot *(Lewisa rediviva)*; members of the celery family, including Desert Parsley *(Lomatium macrocarpum)*; and the aster family, particularly Balsamroot *(Balsomorhiza sagittata)*. Roots were harvested to provide immediate consumption food for deer hunters and other task groups in the spring and fall (Alexander 1992). They were also harvested and preserved as staples for consumption in winter housepit villages (Lepofsky and Peacock, this volume; Peacock 1998; Thoms 1989; Turner 1992). Hayden and Cousins (this volume) also suggest that they may have had an important use as a feasting item.

Archaeological research demonstrates that hunter-gatherer peoples have been present on the Plateau for over 11,000 years (Figure I.2). For much of this time, bands were small and mobile, and social relations were generally egalitarian. Although many specific questions remain, the overall trajectory of the socioeconomic change of hunter-gatherer groups living on the Plateau is relatively well understood by archaeologists. Subsistence strategies have varied from a larger game orientation, as represented at such sites as Marmes Rockshelter and Lind Coulee (Daugherty 1956; Rice 1972), to wide diversity in Middle Holocene housepit sites and the widely recognized salmon- and root-dominated pattern in the late period villages (Chatters 1995a). Highly mobile settlement systems appear to have given way to greater degrees of sedentism after 5000 B.P. throughout much of the Southern Plateau (Ames 1991; Chatters 1989c, 1995a). Conversely, sedentary adaptations were rare in the north until after 3500 B.P. (Stryd and Rousseau 1996). Forager-like (per Binford 1980) mobility/subsistence strategies emphasizing immediate-return subsistence tactics persisted until approximately 3500 B.P., when collector systems,

Time Frame	Period	Adaptive Pattern
4,000-200 b.p.	Late Period	Semi-sedentary collectors, Winter pithouse villages
8,000-4,000 b.p.	Middle Period	Mobile Foragers, First pithouse villages (post-5,000 b.p.)
11,500-8,000 b.p.	Early Period	Mobile Foragers

Figure I.2. Generalized culture chronology of the Plateau.

focused on intensified harvest and storage of salmon and roots, became dominant throughout the region (Chatters 1995a; Kuijt 1989; Prentiss and Chatters 2003; Richards and Rousseau 1987). Characteristic elements of complex hunter-gatherer lifeways, such as entrenched social differentiation, high levels of sedentism, population aggregation, and long-distance trade and exchange of goods, appear to have emerged after 2000 B.P. in many areas of the Plateau (Chatters and Pokotylo 1998), though some suggest earlier appearances at select localities such as Keatley Creek (Hayden 1997; Hayden and Ryder 1991; Hayden et al. 1996a).

Given the wide range of temporal and geographic variability in adaptations and cultural patterns, the Plateau forms an ideal context for the study of hunter-gatherers. The Plateau is a place, like the Northwest Coast, where social complexity, on a scale similar to that of many agriculturalists, emerged within an entirely hunter-gatherer/forager context. It is also important to note that the emergence of complex hunter-gatherer/foragers in the relatively recent past along the Plateau provides a unique case study of the overall trajectory of cultural change and the evolution of complex social systems.

THE CURRENT STATE OF COMPLEX HUNTER-GATHERER STUDIES IN PLATEAU ARCHAEOLOGY

Culture History

The Plateau has witnessed a substantial amount of archaeological investigations in the past 20 years due in no small part to federal (U.S.) and provincial (British Columbia) cultural resource management programs. Despite many large-scale archaeological investigations (e.g., Campbell 1985; Chance and Chance 1982; Chatters 1986; Dumond and Minor 1983; Galm and Masten 1985; Galm et al. 1981; Mohs 1982; Richards and Rousseau 1982; Schalk 1983; Wilson 1992), attempts at developing a synthetic understanding of broad patterns have been rare, and in many ways the analysis and interpretation of these large archaeological research projects have been conducted in isolation from other neighboring projects. In reference to the Columbia Basin, Chatters argues that this is in large part caused by "fragmentation of research on the scale of hydroelectric reservoirs, each investigated by a different group of archaeologists" (1995a: 346). Indeed, Chatters (1995a) lists six subregional chronologies for the Southern Plateau, whereas Richards and Rousseau (1987) outline eight similarly local chronologies from the Northern Plateau. One contributor to this problem has been lack of access to archaeological reports produced during many of these investigations (Lyman 1985a). But Bicchieri, in 1975, also argued that a major problem was the inconsistent use of basic methods for designing culture histories. A final important factor considering the historical genesis of this cultural-historical Balkanization is that there is some degree of variability between the timing and form of archaeological patterns evident within the larger region.

Despite this pattern of seeming archaeological parochialism, it should be noted that many investigators have relatively recently made significant progress in developing regional cultural-historical syntheses (Ames and Marshall 1981; Ames et al. 1998; Chatters and Pokotylo 1998; Fladmark 1982; Hayden and Schulting 1997; Pokotylo and Mitchell 1998; Richards and Rousseau 1987). These syntheses have sought to build and improve on earlier Plateau chronologies (Browman and Munsell 1969; Daugherty 1962; Sanger 1967). Although all recognize the need for regional syntheses, researchers have approached this task from significantly different positions, the results of which may not necessarily correlate because of varying initial assumptions about relationships among artifacts, behavior, culture, and time.

One of the first attempts to synthesize the results of numerous archaeological research projects along the Northern Plateau was undertaken by Fladmark (1982). Noting the obvious geographical gaps in research, especially in northern and eastern areas of British Columbia, he has provided an important chronological overview of material variability and change between different areas. Expanding on this foundation in 1987, Richards and Rousseau published their synthesis of the Middle and Later Holocene archaeology of the Northern Plateau using traditional culture-historical concepts. Some elements of this synthesis have been subsequently refined by Stryd and Rousseau (1996) and Rousseau (this volume). In order to provide a coherent synthesis of the Northern Plateau, Richards and Rousseau (1987) adopted Willey and Phillips's (1958) concept of the cultural tradition in order to identify the temporal persistence of distinctive cultural patterns. They employ the horizon concept to recognize and partition temporal variation within their traditions. Horizons are identified on the basis of polythetic trait lists, assuming that a variety of functional and stylistic traits served as markers of distinctive cultural patterns. Consequently, these researchers have shortened Sanger's (1967) Nesikep tradition to the Early and Middle Holocene and have added the Plateau Pithouse tradition spanning the Middle to Late Holocene. The Plateau Pithouse tradition (PPt) is subsequently divided into three horizons termed Shuswap, Plateau, and Kamloops. Recently, Stryd and Rousseau (1996) have added the late Lochnore phase as an early member of the PPt, on the basis of the enigmatic Baker site, an early housepit settlement on the Thompson River near Monte Creek, B.C. (Wilson 1992). Although this synthesis is not based on archaeological analysis designed to partition adaptive variation (e.g., Chatters 1989c, 1995a), Stryd and Rousseau do comment that the two traditions demarcate distinctly different adaptations: Nesikep being mobile foragers, while PPt represents more sedentary collectors (per Binford's 1980 definitions of foragers and collectors). Because this approach seeks recognition of broad cultural patterns, its users have extended their conclusions to address not only socioeconomic changes but also histories of sociolinguistic groups (Stryd and Rousseau 1996).

Several researchers on the Southern Plateau have sought to develop chronological syntheses based on distinctions in adaptive behavior. In order to accomplish this, these researchers conducted studies of housepit size and contents (Ames 1991), subsistence remains (Ames and Marshall 1981; Chatters 1989c, 1995a, this volume; Schalk 1981; Schalk and Cleveland 1983), and artifact patterns (Ames and Marshall 1981; Goodale et al., this volume). Syntheses of the early to middle 1980s recognize a dichotomy between more mobile, broad-spectrum subsistence foragers living prior to 3500 B.P. and the more sedentary, resource-specialized, winter village collectors of the post-3500 B.P. time frame (e.g., Schalk and Cleveland 1983). By the late 1980s and into the 1990s researchers were recognizing an early (ca. 4000–4500 B.P.) sedentary adaptation associated with broad-spectrum foraging that was replaced after 3500 B.P. by the collector adaptation. Chatters (1989c, 1995a) terms these, respectively, Pithouse I and Pithouse II. Chatters (1995a; Chatters and Pokotylo 1998) and others (e.g., Ames et al. 1998) have variously defined the late period of post-2500 B.P. as the ethnographic or winter village pattern, citing the appearance of the combination of mobility, subsistence, and organizational characteristics also recognized for the historic period. Andrefsky (this volume) divides the Southern Plateau chronology into four major periods including Paleoarchaic and Early, Middle, and Late Archaic. In one of the few attempts to synthesize archaeological excavations from both the Southern and Northern Plateaus, Hayden and Schulting (1997) have explored the distribution of cultural materials through the later periods, arguing that the shared use of these objects is representative of a "Plateau Interaction Sphere." Although this is an important regional synthesis, further work is necessary to understand and clarify how the presence and frequency of different forms of material culture shift within the later prehistoric periods. Ames and Maschner (1999) have developed a chronology that seeks to be inclusive of the Plateau and Northwest Coast by dividing the Middle and Late Holocene into three major periods termed Early, Middle, and Late Pacific.

A final strategy sometimes used in Plateau chronological syntheses has been to divide time into a series of arbitrary segments (e.g., 3000–4000 B.P., 4000–5000 B.P., etc.). Ames (1991) uses this strategy to define variation through time in the construction and occupation of pithouses. Others have divided the Plateau chronology into segments generally conforming to broad cultural and paleoenvironmental periods recognized throughout western North America (Roll and Hackenberger 1998). This external approach has the advantage of viewing Plateau data in light of changes elsewhere but may be problematic in potentially masking local variability.

Regardless of the approach adopted by individual researchers, all syntheses seem to share recognition of the major transitions in Plateau culture history, particularly that associated with the emergence of semisedentary pithouse communities. Despite recognizing this major transition, there continues to be variation in how this transition is interpreted and explained. Echoing earlier arguments by Nelson (1973), Stryd and Rousseau (1996) and Rousseau (this volume) argue that the Plateau Pithouse tradition is different from that of the Nesikep on the grounds of sociolinguistic differentiation. In contrast, Ames (1991) and Chatters (1995a) explain the change as a fundamental restructuring of socioeconomic systems. In a recent analysis, Prentiss and Chatters (2003) have argued that the processes of change on the Plateau were probably complex and at times involved in situ socioeconomic change and at other times resulted from economic collapse, abandonment, and population replacement. Adopting a similar perspective, later in this book we address these issues, arguing that on the Northern Plateau there is no clear gradual transition from the early PPt, as represented at the Baker site, to the Shuswap horizon. Rather, we suggest that a substantial population movement from the coast was responsible for the dramatic differences between the archaeological records of the late Lochnore phase and the early Shuswap horizon. Interestingly, Chatters (1995a) argues for a similar process on the Southern Plateau.

Evolutionary Process on the Plateau

Despite the long history of archaeological and ethnographic research on the Plateau, remarkably few attempts have been made to explore how these data further our general understanding of the evolution of complex hunter-gatherer communities. There are two areas of study, often overlooked, that can provide critical insights into the evolution and organization of complex hunter-gatherer lifeways: the process of subsistence intensification and the emergence of social complexity. Although there clearly are exceptions, contributions exploring resource intensification have generally come from the Southern Plateau, whereas researchers on the Northern Plateau (particularly Hayden and colleagues) have emphasized social complexity.

It is well recognized that subsistence intensification is a fundamental process behind the development of aggregated communities and social complexity on the Plateau. Despite wide acknowledgment of its importance, few have attempted to define the concept. Some see intensification as a process dependent on other factors such as population size and carrying capacity. Schalk (1977, 1981) links the degree of salmon intensification to the structure of that resource. Ames and Marshall (1981) argue similarly for root intensification. Galm (1985) and Thoms (1989) suggest that population packing drove the intensification process whereby the human group shifted from optimal fishing locations to less desirable places, ultimately having to consume large quantities of plant foods. Intensification, in these models, is a process of expanding the range of dietary items, starting with high-ranking resources such as deer or elk, adding anadromous fish and then less desirable fish, and finally intensively harvesting and storing plants. The process of adding progressively lower-utility resources, requiring higher processing costs, is often cited as an example of declining economic efficiency (see Broughton 1994; Chatters 1995a; Janetski 1997). Intensification in this context is thus inefficient and a marker of subsistence stress.

In contrast, other researchers explain the expanded utilization of fish and roots on the Plateau not as markers of stress but, rather, as consequences of technological innovations that make the harvesting of these resources more efficient. Hayden (1981, 1992a) has argued that resource conditions could favor the application of innovations developed earlier, making harvest of "r-selected" resources (such as fish) more productive and palatable. Chatters (1989c, 1995a) presents evidence that salmon intensification after 4000 B.P. was driven by new technological and organizational concepts permitting efficient harvesting and storage of massive quantities of this resource.

Intensification processes clearly played a role in the emergence of complex hunter-gatherer communities (Arnold 1993; Binford 2001; Brown 1985; Lourandos 1988). Plateau researchers have explored explanatory models that fall generally into two groups: pressure versus opportunity. Pressure models assert that competitive behavior associated with complex communities is a consequence of reduced foraging options associated with population rise, packing, or ecological change. Put in evolutionary terms, competitive behavior is rewarded or "selected for" in an environment where resources are patchily abundant and human mobility is restricted. Lohse and Sammons-Lohse (1986), following from Cohen (1977, 1985), explain the rise of winter village–pattern communities as a consequence of gradually increasing population density and resource stress. Galm (1985) explains the complex settlement systems of the late period as a consequence of population packing, requiring increasing use of more marginal spaces. Relying on ethnographic data from the Plateau and elsewhere, Binford (2001) promotes an expanded version of his 1968 model, arguing that patchy environments and population packing promote territorialism, competition for control of labor, resource intensification, and various markers of social complexity.

These packing and pressure models are superficially similar but do imply some differences. Simple population increase requires steady resource stress that presumably drives innovation. In contrast, packing does not necessarily produce resource stress but does rearrange mobility options, thereby favoring new organizational strategies. Simple resource stress need not necessarily enter into the equation. Population pressure models seek to explain all changes within this single model; in essence, stress drives intensification, competition, and complexity. Prentiss and Chatters (2003), however, argue that processes of human population isolation and niche reorganization drove the emergence and expansion of collector systems. Binford (2001) offers a similar argument favoring "niche filling" as a fundamental process associated with new socioeconomic practices. He expands on this and argues that a separate process of packing would be responsible for the more competitive communities of the Northwest Coast and Plateau.

Hayden (1990, 1992a, 1995) explains the emergence of complex societies on the Plateau as a consequence of opportunity. He suggests that once collector-like systems had emerged and people were able to harvest surplus quantities of resources (salmon in particular), then highly competitive individuals sought to elevate their own status within their communities through a variety of strategies centered around the manipulation of labor through the establishment of debt relationships and the accumulation of goods. Hayden (2000a) asserts that in key places such as the Mid-Fraser Canyon or The Dalles, complex permanent communities could arise very quickly following the technological transition. Thus, the large housepits of the Keatley Creek site should date to a time shortly after the appearance of collector systems, perhaps as early as circa 3000 B.P. Hayden also suggests that variability in interhouse storage, food remains, and dog skeletons at the Baker site could reflect status competition in a very early (4000–4500 B.P.) collector context.

In brief, the Plateau will continue to provide important data and fertile grounds for debating evolutionary theories. Clearly, one of the fundamental problems to be resolved with archaeological data concerns the origins of complexity. The first step will be to determine the relevance of the packing versus opportunity models before any more progress can be made. Several chapters in this book, including those by Chatters, Hayden and Adams, Hayden and Cousins, Kuijt and Prentiss, and Arnold, address this problem.

Organization of Complex Hunter-Gatherer Communities

The Plateau provides an abundance of information regarding the organization of complex hunter-gatherer communities. These data derive from ethnographic, ethnoarchaeological, and archaeological sources. This record is critical for archaeologists and ethnologists working in other areas to understand the evolution and organization of complex hunter-gatherer communities. Information from the Plateau can be used to aid in the interpretation of ancient hunter-gatherer communities in a variety of contexts including Mesolithic Europe, the Natufian of the Near East, and the Jomon culture of Japan. But the rich archaeological record of the Plateau is valuable on a local level as well, for it provides the material basis for reconstructing the societies of the indigenous Plateau peoples prior to contact with Europeans. The following discussion outlines archaeological and ethnoarchaeological perspectives on the organization of subsistence and technology, social organization, conflict, and exchange on the Plateau (for related and detailed discussions of these issues, see also Blake, Hayden and Adams, Hayden and Cousins, Lepofsky and Peacock, all this volume).

Researchers working on the Plateau have conducted extensive ethnoarchaeological and archaeological studies of subsistence practices in different areas and periods of time. Ethnographic research is substantial and includes critical early work by Teit (1900, 1906, 1909, 1928, 1930) and important recent work by a number of researchers, including Alexander (1992), Hunn (1990), Kennedy and Bouchard (1978, 1992), Kew (1992), Palmer (1975), Romanoff (1985, 1992), Turner (1992, 1997; Turner et al. 1990), and Tyhurst (1992). The rich Plateau ethnographic record has helped inform archaeologists working within this region but has also been useful in broader cross-cultural studies of hunter-gatherer subsistence organization (Binford 2001).

In contrast to the relatively extensive faunal research and ethnographic descriptions of seasonal plant use, most notably exemplified by the remarkable and extensive works of Nancy Turner, the archaeological study of Plateau paleoethnobotany is still in its infancy. Yet many important studies have been conducted, particularly emphasizing the importance of roots as critical sources of carbohydrates and other nutrients. Pokotylo and Froese (1983) provide an early and important demonstration of the antiquity and nature of root processing on the Canadian Plateau. Developing some of the earliest archaeological arguments for the importance of plant resources on the Plateau, Ames and Marshall (1981) have argued that early Southern Plateau subsistence intensification centered on roots. Thoms (1989) conducted a more in-depth exploration of camas intensification on the Southern Plateau. Most recently, Peacock (1998) studied root intensification and the emergence of social complexity on the Canadian Plateau. Lepofsky and colleagues (Cousins 2000; Hayden and Cousins, this volume; Lepofsky 2000a, 2000b; Lepofsky et al. 1996) have studied root use at the Keatley Creek site and its implications for understanding the complex socioeconomies of late period villages in the Mid-Fraser Canyon. Lepofsky's (2000a, 2000b) contributions have not been limited to the study of roots. Her research at Keatley Creek, in particular, has focused on broad questions of subsistence, social organization, and technology. Lepofsky and Peacock (this volume) provide a detailed overview of the contribution of paleoethnobotanical studies to Plateau archaeology.

Although some argue that the importance of salmon in Plateau subsistence economies has been overstated by researchers (see Hunn 1990; Kuijt and Prentiss, this volume; Peacock 1998), there is no question that salmon and other fish were a critical subsistence resource. Numerous researchers have studied the salmon-related intensification process on the Plateau. Chisholm (1986; Chisholm and Nelson 1983) has used stable isotopes to reconstruct evidence for early use of anadromous fish on the Canadian Plateau. Butler (1993; Butler and Chatters 1994) has assessed the role of taphonomic factors in the formation of salmon bone assemblages. Chatters (1989c, 1995a) and Schalk (1977, 1981) have explored salmon intensification processes on the Southern Plateau. And Hayden and colleagues (Berry 2000; Hayden 1997; Kusmer 2000a, 2000b) have explored how salmon remains serve as markers of variability in the socioeconomic status of households at the Keatley Creek site. Moving beyond anadromous fish, Plateau researchers recognize a variety of additional aquatic resources. Clearly, other fish species such as trout were of seasonal importance on the Plateau (Alexander 1992; Chatters 1995a; Hunn 1990; Lyman 1985b). However, shellfish also provided an important resource in many areas, especially in the earlier periods (Chatters 1987, 1995a; Kusmer 2000a, 2000b; Lyman 1980, 1984).

Mammals were widely exploited by late period peoples of the Plateau, though specific resources varied with the ecological context. All zooarchaeologists working on the Plateau document the use of small mammals (e.g., Chatters 1995a; Kusmer 2000a, 2000b; Lyman 1985b; Lyman and Livingston 1983; Schalk and Olson 1983). A number of sites have provided substantial data for studies of procurement and processing strategies associated with medium to larger mammals including pronghorn (Schalk and Olson 1983), deer (Jaehnig 1984; Kusmer 2000a, 2000b; Lohse 1984; Lyman 1985b), bison (Butler 1978; Chatters et al. 1995; Schroedl 1973), elk (Lohse 1984), and bighorn sheep (Jaehnig 1984; Kusmer 2000a, 2000b; Lohse 1984).

Technological organization, particularly as it relates to mobility strategies, remains an important research topic on the Plateau (Prentiss and Kuijt, this volume). Indeed, the Plateau is an excellent place to study relationships between technology and mobility given the wide diversity in strategies evident during the Holocene (Ames 1991). Further, the ethnographic record from the Plateau provides some of the best insights into aboriginal technology in North America. Teit's (1900, 1906, 1909, 1912, 1930) ethnographies are the most comprehensive. However, various other works discuss technological adaptations on the Plateau (Kennedy and Bouchard 1978; Morice 1893; Smith 1899, 1900; Turner 1998). Alexander (2000) has provided a comprehensive summary of the ethnographic literature concerning technologies associated with Canadian Plateau winter housepit villages. Magne (1985) provides an earlier summary of the ethnographic literature with a narrower focus on the organization of lithic technology.

Several archaeologists have conducted studies of lithic technological organization. Chatters (1987) has outlined strategies for recognizing variation in mobility using lithic artifacts ranging from fire-cracked rock to formed tools. Andrefsky (1995) uses distributions of lithic raw material types in Cascade Phase assemblages to demonstrate high residential mobility. Many investigators have studied the organization of lithic technology associated with late period winter housepit villages. Magne (1985), for example, explores lithic assemblages from a wide range of site contexts in order to better understand settlement patterns from the Canadian Plateau. Rousseau (1992) has conducted an in-depth study of key-shaped, formed unifaces on the Canadian Plateau. Focusing on the site level, Hayden and colleagues (Hayden 1997; Hayden et al. 1996b; Prentiss 2000, 2001; Spafford 2000) have analyzed lithic technological organization associated with the Keatley Creek site. One major result of these studies has been the collective recognition of the abrupt change from the use of highly curated and transported technologies by the more mobile peoples of the Early to Middle Holocene to the more complex systems of the late period winter villages emphasizing greater expediency in chipped-stone production and an increasing reliance on ground stone for woodworking and trade purposes (Prentiss and Kuijt, this volume). Excavations of housepit settlements throughout the Plateau have provided a particularly useful database for future studies of technology (see Brauner 1976; Campbell 1985; Chatters 1986; Dumond and Minor 1983; Galm and Masten 1985; Hayden 2000a, 2000b; Schalk 1983).

As noted above, sociopolitical organization appears to have varied substantially on the Plateau, both spatially and temporally. The most ambitious and prominent research program seeking to reconstruct prehistoric sociopolitical organization has been that of Brian Hayden at the Keatley Creek site. Hayden and colleagues have relied on a variety of data to provide a provocative set of conclusions. Hayden's primary focus has been on intra- and interhousehold variation. Hayden (1997) reasons that if social inequality was present at Keatley Creek, then it should be reflected in a manner consistent with many ethnographic descriptions of complex societies from the Plateau (e.g., Teit 1900, 1906, 1909) and elsewhere (Boas 1966; Burch 1981; Oberg 1973). In other words, the most wealthy and powerful groups would reside in the largest and most well-constructed and -supplied housepits. The interiors of these houses should reflect the distribution of multiple domestic groups similar to that in large houses of the Northwest Coast (Chatters 1989a; Huelsbeck 1989). Further, Hayden suspects that marginal members of the community would have resided in less prominent houses with reduced access to some food sources (deer, chinook salmon) and other goods. Hayden has also explored the possibility that elite groups might have participated in trade networks emphasizing prestige goods from which less prominent community members were excluded. Testing of these predictions has produced a substantial body of household archaeological research into Plateau social organization (Darwent 1998; Hayden 1997, 2000a, 2000b; Hayden et al. 1985; Hayden et al. 1996a; Lepofsky et al. 1996; Prentiss 2000; Spafford 2000). Schulting (1995) has provided an exhaustive overview of burial data from the Plateau and subsequently has used it to test ideas about social inequality. Hayden and Adams (this volume) and Hayden and Cousins (this volume) continue this important research program, offering new strategies, respectively, for recognizing secret societies and for feasting behavior in the archaeological record.

It is, of course, hard to discuss sociopolitical organization without considering exchange. Ethnographers and archaeologists have been interested in exchange mechanisms and practices on the Plateau for some time. Various ethnographers have documented historical exchange systems within the Plateau and between the Plateau peoples and their neighbors (Anastasio 1985; Ray 1939; Spier and Sapir 1930; Teit 1906, 1909, 1930). The archaeological evidence for exchange on the Plateau is very extensive and recently has been summarized by Hayden and Schulting (1997). They emphasize, in particular, the importance of various highly decorated utilitarian items and art objects. Ames and colleagues (1998) highlight the importance of obsidian and shell in Plateau exchange. Darwent (1998) reviews the production and distribution of nephrite artifacts. Chatters (1989a, 1995a) notes that the geographic extent and form of exchange have probably varied over time on the Plateau. Hayden and Schulting (1997) further argue that the most extensive exchange networks featuring elite exchange relationships did not emerge until after 2,400 years ago. Although Hayden and Schulting argue convincingly for a Plateau interaction sphere, Blake (this volume) also points out critical relationships between Plateau communities and those of the adjacent Northwest Coast.

In 1980, Kent debunked the myth of pacifism on the Plateau, at least for the more recent periods. She has demonstrated that conflict was historically endemic throughout the region. Archaeologists have found substantial evidence for violence in the past in the form of skeletal indicators and fortified villages (Chatters 1989b; Lynch 1978; Rice 1978; Schalk 1983; Smith 1977). Hayden (1995) suggests that conflict may have been in part economically motivated, depending on ecological context. Cannon (1992) argues that conflict was more frequent in contexts where opportunities for production and exchange of surplus were limited. Thus, the lowest frequency of conflict occurred in the Mid-Fraser Canyon and The Dalles, where surplus high-quality salmon was easily obtained and trade could be carefully controlled. Importantly, Chatters (this volume) argues that conflict may have played a major role in the emergence of the large aggregated villages in the late period.

FINAL THOUGHTS

As noted at the start of this essay, archaeological research on the Plateau of northwestern North America provides a unique opportunity both to develop a detailed understanding of the heritage and cultural context of prehistoric First Nation members living in this area and to draw on this regional understanding to understand the broader anthropological context of the organization and evolution of complex hunter-gatherers. In contrast to research in many other world areas, this process occurred relatively late and is complemented by a relatively rich ethnographic record manifested through the journals and writings of early explorers and anthropologists, 19th-century photography, and perhaps most importantly, the continued input and perspectives provided by the First Nation members themselves. By over 1,500 years ago, complex hunter-gatherer societies had appeared on the Plateau of northwestern North America. The societies typically used a biseasonal settlement pattern, remaining relatively sedentary in winter housepit villages in the winter and becoming more mobile during the warm season. Foraging strategies varied from broad-spectrum resource gathering, emphasizing a wide array of plant and animal species, to resource-specialization strategies, particularly focusing on salmon and select plants such as camas. Sociopolitical organization varied widely, but at its most complex it featured ranked societies, elite control of resources and trade routes, institutionalized slavery, and endemic warfare. Given its excellent ethnographic and archaeological records, the Plateau offers an ideal context for the study of the evolution and organization of complex hunter-gatherer communities.

I

CHRONOLOGY AND MATERIALS IN PLATEAU ARCHAEOLOGY

1

A CULTURE HISTORIC SYNTHESIS AND CHANGES IN HUMAN MOBILITY, SEDENTISM, SUBSISTENCE, SETTLEMENT, AND POPULATION ON THE CANADIAN PLATEAU, 7000–200 B.P.

MIKE K. ROUSSEAU

The Canadian (Northern) Plateau occupies a vast area of highly varied topography and environments in south-central British Columbia (Figures 1.1–1.4). Its southern boundary lies 15–20 km north and parallel to the Canada–U.S. border at Princeton in the Similkameen Valley, Okanagan Falls in the Okanagan Valley, Rock Creek and Grand Forks in the Kettle River Valley, and Castlegar at the confluence of the Columbia and Kootenay rivers. The Coast Mountains are its western boundary, and the Monashees make up its eastern fringe. Its northwest limit lies near Burns Lake, and Prince George marks its northeast extent. The Canadian Plateau owes its ecological and geographic diversity to many climatic and geographic factors, notably differential latitudinal and altitudinal floral and faunal species zonation, the nature of its post-Pleistocene deposits, major aquatic features (lakes and rivers), prevailing winds, and rain shadows. It is this great natural diversity in land and resources that allowed precontact-period peoples to develop complex and diverse cultural patterns, particularly during the last 3,500 years.

Prehistoric occupation of the Fraser, Thompson, Shuswap, Arrow Lakes, Okanagan, Similkameen, Nicola, and Chilcotin drainages is represented by a suspected 10,000-year-long succession of unique hunter-gatherer-fisher cultures that saw major and minor environmental changes and the development or adoption of a myriad of successful technological, subsistence, and settlement strategies. Some changes in behavior and material traits occurred fairly rapidly (e.g., over 100 years), whereas others were invented or introduced, implemented, refined, and gradually worked into cultural systems over many generations.

The period from 10,000 to 7,000 B.P. is still poorly understood; nevertheless, Rousseau (1993) and Stryd and Rousseau (1996:179–185) summarize what is known. This chapter presents a culture historical synthesis and overview of human sedentism, mobility, subsistence, settlement, and population on the Canadian Plateau over the last 7,000 years. The Nesikep tradition (ca. 7000–4500 B.P.) and subsequent Plateau Pithouse tradition (PPt) (ca. 4500–200 B.P.) are described and discussed. Data and conclusions are drawn from (1) paleoenvironmental reconstructions, (2) site excavation and survey results, (3) modeling of culture change and adaptation, (4) the ethnographic record, (5) oral elder interviews, and (6) consideration of information gained and exchanged among researchers over many decades. The overall conceptual approach for development of the cultural sequence is "normative" (Binford 1965, 1968b). It also draws on aspects of systems theory and cultural ecology. Solid reconstruction of culture histories is required before any problems relating to culture process and complex behavior can be properly addressed. Interregional similarities, differences, and variation are also important factors to consider. The main goals of this chapter are to (1) describe currently defined Canadian Plateau archaeological units, (2) identify evidence relating to culture process as suggested by current data, (3) discuss the emergence and persistence of the PPT, and (4) provide direction for future research.

NESIKEP TRADITION (CA. 7000–4500 B.P.)

The Nesikep tradition was first defined by Sanger (1969, 1970), who has proposed a 7,000-year-long cultural continuum culminating in ethnographic Interior Salish culture. This tradition has been shortened and redefined by Stryd and Rousseau (1996:187–191). The initial

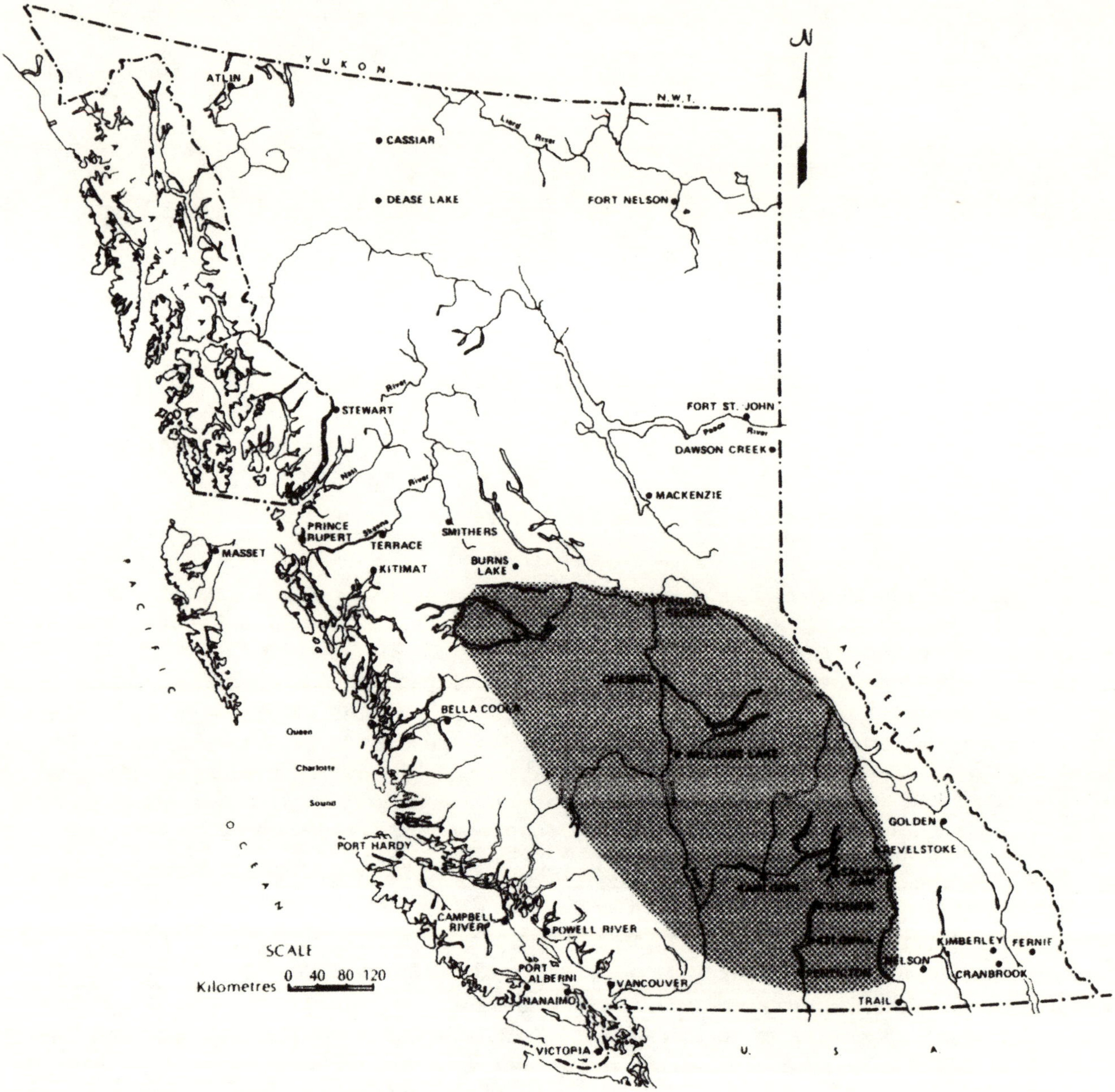

Figure 1.1. The Canadian Plateau culture subarea in British Columbia.

appearance and cultural origin of the Nesikep tradition remains unknown. The earliest component is dated 6650 ± 110 B.P. (I-2367), obtained from bone associated with Zone II at the Lehman site (EdRk 8), with several other problematic dates falling between 6000 and 4500 B.P. (Sanger 1970; Stryd and Rousseau 1996:203). The Nesikep tradition may have emerged in the Fraser and Thompson river drainages as early as 8,000 B.P. If pre-Mazama occupations at the Landels site (EdRi 11) belong to this tradition, then it may have begun as early as 8,500 years ago (Rousseau 1991; Rousseau et al. 1991).

A few excavations and site inventories conducted in the Thompson and Mid-Fraser river drainages permit a basic reconstruction of Nesikep tradition technologies, adaptive strategies, and lifeways (see Gehr 1976; Lawhead and Stryd 1985; Lawhead et al. 1986; Rousseau 1991; Rousseau and Richards 1988; Rousseau et al. 1991; Sanger 1970; Stryd 1972; Wilson 1991). The Nesikep tradition is further divided into the Early Nesikep period (ca. 7000–6000 B.P.) followed by the Lehman phase (ca. 6000–4500 B.P.) (Stryd and Rousseau 1996:203–204).

Early Nesikep (ca. 7000–6000 B.P.)

Excavated data secured from Early Nesikep sites are sparse but allow general reconstruction of subsistence and settlement (see Lawhead and Stryd 1985; Rousseau et al. 1991; Sanger 1970; Stryd 1972; Wilson 1991). Early Nesikep

Figure 1.2. View of the Fraser River about 15 km north of Lytton in the Mid-Fraser River region, looking north. This region has a very high archaeological site density and a long occupational history.

Figure 1.3. View of the Ashcroft-Cache Creek locality in the Thompson River Valley, looking east toward Kamloops. Arrowstone Hills (upper left) was an extensive and abundant source of "Cache Creek basalt" (dacite) intensively quarried for thousands of years.

residential base camps were typically small, were occupied for relatively short periods (e.g., days to several weeks), and were often established along valley sides at or near river–creek confluences in sandy areas protected from winds. Many site settings afford excellent vantage over the surrounding locality and are near extinct or extant sources of potable water close to major salmon fisheries. Field camps were small, numerous, and short term and are found in all ecological niches and altitudes. They are especially common beside upland lakes and streams.

Early Nesikep lithic assemblages often include distinctive, well-made, medium-sized and large lanceolate, corner-notched, barbed, and shouldered formed bifaces

Figure 1.4. The Monte Creek locality in the South Thompson River region, looking south. This locality has been the focus of major investigations, including those at the Baker site (EdQx 43), where the earliest known pithouses have been documented for the Canadian Plateau.

(Figure 1.5 [items 1–29]); a high incidence of formed unifaces, notably tabular oval and circular scrapers (Figure 1.6 [14–15]); microblade technology (Figure 1.7 [1–13]); a variety of thin unformed unifaces and utilized flakes; antler wedges; ground rodent incisors; bone points and needles; and red ochre. Recovered faunal assemblages are dominated by deer remains, with lesser proportions of elk, salmon, steelhead, bird, and freshwater mussel (Lawhead and Stryd 1985; Sanger 1970; Stryd 1972). Various plant resources were undoubtedly consumed when fortuitously encountered or seasonally available, but specific species and their relative contributions to the diet remain to be determined. Current data indicate that Early Nesikep people engaged in a "foraging" subsistence and settlement strategy (Binford 1980).

Regional population densities during the Early Nesikep were low because most residential base sites of this age are typically small and are far less common than those of later periods. It might be argued that low Early Nesikep site frequency can be attributed to low site visibility, but many deflated "blowouts" along terrace edge sites within the semiarid desert Mid-Fraser and Thompson regions lack evidence for Early Nesikep occupations and contain materials relating to subsequent archaeological units.

Early Nesikep components have yielded distinctive formed bifaces (Figure 1.5 [1–29]) that indicate superb technical skill and fairly close adherence to a specific formal theme. Most complete bifaces are well made, relatively thin, lanceolate in outline, and have straight or recurved lateral margins and thin lenticular cross sections. A few specimens (10 percent) have microserrated edges (Figure 1.5 [13, 19–20]), presumably to enhance cutting and hemorrhaging efficiency. Distinctive attributes include (1) V-shaped corner notches and shoulders with slight to pronounced "hooked" lateral barbs, (2) parallel to slightly expanding basal-lateral margins, (3) straight or convex basal margins, and (4) slight to pronounced basal and basal-lateral edge grinding. Intentional basal thinning is evident on many specimens. Viewed end-on, most bifaces have straight or minimally bowed lateral margins. Transversely snapped specimens often have impact damage along break margins, and many shorter examples suggest that they have been reworked (retipped) after distal portions had snapped off. Large bifaces with recurved blade edges (Figure 1.5 [1–6]) were often the optimal intended initial form, with accidental breakage and successive resharpenings resulting in loss of dimensions and reduction in basal-lateral barb size.

Early Nesikep bifaces display a high level of chipped-stone technological proficiency and distinctive traits that Sanger (1970:122, 127) thought were somehow ultimately derived from early "Plano" traditions of the Northern Plains. Although an apparent "lingering" of Plano tradition technological traits is plausible, there is a 1,500–2,000 year gap between these two archaeological constructs, which challenges Sanger's argument for direct ancestral or cultural continuity. Similarities reflected in Plano and Early Nesikep bifaces may be coincidental, the result of parallel technological innovation rather than direct ancestry or Plains–Plateau group interaction.

Tool multifunctionality and flexibility are important and consistent components of effective, highly mobile,

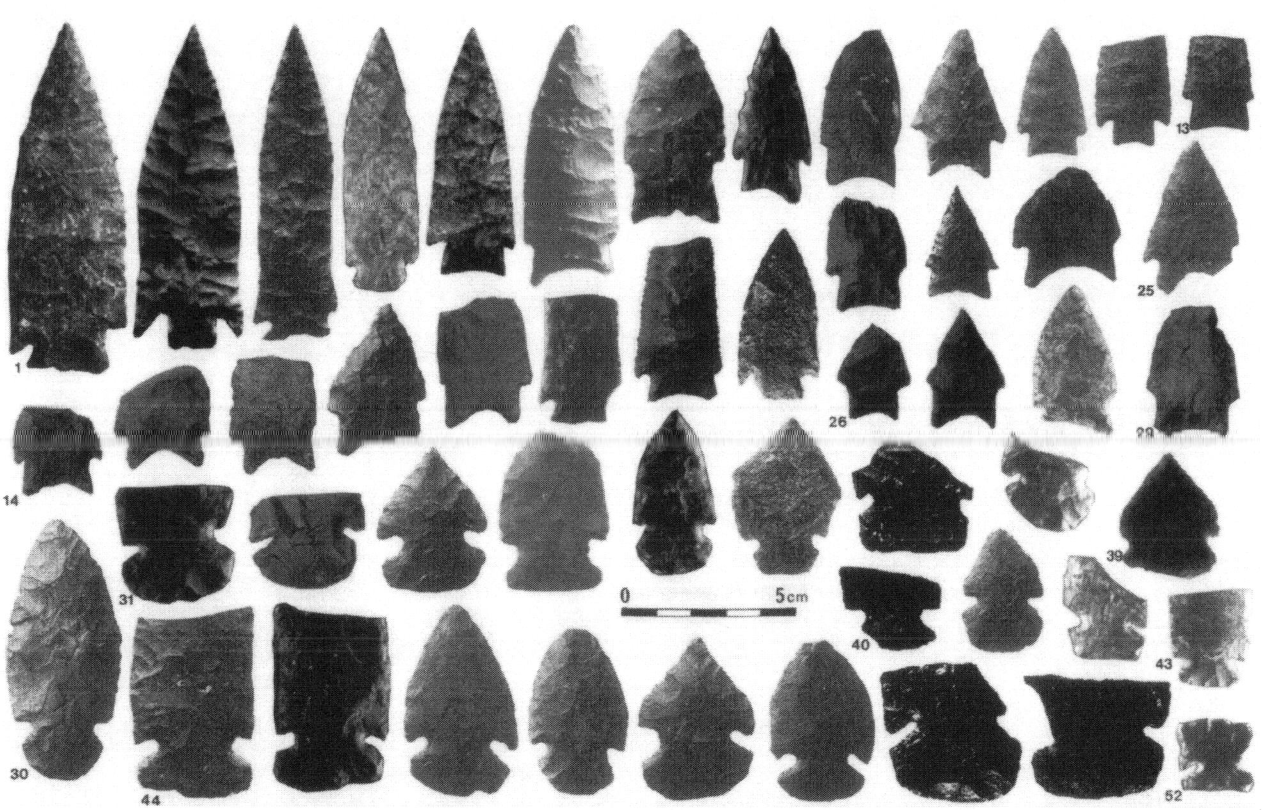

Figure 1.5. Selected examples of diagnostic bifaces from numerous sites containing Nesikep Tradition components. Items 1–29: Early Nesikep Period (ca. 7000–6000 B.P.); 30–52: Lehman Phase (ca. 6000–4500 B.P.).

hunting-oriented, curated technological strategies (Bamforth 1986; Binford 1979; Bleed 1986; Kuhn 1994; Torrence 1983, 1989). Early Nesikep points have been found as "isolated finds" in almost every environmental niche, geological context, and altitude. Their distribution indicates high mobility and frequent loss during hunting-related activities. They almost certainly tipped the ends of throwing spears or atlatl darts and were employed as knives once prey had been dispatched.

Early Nesikep people were avid users of microblade technology, and it was an important and indispensable component of their lithic technological system. Microblade technology is fairly involved, and it requires a high level of technical skill to successfully make microblades in large numbers. All functional applications of microblades still remain largely unknown, and their presence is sometimes offered (albeit perhaps incorrectly) as direct evidence for interregional or interareal ethnic or cultural affiliation or ancestry. Microblade technology was in use by at least 8500 B.P. (Rousseau 1991, 1993:154; Stryd and Rousseau 1996:181), and eventually it may be shown that it was introduced as early as 9000 or 10,000 B.P. via the Central or South Coast regions (Carlson 1983b). It is absent from all components dating later than 3500 B.P. This efficient lithic-reduction system was employed by mobile groups in situations in which extensive cutting tasks (e.g., animal or fish processing) were required but very little good-quality, highly flakeable, sharp-edged stone was immediately available. Microblades are functionally flexible and were used to execute a variety of activities common to mobile groups practicing a basic opportunistic foraging strategy. Additional discussions on Plateau microblade technology are presented by Campbell (1985:299–304), Ludowicz (1983), Richards and Rousseau (1987:57–58), Rousseau (1993:150–151), Sanger (1968b), and Stryd and Rousseau (1996:181–183).

Current paleoenvironmental reconstructions suggest that around 7000 B.P., British Columbia's southern interior began receiving steadily increasing annual precipitation accompanied by warmer-than-present temperatures. Grasslands consisting of sagebrush, bunchgrass, and cactus covered vast regions, and small shallow lakes began to form in previously dry catchment basins, creating a prime habitat for deer, elk, moose, and possibly antelope. These large ungulates provided reliable sources of protein for small, highly mobile Early Nesikep hunter-gatherer-fishers.

The violent eruption of Mt. Mazama in Oregon around 6,800 years ago (Harris 1988:107) was a significant catastrophic geologic event that undoubtedly had immediate deleterious effects on humans, animals, and plants inhabiting the entire Plateau. Studies conducted on the effects of historic volcanic eruptions show that broad-leafed plants, terrestrial animals, and fish are immediately and

Figure 1.6. Selected examples commonly found in Early Nesikep, Lehman Phase, and Lochnore Phase components on the Canadian Plateau. Item 1: a microblade core "blank"; 2–5: selected microblade cores in various stages of reduction to final exhaustion; 6–13: microblades; 14–22: examples of typical formed unifacial scrapers.

severely negatively affected by ashfall, but they also note that periods of environmental recovery were relatively short (e.g., one–four years) (Bilderback and Stone 1987; Blong 1984; Lucas 1986; Mack 1987). Early Nesikep people and other large mammals would have experienced difficulty breathing, eye and nasal irritation, and possibly intestinal inflammation (Bolt et al. 1977:79). Many individuals would have succumbed as a result of starvation or ash-related respiratory complications (Montgomery 1990). Salmon populations would have been impacted if the blast occurred during spawning runs or the early emergence of salmon fry. Montgomery (1990) offers the idea that existing opportunistic foraging patterns allowed groups to shift emphasis on available surviving resources without resorting to any major technological change(s) or exodus from affected regions. Despite our current poor understanding about the origins and development of Early Nesikep culture, it is clear that these people participated in a highly mobile, hunting/gathering/fishing, opportunistic "forager"–type adaptive strategy that developed in situ as a unique and widespread Canadian Plateau cultural and archaeological entity by at least 7000 B.P. and possibly earlier.

Lehman Phase (ca. 6000–4500 B.P.)

The Lehman phase was initially identified and defined on the basis of excavations conducted at the Oregon Jack

Figure 1.7. Selected examples of diagnostic bifaces from Plateau Pithouse Tradition components. Items 1–14: Lochnore Phase (ca. 5000–3500 B.P.); 15–34: Shuswap Horizon (3500–2400 B.P.); 35–68: Plateau Horizon (2400–1200 B.P.); 69–84: Kamloops Horizon side-notched arrow points (1200–200 B.P.); 59–68: late Plateau Horizon arrow points (ca. 1600–1200 B.P.); 75–77, 84: examples of occasionally found Kamloops "multinotched" arrow points (400–200 B.P.).

Creek and Rattlesnake Hill sites near Ashcroft and several sites in the nearby Highland Valley (Lawhead and Stryd 1985; Lawhead et al. 1986; Rousseau and Richards 1988). Several other Lehman phase components have since been investigated and reported (see Stryd and Rousseau 1996: 189–191, 201–204). Radiocarbon dates suggest that it began around 6000 B.P. and ended by 4500 B.P. Lehman phase people were directly descended from Early Nesikep folks, as indicated by clear continuities in technological traits, lithic tool repertoires, subsistence practices, and radiocarbon dates. By all current accounts, transition from the Early Nesikep to the Lehman phase appears to have been gradual and relatively seamless, with notable differences being related to increasing regional familiarity with lithic and subsistence resources by the end of the Lehman phase.

During the Lehman phase, the climate was warmer and drier than it is today, although annual precipitation may have been similar. During this time, vast desert and grassland areas in major valley bottoms extended up onto the Plateau highlands, supporting large ungulate and smaller animal populations that provided a reliable and abundant source of protein for small, highly mobile groups.

Lehman phase components are often small, deeply buried, short-term occupation horizons containing medium- to high-density scatters of lithics, bone, and freshwater mussel shell. Some multistratified sites comprise amalgams of discrete, well-separated (both vertically and horizontally) occupations suggesting long breaks between them. Many occupations are found on flat or gently sloping terrain in protected settings along the sides of main river valleys, at or near junctures of major creek and river valleys, and on extinct river channel terraces 10 m or more above the present river base levels. Countless components have been exposed along deflated terrace edges in Mid-Fraser and Thompson regions. A few mid-altitude and upland Lehman phase sites beside small lakes and streams have also been investigated; these indicate that they were short-term seasonal field camps occupied by a few people (Gehr 1976; Lawhead et al. 1986; Rousseau et al. 1991; Stryd and Rousseau 1996).

Low site densities and the small size of observed Lehman phase sites imply relatively low regional populations compared with those of later cultural manifestations, but there is a greater noted frequency of Lehman phase components compared with the preceding Early Nesikep. This suggests slow steady population growth throughout the Nesikep tradition (Figure 1.8). Seasonally mobile extended family groups consisting of 20–30

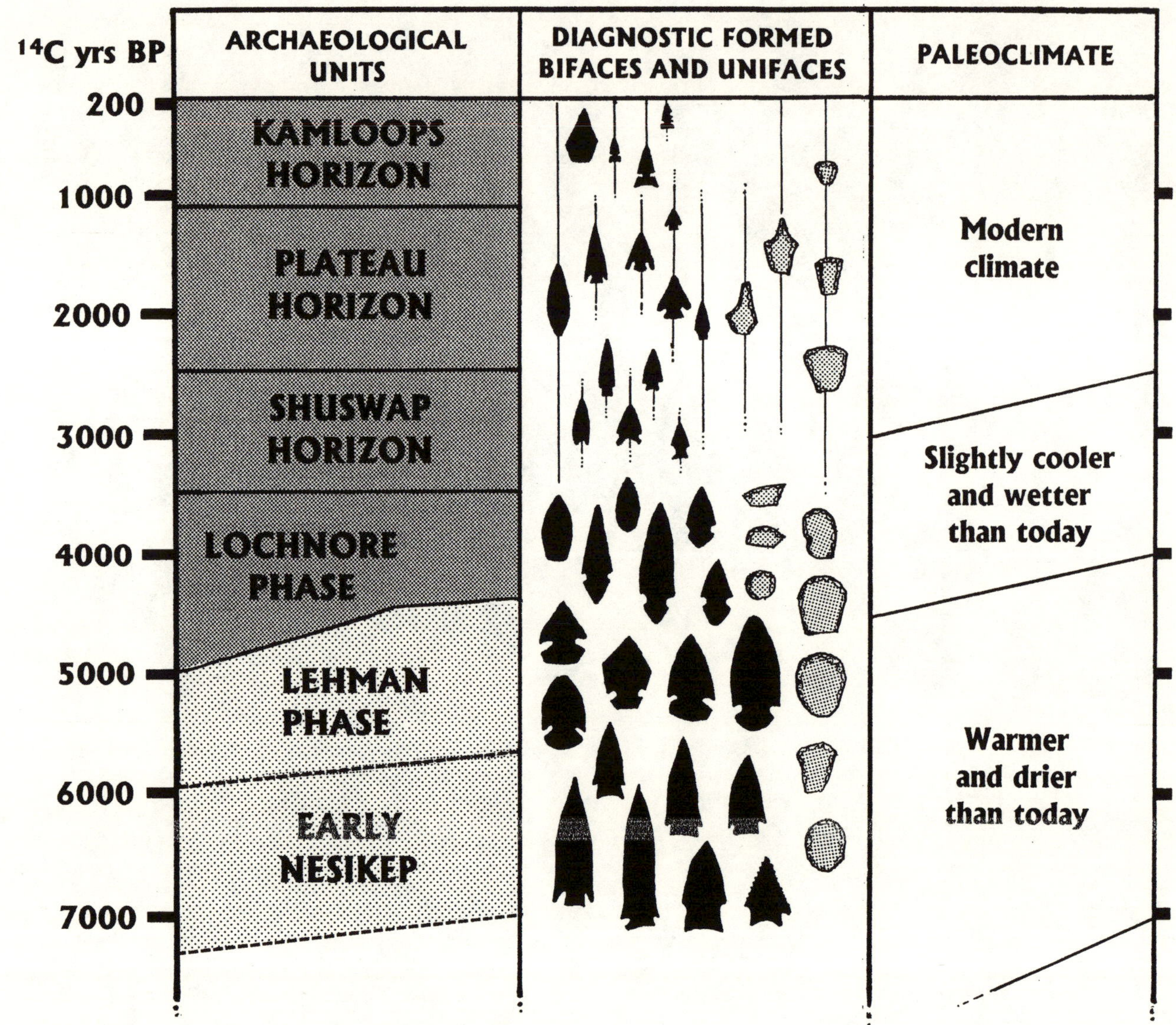

Figure 1.8. Archaeological descriptive units, selected common diagnostic temporal indicator artifacts, and general late Holocene paleoclimatic sequence for the Canadian Plateau.

individuals were common, but regional populations probably rarely exceeded a few hundred souls.

Lehman phase faunal assemblages suggest generalized broad-spectrum opportunistic foraging. There is evidence for emphasis on hunting between about 6000 and 5000 B.P., with elk and deer being preferentially targeted. After 5000 B.P., typical diets shifted to include greater use of salmon, but there is no evidence for intensive salmon consumption or storage for delayed consumption. Freshwater river mussels were collected and consumed along the Thompson and South Thompson river systems. Floral resources were no doubt exploited regularly within residential site catchment areas during daily subsistence routines or while traveling to new locations. They helped offset primary dependence on animal protein and served as "insurance" food alternatives during periods of faunal scarcity (see also Kuijt and Prentiss, this volume; and Lepofsky and Peacock, this volume).

During the Lehman phase, mid-elevation and upland areas were frequented in early spring to exploit spawning nonanadromous fish such as rainbow (Kamloops) trout and suckers. After spring thaw, spawning trout were numerous and were easily harvested at narrows or channels between lakes or in gravely sections of smaller streams where they were easily netted, speared, or clubbed. This abundant and easily harvested protein source would not have been overlooked by mobile, foraging, Lehman phase residential groups, particularly after winter when food was scarce in valley bottoms. Microblades are well suited to cleaning small fish, and their presence in many upland stream and lake contexts may be linked to this activity. Future studies may show that regular intentional spring exploitation of spawning trout began during the Lehman phase and persisted to Euro-Canadian contact.

Lehman phase lithic assemblages often include (1) thin, pentagonal knives/points with obliquely oriented, shallow to very deep V-shaped, U-shaped, corner, or side notches; (2) lanceolate knives with straight cortex-bearing bases; (3) elliptical and leaf-shaped knives (Figure 1.5 [30–52]); (4) tabular circular, oval, and horseshoe-shaped scrapers (Figure 1.6 [14–20]); (5) multidirectional cores with medium to large flake scars; (6) large, thin flake blanks and simple flake tools; (7) unifacially retouched flakes with cortex or steep retouch backing; (8) a high incidence of fine- and medium-grained basalt (dacite); and (9) occasional use of microblade technology. Distinctive *Lehman phase obliquely notched* bifaces (Figure 1.5 [30–52]) (Stryd and Rousseau 1996:189, 194) are diagnostic temporal horizon markers exclusive to Lehman phase occupations and probably functioned both as projectile tips and, most importantly, as knives. Similar bifaces are found during the coeval Cold Springs horizon on the Columbia Plateau, where they are called "Cold Springs Side-Notched points" (Andrefsky, this volume; Womack 1977). A slightly earlier appearance on the Columbia Plateau around 6700 B.P. suggests that this "multipurpose" bifacial tool form may have initially been developed there and was adopted several hundred years later by Lehman phase groups on the Canadian Plateau through direct interaction with southern groups or as a result of interregional information exchange and trait diffusion.

High-quality flakeable lithic materials such as vitreous and fine-grained basalt (dacite) and various silicates from isolated upland sources were in common use during the Lehman phase. Many sites contain unmodified and unused medium-size and large flakes in high densities, indicating that lithic raw materials were abundant in most areas. Major sources of basalt (dacite) and cryptocrystalline silicates around Arrowstone Creek, Cache Creek, and the Hat Creek and Maiden Creek drainages (Leaming 1971; Richards 1988; Rousseau 2000) were known and frequently exploited during subsistence forays.

Presently there is no evidence for use of semisubterranean winter pithouses or any other dwellings. Nevertheless, simple rapidly constructed structures similar to ethnographic "matlodges" or lean-tos may have been used. Such dwelling floors are difficult to identify in the archaeological record, but I suspect that flat or slightly depressed Lehman phase dwelling floors will eventually be encountered. Pithouses were not deemed necessary because it never got cold enough, and their use was contradictory to high residential group mobility.

The Lehman phase adaptive strategy very nicely fits the classic "forager" subsistence and settlement system defined by Binford (1980) and is consistent with that noted for coeval cultures on the Columbia Plateau (Andrefsky, this volume; Chatters 1995a). It seems that even Early Nesikep big game hunters were more organized than Lehman phase people with respect to annual scheduling and movement. In some respects, the Lehman phase can be regarded as a paler version of the Early Nesikep, with most notable differences being a slight decline in lithic technological proficiency and organization and a greater emphasis on nonlocal high-quality lithic materials during the Lehman phase.

The Lehman Phase–Lochnore Phase Transition

The transition from the Lehman phase to the Lochnore phase is a subject of great interest and debate. Between about 5000 and 4500 B.P., the climate was cooler and wetter than it is today, with expanding and lowering pine and Douglas fir forests (Figure 1.8). Highly mobile hunting and opportunistic gathering peoples participating in the latter part of the Lehman phase were confronted by an ever shrinking and lowering grassland habitat with a concomitant expansion of conifer and deciduous forests. How these gradual climatic and environmental changes directly influenced the Lehman phase still remains unclear. This can be partly attributed to the paucity of excavated data from sites dating between 5000 and 4500 B.P.

Several contributory factors were involved in the shift from Lehman phase mobile hunting and intensive foraging to the increased sedentism and greater dependence on a more logistically organized "collector" adaptive pattern characterizing the Lochnore phase. The appearance of small pithouses around 4400 B.P. was not only a direct consequence of, and response to, increased environmental prosperity and resource diversity, abundance, and availability (Kuijt 1989; Kuijt and Prentiss, this volume; Prentiss and Kuijt, this volume); it was also partly caused by greater seasonal climatic variation and external cultural influences originating from coastal regions beginning around 5,000 years ago.

Increasingly cold winters and deeper snowfalls would have eventually reached a critical tolerance level for mobile groups, reducing mobility and necessitating the construction of semipermanent winter dwellings. Shortly after 5000 B.P., intensive foraging in large catchment areas was not productive during winter months. It was more practical to establish semipermanent camps in major valley bottoms near rivers and forest/grassland ecotones where food resources were more abundant, varied, and accessible and snow cover was at its lowest. People of the latter part of the Lehman phase were aware of the existence of, and means to construct, semisubterranean houses, for they were being used as early as 5000 B.P. in the Lower Fraser River region (Matson and Coupland 1995; Ormerod

2002; Schaepe 1998; Sto:lo Nation and Antiquus Archaeological Consultants Ltd. 1999).

Chatters (1989c, 1995a) argues that pithouses were used on the Columbia Plateau during two discrete episodes. "Pithouse I" initially appeared around 4300 B.P., climaxed around 4000 B.P., and ended about 3700 B.P. An apparent hiatus in pithouse use lasting several hundred years was followed by "Pithouse II," which started about 3300 B.P., peaked by 3000 B.P., and ended by 2600 B.P. Chatters (1995a:387–391) comments that the shift from an essentially mobile foraging adaptation to increased semisedentism, use of pithouses, and wide-spectrum food-resource exploitation at the start of Pithouse I around 4400 B.P. can be linked to major climatic and environmental changes. Sharp climatic cooling and greater precipitation increased downslope forest expansion, enhanced biological carrying capacity, and allowed small groups to settle along main waterways near forest fringes where they exploited a variety of resources on a more or less year-round basis within relatively small catchment areas. Chatters also argues that salmon were not an important resource during Pithouse I, and clear evidence for extended food storage is absent. Population growth was rapid, perhaps a result of reduced mobility. He suggests that the switch from foraging to collecting strategies is a ubiquitous, contemporaneous, Plateau-wide phenomenon, and it may be difficult to define it origins and precise causes. In many ways, the overall adaptive strategy described by Chatters for Pithouse I is remarkably similar to that observed for the Lochnore phase and Shuswap horizon (below) on the Canadian Plateau. However, many chronological, behavioral, and material trait disparities are evident between Northern and Southern Plateau subareas.

Several researchers (myself included) maintain that people of terminal Lehman phase times had both direct and indirect contact with people and cultural systems of the South and Central Coast regions between 5000 and 4500 B.P. (Lawhead and Stryd 1985; Lawhead et al. 1986; Stryd and Rousseau 1996). The "Coast Salish incursion model," originally proposed by Lawhead and Stryd (1985), maintains that around 5000 B.P., small, highly mobile groups whose primary winter residency was in the Lower Fraser River and Fraser Canyon regions (and perhaps also the Lower Columbia River region) began venturing upstream and inland along major drainages. Expeditions were routinely dispatched to follow salmon runs, hunt ungulates, and gather freshwater river mussels and edible plants. Such forays were necessary when salmon fishing was poor or when food shortages were experienced or anticipated. Relying on simple, effective, and highly portable technologies developed and refined centuries before on the coast, in late fall these migratory Salish groups returned to permanent winter villages in the Lower Fraser River and Lower Columbia regions.

Direct physical interaction between coastal and Plateau groups between about 5500 and 4500 B.P. resulted in mutually beneficial exchanges of technological traits, knowledge of successful subsistence practices, language, and genetics. Because both groups targeted somewhat different major food sources (salmon by early migratory Lochnore phase people and large ungulates by resident late Lehman phase folks), direct competition for the same major resource(s) was rare or occasional, explaining their apparent 750–1,000-year amicable coexistence as separate cultural entities. The late Lochnore phase (ca. 4500–3500 B.P.) cultural pattern, which includes pithouses, use of sophisticated subsistence technologies, and some scheduled resource collection, represents a mutual acculturation and melding of these two groups. Overall, the Salish incursion model is generally consistent with Elmendorf's (1965) model of Interior Salish origins and migrations based on linguistic considerations.

Alternatively, Prentiss and Kuijt (this volume) and Kuijt and Prentiss (this volume) propose that a seamless cultural and ethnic continuity exists between the Lehman phase and the Lochnore phase, with the latter being directly descended from the former, and the late Lochnore phase being derived from the Columbia Plateau (see also Wilson et al. 1992:189–190). They maintain that differences in material culture traits and patterns of adaptation between these two archaeological entities are not significant enough to infer the existence of any cultural or ethnic disparity. I submit that the differences between them are actually quite marked, particularly with regard to the formal and technological aspects of biface manufacture and use, unifacial scraper forms, the employment of lithic materials, and the presence of edge-ground discoidal cobbles and pebble tools in Lochnore phase components (see below). It could also be argued that these two distinctive assemblage patternings reflect two sets of different activities engaged in by a single group. I submit that this explanation has little merit, for both assemblages are too dissimilar in content and are sometimes found together as discrete alternating occupation episodes at the same site (see Lawhead and Stryd 1985).

Collectively considered, transition from the Lehman phase of the Nesikep tradition to the Lochnore phase can be attributed to several causes. These include (1) the seasonal incursion of Coast Salish peoples and exchange of information, materials, language, and genetics with Lehman phase people; (2) intercultural (Coast–Plateau) exchange of technologies and subsistence practices, which led to greater logistical collecting behavior in interior regions; (3) a prolific, abundant, and varied food-resource base available at this time; and (4) the increasingly cooler climate, with greater seasonal variation and deepening snow falls starting around 5000 B.P., which seriously curtailed winter movement and necessitated the construction and use of simple, shallow pithouses around 4500 B.P.

PLATEAU PITHOUSE TRADITION (CA. 4500–200 B.P.)

The Plateau Pithouse tradition (PPt) was originally defined by Richards and Rousseau (1982, 1987) on the basis of similarities evident among three late cultural horizons represented in the Fraser and Thompson river drainages. Initially, the PPt included the Shuswap horizon (ca. 3500–2400 B.P.), Plateau horizon (2400–1200 B.P.), and Kamloops horizon (1200–200 B.P.) (Figure 1.9). Subsequent excavations at the Baker site (EdQx 43) near Monte Creek in the South Thompson River valley (Wilson 1991; Wilson et al. 1992) encountered two small buried oval housepit depressions, providing ^{14}C dates between about 4200 and 4450 B.P., corresponding with the middle of the Lochnore phase (below).

EdQx 43 provides the earliest dated pithouses on the Canadian Plateau, confirming their use by about 4400 B.P. This is commensurate with the Columbia Plateau, where most early housepits date to about the same time (Andrefsky, this volume; Chatters 1989c, 1995a, this volume). Because pithouses were in use, there was almost certainly some food storage and delayed consumption being practiced midway through the Lochnore phase, and the site occupants were very probably Interior Salish, this site and the latter half of the Lochnore phase have been included in the PPt (Stryd and Rousseau 1996). Given identification of 5,000-year-old housepits in the Lower Fraser River region (Ormerod 2002; Schaepe 1998; Sto:lo Nation and Antiquus Archaeological Consultants Ltd. 1999) and on the Columbia Plateau (Andrefsky, this volume), I am confident that similar early housepits with evidence for some preparation and storage of salmon and other delayed consumables will eventually be found on the Canadian Plateau.

As redefined by Stryd and Rousseau (1996), the PPt now includes the Lochnore phase (ca. 5000–3500 B.P.) and Shuswap, Plateau, and Kamloops horizons (Richards and Rousseau 1987). The PPt is characterized by a lifeway generally similar to that described for the ethnographic Interior Salish, and its salient aspects are the use of semisubterranean pithouses in seasonal (winter) or semipermanent villages; some degree of semisedentism and occasional or full-time participation in logistically organized, seasonally scheduled subsistence and settlement strategies; a hunting and gathering subsistence mode with emphasis on salmon fishing; and the use of food-storage technology and facilities (i.e., drying racks, pits, scaffolds). The emergence and persistence of PPt lifeways constitute a dynamic and evolving cultural continuum, with all the major archaeological units within it representing periods of relative adaptive stability separable by punctuated periods of rapid change.

Lochnore Phase (ca. 5000–3500 B.P.)

Sometime between 5000 and 4500 B.P. there was gradual change from conditions warmer and drier than those at present to those that were significantly cooler and wetter by 3500 B.P. (Hebda 1982; Mathewes 1985; Mathewes and King 1989). This climatic episode corresponds with a major Neoglacial event that climaxed around 3300 B.P. and ended sometime around 2500 B.P., when more or less modern conditions were established (Figures 1.8–1.9). Details about the specific effects that this climatic change had on various aspects of the local environments, ecosystems, and cultural patterns during this time are not yet entirely clear, but as Kuijt (1989; Kuijt and Prentiss, this volume; Prentiss and Kuijt, this volume) correctly points out, its impact was major.

Residential and field camps were often small to medium sized and fairly deeply buried, and they suggest relatively short-term occupation episodes with medium- to high-density scatters of lithics, bone, and freshwater river mussel shells. Many sites lie on the edges of flat upper river terraces along the sides of main river valley bottoms, especially at or near junctures of major tributary creek valleys. Some larger residential sites indicate repeated occupations. Field camps have also been identified in mid-altitude valley contexts beside small lakes and streams and suggest occupation by small groups (10–20 people) for short periods.

Distinctive lithic artifacts and technological traits of the Lochnore phase include (1) large and medium-sized, lanceolate, leaf-shaped, formed bifacial points/knives with wide, shallow to moderately deep opposing side notches, heavy basal edge grinding, and pointed or convex bases (i.e., *Lochnore side-notched point*) (Figure 1.7 [1–9]); (2) unnotched leaf-shaped and bipointed bifaces (Figure 1.7 [10–14]); (3) foliate bifaces with straight or slightly convex basal margins; (4) oval bifaces; (5) small and medium-sized, round and oval, continuously retouched formed unifacial scrapers on thick flakes (e.g., Figure 1.6 [18–22]); (6) concave-edged, cryptocrystalline silica end scrapers; (7) end or side scrapers; (8) microblade technology (at some sites); (9) unifacially retouched backed flake scrapers; (10) flake scrapers with an oblique straight scraping edge; (11) edge-battered, ground, and abraded cobbles; (12) unifacial pebble tools/choppers; (13) notched flat pebbles (net sinkers); and (14) the predominant use of medium-grained to vitreous basalts (dacites) with some use of exotic silicates and, rarely, obsidian. Bone and antler items include bone splinter unipoints (fishhook barbs), antler flakers, antler wedges, unilaterally barbed antler points, worked rodent incisors, drilled animal

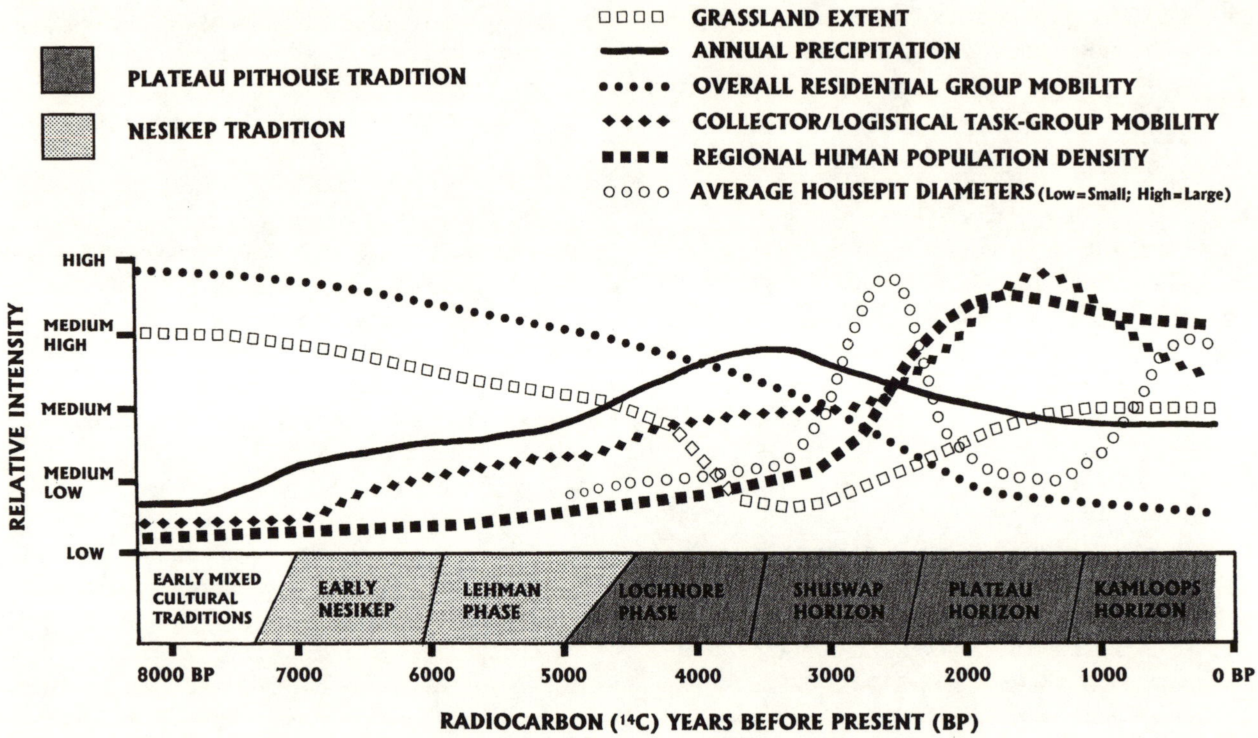

Figure 1.9. Schematic modeling of relative intensities or magnitudes of important climatic events and conditions, important human behaviors, and relative population densities on the Canadian Plateau for the last 8,000 years.

tooth and eagle claw pendants, and marine shell beads. The barbed points and marine shells attest to some kind of interaction with coastal peoples, notably those participating in the Charles culture or Eayem phase cultural system of the Lower Fraser River (Borden 1968; Carlson 1983b; Fladmark 1982; Haley 1996; Matson and Coupland 1995; Mitchell 1990).

Microblade technology is not found in all components, but in some blades number in the hundreds. Around the end of this phase (ca. 4000–3500 B.P.), microblade technology made a conspicuous exit from the Canadian Plateau archaeological record. Whether its discontinuation was abrupt or gradual remains to be shown, but it is evident that this specialized technological system was abandoned with the onset of increased semisedentism, a greater reliance on collected stored food, and scheduled seasonal resource exploitation at about 3500 B.P. This is not surprising, for microblade technology was most practical for people engaged in high mobility and opportunistic foraging. That people living on the Canadian Plateau after 3500 B.P. were not aware of this technology is very unlikely; they simply had no use for it.

Faunal assemblages attest that Lochnore phase peoples practiced a generalized, opportunistic, broad-spectrum subsistence strategy. Included are remains of deer, elk, beaver, migratory fowl, anadromous salmonids, turtles, and freshwater mussels. There is no direct evidence for intensive consumption of anadromous salmon during this phase, but it may have been fairly high given associated proficient fishing technology. The Lochnore phase cultural and adaptive pattern best fits the "forager" description, but undoubtedly some foods (e.g., dried salmon and edible plants) were stored for delayed consumption on a regular basis. An apparent lack of food storage pits may be caused by sampling bias, or perhaps above-ground wooden storage scaffolds similar to those used by Plains groups may have been used.

Mid and latter parts of the Lochnore phase share several commonalities with Chatters's (1995a) Pithouse I period on the Columbia Plateau. These include (1) coincident starting dates of circa 4500 B.P., (2) small dwellings in low numbers at sites consistently established in resource-rich and diverse areas, (3) a primarily broad-spectrum opportunistic foraging subsistence strategy, (4) formal and technological similarities in bifaces, and (5) wedge-core microblade technology. Pithouse I can be linked to major climatic and environmental changes. Sharp climatic cooling and greater precipitation increased downslope forest expansion, enhanced biological carrying capacity, and allowed small groups to settle along main waterways near forest fringes where they exploited a variety of resources on a more or less year-round basis within relatively small catchment areas. Chatters also offers that salmon were not a primary protein source during Pithouse I, and clear evidence for extended food storage is absent. Population growth was rapid, perhaps a result of reduced mobility. Although Chatters observes a hiatus in pithouse use from about 3700 to 3400 B.P., in my opinion, the current dearth of Lochnore phase data does not yet confirm a similar break on the Canadian Plateau. Other viewpoints are presented by Prentiss and Kuijt (this volume).

Shuswap Horizon (ca. 3500–2400 B.P.)

The Shuswap horizon began shortly after 3500 B.P. when cool and wet conditions reached their maximum. At this time increased precipitation enhanced the rearing and spawning habitat for anadromous salmonids (see also Chatters 1995a; Kuijt 1989). Also, delta ^{13}C isotope analyses indicate an increase in salmon consumption along major rivers (Chisholm 1986). Grasslands were at their absolute minimum, forcing large ungulates (deer, elk, moose) to subsist at the bottoms or sides of river valleys and their tributaries. Maximum forest expansion provided an ideal habitat for a wide variety of forest-dwelling animals and plants. The Shuswap horizon ended about 2400 B.P. when a warmer and drier climate similar to that of today was established (Hebda 1982, 1995).

At the onset of the Shuswap horizon, there was a rapid shift from the moderately mobile, seasonally sedentary, foraging and occasional collecting ways of the Lochnore phase to a more logistically organized collector adaptation with some food storage and regular winter residency in pithouses. Low population stress on valley bottoms allowed the adoption of a strategy emphasizing both foraging and scheduled collecting, for a wide selection of readily accessible resource options was available.

The Shuswap horizon was a time of plenty, allowing comfortable subsistence within small catchment areas (e.g., 5 km^2) on valley floors, along side tributaries, and sometimes in mid-altitude areas (Wyatt 1972). Small, moderately mobile bands established winter residential base camps on valley bottoms where food and material resources were abundant and varied. While most winter village catchment areas could support one or two extended families during their stay, serious unforeseen food depletions could be offset by moving to another resource-rich area. There is currently no direct evidence for root-roasting pits, digging stick handles, carbonized floral remains, or any upland or valley bottom intensive floral-resource exploitation. Nevertheless, a very broad range of plant resources was available and routinely collected.

Residential group mobility steadily decreased throughout the Shuswap horizon. This trend corresponds with lessening precipitation, a rise in seasonal temperatures, and the growing frequency of small task-specific groups being dispatched from main villages. Intimate familiarity with local environments gained over many generations included an awareness of where and when certain important food resources were available. As Chatters (1995a) also suggests, steps toward reorganizing "immediate-consumption" subsistence strategies toward a collector or "delayed-consumption" pattern were probably initiated at larger villages where food stresses were common because of constant population growth and reduced child mortality. Extrapithouse salmon storage in pits is not evident, but food storage and refuse pits in house floors have yielded abundant salmon remains (Richards and Rousseau 1982). It seems that intensive salmon drying and storage were unnecessary during much of the Shuswap horizon. A wide variety of other animal food resources was also taken (Richards and Rousseau 1987:29), and there is ample evidence for heavy reliance on meat.

Shuswap horizon regional populations increased slightly relative to the population of the preceding Lochnore phase, with about two–five sites containing from three to ten pithouses in most major valley systems. Growth seems to have been most dramatic from 3000 to 2400 B.P., eventually climaxing during the Plateau horizon (Figure 1.8).

Salient Shuswap horizon characteristics include (1) small seasonal residential sites sparsely distributed in resource-rich valley bottoms, (2) brief occupational episodes (several months) with subsequent reoccupation being uncommon, (3) faunal remains indicating a wide spectrum of local species, (4) a lack of evidence for any heavy reliance on stored food, (5) use of lithic raw materials found near winter villages and field camps, and (6) less overall tool curation behavior than is evident for later horizons. Other Shuswap horizon traits include (1) a variety of stemmed, basally indented and corner-removed projectile point styles (Figure 1.7 [18–34]) (Richards and Rousseau 1987:26); (2) key-shaped formed unifaces (Rousseau 1992); (3) small "thumbnail" scrapers and convex-edged hide scrapers with straight, proximally tapered lateral margins; (4) split-cobble scraping tools; (5) high frequencies of utilized and unifacially retouched flake tools; (6) lithic assemblages that indicate simplicity in composition and moderate levels of technological proficiency; (7) a fairly heavy reliance on the use of locally obtained, fair- to good-quality lithic raw materials (e.g., basalts, dacites, quartzites, siltstones, and rhyolite); (8) well-developed bone and antler technology; and (9) flexed burials in pits within housepit floors. Additional trait information is presented by Richards and Rousseau (1982, 1987:25–31; Rousseau and Richards 1985).

Projectile point forms are similar to Oxbow and McKean-Hanna-Duncan complex atlatl points found during the Middle period on the Northern Plains (Reeves 1969, 1983; Richards and Rousseau 1987:30–31; Vickers 1986). This suggests that during the Shuswap horizon, some form of direct or indirect interaction occurred with Plains groups, inciting adoption of Plains point styles and possibly other traits. Early housepit sites near Banff in the

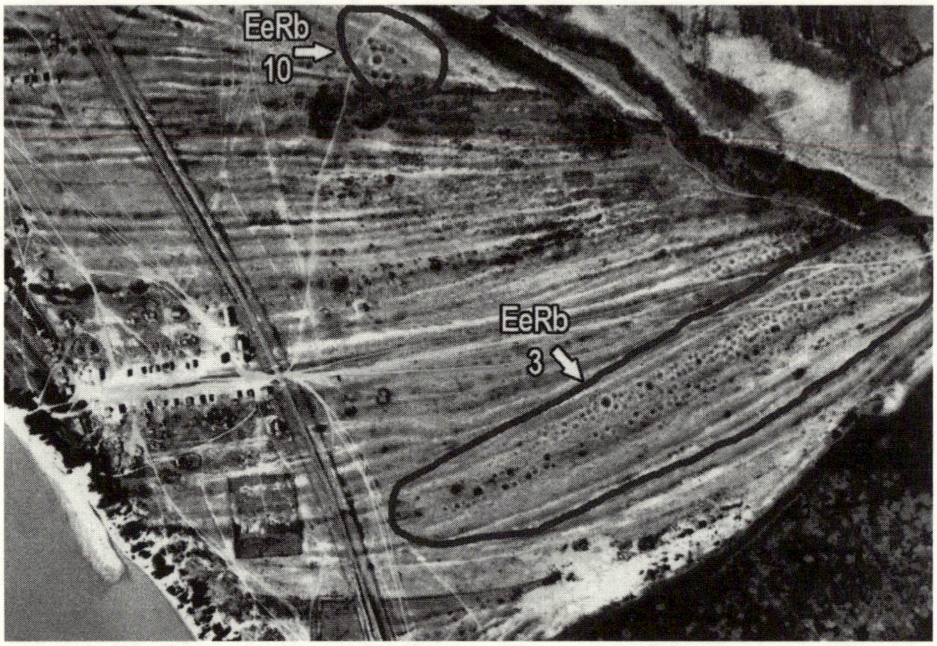

Figure 1.10. A 1920s aerial photo showing large housepits at the small Shuswap Horizon (ca. 3500–2400 B.P.) site EeRb 10 and approximately 100 mostly small housepits at the significantly larger Plateau Horizon (ca. 2400–1200 B.P.) site EeRb 3 nearby at the confluence of the North and South Thompson rivers at Kamloops. These sites no longer exist. EeRb 3 was a major settlement focus from 2200 to 1500 B.P., and its inhabitants were active participants in organized interregional exchange systems and full-blown logistical collector subsistence and settlement strategies.

Rocky Mountains (Langemann 1998, 2002; Langemann and Perry 2002) further attest that Shuswap horizon groups occasionally visited and wintered on the western fringe of the Northern Plains.

The majority of identified Shuswap horizon pithouse sites lie in main valley bottoms or their tributaries beside or near rivers, streams, and large lakes. The villages are relatively small when compared with those of later horizons (Figure 1.10). Pithouses were quite large, averaging 11 m and ranging from 7.5 to 16 m in diameter, and were often deep (up to 2 m). Most lack obvious peripheral heaped rims. Big houses were practical for moderately mobile groups, for they required less time and energy to construct than numerous smaller houses better suited for nuclear families or individuals.

Sometime around 3200 B.P., Mt. St. Helens erupted, depositing ash over most of the Plateau. The effects of this eruption on people during the beginning of the Shuswap horizon were likely similar to those experienced by people of the Early Nesikep with the eruption of Mt. Mazama. It was an abrupt event with some loss of life, but the effects on the regional environments and human adaptive patterns were of minor consequence and short-lived.

Low regional populations suggest that it was unlikely that any sort of formal "elite" or "corporate" group behavior existed during this horizon. Such groups arise under conditions of much greater population density and when important resource acquisition, control, and distribution become necessary to cope with food shortages or technological demands involving large quantities of expendable materials (Hayden 1997, 2000b; Hayden and Adams, this volume; Hayden and Schulting 1997).

On the Columbia Plateau, Chatters (1995a:389, this volume) notes that an abrupt reappearance of pithouses (Pithouse II) around 3500 B.P. was accompanied by the rapid emergence of intensified logistical "collector" behavior, extensive reliance on salmon, and the development and eventual extensive use of food-storage technology. This general pattern is consistent with data gathered for the Shuswap horizon. Efficient harvesting and storage of salmon for later consumption allowed spatial resource inequalities or food shortages to be offset during leaner months, thus sustaining steady population growth. This led to the eventual development of and participation in a logistically organized "full-blown" collector lifestyle at the beginning of the Plateau horizon around 2400 B.P.

Plateau Horizon (2400–1200 B.P.)

Between about 3000 and 2500 B.P., cool and moist conditions gradually changed to warm and dry conditions similar to those of today (Hebda 1982, 1995). Some researchers (Hallett et al. 2003a; Lepofsky and Peacock, this volume) maintain that from 2400 to 1200 B.P., the climate may have been slightly warmer and drier than it is at present. Shortly after 2500 B.P., there were major rapid changes in many aspects of material culture and subsistence and settlement, marking the onset of the Plateau horizon, the period of greatest aboriginal population density on the Canadian Plateau.

Although Plateau horizon pithouse village sizes vary, most were much larger than those of the Shuswap horizon, with up to 100 houses at some sites in the Kamloops (Figure 1.10) and Lillooet localities (Hayden 1997, 2000a, 2000b; Wilson 1980). Larger villages indicate continuous reoccupation over long periods and were situated in resource-rich areas at or near major salmon fisheries and locations where important floral resources were prolific (see Lepofsky and Peacock, this volume). Numerous steep-sided food-storage pit features averaging 1–2 m in diameter by 1.5 m deep are common within winter village confines or clustered nearby.

Small field camps and resource-extraction locations have been identified and investigated in mid- and upland environments (Figure 1.11) (Pokotylo and Froese 1983; Rousseau and Howe 1987; Rousseau et al. 1991). Intensive root exploitation is clearly evident (Lepofsky and Peacock, this volume; Peacock 1998), and digging stick handles appear in the archaeological record at the start of this horizon. Wide site-type variability suggests that numerous economic activities were executed by specialized task groups. Task-specific items such as digging stick handles, key-shaped unifaces (Rousseau 1992), well-made bifacial tools, and unifacial scraping tools are common in Plateau horizon components. These indicate a high incidence of curational behavior, a practice regarded to be an important component of logistically organized collector subsistence strategies (Bamforth 1986; Bleed 1986; Kuhn 1994; Torrence 1983, 1989).

Typical Plateau horizon housepits range from 4 to 8 m in diameter with a mean of 6 m. Most are fairly deep, are circular to oval in plan, and lack raised earth rims. An exception is the Mid-Fraser River region, where housepit diameters range from 8 to 20 m and average 10 m. In contrast to the large pithouses of the preceding Shuswap horizon, there was a widespread shift to smaller houses during the Plateau horizon because of several factors. First, population growth was rapid, which imposed overharvesting stresses that negatively affected availability, abundance, and the regeneration of major local and upland food resources. This would have promoted and encouraged nuclear families (five–ten people) as the basic economic and social unit, for they are much easier to maintain than larger extended-family groups.

Second, increased residential sedentism, exemplified by large semipermanent and permanent villages during the population maximum from 2000 to 1600 B.P., made it practical to live in more private, nuclear family-sized dwellings. These people preferred smaller houses because they provided greater personal privacy and helped reduce the incidence of interpersonal tensions and conflicts common to larger residential groups. Small houses are also easier to construct and maintain and require less fuel to heat.

Plateau horizon mortuary practices are poorly known, but some excavated and incidentally encountered data are available (Richards and Rousseau 1987:38–39; Schulting 1995). Cremation was a common mode of treatment either before or during interment. It was particularly practical in large communities where mortality was frequent.

Proficiency and excellence in lithic-reduction and tool production techniques, a well-developed bone and antler technology, and the development of an Interior Plateau art tradition during this horizon (Stryd 1983) all indicate craft specialization, notably in Mid-Fraser and South Thompson river regions. Whether specialists were influenced by powerful community members or were motivated by the benefits to be reaped by entrepreneurial ventures remains unresolved.

Projectile points are typically barbed with either corner or basal notches (Figure 1.7 [35–68]). Basally notched forms are common from circa 2400 to 2000 B.P.; and corner-notched forms, from circa 2000 to 1200 B.P. Rare leaf-shaped and stemmed points are also present. A progressive reduction in point size is evident during this horizon, particularly after 1600 B.P. Convex-edged chipped-stone end scrapers and "key-shaped" unifaces (Rousseau 1992) are more common during this horizon than in the preceding Shuswap horizon.

An important technological development during the Plateau horizon was the adoption of bow and arrow technology. It was clearly in use on the Northern Plains by about 1700 B.P. (Vickers 1986), spreading westward onto the Canadian Plateau sometime around 1500 B.P. (Richards and Rousseau 1987:34) and into the Great Basin by 1350 B.P. (Bettinger and Eerkens 1999). Chatters (this volume) argues for a 2000 B.P. introduction on the Columbia Plateau but notes that it was not commonly used until several centuries later. This technology is hallmarked by the appearance of small (< 3 cm in length and < 1 cm in neck width), triangular, corner-notched point forms (Figure 1.7 [59–68]). Their appearance corresponds with a steady decline in larger atlatl dart points from 1500 to 1200 B.P., suggesting that the atlatl was used concurrently with the bow and arrow for several hundred years but was phased out shortly after 1200 B.P. Almost exclusive use of the bow and arrow after 1200 B.P. substantially enhanced the ability of people to harvest terrestrial fauna, thereby alleviating intensive exploitation of mid- and high-altitude plant resources and reducing the need to dispatch task groups to do so (see Chatters, this volume). Its regular use resulted in the

Figure 1.11. View of the Upper Hat Creek Valley, looking southwest. Located between Cache Creek and Lillooet, it has been subjected to detailed site surveys and excavations. It is one of several areas in mid-altitude contexts where root foods and other important food plants were gathered and processed in earth ovens from 2400 to 1000 B.P.

major reorganization of hunting strategies during the latter part of the Plateau horizon and lessened the time required for successful hunts. This allowed more time to devote to pursuits relating to art, ceremonialism, and social elaboration.

Many Plateau horizon chipped-stone assemblages contain much higher proportions of good-quality lithic raw materials (e.g., vitreous basalt [dacite], cryptocrystalline silicates, and, rarely, obsidian) compared with previous Shuswap horizon and later Kamloops horizon occupations. There are two main reasons for this. First, intensive resource-procurement activities in mid- and high-altitude areas resulted in the discovery of quarries with high-quality silicates, and regular visits to these sources were embedded into seasonal food forays (see Binford 1979). Second, superior durability and edge longevity provided by these silicates were desirable to people engaging in highly logistical collecting strategies because they could be made into efficient, reliable, and easily maintained tools. For task groups targeting specific resources distant to residential villages, such tools would have been important and necessary inclusions in personal toolkits (Andrefsky 1994; Bamforth 1986; Bleed 1986; Rousseau 1992; Torrence 1983, 1989).

At the onset of the Plateau horizon, the "Plateau Interaction Sphere" (PIS) (Hayden and Schulting 1997) developed and spread, an event coincident with the start of the Marpole phase cultural florescence in the Lower Fraser River and Gulf of Georgia regions (Burley 1980; Carlson 1983b, 1996; Fladmark 1982; Matson and Coupland 1995; Mitchell 1971, 1990). Hayden and Schulting offer that the PIS owes its emergence to the development of an elite class seeking to maximize power, wealth, and access to prestige goods by establishing and maintaining socioeconomic ties with neighboring elites on the Northwest Coast. While focused on communities in the Lillooet and Lytton localities of the Mid-Fraser and Lower Fraser river regions, their discussion does not mention the involvement of large populations around Kamloops and along the South Thompson River.

In contrast, I argue that the PIS developed primarily out of a conscious collective need to establish and maintain interregional movement of important food and raw materials such as dried salmon and meat, root plants, nephrite (Darwent 1998), and high-quality lithic materials (Choquette 1981; Leaming 1971; Rousseau 2000). Nephrite and "jadeite" celts (adze blades) were used extensively by coastal groups for woodworking tasks. Steatite was also of interest for the manufacture of pipes, bowls, and small ornaments and sculptures (Blake, this volume). Ceremonial, prestige, decorative, personal, and art objects may have acted as "systemic regulators" to ensure that food-exchange networks were maintained and important consumables were distributed as needed throughout the Canadian Plateau and Lower Fraser and Gulf of Georgia regions. Hayden and Schulting submit that nephrite celt manufacture is possibly indicative of slavery because it is labor and time intensive. I offer that the personal economic rewards gained by making unfinished blanks or completed celts and involving them in exchange systems with coastal groups were sufficient to encourage willing participation in this endeavor.

Did the impetus for the development and maintenance of the PIS grow out of the conscious need for certain individuals or families to establish themselves as a wealthy elite, or was it an insurance or "risk-pooling" mechanism (Weissner 1982) promulgated by independent, self-motivated, entrepreneurial members of major communities to help ever-growing populations offset local food and material shortages during difficult periods? As hunger and personal gratification are powerful motivators, I suspect the latter. It is logical that once formal interregional exchange became established, a regulatory "elite" involving certain families would have emerged and evolved from it.

When compared with the numbers during earlier and later horizons, regional populations were greatest during the Plateau horizon. This is inferred from the presence of many large winter village sites, extensive and intensive use of upland resources, and the high frequency of observed Plateau horizon sites. Data suggest that populations were most dense between about 2000 and 1600 B.P. Feeding these populations imposed considerable harvesting stress on valley floors and sides that was compensated to some extent by expanding the repertoire of resource options and by intensifying the use of secondary foods, such as mid- and high-altitude edible roots and berries (see Lepofsky and Peacock, this volume) and upland game.

It is during this horizon that medium-sized stocky dogs appear in the archaeological record on both the Plateau and the Northwest Coast (Crellin 1994, Crellin and Heffner 2000, Crockford and Pye 1997). Beyond providing companionship and protection, dogs assisted in hunting, served as pack animals, and helped dispose of unwanted domestic waste in villages. In the Mid-Fraser River region, dogs regularly transported huge quantities of salmon hundreds of meters up steep valley sides to winter villages. Pack dogs were very valuable to people participating in a "collector"-type subsistence pattern and delayed-consumption food storage because they would repeatedly transport heavy loads and are more easily motivated than people for this task. Dogs also assisted in amassing and conveying food and other material surpluses for intra- and interregional exchange.

In sum, the Plateau horizon saw a fairly steady and rapid population growth that climaxed around 2000 B.P., intensive seasonal mid- and high-altitude resource procurement, low residential group mobility during winter months, high task group mobility, and a collector subsistence and settlement pattern that was more logistically organized than in preceding Shuswap and later Kamloops horizons (Figure 1.8). The Plateau horizon truly represents the maximum florescence of Canadian Plateau hunter-gatherer-fisher cultures, and importantly, it was coincident with a similar peak in cultural development during the Marpole phase on the South Coast (Burley 1980; R. Carlson 1996; Fladmark 1982; Mitchell 1971, 1990).

Kamloops Horizon (1200–200 B.P.)

Some important aspects of subsistence and settlement remained constant or similar during the Plateau and Kamloops horizons, including (1) a highly logistically organized subsistence and settlement strategy, (2) the continued permanent and semipermanent occupation of medium-sized and large winter pithouse villages, (3) the use of upland base camps in locations proximal to major food resources, (4) the continued extensive use of mid-altitude and upland plant resources (especially during the first 200 years), (5) a heavy reliance on salmon supplemented by deer and small animals, (6) active participation in well-developed interregional exchange networks, and (7) the continuation of a unique Plateau art tradition (Stryd 1983). Outstanding differences include (1) the use of medium-size and large housepits with a variety of floor plan configurations; (2) the appearance and persistence of "Kamloops side-notched" arrow points (Figure 1.7 [69–84]) and complete absence of small corner-notched point forms after 1000 B.P.; (3) significant elaboration in mobile art and the decoration of utilitarian items; (4) a marked decline in the frequency and intensity of the exploitation of upland plant resources (Lepofsky and Peacock, this volume; Peacock 1998); and (5) a widespread reduction in regional populations densities, particularly after 1000 B.P. (Hayden and Ryder 1991; Kuijt and Prentiss, this volume).

Housepit diameters range from 6 to 20 m, with a mean of 8.5 m. They are either oval, circular, rectangular, or square in plan and often have prominent or fairly well-defined raised peripheral earth rims (Figure 1.12). Side entrances are sometimes evident. Many have bowl-shaped, saucer-shaped, or basin-shaped interiors, and depths vary from 0.1 to 1.5 m. A return to medium-sized and large pithouses may again reflect extended family groups constructing and occupying a single residence. This is consistent with ethnographic accounts of winter residential behavior (Alexander 2000; Teit 1900, 1909). Larger houses were used by families with many members or possibly by wealthy elite corporate groups (Hayden 1992b, 1997, 2000a, 2000b; Hayden et al. 1985). Variation in house sizes during the PPt probably simply reflects the relative number of people in a close-knit family or economic group, intended duration of occupation, and availability of suitable construction materials.

In warmer months, matlodge dwellings ranging from 4 to 7 m in diameter were erected in upland locations proximal to important seasonal food resources and water

Figure 1.12. Typical Kamloops Horizon housepits beside the Stein River near its confluence with the Fraser River, looking south. Note the circular plan, well-defined heaped rim, peripheral storage and earth oven pit depressions, and past and recent evidence for pot-hunting activity. These housepits no longer exist.

(Alexander 1992:135; Ray 1939:137–140; Teit 1900: 195–196, 1909:494). These temporary dwellings were used during the Kamloops horizon, but identification of their floors is difficult because little or no intentional soil displacement was involved in construction. Excavated matlodge depressions at Botanie Lake near Lytton (Antiquus Archaeological Consultants Ltd. 1999) yielded an assemblage resulting from the production and resharpening of flake tools used to harvest and process abundant plant food resources (Turner et al. 1990:15). It is not known when matlodges were first used on the Canadian Plateau, but it may have been during the Lochnore phase, with their use persisting through the PPt until Euro-Canadian contact in the mid-1800s.

Projectile points are typically small, triangular, side-notched forms known as "Kamloops side-notched" points (Figure 1.7 [69–84]). Larger points of identical style are also occasionally found. Multinotched variants with two or more deep, narrow, U-shaped notches along one lateral blade margin (Figure 1.7 [75–77, 84]) and occasional large side-notched specimens appear in the last 400 years of this horizon. A variety of formed chipped-stone tools is common, including well-made formed scrapers, gravers, and perforators. Of note are distinctive pentagonal formed bifaces (Figure 1.9), which are exclusive to the Kamloops horizon. "Key-shaped" unifaces (Figure 1.9) are absent after about 1000 B.P. (Rousseau 1992).

Kamloops horizon burial practices varied widely, particularly during the last 500 years. The dominant pattern is primary flexed interments in unmarked shallow pits. Others include wooden cist inhumations marked with cobble cairns, multiple "tomb" burials along sandy ridges, talus slope burials, and graves with fires built over them (Dawson 1891; Pokotylo et al. 1987; Richards and Rousseau 1987; Sanger 1968a, 1968c; Schulting 1995; Skinner and Copp 1986; Smith 1900).

Groups participating in the Kamloops horizon were clearly engaged in a "collector"-type subsistence and settlement strategy, but they appear to have been less logistically organized than people of the preceding Plateau horizon. While organized task-specific forays into mid- and upland areas to harvest floral, faunal, and lithic resources continued to be important, the need to initiate such expeditions declined. This is indicated by fewer and smaller Kamloops horizon field camps and root-processing oven sites in uplands where Plateau horizon sites are more common and much larger.

Climatic conditions have been somewhat similar over the last 2,500 years on the Canadian Plateau (Hebda 1982; Mathewes 1985; Mathewes and King 1989), thus significant cultural changes evident between about 1,200 and 1,000 years ago cannot be blamed on any major climatic or paleoenvironmental changes. Hayden and Ryder have postulated that the Texas Creek landslide 16 km south of Lillooet blocked the Fraser River 1,200–1,000 years ago, significantly reducing salmon runs, which led to abandonment of the Mid-Fraser River region (Hayden and Ryder 1991, 2003). There are no radiocarbon dates for either main slide event (Ryder et al. 1990). Kuijt (2001) has questioned this model, arguing that the slide events predate 4200 B.P. based on excavations at site EeRl 171, which is now only 30 m above the Fraser River (Richards 1978). I concur with Kuijt that there is no direct evidence for a major flooding event or short-term lake that might have affected local populations in the Lillooet locality. The reduction of populations around 1000 B.P. was characteristic of many regions of the Canadian Plateau.

Alternate models explicating apparent population decline on the Canadian Plateau around 1000 B.P. remain to be rigorously explored. One hypothesis is that earlier Plateau horizon people were so heavily dependent on mid-altitude and upland resources that relentless harvesting stress between about 2000 and 1200 B.P. gradually reduced the distribution and quantity of important plants and animals (see Kuijt and Prentiss, this volume; Lepofsky and Peacock, this volume). Some species may have been completely extirpated in some regions (e.g., elk). Bow and arrow technology certainly had a serious impact on deer populations between 1500 and 1200 B.P. and may have played a major role in animal depletion. Overharvesting stresses imposed in lowland areas adjacent to main villages would have rendered food resources to critically low levels. If the maximum human carrying capacity of Canadian Plateau environments was exceeded, and terrestrial food resources became scarce, then it stands that human populations would have declined as a result.

Along a similar vein, another possible explanation for population decline may be related to long-term changes in salmon ecology and habitat. Salmon runs can be either destroyed or seriously impaired and disrupted by large landslides blocking major rivers, extended periods of extreme drought that affect reproductive and rearing habitats, overharvesting, and fatal contagious piscine disease. Assuming that people would ingest less salmon during the period of scarcity than before and after, then the relative proportion of marine protein in their skeletons would indicate this. Delta ^{13}C isotope analyses conducted by Chisholm (1986) do not indicate any obvious proportional differences or discontinuity between 1200 and 700 B.P. Prehistoric overexploitation of salmon is an unlikely scenario, but harvesting pressure imposed on naturally weakened salmon populations would have only made matters worse.

Marked reduction in human populations throughout the Plateau between 1200 and 1000 B.P. could also have been caused by a highly contagious fatal biological pathogen that caused a widespread epidemic. The devastating effect on Native populations during the smallpox epidemic of the mid-1860s (Teit 1900:175–177) clearly indicates that virulent and potentially deadly communicable diseases can rapidly infect and kill many people over vast areas, especially along major travel routes. The existence and effects of any prehistoric epidemics remain to be identified in the archaeological record or in oral histories on the Canadian Plateau. However, there are many examples documented in world histories (Diamond 1992, 1997).

The reduced use of upland plant and animal resources during the Kamloops horizon may also be attributed to the adoption of bow and arrow technology, as it enabled people to refocus their attention on previously unattainable protein resources (e.g., deer, birds, hare, and other small animals) available on valley bottoms near permanent villages. This would have negated a need to maintain continued intensive reliance on upland resources to supplement dietary needs and offset food shortages. Presently, excavated Kamloops horizon assemblages lack any clear evidence for major changes or improvements in fishing technology compared with that available during the Plateau horizon, but any such technological advancement could certainly contribute to changes in or the reorganization of subsistence routines.

We have more data on the Kamloops horizon than on any other archaeological unit, and yet a great deal remains to be learned. By all standards the Kamloops horizon was a great time to be alive on the Canadian Plateau, but its character and overall level of cultural sophistication suggest that it was less grand than the Plateau horizon. The imposition of Europeans about 200 years ago marks the end of this horizon and the PPt. Ethnographic accounts for the end of the Kamloops horizon are provided by Boas (1890, 1895), Dawson (1891), Lane (1953), Morice (1893), Ray (1939), and Teit (1900, 1906, 1909, 1930).

SUMMARY REMARKS AND DIRECTIONS FOR FUTURE RESEARCH

The culture history of the Canadian Plateau during the last 7,000 years is characterized by a remarkable series of social, economic, technological, and behavioral achievements and transitions. From early big game hunting, to opportunistic foraging, and on to the eventual emergence and intensification of logistical collecting, cultures of this unique culture subarea engaged in a broad range of diverse strategies and technologies that were developed both in situ and in concert with adjacent regions. It is indeed one of the last archaeological research frontiers, and we are fortunate that there are still many undisturbed sites of all ages and types. Most of these have the potential to further our knowledge about past human occupation of the Canadian Plateau, provided they are properly managed, investigated, and reported.

In conclusion, I offer several important topics and goals for future investigation. They include (1) determining onset and terminal dates for Early Nesikep and gathering more subsistence and technological data pertaining to it; (2) disclosing whether or not microblade technology and dwellings are indeed absent during the Lehman phase; (3) improving our understanding of the "Lehman–Lochnore" transition; (4) securing more subsistence data for all archaeological units; (5) initiating an attempt to secure human skeletal data that can be used to verify or refute the Coast Salishan incursion model for the Lochnore phase; (6) further developing models that attempt to explain the rapid emergence of full-blown logistical strategies and population growth at the start of the Plateau horizon; (7) investigating the nature, extent, and social implications of exchange system networks that existed during the Plateau and Kamloops horizons; (8) determining and exploring the cultural impact of bow and arrow technology on subsistence systems around 1600 B.P. and thereafter; (9) determining whether or not a population decline actually occurred during the beginning of the Kamloops horizon; (10) reconstructing the nature, degree, duration, and possible effects of interaction with Columbia Plateau groups; (11) continuing attempts to solve problems related to ethnicity, notably Athapaskan and Salish migration, dispersal, and settlement; (12) gathering and synthesizing more paleoenvironmental data for the detailed reconstruction of past climates and environments; and (13) securing information about modes of interment for the Nesikep tradition and the initial half of the Lochnore phase. The list of interesting and intriguing problems worthy of detailed exploration is virtually endless, and some of these issues are addressed in the following chapters.

2

MATERIALS AND CONTEXTS FOR A CULTURE HISTORY OF THE COLUMBIA PLATEAU

William Andrefsky Jr.

This chapter is an overview of the prehistoric occupation of the southern part of the Plateau cultural area (hereafter called the Columbia Plateau). It is important to remember that the Plateau in general and the Columbia Plateau in particular were defined as culture areas by anthropologists observing and working with relatively recent Native American inhabitants of the region (Driver and Massey 1957; Kroeber 1939; Murdock 1941). As such, the boundaries of culture areas were defined partially on the lifeways, economy, cultural traits, and language of inhabitants and partially on the geography and physiography of the region those people inhabited. Although the prehistoric picture of occupation in the Columbia Plateau is incomplete, it is apparent that artifacts, mode of habitation, subsistent practices, and human use of the land were dynamic and changed through time. It is also apparent that the environmental conditions of the regions shifted with regard to effective moisture, biotic communities, and even landforms (Daubenmire 1969; Wigand 1987). This necessarily means that the boundaries of the Columbia Plateau culture area may also have shifted over time as humans adapted to different social and environmental conditions. In fact, the Columbia Plateau culture area (defined by cultural traits) may have been drastically different 1,000 or 8,000 years ago than when it was originally defined by those anthropologists first working in the area. For this reason, the Columbia Plateau is defined for the purposes of this overview as primarily a geographic area, and the archaeological overview explores the human occupation of this geographic area even if such habitation does not conform to the Columbia Plateau culture area traits as originally defined by contemporary anthropologists.

However, the coarse-grained scope of this overview in both time and space provides a platform from which more questions are generated than answered. As such, this coarse-grained culture historical overview will be presented as a data set of prior knowledge about select aspects and areas of the Columbia Plateau. Prior knowledge helps guide researchers toward relevant questions and issues directly related to the data at hand. The topics to be discussed are quite broad, for without prior knowledge, our questions may or may not be relevant. This culture historical overview lends context to the issues, arguments, and concerns of many of the chapters to follow.

The Columbia Plateau includes those lands drained by the Lower and Middle Columbia River and its tributaries. Some of the more significant drainages of the Columbia River included within the Columbia Plateau geographic zone include the Snake, Clearwater, Salmon, Deschutes, John Day, Yakima, Grande Ronde, and Tucannon rivers. This is a relatively large area with a diverse environmental mosaic. As the prehistoric record of the Columbia Plateau is presented below, I refer sometimes to the entire region and at other times to specific drainages. I draw on information from specific drainages and particular sites to make interpretations about the entire Columbia Plateau. However, the specificity for which such interpretations can be made will vary from location to location based on the extent to which we can rely on the accuracy of our prior knowledge. Before reviewing the prehistoric occupation of the Columbia Plateau, it is necessary to discuss the contemporary and prehistoric environment.

ENVIRONMENTAL SETTING

The Columbia Plateau covers an area of about 500 km east to west, bounded on the east by the Bitterroot Range and on the west by the Cascade Range, and about 700 km north to south, bounded on the north by the Okanogan

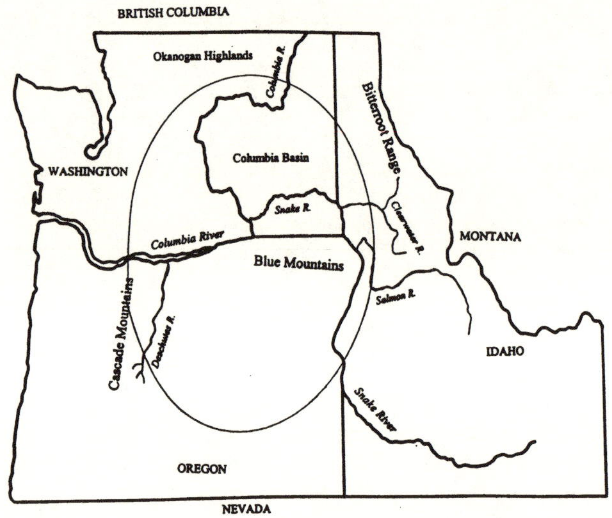

Figure 2.1. Generalized location of the Columbia Plateau culture area.

Highlands and on the south by the intermountain basin and range physiographic zone (see Figure 2.1). The Blue-Ochoco Mountains, which rise to 3,000 m above sea level are near the center of this 350,000 km^2 area. Almost completely encircling the Blue-Ochoco Mountains are the deeply incised river canyons of the Snake and Columbia, with the elevation of some areas of the Columbia Plateau at less than 100 m above sea level. Tributaries of the Columbia and Snake rivers drain the Blue-Ochoco Mountains as well as the slopes of the Cascade Range to the west and the Bitterroot Range to the east. The Columbia Plateau also contains an extensive basin (Columbia Basin) as large as the Blue-Ochoco mountain range. Variability in elevation combined with the orographic effect of the Pacific Ocean air masses and the high Cascade mountain range produces a wide diversity of environmental conditions in the Columbia Plateau. Kimberling and Jackson (1985) provide additional details on the physiography of the region.

The lowland areas of the Columbia Plateau are primarily populated by shrub steppe and bunchgrass steppe habitat, while the higher elevations in the center of the region are populated by xeric montane forests (Daubenmire 1969; Franklyn and Dyrness 1973). However, parts of the Columbia Plateau, particularly in mountains surrounding the region, contain mesic montane forests, subalpine forests, alpine meadows, and woodland transition forests. This diversity of habitat supports a wide range of ungulates, including but not limited to elk *(Cervus elaphus),* mule deer *(Odocoileus hemionus),* and mountain sheep *(Ovis canadensis)* (Dalquest 1948; Hall 1981). In the recent past bison *(Bison bison)* were also found in the region (Van Vuren 1985). Resident fish of the Columbia Plateau include northern pike minnow *(Ptychocheilus oregonensis),* chiselmouth *(Acrocheilus alutaceus),* mountain whitefish *(Prosopium williamsoni),* and bridgelip *(Catostomus columbianus).* Anadromous species of economic importance include Pacific lamprey *(Entosphenus tridentatus),* chinook salmon *(Oncorhynchus tschawytscha),* sockeye salmon *(O. nerka),* and steelhead trout *(O. mykiss).* Schalk (1977) provides a detailed overview on salmon habitat and migrations into the region. Important edible plants found in the Columbia Plateau include Indian ricegrass *(Oryzopsis hymenoides),* bitterroot *(Lewisia rediviva),* common camas *(Camassia quamash),* and many, many more root, seed, and berry species (see Daubenmire 1970; Hunn 1990; Lepofsky and Peacock, this volume; Statham 1975).

Latitude, elevation, and coastal moisture are among the most important characteristics that define the climate of Columbia Plateau today and in the past. Another of these characteristics is the high level of yearly and seasonal variability in effective moisture and prevailing winds. As such, the local environment in different areas of the Columbia Plateau is both dynamic and changing. Primary evidence used as a proxy for climatic change comes in the form of plant and animal identification at specific times (i.e., Gustafson 1972; Lyman and Livingston 1983; Schroedl 1973). These proxy data are gathered from archaeological sites, zoological sites such as pack rat middens and shell middens, and geological contexts such as bog and ice cores (Mehringer et al. 1977). Unfortunately, this evidence is often specific to isolated locations. It is now apparent that biotic evidence taken from different locations but in relatively close proximity to one another often suggests different climatic contexts (Blinman et al. 1979; Foit et al. 1992). The variability in climatic proxy data may be caused in part by true climatic differences over small or microenvironmental areas. Other factors such as the invasion of insects and natural and human-induced fires may also be responsible for localized changes in the biotic communities. These factors make it difficult to determine regionwide climatic regimes during the course of prehistory. Although localized and regional climatic reconstructions for the Columbia Plateau have been published (Table 2.1; see also Chatters 1998) it is important to note that each of these local reconstructions is unique.

CULTURE HISTORY

Introduction

The prehistoric culture history of the Columbia Plateau can be divided into four broad periods: Paleoarchaic (pre-11,000–8000 B.P.), Early Archaic (8000–5000 B.P.), Middle Archaic (5000–2000 B.P.), and Late Archaic (2000 B.P.–A.D. 1720). These dates are generalized for

TABLE 2.1. Columbia Plateau Environmental Generalizations.

Date B.P.	Environmental Generalization	Source
approximately 18,000	The last glacial maximum, bringing continental ice sheets into the northern border of contemporary Washington State	Kutzbach et al. 1993
approximately 15,000	Noticeable increase in solar radiation resulting in glacial retreats and warming oceans	Kutzbach et al. 1993
11,700	Mount Saint Helens (J) in western Washington erupted and spread tephra over much of the Columbia Plateau	Foit et al. 1992
11,200	Glacier Peak in northwestern Washington erupted and spread tephra over much of the Columbia Plateau	Foit et al. 1992
11,000–10,000	A pulse of colder weather caused an advance in ice sheets. This event has come to be known as the Younger Dryas	Mathewes 1993
9000–6000	The period (Altithermal) produced the greatest amount of summer insulation in the past 20,000 years, causing extreme seasonal climatic differences	Thompson 1984
approximately 6700	Mount Mazama (Crater Lake) in western Oregon erupted and spread tephra over much of the Columbia Plateau and Great Basin	Mehringer et al. 1977
approximately 6000	There is evidence for widespread cooling and increased moisture. Alpine glaciers begin to advance in the Cascades and northern Rocky Mountains	Ryder and Thompson 1986
approximately 4500	The Columbia Plateau became abruptly cooler and continued to get more moisture than today. Alpine glaciers advanced in all higher mountain ranges	Chatters 1998
2800–2500	Temperatures warmed, and vegetation communities approached modern distributions	Chatters 1998
approximately 700–600	Temperatures became much cooler, summers became shorter and wetter, sea ice spread southward, and alpine glaciers advanced. The "Little Ice Age" caused famine and halted northern latitude human colonization	Grove 1988

the entire Columbia Plateau, of course, and may differ slightly for any specific local area. They do, however, tend to follow culture historical trends across the entire Columbia Plateau. Table 2.2 cross-lists these four periods with various culture historical sequences from specific locations on the Columbia Plateau.

Early cultural chronologies on the Columbia Plateau were synthesized by Browman and Munsell (1969), Butler (1961, 1965), Cressman et al. (1960), Daugherty (1962), and Swanson (1962). Daugherty felt that the Columbia Plateau was part of a larger "Intermontane Western Tradition" that covered an area from British Columbia to Mexico and from the Cascades to the Rocky Mountains. He proposed that the area encompassed by the Columbia Plateau consisted of five periods that roughly correspond to environmental shifts proposed by Antevs (1955). Butler (1961) viewed the Columbia Plateau culture area as consisting of four traditions within what he called the "Old Cordilleran Culture," which emerged in different areas and had a distinctive identity throughout most of prehistory. These four traditions eventually overlapped in various regions of the Columbia Plateau. Swanson's synthesis is similar to Butler's Old Cordilleran Culture of hunting and gathering but more refined and specific for the Middle Columbia River. Browman and Munsell's culture history attempts to combine Daugherty's and Butler's ideas into a new sequence of seven periods. The Browman and Munsell synthesis added the notion of outside influences into the Columbia Plateau at different times in the prehistoric past, from both the Great Basin and the Canadian Plateau.

Since the 1960s there have been a number of new syntheses for specific regions of the Columbia Plateau. Several culture historical sequences have been suggested for the Lower Snake River (Ames et al. 1998; Leonhardy and Rice 1970; Reid 1991; Warren 1968). There have been numerous culture historical sequences for the lower section of the Middle Columbia River (Andrefsky et al. 1996; Galm et al. 1981; Greengo 1982; Nelson 1969; Swanson 1962) and the upper section of the Middle Columbia (Campbell 1985; Chatters 1984, 1986; Gough 1990). Cultural overviews for the Lower Columbia River and its tributaries (Deschutes and John Day rivers) can be found in Butler 1959, Cressman et al. 1960, Minor et al. 1987, and Toepel et al. 1980. Archaeological overviews of the northern Great Basin and Columbia Plateau boundary areas are available in Aikens 1993, Aikens and Jenkins 1994, and Connolly 1999. The culture history of the Blue Mountains, Hell's Canyon, and major tributaries above Hell's Canyon can also be found (see Andrefsky and Nauman 2003; Andrefsky et al. 1999; Burchard 1998; McPherson et al. 1981; Plew 2000; Schmeller 1999).

TABLE 2.2. Select Columbia Plateau Culture Historical Sequences.

Period	Phase Names in Various Regions
Late Archaic 2000 B.P.–A.D. 1720	Piqunin and Harder phases from the Lower Snake River; Big Bar I and Big Bar II phases from Hell's Canyon; Cayuse phase on the lower Middle Columbia River; Coyote Creek phase on the upper Middle Columbia River; Wildcat phase on Columbia River near Wildcat Canyon; Ahsahka Phase on the Clearwater River
Middle Archaic 5000–2000 B.P.	Tucannon phase on the Lower Snake River; Squaw Creek II and part of Squaw Creek I phases in Hell's Canyon; Frenchman Springs phase on the lower Middle Columbia River; Hudnut and part of Kartar phases on the upper Middle Columbia River; Hatwai phase on the Clearwater River
Early Archaic 8000–5000 B.P.	Cascade phase on the Lower Snake River; Hell's Canyon Creek and part of Squaw Creek I phases in Hell's Canyon; Vantage phase on the lower Middle Columbia River; part of Kartar phase on the upper Middle Columbia River; Canyon phase on the Columbia River near Wildcat Canyon; part of Cascade phase on the Clearwater River
Paleoarchaic pre-11,000–8000 B.P.	Windust phase on the Lower Snake River; Windust phase on the lower Middle Columbia River; Philippi phase on the Columbia River near Wildcat Canyon; Windust phase and part of Cascade phase on the Clearwater River

Paleoarchaic (pre-11,000–8000 B.P.)

The Paleoarchaic is a period of time that represents the earliest undisputed occupation of the Columbia Plateau. There are two recognized artifact "traditions" for this period of time, the fluted-point tradition and the western stemmed-point tradition. The fluted-point tradition is defined by lanceolate bifaces with collateral flaking and usually with an end flake or flute taken from the base. These points have often been called Clovis or Folsom and have been found as isolates and with associated assemblages in Washington, Oregon, and Idaho (Aikens 1978; Butler 1986; Carlson 1983a; Fagan 1988; Willig 1988). The stemmed-point tradition includes lanceolate, stemmed, and shouldered bifaces. These bifaces are often found associated with crescents. Stemmed-point specimens have been called Haskett, Windust, Lind Coulee, Cascade, and Cougar Mountain, among others (Aikens 1993; Bryan 1980; Daugherty 1956; Davis 2001; Galm and Gough 2000; Leonhardy 1970; Rice 1965; Sanders 1982). Figure 2.2 illustrates examples of these artifact forms.

Many archaeologists in North America believe that fluted-point traditions represent the earliest occupation in the Western Hemisphere. However, recent studies disagree with this notion and have postulated a pre-fluted point occupation in some parts of North and South America (Bonnichsen et al. 1996; Dixon 1999; Overstreet 1993). Fluted-point assemblages from locations in and around the Columbia Plateau are not well dated. Jaguar Cave in Idaho produced a date of 11,580 ± 250 B.P. (Butler 1986). Connley Cave from Oregon produced a date of 11,200 ± 200 B.P., and Cougar Mountain, also from Oregon, produced a date of 11,950 ± 350 B.P. (Bedwell and Cressman 1971). In each of these cases, however, there is no clear undisputable evidence that the dates were associated with fluted points. The East Wenachee Clovis site in Washington contained fluted points and other artifacts found resting on top of Glacier Peak ash. This suggests to some (Mehringer and Foit 1990) that the fluted-point assemblage dates to just after the fall of Glacier Peak ash at approximately 11,200 years ago. Unfortunately, when bone from the same assemblage at East Wenatchee was dated, it produced an age of 5,215 ± 90 B.P. (Gramly 1996). Other important fluted-point tradition sites in the region include the Dietz site from Oregon (Fagan 1988; Willig 1988) and the Simon Cache from southern Idaho (Butler 1963; Butler and Fitzwater 1965). Neither of these two sites had its fluted-point assemblage radiocarbon dated.

The Dietz site is notable because in addition to the fluted-point assemblage it also contains a stemmed-point assemblage (also not dated). Both assemblages are found on the dried pluvial lake margins of Greater Alkali Lake in multiple scatters. In general, the stemmed-point assemblages are found at higher elevations than the fluted-point assemblages (Willig 1988), but at times the "Clovis artifacts . . . overlap the occurrence of Western Pluvial Lakes Tradition artifacts in places" (Fagan 1988:390). It is not

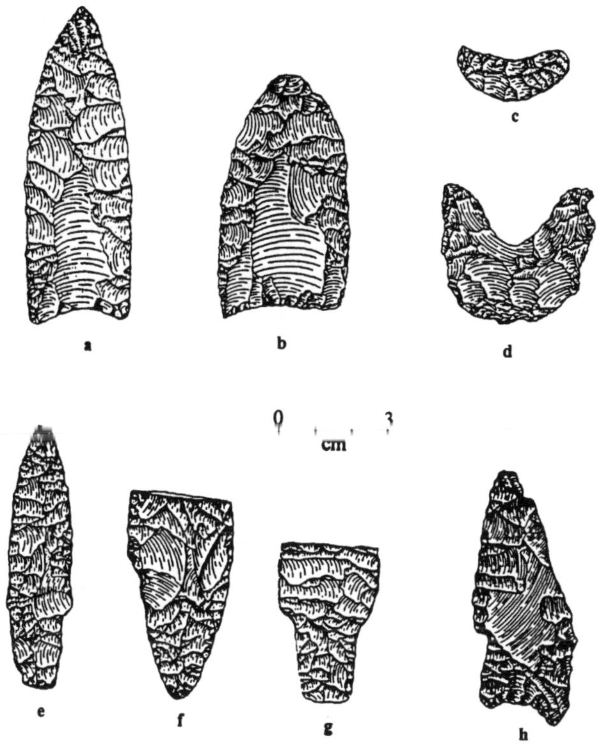

Figure 2.2. Select Paleoarchaic artifacts. Items a–b: fluted points from site 35LK1529; c–d: crescents from site 35LK1529; e–h: western stemmed points from 35LK1529 (adapted from Willig 1988).

therefore clear if the western stemmed-point tradition is earlier than, later than, or coeval with the fluted-point tradition at the Dietz site. There are, however, multiple locations in and around the Columbia Plateau where the western stemmed points are dated after about 11,000 years ago. For instance, the western stemmed-point assemblage at Fivemile Rapids is dated between 9,700 and 7,600 years ago (Cressman et al. 1960); that at Wildcat Canyon is dated between 10,600 and 7,300 years ago (Aikens et al. 1977; Hanes 1988); that at Connley Cave is dated between 9,500 and 7,400 years ago (Bedwell 1970, 1973); that at Marmes Rockshelter is dated between 10,800 and 7,500 years ago (Sheppard et al. 1987); that at Hatwai is dated between 10,800 and 9,300 years ago (Ames et al. 1981); that at Sentinel Gap is dated between 10,600 and 10,100 years ago (Galm and Gough 2000); and that at Bison Rockshelter is dated to approximately 10,300 years ago (Swanson 1972).

It should be noted that the age of the fluted-point tradition in the Columbia Plateau is not well established, and it appears that there are several instances where western stemmed-point assemblages may be older than the oldest well-dated fluted-point assemblages from the Columbia Plateau and other places in North America. For instance, the Cooper's Ferry site located along the Lower Salmon River in Idaho contains several varieties of western stemmed points (e.g., Lind Coulee, Windust, Cascade) (Davis 2001). Two accelerator mass spectrometry dates, one on bone and the other on charcoal, produced dates of 12,020 ± 170 B.P. and 11,370 ± 70 B.P. (Wisner 1998). A freshwater mussel shell taken from the top of a cobble bed and associated with a western stemmed-point assemblage at Granite Point was dated to 14,100 ± 1160 B.P. This date was discarded as being "too early" (Leonhardy 1970). An average date of 12,830 ± 1050 B.P. was taken on a bison scapula from the Lind Coulee site. This date was discarded because of the minimal amount of collagen from the poorly preserved bone (Irwin and Moody 1978: 224). However, this specimen was recovered stratigraphically below Mt. St. Helens J ash presumed to have been deposited approximately 11,700 years ago. Western stemmed points have also been found at the earliest occupation levels of Fort Rock Cave in Oregon. While a radiocarbon age of 13,200 B.P. was recovered in association with human artifacts, there is some confusion about the context partially because of the early age (Aikens and Jenkins 1994:7). These anomalous dates have led some researchers to argue that the western stemmed-point tradition predates the fluted-point tradition in the Columbia Plateau region (Bryan and Tuohy 1999).

The lack of fluted points in an unquestionable dated context in the Columbia Plateau coupled with the anomalous early dates for some western stemmed points suggests that the relationship between these two traditions is not fully understood at this time. Part of the problem might be clarified by a more detailed examination of the styles and chronology of the western stemmed points. Currently, various shapes and sizes of points are encompassed into this single tradition with limited consideration of the possibility that certain point styles may occur earlier than other styles. In fact, this appears to be the case at Cooper's Ferry, where the Lind Coulee points appear to be earlier than the Windust points, which are followed by Cascade points (Davis 2001). Leonhardy's (1970) work at the Granite Point site clearly shows Windust points occurring before Cascade points. New analysis of materials from the Lind Coulee site (Craven 2003) shows that Daugherty's original sequence of Haskett to Lind Coulee 1, 2, and 3 appears to follow a trend through time. The 10,000-year-plus dates from Sentinel Gap (site 45KT1362) do not include Windust or Lind Coulee points (Stan Gough, personal communication, 2003). Clearly, there is some additional work yet to be done on the culture historical sequence and technological styles related to the earliest human occupation of the Columbia Plateau.

The early human occupation of the Columbia Plateau does not appear to be restricted to a single environmental zone or to a single key subsistence resource. Both western stemmed-point tradition and fluted-point tradition sites are found in the southern Columbia Plateau along drying pluvial lake margins and marshes (Dietz site). This same kind of lake margin environment is found farther north into the Columbia Basin, where the Lind Coulee site is located. At such locations it is assumed that the inhabitants were not necessarily hunting large megafauna such as mammoth and mastodon but, instead, may have been taking a variety of game such as bison, deer, waterfowl, fish, and various plants. Pluvial lake margins are not the only place these earliest inhabitants of the Columbia Plateau were camped. Sites have been found in rock shelters and caves (including Marmes Rockshelter, Fort Rock Cave, Windust Caves, and Owl Cave), where evidence suggests that chipped-stone and bone technologies were used extensively by early Columbia Plateau populations. Open-air sites above major rivers (Hatwai site, East Wenatchee site, Cooper's Ferry site) were also occupied by people of the Paleoarchaic. Although the data are few, we also find initial archaic occupants using higher elevation locations such as Weitas Creek and Swamp Creek (Keeler 1973; Sappington 1994). It is not known if one tradition grew from the other or if both were using the Colombia Plateau in an asynchronous pattern. It is evident, however, that these early traditions were widespread over the Columbia Plateau's diverse environment.

Early Archaic (8000–5000 B.P.)

The Early Archaic period is represented widely throughout the Columbia Plateau and as a result can be recognized by multiple phase names, stage names, and tradition names depending on the location within the Plateau. This period is roughly coeval with the early Holocene environmental period known as the Altithermal. This environmental period is hypothesized as a time of very widespread arid conditions (Antevs 1955). The Early Archaic of the Lower Snake River in Washington is known as the Cascade phase (Leonhardy and Rice 1970). Based on excavations from ten sites along the Snake, including but not limited to Thorn Thicket, Marmes Rockshelter, Windust Caves, Votaw, Granite Point, and the Tucannon site, Leonhardy and Rice (1970:23) see this phase beginning approximately 8000 B.P. and ending around 5500 B.P. Although others have slightly different beginning or ending dates for the Cascade phase, they cover roughly the same period of time (e.g., Ames et al. 1998; Andrefsky 1995; Bense 1972; Galm et al. 1981; Reid 1991).

The Early Archaic on the Lower Snake River (Cascade phase) is characterized by the occurrence of leaf-shaped bifaces or bipoints (Cascade points), edge-ground cobbles, large cobble spalls, pounding stones, tabular end scrapers, bone needles, and Olivella beads. The complex cobble tool industry, with cobble spalls, edge-ground cobbles, and pounding or battering stones of various types, is especially noticeable. Some believe that such a technology may be related to salmon processing or bone grease extraction (e.g., Andrefsky in press; Bense 1972; Grater 1966; Muto 1976).

The period is separated into early and late subperiods that are partitioned at the time of the Mazama ashfall at approximately 6700 B.P. Artifact assemblages are identical for the early and late periods with the exception that large side-notched points are found after the fall of Mazama ash (see Figure 2.3). These points have been variously called "Northern Side-Notched" or "Cold Springs Side-Notched" points. It is not certain why or under what conditions the large side-notched points were added to the Early Archaic assemblage. This pattern is widely recognized by site excavations in areas outside of the Snake River canyon as well. The Stockhoff Basalt Quarry in the Blue Mountains of Oregon, for example, reveals the production sequences of the Cascade point before the Mazama ashfall and also reveals the production of Northern Side-Notched points after the ashfall (Womack 1977).

Early Archaic sites along the Middle Columbia River have been grouped into the Vantage phase by Nelson (1969). Nelson's Vantage phase is based on his work at the Sunset Creek site (45KT28) and previous work done by Earl Swanson (1962) at Cedar Cave and Duck Cave. Artifact traits and the temporal span of the Vantage phase were modified by Galm et al. (1981) after more sites were examined. According to Galm and associates' study (1981:60), the Vantage phase corresponds in time to the Cascade phase of the Lower Snake River, with early and late subperiods. The Vantage phase also contains the diagnostic leaf-shaped points, with the occurrence of large side-notched points after about 6700 B.P. Olivella beads, cobble tools, and microblades are also found during this period along the Middle Columbia River.

Robert Greengo's (1982) work in the Middle Columbia River has produced a similar Early Archaic chronology based on the excavation of some 20 sites. Greengo's Early "Prehistoric Period 1" and "Early Prehistoric Period 2" correspond to Leonhardy and Rice's "Early Cascade Phase" and "Late Cascade Phase," respectively. As such, they also correspond to Galm's early and late Vantage phases. Excavations at Rye Grass Coulee and Sourdough Creek were significant in Greengo's culture history for the Middle Columbia River (Munsell 1968). Several large archaeological projects were conducted farther upriver on the Middle Columbia in the 1980s—Chief Joseph (Campbell 1985) and the Wells Reservoir (Chatters 1986) projects. The Early Archaic period is known in this stretch of the Columbia River as the Kartar phase and the Okanogan phase. These phases are also characterized by leaf-shaped lanceolate points, cobble spall tools, edge-ground cobbles, and microblade technology. The Middle Columbia River assemblages differ slightly from Early

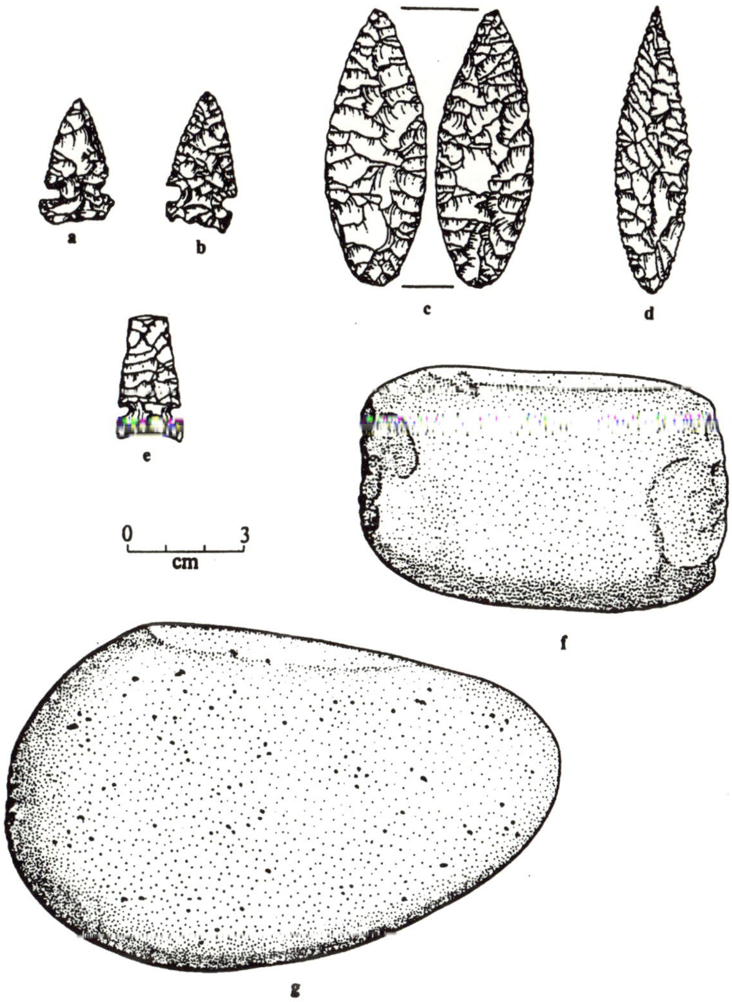

Figure 2.3. Select Early Archaic artifacts. Items a–b, e: large side-notched points from site 10CW30; c: Cascade point from site 10CW548; d: Cascade points from site 10CW584; f: edge-ground cobble from site10CW289; g: edge-ground cobble from site 10CW30 (adapted from Draper 1993; Sappington 1994).

Archaic assemblages on the Lower Snake River primarily because of the inclusion of microblade technology.

The Columbia River and its tributaries below the confluence of the Snake River contain a number of important sites occupied during the Early Archaic period. Within the Columbia Gorge, excavations at the Indian Well Site, Wakemap Mound, and Fivemile Rapids were significant in defining this cultural historical phase (Butler 1959, 1965; Cressman et al. 1960). During the Early Archaic period sites in this end of the Columbia Gorge tended to have few stylistically diagnostic artifacts; however, there is evidence for fish and bird exploitation (Hansel 2003). Sites farther upstream such as Bob's Point, Wildcat Canyon, Hat Creek, and Cold Springs contain artifact assemblages similar to those of the Middle Columbia and Lower Snake rivers. Here, again, there is evidence for the edge-ground cobbles, cobble spall tools, and large side-notched points near the end of the period (Cole 1968; Cole and Cressman 1961; Minor and Toepel 1986; Shiner 1961; Toepel et al. 1980). At Wildcat Canyon this period is known as the Canyon phase and included leaf-shaped points as well as large side-notched points after the fall of Mazama ash (Dumond and Minor 1983). On the southern reaches of the Columbia Plateau (Fort Rock Valley, Connley Caves) the Early Archaic period is represented primarily by Northern Side-Notched points and some Elko series points as diagnostic artifacts (Bedwell 1973; Oetting 1994). The leaf-shaped point does not appear to be temporally diagnostic for this edge of the Columbia Plateau. Lake margins and marsh environments were still being used during this period. Evidence of fish, bird, and small mammal consumption is also found in these locations (Dean 1994; Greenspan 1985, 1994).

Significant Early Archaic occupations in the Blue Mountains and Hell's Canyon include the Stockhoff

Basalt Quarry (Bryan and Tuohy 1960; Womack 1977), Pilcher Creek (Brauner 1985), and Bernard Creek Rockshelter site (Randolf and Dahlstrom 1977). Reid (1991) reports that 21 sites from the Wallowa-Whitman National Forest have been attributed to the Early Archaic period based on the presence of Cascade and Northern Side-Notched points. The Cascade bipoint followed by the large side-notched point is the same sequence evident in most parts of the Columbia Plateau. Hell's Canyon at Bernard Creek Rockshelter also shows clear signs of fish (salmon and local species) and freshwater mussel use as a food source during the Early Archaic.

Early Archaic material culture shows a surprising amount of uniformity over an extensive geographical range. The kinds of interactions and communications needed to maintain such cohesion in the material assemblages have not been well studied, but certainly they may relate to sparse population densities, extensive mobility ranges, and similar adaptive strategies.

Middle Archaic (5000–2000 B.P.)

Unlike the preceding Early Archaic period, the Middle Archaic does not have a uniform "signature" of artifacts across the Columbia Plateau at simultaneous times. One of, if not the, most important and recognizable characteristics of this period is the first appearance of semisubterranean pithouses. On the Middle Columbia River the earliest pithouse was used at approximately 5200 B.P. (Lohse and Sammons-Lohse 1986). A date of 5050 B.P. was taken from house #6 at Hatwai Site on the Clearwater River (Ames and Marshall 1981). By about 4500 B.P. small pithouse villages were located extensively throughout the Columbia Plateau (Chatters 1995a). The Middle Archaic period on the Lower Snake River was originally characterized by Leonhardy and Rice (1970) as the Tucannon phase. They characterize the artifact assemblage as containing sinkers (notched cobbles and pebbles), hopper mortars and pestles, cobble spall tools, a short contracting stemmed projectile point, and a short expanding stemmed projectile point. Again, there seems to have been a broad spectrum of small and large game included in the diet, as well as the use of salmon and freshwater mussels (Leonhardy and Rice 1970). Harder's (1998) analysis of the Tucannan phase sites along the Lower Snake River reveals that hopper mortar bases, notched sinkers, corner-notched points, small side-notched points, and ground-stone smoking pipes were first introduced during the Middle Archaic period (see Figure 2.4). Important sites along the Lower Snake River at this time include the Marmes Rockshelter, Granite Point, Alpowai, Hatiuhpuh, Three Springs Bar, Votow, and Tucannan Site (Brauner 1976; Brauner et al. 1990; Grater 1966; Harder 1998; Leonhardy 1970).

The Middle Archaic period on the Middle Columbia River is recognized as the very late Vantage phase and the Frenchman Springs phase (Galm et al. 1981), as well as the late Kartar and Hudnut phases (Jaehnig 1983). Pithouse sites on the Middle Columbia River often consist of one to three or four contemporaneously occupied structures. Site 45OK11 contained "three to four households, living in pit houses year round" (Lohse and Sammons-Lohse 1986:116). Other sites such as Cox's Pond suggest a single pithouse occupation (Hartman 1975). Chatters (1995a) suggests that the early part of the Middle Archaic period on the Columbia Plateau was characterized by a relatively mobile residential pattern similar to that of the Early Archaic period (see also Rousseau, this volume). This relatively mobile existence, which utilized pithouses seasonally in some areas, was followed by an occupational hiatus (3900 B.P.). Then at approximately 3500 B.P. a more sedentary lifestyle was adopted. Chatters characterizes these two periods as "Pithouse I" and "Pithouse II," respectively. One of the primary differences between Pithouse I and Pithouse II is the inclusion of storage features after 3500 B.P. According to Chatters, Pithouse I did not exist on the Lower Columbia River and it is not until 3000 B.P. that Pithouse II occupations are recognizable there.

Ames et al. (1998) argue that the Lower Columbia River cultural chronology for the Middle Archaic period is not well understood. Wildcat Canyon site and Hobo Cave appear to have a Middle Archaic component, but there is evidence of disturbance in the form of artifact mixing (Ames et al. 1998:110–111). Dumond and Minor (1983:157–162), moreover, suggest an occupational hiatus at the Wildcat Canyon site between approximately 5000 and 2000 B.P. The Fivemile Rapids area near The Dalles, Oregon, appears to have been abandoned during the Middle Archaic period, with human occupation before and after this period (Ames et al. 1998; Minor et al. 1987:40). However, sites just to the south of the Columbia River on the Deschutes River (Jenkins and Connolly 1996) and the John Day (Endzweig 1994b) show evidence of extensive habitation during this period of occupational hiatus along the Lower Columbia River. The proximity of these areas and the concordance of occupation and abandonment suggest a potential cultural relationship. More research must be completed among the sites and assemblages in these occupations to better understand these potential relationships.

The culture historical sequence in the Hell's Canyon region of the Columbia Plateau for the Middle Archaic period appears to conform to the sequence on the Lower Snake and Middle Columbia rivers. The Middle Archaic in this region is referred to as Squaw Creek I phase and Squaw Creek II phase (Pavesic 1971). Squaw Creek I began at approximately 6500 B.P. and lasted until 3500

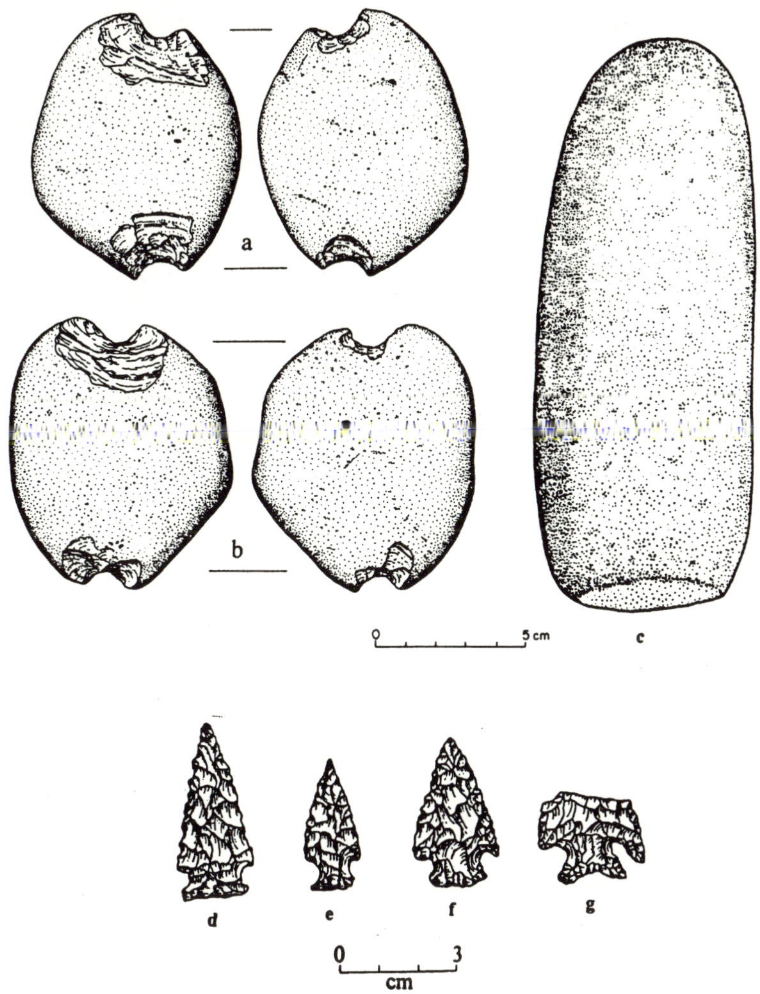

Figure 2.4. Select Middle Archaic artifacts. Items a–b: notched net weights from site 45FR32; c: pestle from site 10CW536; d–g: corner-notch projectile points from 10NP143 (adapted from Ames et al. 1981; Andrefsky in press; Draper 1993).

B.P. This was followed by Squaw Creek II, which lasted until 2500 B.P. (Warren et al. 1968). These phases were established primarily on the occurrence of various hafted biface forms. The early end of the Squaw Creek I phase intersects chronologically with the late Cascade phase of the Lower Snake River. Large side-notched bifaces are found for this time simultaneously in Hell's Canyon and along the Lower Snake River sites. The remainder of the chipped-stone assemblage of the Squaw Creek I and II phases is very similar to those of the Tucannan, Kartar, and Hudnut phases of the Lower Snake and Middle Columbia rivers.

Drawing on available evidence, and following the work of Binford (1980), I argue that the early end of the Middle Archaic period might be characterized as a forager economic strategy. Even though some pithouses were used at approximately 5000 B.P., they probably were occupied by people foraging for seasonally available food resources. Lohse and Sammons-Lohse (1986) note that occupants of site 45OK11 on the Middle Columbia River positioned themselves to exploit a wide range of subsistence resources (large and small game, fish, shellfish, root plants, etc.) from one central base. It is important to note that the exploitation of a single critical resource such as salmon or camas roots has not been established across the Columbia Plateau for the early end of the Middle Archaic period, despite sedentary and semisedentary occupations (but see Ames and Marshall 1981; Thoms 1989). Chatters (1995a) believes that it was only after 3500 B.P. that a collector economic strategy was adopted by Columbia Plateau groups. Evidence for intensive root crop exploitation seems to correspond to this age (Andrefsky 2000). Detailed excavations on the camas-processing and residential sites along the Pend d'Oreille River in northeastern Washington provide a clear history of camas root exploitation from Middle Archaic times through recent history (Andrefsky et al. 2000). Although camas acquisition and processing began as early as 5500 B.P., exploitation seems to have been most intense between 3500 and 2500 B.P. (Andrefsky 2000:19.5). This intensive exploitation appears to coincide with increased salmon availability on the Columbia River system between 3300 and 2200 B.P. (Butler and Schalk 1986; Chatters et al. 1995). Studies imply that intensive critical resource exploitation did not occur until approximately 3500 B.P. on the Columbia Plateau. Clearly, more research is needed to clarify the timing of critical resource intensification in different regions of the Columbia Plateau.

Late Archaic (2000 B.P.–A.D. 1720)

To many, the Late Archaic period represents an archaeological extension of the settlement and subsistence practices of indigenous peoples observed by early researchers. The Late Archaic period terminates at A.D. 1720 because this is the date at which most Columbia Plateau archaeologists believe that the horse was initially introduced into the region (Presler 2000). There are many phase names associated with the Late Archaic period (Lower Snake River uses Harder and Piqunin phases, Middle Columbia uses Cayuse phase, Clearwater River uses Ahsahka phase, Hell's Canyon uses Big Bar I and II phases, Wildcat Canyon uses Wildcat phase, etc.). Regardless of the phase name used, the Late Archaic period is roughly similar in all areas of the Columbia Plateau. All areas of the Columbia Plateau show evidence by approximately 2000 B.P. of human occupation along all major and minor river valleys, in upland areas, and in dry basin areas. There is also evidence for the use of a great variety of nonlocal raw materials in artifact form not common in earlier periods. Obsidian artifacts traced to sources from southern Idaho and southern Oregon can be found in assemblages from central and northern Washington (Galm 1994). Marine shell from the coast of British Columbia and from the coast of California is also found in Columbia Plateau assemblages (Erickson 1983). The nature of the contact among different areas within and outside of the Columbia Plateau is in need of further exploration by researchers.

One of the most recognizable traits of a Late Archaic period occupation is the occurrence of pithouse villages. Pithouse villages with as few as a dozen pit features and as many as 100 or more are found on all the major river drainages of the Columbia Plateau in this period (Brauner 1975; Jenkins and Connolly 1994; Kenaston 1966; Reid 1991). Pithouse villages are also located on small tributary canyons away from the major rivers (DiScipio 1997; Reid and Gallison 1993), and they are found in higher upland areas (Endzweig 1994a; Gough 1990; Reid and Gallison 1992). Pithouse villages reveal a great amount of individual pithouse variability in size and depth. Some pit structures are as small as 4–5 m in diameter, and others are over 20 m in diameter (Green 1993). There is a strong possibility that the smaller pithouse features were used as nonresidential structures (sweat houses, storage pits, menstrual huts, etc.) and that the larger pit structures were used as habitation structures (Kennedy and Bouchard 1998; Smith 2000).

Some Columbia Plateau archaeologists believe that the ethnographic settlement pattern documented at the time of Euro-American contact actually began in the Late Archaic period 2,000 years earlier. This "ethnographic pattern" is characterized as large winter villages established in deep canyon bottoms where winter temperatures were relatively warmer; as spring arrived the large winter villages would begin partitioning into smaller groups to exploit seasonally available resources (Ray 1936). People in winter villages relied primarily on stored food materials that were supplemented with freshly killed game and fish catches. Although this ethnographic pattern is widely accepted by researchers, it is interesting to note that pithouse villages were not directly observed by the first Euro-American explorers into the Columbia Plateau. By the time Lewis and Clark had arrived into the region the indigenous Columbia Plateau peoples were living in rectangular mat-covered longhouses with no occupation of circular pithouse villages. It is not known for certain when pithouses were replaced by rectangular longhouses; nor are the conditions under which this transition occurred known. However, several studies have provided evidence that rectangular houses might be considerably older than originally suspected. Galm and Masten (1985), for example, have dated a rectangular longhouse found in the East Wenatchee, Washington, area to approximately 1,200 years ago. Evidence from site 45PO137 on the Pend d'Oreille River indicates that a large rectangular feature (perhaps a longhouse) was occupied at around 1,150 years ago and possibly as early as 1,700 years ago (Andrefsky et al. 2000). Nakonechny's (1998) study of house structures at the Wexpusnime site on the Lower Snake River reveals that these structures were very shallow pits, subrectangular in shape, dating to between 1,000 and 1,200 years ago. Some archaeologists believe that deeply excavated circular pithouses were gradually replaced by shallowly excavated and surface rectangular longhouses during the course of the Late Archaic period (Ames et al. 1998).

Relative to earlier periods, the Late Archaic period showed significant population increases and higher population densities. There is a clear association with anadromous fish harvesting and processing (Campbell 1985; Schalk 1977). There is also evidence, associated with the intensification of fish harvesting, for storage technology in the form of pits and dry rock shelters (Draper and

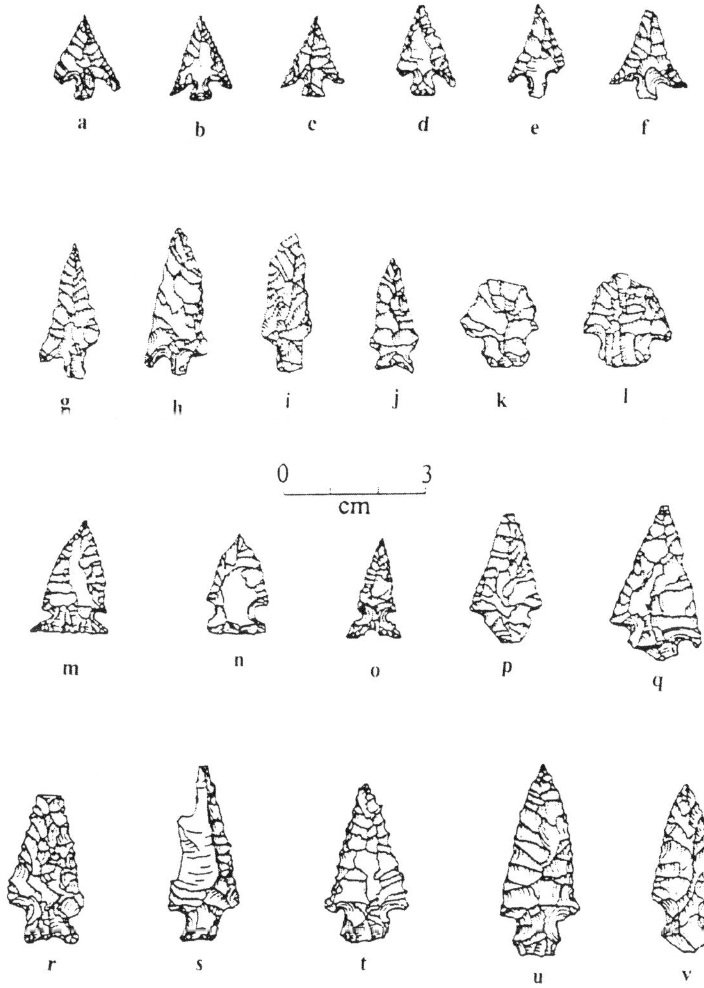

Figure 2.5. Select Late Archaic artifacts. Items a–l: corner-notched and stemmed arrow points from 10IH1017; m–v: notched arrow and dart points from North Fork of the Clearwater River (adapted from Draper 1991, 1993).

Brauner 1989; Draper and Morgenstein 1993; Endacott 1992). Test excavations in the Palouse Canyon Archaeological District near the confluence of the Palouse and Snake rivers have revealed that shallow rock shelters had as few as one storage pit and that deep rock shelters such as McGregor Cave contained dozens of storage pits (Hicks and Morganstein 1994).

Evidence for bow and arrow technology first appears with certainty during the Late Archaic period. Often bow and arrow technology is identified archaeologically by the occurrence of small (< 2 cm long) chipped-stone projectiles with narrow neck widths (Christenson 1986; Shott 1997; see also Chatters, this volume; Rousseau, this volume; and Figure 2.5). Some of the earliest arrow points from the Columbia Plateau were found at Strawberry Island on the Lower Snake River (ca. 2400 B.P.) (Schalk 1983) and at Alpowai near the confluence of the Snake and Clearwater rivers (ca. 1900 B.P.) (Brauner 1976). Early in the Late Archaic period arrow technology was found mixed with dart point technology (Cannell 2001; Leonhardy and Rice 1970). However, by approximately 1,000 years ago arrow point technology had almost completely replaced dart or spear technology in all parts of the Columbia Plateau (DiScipio 1997; Endacott 1992; Jenkins and Connolly 1994; Sappington 1994:383). Although it can be argued that bow and arrow technology reflects a greater efficiency for hunting compared with dart technology, the rise of bow and arrow technology and ultimately the complete replacement of dart technology by the bow and arrow might also be related to an increase in warfare on the Columbia Plateau during the Late Archaic. In comparison to dart technology, bow and arrow technology is effective for fighting from safe distances and for providing rapid deployment of projectiles. The Late Archaic period shows evidence of large aggregations of people into villages, the isolation of villages on islands, the concealment of villages in deep side canyons, and inevitably more competition for limited or valuable resources. These factors suggest that the adoption of the bow and arrow may be related as much to hostilities among humans as to more effective hunting methods.

CULTURE HISTORY AND RESEARCH CONTEXTS ON THE COLUMBIA PLATEAU

This brief culture historical overview of the Columbia Plateau raises important questions about the extent and content of regional prehistory. I argue that culture histories provide the foundation of prior knowledge that allows researchers to ask relevant questions about past human conditions. Coarse-grained culture histories (like the one presented above) are helpful for defining coarse-grained questions about a region. As culture histories become more fine-grained (scaled by space and time) they become more effective measures of prior knowledge and allow researchers to ask increasingly more relevant anthropological or behavioral questions about the data and patterning under investigation (see Goodale et al., this volume; Rousseau, this volume). This chapter concludes with a discussion of some of the important questions suggested in the culture historical overview presented above.

Archaeologists often assume that residential sedentism can be recognized in the archaeological record by the use of pithouse structures because pithouses are intellectually linked by researchers to increased residential sedentism and perhaps a more "collector-like" economic strategy. This assumption of course needs to be systematically tested and demonstrated. If this is true, however, then it is important that we develop a better understanding of the temporal and spatial ranges of Columbia Plateau sedentism. Culture history tells us that pithouse use was not uniform in time and space across the Columbia Plateau or the greater Plateau region (see Chatters, this volume; Kuijt and Prentiss, this volume). A tally of pithouse dates from the 350,000 km^2 Columbia Plateau may not provide a reliable understanding of prehistoric sedentism. Different locations on the Columbia Plateau may have adopted residentially sedentary practices at much different times. Without refined spatial segregation of such data, it would be difficult to understand the potential regional differences in Columbia Plateau sedentism. Could the same cultural group be moving from one location to another over the centuries? Could specific locations holding sedentary peoples have been abandoned for more productive locations as microenvironments changed because of natural and human perturbations (see Kuijt and Prentiss, this volume)? Such questions are generated from our more detailed understanding of Columbia Plateau culture history.

Columbia Plateau culture history reveals that residential sedentism was practiced at multiple locations on the Columbia Plateau simultaneously. For instance, sedentary villages appear to have been occupied on the Middle Columbia River and on the Clearwater and Deschutes rivers at the same time. We do not yet understand this relationship between the different spatially distinct areas; nor do we understand the conditions under which we might expect different groups to adapt to a sedentary lifestyle at approximately the same time. This leaves us with a number of important questions. For example, do these different sedentary villages represent different cultural groups? Could there have been contact among the various groups that might have led to similar adaptations? Can any or all of the sedentary groups be historically traced to a common geographic or cultural origin? These are important questions related to human culture change and continuity not only for the Columbia Plateau but for a much wider anthropological audience (see Prentiss and Kuijt, this volume). Prior knowledge helps us craft these questions for our regional studies.

The later end of the Late Archaic period on the Columbia Plateau shows clear evidence of population aggregation. Culture histories from all corners of the Columbia Plateau reveal multiple settings for these aggregated communities (islands, hidden side canyons, upland meadows, etc.) (see Chatters, this volume). Refined culture histories help us pose relevant questions about larger issues of human organization, cultural evolution, and social formations, and they direct us toward meaningful data sets in the archaeological record that may be useful for addressing specific questions (see Hayden and Cousins, this volume; Prentiss and Kuijt, this volume). To what extent was Columbia Plateau population aggregation related to coalition formation? How might this be related to the emergence of warfare, trade, and the centralization of power (see Chatters, this volume)? Along different lines, we might ask if prior knowledge about raw material sources and particular technologies helps define specific components of the archaeological record that might help support or refute competing hypotheses related to warfare, trade, and power (see Blake, this volume).

The intensification of food acquisition and processing has been an important archaeological issue on the Columbia Plateau for over 20 years. Most researchers attribute food intensification to greater population densities, or they attribute increased population densities to increased food intensification. In either case, we know that increases in human populations occur with a shift (even a slight shift) toward greater female-to-male survival ratios and potentially shifts in the economic roles of females and males. Female-to-male sex ratios in the majority of known hunter-gatherer populations worldwide tend to positively correlate with the economic contribution of females and males. When considering how labor was allocated in these communities, we should ask if our broad understanding of culture history illustrates a shift in food-production effort from males to females on the Columbia Plateau (see Lepofsky and Peacock, this volume). If so, when and where did this occur? Does it correlate with increased population aggregation? From the standpoint of material correlates, what data sets can be used to asses food-production and -processing efforts in the archaeological record (see Goodale et al., this volume; Hayden and Adams, this volume)?

If nothing else, this overview of Columbia Plateau culture history illustrates that there is a whole series of significant anthropological and evolutionary questions that have yet to be fully addressed by researchers. In addition to the issues of sedentism, aggregation, coalition formation, and food-resource intensification, there are a number of important unresolved cultural-historical topics. For example, how should the phrase "Plateau ethnographic pattern" be used by researchers, and to what extent was it characteristic of the Columbia Plateau at different points of the past? How do we account for the aggregated Late Archaic pithouse villages found in upland areas away from major river canyons (so uncharacteristic of the "Plateau ethnographic pattern")? How do we explain the replacement of pithouses and perhaps pithouse villages by rectangular lodge houses? How extensive was this "replacement" pattern, and what does this tell us about prehistoric settlement systems? Does it represent a new adaptive strategy adopted by extant Columbia Plateau groups, or does it mark the migration (or invasion) of a different cultural group into the Columbia Plateau?

Culture histories provide important material patterning over time and across space. Such patterning affords the contexts for which archaeologists begin to synthesize archaeological "facts." It is important to remember that even though culture histories cannot often help answer questions about cultural evolution and human organization, these histories provide the contexts that allow us to pose relevant questions about complicated human conditions. Detailed culture histories yield pertinent questions and help archaeologists identify data useful for addressing our questions. It is both necessary and important that a book on the evolution of hunter-gatherer complexity, such as this one, devotes the first third of its contents to discussing preexisting social and economic systems and establishing how these regional patterns change through time.

3

CULTURAL COMPLEXITY

A NEW CHRONOLOGY OF THE UPPER COLUMBIA DRAINAGE AREA

Nathan B. Goodale, William C. Prentiss, and Ian Kuijt

The Upper Columbia drainage contrasts significantly with that of the Middle and Lower Columbia. For the purposes of this chapter, the area includes the Columbia River drainage extending from Kettle Falls in the south through Upper Arrow Lake. It also includes the Lower Kootenai and Slocan river drainages (Figure 3.1). First, from an environmental standpoint, this landscape features substantially forested contexts including a significant interior rain forest. Second, human adaptations in this place were often quite different from those in nearby regions of the Plateau. Ethnographic research documents a complex hunter-gatherer society (Lakes Salish or Sinixt) whose principal subsistence resources included not just salmon and roots but also a very significant investment in larger game including mountain goat, bighorn sheep, and elk. No other Eastern Plateau society exhibited the same degree of cultural complexity as that of the Sinixt. As this study demonstrates, densely aggregated communities appear to have emerged in this area more than once, implying cycles of aggregation and possible socioeconomic complexity. The following analysis seeks to review current cultural chronologies developed for the Kettle Falls, Arrow Lakes, and Slocan areas and then to develop a comprehensive chronology for the region based on archaeological data primarily reflecting settlement and subsistence behavior but also considering limited indicators of variability in social organization. Implications for archaeological explanation are considered at the end.

KETTLE FALLS CHRONOLOGY

The cultural chronology of the Kettle Falls area derives primarily from the extensive cultural resource management investigations of Chance and Chance (1977, 1979, 1982, 1985). Their research has been particularly important for defining variability in settlement and subsistence during the past 4,000 years. The first evidence for human occupation of the Kettle Falls area is the Pre-Takumakst period and dates from 3500 to 2700 B.P. This time period in the Kettle Falls region is not well understood at this time. There is evidence for low densities of human populations at the Fishery, Ksunku, and Kwilkin sites. Currently, no pithouses have been discovered in this region that date to this time. However, two hearths from the Fishery site have been excavated that date to the Pre-Takumakst period (Chance and Chance 1982). Lithic assemblages of this time period contain high frequencies of cryptocrystalline artifacts, featuring contracting and square stemmed projectile points and a few cobble cutting tools. Based on limited aquatic faunal remains, the Kettle Falls area seems to have been used for limited fishing activities during this early time period (Chance and Chance 1982).

The Takumakst period dates from 2700 to 1600 B.P. and is characterized by a quartzite technology that is "clumsy" when compared with that of the later periods of occupation in the Kettle Falls. However, this raw material can be expediently flaked along the dominant cleavage planes. The most diagnostic element of this assemblage is the "Takumakst chopper," which functionally may actually have been a core. Flakes removed from this core would probably have been intended for fish butchering or to aid in the construction of fish traps. Chance and Chance (1982) argue that the first extensive period of occupation at the Fishery site seems to have been during the Takumakst period by Salish peoples. The China Bend site is a possible residential context, containing lithic artifacts, but, as yet, no pithouses firmly dated to this time frame.

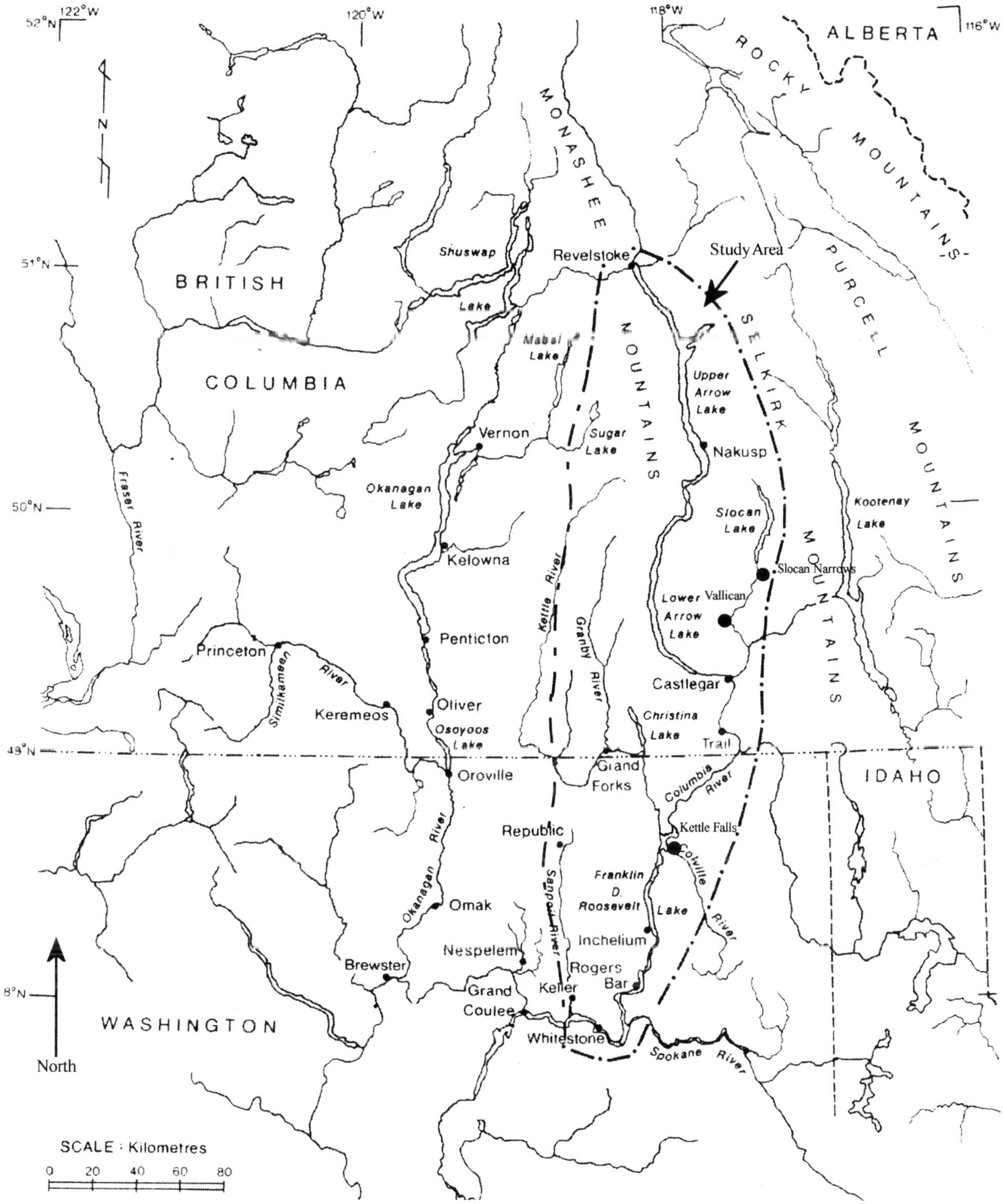

Figure 3.1. Map of the Upper Columbia.

The Sinaikst period dates from 1600 to 600 B.P. and shows wide variation in projectile point style. Chance and Chance (1982) suggest that the variation in the assemblage at the Fishery site is a consequence of many different groups of people using the site. Exotic lithics entered the Kettle Falls area in substantial quantities during this time frame, peaking at 1150 B.P. Chance and Chance suggest that this peak in exotics corresponds to peak trade in the area. During the Sinaikst period, deep pithouses were occupied at the Ilthkoyape and Chaudiere sites. A medium-sized house (10–14 m in diameter) at the Ilthkoyape site is dated with multiple occupations at

770 ± 90 and 1190 ± 70 B.P. Relying on botanical data, Chance and Chance argue that these pithouses were occupied during the summer months and reflect the largest population densities in the Kettle Falls area.

The Shwayip period dates circa 600–200 B.P. and was dominated by side-notched projectile points and miniature quartzite knifes (Chance and Chance 1982). These assemblages are found at the Fishery, Ksunku, Ilthkoyape, Chaudiere, Shonitkwu, Kwilkin, and Nancy Creek sites. Chance and Chance (1982) argue that this time period reflects a reduction in human populations in the area. The Ilthkoyape site also produced a medium-sized pithouse that has produced a date of 370 ± 70 B.P.

THE ARROW LAKES/SLOCAN VALLEY CHRONOLOGY

The sequence developed for the Upper Columbia Drainage/Arrow Lakes area is primarily also the consequence of cultural resource management archaeology conducted for hydrologic dam- and road-construction projects. Excavations in the 1970s by Turnbull and in the 1980s by Mohs provide the basis for the literature that has been available for the area. Cultural historic frameworks for the area have been constructed based on stylistic changes in artifacts, housepit morphologies, and their arrangement in the landscape. This section presents the Arrow Lakes chronology from Turnbull (1977), the Slocan Valley variants of Mohs (1982), Rousseau (1982), and Eldridge (1984) and recent additions by Prentiss et al. (2001) and Goodale (2001).

The first substantial evidence of settlement in the Arrow Lakes region has been termed the Deer Park phase (Turnbull 1977) or the Winlaw phase (Eldridge 1984; Mohs 1982) and dates to 3500–2450 B.P. The pithouses contained in this phase follow a distinct distribution along the immediate riverbanks and lakeshores in a linear fashion. The housepits excavated by Turnbull and Mohs assigned to this phase are small in size, ranging from 7 to 10 m in diameter. However, the Slocan Narrows site (DkQi 1) has revealed two large houses that date to this time period and measure 16 m and 22 m in diameter (Prentiss et al. 2001). These housepits are circular to oval in plan, and Mohs (1982) describes them as lacking raised earth rims. This may only be a characteristic of the small-sized pithouses because the large house in DkQi 1 has an obvious raised rim. Mohs (1982) also notes that this cultural phase is not well represented at the Vallican site. This early occupation at the Slocan Narrows site provides the best example of pithouse architecture from this early phase. The Slocan Narrows site contains over 60 housepits, featuring two clusters of exceptionally large houses, many of which could date to this early time frame.

The lithic tool assemblage of the Deer Park/Winlaw phase is marked by the presence of medium-sized stemmed and shouldered projectile points that are similar to Shuswap horizon points of the Fraser–Thompson Plateau area (Richards and Rousseau 1987; Rousseau, this volume). The most frequently recovered raw materials include Kootenay argillaceous chert, siltstone, schistose mica quartzite, and basalt. The lithic assemblage at the Slocan Narrows site associated with this cultural phase is very limited. Faunal remains are limited to unidentifiable mammal with fish and shell completely absent, primarily because of acidic soils.

The next cultural phase in the Upper Columbia region is the Vallican phase, which dates to 2450–1250 B.P. Housepits average 11 m in diameter from the Vallican site (Mohs 1982). No pithouses associated with this time period have been discovered at the Slocan Narrows site or in the Turnbull (1977) excavations. Diagnostic lithic artifacts include corner- and basal-notched points and crescent- or key-shaped scrapers/perforators. This stylistic variation in the lithic technology is similar to that found in the later Takumakst and early Sinaikst periods at Kettle Falls, the Okanagan Chiliwist phase (Grabert 1974), and the Plateau horizon of the Fraser–Thompson region (Richards and Rousseau 1987; Rousseau, this volume). The Vallican phase artifacts differ from those of the Takumakst in the quality of stone working. The Takumakst period in the Kettle Falls region contains hastily made lithic tools, whereas the Vallican phase features high-quality tools and exotic goods such as nephrite adzes. Although no housepits dating to this time period were found at the Slocan Narrows site, numerous (relative to the lithic assemblage size) Plateau horizon-style projectile points were recovered in addition to one key-shaped scraper. Faunal remains are rare for reasons discussed previously. However, when they are recovered, assemblages include mammal bones and the shells of freshwater mussels (Mohs 1982).

The final cultural phase defined by Mohs (1982) and Turnbull (1977) is termed the Slocan phase and dates from 1250 B.P. to contact. The housepits that date to this time period have been excavated at the Slocan Narrows and Vallican sites. The houses excavated at the Vallican site average 8.7 m in diameter. However, there is variability, with medium and small-sized pithouses occurring together. This average was determined by the data set provided by Mohs (1982) and only includes those cultural depressions with a diameter greater than 5 m. The second occupational phase of Housepit 1 at the Slocan Narrows site (DkQi 1) dates to this time period, suggesting that very large houses (e.g., 16 m in diameter) do date to the phase. This phase employs a wide variety of housepit styles, including circular, oval, and rectangular outlines with top and side entrances. Cache pits were also used during this time and are external to the housepits, along with extramural hearths and activity areas.

Lithic artifacts of the Slocan phase include small side-notched points, occasional Columbia corner-notched points, and frequent ground-stone items (Eldridge 1984; Mohs 1982; Rousseau 1982). These points are characteristic of the Kamloops horizon in the Canadian Plateau (Rousseau, this volume). However, the Kamloops multi-notched variety has remained undiscovered in the Slocan Valley and Upper Columbia region. The material culture from during this time also closely resembles materials recovered in the Kettle Falls area.

DEVELOPING A COMPREHENSIVE CHRONOLOGY BASED ON ADAPTIVE PATTERNS

The preceding chronologies have provided important frameworks for the collection and organization of Upper Columbia Plateau archaeological data. However, they are not based on a formal assessment of data designed to provide indicators of variability in adaptive behavior. The following analysis provides a first step toward defining temporal variability in human adaptations in the Upper Columbia, similar to that undertaken by Chatters (1995a) for the middle and lower portions of the Columbia and Snake river basins.

The data set used in this analysis is derived from 116 ^{14}C dates compiled by Goodale (2001) from the published and unpublished literature for the area. These dates are representative of housepit occupations, root-processing ovens, cultural earthworks, storage features, hearths associated with nonresidential sites, and dated faunal assemblages. Each date was calibrated via CALIB 4.3 and then plotted with respect to the date's mean in age by a series of graphs presented below. A strict review of provenience was conducted in order to assess which dates are appropriate for this data set. Dates that were not used either lacked adequate provenience data or were considered to be associated with other unrelated cultural or noncultural events (i.e., rim dates from pithouses).

The calibrated dates were then used to examine changes in the settlement systems of the prehistoric inhabitants of the Upper Columbia. By looking at the distribution of ^{14}C dates from multiple sites and feature contexts, we were able to provide preliminary proxy measurements of settlement and subsistence behavior and population densities. Differences in time periods were then subdivided into six distinct phases based on cultural material. Characteristics were then grouped together under a date range, adaptive pattern, and cultural phase name for the Upper Columbia, distinguishing differences in settlement pattern and socioeconomic organization.

DATA PATTERNS

Housepits

In the Upper Columbia region the first pithouses appear circa 3400–3200 B.P. (Figure 3.2). The early houses, dating between 3400 and 1800 B.P., range in size from small to large. The Slocan Narrows site contains houses that are 16 m and 22 m in diameter, dating prior to 2700 B.P., which are the largest pithouses recorded on the Plateau at this early date. Between 1200 and 200 B.P. the greatest concentration of occupations occurred as small, medium, and large pithouses. In this region, small pithouses occurred between 3400 and 600 B.P., medium pithouses occurred between 3400 and 200 B.P., and large pithouses occurred between 2800 and 600 B.P.

Root Processing

In the Upper Columbia region the root-processing record begins at circa 6200 B.P. (Figure 3.3). The dated root-processing ovens were obtained entirely from sites in the southern part of the study area at Kettle Falls and in the Calispell Valley. The interval from 6200 to 3800 B.P. is characterized by limited use of root-processing ovens. Two periods of intense root processing appear to correlate with increasing use of pithouses after circa 3800 B.P. The first peak in oven frequencies occurred at circa 3800 B.P. and continued until 2400 B.P., and the second occurred between 1200 and 600 B.P.

Storage Pits

The calibrated data for the use of storage pits in the Upper Columbia (Figure 3.4) are very limited ($n = 5$). The storage pit features that have been dated for this region may have been used for storing edible plants such as camas, but much further research is needed to fully understand variability in storage technologies in this area. All dates come from sites in the Kettle Falls and Calispell Valley areas. Storage pit features occur during the same intervals as the most frequent indicators of root processing. Pit features contain a variety of stone tool artifacts, mammal bone, and some camas root remains (Andrefsky et al. 2000).

Cultural Earthworks

Cultural earthworks have been identified at the Slocan Narrows and Vallican sites in southeastern British Columbia ($n = 4$). Cultural earthworks appeared in the late prehistoric during 800–0 B.P. (Figure 3.5). These dates bracket the earliest and latest times for the possible con-

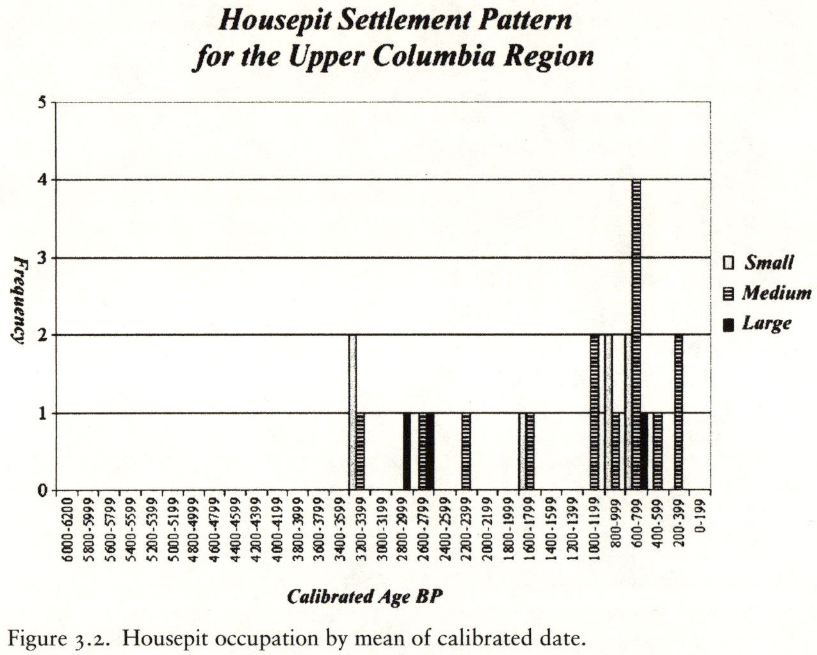

Figure 3.2. Housepit occupation by mean of calibrated date.

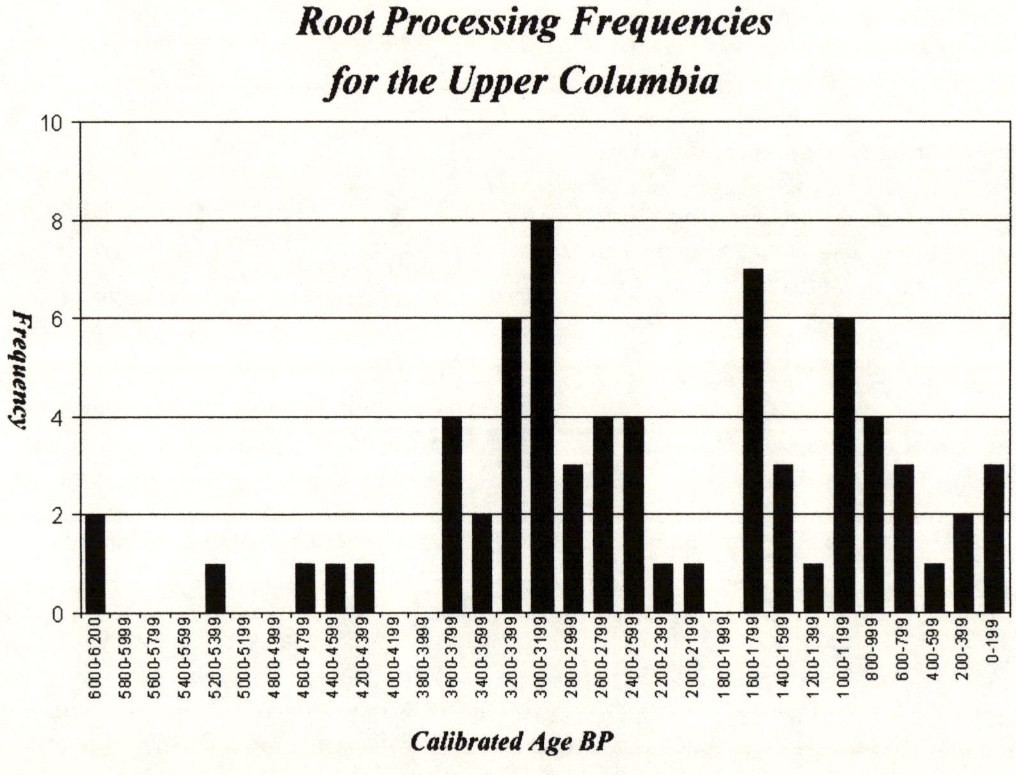

Figure 3.3. Root processing use by mean of calibrated radiocarbon date.

struction of these features. Earthwork functions are not well understood. A 60 m earthwork at the Slocan Narrows site (Prentiss et al. 2001) may have been used for defensive purposes. Platforms at the Vallican site may have had defensive functions as well, though other functions, such as housing, are also possible. It should be noted that the appearance of these features corresponds with changes in aspects of the environment and behavior corresponding to the onset of the "Little Ice Age" and a decline in root-processing activity.

Nonresidential Sites

The dates of hearths from contexts inferred to be nonresidential (not from housepit sites) in nature ($n = 17$) show a bimodal distribution (Figure 3.6). The first peak

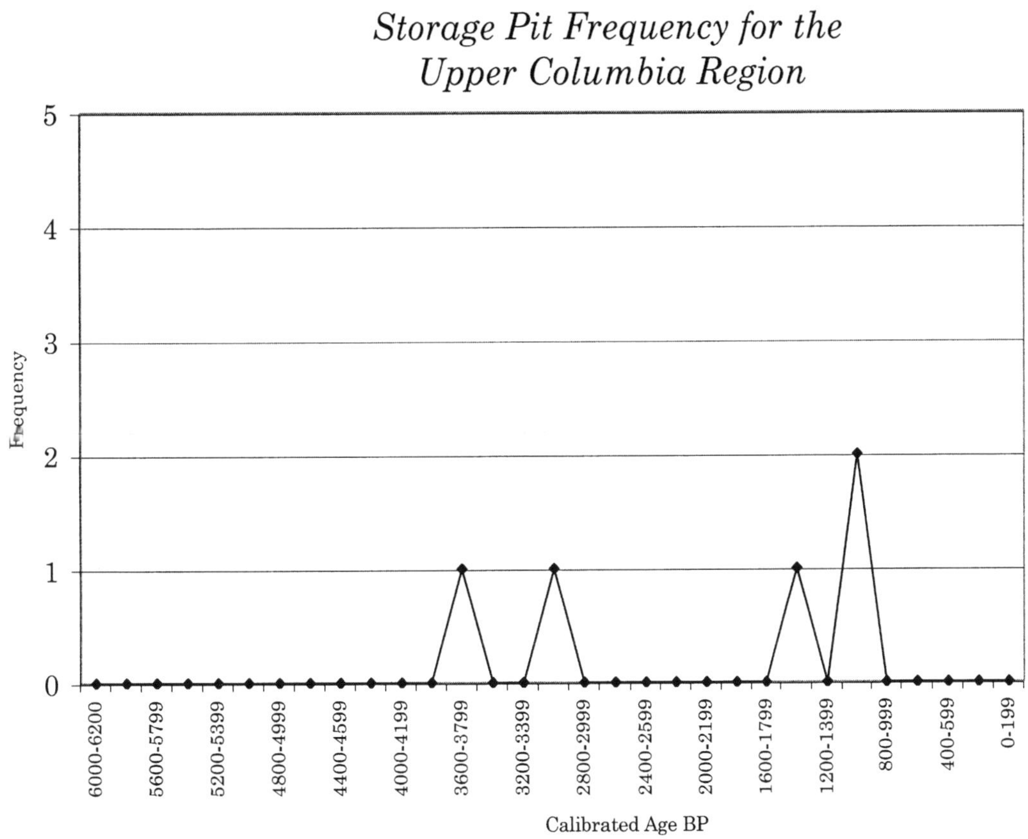

Figure 3.4. Storage pit use by mean of calibrated radiocarbon date.

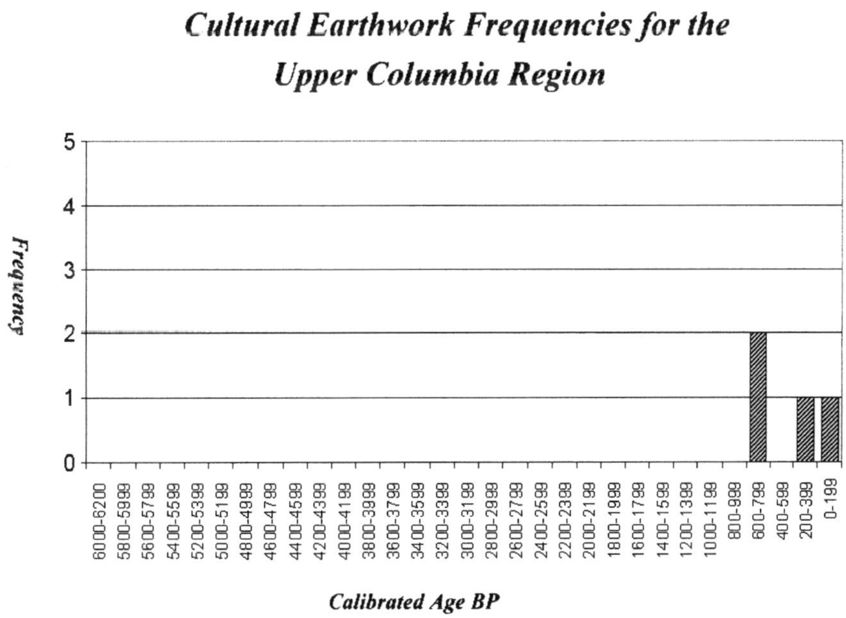

Figure 3.5. Cultural earthwork use by mean of calibrated radiocarbon date.

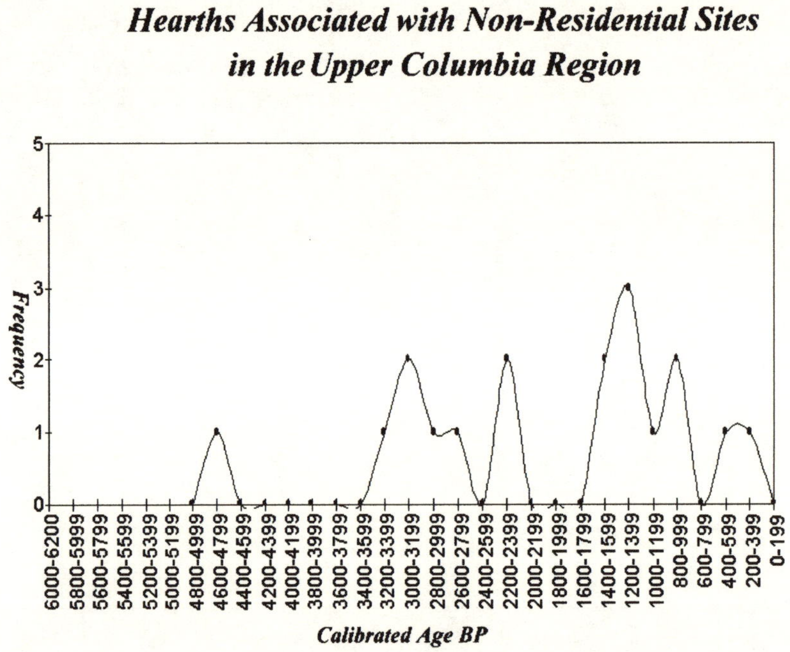

Figure 3.6. Nonresidential site use by mean of calibrated radiocarbon date.

occurred between 3600 and 2200 B.P., and the second occurred between 1600 B.P. and the present (A.D. 1950). These intervals correspond to a temporal peak in housepits, storage pits, and root-processing ovens.

Dated Faunal Assemblage

Highly acidic soils have left faunal assemblages very scarce in the Upper Columbia. Site 45PO137 in the Calispell Valley contains the only dated faunal assemblage with substantial numbers of faunal remains (Figure 3.7). This site reveals stable use of mammalian and fish resources after 1600 B.P. Ethnographically, mammals were a critical resource for the Sinixt people. The calibrated evidence supports this assumption and suggests that mammals were a relatively intensively utilized food staple during the latest prehistoric period. However, this difference may also be a consequence of preservation factors, with larger mammal bones withstanding acidic soils more frequently than small fish remains.

A NEW CHRONOLOGY FOR THE UPPER COLUMBIA

The calibrated evidence suggests a revised view of the evolution of hunter-gatherers in the Upper Columbia region. Six intervals appear to be evident during the past 6,200 years of occupation (Figures 3.8–3.9, Table 3.1). Most obvious are the two periods of heightened pithouse construction and root intensification (see also Thoms 1989), followed in each case by indicators of population dispersal and possible subsistence diversification. We use Binford's (1980) terminology *(collectors* and *foragers)* throughout this discussion as a means of conveying our understanding of the most likely and frequent mobility and subsistence strategies employed by hunter-gatherers of each phase. Our inferences are not intended to reflect the definition of essentialist cultural entities. Rather, we view these patterns as starting points for further analysis of organizational variability.

The Upper Columbia Forager (6200–4200 B.P.)

The Upper Columbia Forager represents a high-mobility forager adaptation that is suggested by the lack of evidence for any permanent residential structures. This period contains dates for the first uses of root processing in the Upper Columbia region, and these are represented by six dates in the Calispell Valley: five from 45PO139 and one from 45PO141. Roots seem to have been a fairly stable resource base during this time and were probably used in a limited manner. The Upper Columbia Forager period also contains one date from the Fishery site in the Kettle Falls area that is in association with a nonresidential site. This period represents a "forager" adaptation similar to those in the Middle Holocene Nesikep tradition of the Canadian Plateau and the Cascade phase in the Columbia Plateau (Chatters 1995a; Prentiss and Chatters 2002; Stryd and Rousseau 1996).

"Hiatus" (4199–3800 B.P.)

Currently, this interval lacks calibrated radiocarbon evidence and represents a brief archaeological gap that separates the forager and collector adaptations. This hiatus

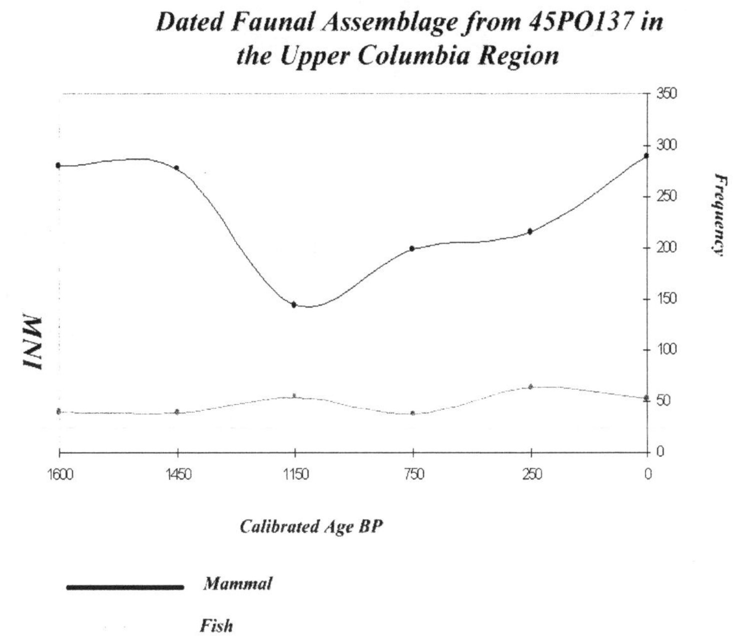

Figure 3.7. Faunal assemblage data by frequency.

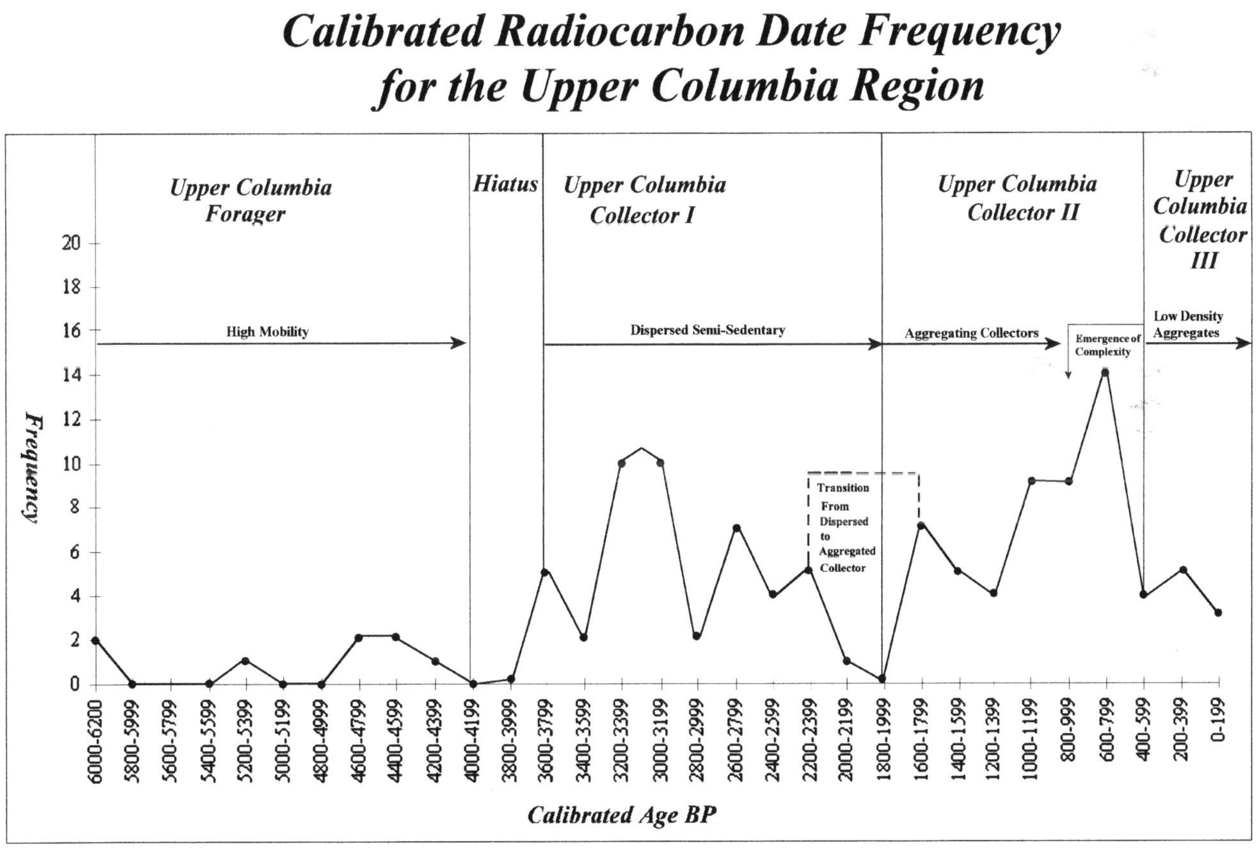

Figure 3.8. Calibrated radiocarbon data for the Upper Columbia region.

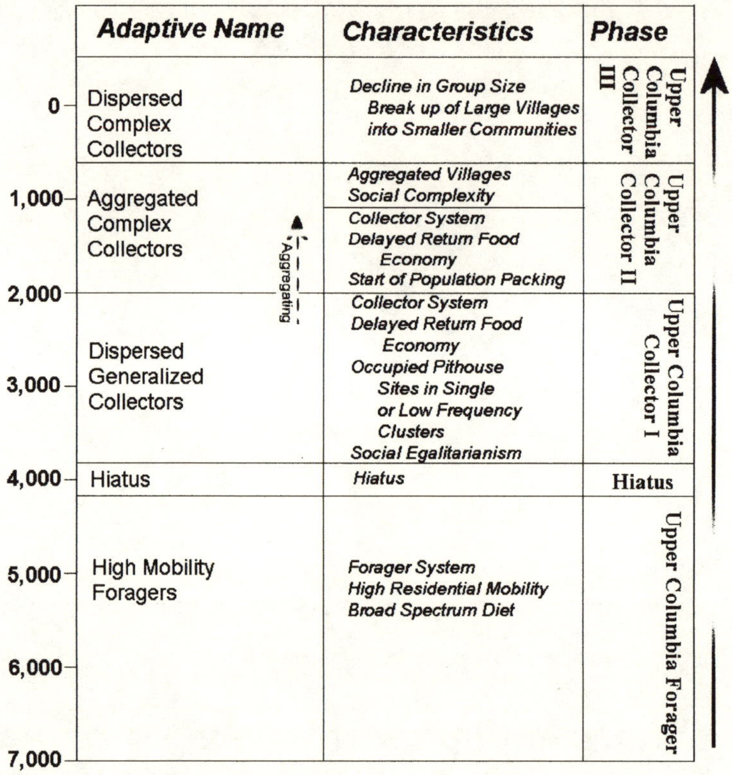

Figure 3.9. Adaptive Interval Summary for the Upper Columbia region.

TABLE 3.1. Time Period Characteristics of the Upper Columbia Regional Chronology.

Time Period	Adaptive Name	Characteristics
6200–4200 Cal B.P.	Upper Columbia Forager	Limited root-processing and nonresidential sites. High-mobility forager adaptation.
4199–3800 Cal B.P.	Hiatus	Hiatus in the archaeology record with a 400-year lapse in radiocarbon dates.
3799–2000 Cal B.P.	Upper Columbia Collector I	Small, medium, and large pithouses are occupied; there is extensive root processing; storage pits appear; and nonresidential site use rises in frequency. Advent of semisedentary dispersed collector system.
1999–600 Cal B.P.	Upper Columbia Collector II	Small, medium and large pithouses are occupied; there is extensive root processing; storage pits are used; nonresidential site use rises in frequency; fish and mammal resources appear to be consistent subsistence contributions throughout the interval. The advent of the aggregated collector adaptation and complex hunter-gatherers exists from 1200 to 600 cal. B.P.
599–0 Cal B.P.	Upper Columbia Collector III	Onset of the "Little Ice Age," only medium-sized pithouses are occupied with a decline in root processing, storage pit frequencies, and nonresidential sites. Cultural earthworks as a possible defense mechanism appear during this interval. Fish and mammal appear to be constant throughout this interval. Dispersed complex collectors.

temporally corresponds to a similar pattern throughout the Canadian and Columbia Plateaus (Chatters 1995a; Prentiss and Kuijt, this volume). Although the pattern, as recognized in the Upper Columbia area, can be partially explained by the presence of a "flat place" on the radiocarbon curve at 3950–4050 B.P. (Stuiver et al. 1998), it is not adequate as an explanation when examining the larger Plateau region. As noted by Chatters (1995a) and Prentiss and Kuijt (this volume), the evidence for near to complete abandonment is much longer than 100 years and generally occurs after this time. Thus, it still remains possible that a short occupational hiatus occurred after 4000 B.P.

The Upper Columbia Collector I (3799–2000 B.P.)

The Upper Columbia Collector I represents the first of two peak occupational horizons and the advent of the collector-type system in the Upper Columbia. The first semisubterranean pithouses were established and occupied during this interval and vary in size from small to large. Pithouses dating to this time are found in single or low-density clusters in the Upper Columbia landscape and are generally representative of a dispersed collector adaptation. The Slocan Narrows site may provide an exception to this pattern, for it contains two clusters of extremely large houses, two of which now date to this time frame (Prentiss et al. 2001). Further research could demonstrate an early aggregated community in this context. The first indicators of intensified camas root processing occur in conjunction with an expansion in the frequency of storage pits. Faunal and floral data are still lacking at this point, but given the present indications of dispersed and possibly occasional aggregated pithouse communities in optimal fishing locations, evidence for camas intensification, and data on the use of storage tactics, this period likely marks the beginning of the dispersed generalized collector adaptation in the Upper Columbia and is concurrent to similar behaviors at the advent of Pithouse II (Chatters 1995a, this volume) and the Shuswap horizon (Richards and Rousseau 1987; Rousseau, this volume).

Transition

Between the Collector I and Collector II adaptations there is a decline in the frequencies of radiocarbon dates. Although this could be explained, at least in part, by sampling bias, a similar pattern has been recognized by Chatters (1995a) for the entire Columbia Plateau. This suggests the possibility of short-term population decline in the region prior to the advent of the next broad adaptive period. Clearly, further research is required into this important but little understood period.

The Upper Columbia Collector II (1999–600 B.P.)

The Upper Columbia Collector II corresponds to a second high-density occupation of the Upper Columbia. Archaeological evidence supports the emergence of aggregated pithouse villages by late in this period (ca. 1200–600 B.P.). Large sites, such as Vallican, Slocan Narrows, and Ilthkoyape, feature the highest-density clusters of houses in all size ranges. This period also corresponds to the late peak in root processing and storage pits. Hearths associated with nonresidential sites also peaked at this time. Some of these could be the consequence of logistical or task group mobility strategies. Specialized sites such as the Fishery at Kettle Falls (45ST94) clearly reflect specialized resource-harvesting strategies, typical of collectors (Chance and Chance 1977). Intensified harvesting of shellfish is also known from the Vallican site (Mohs 1982). Faunal remains from 45PO137 in the Calispell Valley demonstrate the continuous use of both fish and mammalian resources during this time, with a relatively more intensive use of mammals over fish.

The Upper Columbia Collector III (599–100 B.P.)

The beginning of this interval corresponds to the start of the Little Ice Age (Pielou 1991) and marks the expansion of glaciers in the high-altitude contexts of the Rocky Mountains and Cascade Range. This interval is indicated by a decline in the frequency of radiocarbon dates; however, pithouse occupations are still present, and medium-sized structures dominate the record. The use of root-processing ovens appears to have declined and may have been consequent to the onset of the Little Ice Age and the associated effects on the availability of resources in some areas. During this time, cultural earthworks appear in the archaeological record. If these features do reflect heightened attention to territorial defense, then they could be linked to an increasingly patchy environment brought on by cooler conditions. Interestingly, warfare increased in many other areas of western North American during the final several hundred years of the prehistoric period and into historic times (Chatters, this volume). Simultaneously, burials from the Vallican site provide indicators of the distinct presence of complex social organization. Burial 2, for example, included an infant and a fetus, wrapped in animal skins, interred with 2,102 glass trade beads, 138 rolled copper-tube beads, 595 dentalia shell beads and pendants, 59 drilled elk-tooth pendants, 16 perforated copper-slate pendants, nine copper-alloy buttons, three copper-alloy rings, one iron pendant, one coiled copper-tube bead, and various other small items (Mohs 1982). Clearly, this reflects a high degree of material investment in the status of children, typical behavior for complex hunter-gatherers, whom Hayden (1995) calls entrepreneurs. Overall, these data suggest generally reduced or at least more dispersed populations, yet increased attention to the marking of territory and social status, particularly during the early historic period.

TESTING THE ADAPTIVE MODEL

The data discussed above appear to reflect some important past dynamics. First, populations appear to have strongly increased and declined twice in the past 4,000 years. This pattern appears to correlate with the emergence and decline of aggregated pithouse communities and various markers of socioeconomic complexity. Our

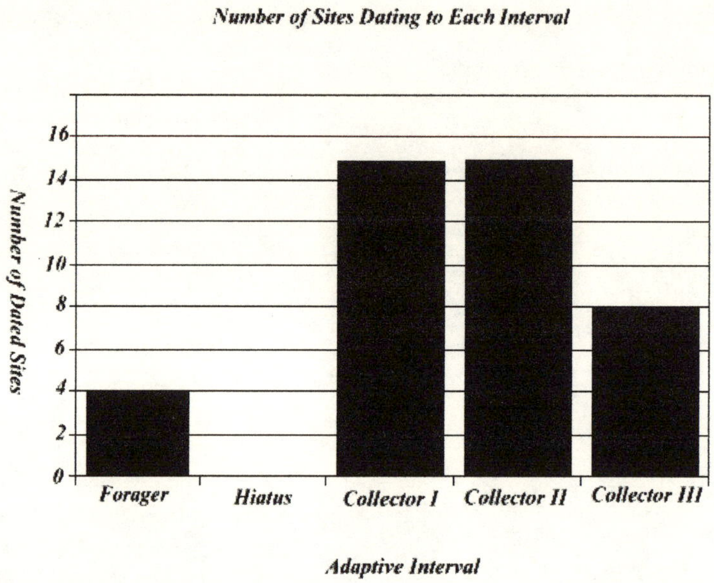

Figure 3.10. Sites per interval.

question is, Does the radiocarbon record reflect actual population dynamics, or is this merely a mirage created by a record biased toward more frequent dates at the largest sites? If the data do reflect population dynamics, then this will have implications for our explanations of cultural variability. The second problem concerns abandonments. Chatters (1995a), Prentiss and Chatters (2003), and Prentiss and Kuijt (this volume) assert that near to total abandonment of many parts of the Plateau occurred at circa 4000 B.P. These researchers argue that abandonment was associated with climate change and cultural maladaptation and may have opened the region to an influx of populations from the Northwest Coast and possibly elsewhere, bringing new adaptations (namely, the collector system). Data presented in this study so far point to this period and one other (ca. 1800–2000 B.P.) as possible periods of low population or even abandonment. However, a more rigorous evaluation of the error distributions around the calibrated dates must be undertaken to justify this conclusion.

Population Dynamics

First, to support the data expressed in Figure 3.8 as a proxy for population, the calibrated evidence should indicate that the percentage of radiocarbon dated sites is roughly equal to the percentage of sites occupied for each given adaptive interval. In this model, higher site frequency should represent higher population densities. Therefore, the highest density of occupied sites should correspond to the Upper Columbia Collector I and II, with relatively lower densities during the Collector III adaptation and even lower ones during the Forager adaptation. Site frequency data (Figure 3.10) do indeed provide a similar pattern to that of Figure 3.8, tentatively supporting its use as a population proxy. Interestingly, Figure 3.10 also shows that the site densities for Collector I and II are roughly the same. However, merely counting the frequency of sites in each interval is an insufficient test. A more accurate approach is to consider the relationship between total time span in each interval and the frequency of sites. The data from this analysis (Table 3.2) suggest generally low populations during the Forager and Collector I periods, followed by a substantial increase during Collector II and III. Further, despite seemingly reduced frequencies of aggregated pithouse villages and root-roasting and storage pits, these data suggest that Collector III may not have featured significant population reduction but, rather, a more even pattern of dispersal on the landscape.

Abandonment and Change in the Upper Columbia

Another way to test the conclusions illustrated in Figure 3.8 is to assess patterning in calibrated dates at two-sigma (95 percent confidence interval) error ranges. Points where major adaptive changes occurred that were accompanied by breaks in occupation sequences should be recognizable as significant disjunctions in the radiocarbon record. Figure 3.11 illustrates the full range of calibrated dates (n = 116), plotted and coded by cultural interval. This picture reveals a fairly continuous distribution spanning 7200–0 B.P. This is especially evident during the Collector I, II, and III intervals where the centroids (means) overlap in many instances. A couple of exceptions occur. First, between the Forager and Collector I adaptations, the high two-sigma range of the youngest Forager date and the oldest Collector I date explains the overlap.

TABLE 3.2. Adaptive Interval and Site Density in the Upper Columbia.

Adaptation	Total Time/Years	Number of Sites	Percent of Sites	Site : Year
Forager	2,000	4	9.5	1 : 500
Hiatus	400	0	0.0	0 : 0
Collector I	2,000	15	35.7	1 : 133.3
Collector II	1,200	15	35.7	1 : 93.3
Collector III	500	8	19.0	1 : 62.5
Total	6,100	42	100.0	42 : 6,100

Although this may be partially explained by variability in the calibrated radiocarbon curve, comparisons with data from other areas of the Plateau (Chatters 1995a; Prentiss and Kuijt, this volume) still support the possibility that a significant population reduction or even full abandonment occurred during the period 4200–3800 B.P.

Second, Figure 3.11 reveals that there is another break during the transition from Collector I to Collector II. This would be a major disjunction if not for the presence of a single date from a root-roasting pit considered for the purposes of this study to be the final event in the Collector I sequence. The time period from 2200 to 1800 B.P. appears to represent some form of cultural transition, perhaps associated with a brief population dispersal. The radiocarbon record does not appear to reflect abandonment, however. Chatters (1995a) recognizes a similar pattern on the Middle Columbia and Lower Snake.

Finally, Figure 3.11 presents a continuous overlap of dates associated with the transition from Collector II to Collector III. This supports the argument that no major population disjunction occurred between Collector II and III. It appears likely that there was little cultural change between these intervals other than in the scale and frequency of large group aggregation in pithouse communities.

DISCUSSION

The results of this research present a number of implications for understanding the evolution of complex hunter-gatherer societies. First, this research provides another indicator of dramatic cultural change at circa 4200–3800 B.P. A small-scale mobile society appears to have existed in the Upper Columbia prior to the onset of the full Neoglacial climatic period. Rapid cooling at 4200 B.P. may

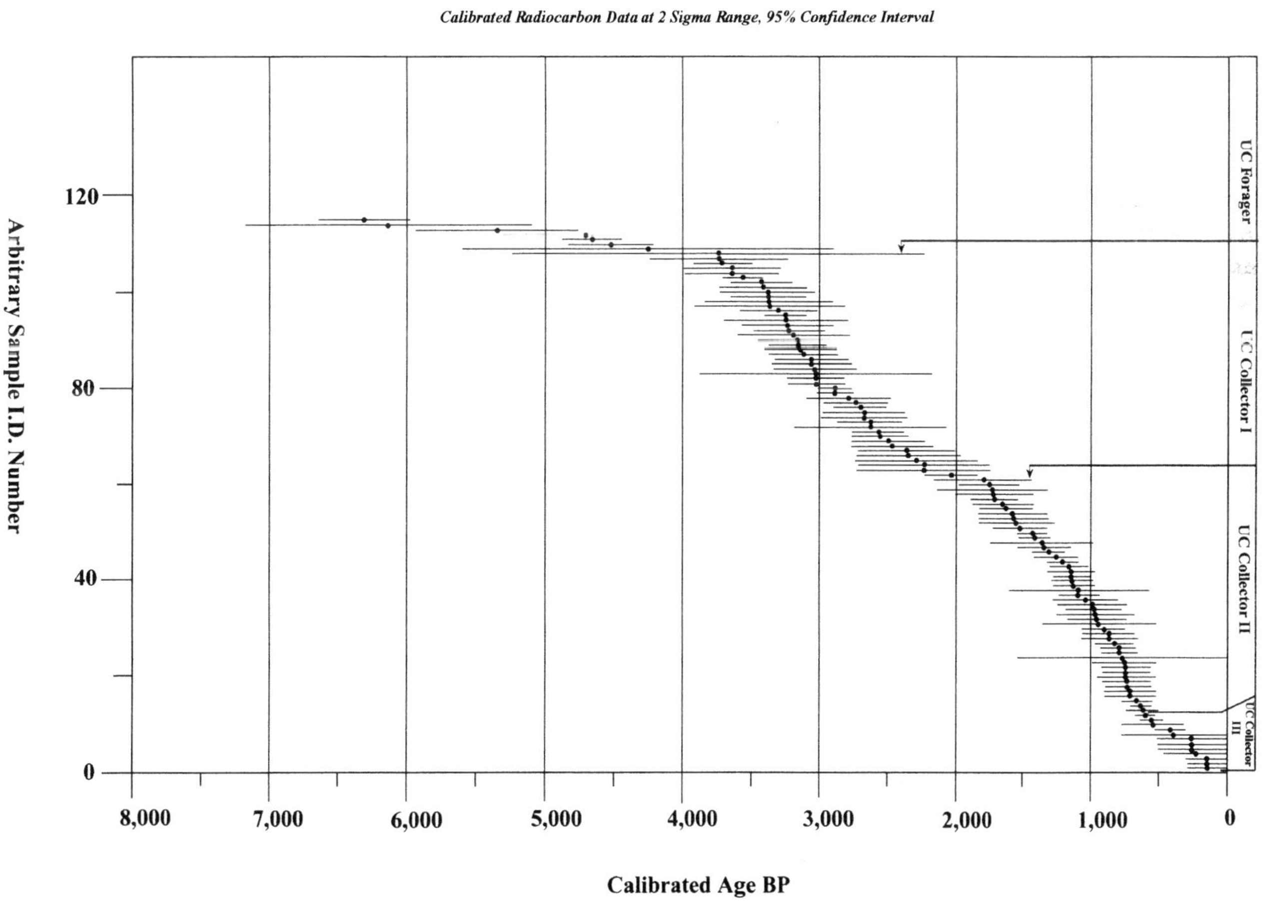

Figure 3.11. Two-sigma range of calibrated radiocarbon dates.

have caused population reduction until at least 3800 B.P., after which populations bringing a collector-like adaptation emerged in the area. We argue that this process was not one of simple social change but, rather, a wholesale transformation of the basic socioeconomy. Prentiss and Chatters (2003) propose that the interior Plateau collector system emerged on the Northwest Coast at a much earlier date, spreading into the former region after the climate change had largely emptied the area. This will be an important problem to test with future research in the Upper Columbia.

Second, it would appear that, at least as represented by the Slocan data, aggregated pithouse communities emerged and declined twice in the Upper Columbia. The village at Slocan Narrows featured the largest early pithouses on the entire Plateau (Prentiss et al. 2001). Although only two of the large houses have been radiocarbon dated, it is likely that the two clusters of these houses will reveal numerous other early dates. These houses are equivalent in size to the largest houses found at sites such as Keatley Creek in the Mid-Fraser Canyon (Hayden 1997). They are large enough to have housed groups potentially as large as 30–40 people per house (cf. Hayden et al. 1996c). The management of groups this large may have necessitated at least some form of achievement-based ranking (Ames 1985; Binford 2001). Researchers now need to look for additional data to explore this issue and to ask how and why this occurred. Our radiocarbon record suggests a rapid and relatively short-lived process of aggregation in this locale that started elsewhere with small houses but very quickly favored the unusually large houses at Slocan Narrows. Without better control over changes in subsistence and technology it is impossible to fully evaluate the processes that gave rise to this pattern. A much larger scale process of aggregation occurred late in the Collector II period, producing major villages at Slocan Narrows, Vallican, Ilthkoyape, and probably many other locations now destroyed by development. In this case, the occupation of exceptionally large housepits followed hundreds of years of buildup in small to medium houses. This pattern provides some tentative support for Binford's (2001) ideas linking social complexity to population packing and territorial behavior in patchy environments.

The final issue most prominently raised by this project is that of community decline and abandonment on the Plateau. Debate between Hayden and Ryder (1991) and Kuijt (2001) highlights the importance of identifying the processes leading to the collapse and reorganization of large-scale interior Plateau communities. Archaeologists must consider local factors such as landslides and temporary dams as well as larger-scale processes such as those associated with climatic change and regionally altered resource conditions. The decline of the Slocan Narrows and Vallican site villages coincided with similar processes in the Fraser–Thompson drainages (Hayden and Ryder 1991; Kuijt 2001) and to the south on the Middle Columbia and Lower Snake rivers (Chatters, this volume). This provides some tentative indicators that this process was regionwide, as suggested by Kuijt (2001). Attention to the construction of earthworks suggests that abandonment may have been preceded by territorial defense (see also Chatters, this volume).

CONCLUSION

The calibrated evidence reveals a bimodal distribution for occupation in the Upper Columbia. The collector-type adaptation was present shortly after 3799 B.P. and continued until ethnographic times with a pattern of population increase extending from during Collector I through II and possibly III. We have argued that population aggregation started to appear as early as 3000 B.P. Complex hunter-gatherers appear to be widely visible between 1200 and 600 B.P. After 600 B.P. most of the high-density villages dispersed into smaller aggregates occupying the drainages of the Upper Columbia. However, they appear to have retained the settlement characteristics and complex social organization of earlier times as the Collector III adaptation.

4

THE EVOLUTION OF COLLECTOR SYSTEMS ON THE CANADIAN PLATEAU

William C. Prentiss and Ian Kuijt

Canadian Plateau societies of the late prehistoric and contact periods were typified by a pattern of economic organization that archaeologists, following Binford (1980), call the "collector" system. On the Plateau, the collector system allowed foragers to harvest excess quantities of anadromous fish, roots, berries, deer, and other resources and preserve enough to provide survival food for long winters (Chatters 1995a; Chatters and Pokotylo 1998; Hayden 1992). Some communities transformed resources into surplus production that could be used in exchange and feasting. This, in turn, helped to increase some household sizes, as reflected in large housepits in some villages (e.g., Hayden 1992, 1995, 1997). It is abundantly clear, however, that the complex societies of the late period, particularly in the Middle Fraser and Thompson river areas, would not have appeared without the economic foundation provided by logistically organized collecting.

The evolutionary origin of collecting on the Canadian Plateau (also termed the Northern Plateau; see Prentiss and Kuijt, this volume) is still not clear. We do know that by circa 3000 B.P. a collector system was present, termed by Richards and Rousseau (1987) the Shuswap horizon (see also Rousseau, this volume). However, excavation of the Baker site, in the South Thompson Valley, has suggested to some (Hayden 2000; Stryd and Rousseau 1996; Wilson 1992) that a collector-like system was in place by about 4500 B.P. Stryd and Rousseau (1996) now argue that collecting developed in situ on the Plateau beginning at this time, arising out of the Lochnore phase. Hayden (2000) agrees, suggesting that the complex Plateau and coastal societies of the later Holocene had their origin in these developments on the interior Plateau. In contrast, Prentiss and Chatters (2003a) have argued that the Baker site does not provide strong evidence for a winter village collecting system and that it is more likely that collecting arose shortly after 5000 B.P. on the central or northern Northwest Coast and spread to the interior after 4000 B.P. This acknowledges that climatic change was fundamentally important in restructuring the foraging environment of the Plateau, apparently driving some cultural systems to extinction while eventually favoring the spread of collector-like adaptations (Chatters 1995a; Prentiss and Chatters 2002).

This chapter provides a test of these alternate models relying on radiocarbon dates and lithic assemblages from the Middle Fraser, Thompson, South Thompson, and Nicola regions (Figure 4.1) of the Canadian Plateau (per definitions in Richards and Rousseau 1987). In our data analysis, we make the assumption that the collector system required a distinctive pattern of energy management necessitating integrated behavior that can be quantified archaeologically as different from other, more forager-like systems (Chatters 1995a; Prentiss and Chatters 2003a, 2003b). Further, we make the assumption that if cultural systems do indeed evolve, then ancestor–descendant relationships should be recognizable in inherited adaptive and stylistic patterns of artifact manufacture and use (O'Brien and Lyman 2000). Finally, evolution of one cultural pattern from another must also be demonstrable through dating. If ancestor–descendant relationships are present, then, ideally, they should be demonstrable through overlapping date ranges.

ALTERNATE MODELS: INDIGENOUS OR EXOGENOUS ORIGINS OF PLATEAU COLLECTORS

Indigenous Evolution of the Collector System

The first model states that the Plateau collector system evolved in situ from within the Lochnore phase (Stryd and Rousseau 1996). Stryd and Rousseau (1996) argue

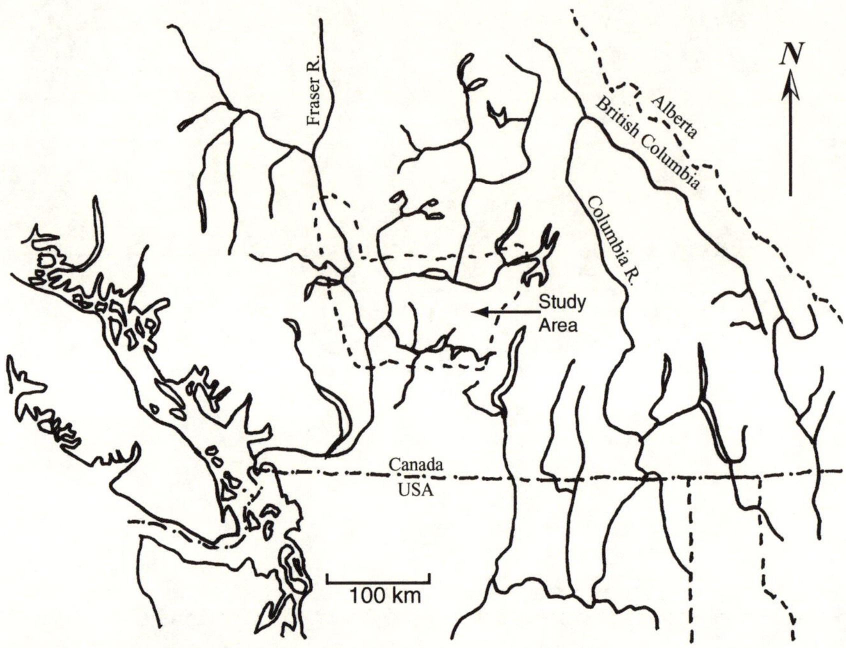

Figure 4.1. Study area on Canadian Plateau.

that Lochnore populations entered the Canadian Plateau with a cultural origin in the Old Cordilleran tradition of the central Northwest Coast (per Matson and Coupland 1995), eventually overwhelming indigenous Lehman phase foragers. Lochnore lithic assemblages are highlighted in particular by notched, leaf-shaped bifaces and a variety of specialized unifaces, including circular, crescent, and end scraper styles, notched pebbles, and microblades. Stryd and Rousseau include the Baker site as Lochnore, thereby expanding the inventory of Lochnore cultural items to include an array of bone/antler tools and large foliate bifaces produced on end-struck flakes. They suggest that a process of cultural change can be recognized from early (ca. 5500–4500 B.P.) to late Lochnore (4500–3500 B.P.). Early Lochnore is represented entirely by ephemeral camps containing lithic artifacts, occasional faunal remains, and scattered hearth features. Faunal remains are diverse but favor mammals, particularly deer, over fish or shellfish. However, salmon remains are found in some early Lochnore contexts. Stryd and Rousseau conclude that early Lochnore represents a mobile foraging adaptation, derived from the coast. This conclusion is based primarily on the association between leaf-shaped (albeit notched) points and salmon, a pattern well defined on the coast during the late Old Cordilleran culture (Ames and Maschner 1999; Matson and Coupland 1995). Late Lochnore, according to Stryd and Rousseau, witnessed the development of a collector-like system beginning at 4500 B.P. The researchers suggest that the classic Lochnore notched leaf-shaped bifaces declined at this time, largely replaced by unnotched leaf-shaped bifaces. Proposed evidence for collector behavior comes entirely from the Baker site and consists of a large salmon bone assemblage and a variety of small storage pits within and, more commonly, outside of three small housepits (Wilson 1992).

Stryd and Rousseau argue further that Lochnore is ancestral to the Shuswap horizon, the first of the three late prehistoric horizons on the Canadian Plateau. They suggest continuity in artifact types, lithic technology, housepits, and use of salmonids. The Shuswap horizon dates to circa 3500–2400 B.P. and is characterized by a wide variety of projectile points, particularly stemmed varieties, but a contrasting low variety of other formally shaped chipped-stone tool types. Richards and Rousseau (1987:27) describe Shuswap lithic technology as "crude" in comparison to later Plateau horizons, as it was often conducted using low- to medium-grade raw materials, resulting in largely expedient flake tools. Housepits of various sizes are present, often containing small to medium storage pits and evidence for increasingly intensive use of salmon (Richards and Rousseau 1987; Stryd and Rousseau 1996).

Hayden (2000) also includes the Baker site within the Lochnore phase, agreeing with Stryd and Rousseau (1996) that Lochnore populations developed a collector adaptation, which ultimately gave rise to the larger and more complex villages of the late period. Hayden suggests that the origin of Lochnore is not well established but that late Lochnore populations probably expanded out of the interior to help establish the early complex societies of the Northwest Coast. He argues that interior contexts would provide a better selective environment for successfully developing storage technology and using this to gain military advantage over indigenous coastal dwellers.

A cornerstone of this argument is that the Baker site is representative of the late Lochnore phase and that Lochnore gradually transformed into Shuswap. If Stryd and Rousseau (1996) and Hayden (2000) are correct, then the Baker site should reflect a winter village collector system with little difference from the subsequent Shuswap horizon sites. If Lochnore, inclusive of the Baker site, is ancestral to Shuswap, then we should also expect relatively significant continuity in the stylistic elements of tool design (O'Brien and Lyman 2000). More specifically, Lochnore artifacts should have greater stylistic similarities to those of Shuswap than to other similarly dated Pacific Northwest traditions such as those of the Charles Culture of the Lower Fraser Valley and Central Coast or Pithouse I of the Columbia Plateau. Tangentially, if the Lochnore phase was intrusive to the Plateau circa 5500 B.P., then Lochnore artifacts should also show greater stylistic similarities to those of the Old Cordilleran Culture but not to those of Early Nesikep or Lehman phase sites. Finally, there should be continuity in dates between late Lochnore and early Shuswap. In particular, there should be no indicators of abandonment on the Canadian Plateau after 4000 B.P., similar to the case on the Columbia Plateau.

Coastal Origin for the Plateau Collector System

A second model suggests that the collector system recognized for the Shuswap horizon has its evolutionary origin outside of the Plateau and was transported into this area by new populations following the abandonment of the area at the Neoglacial temperature downturn of 4000 B.P. (Chatters 1995a; Prentiss and Chatters 2003a, 2003b). This does not mean, however, that earlier experiments with alternative settlement and subsistence systems did not occur. The Baker site could reflect a short-term adaptation to the interior Canadian Plateau by peoples either from the coast or, per Wilson (1992), from the Columbia Plateau (also termed the Southern Plateau; see Prentiss and Kuijt, this volume). Prentiss and Chatters (2003a) leave open the possibility that Baker is also a consequence of Lochnore experimentation with sedentism.

Prentiss and Chatters (2003a, 2003b) have argued that mild temperatures and high moisture, combined with sea-level stabilization, led to optimal resource conditions for interior and coastal foragers of the Pacific Northwest region between 5000 and 4000 B.P. Reduced subsistence constraints led to more intensive and permanent use of formerly marginal environments by growing populations. Geographic and effective isolation and low competitive conditions led to the rapid diversification of cultural systems, resulting in a wide array of mobile to sedentary forager-like adaptations and at least one example of a collector system on the coast. Shortly after 4000 B.P. temperatures declined, seasonality increased, and resource access became temporally constrained. Salmonid populations probably increased, but access was constrained by shorter periods of availability. Winter terrestrial foraging became more costly and risky because of increased forest density and the quantity of snow. Populations without the capacity to harvest surplus food and store it for winter use could not maintain their prior numbers under these conditions. Nearly every cultural variant between southern Alaska and Oregon disappeared between 4000 and 3000 B.P. The collector system had likely appeared on the Queen Charlotte Islands by 4500 B.P. and possibly at the Namu site equally early. It appears to have spread throughout the central coast and into the interior at around 3500 B.P. and then, shortly after, on to the north and south coasts. Under this model, the Lochnore phase, like Pithouse I on the Columbia and the Eayam phase of the Lower Fraser Valley in British Columbia, succumbed to the early Neoglacial and resulted in near or complete population abandonment. The Shuswap horizon reflects a new colonization of the interior by successful populations from the coast in possession of the organizational and technological means for implementing a collector strategy in an interior context.

If this model is correct, then the Lochnore phase sites will reflect adaptations fundamentally different from those of Shuswap. If Lochnore was the end of a long tradition of mobile hunting and gathering on the Canadian Plateau, then Lochnore sites will show similar patterns to those of the Lehman and Early Nesikep phases. If the Baker site was a short-lived experiment in housepit use and food storage, then Baker could reflect elements of a collector system. Next, if Lochnore was indigenous to the Plateau, whereas Shuswap was more strongly linked to coastal cultures, Lochnore artifact styles will be more strongly linked to earlier Plateau patterns, whereas Shuswap will have direct antecedents on the coast. Baker site artifacts will pattern most closely to coastal or Columbia Plateau patterns if they were produced by peoples from either of these places. Finally, if Baker and Lochnore are cultural evolutionary dead ends consequential to Neoglacial climate change, then there should be a hiatus in radiocarbon dates circa 4000–3500 B.P., similar to the pattern seen on the Columbia Plateau for the Pithouse I–II sequence.

ANALYSIS

Three analyses are undertaken to provide tests of the proposed models. First, we assess interassemblage variability in lithic artifacts in order to ascertain if, indeed, there are major differences in adaptive/organizational behavior (per Binford 1979) between and also within the major cultural phases and horizons of the Middle Holocene

Central Coast and Plateau. Second, we examine variability in manufacture style associated with formally shaped artifacts of the same contexts. This permits us to explore issues of cultural inheritance. Finally, we assess patterning in calibrated radiocarbon dates as a final test of cultural relationships.

Lithic Interassemblage Variability

This analysis seeks to examine intersite variability in lithic artifact assemblage contents as a means of assessing similarities and differences in mobility and subsistence adaptations. This requires a number of basic assumptions about the nature of cultural systems and their archaeological markers that must be considered before moving forward with the data analysis. Cultural systems can be viewed from genealogical and ecological standpoints (Rosenberg 1994). When defined from a genealogical standpoint, cultural systems are self-replicating ideational systems that guide and constrain human behavior. Economically successful human behavior supports the ecological hierarchy that consists of actual human beings and groups (Prentiss and Chatters 2003a). Those portions of the behavioral range interacting most closely with the environment can be called energy or resource management systems (Chatters 1995a; Prentiss and Chatters 2003b) and are consequently most influenced by selection and selection-like processes (Boyd and Richerson 1985). Fortunately, those forms of behavior most critical for survival are also most readily recognized archaeologically (Dunnell 1973, 1980; O'Brien and Lyman 2000). We now have the benefit of over 30 years of focused methodological research designed to allow us insight into relationships between the organization of hunter-gatherer resource procurement and mobility and its archaeological indicators (e.g., Binford 1977, 1978, 1979, 1980; Chatters 1987; Hayden 1979; Kelly 1983, 1988; Torrence 1983). These studies permit us to recognize variability, not just in idiosyncratic behaviors but also in integrated systems of behavior. Recognition of variation in integrated systems is the focus of this analysis.

Binford (1980) has offered two distinctly different forms of hunter-gatherer mobility and subsistence organization, termed "collector" and "forager." When applied to archaeological cultures these represent analyst-defined structural patterns or *Baupläne* (per Rosenberg 1994; see also O'Brien and Lyman 2000). As cultural *Baupläne* can be defined at more than one scale and represent a general structural pattern, it is not hard to imagine many variants within either collector or forager. Indeed, Binford intends the concepts to reflect ends of a continuum and a wide array of variation between. The primary difference between the two is in the degree of storage required annually by a given group.

Collectors practice a delayed-return tactic whereby food resources are often collected in one season for consumption during a subsequent season. This is accomplished with task group or logistical mobility, allowing specialists to mass harvest and process specialized food sources (e.g., Alexander 1992; Binford 1978). Archaeologically, collector-like systems are marked by a variety of distinctive characteristics including complex settlement patterns (Binford 1980), variable and often staged food-preparation strategies (Alexander 1992; Binford 1978), storage facilities (Testart 1982), and artifact assemblages marked, in particular, by intensive downtime "gearing-up" (Binford 1979) procedures. In the Canadian Plateau region, gearing up was particularly prevalent in late period winter villages where various activities were conducted to prepare for intensive warm season subsistence activities, including preparation of nets, traps, weapons, digging sticks, baskets, and clothing (Teit 1900, 1906, 1909). Lithic tool assemblages associated with these contexts are typically dominated by expedient tools produced from curated block cores, combined with lesser numbers of ground-stone tools such as axes, adzes, and abraders and formally shaped chipped-stone tools constituting a portable technology used primarily during the warm season under conditions of higher residential mobility (Prentiss 2000). These patterns make significant economic sense. Expedient flake tools are common in more sedentary contexts (Parry and Kelly 1987), particularly in the north, where lithic resources were easily acquired in the summer but not in winter. In the latter context, tool stone was acquired and transported to residential sites for winter use. The transported cores served as a winter source for flake tools used in the production of more complex tool systems necessary for the warm season harvesting of fish, roots, bark, berries, and larger game. Ground-stone tools were also fundamentally important in this regard. As Hayden (1989) has argued, ground stone provides an energy-efficient technology for intensive resource-processing tasks, such as salmon processing or woodworking.

Foragers, in contrast, relied primarily on immediate-consumption tactics. This required frequent, often daily, forays aimed at acquiring and delivering food and other resources. Foragers were often residentially mobile, though this is not required (Bamforth 1997). There are archaeological examples of foragers who moved residential camps as infrequently as once per year by making optimal use of ecotones, providing access to different resources throughout the year (Chatters 1995a). The archaeological record of foragers consists of less variable settlement patterns with little evidence for specialized resource-gathering and -processing sites or storage facilities. Faunal and floral remains will usually show high diversity and little specialized processing associated with storage. Lithic artifacts will typically be organized to permit the transport of tool systems, and although evidence of gearing up will be present in many contexts, the intensive pattern seen in the late prehistoric winter villages of the Plateau will be unlikely. For foragers in northern contexts, highly reliable and maintainable technologies are common (e.g., Myers 1989; Torrence 1983, 1989). In these contexts, lithic tools served as parts of more complex hafted-tool systems and may include formally shaped bifacial and unifacial scrapers, knives, and projectile points. Blades are often also important in these contexts as insets for spears, arrows, and knives. Modular parts in mobile tool systems were particularly critical for these foragers, as failure without adequate tool backups can quickly lead to food shortage.

Hayden et al. (1996) have offered a system for sorting lithic tool types into strategy groups that has great potential for use in understanding interassemblage variability. They identify five tool-production and -use strategies at the late prehistoric Keatley Creek winter village site: expedient block core, biface, portable long use (shaped scraping tools and drills), quarried bipolar, scavenged bipolar, and ground-stone cutting (e.g., nephrite adzes). The Keatley Creek assemblage is dominated by expedient tools with much lesser numbers of all other tool types. Hayden et al. point out that bifaces and portable long-term-use tools are particularly infrequent (3.6 percent and 0.6 percent, respectively) as they are more typically associated with mobility and activities conducted away from the winter village. Ground-stone cutting tools such as adzes are present in very infrequent numbers likely because they were not only valued tools but also prestige items (Hayden 1998).

We adopt a modified version of the Hayden et al. (1996) strategy sets in order to help quantify and sort Middle Holocene lithic assemblages into groups. We retain the expedient block core, biface, portable long-term use, and ground-stone cutting strategies, including within the latter ground-stone adzes, axes, and saws. Within the biface category we add bifacial projectile points because their organizational role and function are often equivalent to those of other more generalized bifaces. We exclude the bipolar categories, not because they are not useful but, rather, because they require the collection of data generally not available in many excavation reports. We add two strategies: blade and abrader. Middle Holocene assemblages are often characterized by microblades used as insets in portable technologies, thereby offering a distinct contrast to later nonmicroblade assemblages. Abraders are important to mobile and more sedentary peoples, though we suspect that the scale of abrader production and use will be seen to have been far higher in more sedentary contexts where downtime activities were most intense. This system is useful for two reasons. First, it is adaptively meaningful. These categories allow us to organize our descriptions of prehistoric artifact assemblages along organizational lines associated with mobility regime and subsistence strategy. More sedentary hunter-gatherers of the Pacific Northwest region, who processed large quantities of specialized resources, will tend to have had more expedient tools, ground-stone cutting tools, and abraders, whereas the more mobile foragers will tend to have had more bifaces, portable long-use tools, and blades. Second, these categories are sufficiently broad that data from most excavation reports can be used despite differences in data presentation.

We chose 23 site components for this study of interassemblage variability (Tables 4.1–4.2). We attempted to include all Shuswap, Lochnore, Lehman, and Early Nesikep sites from the study area that had adequate numbers of artifacts (greater than 50), adequate published descriptions, and minimal indicators of component mixing. We do include several differentially mixed Lehman, Lochnore, and Early Nesikep components but suggest that these form an important part of the record. They do not compromise the goals of this analysis as there has been no formal demonstration of differentiation in the Nesikep tradition. We also include several important Charles Culture and Pithouse I site assemblages following the same criteria.

We used principal components analysis to help identify major sources of variability. In order to eliminate sample size and to avoid structural correlations as factors influencing the results of multivariate analysis, we rescaled all scores (Table 4.2) by converting the largest score to "100" and scaling all other scores in a given data set in relation to this number (see Binford 1978, 1981; Prentiss 1993). A correlation matrix (Table 4.3) was derived from the rescaled data set, from which two principal components were extracted (Tables 4.4–4.5) and "varimax" rotated using an eigenvalue criterion of 1.0 (Kim and Mueller 1978). Component loadings were interpreted as significant using a criterion of 0.4 (Rummel 1970:477). We use factor scores as markers of each case's (site assemblage's) contribution to the factor solution (Table 4.6, Figure 4.2). This serves as the means for developing an understanding of interassemblage variability.

Principal component 1 scores significantly in the positive dimension on the expedient block core, ground-stone, and abrader strategies. Assemblages identified as critical to this group are likely those resulting from higher degrees of sedentism and more intensive gear-up activities. They include several Charles Culture (Glenrose Cannery, St. Mungo, Hatzic Rock), two Shuswap horizon (Guichon Slough, EdRk 7-1), and two Pithouse I (45OK382, 45OK383) sites. The remaining Shuswap, Pithouse I, and Charles Culture sites, as well as the Baker site, score weakly positive for this component.

TABLE 4.1. ARCHAEOLOGICAL SITES AND COMPONENTS.

Site	Component	Sources
	Charles Culture	
Glenrose Cannery DgRr 6	St. Mungo	Matson 1976; Matson and Coupland 1995; Schaepe 1998
St. Mungo DgRr 2	St. Mungo	Matson and Coupland 1995; Schaepe 1998
Hatzic Rock DgRn 23	Eayam (single component)	Schaepe 1998
Mauer DhRk 8	Eayam (single component)	Schaepe 1998
	Lochnore Phase	
Landels EdRi 11	Stratum II	Rousseau et al. 1991
Keatley Creek EeRl 7	Stratum XVIII and XX	Prentiss et al. 2000
Baker EdQx 43	Zone 3	Wilson et al. 1992
Baker EdQx 41	Zones 2 and 3	Wilson 1991
Baker EdQx 42	Zone 2	Wilson 1991
Lochnore Creek EdRk 7	Zones II and III	Sanger 1970
Highland Valley Mine EcRg 1b	Component II	ARCAS Consulting Archeologists, Ltd. 1986
	Shuswap Horizon	
Lochnore Creek EdRk 7	Zone I	Sanger 1970
Guichon Slough EbRc 6	Shuswap (single component)	Wyatt 1972
Mitchell EeRl 22	Components 5 and 6	Stryd 1973
	Lehman Phase	
Rattlesnake Hill EeRh 61	Levels 2 and 3	ARCAS Consulting Archeologists, Ltd. 1985
Oregon Jack Creek EdRl 6	Lehman (single component)	Rousseau and Richards 1988
	Early Nesikep Phase	
Rattlesnake Hill EeRh 61	Level 4	ARCAS Consulting Archeologists, Ltd. 1985
Nesikep Creek EdRk 4	Zone VII	Sanger 1970
Nesikep Creek EdQx 42	Zone 1	Wilson 1991
Lehman EdRk 8	Zone II	Sanger 1970
	Pithouse I	
45OK11	Pithouse I (single component)	Lohse 1984
45OK382	Pithouse I (single component)	Benson 1986a
45OK383	Pithouse I (single component)	Benson 1986b

The negative dimension of component 1 is loaded significantly on the blade strategy. Assemblages contributing here are entirely associated with the Lochnore phase (Landels, Keatley Creek, EdQx 42-2/3, EdRk7-2/3) and Early Nesikep tradition (EdRk 4-7, EdQx 42-1, EdRk 8-2). Lochnore component EdQx 41-2/3 scores weakly negative on this component. Principal component 2 only contains significant loadings in the positive dimension, in this case on the biface and portable long-use strategies. This identifies an array of assemblages with high biface and formally shaped uniface scores, including Lochnore (EdRk 7-2/3), Lehman (Oregon Jack Creek), Early Nesikep (EdRk 4-7), and Pithouse I (45OK11). The Baker site loads weakly in the positive dimension on this component. Several sites fail to score strongly on either component, including Mauer (Charles Culture), Rattlesnake Hill (Lehman and Early Nesikep phases), and Highland Valley Mine (Lochnore phase).

These data suggest several implications. First, from an adaptive standpoint, site assemblages from the Shuswap horizon, Charles Culture, and Pithouse I are virtually identical. All suggest an organization of technology oriented around the production and use of expedient tools coupled with the regular production and use of ground

TABLE 4.2. FUNCTIONAL LITHIC ASSEMBLAGE RESCALED AND (RAW) DATA BY STRATEGY GROUP.

Site	Expedient	Biface	Portable Use	Ground Stone	Blade	Abrader
Glenrose	100 (310)	16.7 (52)	0 (0)	1.0 (3)	1.2 (4)	5.8 (18)
St. Mungo	100 (226)	20.8 (47)	0 (0)	0.4 (1)	0 (0)	5.3 (12)
Hatzic Rock	100 (235)	18.3 (43)	0.4 (1)	2.1 (5)	0.4 (1)	4.3 (10)
Mauer	100 (199)	5.5 (11)	1.5 (3)	0 (0)	1.0 (2)	0 (0)
Landels	7.9 (57)	1.2 (9)	1.3 (10)	0 (0)	100 (721)	0 (0)
Keatley Creek	38.7 (12)	29.0 (9)	12.9 (4)	0 (0)	100 (31)	0 (0)
Baker	100 (455)	31.6 (144)	12.7 (58)	0 (0)	2.0 (9)	1.1 (5)
EdQx 41-2/3	100 (124)	25.0 (31)	12.1 (15)	0 (0)	50.0 (62)	0 (0)
EdQx 42-2	30.5 (22)	10.6 (12)	15.9 (18)	0 (0)	100 (113)	0 (0)
EdRk 7-2/3	100 (112)	37.5 (42)	38.4 (43)	0 (0)	69.6 (78)	0 (0)
Guichon Slough	100 (319)	34.2 (109)	6.2 (20)	0.3 (1)	0 (0)	2.2 (7)
EeRl 22	100 (137)	10.2 (14)	0 (0)	0 (0)	0 (0)	0.7 (1)
EdRk 7-1	100 (416)	46.6 (194)	12.7 (53)	2.4 (10)	1.4 (6)	0.5 (2)
Rattlesnake Hill 2/3	100 (187)	19.3 (36)	7.4 (14)	0 (0)	1.6 (3)	0 (0)
Oregon Jack Creek	100 (21)	66.7 (14)	66.7 (14)	0 (0)	0 (0)	0 (0)
EdRk 4-7	84.2 (16)	57.9 (11)	100 (19)	0 (0)	21.0 (4)	0 (0)
Rattlesnake Hill 4	100 (43)	20.9 (9)	4.7 (2)	0 (0)	0 (0)	0 (0)
Highland Valley Mine	100 (586)	3.4 (20)	2.4 (14)	0 (0)	2.6 (15)	0 (0)
45OK11	100 (535)	65.1 (348)	4.5 (24)	0 (0)	0.7 (4)	0.2 (1)
45OK382	100 (130)	6.9 (9)	6.2 (8)	1.5 (2)	1.5 (2)	0 (0)
45OK383	100 (472)	15.4 (73)	10.0 (47)	0.8 (4)	0 (0)	0 (0)
EdQx 42-1	68.0 (149)	20.5 (45)	5.0 (11)	0 (0)	100 (219)	0.5 (1)
EdRk 8-2	14.3 (69)	14.0 (68)	12.4 (60)	0 (0)	100 (484)	0 (0)

stone. These data combined with other archaeological data from these contexts, including such elements as middens and house features (Benson 1986a, 1986b; Matson 1976; Sanger 1970; Schaepe 1998; Wyatt 1972), imply the possibility of at least seasonally sedentary occupations. However, the presence of sedentism does not mean that a collector strategy was present. Charles Culture and Pithouse I do, indeed, show characteristics of sedentism yet little direct evidence for collector behavior (Chatters 1995a; Prentiss and Chatters 2003b). Shuswap sites, in contrast, indicate some degree of sedentism combined with delayed-return economies as indicated by the presence of significant storage features.

Second, from this perspective, site assemblages from the Lochnore phase (excluding Baker) and Early Nesikep tradition are substantially similar from the perspective of the high frequencies of blades, coupled with the relatively frequent bifaces and portable long-use tools. Interestingly, some Lochnore, Lehman, and Early Nesikep assemblages contain few blades and large numbers of expedient tools. In essence, there is interassemblage variability within the archaeological record of circa 7000–4000 B.P. Underlying this pattern is a set of strong differences between these patterns and those of the Columbia Plateau and Coast during post-5,000 B.P. times and the Canadian Plateau after 3,500 B.P. Lochnore, Lehman, and Early Nesikep clearly represent a forager-like model, with technological organizations emphasizing the formally shaped, modular parts of transportable tool systems. Other evidence for forager behavior comes from a diverse array of exploited fauna and a feature inventory from individual sites consisting entirely of hearths.

The Baker site falls in an intermediate position between the Lochnore/Early Nesikep group and the Charles

TABLE 4.3. CORRELATION MATRIX.

	Expedient	Biface	Portable Use	Ground Stone	Blade	Abrader
Expedient	1.0					
Biface	0.283	1.0				
Portable Use	0.022	0.65	1.0			
Ground Stone	0.278	−0.017	0.195	1.0		
Blade	−0.863	−0.203	0.033	−0.353	1.0	
Abrader	0.247	−0.078	−0.268	0.411	−0.305	1.0

TABLE 4.4. Principal Components Analysis Initial Statistics.

Component	Initial Eigenvalues		
	Total	% of Variance	Cumulative % of Variance
1	2.322	38.697	38.697
2	1.820	30.334	69.031

TABLE 4.5. Rotated Component Loadings.

	Component 1	Component 2
Expedient	0.853	0.277
Biface	0.179	0.863
Portable Use	−0.155	0.872
Ground Stone	0.629	−0.264
Blade	−0.889	−0.182
Abrader	0.591	−0.371

TABLE 4.6. Factor Scores.

Site	Factor 1	Factor 2
Glenrose	1.403	−1.079
St. Mungo	1.127	−0.788
Hatzic Rock	1.62	−1.084
Mauer	0.134	−0.441
Landels	−1.889	−1.213
Keatley Creek	−1.448	−0.132
Baker	0.348	0.309
EdQx 41-2/3	0.121	0.155
EdQx 42-2	−1.625	−0.574
EdRk 7-2/3	−0.479	0.956
Guichon Slough	0.67	0.057
EeRl 22	0.159	−0.352
EdRk 7-1	1.243	0.254
Rattlesnake Hill 2/3	0.163	0.023
Oregon Jack Creek	0.172	2.414
EdRk 4-7	−0.344	2.743
Rattlesnake Hill 4	0.191	0.013
Highland Valley Mine	0.109	−0.479
45OK11	0.381	1.094
45OK382	0.696	−0.627
45OK383	0.461	−0.187
EdQx 42-1	−1.029	−0.423
EdRk 8-2	−1.798	−0.637

Culture/Pithouse I/Shuswap horizon group. As in the latter group, the Baker site lithic assemblage is dominated by expedient tools and is nearly lacking in indicators of blade technology. Baker's large biface and scraper assemblage is reminiscent of some Pithouse I and Shuswap assemblages. The Baker site lithic assemblage is also very similar to expedient tool-dominated Lochnore, Lehman, and Early Nesikep assemblages (e.g., Rattlesnake Hill levels 2/3 and 4, Highland Valley Mine) and the Mauer site from the Lower Fraser Valley. Although not formally quantified in this study, each of the three housepits excavated at Baker produced over 20,000 lithic flakes (primarily small retouch flakes), suggesting a very substantial investment in tool maintenance rather than the production of tools from cores (as at later winter villages). Moving beyond lithics, the Baker site does indeed contain a large array of fauna, with a dominance of salmon, bone tools, and numerous pits, interpreted by Wilson (1992) as storage features. However, the storage capacity of these features is quite low. Indeed, the ratio of pit volume to square meters of floor is in the range of the smallest houses at Keatley Creek, thought by Hayden (1997) not to have had a serious investment in food storage. The features present probably would not be adequate for long-term food storage in a winter village situation. Bone tools are similar to those from coastal contexts, including points, awls, and wedges. Faunal remains are very rich with at least 16 taxons, but a significant emphasis is on salmon (Wilson 1992). Other indicators often used to mark storage, such as a near or total dominance in salmon bone assemblages by postcranial parts (Matson and Coupland 1995), are ambiguous. These data do suggest that some degree of delayed consumption may have occurred at Baker. However, low storage capacity and the presence of numerous salmonid cranial parts argue against substantial reliance on this tactic. Further, the lithic assemblage lies uncomfortably between the extremes thus far identified in this study. From an organizational standpoint, Baker site lithic technology appears to have been quite different from later housepit village assemblages in its emphasis on long-term tool maintenance rather than expedient production and recycling (e.g., Hayden et al. 1996). From the perspective of economic adaptation, the Baker site must remain enigmatic, with some indicators of collector-like behavior and yet other indicators of Middle Holocene forager strategies.

In conclusion, this analysis indicates two different patterns of technological organization. The Charles Culture/Pithouse I/Shuswap group represents a more sedentary adaptive pattern with strong emphases on relatively intensive resource processing including woodworking. The Early Nesikep/Lehman/Lochnore group reflects a less sedentary strategy, likely favoring broad-spectrum foraging, benefiting from highly curated and transportable tool systems. The Baker site evinces characteristics of both but is most similar to the former. Nonlithic data presented elsewhere draw a distinction between the Shuswap sites versus those of the Charles Culture and Pithouse I, in its likely employment of a collector strategy, as opposed to the semisedentary forager-like system associated with the latter (Chatters 1995a; Prentiss and Chatters 2003a;

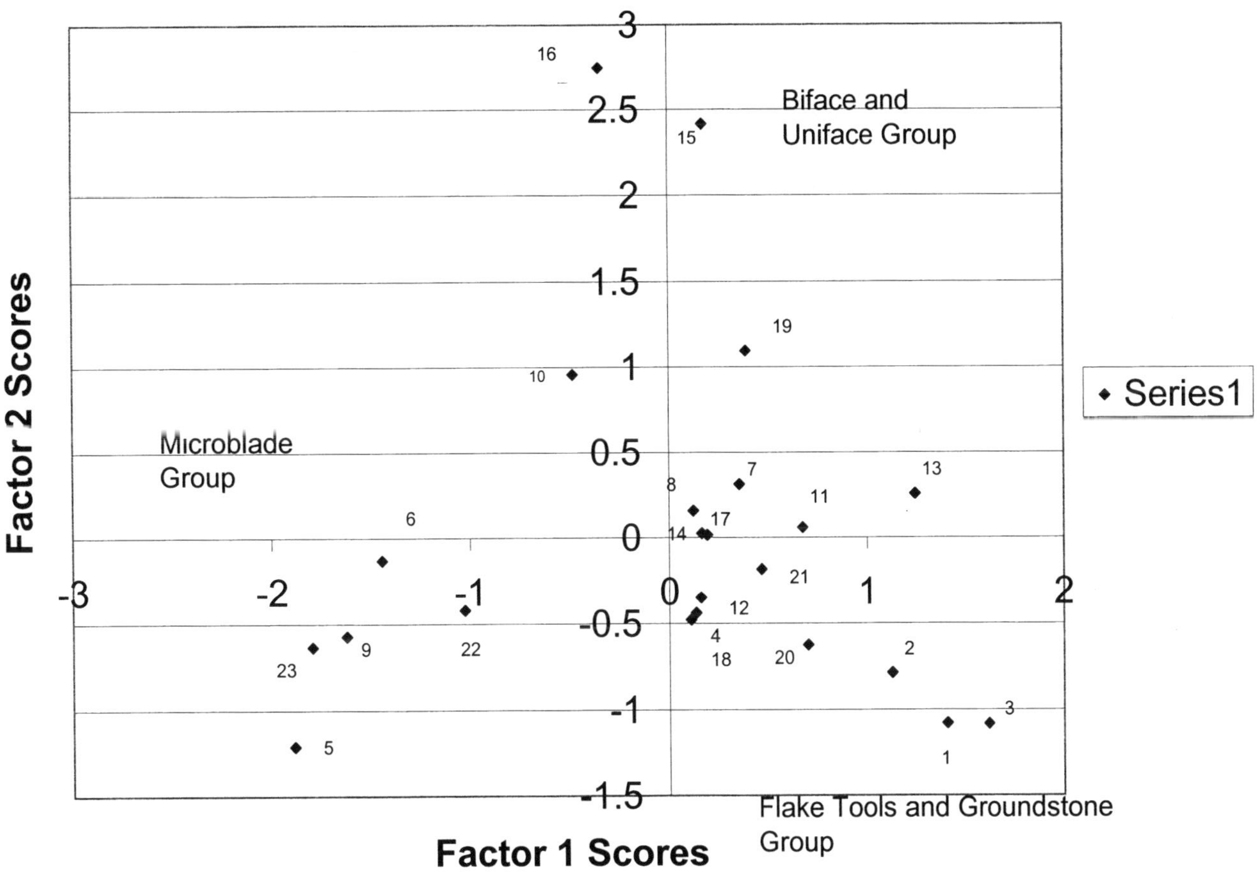

Figure 4.2. Plot of factor scores.

Richards and Rousseau 1987). Despite this distinction, from the perspective of inherited adaptive patterns, Charles Culture, Pithouse I, and Baker assemblages offer relatively equal possibilities as ancestors to the Shuswap horizon, as they do contain similar characteristics. Exclusive of the Baker site, Lochnore, Lehman, and Early Nesikep assemblage patterns show little similarity to this group. Our next problem is to address the important issue of inheritance.

Style and Inheritance

O'Brien and Lyman (2000) have pointed out that archaeologists seeking to clarify ancestor–descendant relationships must, like paleobiologists, be concerned with the issues of analogous versus homologous characters. They provide the example of the bird and bat wing. Both solve the same problem and are superficially similar, but they are unrelated from an inheritance standpoint. They are thus analogous characteristics of those organisms. In contrast, the vertebral column is held in common by mammals, birds, reptiles, and fish because of inheritance. It is thus a homologous character. In archaeology, we seek to establish similar relationships between archaeological manifestations of past cultures. In reference to the Middle Holocene Canadian Plateau, the Shuswap horizon may demonstrate adaptive characteristics, such as semisedentism and resource intensification, similar to those of the Charles Culture, Pithouse I, and the Baker site. This could mean that all are related through either cultural transmission or actual population movement. But it could also mean that some or all commonalities held are consequences of evolutionary convergence and are, thus, analogs. Because of this problem we need to apply independent criteria in a test designed to clarify these relationships.

O'Brien and Lyman (2000) recommend the construction of artifact lineages as a means of defining heritable continuity within artifact sequences. They most strongly recommend the use of phyletic and frequency seriation techniques as these are well-tested strategies used in paleontology to solve similar biological problems. They (2000:286–287) outline three requirements that must be met to successfully conduct seriation in this way. First, assemblages must come from contexts accumulated over similar durations in time. Second, assemblages must come from the same geographic region. Finally, assemblages must belong to the same tradition. Considering the data sets available in this study, requirement two is most closely met. All data are derived from the Plateau and nearby central Northwest Coast regions. However, this is not the same local area but, rather, a much larger region. The first requirement is difficult to establish with many sites, as duration of occupation is not always known, and in some cases (e.g., Keatley Creek, Rattlesnake Hill, Landels, Highland Valley) multiple reoccupations may have occurred. The third requirement is also problematic. This study seeks to explore the relatedness of assemblages derived from a number of independently defined traditions including the Pithouse I–II sequence of the Columbia Plateau (Chatters 1995a); the Old Cordilleran–Charles Culture sequence or Middle Pacific period (Ames and Maschner 1999); the Nesikep tradition, inclusive of the Early Nesikep tradition, Lehman phase (Stryd and Rousseau 1996), and possibly the Lochnore phase (Pokotylo and Mitchell 1998); and the Plateau Pithouse tradition, including the Shuswap horizon and possibly the Lochnore phase (Stryd and Rousseau 1996).

Because of the outlined problems, we did not attempt a formal seriation. This is a potentially useful technique that will require substantially more controlled data. Instead, we examine three broad patterns as potential indicators of inheritance similar to O'Brien and Lyman's assessment of the Clovis–Dalton lineage. Our goal here is to point out likely relationships without the rigorous testing advocated by O'Brien and Lyman (2000; Lyman and O'Brien 1998), Dunnell (1970, 1980), and others. Lithic artifact manufacture style provides a potentially useful indicator of inheritance patterns (Dunnell 1978; O'Brien and Lyman 2000) if functional characteristics can be largely factored out. We acknowledge, however, that processes of cultural transmission regarding style can be complex and certainly require substantially more study (Bettinger et al. 1996).

We explored projectile point style as indicated by general point shape and hafting mechanism. Following recommendations in O'Brien and Lyman (2000), which follow in part from Dunnell (1970, 1986), we created a simple paradigmatic key for sorting projectile points (Table 4.7). This relies on general shape (leaf, triangle, teardrop) and hafting mechanism (no notch, corner notch, side notch, split or concave base stem, flat or convex base stem). A preliminary assessment of assemblage similarity was undertaken using hierarchical cluster analysis. This required that we review the site database used in the study of interassemblage variability for potential candidates for cluster analysis of projectile point style. Most sites could not be used because of low sample size (generally fewer than eight projectile points). Lochnore, Lehman, and Early Nesikep sites are particularly lacking in projectile points. In addition, several sites had to be excluded because of potential mixing of later stylistic traditions (e.g., EdRk 7, Level 1). Nonetheless, a small group of sites was identified for analysis. Bifaces were only called

TABLE 4.7. PROJECTILE POINT STYLE KEY.

Haft Morphology	Preform Morphology		
	Triangle	Leaf	Teardrop
Notch			
Corner	1	2	3
Side	4	5	6
No Notch	7	8	9
Flat/Convex Base Stem	10	11	12
Split/Concave Base Stem	13	14	15

projectile points if they were identified as such in the original excavation reports. In all cases this required direct evidence of an early stage of point manufacture using hammer stone and billets, followed by at least one final stage of pressure flaking for final artifact shaping and haft creation. Raw artifact frequency data were transformed as described above to eliminate sample size as a defining factor in the clustering process. Then the rescaled matrix (Table 4.8) was subjected to a hierarchical cluster analysis using squared euclidean distance and average linking. The resulting dendrogram (Figure 4.3) illustrates a small but strong Lehman and Lochnore cluster on the basis of the shared presence of Lochnore notched leaf-shaped points at Highland Valley Mine and Rattlesnake Hill. A much larger cluster includes two very tight subgroups of Charles Culture and Pithouse I assemblages and the Baker site. Linkage here is clearly related to the strong presence of unnotched leaf-shaped points in all cases. Attached to these groups at a slightly greater distance is Guichon Slough, the only Shuswap horizon site with adequate artifacts and a lack of stylistic mixing. Similarity is based on the common presence of leaf-shaped points and, in particular, stemmed points. Finally, a single Early Nesikep assemblage was included that falls widely on the outside of the latter cluster. It has no overlapping characteristics, however, other than a coincidental similarity in projectile point shape.

Significantly, there is no tradition of stemmed point manufacture within the Lochnore or Lehman phases, whereas stemmed points are common in Shuswap, Charles Culture, and Pithouse I contexts. A question requiring further research concerns the range of variation in Shuswap horizon projectile points and, in particular, their similarities to those of the Great Plains McKean complex. In addition, though we divide Lochnore and Lehman projectile points into two distinct "types," the reality is that they grade from one to the other. Lehman points have a generally greater width to thickness ratio, with a higher degree of facial billet flaking and a more rounded base (Figure 4.4). Lochnore points are more narrow, with reduced width–thickness ratio and a pointed base (Figure 4.4). However, production of a Lochnore from a Lehman

TABLE 4.8. Style in Projectile Points: Rescaled and (Raw) Data.

Site	Type 4	13	10	8	5	6	1
EdRk4-7	0	0	0	0	0	0	100 (10)
Rattlesnake Hill 2/3	0	0	0	0	100 (5)	100 (5)	0
Highland Valley Mine	0	0	0	0	100	0	0
Baker 3	0	0	0	100 (50)	0	0	0
Glenrose	0	0	21.1 (4)	100 (19)	0	0	0
45OK383	0.4 (1)	0	7.1 (2)	100 (28)	0	0	0
St. Mungo	0	0	100 (13)	53.8 (7)	0	0	0
Hatzic Rock	0	0	100 (13)	69.2 (9)	0	0	0
45OK11	0	0	100 (38)	79 (30)	0	0	0
Guichon Slough	28.6 (6)	100 (21)	61.9 (13)	28.6 (6)	0	0	0

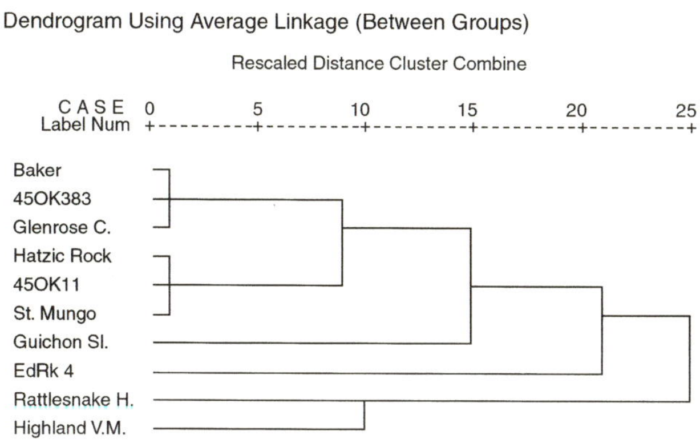

Figure 4.3. Hierarchical cluster analysis dendrogram using average linkage (between groups).

point is not difficult and can be accomplished by one or at most two additional stages of pressure flaking.

Although the cluster analysis suggests a clean break between the Lochnore/Lehman group and the Charles Culture/Pithouse I/Shuswap/Baker group, data from lower sample size contexts suggest a less clear distinction. Stryd and Rousseau (1996) note that unnotched leaf-shaped points are found in low numbers in some Lochnore contexts including possible Lochnore components at the Moulton Creek (Eldridge 1974) and Terrace sites (Richards 1978). Their primary argument, however, for the linkage between unnotched leaf-shaped points and the Lochnore phase is the Baker site, where leaf-shaped points are dominant and notched Lochnore points are lacking other than one in zone 2, not associated with the housepits of zone 3.

Moving beyond projectile points, we suggest that other data sets still corroborate the distinction in stylistic traditions between the Charles Culture/Pithouse I/Shuswap/Baker and Lochnore/Lehman/Early Nesikep groups. Assemblages of the latter group are frequently characterized by distinctive oval to circular formed unifaces, notched oval scrapers, end scrapers, and occasionally, specialized scrapers such as crescents. In contrast, Charles Culture, Pithouse I, Shuswap, and Baker assemblages are characterized by extremely low frequencies of formed unifaces, which, if present at all, tend to be end scrapers and, rarely, circular scrapers in some Shuswap contexts. The Baker site contains a very limited number of formally shaped unifaces, some resembling Lochnore types. Otherwise, the Baker assemblage is little different from Shuswap, Charles Culture, or Pithouse I.

Lochnore, Lehman, and Early Nesikep artifacts are found in association with well-developed microblade technology. Microblade production in Early Nesikep contexts is similar to that of the North Coast Microblade tradition, including types similar to both "Richardson" and "Kasta" variants from Haida Gwaii, produced primarily on tabular raw material (e.g., Magne 1996). Later Lochnore and possibly Lehman associated cores are smaller but remain generally similar to the earlier types. Microblades are extremely rare in Charles Culture and Shuswap assemblages, as well as at the Baker site. They are found in Pithouse I contexts, however. We suggest that there is a stylistic tradition of microblade manufacture that strongly links Early Nesikep, Lochnore, and possibly Lehman (e.g., Rattlesnake Hill).

Clearly, significant additional analysis of stylistic factors in Plateau lithic assemblages would be of great benefit. This study has suggested three lines of evidence to promote two distinctive traditions. First, the Early Nesikep tradition and the Lehman and Lochnore phases are clearly linked along stylistic lines. Projectile point styles suggest typological and technological overlap between Lehman and Lochnore types. Early Nesikep points are stylistically distinctive from either of the latter types. However, there is substantial evidence to suggest relatedness in other areas of lithic technology, particularly uniface morphology and microblade manufacture style.

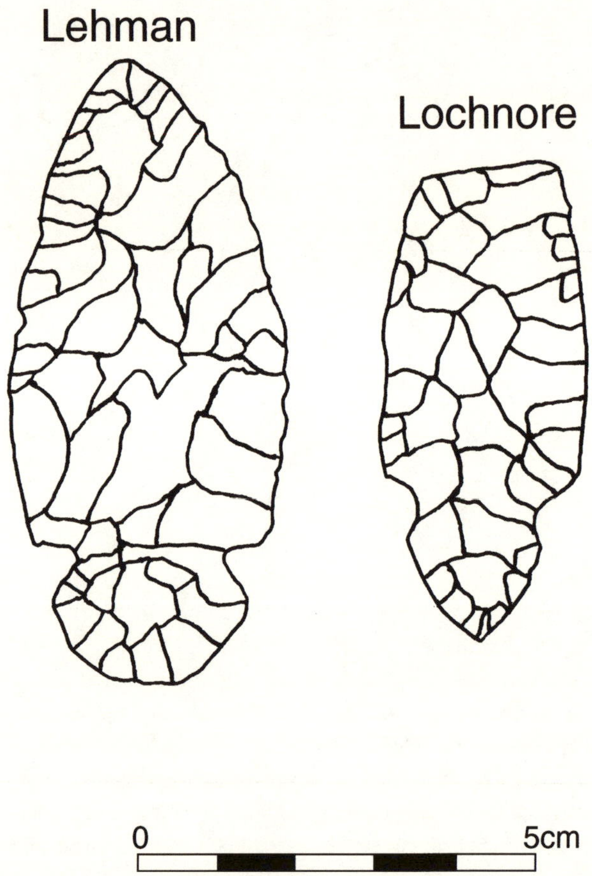

Figure 4.4 Lehman and Lochnore projectile points.

Second, the dominant presence of stemmed and leaf-shaped projectile points in Pithouse I, Charles Culture, and Shuswap assemblages overwhelmingly supports the likelihood of a lineage-like relationship among these groups. Further, they appear almost completely distinct in stylistic attributes from the Nesikep tradition (inclusive of Lochnore). Finally, the Baker site lies once again in the middle between each group. However, we suggest that, given the overwhelming presence of unnotched leaf-shaped points, the lack of microblades, and the extremely low frequencies of distinctly Lochnore-style shaped unifaces, the Baker artifacts are most similar stylistically to those of the Charles Culture/Pithouse I/Shuswap group. The few circular and end scrapers are of limited significance and could be explained in a myriad of fashions, including convergence, mixing, scavenging, trading, or imitation of indigenous (Lochnore?) knappers.

Dating and Population Dynamics

Thus far, we have argued for the presence of two major traditions: a long-term mobile forager pattern on the Canadian Plateau interior, termed most broadly the Nesikep tradition; and a more sedentary forager and, in later times, collector tradition linking the central Columbia Plateau (Pithouse I) with the central Northwest Coast (Charles Culture) and the Canadian Plateau Shuswap horizon. The Baker site defies precise classification but appears to have formed as a consequence of elements of both forager and collector-like behavior. Stylistically, it has characteristics of both, but overall it appears closest to sedentary forager groups. If these distinctions reflect patterns of cultural evolution, then they may also have implications for human population movements. The Nesikep tradition appears to have been entirely indigenous to the Canadian Plateau. If the Nesikep tradition indeed includes Early Nesikep, Lehman, and Lochnore as part of a single lineage, then there should be overlap in dating between assemblages from each. The Shuswap horizon, in contrast, appears not to be stylistically or adaptively related to the Nesikep tradition, offering potentially stronger links to the south and the coast. If the latter is the case, then there should be overlap in dates between these entities.

Although radiocarbon dates are now commonly used as markers of occupation patterns, population movement, and cultural change in Americanist archaeology (Gerlach and Mason 1992; Mason 1998; Rick 1987; Shott 1992), there has been very little use of calibrated radiocarbon dates on the Canadian Plateau to address these issues. However, as noted by Gerlach and Mason, we cannot begin to make statements regarding "independent invention, population movements by different groups . . . through time" without careful control of dating (1992:55). Further, we must also not fall into the trap of viewing radiocarbon dates as precise points in time to be rejected or accepted depending on their degree of fit with our prevailing taxonomies and culture histories. Rather, we must view radiocarbon dates as providing probabilistic estimates of occupation dates requiring calibration from radiocarbon to calendar years.

With these thoughts in mind, we used calibrated dates to explore the dating relationships between Pithouse I, Charles Culture, Shuswap horizon, and Nesikep tradition sites and the Baker site. Our strategy, following Gerlach and Mason (1992), was to simply calibrate the oldest and youngest acceptable dates from the Canadian Plateau groups, to plot them at two sigmas or at the 95 percent confidence interval, and then to examine the presence or absence and, as appropriate, degree of overlap in ranges. In collecting our database (Table 4.9), we rejected all freshwater shell dates, as these are known to be highly error prone (Stryd and Rousseau 1996). We also rejected dates with extremely high uncalibrated error ranges (greater than 200 years). The latter had little impact on the analysis as the error ranges of nearly all Mid–Late Holocene Canadian Plateau dates lie in the 100–200 radiocarbon year range. Finally, all calibrations were conducted using the Calib 4.3 program (Stuiver et al. 1998),

TABLE 4.9. Radiocarbon Data Illustrating Maximum Range by Group.

Site	Uncalibrated Date	Calibrated Date (2-Sigma Maximum Range)
	Early Nesikep Phase	
EdRk8-2	6650 ± 110	7684–7321
EdRk4-7	5635 ± 190	6855–5692
	Lochnore Phase	
Highland Valley Mine EcRg1b-2	5490 ± 190	6724–5785
Highland Valley Mine EcRg1b-2	3930 ± 100	4804–4016
	Lehman Phase	
Oregon Jack Creek EdRi6	4850 ± 100	5879–5321
Rattlesnake Hill EeRh61-2b	4470 ± 110	5450–4837
	Shuswap Horizon	
EdRk7-1	3280 ± 125	3681–3213
EfQu3	2540 ± 100	2839–2351

and dates are presented in years before the present counting from A.D. 1950.

Results (Figure 4.5) can be interpreted as follows. First, Early Nesikep overlapped with both Lochnore and Lehman at 95 percent confidence. Indeed, there appears to have been a short period of high diversity in projectile point manufacture between 5500 and 6000 B.P. that could represent not so much interacting independent traditions but, rather, the diversification of interior Plateau styles. Second, the most recent Lochnore date (3983–3832 cal. B.P.) is from the Landels site (Rousseau et al. 1991) and consists of a single bone from the middle of stratum II, stratigraphically associated with a hearth charcoal date of 5480 ± 70 B.P. (6410–6002 cal. B.P., two sigmas) and another bone date from a slightly lower stratigraphic level in stratum II of 6000 ± 80 B.P. (7155–6644 cal. B.P., two sigmas). Because of its association with much older dates, the late date does not seem to be a reliable indicator of the termination of the Lochnore phase. If this date is rejected, then the next oldest date comes from Highland Valley (ARCAS Consulting Archeologists, Ltd. 1986) and falls at 4804–4010 cal. B.P. (two sigmas). Consequently, the last Lochnore dates are minimally 151 years (Landels) and, more likely, at least 329 years from the very earliest Shuswap materials (3681–3213 cal. B.P.) from EdRk7-1 (Sanger 1970). The current data support a very clear disjunction between the timing of the latest Lochnore and earliest Shuswap occupations. As noted by Goodale et al. (this volume), the apparent hiatus is not an artifact of flat places on the calibrated radiocarbon curve (Stuiver et al. 1998). Interestingly, they match almost exactly the Pithouse I–II sequence on the Columbia Plateau, suggesting the distinct possibility that the Lochnore foraging system vanished around 4000 cal. B.P., to be replaced several hundred years later by Shuswap horizon collectors.

Calibrated dates at two sigmas from the Baker site span 5430–4423 cal. B.P. These fall within the two-sigma range of Lochnore, Lehman, Pithouse I, and the Charles Culture. Of this group, only the Charles Culture overlaps with the Shuswap horizon. Two sigma dates from the St. Mungo phase component at Glenrose Cannery span, for example, 5254–3264 cal. B.P. (Matson 1976; Matson and Coupland 1995). Interior Charles Culture or Eayam phase components fall within an almost identical range to that of Baker. For example, the Mauer site is dated 5034–4444 cal. B.P. at two sigmas. These dates eliminate the Eayam phase and Pithouse I as potential direct ancestors to the Shuswap horizon. This also suggests that patterns seen at Baker are not likely to be directly ancestral to those of the Shuswap horizon. However, they could be tangentially related. If Component 3 at Baker is linked to pioneers originating on the coast (perhaps associated with the Eayam phase) or the Mid-Columbia, then Baker could conceivably be a consequence of early interior exploration that was successful only in the short term. In contrast, nearly 800 years later, the Shuswap expansion did indeed result in the establishment of a permanent and new cultural tradition. From the perspective of these studies, its cultural origin is most likely on the central Northwest Coast as reflected in the components of the St. Mungo phase of the Charles Culture.

DISCUSSION

In 1989, Kuijt argued that climate change had played a major role in the emergence of the more sedentary communities of the late prehistoric period. In particular, he

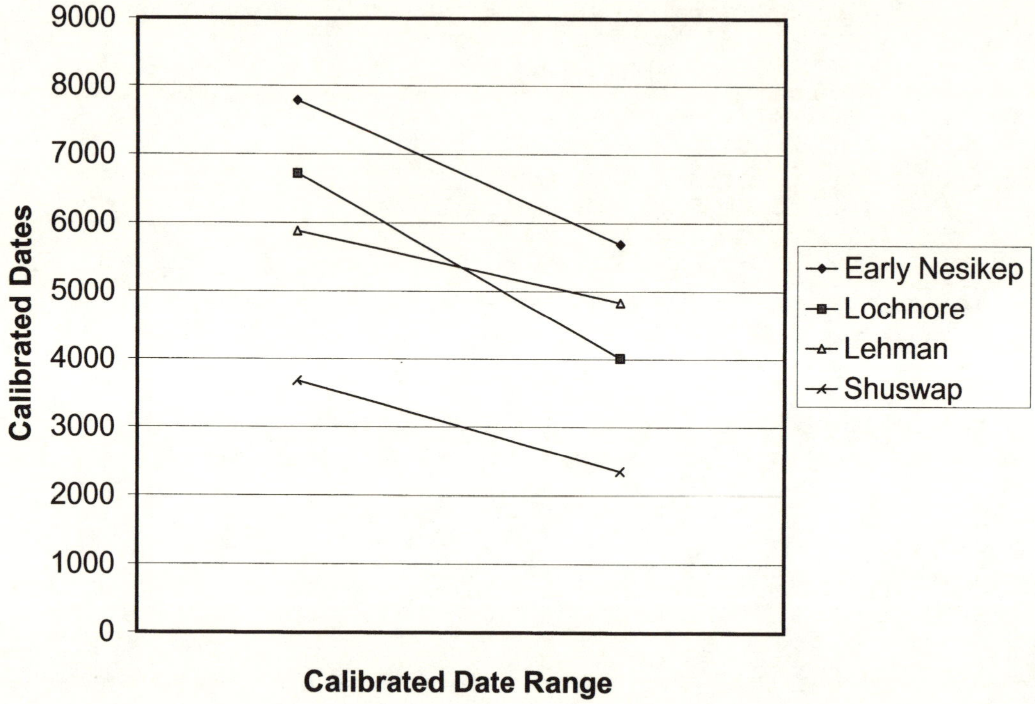

Figure 4.5. Distribution of calibrated radiocarbon dates from Middle Holocene Canadian Plateau.

suggested that a reduction in deer access coupled with expanding salmon populations required major changes in hunter-gatherer economies between 4,500 and 3,500 years ago. While demonstrating the importance of changing ecological conditions for the human group, Kuijt (1989) leaves open the possibility that one consequence of dramatically restructured environments was human population movement. This study suggests that the process of culture change during the Middle Holocene was not subtle and that population movement was of vital importance. From this vantage point, the Lochnore phase is the terminus of a long tradition of mobile foraging on the Canadian Plateau. It appears to have been a system fundamentally adapted to Hypsithermal interior environments featuring relatively optimal access to mid-size ungulates and a wide range of smaller game. Fish appear to have gained limited importance during the final centuries of this system's existence. There is little evidence to suggest any significant degree of population growth, other than perhaps during a brief period associated with projectile point diversification at circa 5500–6000 cal. B.P. Meanwhile, human populations on the Central Coast and to the south on the Columbia Plateau do appear to have grown in size while experimenting with a variety of new adaptive strategies (Ames and Maschner 1999; Chatters 1989, 1995a; Matson and Coupland 1995). In particular, populations explored varying degrees of sedentism and intensified resource and processing harvesting strategies. Interestingly, there is little evidence that any developed long-term storage technologies prior to 3500 cal. B.P. Population growth and fissioning probably occurred, likely resulting in incursions into new territories. We suggest that the anomalous patterns seen at the Baker site owe much more to developments on the coast or on the Columbia than those of the Lochnore or Lehman phases of the Canadian Plateau.

Temperature downturn after 4000 B.P. produced dramatic change throughout the region. All data collected to date point to economic collapse and abandonment in the interior environments of the Plateau and coastal region. Chatters (1995a) has demonstrated the abrupt extinction of the Pithouse I pattern. This study suggests a sudden disappearance of the archaeological pattern defining the Lochnore phase. Current data also suggest a lack of direct continuity between the interior Charles Culture or Eayam phase and later interior Fraser Valley developments. In contrast, it is well known that despite a lack of obvious breaks in the coastal sequence, there was a rapid shift to a collector-like system after 3500 B.P. The abrupt appearance of the Shuswap horizon by circa 3500 B.P. implies to us the movement of a new population into the Fraser–Thompson drainages. It is adaptively and stylistically unlike earlier Plateau patterns while remaining quite similar in many adaptive and stylistic traits to Charles Culture patterns. It overlaps only the coast sequence but not any other of the interior patterns, which declined around 4000 B.P. If the Shuswap horizon does represent colonization of the interior by coastal populations, then we must ask, Did this occur in a rapid wavelike advance or by a less dramatic process of periodic band fission and movement into the interior? If the latter model is correct, then it may be that not all attempts at interior colonization were successful and that it may even have taken some time for the full-scale winter village model to take hold. Indeed, Richards and Rousseau (1987) note that external storage and cooking pits are rare in Shuswap residential sites prior to the final 500 years of the horizon (post-2900 B.P.).

Our model proposes that the emergence of the Plateau Pithouse tradition did not come about as a consequence of gradual evolutionary processes. Rather, it appears to have been a consequence of a major population shift. Current data suggest abandonment of the interior Canadian Plateau for several hundred years after about 4000 B.P. Successful permanent colonization during this time was probably not possible without the technological and organizational tactics required for a collector system. Once this was available, human populations spread again into the Plateau. Populations then began to grow, and large communities developed in places such as the Mid-Fraser Canyon (Hayden and Adams, this volume; Hayden and Cousins, this volume). Although this model is different from some previous hypotheses, we argue that it is in line with what we know about major cultural shifts in many other contexts in North America. Examples of abandonment and replacement abound in the Arctic, particularly associated with major climatic transitions (Fitzhugh 1978; Maxwell 1985; McGhee 1996; Park 1993). Other examples are known from the Great Plains (Bamforth 1993; Toom 1992; Winham and Calabrese 1998), the Great Basin (Bettinger and Baumhoff 1982; Kaestle 1997; Parr et al. 1996), and the Columbia Plateau (Chatters 1995a).

CONCLUSION

This chapter has examined two models designed to explain the evolution of collector behavior on the Canadian Plateau. Analyses of lithic artifacts from functional and stylistic vantage points suggest that human occupation patterns after circa 3500 B.P. have little resemblance to those of earlier Plateau cultures. Rather, they most strongly reflect a coastal adaptation featuring higher degrees of sedentism and the intensive production of larger residential structures and complex food-procurement technologies, particularly associated with fishing. The controversial Baker site falls most closely also within the coastal/Columbia Plateau group on functional and stylistic grounds. It may reflect a short-term expansion of people from these areas. Assessment of radiocarbon dates indicates Plateau abandonment after about 4000 B.P. Given a similar abandonment process in the Mid-Columbia and a pattern of coastal continuity throughout this period, the expansion of coastal populations around 3500 B.P. seems to be the most reasonable argument. Thus, collecting appears to have emerged on the coast and only developed on the Plateau with the expansion of those coastal populations possessing this important techno-economic system.

II

HOUSEHOLDS, SOCIAL COMPLEXITY, AND THE FORMATION OF AGGREGATE HUNTER-GATHERER COMMUNITIES

5

SAFETY IN NUMBERS

THE INFLUENCE OF THE BOW AND ARROW ON VILLAGE FORMATION ON THE COLUMBIA PLATEAU

James C. Chatters

The winter village was the central place in the subsistence–settlement system of ethnographic Plateau peoples. It was the point of departure and return for an annual seasonal round that saw people disperse into upland root-gathering grounds in winter, coalesce at salmon-fishing localities in summer, and climb into nearby mountains in the fall for berries and big game (e.g., Ray 1932). Foods amassed during the productive, warm seasons of the year were transported to the permanent villages, where they were either cached in unoccupied pithouses, placed on extramural racks, or hidden in nearby caves and talus slopes. Archaeologically, these villages are evident as concentrations of housepits, around which are typically found cemeteries, heavily used panels of rock art, and clusters of storage facilities (Chatters and Langdon 2002; Reid 1991a). Some are quite large, containing more than 100 house depressions (e.g., Osborne 1957; Schalk 1983a), but groups of 5–20 are closer to the norm.

Winter villages, by which for the purposes of this chapter I mean groups of more than three simultaneously occupied housepits, are a late development in Southern (or Columbia) Plateau prehistory, although housepits themselves were in use as early as 4300–5000 B.P. (Ames and Marshall 1980; Ames et al. 1998; Chatters 1995a; Chatters and Pokotylo 1998; Lohse and Sammons-Lohse 1986).

Most attempts to explain the "Winter Village Pattern," "Plateau Culture," or "Plateau Pattern," as the ethnographic subsistence settlement system has long been called (e.g., Nelson 1973; Swanson 1962; Warren et al. 1968), have focused on the onset of pithouse living, not on the development of village life in the sense I mean it. The existence of pithouses has been taken as a proxy indicator of the full suite of behaviors that characterized historically documented adaptive strategies, including a heavy reliance on food storage, although scholars have recognized that the system became more territorially expansive as time progressed (e.g., Galm 1985). Explanations have included the immigration of Salish speakers from the Northwest Coast (Nelson 1973), salmon intensification enabled by a growing population (Schalk 1981b and elsewhere; Schalk and Cleveland 1983), population growth and attendant resource stress leading to territorial restriction and increased emphasis on storage (Lohse and Sammons-Lohse 1986), and an increased emphasis on the exploitation of plant foods in whole or in part as a result of population stress (Ames and Marshall 1980; Thoms 1989). The onset of pithouse dwelling was not, however, the beginning of the Plateau Pattern, as I shall refer to it here.

What concerns us here is not the initial settlement in semisubterranean dwellings, which I have addressed elsewhere (Chatters 1995a), or the development of the collector strategy that later become so integral to Plateau subsistence. I am concerned here with what caused people to abandon their scattered pithouse hamlets and nucleate into villages of dozens to hundreds of dwellings and hundreds of inhabitants. The issue I consider here is whether defensive considerations, specifically defense from a new weapon, the bow and arrow, were the impetus behind nucleation. Before I address that question, however, a brief overview of the development of Plateau settlement systems is warranted.

A BRIEF PREHISTORY OF SOUTHERN PLATEAU SETTLEMENT SYSTEMS

The early cultures of the Southern Plateau, like those of the Canadian Plateau to the north (Rousseau, this volume), were characterized by small, dispersed, highly mobile bands that appear to have remained in one camp for no more than a month or two at a time during any season. For the period between about 10,000 and 4300–5000 B.P., the only indications of dwellings are two small circles of stones that probably held down the edges of mat- or hide-covered shelters and one small, expediently utilized pit feature (Chatters 1986; Draper 1986a, 1986b). People lived by foraging (sensu Binford 1980), exploiting one or a few primary resources or resource types from each of many sequential, temporary encampments. This high-mobility foraging existence was followed by a series of developments I have previously identified as sedentary foraging, tethered collecting, and networked collecting (Chatters 1995a). Each of these adaptations included at least winter season habitation in semipermanent, semi-subterranean dwellings.

Sedentary foraging was practiced by the people of Pithouse I (ca. 4300–3900 B.P.), which was characterized by the establishment of small hamlets of one or two pithouses at the forest–steppe ecotone, usually at the mouths of large canyons or drainage systems tributary to the area's major rivers (Chatters 1995b; see also Lohse and Sammons-Lohse 1986). They would occupy these pithouses year-round for one to a few years, exploiting foodstuffs available in the rich ecotonal setting. Because this strategy led to the rapid depletion of the catchment area, however, people would relocate their settlements frequently or revert to the mobile foraging of their predecessors. Populations grew under favorable climatic conditions, but around 3900 B.P. a sharp downturn in regional temperature and the onset of markedly seasonal patterns of resource availability caused this system to collapse; people reverted to the mobile foraging of their ancestors.

After a 400-year hiatus, during which people rarely settled in pithouses, the foraging lifeway was replaced by the tethered collecting strategy of Pithouse II. Pithouse II was a full-blown collector adaptation from its first appearance, making it likely that, as Nelson (1973) has suggested on the basis of far less evidence, it represents the immigration of a new group of people with a developed strategy for coping with the markedly seasonal environment that brought Pithouse I lifeways to an end. During this period, people occupied small hamlets of from one to three dwellings, scattered along the river terraces throughout the Southern Plateau. Staying close to their winter dwellings, Pithouse II peoples made forays to temporary food-processing camps a short distance from their primary habitations, rarely straying more than a few kilometers away. Activities at these temporary camps appear to have been highly organized and efficient (Chatters 1995b). Food must have been stored in the pithouse hamlets, either within houses or in extramural facilities; storage features representing this time period are rare (see Reid 1991a; Swanson 1962). Territories were small and circumscribed, and there is little evidence of extensive trade or long-distance travel for food or raw materials during this period. During Pithouse I and II, as well as the preceding millennia, the great expanse of upland plains and scablands that lay between the Snake and Columbia rivers and the highlands of the nearby Cascade, Blue, and Rocky mountains were infrequently visited.

This changed by around 2500 B.P., when people began making longer-distance moves into the uplands away from the region's primary watercourses (see, e.g., Reid 1991a). Pithouse clusters became larger, frequently arriving in the range of "village" as defined above, and increasing numbers of temporary resource-gathering camps were established at greater distances from the river valleys. The systematic tactic of storing food in caves, rock shelters, and talus pits appeared first during this period, and rock art and cemeteries became common. Increasing quantities of exotic stones, shells, and other raw materials evince increased trade, expanded foraging territories, or both. It is at this time that nearly all local chronologies show the inception of new cultural patterns, including settlement patterns, burial practices, and artifact styles (Daugherty 1962; Leonhardy and Rice 1970; Nelson 1969; Rousseau, this volume; Salo 1985; Warren et al. 1968; cf. Sappington 1995). The Plateau Pattern had become established (Nelson 1973).

THE PROS AND CONS OF VILLAGE LIVING

What was it that led the people of Pithouse II, assuming that we are talking here about a cultural transformation and not a cultural replacement, to abandon their dispersed hamlets and aggregate into larger, more widely separated groups to wait out the winter? Clearly, there are potential benefits to such a move, but nucleation also entails significant costs.

Among advantages, we might count increased access to mates (at least in the larger villages), increased access to craft specialists, increased communication and consequent increases in the ease of mobilizing the labor force, and increased social/political cohesion and defense. Several of these potential advantages can be quickly dispelled as largely irrelevant on the Plateau. Access to potential mates would have been limited in all but the largest villages because of the relatedness of village occupants, and, indeed, ethnographic accounts and living elders have spoken of ceremonials that brought multiple village groupings together as key times of matchmaking (e.g., Spinden 1908). Craft specialization, although present to a minor degree in highly skilled makers of arrows, baskets, and other items, was not the critical economic factor that it was on the Northwest Coast and probably played little part in the nucleation process. Labor management is not likely to have been much of a factor either. Individual families saw to their own food needs, and the only time of year when the cooperative action of a large labor force might have been needed was during the salmon harvest, when large fish traps and netting platforms had to be constructed (see Schalk 1977, 1981b). People from multiple villages converged on the primary salmon intercept points and worked cooperatively on facilities, so group living in winter seems irrelevant to the organization of labor in summer. Safety increases with nucleation; however, because a larger settlement means a bigger pool of able-bodied males to defend the community and its stores of food; dispersed families are highly vulnerable to attack by even small parties of assailants. An elderly Okanogan woman I once interviewed brought this into sharp focus as she related the events behind a small cemetery that had been disturbed by irrigation developments. She told me in simple terms that whenever people were traveling through another group's territory and had the opportunity to kill someone, they did (Chatters and Zweifel 1987). Life away from the village could be extremely hazardous.

The costs of nucleation are high. A move from small, scattered hamlets to large, more widely spaced villages would have increased the cost of transporting harvested foods, as the larger community population required a larger food-gathering territory (for additional discussion of these topics, see Hayden and Cousins, this volume; Kuijt and Prentiss, this volume; Lepofsky and Peacock, this volume). A larger wintering group would quickly deplete locally available food and fuel resources, increasing the cost of heating and cooking and further raising the cost of feeding the community. They could, over time, place a strain on the local availability of building materials as well, and these would have to be transported ever-greater distances. In addition, a larger group meant more health risks, as vermin and wastes from people and dogs would build up around the camp. There would also be a greater risk of communicating infectious diseases, such as tuberculosis, which was present locally for at least 1,000 years (Chatters 2002), and treponematoses, which was already widespread in the Pacific Northwest by this time (Skinner 1994). Finally, the advantages of social cohesion would be negated at least in part by the increased potential for interpersonal conflict that inevitably develops in cohabiting groups.

After this brief consideration of the pros and cons of nucleation, what remain are higher resource-transport costs, health risks, and internal conflict on the con side, balanced on the pro side only by social cohesion and the increased ability of the community to defend itself. There is extensive evidence that, despite the costs, defense was often an overriding consideration.

Villages as Strongholds

Some of the largest villages occupied defensive locations on islands or in difficult-to-reach landscapes. Strawberry Island, which is situated near the confluence of the Snake and Columbia rivers, had 133 housepits on its upstream end (Osborne and Crabtree 1961; Schalk 1983a) (Figure 5.1). Site 45BN53, 37 km downstream on the Columbia at Berrians Island, had 182 (Osborne 1957); and Locke Island, 74 km upstream, had as many as 100. Villages were also found on Martindale, Techumtas, and Miller islands on the Columbia and Fishhook Island on the Snake, to name a few. In Hell's Canyon, which lies on the border between Oregon and Idaho, the largest housepit groupings are situated in the deepest, most inaccessible part of the 2,100 m-deep canyon (Chatters and Langdon 2002). The largest group of housepits (19) occurs on a small, steep stream, where it is bounded on two sides by sheer bedrock cliffs, on a third by steep canyon slopes, and on the fourth by the Snake River (Chatters and Root 2002). Although its higher, northerly cliff would gather some of the sun's heat, the site itself lies in shadow throughout the winter, making it a poor location for staying warm.

Although island living and the remote, canyon villages might have other advantages—ready access to the immense salmon resources of the Middle Columbia River in the case of islands, warmth and access to game pushed downslope by snow cover in the deepest canyons—so defense may not have been the only or even the principal reason for the placement of villages in hard-to-reach localities. Village settlement on islands or in remote rock clefts, however, must have been defensively motivated, at least in part, because such placement further elevates the cost of nucleation. Islands would be a particularly costly choice. Access to most of the island sites mentioned above (45BN53 is the exception) could only be achieved by boat, further increasing the cost of resource transport. In addition, many of the islands were subject to flooding during winter rain-on-snow events, and, in fact, most were inundated during severe floods of the late 19th and mid 20th centuries. This means that homes, storage facilities, and their contents could have been washed away, leaving people destitute. Finally, on an individual level, the risk of drowning would have been great, even during nonflood seasons, especially for children. The costs of canyon living also involve transport time and energy, plus the risk of death and injury from falls or drowning.

Figure 5.1. The upper end of Strawberry Island on the Lower Snake River, as it appeared in 1952. The dark circles lining both sides of the island are housepits. Photo by U.S. Army Corps of Engineers.

Whereas island and canyon villages might have been situated for multiple reasons, defense is the only explanation for fortified mesa-top camps in the root-gathering areas of the channeled scablands, a vast area that lies between the Snake and Columbia rivers in eastern Washington. Sheer-walled basalt mesas that sometimes stand near springs or vernal pools in this near-desert landscape frequently sport walls, redoubts, and guarded access routes. In some cases, housepits occupy the mesa tops (Smith 1977; Swanson 1962). One such locality, the Lee site, is a cluster of five housepits on a 12 × 50 m mesa, situated 300 m above and 1.6 km from the Columbia River, 0.8 km from the nearest spring. Such sites are numerous. Between 1964 and 1972, amateur archaeologist Nat Washington (1973) identified 55 such mesas stretching from the Columbia River near the town of Vantage, Washington, nearly to the city of Spokane. Interviewing Billy Curlew, an aged Sincayuse informant who was one of the last people able to recall life before the reservation, Washington learned that these mesas had indeed been used for defense, most recently from marauding bands of Blackfeet warriors.

CONFLICT ON THE PLATEAU

In his seminal work on the cultures of the Plateau, Ray (1932 and elsewhere) observed that the Sanpoil and Nespelem had a pacifist ethic. Believing them to have been less influenced by European contact and the equestrian lifeways of the Great Plains than their neighbors were, he posited that peace had been the rule among the pre-equestrian peoples of the Southern Plateau. In the past two decades, however, repeated discoveries of brutalized individuals and families along with extensive evidence for club warfare have come to light, effectively dispelling Ray's idyllic vision (Chatters 1989; see also Kent 1980). In fact, there is no time in the prehistory of the region for which recovered human skeletal remains have entirely lacked evidence of conflict. Wounds apparently inflicted by clubs and projectiles occur as early as Kennewick Man (ca. 8400 B.P.) and the 10,100 B.P. Marmes discoveries (Chatters 2000; Krantz 1979). I address this issue in more detail below.

If conflict was endemic on the Plateau from earliest times, then there would have to be some additional element that entered the picture and raised the importance of defense in people's strategic decisions about settlement placement and size. One possible explanation is that the population had grown to the point that territorial circumscription, and the defensive posture that attends it, had begun. A second possibility is that the introduction of bow and arrow weaponry increased the effectiveness of raiding parties, allowing them to inflict damage at a distance and placing dispersed populations at greater risk of successful assault. In reviewing these two possible explanations, I consider the chronological relationships among several variables: the onset of the Plateau Pattern; evidence for or against population growth; the introduction of the bow and arrow; the inception of island villages, fortified mesa tops, and extramural storage in caves and rock shelters; and the incidence of club wounds versus projectile wounds in human skeletons.

Beginnings of the Winter Village Pattern

It is now generally accepted that the Plateau Pattern had its inception shortly after 2500 B.P. (Ames et al. 1998; Chatters and Pokotylo 1998). The earliest dated housepits attributable to this lifeway, whether they occur singly or in groups, consistently date between 2500 and 2000 B.P. These sites are scattered throughout the Southern Plateau, indicating that the Plateau Pattern spread rapidly following its inception (for additional discussion, see also Rousseau, this volume).

The earliest sites with house groupings are Wildcat Canyon on the Middle Columbia River; Old Umatilla at the mouth of the river by that name; Bone-in-the-Throat on the Lower Snake River; Game Farm on the Upper Columbia near its confluence with the Okanogan River; Alpowai, near the confluence of the Clearwater and Snake rivers; Hasotino, at the mouth of the Grand Ronde River; and Knight Creek in Hell's Canyon of the Snake River (Table 5.1). In addition to the sites listed in Table 5.1, single early houses associated with the Plateau Pattern have been found at the Clearwater Fish Hatchery in northern Idaho at 2430 ± 60 B.P. (Sappington 1995), at Salishan Mesa in the Grand Coulee with a mean date of circa 2350 B.P., and at Metamooteles Spring near the Upper Columbia at 2310 ± 110 B.P. (Beta 33659; J. R. Galm, personal communication, 2001). None of the sites with multiple housepits can be construed as a large village, but five appear to contain four or more structures that may be contemporary. At the Game Farm, for example, radiocarbon dates identify at least three and probably four houses as contemporaneous (Moura 1986), and the site appears to contain many more; house depressions are not visible at the surface, and less than half of the site area has been explored. Bone-in-the-Throat is an assemblage of eight presumably contemporaneous house depressions, only three of which were radiocarbon dated (Schalk 1983b). A similar situation exists for Knight Creek, where only four of 11 house depressions were explored. Multiple, apparently contemporary, early house depressions also occur at the Umatilla and Wildcat Canyon sites, although few have been dated by radiocarbon analysis (Dumond and Minor 1983; Schalk 1981a).

Isolated house structures are an interesting contrast, but at least one (Metamooteles Spring has not yet entered the literature) seems to accentuate the importance of defense at this time period. House 1 at Salishan Mesa is situated beside a spring on a broad ledge that overlooks the Grand Coulee. Within less than 100 m is the fortified mesa that gives the site its name. Occupants of this single house had ready access to this defensive feature if under threat of attack.

Population

As I note in the introduction, many of the models that Plateau archaeologists have advanced to explain the development of semisedentary living, and thus the Plateau Pattern, rely primarily on population as the prime mover. That is, they see the process as demogenic (Chatters 1995b)—driven by population pressure. It is reasonable to presume that nucleation and increasing village size might be seen as a continuation of that process, and, in fact, we see allusions to that effect (e.g., Reid 1991a).

To explore the role of population, we can use the frequency of radiocarbon dates in the Southern Plateau, adjusted for decay, as a proxy for regional population size (Chatters 1995a) and compare it with the appearance of the first village settlements (Figure 5.2). The graph shown here is an integral of the normal distributions of uncalibrated radiocarbon age estimates displayed in 20-year increments. That is, for each date, the proportion of 1.0 that falls under the probability curve for the sample is added to the proportions of all other dates that include that segment under their probability distributions. From this graph, it is evident that populations were relatively high, in fact, near their highest levels if we use the corrected curve, between 3000 and 2600 B.P. A decline is indicated between 2600 and 2400 B.P.., and a subsequent second peak occurs between 2200 and 2400 B.P., but this fluctuation is probably caused by the major radiocarbon anomaly that occurred at this time (e.g., Pearson and Stuiver 1986). Because of the anomaly, which results in few dates during the earlier interval and an inordinate number during the later, many of the samples dated between 2200 and 2400 B.P. should actually fall between 2600 and 2400 B.P. If the two periods are averaged, the result indicates a decline in population that continued until 2000 B.P., well after the influence of the anomaly had come to an end. Indications are that, whether we use the corrected or uncorrected curve, populations were not on the rise at the time the Plateau Pattern emerged but, rather, on the decline.

It is possible, however, that we are looking here not at a decline in human numbers but, rather, at an artifact of changing settlement pattern. If people were nucleating, then they would have occupied fewer winter base camps and would thus potentially have produced fewer radiocarbon-dated samples (especially if excavators of the

TABLE 5.1. Radiocarbon Ages of Early Pithouse Groups Associated with the Plateau Pattern, Located in the Southern Plateau.

Site	Housepit	Radiocarbon Age	Source
Wildcat Canyon			Dumond and Minor 1983
	Fea. 217	2460 ± 110	
	2	1860 ± 60, 1790 ± 275	
Umatilla	Numerous	1900–2400	Schalk 1981a
Knight Creek			Hackenberger 1990
	1	2240 ± 60	
	11	2050 ± 140	
Game Farm			Moura 1986
	23	2400 ± 80	
	52	2340 ± 80	
	45	2350 ± 120	
	55	2200 ± 60	
Bone-in-the-Throat			Schalk 1983a
	5	2435 ± 65	
	2	2080 ± 55	
Hasotino	Big House	1970 ± 90	Sappington 1985
Alpowai			Brauner 1976
	4c	1940 ± 60	
	2a	1910 ± 80	

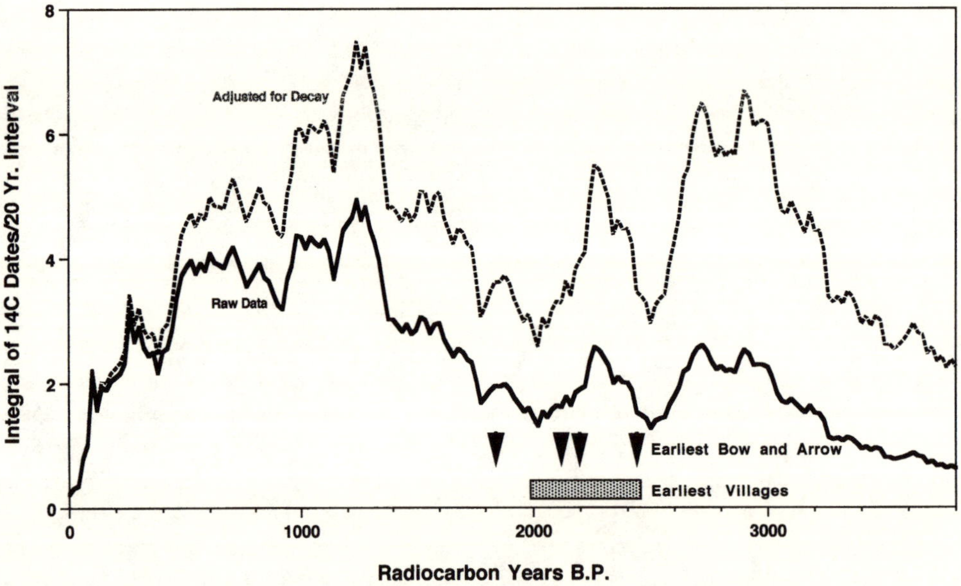

Figure 5.2. The relationship among population change, represented by numbers of radiocarbon dates, the initiation of village settlements, and the introduction of the bow and arrow on the Southern Plateau.

sites were not well funded, which was the case for many of the sites listed in Table 5.1). However, evidence from two other sources—bison kills and root-gathering sites—supports the interpretation of a population decline.

Bison were present in the Southern Plateau throughout the Holocene, but they have rarely been abundant in the archeological record (Chatters et al. 1995a; Lyman 1985) and generally occur only as a few foot bones or teeth in much larger mammalian archaeofaunas. One botanist (Daubenmire 1985) posits that bison were rare because the summer grasses that they depended on for successful rearing of young are not a significant part of the region's flora. Wildlife biologist Van Vuren (1987), however, counters that bison seem to have been rare on the Plateau because their numbers were kept low by human predators. He cites historic records in asserting that bison that strayed into the Columbia Basin from western Montana or the Snake River Plain would have been quickly dispatched by local hunters. Bison simply offered too large and easily followed a food package to be ignored. If this were true, then we should expect to see an increase in the frequency of bison in regional archaeofaunas coinciding with the decline in human populations as indicated by the radiocarbon record. This is exactly what we see (Figure 5.3). All but one of the eight sites in which bison number more than 10 percent of the mammalian archaeofauna date between 1800 and 2400 B.P., reaching their peak around 2000 B.P., when human populations appear to have been at their minimum (Chatters 1993; Chatters et al. 1995a; Harkins 1980; Lyman 1985; Schroedl 1973).

Activity in at least one prime root-gathering ground declined at the same time that bison numbers appear to have surged. In his study of root-processing ovens in the Calispell Valley of the Pend d'Oreille River, northeastern Washington, Thoms (1989) found that camas-exploitation intensity followed a pattern very similar to the radiocarbon record of (presumed) population intensity shown in Figure 5.2. Camas was used occasionally between 5500 and 3500 B.P.; then its exploitation increased sharply to a peak during Pithouse II (3250–2500 B.P.). Use plunged thereafter to one-fourth its former levels at 2000 B.P. and climbed again to a second high between 1250 B.P. and historic times. Thoms attributes what he refers to as the "intensification nadir" to people abandoning root harvest for the more efficiently acquired (from a caloric standpoint) bison that were irrupting in the interior Columbia Basin (for further discussion of shifting plant uses and harvesting/processing, see Lepofsky and Peacock, this volume). When we compare Thoms's data with the pattern of bison occurrence and the population proxy for the entire Southern Plateau (Figure 5.3) his argument does not hold. First, bison were not so abundant that people could abandon their other subsistence pursuits in favor of the large, hoofed meat packages—only eight sites contain many bison bones, and only one of these has been found in the interior of the Columbia Basin. Second, and more importantly, the pattern of radiocarbon dates from camas harvest is almost identical with the Plateau-wide pattern. The latter includes dates from both riverine and upland sites. It appears, therefore, that bison were not the cause of the decline but, rather, its beneficiaries. I have argued elsewhere that declining riverine resources brought a drop in human numbers and that the subsequent irruption of bison combined to draw people into upland regions and at least helped trigger the development of the Plateau Pattern (Chatters 1993; see also below).

The available evidence thus seems to contradict the suggestion that nucleation, at least in its nascent form, was strictly demogenic. In fact, populations were on the

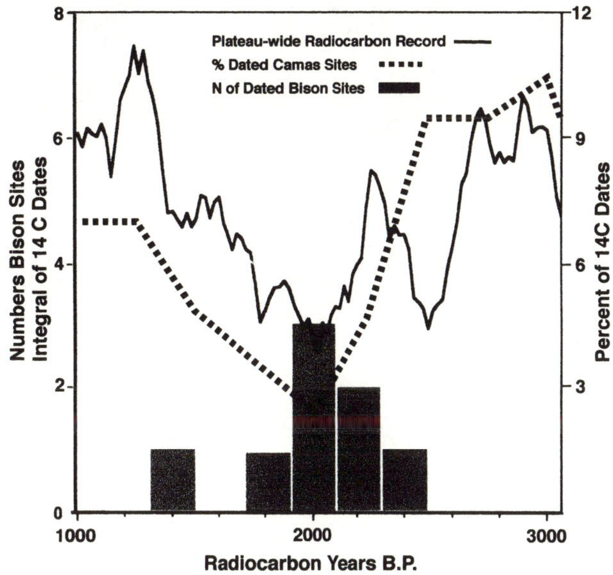

Figure 5.3. Graphs comparing the decay-corrected radiocarbon curve for the entire Southern Plateau, shown in Figure 5.2, with the numbers of sites per 200-year period that contained more than 10 percent bison in their vertebrate archaeofaunas; and a portion of a graph (after Thoms 1989), showing the percent of radiocarbon-dated camas-processing features per 250-year period in the Calispel Valley of northeastern Washington.

decline when the nucleation process began. This does not mean that the increase in village sizes we see in later periods was not a manifestation of population growth; it almost certainly was, at least in part.

Introduction of the Bow

Blitz (1988) has suggested that the North American spread of bow and arrow weapon technology was driven by its efficiency as a weapon of war. Its greater utility as a weapon, when compared with the atlatl and dart technology that preceded it, is readily apparent. With an atlatl, a warrior has access to only one or a literal handful of darts and can readily find himself without a projectile weapon if a battle rages for more than a few minutes. To use this weapon accurately and with force, he must stand and show himself, making ambush by atlatl largely ineffective. For this reason, osteoarchaeological evidence from many parts of the continent indicates that clubs were the preferred weapons of battle before the bow was introduced (e.g., Cybulski 1992; Walker 1989). To use them, however, one must close with the enemy, increasing one's chance of personal injury. In contrast, a bow user has multiple projectiles (sometimes up to 100) in his quiver and can unleash a rain of projectiles on his intended victims from safety and distance. Blitz suggests that bow warfare had a strong influence on settlement characteristics, settlement locations, and the prevalence of warfare, particularly in eastern North America (see also LeBlanc

TABLE 5.2. Earliest Records of Arrow Points in the Southern Plateau.

Site	Associated ^{14}C Date	Discussion	Source
Bone-in-the-Throat	2435 ± 60	Date is from hearth above feature containing a single arrow point	Schalk 1983a
Game Farm	2200 ± 60	Arrow points and ^{14}C date from same house floor	Moura 1986
Tsulim	2100 ± 90	Two arrow points among an assemblage of dart points found at an isolated bison kill	Chatters et al. 1995b
Alpowai (45AS82)	1910 ± 80	Found in house 2A, where arrow and dart points were found on different portions of the floor	Brauner 1976

1997; Maschner and Reedy-Maschner 1998). Among the settlement changes were the choice of defensive locations for villages and the construction of stockades with bastions, which not only protected the warriors and noncombatants from arrows but also allowed warriors to shoot from between stockade posts with less risk of personal injury.

Although I take umbrage with many of Blitz's assertions, including his chronology, his argument is not without merit. It is possible that safety from bow and arrow attack influenced nucleation into villages and chosen village locations in many parts of the continent. Evidence from coastal California strongly suggests heightened levels of conflict after the introduction of the bow (Lambert and Walker 1991). I explore this possibility for the Southern Plateau, first by looking into the relative timing of nucleation and bow introductions and then by considering physical evidence from the bow's victims.

Bow and arrow technology, as indicated by the appearance of small, thin, narrow-necked projectile points (Thomas 1978), arrived earlier on the Plateau than anywhere else in temperate North America (cf. Blitz 1988; Rousseau, this volume). Use of this new technology started slowly at first, representing a small part of the weapon inventory beginning shortly before 2400 B.P. (Table 5.2). The earliest find reported thus far is from the Snake River site of Bone-in-the-Throat, where Schalk (1983b) found a single arrow point in a feature that lay beneath a hearth dated 2435 ± 60 B.P. Small arrow points are well represented at the Game Farm site in house floor deposits dating 2200 ± 60 B.P. (Moura 1986) and occur 2100 ± 90 B.P. at the Tsulim Bison Kill site, along with dart points (Chatters et al. 1995b). It is possible in all of these instances to argue for the mixing of later isolates with earlier deposits, but this is not the case at Alpowai site 45AS82, where arrow and dart points occupied different parts of a house floor dating 1910 ± 80 B.P. (Brauner 1976). Bow and arrow technology was certainly established by 2000 B.P. and arguably as much as 400 years earlier. It was introduced at the same time that people were shifting to the Plateau settlement subsistence pattern and beginning to nucleate small hamlets into villages. A potential link to the process of nucleation is established.

Defensive Settlement Strategies

If defensive actions other than nucleation followed bow and arrow introduction, then the link between changing weapon technology and village living is strengthened. Three aspects of the Plateau settlement pattern are arguably or demonstrably associated with defense, and all postdate the introduction of the bow and arrow. These are the occupation of fortified mesas, the placement of large villages on islands, and the use of caves for storage (Table 5.3).

Mesa Fortifications. Smith (1977) has produced the only published data on the age of mesa-top fortifications, having excavated campsites on four of the 55 identified by Washington. Fortifications included rock wall ramparts along all or portions of mesa rims, walled access routes, and, in some cases, small bastion-like structures overlooking access routes. Many mesas could be reached only through a single, narrow defile once wall construction had been completed. Settlements occurred on the tops of mesas and at their feet; sometimes the outer settlements were situated directly in front of the route to the fortified mesa tops. Smith found that artifacts associated with the mesas were all attributable to the latest phases of local prehistory—Harder phase on the Snake River and Cayuse phase on the Columbia—both of which postdate 2500 B.P. (Leonhardy and Rice 1970; Nelson 1969). Radiocarbon dates (Table 5.3) show that Mesa 12 (45GR144), one of the highest and most difficult mesas to reach (Figure 5.4), was first used around 2100 B.P. Mesa use seems to have accelerated between 900 and 1250 B.P. and continued into the historic era. Swanson (1962) excavated the mesa-top village at the Lee site,

TABLE 5.3. Examples of Fortified Mesas, Villages on Islands, and Earliest Storage Caves.

Site Name	Radiocarbon Age	Source(s)
	Mesa Fortification	
45GR144	2070 ± 90	Smith 1977
	1605 ± 90	
	1240 ± 80, 1230 ± 95, 1100 ± 90	
	565 ± 80	
45GR145	1015 ± 90, 945 ± 80	Smith 1977
45GR162	615 ± 145	Smith 1977
	305 ± 75, 220 ± 115	
Lee	Cayuse III Phase (ca. 350–150)	Swanson 1962
	Island Villages	
Strawberry Island	1395 ± 80	Schalk 1983a
	610 ± 90–140 ± 80[a]	
Techumtas Island	Cayuse Phase (ca. 2000–150)	Shiner 1961
45BN53	Cayuse Phase (ca. 2000–150)	Osborne 1957
	Storage Caves	
McGregor Cave	1970 ± ?	Unconfirmed report
Squirt Cave	1750 ± 150	Endacott 1992
	1070 ± 200	
	405 ± 80, 410 ± 80, 570 ± 80	
Marmes Rockshelter	1940–1300	Rice 1969; Sheppard et al. 1987
	1660–660	
Allison Creek Rockshelter	Early Harder Phase (ca. 1500–2500)[b]	Caldwell and Mallory 1967

[a]Multiple dates fall between 610 and 400 B.P., which probably represents the primary later period of occupation.

[b]Associated projectile points are Snake River corner-notched dart points, which lasted until 1000 B.P. They are, however, more common relative to arrow points between 2500 and 1500 B.P., making this the likely age range for the storage features in this site.

which he describes as belonging to the early Cayuse III phase, although he obtained no radiocarbon dates.

Island Villages. Excavations have been conducted at three island villages (Table 5.3), and, although there is occasional evidence of habitation during Pithouse II, only the latest phases of prehistory are represented by the dwelling features (Osborne 1957; Schalk 1983a; Shiner 1961). Radiocarbon dates are only available for Strawberry Island and show that this village was used at least twice, once at around 1400 B.P. and again between about 600 and 400 B.P.

Concealed Storage Facilities. Stored provisions were critical to the subsistence systems of Southern Plateau peoples from Pithouse II through the Plateau Pattern. Explorers, military men, and early ethnographers made a number of observations about storage behavior and storage facilities on the Plateau. In most cases, writers describe storage platforms or houses in villages (e.g., Ray 1932), large pits dug into the riverbanks in or near villages (Lewis 1961), and pits in talus slopes (Walker 1973). Ross (1956), who lived among the Southern Okanogan during the early 19th century, observed that food caches were often placed outside the villages and were kept secret by their owners to prevent pilfering. Caves were also used and contained substantial quantities of food. Wilfong (1990) reports that federal troops chasing the Nez Perce in 1877 found a cave containing two tons of dried roots, which they removed and burned.

Some authors consider the use of caves and subterranean pits as storage features to be an indicator of the need for defense, in this case defense of one's food supply. In a study of ethnographic reports and chronological relationships between subterranean storage and village fortification, DeBoer (1988) concludes that concealment of foodstuffs was regularly practiced by peoples who were plagued by chronic, persistent warfare and followed a

Figure 5.4. Fifty-five fortified mesas have been documented in the channeled scablands that lie between the Columbia and Snake rivers in eastern Washington. This is Mesa 12 (45GR144), the earliest of the mesas to be occupied and the most difficult to reach. The only access to the top is through the narrow defile at the lower left of the landform. Photo courtesy of William C. Smith.

settlement pattern that was often semisedentary. On the Great Plains, for example, Plains Village farmers, who left their homes in winter to hunt bison, used subterranean storage more frequently during times when their villages were also fortified, indicating that increased threat of attack caused more cautious caching of provisions. DeBoer also notes that early observers saw the Miami and other Eastern Woodlands peoples concealing their provisions when intertribal hostilities erupted. The use of subterranean and cave storage by Plateau peoples, therefore, probably indicates that food was being buried and separated from the main settlement in an effort to hide it from enemies. Storage outside the village would have had the secondary effect of separating food stores from vulnerable occupants of the villages when marauders came to steal food.

Storage caves and talus pits have been documented in large numbers on the Middle Columbia (e.g., Swanson 1962) and Lower Snake rivers (Chatters and Langdon 2002; Mallory 1966; Reid 1991a, 1991b). When investigated, the storage pits in these caves contain artifacts attributable to the Plateau Pattern, with few exceptions. The exceptions to date are Cedar Cave and Burr Cave. Swanson (1962) has documented one grass-lined pit (but no foodstuffs) at Cedar Cave on the Mid-Columbia River in strata attributable to his Frenchman Springs phase, a local manifestation of Pithouse II. A storage basket was found in Burr Cave, on the Lower Snake River, and dated 2660 ± 90 B.P. (Gilbow 1978). Some of the sites, including the large Porcupine and McGregor caves of the Lower Palouse River, were used into the historic period for storing fish, lampreys, and roots (Mallory 1966).

Larger storage caves are often widely separated from the nearest known villages. McGregor Cave, an immense shelter near the mouth of the Palouse River that contains 34 distinct storage pits, is nearly 10 km from site 45FR36, the Palus Indian village that probably maintained it.

The earliest dates that have thus far been obtained on large storage caves, and in fact virtually the only dates on these sites, come from Marmes Rockshelter, McGregor Cave, and Squirt Cave, all of which are located in the Lower Snake River region (Table 5.3). There are unverified reports of a radiocarbon date of 1970 B.P. at McGregor Cave, and storage pits were found at Marmes Rockshelter in Stratums VI, which is dated between 1940 and 1300 B.P., and VII, with dates between 1660 and 660 B.P. (Rice 1969; Sheppard et al. 1987). In addition, projectile points found along with storage pits at Allison Creek

Rockshelter in Hell's Canyon (Caldwell and Mallory 1967) date that site to the early Harder phase or sometime between 2500 and 1000 B.P. However, precise dates on cave storage come only from Squirt Cave, where Endacott (1992) found at least three episodes of cache building: 1750 B.P., 1070 B.P., and 570–405 B.P. This record indicates that people were regularly using caves to store food as early as 2000 B.P. and that cave use waxed and waned thereafter.

Physical Evidence for Conflict

For the purposes of this analysis, I use two kinds of skeletal trauma as indictors of conflict: projectile wounds and cranial injuries. It may be argued that either form of trauma might result from accident, but both are more likely to be the result of intent (regarding cranial injuries, see Walker 1989).

CRANIAL TRAUMA. Cranial injuries have occurred throughout the prehistory of the Southern Plateau, although with varying frequency (Table 5.4). A healed, depressed fracture appears in the skull of Marmes 3, a young adult male who is one of the earliest individuals yet found on the Plateau (Krantz 1979). Healed cranial trauma is also present in the skull dubbed "Stick Man," which is dated to the Early–Middle Holocene transition (Chatters et al. 2000), and is arguably present in the 8400 B.P. skeleton known as Kennewick Man (Chatters 2000). We have few human skeletons dating between 8000 and 3000 B.P., and most of these are in very poor condition (e.g., Breschini 1977). The only well-preserved remains that have received a thorough examination come from the Braden and Damoss sites of west-central Idaho, at the southeastern periphery of the Southern Plateau. Just two skulls are present in the 6,400-year-old Damoss collection, and neither exhibits injury; but one of nine individuals, again a male, from the 6,600-year-old Braden site has a massive, healed, depressed fracture to the right posterior parietal region (R. Yohe, personal communication, 2001). The next-most recent individual of which I am aware is a skull from Priest Rapids dated 2850 ± 60 B.P., which has extensive new bone formation on his left parietal, possibly from one or more blows to the head. Eleven other skeletons of this approximate age range (Pithouse II) were excavated on Rabbit Island in the Columbia (Osborne 1957), and one of similar age was found at Lenore, on the Clearwater River (Toups 1967), but reports on the osteology of these individuals are unavailable.

The largest skeletal collection from the Southern Plateau that predates the nucleation into villages comes from the Congdon site (45KL41), located just upstream of The Dalles, Oregon, and thus just inside the geographic limits of the Plateau. During the early 1960s, Butler (1963) recovered skeletal remains from this ossuary as it was being looted by collectors and destroyed by a railroad building crew. I was able to analyze 35 crania and postcranial material representing at least 80 individuals that were housed at Central Washington University.[1] Of the 28 crania complete enough for me to assess whether trauma had occurred, 16 exhibited cranial trauma and additional individuals had button osteomas that might have resulted from less severe trauma. The injuries, which ranged from small depressed fractures to massive fractures to the facial bones and brows (Figure 5.5), had in most cases healed completely before death. This assemblage dates between 2280 and 2370 B.P., the time of transition between Pithouse I and the Plateau Pattern and also at or just before the introduction of the bow and arrow.

Cranial injury became much less common after 2200 B.P. Although my review for this variable may have missed potentially pertinent gray literature, I am familiar with only three widely spaced incidences of cranial trauma that postdate 2000 B.P. (Table 5.4; e.g., Figure 5.5).[2] Additionally, of 280 late prehistoric crania recently received by Central Washington University from the descendants of eastern Washington collectors, less than 2 percent show any sign of cranial trauma. This collection had been assembled primarily by physicians, who were interested in the incidence and characteristics of pathology. They not only made collections themselves but also purchased skulls from other collectors in part because the skulls possessed defects, so this lack of cranial injury is particularly noteworthy.

PROJECTILE WOUNDS. The chronological distribution of projectile wounds is nearly inverse that of cranial traumas (Table 5.5). While Kennewick Man, with a dart point in his ilium, is the earliest example at circa 8400 B.P. (Chatters 2000), he is the only confirmed case that predates the beginning of the Plateau Pattern.[3] I know of only one other dart point wound, which consists of a Snake River Corner-Notched point embedded in an isolated sacrum.[4] The Snake River Corner-Notched projectile point style postdates 2500 B.P. and remained common for 1,500 years after the introduction of the bow. Projectile point wounds, all produced by arrows, have been found in the remains of 12 individuals postdating 1700 B.P. An additional eight individuals who either were found in mass graves beside skeletons with arrow point injuries or had shattered projectile point blades among "ibones" are inferred to have been killed by those projectiles. These radiocarbon-dated incidences of death by arrow begin with the cremated remains of five individuals—a young female, two males, and two children—from Ellisford, on the Okanogan River, who died circa 1620 ± 160 B.P. and were buried in an isolated mass grave (Chatters 1986).

TABLE 5.4. Incidence of Cranial Injuries (Club Wounds) in Skeletal Remains from the Southern Plateau (Remains Are from Washington Unless Otherwise Indicated).

Site/Find	Radiocarbon Age	Description	Source(s)
Marmes Rockshelter	10130 ± 300, 9840 ± 300	Male skeleton with healed cranial injury	Krantz 1979; Sheppard et al. 1987
Kennewick Man	8410 ± 60	Male with possible healed cranial injury	Chatters 2000
Stick Man	8040 ± 50–8140 ± 50	Male with healed depressed fracture	Chatters et al. 2000
Braden Site, Idaho	6590 ± 90	Male with healed depressed fracture	R. Yohe, personal communication, 2001; Beta-90555
Priest Rapids	2850 ± 60	Male with extensive, healed cranial damage	Author's notes; CAMS-38950; UCR-3566
Congdon	2280 ± 50, 2370 ± 40	Of 28 individuals, 9 males (69%) and 7 females (50%) with cranial trauma, usually healed	Author's notes; CAMS3899; CAMS 46954; UCR-3564; UCR-3626
Jaeger Island	1880 ± 110	Male with healed cranial trauma	Chatters and Pasternack 1992
45OK112	650 ± 80	Male from small cemetery with healed, depressed fracture	Chatters 2003
Sntlexwenewixwtn	650 ± 100	Male in mass grave with penetrating cranial injury	Chatters and Zweifel 1987

Like the Ellisford group, most of the individuals with projectile wounds were found outside of cemeteries, far from any known villages. A second mass grave, containing skeletons of six able-bodied males, was found by amateurs in a hillside roadbed near the Grand Ronde River in southeastern Washington. Three had arrow wounds, and two, including one of the arrow victims, had been scalped. The bodies of the individuals in the Ellisford and Grand Ronde graves had been partially scavenged by carrion eaters before burial, indicating that their relatives did not immediately find or retrieve the remains. Two other males (45OK197 and Bonaparte Creek; see Figure 5.6), both shot with multiple arrows and both apparently foreign to the region where they died, were also found in isolated graves.

Arrow wounds have been found in a small number of individuals from cemeteries, most notably those located along the Okanogan River in north-central Washington (Chatters 2003; Chatters and Zweifel 1987).[5] Most are from single graves, but two are from a mass grave at a cemetery called Sntlexwenewixwtn (The Place Many Killed One Another in Battle). There, a young man and teenaged girl, both with evidence of death from arrows, were interred with a young child and another young man who had died from a head wound inflicted by a club or cylindrical arrow point (the cranial injury reported in Table 5.4). That cemetery had, according to legend, been placed around the bodies of a family who had been killed by marauders while picking berries away from camp (Chatters and Zweifel 1987). This case, along with the homicide victims from isolated graves, brings into sharp focus the danger of being away from the security of the village during the later periods in Plateau prehistory.

The mass graves are particularly instructive on this issue. Two, Ellisford and Sntlexwenewixwtn, consist of what appear to be families, with young adult males, young adult or adolescent females, and small children. The third, from the Grand Ronde, consists entirely of young males, who incidentally were remarkably uniform in size and appearance, suggesting members of a single band or extended family. The first two groups were probable victims of attack by small bands of young men like those found at the third group. In the latter case, it was the war party that did not make it home.

Another undated case, again discovered by a collector, is also instructive. Found in central Washington, in the region of the fortified mesas, it consists of a cervical vertebra with an embedded arrow point (*Wenatchee Daily World* 1962). A photograph of the find shows that the point entered through the throat, penetrating from above, and was embedded in the anterior surface of the vertebral body. The individual was apparently looking up, with head tilted back, when the point struck, perhaps looking at intended victims who had taken refuge on a mesa top.

Arrow wounds seem to differ from the previously common cranial injuries in one important respect. Whereas most people seem to have survived their head injuries, few survived being shot by arrows. Only two cases, a female from 45OK112, near the mouth of the Okanogan River (Chatters 2003), and one of the males from Ellisford, had healed wounds. The older Ellisford male had a healed cut in one vertebra but did not survive the second

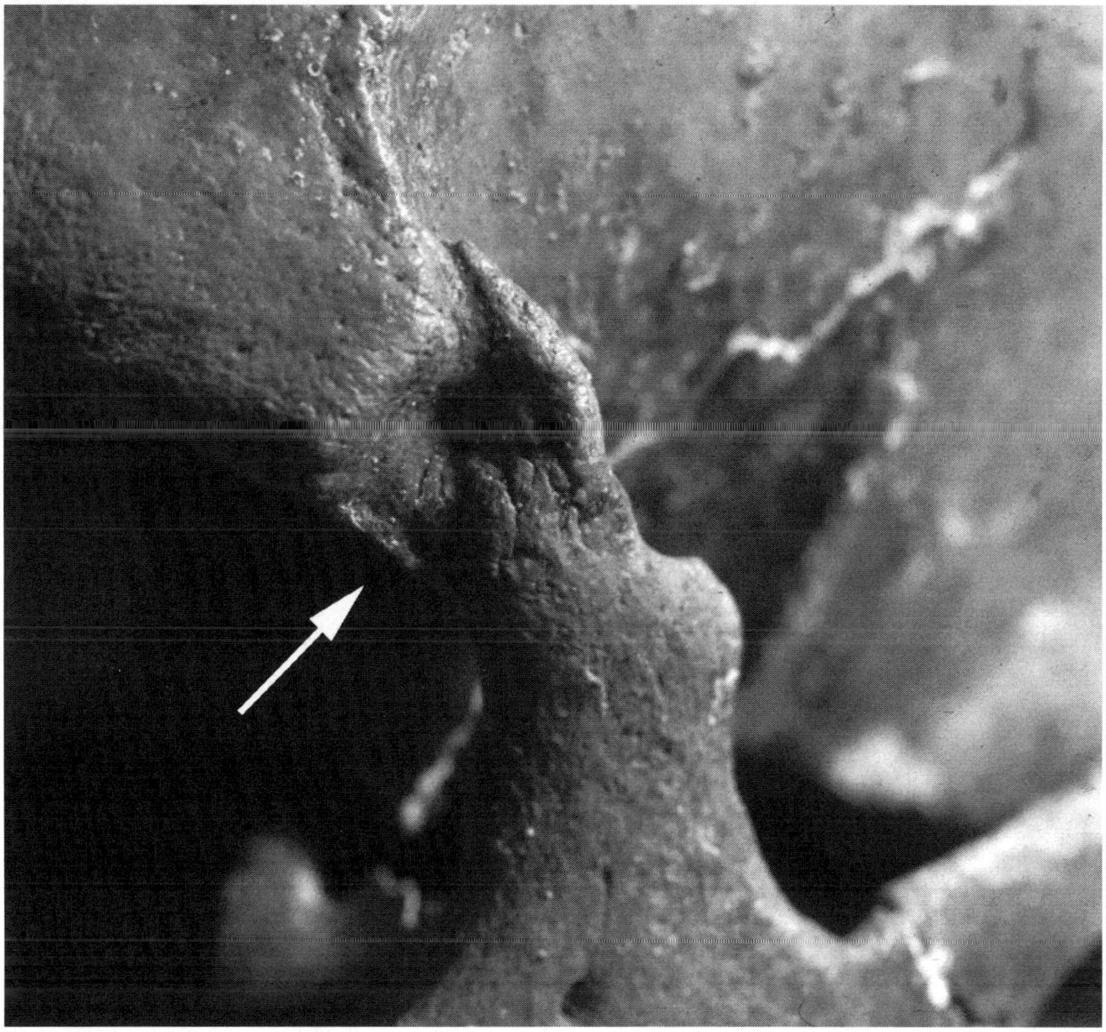

Figure 5.5. An example of the cranial trauma that was so commonplace on the Southern Plateau before the introduction of the bow and arrow. This male, from the Congdon site near The Dalles, Oregon, received a crushing blow to the lateral rim of his eye socket.

attack. This difference between cranial and projectile injuries demonstrates that the lethality of conflict increased markedly with the introduction of the bow.

DISCUSSION

If we look at all these lines of evidence together (Figure 5.7), excluding for the moment the population diagram, then a relationship among many of the variables is clearly evident. The Plateau Pattern, with its nucleated winter villages, emerged at the same time as the bow and arrow first appeared, between 2500 and 2100 B.P. By around 2100 B.P., we see the first use of mesa-top fortifications. By about 2000 B.P., extramural storage in caves commenced. The movement of villages to islands began by at least 1400 B.P., but that information comes from only one site, and I have no doubt that some island villages, if ever radiocarbon dated, will prove to be earlier.

Signs of conflict, or at least of the need to defend oneself and one's food supply, are ubiquitous. The coincidence of defensive behavior with the introduction of the bow and arrow weapon system is evident, and it is tempting to suggest that this new ability to inflict damage at a distance through a rain of projectiles or by ambush brought increased intergroup strife. However, conflict clearly did not begin with the winter village pattern but, rather, was a component of human behavior in the region for as long as 10,000 years. In fact, if the Congdon site is any indication, conflict appears to have been escalating as the Plateau Pattern began. What did change after the introduction of the bow was the lethality of the conflict. Isolated families were at greater risk, as we see from the murdered bodies of men, women, and children who were so unfortunate as to be caught away from the village during foraging excursions. This means that larger groups were less vulnerable to attack and that there was strong

TABLE 5.5. PROJECTILE WOUNDS IN SOUTHERN PLATEAU SKELETONS.

Site/Find	Radiocarbon Age	Description	Source(s)
Kennewick Man	8410 ± 60	Male with dart point healed in pelvis	Chatters 2000
Mid-Columbia[a]	ca. 2500–1000	Dart point in the sacrum	Author's notes
Ellisford	1620 ± 160	Mass grave (5) of mixed sex and age, two with arrow wounds	Chatters 1986
45OK66[b]	1070 ± 80	Male with apparent perimortem arrow wound	Chatters 2003
Attrocity	910 ± 40	Mass grave (6) of males: three with stone arrow wounds, two scalped	Author's notes; CAMS-76744; SR-5881
Bonaparte Creek[c]	850 ± 70	Isolated male with multiple perimortem arrow wounds	Chatters 1995a
Sntlxwenewixwtn	650 ± 100	Mass grave (4) of mixed sex and age, two with perimortem arrow wounds	Chatters and Zweifel 1987
45OK112	650 ± 80	Female with arrow tip healed in the humerus	Chatters 2003
45OK52[b]	550 ± 60	Two males with perimortem arrow wounds	Chatters 2003
45OK197[d]	170 ± 110	Isolated male with multiple perimortem wounds	Chatters 1982
45OK66	protohistoric	Female with perimortem arrow wound	Chatters 1982
Waterville Plateau[e]	post-2500	Arrow point in body of cervical vertebra	*Wenatchee Daily World* 1962

[a]Found by a collector and housed in a local museum; precise provenience unknown, age estimate based on dart point style.

[b]One individual had impact-shattered projectile point blade(s) but no perimortem wound.

[c]This individual had cranial deformation that is uncharacteristic of the region in which he was found.

[d]This young male had 11 arrow points associated, six of a local style in his torso (all broken; one embedded in the humerus) and five of a different, nonlocal style beside him.

[e]Found by a collector, reported (with photo) in the local newspaper.

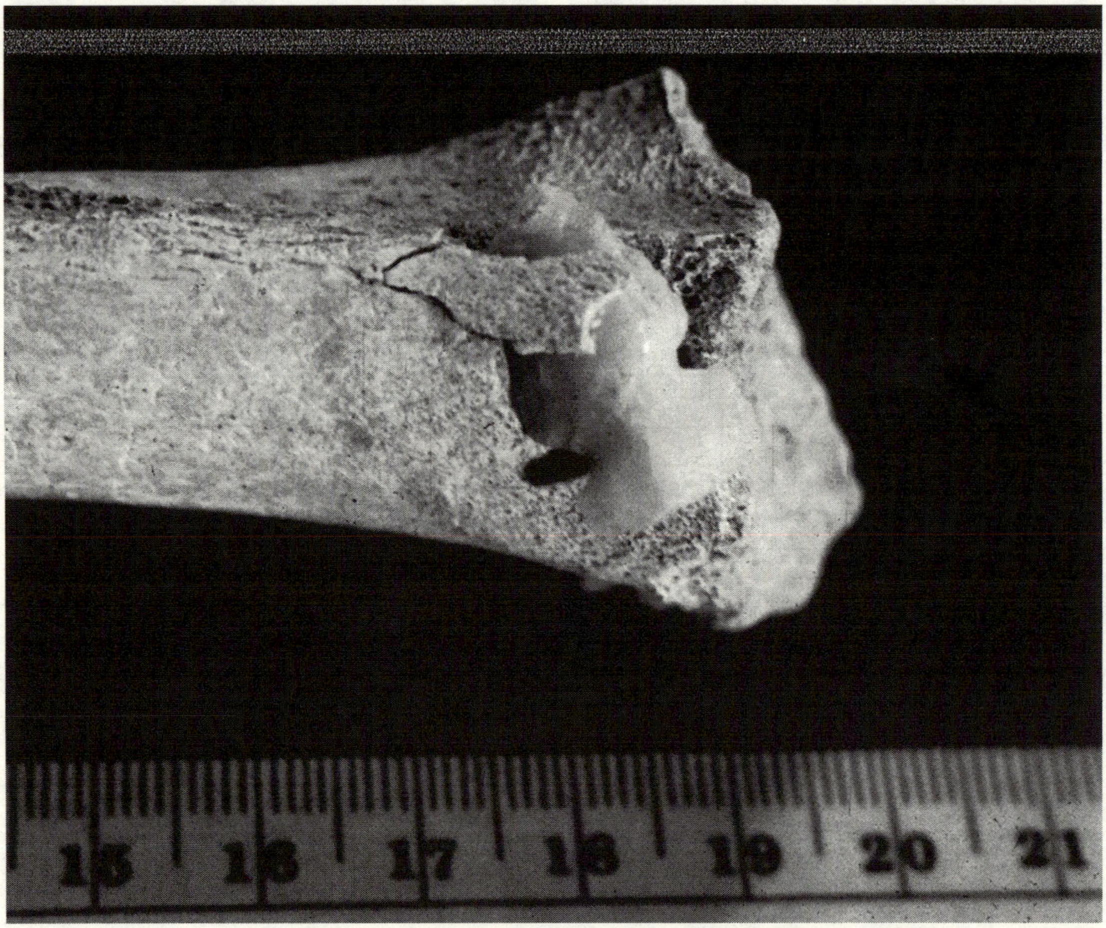

Figure 5.6. An arrow point lodged in the humerus of an adolescent male from site 45OK197, on the Upper Columbia River.

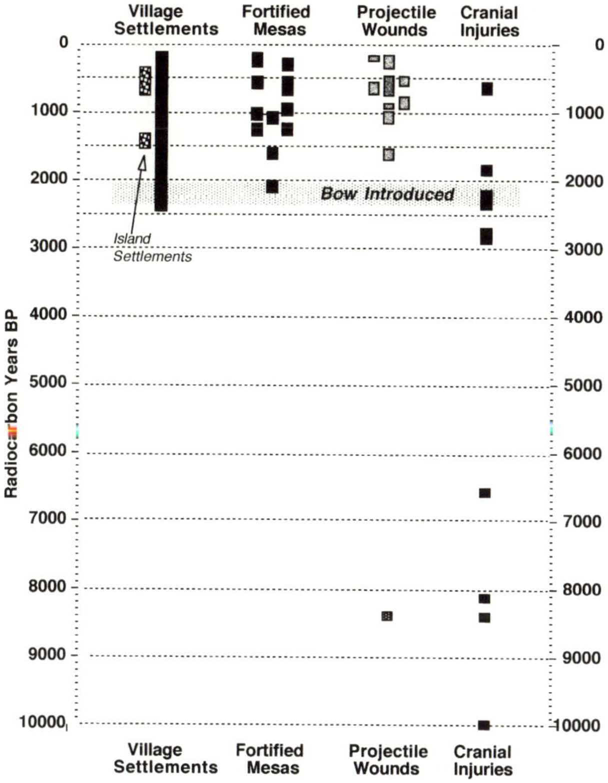

Figure 5.7. Changes in settlement, storage tactics, and injury patterns on the Southern Plateau and their association with the introduction of the bow and arrow.

pressure, at least during periods of heightened tensions, for nucleation into villages.

It is clear from a comparison between Figures 5.2 and 5.7 that, whereas population growth does not seem to have influenced the development of the winter village pattern, it may have played a part in the escalation of conflict associated with that pattern and in the increasing sizes of villages. Regional populations appear to have reached their peak between 1400 and 1000 B.P. and to have remained high until around 500 B.P. It is during this time that we see greater use of mesa tops, the first use of Strawberry Island, the second use of Squirt Cave, and the highest incidence of arrow wounds.

Alternative Explanations

Although the scenario I have laid out is seductive, with a certain Hollywood appeal, there is an equally attractive explanation for many of the components of the story. Regarding the use of caves and talus pits for storage, Reid (1991a), also citing DeBoer's (1988) work, suggests that it was increased mobility range—a greater distance from the villages to the seasonal food-gathering areas—that led people to conceal their foodstuffs. Noting that the irruption of bison coincided with the first use of these storage facilities, he sees the inception of the Plateau Pattern as a response to a change in the availability of large food packages (bison). The attraction of the bison pulled people away from their riverine homes into the little-used uplands, causing them to leave their homes and food stores behind (as discussed above, for a similar argument regarding the abandonment of camas fields, see Thoms 1989). To minimize the risk of temporary abandonment, they concealed their food supplies. We might carry the argument further and suggest that this expansion of peoples' ranges brought them into contact with new, nonbison food patches and raw materials on which they eventually became dependent. I have made a similar argument (Chatters 1993), observing that the bison irruption coincided with geologic evidence for drier climatic conditions and a summer-dominant precipitation pattern (Chatters 1998). This change, which led to floodplain degradation, alluvial fan building, and increased stream turbidity, would have caused salmon productivity to decline (Chatters 1998; Chatters et al. 1995a). The simultaneous decline in riverine productivity and increase in terrestrial productivity pushed and pulled people away from the rivers.

Both of these scenarios, which differ only in the relative strength of ecological factors, would have created conditions that Smith (1977) believes led to the need for fortifications in the root-gathering grounds of the channeled scablands. Citing the expansion of Salish speakers onto the Plateau as the initial trigger, Smith reasons that the scablands lay between the Snake and Middle Columbia river canyons, with their Sahaptian-speaking populations, and the Upper Columbia River, with its Salish inhabitants. This food-rich area was contested and became a zone of conflict between these distinct ethnic groups. If the three of us are correct (with or without the Salishan expansion argument), then the primary cause of the conflict—resource competition under times of stress—led to the pattern of violence, defensive settlement positioning in the root grounds, and, potentially, the nucleation of hamlets into villages along the river corridors. As is discussed by others below (see Lepofsky and Peacock, this volume; Hayden and Cousins, this volume; Kuijt and Prentiss, this volume), issues of resource competition, as manifested through feasting, available labor, ownership, and resource selection, may have been an important consideration in the Northern Plateau as well.

We are left with one nagging gap in this argument. As strife was clearly present throughout Plateau prehistory, why didn't people nucleate sooner? Again, it may have been the ability to do battle and kill effectively at a distance that the bow and arrow provided that triggered this final increase in settlement size, the use of fortifications with ramparts, and the occupation of islands.

In the absence of radiocarbon dates for many of the larger villages on the Lower Columbia River, including Locke, Berrians, Miller, and Techumtas, we are left not knowing when these large villages were first or most intensively occupied. If their formation coincided with the second occupation of Strawberry Island, at around 400–600 B.P. or later (a conclusion that illustrated artifacts would support—see Osborne 1957; Shiner 1961), then there are at least two possible explanations. The first, based again on climate, is that a severe drought at around 450 B.P., documented in a small lake north of the Snake River (Bartholomew 1982), might have heightened resource competition. It is interesting that the intensity of storage in Squirt Cave and the number of arrow killings both increased at this time. Another possibility is that the expansion of the Numic-speaking Paiute, documented by Lewis and Clark as a cause for village relocation by the Umatilla between 1805 and 1806 (Lewis 1961), was already under way. These scenarios again emphasize community defense as a motivation for nucleation and village location.

The Risk of a Regionwide Analysis

One advantage of looking at the past on a regional scale is that it reduces the problems of sampling error that so beset an attempt to understand patterns at a local level. If we lack information from one time period in one locality, then we can supplement the record with data from another. The problem with regional-scale analysis is that local variations in behavior are masked. So it is with the study described above (Figure 5.8). Whereas early villages have been found throughout the Southern Plateau, island villages are confined to the Middle Columbia and lowermost Snake rivers, where large islands exist. Mesa-top fortifications are primarily north of the region that contains the islands and probably did not play a part in the seasonal rounds of most of those islands' inhabitants. What we know about storage in caves comes from the Lower Snake River. Evidence about the abandonment of camas grounds comes from the northeastern part of the region; bison were in the south. Skeletons with club wounds (not including those earlier than 3000 B.P.) come primarily from the Mid-Columbia, where earlier human remains have been found, whereas most skeletons with arrow wounds have been found on the Upper Columbia and Okanogan rivers. The Congdon site, where cranial injuries are most common, lies at the frontier between

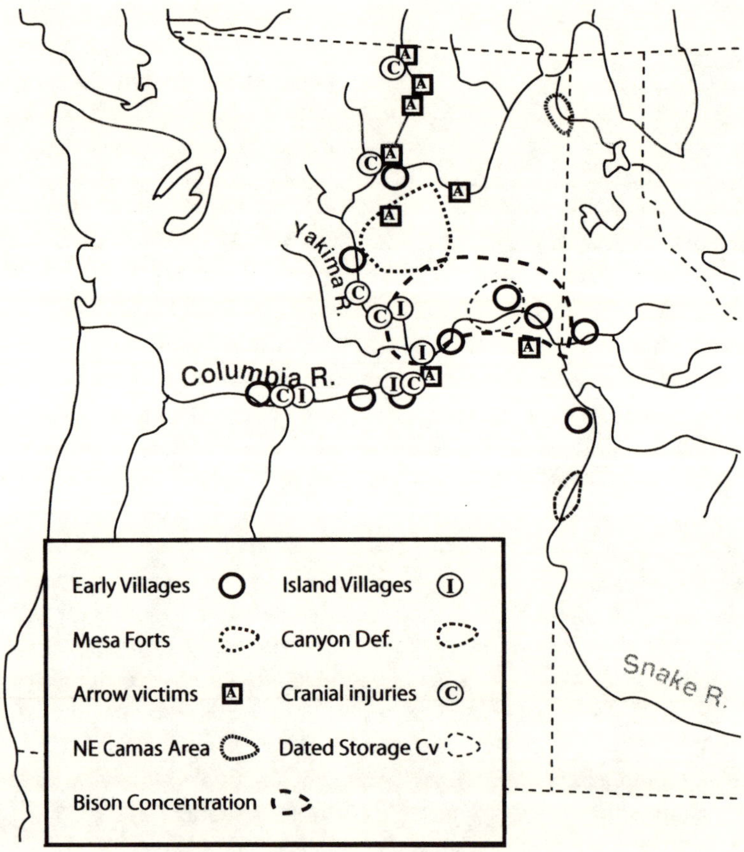

Figure 5.8. Each of the lines of evidence discussed in this chapter comes from a different part of the Southern Plateau, leaving open the question of whether defensive developments, including island villages, mesa-top forts, canyon villages, and underground and cave storage are in fact related to changes in injury patterns. This map illustrates how much we need to learn before a thorough understanding of this issue can be achieved.

Northwest Coastal and Plateau culture areas and is from a location I have long considered the Troy of the Columbia River Basin. Excavators of later cemeteries on the Lower Columbia and Snake rivers operated under the concept of Plateau pacifism and make no note of trauma patterns, if any existed; many of those collections have not been analyzed or at least are not yet reported. Therefore, these coincident variables may be part of a pattern of conflict and defensive behavior, or they may not. We will need a great deal of additional information before this picture becomes clear.

CONCLUSION

Strong chronological correlations exist among the introduction of the bow and arrow, evidence for lethal conflict, and the settlement and storage tactics of the Plateau Pattern. Evidence for the bow and arrow first appears between 2,000 and 2,400 B.P., at the same time as the first larger groupings of houses that can properly be referred to as villages and at the beginning of the networked collecting strategy that persisted in the Southern Plateau into historic times. Within the next few centuries mesa-top fortifications, concealed food storage, episodic settlement on islands, and skeletons with arrow wounds began to appear. The overall pattern of settlement change, including nucleation, fortification, defensive village positioning, and cave and pit storage of foods, is consistent with an increasing need for defense from one's neighbors or from external enemies. Arrow wounds and particularly the mass killing of isolated families confirm that conflict and highlight the danger that small social groups faced. Nucleation into villages, it appears, was one of the solutions to this heightened risk. With the additional dating of villages, fortifications, and storage and greater attention to patterns of trauma in those skeletal populations that are still available for study, we might evaluate this proposition and ultimately learn whether intergroup tensions were episodic and, if so, what the climatic and social triggers for those tensions might have been.

NOTES

1. A few additional crania are held at the University of Washington's Burke Museum, which has refused access for study despite the fact that it has determined the remains to be unaffiliated. Even if none of those crania exhibit trauma, the frequency of injury is still unusually high. Because most of the smaller long bones appear to have been destroyed by carnivores before the burials took place, we lack ulnae and radii, which might exhibit parry fractures and confirm whether or not the head wounds are from accident or attack.

2. Amateurs who excavated at the cemetery at Old Umatilla (35UM) report finding an individual with a severe perimortem cranial injury, but no report is available on the osteology or age of this individual or any other from that site.

3. Douglas Owsley (personal communication, 2000) of the Smithsonian Institution interprets a lytic area in a female vertebra from Braden as a projectile wound, but no cut or projectile fragment is present. Although the lytic lesion might have resulted from a penetrating wound and ensuing infection, it is not possible to state with certainty that it was produced by a projectile.

4. This item was, at least until recently, held in the Sacajawea State Park Museum. Having come from an amateur collection, it is unprovenienced.

5. Most cemeteries were excavated when the idea of Plateau pacifism held sway, so I wonder if this influenced the excavators' quest for evidence of projectile wounds and other evidence of trauma.

6

RITUAL STRUCTURES IN TRANSEGALITARIAN COMMUNITIES

Brian Hayden and Ron Adams

In this chapter, we explore the possibility that certain structures at the Keatley Creek site in the British Columbia interior had specialized functions involving rituals and feasting. The Keatley Creek site was a large prehistoric pithouse village of complex transegalitarian hunter-gatherers. Feasting tends to be common in complex transegalitarian hunter-gatherer societies, and there are strong indications that feasting was a key element in the emergence of socioeconomic complexity (Hayden 1994, 1995, 1996). Secret societies also typify the most developed transegalitarian hunter-gatherer societies cross-culturally, and in some instances, there are structures built specifically to house secret society rituals and feasts. Thus, comparative studies of developed transegalitarian hunter-gatherer societies lead us to expect the existence of secret societies at Keatley Creek and the use of restricted spaces (e.g., caves or special structures) for the most secret meetings and rituals of these groups (Owens and Hayden 1997; see also Wason 1994:150–151). However, archaeologists dealing with complex hunter-gatherers rarely consider the possibility that specialized ritual structures might exist, and in the few cases where such possibilities have been considered, researchers have looked for special purpose structures among the largest buildings in the centers of sites. Our research indicates that in many cases small remote structures are more likely to have been used for ritual and feasting purposes. This is a pattern that is consistent with the emergence of special ritual structures in transegalitarian communities elsewhere in the world.

At Keatley Creek, there are at least two pairs of housepits that may have been used for such purposes as well as several isolated structures. The remote locations of these structures in addition to their unique cultural remains indicate their function as ritual structures. They may be the first examples of secret society ritual structures archaeologically documented among hunter-gatherers of the Northwest. We argue that the existence of these structures is critical to understanding the emergence of sociopolitical complexity in the region.

THE KEATLEY CREEK SITE

The Keatley Creek site is located near Lillooet, approximately 300 km from the Pacific coast in the British Columbia interior. It is a winter village site consisting of about 120 structural depressions located on a moraine terrace along the Fraser River (Figure 6.1—see also Hayden 1997:281). Most structures visible on the land surface were occupied from about 2600 B.P. to 1000 B.P., although there is a small cluster of structures on the upper terraces that were used in protohistoric times, about 200–300 years ago (Hayden 2000b).

The archaeological indications at Keatley Creek are clearly of a transegalitarian society in which wealth and power were unequally distributed. Substantial variations in house size, storage facilities, architecture, stone tools, stone raw materials, faunal remains, botanical remains, hearth development, and prestige items all indicate inequalities typical of transegalitarian societies. In particular, there is a dichotomy of small and large structures at the site. In small structures, with sizes up to 9 m in diameter, there is substantial variation with regard to cultural materials. The remains from some of the small structures are indicative of relatively poor households, lacking prestige items and valued food remains. Other small structures, including some of those examined in this chapter, are characterized by an abundance of prestige items or a conspicuous lack of faunal or lithic remains (Hayden 2000b:3–10). There appears to be much less variability among the larger structures, with sizes up to 22 m in diameter. These structures typically contain large storage pits, a higher density and quantity of fish and mammal bones (compared with the smaller structures), the remains of specialized fauna (short- and long-tailed hawks, freshwater shells, and dog), and prestige lithic items (e.g.,

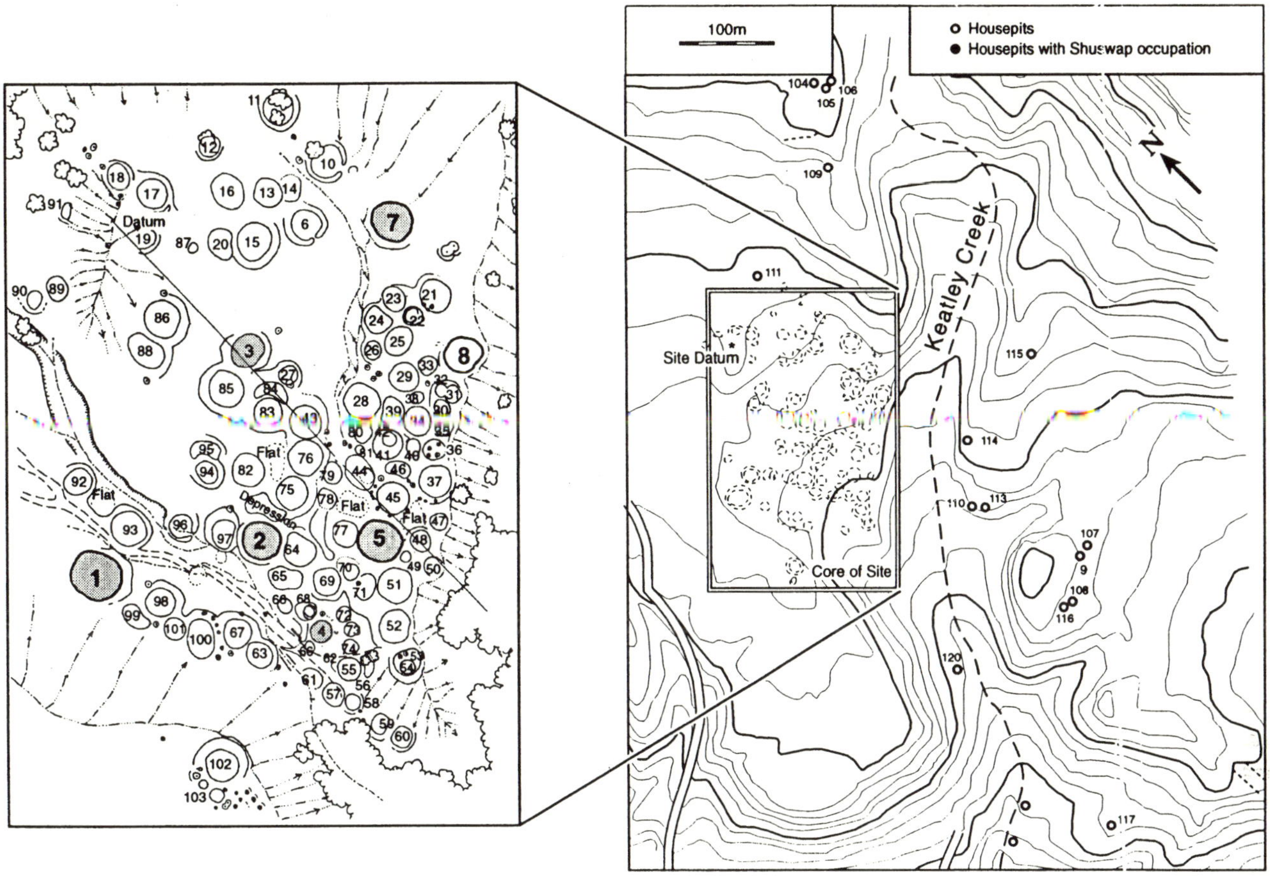

Figure 6.1. A map of the Keatley Creek site showing the core area (left) and the peripheral structures located on terraces to the east (Terraces 1–2) and south as discussed in this analysis (right).

nephrite adze fragments, copper items, pipe fragments, graphite, obsidian, and substantial indications of hide working). In the larger structures, the types of salmon bone remains also indicate a higher proportion of more valued salmon species as well as significantly greater access to a larger variety of salmon in comparison with the smaller structures (Hayden 2000b:10–14).

The Keatley Creek housepit remains indicate a socio-economic organization in which large residential corporate groups were the major economic powers of the community and controlled prime hunting areas, fishing locations, root-collecting areas, and access to lithic sources. The prestige items, raw materials from distant sources, and valued food remains recovered in the largest structures are evidence for such differential access to resources.

Some poor families probably also lived in the larger corporate group households as laborers for the wealthier noble members of the groups. However, other poor families evidently preferred to live independently in small pit-houses (Hayden 2000b:16). On the Northwest Coast, such poor families needed to wait until the owners of the resources or land had finished gathering resources for themselves, after which the poor could procure what was left for a fee (Swanton 1975:71). The presence of small houses at Keatley Creek lacking valued faunal remains and prestige items fits this pattern.

CRITERIA FOR IDENTIFYING RITUAL STRUCTURES

Our focus in this analysis is on the ritual structures in transegalitarian societies. This includes complex hunter-gatherers (such as those at Keatley Creek) as well as simple horticultural groups, such as the early Neolithic communities of the Near East. The basic similarities among these types of cultures have been noted elsewhere. In other parts of the world, it is among transegalitarian communities that the first ritual structures appear (Hayden 2003b). We have therefore assembled a preliminary list of criteria for the identification of ritual structures based on an initial comparative study of transegalitarian archaeological and ethnographic examples. These criteria include the following characteristics.

Location

There are numerous types of locations for group ritual activities in traditional communities, including the *interiors of large households* or residential corporate structures, *lineage structures* near lineage households, *central locations* within communities (e.g., great kivas or the plaza-related structures at Çayönü, Jerf el-Ahmar, San José Mogoté, and Hallan Çemi), *peripheral or remote locations* for secret societies (especially caves or special structures [Bar-Yosef and Schick 1989; Hampton 1999]), and *special geographic locations* in the landscape (especially caves or mountain tops). At Keatley Creek, the large residential corporate group structures were almost certainly used for impressive rituals and feasts. For instance, at one large housepit (Structure 7), there were large roasting pit features EHPE 1 and 2, an external hearth with numerous dog bones, a large internal roasting feature, large episodically used hearths, impressive dog sacrifices, and a number of prestige or ritual items (see Crellin and Heffner 2000; Hayden 2000a, 2003a: chaps. 11.2–11.3; Prentiss et al. 2003b). The use of large corporate group residences for rituals probably obviated the need for any central, community-based ritual structures at the site. In contrast, communities composed of nuclear family household structures probably required some centrally located, specialized structures for major ritual gatherings.

Moreover, given that Keatley Creek sociopolitical organization appears to have been "heterarchical" rather than centralized, we should not necessarily expect any centralized special ritual structures at the site. However, specialized structures for secret societies may have existed, and given a basic heterarchical organization, there may well have been more than one secret society organization, just as on the Northwest Coast there were the Cannibal Society, the Wolf Society, and others. Secret society structures can be expected to occur in peripheral or remote locations, but more central locations cannot be automatically excluded without further detailed ethnographic and archaeological studies.

In the ethnographic literature, the existence of secret societies with remote ritual houses, each containing a resident custodial "guard," has been documented among the transegalitarian societies in the western New Guinea Highlands (Hampton 1999:208–209). Hampton's description is particularly useful:

> With the exception of the house where the guard lived and the sacred men's house, the other buildings of both compounds were void of material goods normally related to inhabited living sites. The designs of the compounds and their various structures are all within normal size, shape, and material variance of compounds being lived in with the exception of the sun house compound, where one house built on stilts is rectangular in shape with a board slat roof. [1999:138]

Special temporary community ritual dance structures erected for the Sun Dance of the Kutenai and the Spirit Dance of the Flathead in the Plateau of northwestern North America have also been reported ethnographically. For the Sun Dance structures, the members of the Kutenai Crazy Dog Society collected the coverings of three tipis to use as the structure cover (Ray 1939:125–131). Among the Tlingit on the Northwest Coast, bathhouses, some of which were reportedly quite large, located adjacent to a high-ranking household were used as gathering places for political elites (de Laguna 1972:305–306). Although it is not specifically stated that bathhouses were used by secret societies, they are indicative of a similar pattern of exclusive gatherings for some of the elite members of society who typically form secret societies.

Some ritual structures in transegalitarian societies were often situated outside of villages. This was the case in New Guinea, and Tlingit shamans also reportedly lived in separate houses with a shrine in the forest near the village (Oberg 1973:19). Ritual enclosures used for ceremonies by the Nisenan of Northern California were located some distance from the main villages (Wilson 1957–1963, cited in Wilson and Town 1978), as were ritual structures in which special whaling ceremonies took place among the Nootkans of Vancouver Island (Arima and Dewhirst 1990:395; Boas 1969:266–269). In some of the transegalitarian Neolithic communities of the Near East, specialized ritual structures occur 300 m from the nearest contemporary habitations (Garrard et al. 1994:79–81, 93), whereas the specialized ritual structure at the Upper Paleolithic site of Dolni Vestonice (a complex hunter-gatherer occupation) was 100 m from the residential area. These are distances comparable to the distance from the core of the Keatley Creek site to the proposed ritual structures that we will be discussing located on the periphery of the site.

Assemblage Characteristics

Because ritual structures can play a number of roles (e.g., sanctuaries, dancing or performances, food preparation, feasting, storage, custodian residences, meeting halls), there is no single distinctive assemblage type for specialized ritual structures. Thus, some structures, such as the earliest ritual structures at San José Mogoté (Flannery 1976:334–335), are devoid of any artifacts or lack any signs of domestic use. The younger layers of the ritual structures at Göbekli Tepe in Turkey provide another example (Schmidt 2001:49). This was also the case in some New Guinea shrines recorded by Hampton and at several tribal community shrines and regional sanctuaries that Hayden investigated in Laos (Figures 6.2–6.6). However, associated with these structures generally were nearby feasting and food-preparation areas or structures (Figure 6.4) or custodian/priestly residences. In some instances, all these functions might be combined in one structure. For instance, in the transegalitarian early Neolithic com-

Figure 6.2. The shrine structure of Ton Wai in northern Laos (in the region of Meung Meung and about 5 km from the Mekong River).

Figure 6.3. Food preparation area associated with the shrine structure of Ton Wai in northern Laos. Note the minimal contents of the shrine.

Figure 6.4. Feasting area (about 50 m away) associated with the shrine structure of Ton Wai in northern Laos.

munity of Jerf el-Ahmar, the assemblage of the centrally located, rather spectacular ritual building is described as "domestic" in character, probably reflecting meal preparation and consumption in the building as well as the performance of basic maintenance tasks involving the construction of paraphernalia for rituals. Large storage facilities were also present (Stordeur et al. 2001). Similarly, most kivas in the Southwest United States typically have assemblages that are difficult to distinguish from domestic pithouse assemblages (Feinman et al. 2000: 461; Muir 1999), and other ritual buildings, such as the "D"-shaped structures, have abundant storage areas against their outside walls (Bob Muir, personal communication, 2003). Even in modern industrial contexts, most churches have one room or one building for religious services (where refuse is minimal) and another for feasting and other activities (where food and other refuse production is significant).

On the other hand, some structures, such as great kivas, have very clear feasting-dominated or specialized faunal assemblages (Muir 1999:78–81). In other cases, although relatively rare for the archaeological remains of ritual structures in most transegalitarian communities, the most convincing assemblages include clearly ritual items such as those recovered at 'Ain Ghazal (Rollefson 1983, 1986). Such ritual items generally involve the use

Figure 6.5. An example of a religious shrine in Ban Sop Fan, Laos, (the building at right) with its caretaker's/priest's residence only a few meters away (the building on the left).

Figure 6.6. The religious shrine in Ban Sop Fan, Laos, has paraphernalia inside, probably because of the proximity of a caretaker in residence.

of exotic materials such as precious skins, feathers, and other decorations. These can often be similar to prestige items used in secular promotional displays. Their status can thus be somewhat ambiguous when considered in isolation; but where other indicators of ritual activity are present, their presence certainly supports ritual interpretations.

Remains from *the manufacture* of prestige/ritual items also can characterize ritual areas. Ethnographically, a similar pattern is reported in kivas among the Hopi-Tewa, where men engaged in "leisure" activities such as stone flaking and weaving (Fewkes 1899:265; Parsons 1940; Stephen 1936). In the Near East, at Hallan Çemi, Rosenberg and Redding (2000) have noted that the "public" architecture is similarly associated with the manufacturing of prestige items such as copper and obsidian articles, whereas European Neolithic ritual enclosures such as Dösjebro (Svensson 2002) can be associated with axe manufacturing. Similarly, at Cahokia, ground-axe manufacturing and biface knapping were associated with feasting and rituals (Pauketat et al. 2003:271, 275). In perhaps an analogous vein, in the remote Maya Highlands, Hayden observed that it is common to find municipal officials in public buildings spending large parts of their slow days engaged in some relatively simple craft activity, such as basket or bag making with local sisal fibers.

Indications of wealth and status should be expected to characterize the artifact assemblages of many ritual structures, for rituals are frequently used as arenas for displaying group power, success, and wealth. Moreover, secret societies typically have a pronounced hierarchy, with the rich and politically powerful elites, in particular, occupying the most important positions, although lower-ranking membership is usually open to members of various socioeconomic standings (Owens and Hayden 1997). Thus, the leaders of these societies control significant labor and resources (drawn from members) in order to conduct their rituals and other activities, and they requisition members or society resources to put on lavish displays to impress other members, guests, and spirits. Because of this, elements of costumes (e.g., bird wing bones, shell or bone beads) and musical instruments sometimes form part of these assemblages. More rarely, cult paraphernalia (e.g., sacred vessels, figurines, drinking tubes) are recovered. In the American Southwest, objects, such as crystals and dog skulls, appear to have been deliberately placed within some kivas prior to the apparent ritual burning of the structures (Walker 1995; Walker and Lucero 2000: 137). Similarly, the ritual deposition of items, such as jade ornaments, appears to have been associated with the destruction rites of ancient Maya temples (Garber 1986, 1989:98; Walker and Lucero 2000:139). However, most items of value or ritual importance are generally removed from structures before abandonment.

Storage and Cult Property

Special or unusual storage areas for food or cult property are relatively common features in many types of ritual structures. Such features containing ritual paraphernalia and foods consumed at feasts should also be expected in secret society structures or in adjacent custodian residences. Archaeologically, special storage areas occur in or close to Near Eastern central community structures (Rosenberg and Redding 2000; Stordeur et al. 2001) and centrally located Hohokam ritual structures or mounds (Bostwick and Downum 1994:341; Seymour 1994:393; Wilcox et al. 1981), as well as "D"-shaped structures in the Southwest (Muir, personal communication, 2003). They also characterize the proposed ritual structures at Keatley Creek (see below).

Hearths and Ritual Structures

Fires are frequently central elements in rituals and feasts or at least occupy a central place in spaces used for rituals or feasts. In order to provide equal viewing, access, heat, and lighting for everyone in attendance, hearths in transegalitarian ritual structures frequently are located in the exact center of floor areas or at one end of structures, whereas in domestic structures, hearths are located to one side and tend to be simple affairs, often merely being an area on the floor. Ritual hearths can be more elaborate than domestic hearths or can display other unique qualities. This pattern has been documented archaeologically in the Levant, where Byrd (1994:656) notes that one of the distinctive features of ritual structures at Beidha was their central and rimmed hearths while domestic hearths were located to one side and were unrimmed. This same pattern occurs at Keatley Creek. Structures identified as kivas in the Southwest also have centrally located hearths (Hibben 1937; Luebben 1953; Mindeleff 1891:118–136; Peckham 1974; Stephen 1936:719–720; Vivian 1965:12).

Floor and Roof Characteristics

Because ritual structures are generally meeting places where socially pleasurable interactions take place and social status is displayed, it is common to find more comfort and status-display features in ritual structure construction. In transegalitarian ritual structures, such features often take the form of formal benches (e.g., Hauptmann 1999:74; Stordeur et al. 2001; Wilcox et al. 1981:182), special flooring materials (fine sand or plaster), floor coverings (mats, boughs, or carpets), specially decorated roof supports, or special roofing. Özdogan (1999:47) lists special attention to floors as one of the characteristics of Neolithic Anatolian cult buildings.

Special Floor Plans

Because the logistics and proxemics of rituals are considerably different from those of domestic activities, ritual structures generally exhibit different floor configurations and use of space from domestic structures. Ritual structures can be arranged so that all attention and viewing is focused either at one end of a building (especially square buildings with altars or platforms) or at the center of the floor area (an arrangement that seems more common in round buildings). In either case, it is important to provide unimpeded viewing of the focal area. This generally entails special efforts to move roof supports as close to the walls as possible or to eliminate central supports entirely, as noted at Jerf el-Ahmar (Stordeur et al. 2001:42–43). The size of the floor space is obviously a function of the number of people participating in the rituals and the nature of the activities involved. It is also not uncommon to find ritual structures dug significantly deeper into the ground in the form of deep semisubterranean buildings or, at the extreme, completely buried sanctuaries (e.g., Neolithic tombs and sanctuaries in Europe) or caves. Jerf el-Ahmar, Göbekli, Hallan Çemi, and the southwestern kivas all provide good examples.

Intentional Destruction of Structure

Precisely why ritual structures should be intentionally burned or destroyed is something of a mystery. However, there is abundant evidence that this was a common practice in archaeological and ethnographic transegalitarian societies. Intentional and complete destruction can therefore be used as one further identifier of the ritual status of structures, although by itself it is clearly an insufficient criterion. Ethnographically, some groups in New Guinea burned certain types of ritual structures after use (Wiessner 2001:133). Intentional burning of specialized buildings also appears to have been practiced frequently in early Neolithic Anatolian settlements (Özdogan 1999:47), in the Neolithic of the Euphrates Valley at Jerf el-Ahmar (Stordeur et al. 2001:37), and in the American Southwest (Wilcox et al. 1981:138; Wilshusen 1986).

Filling of Structures

In a similar vein and often as a part of the act of demolition, ritual structures often have their floors filled with sediment and debris. As part of the termination ceremony for Maya temples, fill and caches were laid on top of the floor over which a new temple was subsequently constructed (Freidel and Schele 1989:237–238; Schele and Freidel 1990:104–108; Walker and Lucero 2000:135). Archaeologically, at Göbekli Tepe in Turkey, Neolithic structures interpreted as being used for rituals were intentionally buried (Schmidt 2001:46). In Europe, megalithic tomb chambers were frequently filled with earth at the end of their use lives. At Navan, the largest known Celtic structure was completely filled with stones shortly after construction and then burned down (Lynn 1993).

Rebuilding

Archaeologists have often noted that ritual structures are frequently rebuilt in exactly the same place as previous ritual structures and often even incorporate some of the same architectural elements (e.g., Garrard et al. 1999; Özdogan 1999:47). This is undoubtedly because of the sacred nature of the specific locations. For example, archaeological evidence indicates that destruction and subsequent rebuilding were characteristic of ceremonies for ancient Maya temples (Haviland 1981, 1988; McAnany 1995:97; Walker and Lucero 2000:139; Willey et al. 1965).

Feasting

In transegalitarian societies, feasting is a pervasive part of most ritual activities wherever groups of people are involved (e.g., Figures 6.2–6.6). Feasting can be defined as a sharing of special foods (or special quantities of food) between two or more people. Hayden (2001:40) provides a list of 29 material correlates of feasting behavior. The most pertinent correlates for the present discussion involve special food items (especially meat and root foods) in unusual quantities, indications of waste, the unusual size of food-preparation facilities, unusual storage facilities, and special refuse areas. Therefore, we might well expect to find indications of feasting in terms of both food remains and food-preparation facilities associated with ritual structures.

Human or Animal Sacrifices

Human sacrifices occurred sporadically in Neolithic ritual structures of the Near East (Stordeur et al. 2001) and in proto-kivas of the American Southwest (Wilshusen 1986:248) but do not occur at Keatley Creek. Animal sacrifices occurred primarily among groups with domesticated animals and thus are rare in hunter-gatherer contexts, although some examples do exist such as the Ainu bear sacrifices.

THE HOUSEPITS IN QUESTION

According to the model developed by Owens and Hayden (1997), it is highly probable that secret societies would have been present at Keatley Creek because it was clearly a large and quite socially complex type of transegalitarian community (Hayden 2000b). The most secret rituals of such societies were often held in relatively secluded and remote areas where concealment could be most easily maintained (Wason 1994). For example, Blackburn (1976) notes that among the Chumash complex hunter-gatherers of California, the elite secret society structure shrines were often located on hilltops or other remote locations. Other examples of remote ritual structures are discussed above. Especially relevant are the Tlingit, Nootkan, Chumash, and New Guinea examples with remote ritual structures as well as the Dolni Vestonice site. We therefore decided to examine some of the most remote structures at the Keatley Creek site for indications of ritual or feasting use. Of particular interest as possible specialized ritual structures were two pairs of structures, one occupied mostly during the Protohistoric Period (200–300 B.P.) and the other during the Plateau Horizon (1200–2400 B.P.). Both pairs of structures exhibit unique cultural remains, in that one structure is almost devoid of artifactual remains, while the other has an unusual abundance of remains and storage capacity. Assemblage characteristics provide further unique elements. In addition, both pairs were situated in isolated locations over 200 m from the main habitation zone of the site. We will describe the indications of feasting and ritual behavior in each of these pairs to the extent possible given the present status of our research. Because of the ongoing nature of this research, all lithic and faunal analyses have not yet been completed; however, we can offer an assessment of work in progress and provide some preliminary results.

The Protohistoric Structures (Structures 104 and 106)

The Protohistoric structures are situated in the northeastern part of the site. Structures 104 and 106 are located on a small terrace (Terrace 2) about 200 m from the site core and 60 m above the rest of the site in a very secluded natural enclosure formed by glacial embankments along the south and west edges of this terrace remnant (Figure 6.7). The Terrace 2 structures appear to have had contemporaneous occupations dating to the Protohistoric Period (ca. 250 B.P.).

STRUCTURE 104. Structure 104 is about 7 m in diameter. A charred piece of coiled basketry found directly on the floor was dated by accelerator mass spectrometry to 250 ± 60 B.P. (CAMS 32253). In terms of its construction, the positioning of posts near the walls of Structure 104 is unusual for such a small structure (Figure 6.8). It is possible that this extra reinforcing was employed either because of the heavy use of the smoke hole as an entrance or in order to open up central spaces for ritual performances or addresses as noted for ritual structures in the Near East (Stordeur et al. 2001:42–43). Additionally, most of the five major postholes of the structure contained the remains of posts burnt in situ. This is an unusual occurrence at Keatley Creek, where most posts were removed prior to the burning of the roof superstructure. As already noted, the intentional burning or destruction of ritual structures tends to be a recurring practice in many parts of the world, and the intentional burning of this structure is consistent with its suggested role as a ritual structure.

The features at Structure 104 include a centrally located hearth that seems to have also been used after Structure 104 collapsed. Ash and rubified floor deposits as well as an unusual abundance of burnt bones indicate that the hearth was used when the structure was occupied. A storage pit was also present in Structure 104. This pit was 130 × 40 cm deep and contained a long spatulate bone object with lightly incised "X." A broken lahal bone gaming piece was also found in the topmost fill of the pit. These two items indicate that the storage pit may have been used as a place to store ritual or feasting paraphernalia.

Concerning the lithic artifacts in Structure 104, the relative abundance of sandstone is of particular interest. There were more sandstone abraders and more pieces of sandstone debitage recovered from Structure 104 than at any other Keatley Creek structure. The occurrence of several sandstone saws, including perhaps the largest and most complete specimen in the Northwest, further indicates that this sandstone was being used to an unusual extent, probably to work nephrite (Figure 6.9). Chipped-stone artifacts were relatively sparse. This may be an indication of either ritual use or the availability of metal tools (Heffner 2000; Spafford 2000). However, the debitage from this structure exhibits an unusually high proportion of billet flakes when compared with assemblages

Figure 6.7. A view of Terrace 2, looking west. This picture encompasses the entire terrace remnant, with Structure 104 visible in the center closest to the foreground and Structure 106 behind it slightly to the left, with Structure 105 directly behind it (less distinctly visible). Note also the raised terrace rim behind Structures 105 and 106 and to the right (it appears as a mound) on which a number of smaller depressions (cache pits) are discernable. Views of the trees behind the terrace indicate the steep slopes extending down toward Terrace 1.

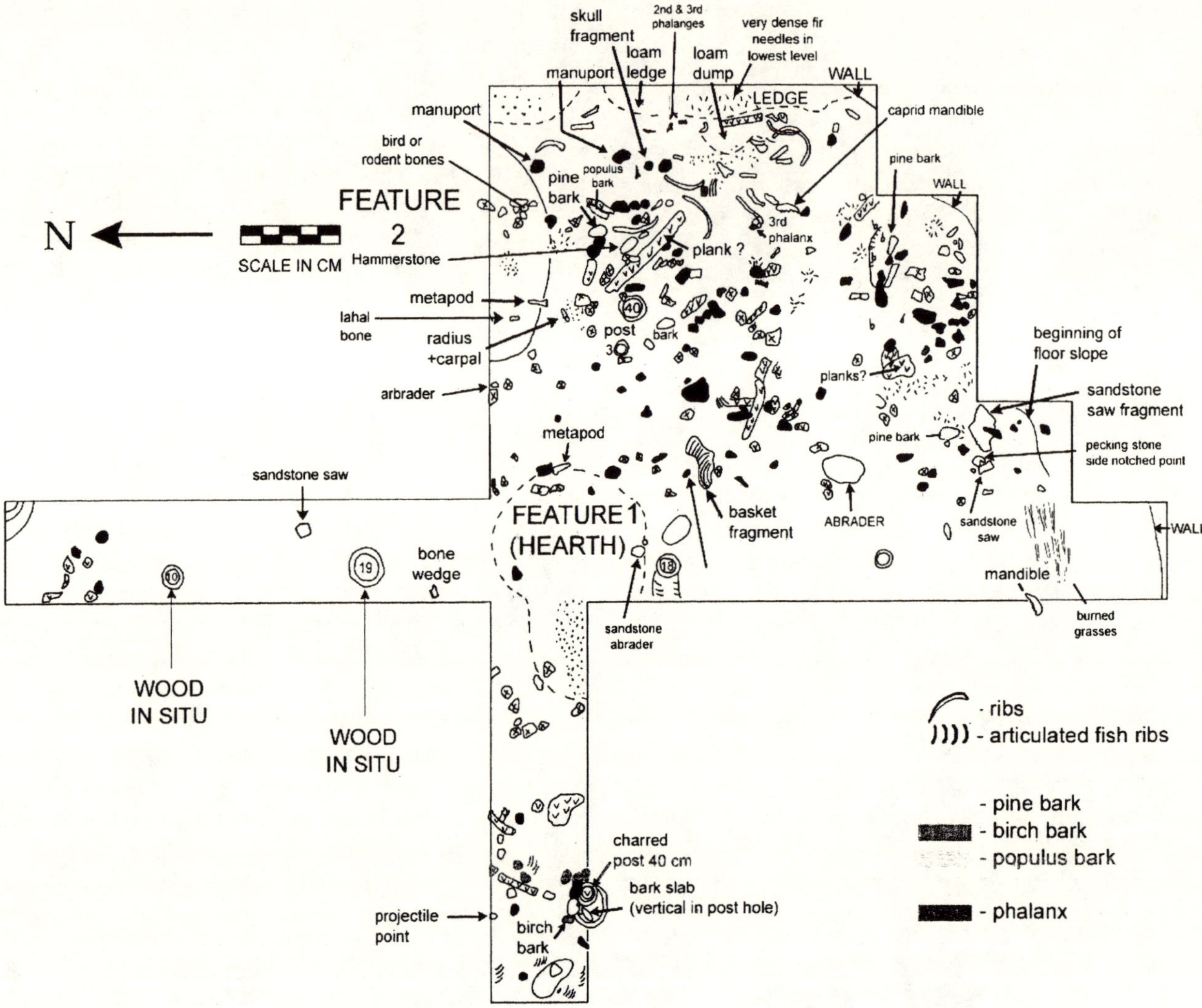

Figure 6.8. The floor plan of Structure 104. Note the dense bone remains that cover much of the floor and may be related to feasting activities. The peripheral support posts are unusual for a structure of this size and may reflect unusual rooftop activities or access or attempts to replace more centralized posts in order to provide more open spaces in the center of the floor.

from clearly residential structures (Table 6.1). Among the modified tools recovered from Structure 104 there appears to be a slightly higher proportion of bipolar cores, more piercers, and more bifaces than in other well-documented residential structures such as Structure 3, Structure 7, and Structure 90.

In Structure 104, there is a much higher density of bone, particularly on the floor, than in most of the other clearly residential housepits at Keatley Creek. Many of these bone pieces are significantly larger than those found at other housepits (Kusmer 2000: appendix 1). The bone assemblage includes articulated leg segments of deer and a number of articulated salmon vertebrae, fins, heads, and ribs. The frequent occurrence of articulated fish elements, especially fins, ribs, tails, and heads, does not seem to occur in most domestic structures, but they frequently occur in the few faunal-rich structures suspected of having served ritual feasting functions. This is therefore a potentially important indicator of ritual use. The fact that the delicate bones of salmon were articulated over large areas of the floor of Structure 104 indicates that they were not heavily disturbed after deposition, implying the intermittent use of the structure rather than a normal residential use.

Most notable among the other cultural remains from Structure 104 is a coiled basketry fragment. This appears to represent the only reported archaeological occurrence of coiled basketry from the Canadian Plateau or Northwest Coast. Dale Croes (1977) has observed that coiled baskets were highly valued and were sometimes cut into pieces, like other valuables, and given away at feasts. There were also abundant charred fir needles and unique thick deposits of grasses near the walls of this structure, as well as indications of a loam covering of the floor.

TABLE 6.1. Comparison of the Proportion of Billet Flakes in Debitage Assemblages of the Proposed Ritual Structures and the Assemblages of Regular Domestic Structures.

Debitage	% Billet Flakes
Proposed Ritual Structures	
Structure 104	
Floor (n = 32)	13
Nonfloor (n = 128)	30
Structure 105	
All strata (n = 2,970)	13
Structure 106	
Floor (n = 20)	45
Nonfloor (n = 335)	51
Structure 107	
Floor (n = 21)	52
Roof (n = 112)	62
Pit (n = 60)	50
Structure 109	
Floor (n = 12)	25
Nonfloor (n = 2,123)	38
Regular Domestic Structures	
Structure 3	
Floor (n = 2,300)	5
Housepit 7	
Floor (n = 5,222)	10
Housepit 12	
Floor (n = 589)	5
Roof (n = 551)	4

Structure 106. The other member of the pair of Protohistoric structures is Structure 106 and is located only 6 m to the south of Structure 104. It is 11 × 9 m in size, and a piece of pine bark from the roof/floor contact has been dated to 220 ± 70 B.P. (Beta 106611). Structure 106 is unique, in that a large boulder forms part of the southern inside wall, and smaller boulders line the wall in the southeast and northeast. It also has an unusual rectangular plan shape and exhibits the most pervasive and deep fire reddening of sediments inside the structure of all the structures tested at Keatley Creek. An unusual funnel-shaped central fire pit was uncovered during the 2003 excavation season.

As in Structure 104, Structure 106 contains the remains of a burned post, indicating that the structure was intentionally burned. Also, many of the charred roof elements found in Structure 106 seem to have been split poles or planks. This split-pole or plank roofing technique was not noted in earlier structures at the site and may represent a special labor-intensive roofing technique used for special function or high-class structures. There is also

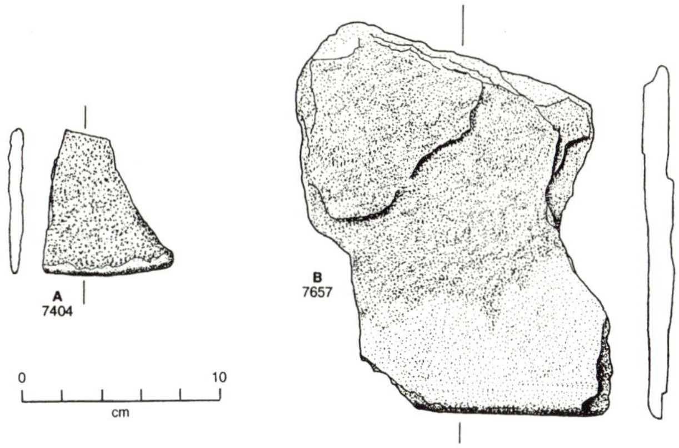

Figure 6.9. Two sandstone saws from Structure 104 probably used for working nephrite, the larger being a remarkably complete specimen.

clear evidence of a special loam flooring and copious use of fir boughs.

Little cultural material of any kind was found in Structure 106 aside from a few faunal remains, flakes, and an antler wedge that had been entirely buried vertically in the floor near a posthole. However, the recent and ongoing excavations undertaken by Jesse Morin and Suzanne Villeneuve have resulted in the recovery of a number of unusual items, including a goose bone drinking tube (ethnographically a ritual item), a cervid tooth bead, and what appears to be a chipped-stone tomahawk. As can be seen in Table 6.1, debitage was heavily dominated by pressure and bifacial thinning flakes (in contrast to domestic assemblages). This antler wedge and some mammal bones in another possible ritual structure (Structure 105) were the only vertically oriented bones found in floor deposits anywhere in the entire site. However, similar occurrences from other complex hunter-gatherers are documented from elsewhere in the world. Particularly notable are the vertical bones found in the floors of the Salle du Fond in the Grotte d'Enlène in southern France and in El Juyu in northern Spain. In both of these cases, vertically buried bones were clearly associated with ritual contexts and behaviors (Bégouën et al. 1993; Freeman and Edhegaray 1981). Structure 106 also contained an unusual pit directly under the large boulder in its south wall. The bottom of this pit contained a very soft organic mold unlike the fill of other pits at the site, raising the possibility that it may have been used for ritual purposes. If the structure was burned intentionally, then this may also reflect ritual use as indicated in our discussion of Structure 104.

The Plateau Horizon Structures (Structures 9 and 107)

The Plateau Horizon structures (Structures 9 and 107) are located about 200 m south of the site core on a terrace south of Keatley Creek (i.e., on the opposite bank from the main part of the site). The structures are only 15 m apart and were occupied during the Plateau Period (1200–2400 B.P.) judging from the style of projectile points associated with both structures and the general appearance of the faunal remains. They are similar to the Protohistoric pair of structures (104 and 106) on Terrace 2, in that one of the pair is full of fauna (especially articulated fish fins and other fin elements), whereas the other structure is almost devoid of artifacts.

STRUCTURE 9. Structure 9, like the other structures discussed here, is a relatively small structure with a diameter of 7.8 m. The general characteristics of the floor assemblage are remarkably similar to those of its Protohistoric counterpart on Terrace 2 (Structure 104). Although the structure is small, the artifacts found in the structure are unusual, indicative of high social or ritual standing, and include the largest collection of dentalium shells found at the site, the only loon bones found at the site, a number of beaver incisors, shell beads, a mussel shell adze, pipe fragments, two pieces of a nephrite adze, abundant fish bones (especially articulated fin and head elements on the floor), an antler digging stick handle, the largest number of worked elk and deer antler pieces of any structure, and a variety of lithic tools (Hayden 2000a; Kusmer 2000). The loon bones are of particular interest with regard to the use of the structure for ritual purposes, as they were ethnographically only worn by shamans (Teit 1900:381, 1909:607). The features include two central, superimposed hearths (one of which was rock lined) and an unusually large storage pit (for a house this size) that contained an abundance of fish bones (Alexander in press). The only other structure in the site with a rock-lined hearth is Structure 107, immediately adjacent to Structure 9. There is good evidence that a special loam was used to cover the floor. In addition, the reconstructed floor-use plan for Structure 9 is remarkably similar to those of the early Neolithic ritual structures at Jerf el-Ahmar in Syria, where a platform bench occupies half the structure with a major storage facility opposite the bench area (Alexander in press; Middleton 2000; Stordeur et al. 2001) (Figure 6.10). Unfortunately, the debitage from the structure has not been analyzed as yet.

STRUCTURE 107. Structure 107 has a diameter of 8 m and, like its Protohistoric counterpart (Structure 106), is characterized by a conspicuously small number of cultural remains for a residential structure. It also contained a storage pit that was uncharacteristically large for a house of this size. The bottom of the pit was filled with cobbles before abandonment, as was the central floor area around the hearth. An unusual circle (about 90 cm in diameter) of large cobbles was found almost in the exact center of the structure (Figure 6.11). The cobbles themselves were not fire stained, and there was no built-up ash inside the ring of rocks, suggesting that the rocks were part of a rarely used hearth in which only fires of minimal duration were lit or perhaps were not part of a hearth feature at all. However, dense charcoal-stained soil did underlie the ring of rocks, indicating the use of a hearth in that location. As in Structure 106, the lithic debitage in the limited tested area (ca. 3 m^2 was heavily dominated by pressure and bifacial thinning flakes (Table 6.1), while tools included bifaces and, in particular, an unusual form of thin, fan-tailed biface. These are all unusual characteristics for domestic assemblages. Aside from a few fish spines and vertebrae, almost no faunal remains were found on the floor of the structure. Investigations are continuing at this structure under the direction of Suzanne Villeneuve.

Other Possible Ritual Structures

We have tested two other structures at Keatley Creek that we believe may have also served ritual functions. There are also a few untested structures on the southern terrace near Structure 9 that should be investigated from this perspective. Both of the two tested structures have Protohistoric and Plateau Horizon occupations, and both are located on the eastern terraces near the Protohistoric pair previously discussed (Structures 104 and 106). They may have functioned separately or as a pair during their Plateau occupations. During the Protohistoric occupation, they may have constituted a larger ritual complex in conjunction with Structures 104 and 106 (similar to the ritual complexes recorded by Hampton in New Guinea or at the Neolithic ritual site of Göbekli Tepe); or, over time, they may have replaced one or both of the pair of structures (104 and 106) already discussed. We provide a brief description of these additional structures.

STRUCTURE 105. Structure 105 is the only other structure on Terrace 2 and clusters together with Structure 104 and 106. Structure 105 is slightly larger, being 9 × 10 m in diameter. There was an earlier (Plateau Horizon) occupation, the only remnant of which is a large storage pit containing 72 bone buttons (the largest and oldest prehistoric collection of such items found in the Northwest). Wood charcoal from this pit yielded a conventional radiocarbon date of 2170 ± 60 B.P. (SFU 642). The concentration, orientation, and distribution of these bone buttons seem to indicate that they were attached to some sort of garment, costume, or blanket—the earliest indications we have of a button blanket or garment (Figure 6.12).

The later, Protohistoric occupation of the structure is marked by the presence of a hearth feature. Unburned wood lying on the floor was dated by conventional means

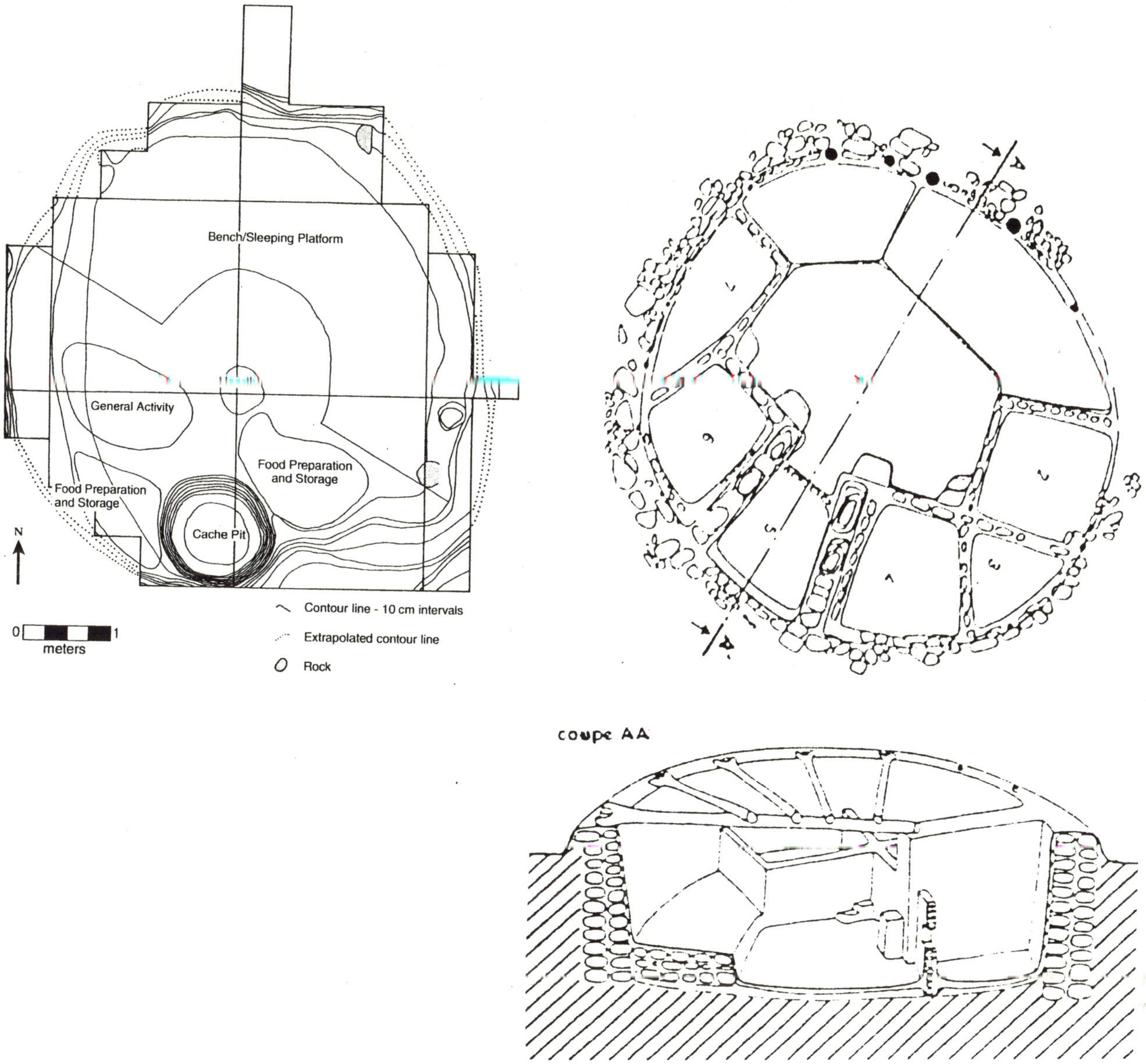

Figure 6.10. The activity areas of the floor of Structure 9, as reconstructed by Diane Alexander (in press), bear a remarkable resemblance to the use of space revealed in the early Neolithic ritual structure at Jerf el-Ahmar (Stordeur et al. 2001). In both cases, a wide bench or platform occupies one side of the structure and faces huge storage facilities or food-preparation areas on the opposite side of the structure.

to 270 ± 55 B.P. (SFU 641). As in Structure 104, numerous salmon bones (especially articulated heads, fins, ribs, and backbones) were found near the hearth as well as in the reddened sediments comprising the hearth. People who were present at illegal excavations at this structure in the 1960s remarked on the great quantities of bones that were found in the structure. High densities of head bones and fins are extremely unusual in other housepit floor deposits at the site, and these parts may have been used for special soups or snacks. In addition, as in Structure 106, which 105 abuts, several long deer bone splinters were thrust vertically completely into the upper Protohistoric floor of Structure 105.

STRUCTURE 109. Structure 109 is 9 m in diameter and is the only semisubterranean structure on Terrace 1. It is located just below Terrace 2 (Figure 6.1). The upper floor, dated to 220 ± 50 B.P. (Beta 125907) from charred roof beams on the floor, is contemporaneous with the Terrace 2 structures discussed above, whereas the lower floor represents an earlier structure, the fill of which seems to be associated with a point that falls within the range of known Shuswap Horizon (2,400–3,500 B.P.) or earlier Plateau Horizon styles. No dates have been obtained from the lower floor. There is almost no charcoal. The structure contains a large storage pit dug down about 80 cm from the upper floor. The size and shape of the pit are

Figure 6.11. Photograph of the floor exposed in the test trench excavated in Structure 107. The large storage pit (Feature 2) is visible at the bottom against the structure's wall, and the ring of rocks surrounding dense charcoal deposits (Feature 3) is evident at the center of the structure. The almost complete lack of bone or stone remains on this floor contrasts markedly to the debris on the floor of Structure 9 and indicates a probable exclusive use for ritual purposes.

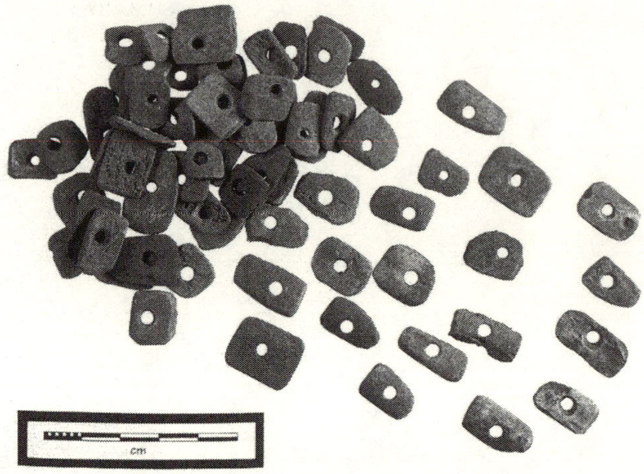

Figure 6.12. Some of the 72 bone buttons recovered from the bottom of a large storage pit inside Structure 105. These buttons appear to have been sewn onto a garment, in the fashion of later button blankets used in rituals, and represent the oldest evidence for such forms in the Northwest. Photo by Phil Hobler.

consistent with those found in other structures that may have been used for ritual purposes mentioned above (Structures 9, 105, and 107).

One of the most peculiar features of Structure 109 is the unusual depth of its early floor (ca. 180 cm below the original ground surface) as well as the considerable effort that a group of individuals expended in order to subsequently fill in this structure with 80 cm of dirt apparently shortly after the first occupation was terminated—perhaps as part of a termination ritual. The lithic assemblage of the construction fill consists almost entirely of exotic cherts and chalcedonies. This contrasts sharply with the lithic assemblages of every other structure at the site, all of which are made up of 80–95 percent local vitreous trachydacites. None of the chipped stone in the construction fill of Structure 109 appears to have been used or modified. Instead, it occurs very abundantly in local pockets, sometimes as piles of flakes touching each other. Some of this chipped stone seems to have been thrown into the construction fill as coherent dumps of flakes, perhaps by an individual flintknapping adjacent to the structure producing bifaces (given the seemingly large scale of production, as gifts for the workers?) during the filling in of the structure. On the other hand, these exotic flakes may have been ritual offerings similar to the copious flint flakes that occur in northern European Neolithic ritual features. It is possible that the abundance of these exotic lithics may reflect a situation in which the structure was filled in just prior to its Protohistoric occupation. Exotic raw materials may have been more accessible in Protohistoric times than in previous times because of the use of the horse. Horse remains were found in a cache pit at the southern end of the site in association with two Kamloops side-notched points. These indicate that horses were present during the Protohistoric Period at Keatley Creek. However, the stratigraphy within Structure 109 indicates that the fill episode occurred much earlier—immediately after the initial occupation ended.

In the lower floor of Structure 109, there were very few lithics found, and these were almost all vitreous trachydacites. According to field observations and our preliminary analysis, this assemblage, too, was dominated by a prevalence of pressure and billet flakes and bipolar flakes/cores (Table 6.1). This appears to represent an unusual composition compared with almost every other domestic floor assemblage at the site. A sandstone abrader or saw was also found on the lower floor as well as an unusually high number of large cobbles and boulders. One uncommonly smooth, round cobble in the southeast corner of square B is similar to some special cobbles venerated by New Guinea highlanders in their ritual sanctuaries (Hampton 1999).

TABLE 6.2. SUMMARY OF TYPES OF EVIDENCE FOR RITUAL USE.

Type of Evidence	Structure 9	104	(Plateau Period) 105	(Protohistoric Period) 105	106	107	(Early) 109	(Protohistoric Period) 109
Remote/Special Location	x	x	x	x	x	x	x	x
Unusual Storage Facilities	x	1/2	x	?	?	x	?	x
Assemblage Characteristics								
Artifacts Are Rare			?		x	x	x	
Pressure/Billet Debitage Dominates	x	x	?	x				?
Feasting Remains								
Deer		x						
Fish Heads/Fins	x	?		x				
Dog								x
Ritual/Prestige Items	x	x	x	x	x		x	
Associated with Roasting Pits	x	x	x	x	x		x	
Prepared Silt Floor	x	x	?	?	x	x	x	?
Destruction/Burning		x			x			
Central Hearths	x	?				x		
Extensive Hearths					x			
Open Central Spaces	?	?	?	?	?	?	?	?
Rebuilding	x		?	x				x
Deep Floor							x	

The most notable of all of the faunal remains from Structure 109 are a sacrum and a few articulating lumbar vertebrae from a dog associated with salmon bones covered with a thick layer of fir needles. The dog sacrum was wrapped in birch bark and found under a rock in the upper (Protohistoric) floor of the structure. These remains appear to represent a special meal and the best evidence for the consumption of canids at Keatley Creek.

DISCUSSION

Using the criteria that we initially identified as indicative of ritual structures, we can identify a number of correspondences with the structures suspected of being used for ritual purposes at Keatley Creek. These are summarized below and in Table 6.2.

Location

As previously outlined, ritual structures have been ethnographically and archaeologically documented in a variety of locales in relation to village cores. In some cases, these structures occupy central locations within villages, whereas in others, they are found in isolated areas outside of villages. At Keatley Creek, large corporate residential structures were undoubtedly used for public rituals. In addition, two clusters of proposed ritual structures are situated in remote locations about 200 m from the site core. The location of several of these structures outside of the central village areas conforms to the heterarchical, as opposed to centralized, sociopolitical organization proposed for Keatley Creek. Additionally, the isolated locations of the structures correspond to the expected occurrence of secret societies in complex transegalitarian hunter-gatherer societies (based on cross-cultural data) and a desire for secret societies to conduct ritual proceedings in secrecy. We would like to emphasize that the setting of Terrace 2 is unusually suited for such purposes. It is a small, secluded, tightly bounded bit of glacial landform high above the settlement core. That it was considered a ritual location prehistorically is strongly indicated by the remains of a bone button garment/costume (in Structure 105) and by an offering deposit of a highly unusual crescentic biface in a meat-roasting pit associated with Structure 106 (Figure 6.13).

Assemblage Characteristics

At Keatley Creek, there are similar patterns indicative of ritual use in the assemblage characteristics of both the Protohistoric Period and the Plateau Period pairs of structures. Structures 9 and 104 contain evidence of having been used by people of status and wealth, making them

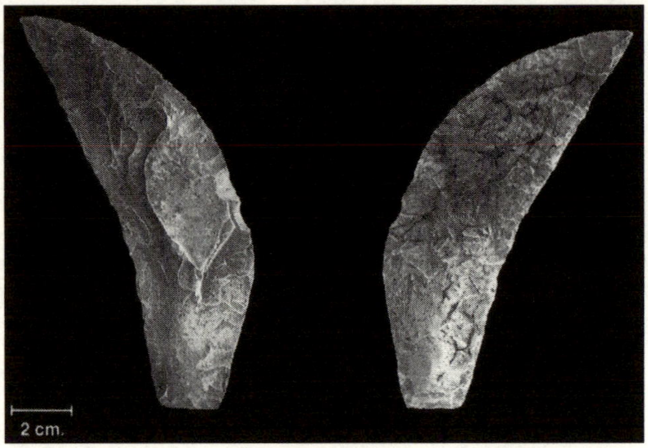

Figure 6.13. The exceptional and unique crescent biface recovered in a meat-roasting pit under the rim of Structure 106, indicating some form of ritual item and offering.

unique considering their small size. Structure 9, in particular, contained an abundance of fish bones and dentalium shells as well as other unique faunal remains and a notably large storage pit. The loon bones are especially interesting because they are ethnographically recorded as having been worn by shamans (Teit 1900:381, 1909:607). In addition, although only a small test trench was excavated from Structure 105, the large number of bone buttons as well as the lithics and fish bones found certainly indicate a Keatley Creek structure used by wealthy individuals. Both the bone buttons and the bones embedded vertically in the floor of this structure imply important ritual functions. Abundant, *articulated* fish segments (especially fin, head, rib, gill, and tail elements—all of which occur in low frequencies on most domestic house floors) also indicate episodic rather than continual use of these structures; they most plausibly represent discarded bits from fish fin and fish head soups, as are found when contemporary tribesmen in Southeast Asia throw the chopped-up pig or chicken bones from the broths on their dirt floors today (Hayden, field observations).

What makes Structure 104 especially interesting is the evidence of specialized nephrite working, as represented by an unusual number of sandstone saws and abraders. This could either reflect the specialized activities of the residents (or slaves), or it could represent activities of secret society members who wanted to "while away" downtime during their meetings or in waiting for feasts to begin, as seems to be the case at other ritual sites like Cahokia, Dösjbro, and Hallan Çemi. The evidence of gaming (a lahal bone) and the use of coiled basketry in Structure 104 is also unique at Keatley Creek.

In contrast to the dense faunal assemblages that characterize one structure in each pair (Structures 9 and 104), the other adjacent structures of each pair (Structures 107 and 106) contain very few faunal remains and are thus more enigmatic. These structures with depauperate assemblages display signs of being the locations of ritual or other specialized activities. The general lack of cultural material in Structures 106 and 107, as well as the unusual nature of the modified artifacts and debitage, seems to imply infrequent use of the structures and a function reserved for periodic ritual occasions. In particular, the occurrence of a bone drinking tube, tooth bead, vertically embedded antler wedge, and tomahawk in Structure 106 indicates a special status. A similar paucity of artifacts was notable at the community shrines and regional sanctuaries in Laos observed by Hayden. Although it may be true that many housepits on the Northern Plateau are often characterized by sparse artifact assemblages, the essentially contemporaneous adjacent structures in each pair (104 and 9) display dramatically different, very dense faunal assemblages. Moreover, the limited lithic assemblages of all these structures, but of 106 and 107 in particular, are heavily dominated by pressure flakes and biface thinning flakes (Table 6.1), a feature of ritual deposits also noted by Pauketat et al. (2003:271, 275). It is especially interesting that this unique pattern seems to persist from the Plateau Period (Structure 107) to the Protohistoric Period (Structure 106). In fact, these two structures appear to be very similar in many respects. All the preceding observations are difficult to account for in terms of ordinary domestic structures.

Other suspected ritual structures, too, have unusual assemblage characteristics. Structure 105 has an unusual bone button assemblage. In Structure 109, the unusually high frequency of cherts and chalcedonies—in comparison to the occurrence of vitreous trachydacites (which dominate in other structures at the site) in the fill and perhaps the upper, Protohistoric floor of the structure—is unusual, as is the presence of the dog remains associated with salmon bones, implying the ritual consumption of dogs at Structure 109. The predominance of exotic debitage has been notable in other ritual contexts, such as at Cahokia (Pauketat et al. 2003:271, 275).

Storage and Cult Property

Structures 9, 104, 105 (the Plateau Horizon occupation), 107, and 109 (the Protohistoric occupation) all contain storage pits. The storage pits in Structures 9, 104, and 105 (Plateau Period occupation) have particularly good indications of use as storage places for food and possible secret society possessions. The long bone object incised with an "x" in the storage pit of Structure 104 and the lahal gaming piece found in its fill imply the storage of ritual paraphernalia. Interestingly, bone "gaming pieces" were also reported from ritual structure contexts in the Southwest (Wilshusen 1986:248). The presence of 72 bone buttons in the Plateau Horizon storage pit of Structure 105 is also indicative of a storage function for cult paraphernalia. In Structure 9, the storage pit was clearly used to store large amounts of salmon as well as antler artifacts. In addition to these internal storage pits, there are a number of large exterior food cache pits on Terrace 2, probably associated with Structures 104, 105, and 106, and a similar cluster of large storage pits occurs on Terrace 1, not far from Structure 109. The sharpness of their contours and the fresh appearance of the artifact contents indicate probable Protohistoric origins. It seems interesting that the earlier structures had interior storage pits, whereas the later ritual structures seem to be associated with external storage facilities. A similar shift clearly took place in Near Eastern early Neolithic ritual structures, such as those documented at Jerf el-Ahmar. These external storage pits associated with probable ritual structures at Keatley Creek constitute the most distinctive clusters of storage pits at the site, with the exception of a very remote Protohistoric cluster on the northern edge of the terraces south of the creek bed.

Hearths and Ritual Structures

The hearths in Structures 9, 104, 106, and 107 all have relatively peculiar characteristics that seem to indicate ritual use. A quite unusual ash-filled and deeply rubified pit hearth occurs in the center of Structure 106. Its pit-shaped center and the sloping (funnel-shaped) surrounding floor make it unique at the site. After the collapse of the roof, there are indications of very intense and large fires on the surface associated with broadcast deposits of fire-cracked rock and bone, creating a pattern of fire use at that structure that is also unique among all the structures at the site, in terms of both pervasiveness and location. In contrast, there is little evidence that, when it was standing, the structure was used either very frequently or for a very prolonged period of time. As in the Near East, the presence of centrally located hearths in Structures 9, 104, 106, and 107 and the low level of use of the hearth in Structure 107 also fit a scenario of ritual use. None of the other small, excavated residential housepits at Keatley Creek had a central hearth; rather, the hearths were offset to the side and were usually minimally developed or difficult to identify (e.g., Structures 12 and 90, and tests of Structures 4, 5, 47, 58, and 101 failed to disclose any evidence of hearths and certainly no central ones). Moreover, the hearth in Structure 107 seems to have been filled in shortly after the ring of stones around it had been put in place. This seems like a curious behavior and may have been part of a ritual action.

Floor and Roof Characteristics

The covering of the floors of Structures 9, 104, 106, 107, and 109 with a fine tan loess may be associated with the ritual use of these structures. Al Mackie (personal communication, 1988) has recorded that loessial "clay" was spread over structures that were used for dancing in the B.C. interior. The thick concentrations of fir needles associated with many parts of the floor in Structures 104 and 106 as well as thick grass coverings along the south wall of Structure 104 are unique. These features seem more consistent with special ritual coverings of floors with fir boughs and the padding of seating areas for greater comfort to an extent not generally taken in normal domestic structures, especially the small structures that were generally used by poorer households at the site.

The possible smoke hole entrance through the roof of Structure 104 may also indicate its use as a ritual structure. As previously noted, there were posts positioned near the wall of Structure 104. This extra reinforcing may reflect the use of a smoke hole entrance through the roof, which would be unusual for such a small structure (MacDonald 2000). A smoke hole entrance in Structure 104 could reflect the preferred mode of entry into ritual structures, just as was the case in Northeast Asia (Condrashoff 1980). Smoke hole entrances also are prevalent in kivas of the Southwest (Ellis 1945–1953, cited in Ellis 1979; Mindeleff 1891:117, 121, 123, 135; Parsons 1962:6; Stephen 1936:151; Titiev 1944:103–104) and in lodges used for shaman initiation and male gatherings among the Wintu of Northern California (Du Bois 1935). The unusually deep floor of Structure 109 (and to a lesser extent Structure 107, with its unusually thick roof) may also reflect ritual construction.

Special Floor Plans

Because of incomplete but ongoing excavations, the indications of special floor plans are not clear in many of the proposed ritual structures at Keatley Creek. However, as noted previously, roof support posts were positioned near the wall of Structure 104, which is an unusual occurrence for a domestic structure of its size and could reflect a desire to open up the central space of the structure for ritual performances. A similar construction pattern has been noted in ritual structures at Jerf el-Ahmar (Stordeur et al. 2001:42–43). There is also a remarkable similarity between the floor plan of Structure 9 and the clearly ritual early Neolithic structures of Jerf el-Ahmar (Figure 6.10).

Intentional Destruction and Filling of Structures

The evidence for the intentional burning of Structures 104 and 106 and the intentional burial of Structure 109 is certainly consistent with the pattern of intentional burning or burial of ritual structures. As previously discussed, the intentional destruction of ritual structures is not completely understood, but it has been documented ethnographically among groups in New Guinea and archaeologically in the Neolithic Near East and Europe, in Mesoamerica, and in the American Southwest. Filling ritual structures with rocks and other debris occurs elsewhere in the world (see above) and may be represented in the cobble deposit of the storage pit and the rock deposit covering the central floor of Structures 107 and, perhaps, 109.

Feasting

Much of the evidence for feasting at the proposed ritual structures comes in the form of roasting pit features. At Keatley Creek, all of the meat- and root-roasting pits that we have located are close to the proposed ritual structures with one or two exceptions (associated with Structure 7, where large feasts also undoubtedly took place). There was an unusual meat-roasting pit that had been dug under the eastern rim of Structure 106 prior to construction. It is possibly contemporaneous with the Plateau Horizon (1200–2400 B.P.) occupation of Structure 105. A significant number of artiodactyl bones (ribs, radius/ulna, astragalus, phalanges, metadopials, thin bone) and a variety of lithic tools were found at the base of this feature. In particular, deer limb bones have been interpreted as evidence for high-status or feasting contexts (Bogan 1983; Cleland 1965; Jackson and Scott 1995; Junker et al. 1994:348; Welch and Scarry 1995:405). An entirely unique, finely made crescent-shaped biface was also recovered at the very bottom and center of this roasting pit (Figure 6.13). The crescent-shaped biface was found lying almost perfectly horizontally, as if it had been purposely placed there as an offering. In addition to the roasting pit underneath the rim of Structure 106, a large meat-roasting pit from the Plateau Horizon was excavated just to the west of Structure 105. There are two other meat-roasting pits on Terrace 2, probably associated with Structures 105 and 106, indicating feasting activity in addition to unusually large quantities of fire-cracked rock and bone remains in the postcollapse deposits of Structure 106.

Root-roasting pits associated with the proposed ritual structures include an 8-m-diameter pit dating to the Plateau Horizon and two smaller Protohistoric root-roasting pits situated in the Keatley Creek streambed just upstream from the Terrace 2 structures. The only structures anywhere near these features are those situated on Terrace 2 (Structures 104, 105, and 106). Given the paucity of root resources in the vicinity and the small number of inhabitants that could have used, or even lived in, the Terrace 2 structures, these root-roasting pits seem to indicate feasting activities, particularly the 8-m-diameter roasting pit. Large root-roasting pits also occur on the South Terrace in the vicinity of Structures 9 and 107 (see Hayden and Cousins, this volume).

Among the proposed ritual structures, faunal evidence of feasting activities is particularly apparent in Structures 9, 104, and 109. The canid and salmon bones found in the upper floor of Structure 109 are very probably the remains of a feast. In Simon Fraser's journals, dogs seemed to have been used as delicacies and were consumed primarily at feasts. This is consistent with the special role of dog consumption in other traditional societies in the world (Schwartz 1998). In Structures 9, 104, and 105, high densities of bone, the low level of bone reduction, and the articulated sections of artiodactyl legs and salmon are indicative of feasting because there is generally more waste in feasting contexts (Wilson and Rathje 2001). The same factors may explain the high numbers of articulated salmon elements in these structures. On the other hand, the intensely burned and fragmented bone remains associated with the central hearth of Structure 104 may well be viewed as ritual sacrifices of food remains (either during or after the main occupation of the structure), not unlike some of the ritual sacrifices of the Chumash, which were intentionally stirred to maximize the destruction of items placed into fire pits. Maxwell (2000), for example, interprets a highly burned deposit of bone in the Gabriel/Tongva area as a deposit of ritually burned remains. Some groups in New Guinea also cremate bone remains from their ritual feasts (Wiessner 2001:133).

SETS OF RITUAL STRUCTURES

If the two pairs of structures being considered above did play a specialized role in community ritual activities, there are three roles that we view as most likely for one or the other structure in the pair: (1) as strictly ritual locations where no other activities took place, (2) as ritual *and* feasting structures used episodically, or (3) as residences for ritual specialists who might be guardians of nearby ritual facilities and hosts for ritual feasts. Considering this last possibility, the more intensively used structures of the Protohistoric Period (Structure 104) and the Plateau Horizon (Structure 9) could have been places of residence for custodians or perhaps some of the leading cult members of secret societies, such as shamans or wealthy secret society leaders, as documented in Vanuatu (Speiser 1996:92–95). Alternatively, these structures may have been used for episodic ritual feasting events. The abundance of articulated small salmon bones on the floors of these structures would seem to favor this latter scenario. It seems more certain that the less intensively used structures of each pair (Structures 106 and 107) were most likely special meeting places for rituals held by secret societies. This was probably true of the early occupation in Structure 109 as well.

At Keatley Creek, combinations of ritual structures associated with custodian residences (as described for the

Tlingit in Oberg 1973:19) can be most strongly argued for the Plateau Horizon pair of structures (Structures 9 and 107), where assemblage and feature characteristics are the most extreme and the most distinctively different from those of domestic structures. During winters, Structure 107 may have been used for the most secretive rituals reserved for the highest-ranking elite secret society members. Once the secretive ritual and political business of these members had been concluded in their special ritual structure (Structure 107), they may have adjourned to the nearby feasting structure or residence of the ritual custodian or shaman (Structure 9), where secret society members' families may have prepared a feast. The very large storage facilities inside Structures 9 and 107 make sense in terms of this scenario, for storage places for secret society food resources and ritual paraphernalia would be required. The differences in food remains between the two structures seem to reflect a situation in which small tidbits of meat or fish may have been consumed in the ritual structure as snacks but not as formal meals. The small size of the two structures would be consistent with their use by a small, very select number of high-ranking secret society members, whereas the large storage facilities and relatively rich prestige items in Structure 9 seem uncharacteristic for small structures used as normal residences.

Although the evidence may not yet be as clear-cut for the pair of Protohistoric structures on Terrace 2, the remains from Structures 104 and 106 appear to represent activities similar to those of the Plateau Horizon ritual structures on the Southern Terrace. It is worth iterating that the small, secluded nature of Terrace 2 and its unusual topography provide grounds for thinking of this location in ritual terms. Excavated features on the terrace dating from the Plateau Horizon seem to confirm its use as a location for rituals, ritual feasts, and ritual structures. The button blanket in the large pit from the Plateau occupation of Structure 105, the large meat-roasting pit associated with Structure 105, the smaller meat-roasting pit under the rim of Structure 106 containing a ritual-like biface, and the exceptionally large root-roasting pit in the vicinity of Terrace 2 all indicate ritual and feasting use of this location from at least 1500 B.P. The same locational characteristics, as well as perhaps local traditions, could have very likely made Terrace 2 a focus of ritual activities in Protohistoric times as well. There is a dramatic difference in artifact content between Structures 104 and 106, as is the case with the earlier Plateau Period pair of structures on the South Terrace (Structures 9 and 107). Specifically, Structure 104 has an unusually large amount of animal bones, fish remains (especially head parts and fins, as is the case in Structure 9), and other artifacts. In all cases, there is an unusual emphasis on billet and pressure flaking, which, together with the presence of animal bones, seems to indicate a male-dominated use of these structures. In addition, hearth locations in all these structures are central, and the hearths exhibit unusual characteristics. We suggest that, as with ritual bone insertions into floors in Europe, the antler that was stuck vertically into the floor of Structure 106 (and 105) indicates ritual behavior.

While there are many residential structures in the core areas of the Keatley Creek site contemporaneous with occupations in the proposed Plateau Horizon ritual structures (Structures 9, 105 [early occupation], 107, and 109 [early occupation]), we have so far not found any good candidates for Protohistoric residential structures at the site (unless, of course, the Protohistoric occupations of Structures 104, 105, and 109 were actually residential in function). If our ritual and feasting interpretations are accurate, then where did the people using these Protohistoric ritual structures live? There are two possibilities. First, Terrace 2 could have had a regional reputation as a particularly sacred area, and people from the surrounding communities (especially Pavilion and Fountain) could have used the location for secret society or other kinds of ritual meetings. Such isolated regional ritual centers have been documented ethnographically in New Guinea (Hampton 1999) and Southeast Asia (Figures 6.2–6.4) and archaeologically at early Neolithic sites such as Göbekli Tepe and Nahal Hemar. Alternatively, there is considerable evidence for many of the collapsed structural depressions having been used as temporary camps in Protohistoric times, and it seems possible that a number of such groups may have cooperated to construct a ritual center during their encampments at the core of the site.

The Terrace 1 Structure and Structural Reuse

On Terrace 1, the possibility that ritual activities related to those occurring on Terrace 2 during the Protohistoric Period appears to be significant. Perhaps the strongest evidence for such a ritual function comes from the canid remains that appear to have been part of a feast in Structure 109. However, the exact role of Structure 109 in any ritual activities associated with the Terrace 2 structures is not clear. It may be that, as in some areas of New Guinea and as seems to be the case at Göbekli Tepe, all the structures used constituted an entire ritual site composed of a number of structures used for different functions (see Hampton 1999; Schmidt 2001).

The earlier Plateau or Shuswap Horizon occupation of Structure 109 seems more clearly to be exclusively ritual in nature, given the very deep excavation and the rarity of faunal or lithic remains. The fact that, like Structure 105, Structure 109 shows evidence of being reused and modified at different times is also interesting. In the Maya area and at Jerf el-Ahmar in the Euphrates Valley, ritual structures were reused and remodified at different times (Stordeur et al. 2001:38). The substantial filling in of the lower floor of Structure 109, and the potential feasting implied by the presence of a hearth associated with the filling, also seems indicative of a specialized status for the structure.

CONCLUSIONS

Although it is unfortunate that there were not even more distinctive material remains associated with Structures 106 and 107 and the earlier occupation of Structure 109, which would enable us to confirm their use as special structures for rituals or secret society meetings on the basis of positive artifactual evidence rather than inferences from broader patterns (including the lack of artifacts in some cases), we feel that there are enough peculiarities, enough indications, and enough distinctive patterns in the data as discussed above to warrant a tentative interpretation of these structures as ritual or secret society meeting structures that conform to a basic pattern among large, complex Northern Plateau villages. This ritual pattern appears to have been established at least during the Plateau Horizon, if not before, and to have persisted at least up until the Protohistoric Period. In the most developed form, this pattern consists of a pair of specialized ritual structures. At least one of these structures was used for the most secret rituals and meetings of the highest-ranking members of cults or secret societies, whereas the other structure was used for somewhat more public feasting after the secret rituals. The adjoining feasting structures were probably open to lesser-ranking cult or secret society members, and it seems most likely that feasts would have been held in order to promote solidarity among secret society members as well as to display the economic success and political power of society leaders to other members and guests. Therefore, special foods such as deer, fish soups, dog, and roasted roots seem to have been prepared. Given the quantity of roots prepared, large amounts of food were probably also sometimes given away.

A similar pattern of special ritual structures reserved for the most important members of the communities apparently also existed on the Northwest Coast, although it is not clear from ethnographic accounts where any feasting associated with these cult structures may have taken place. On the Plateau, the feasting structures associated with exclusively ritual structures may have been used only on ritual occasions, or they may have been the residences of secret society shamans or priests and their families. Either one or both structures may have been used for the storage of society food resources, wealth, and ritual paraphernalia, as in the Southwest and Near East (Bostwick and Downum 1994:341; Seymour 1994: 393; Stordeur et al. 2001; Wilcox et al. 1981). However, there are some taphonomic indications that the feasting structures were used only intermittently and were not used as permanent residences. Considerably more excavation will be necessary in order to determine if this constitutes a genuine pattern at Keatley Creek as well as elsewhere on the Plateau or if this is only a fortuitous coincidence of remains and observations at Keatley Creek. If the pattern does hold up, then there are a number of possible scenarios of ritual life that emerge. One of the most intriguing research projects of the future will be to pursue these scenarios through excavations, wherever they may lead.

Acknowledgments. Initial funding for this research was provided by the Social Sciences and Humanities Research Council of Canada, which we gratefully acknowledge. We would also like to thank Suzanne Villeneuve and Jesse Morin for allowing us to include results from their recent excavations at the site, and we would like to thank the Ts'kw'aylaxw and Xaxli'p First Nations for their support of our research at Keatley Creek, as well as the Diamond S. Ranch for its permission to use this part of the ranch for our research. Thanks go to Bob Muir and Mike Rousseau for comments on an earlier draft.

7

FRASER VALLEY TRADE AND PRESTIGE AS SEEN FROM SCOWLITZ

MICHAEL BLAKE

Archaeological evidence for interaction among ancient communities has long been a central focus of research in North American archaeology. Many studies exist demonstrating the vast range of interaction patterns, including trade, warfare, emulation, and ritual aggregation to name a few. Among these, archaeologists have paid particular attention to understanding prehistoric patterns of trade (see Baugh and Ericson 1994)—partly, I suspect, because traded material remains are relatively easy to identify in the archaeological record and also partly because trade is an essential part of our modern, everyday experience. In the last few decades, however, renewed interest in trade has been sparked by models linking it with changing social organization and the evolution of social and political complexity (Arnold 1991; Price and Brown 1985; Renfrew and Shennan 1982). Trade is often seen as one of several mechanisms whereby communities and individuals can, in the absence of market economies, acquire goods that are exotic, valuable, and correlated with prestige. Given the valuable contributions that such studies have made to our understanding of social and political evolution, it is surprising that so little attention has been paid to trade in the Coast Salish region of the Northwest Coast. Several researchers have tried to remedy this situation during the past few years, and it is in the spirit of contributing to this line of study that the present research is aimed (Ames and Maschner 1999:170–171; Carlson 1994).

In this chapter I examine the contexts and types of exchange goods found at the Scowlitz site located at the junction of the Harrison and Fraser rivers, about 100 km east of the present-day city of Vancouver (Figure 7.1). A rather restricted range of nonlocal exchange goods has been found in recent excavations at the site (Lepofsky et al. 2000). Their contexts of deposition and comparisons with similar materials from other sites ranging from Vancouver Island to the interior Plateau may help us to understand some of the changes that took place in ancient Stó:lō–Coast Salish society and economy between about 3000 and 1000 B.P. I briefly discuss the kinds of materials found, their contexts, distributions in other sites throughout the region and beyond, and some of the implications of these patterns.

The Scowlitz site is one of the hundreds of archaeological sites so far discovered along the Fraser River Valley between Vancouver and the Fraser Canyon. The site is located in the traditional territory of the Scowlitz people, one of many Coast Salish communities that make up the greater Stó:lō Nation. At the suggestion of the chief of the Scowlitz First Nation, as well as heritage advisers from Stó:lo Nation, the University of British Columbia began an archaeological field school at the site in 1992. We later joined forces with archaeologists from Simon Fraser University and, together, have worked at the site for six field seasons (Lepofsky et al. 2000).

CURRENT POLITICAL IMPLICATIONS

Many Stó:lō leaders and community members maintain that they have always engaged in a wide range of trade and that their increasing exclusion from the postcontact economy is predicated on a widely held belief in Euro-Canadian society that little, if any, trade for profit occurred in the past. This belief has been solidified by recent court decisions that have ruled that prior to European contact, the Stó:lō only traded and exchanged goods as part of ceremonial gift-giving activities within and between households. As Keith Carlson has recently put it, federal and provincial governments, through the courts, "have maintained that the concept of market exchange—where one good is traded for another with an eye to maximizing profit and without future obligations to trade—was never a part of the Stó:lō experience until it was taught to them by Europeans" (2001:56). Carlson documents that in the Halq'eméylem language, the language of upriver Stó:lō people, there are at least ten

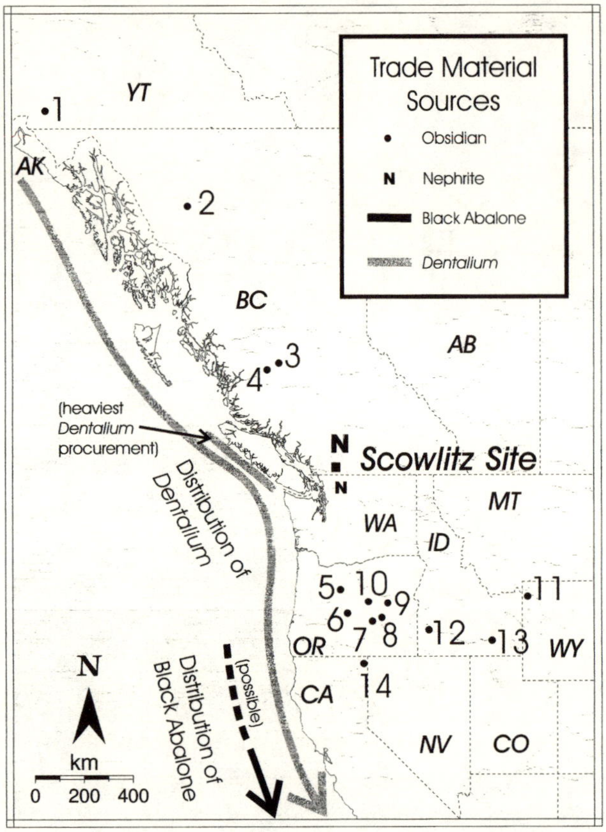

Figure 7.1. Map of the Pacific Northwest region showing the location of the Scowlitz site, obsidian sources for samples found at Scowlitz, black abalone *(Haliotis cracherodii)* distribution, dentalium *(Dentalium pretiosum)* distribution, and main sources of nephrite.

indigenous verbs associated with both labor exchange and market exchange, including bartering, trading, and selling. For example, he lists the verbs *alqá:ls* (al-kalse) and *iléqet* (ilay-ket) as terms meaning "to buy or exchange for money or items with nonfamily members." The verb *xwoxwíyém* (shwoshwee-am) means "to sell something to nonfamily." There are many other examples. Carlson points out that in a spectrum of social and spatial distance, gift exchange and potlatching were reserved for family members, in-laws, and close friends. Contract labor and gambling exchanges took place among trusted nonfamily members. Market exchanges where profit could be maximized took place among unrelated people—presumably those from much more distant villages (K. Carlson 1996).

Any consideration of the archaeological evidence for exchange prior to European contact is ultimately going to play a role in the definition of aboriginal rights and title in British Columbia. First Nations, the provincial government of British Columbia, and the Canadian government are actively engaged in treaty negotiations that will define economic relations in the province for generations to come. As court cases over the past 20 years have shown, traditional practice (i.e., aboriginal activities prior to 1846—the year British sovereignty in the region was no longer contested by other European nations [Carlson 2001:56; see Kew 1990]) is often defined for use in these negotiations by a combination of current practice and historic, ethnographic, and archaeological data.

Unfortunately, however, the archaeological record in Stó:lō traditional territory has, for a number of reasons, had little to say about the role of exchange in past times. One reason for this is the relatively small amount of archaeological work that has taken place at village sites in the region. Another is the relatively poor preservation of many archaeological materials in the highly acidic soils of the Fraser Valley region as compared with the good preservation in the shell middens along the coast or in the arid interior Plateau. Even so, there are some tantalizing glimpses of ancient exchange both within the region and well beyond the confines of the Fraser Valley. One of the keys to this exchange is the central importance that the Fraser River has always had both in terms of its hugely abundant salmon runs and in terms of its role as the main transportation corridor between coast and interior.

EXCHANGE ITEMS IN THE ARCHAEOLOGICAL RECORD

At Scowlitz we have several types of artifacts that clearly demonstrate the import of exotic nonlocal materials, including (1) obsidian, (2) nephrite, (3) dentalium shells, (4) abalone shells, and (5) copper. All of these items appear to have been imported as finished goods, and there is no evidence at the site of working any of these materials. Obsidian occurs in small numbers in the form of microblade segments and small flakes. It came from many sources, none closer than 450 km, and some as far as 800 km distant (Figure 7.1, Table 7.1). Nephrite artifacts at Scowlitz occur as very small, much-worn celts. This stone came from the Fraser Canyon, a few days' journey upriver from Scowlitz. The dentalium, abalone, and copper artifacts all occur in a single burial (Mound 1—dating to 1400 B.P.) and are found nowhere else on the site. The dentalium, used to make shell beads, most likely came from the west coast of Vancouver Island, but suitable species are found all along the Pacific coast of North America. The abalone likely came from coastal California, but the particular species found at Scowlitz can occasionally be found as far north as southern Oregon. The origin of the copper remains a mystery, but sources are known from the interior Plateau.

Perhaps the main local commodity that was exchanged for these imported goods was salmon. The region between Scowlitz and Yale on the Fraser River was renowned throughout the Northwest Coast as being the best salmon fishing place on the river, and both salmon

TABLE 7.1. X-Ray Fluorescence Determinations of Obsidian Artifacts from Scowlitz (DhRl 16).

Artifact Number	Type	Source I.D.	Source Location (North–South)	Source Number on Figure 7.1	Linear Distance to Scowlitz Site (km)	Weight (g)	Length (cm)	Width (cm)	Thickness (cm)
586	Microblade	Anahim Peak	B.C.	3	500	0.20	1.10	0.80	0.20
6892	Microblade	Three Sisters	Oregon	5	450	0.30	1.37	0.55	0.16
8504	Microblade	Newberry Caldera 1	Oregon	6	550	0.30	2.44	0.72	0.16
265	Microblade	Glass Buttes B	Oregon	7	600	0.20	1.10	0.70	0.10
421	Microblade	Glass Buttes B	Oregon	7	600	0.10	0.90	0.60	0.10
6195	Microblade	Glass Buttes B	Oregon	7	600	0.20	1.01	0.83	0.14
6813	Microblade	Glass Buttes B	Oregon	7	600	0.10	1.03	0.42	0.13
6931	Flake	Glass Buttes B	Oregon	7	600	0.40	1.42	1.04	0.26
7345	Microblade	Glass Buttes A	Oregon	7	600	3.00	0.99	0.81	0.18
8489	Flake	Glass Buttes A (?)	Oregon	7	600	0.10	0.81	0.74	0.10
9163	Microblade	Glass Buttes A	Oregon	7	600	0.20	2.32	0.63	0.18
6370	Microblade	John Day	Oregon	9	500	0.20	1.20	0.76	0.12
6445	Microblade	John Day	Oregon	9	500	0.20	1.60	0.64	0.16
6549	Flake	John Day	Oregon	9	500	0.20	1.39	1.05	0.61
8983	Microblade	John Day	Oregon	9	500	0.70	1.22	0.55	0.17
235	Microblade	Hampton Station (?)	Oregon	10	550	0.30	1.40	0.90	0.30
264	Microblade	Hampton Station	Oregon	10	550	0.04	0.80	0.50	0.10
583	Microblade	Hampton Station	Oregon	10	550	0.10	1.00	0.80	0.20
589	Microblade	Hampton Station (?)	Oregon	10	550	0.20	1.10	1.00	0.10
8378	Microblade	Hampton Station	Oregon	10	550	0.20	1.10	0.72	0.07
834	Microblade	Owyhee 1 (?)	Idaho	12	750	0.20	1.80	0.67	0.14
6848	Flake	Sugar Mountain 2	California	14	800	0.20	1.14	0.81	0.22
267	Microblade	Unknown				0.10	1.30	0.60	0.10
359	Flake	Unknown				2.60	2.50	1.40	0.90
584	Microblade	Unknown				0.04	0.70	0.60	0.10
585	Flake	Unknown				0.10	0.80	0.80	0.20
587	Flake	Unknown				0.05	0.70	0.70	0.10
588	Flake	Unknown				0.90	2.10	1.30	0.40
6498	Flake	Unknown				0.20	0.90	0.64	0.25
6795	Microblade	Unknown				0.20	1.71	0.74	0.13
7485	Flake	Unknown				n/a	n/a	n/a	n/a
8849	Microblade	Unknown				n/a	0.67	0.50	0.09
8934	Microblade	Unknown				0.20	1.08	0.49	0.09

and the rights to fish for salmon were actively traded for many centuries. Even so, we still cannot say for certain what goods, besides salmon, moved out of the region around Scowlitz; this is a topic for future research.

Obsidian

The obsidian artifacts from Scowlitz represent a wide range of sources extending from central British Columbia in the north to Northern California in the south (Figure 7.1). Approximately 50 obsidian artifacts have been found at Scowlitz so far, and 33 of these have been analyzed using x-ray fluorescence (XRF) spectrometry (Fraser 1994; James 1995, 2003) (Table 7.1). Of this sample, 19 pieces come from six central Oregon sources (including Glass Buttes A and B, John Day River, Hampton Station, Three Sisters, and Newberry Caldera). One artifact closely matches southern Idaho's Owyhee1 source and may come from there. Another piece is identified as coming from the Sugar Mountain 2 source located in the northeastern corner of California. Surprisingly, only one obsidian artifact is positively matched to a B.C. source—it is from Anahim Peak in the northern interior. Eleven samples total have been analyzed, but their sources are still unknown because their chemical fingerprints do not clearly match any of the reference samples in the Simon Fraser University obsidian library collection (James et al. 1996).

Only ten of the analyzed obsidian artifacts are flakes (or in some cases very small core fragments); the other 23 are microblade fragments that were likely brought to the site in finished form (Figure 7.2). It is possible that the blades were brought to the site already hafted on wooden handles, as illustrated in the hafted microlith and micro-

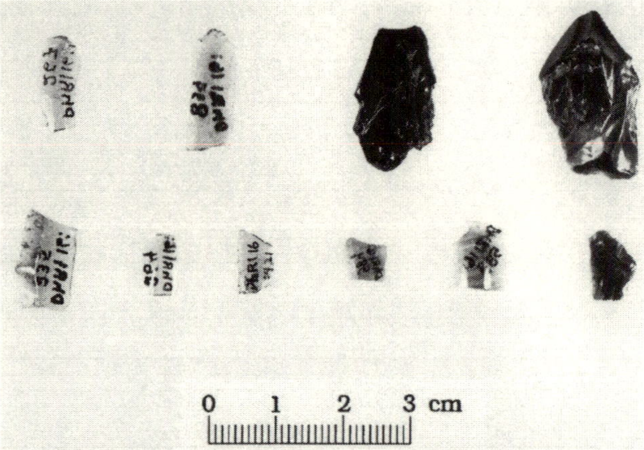

Figure 7.2. Examples of obsidian artifacts from 1992 excavations at Scowlitz. From upper left to lower right: DhRl 267, 839, 588, 359, 235, 264, 421, 584, 583, 585. See Table 7.1 for descriptions and sources.

blade specimens recovered from the Hoko River site in Washington State (Croes 1996).

Roy Carlson (1994) has recently presented an extraordinarily comprehensive analysis of obsidian exchange in British Columbia. He and his colleagues have also used XRF spectrometry to analyze 1,302 obsidian artifacts from 121 sites. This research provides an ideal foundation for understanding the obsidian source variation at Scowlitz.

Of 121 sites in Carlson's sample, only four are located along the Fraser River between its mouth at Vancouver and the Fraser Canyon. They include, from oldest to youngest, Milliken (five artifacts), Maurer (nine), St. Mungo (four), and Marpole (28), for a total of 46 artifacts from nine different obsidian sources (Carlson 1994: 316–317). Seven of these sources are in central Oregon, whereas the remaining two are from Garibaldi (Figure 7.3) and an unknown source on the central coast of British Columbia. The two most common sources for the Marpole site are Garibaldi obsidian (n= 13—this source is located about 100 km north of the Marpole site) and the central Oregon sources (n= 13—these sources are about 500–600 km south of the Fraser Valley). More recently, Reimer (2000:7–8) has presented a summary analysis of a collection of obsidian from the part of the Marpole site excavated in 1973. His analysis focuses solely on the 1,366 artifacts of Garibaldi obsidian, which constitute 52 percent of the chipped-stone assemblage (identified by both XRF analysis and visual inspection). He does not mention how much non-Garibaldi obsidian is present in the collection. Both Carlson's and Reimer's studies of the Marpole site show that it had a much more restricted range of obsidian sources than that exhibited at Scowlitz, even though many more obsidian artifacts are present.

Complementing these studies is another detailed XRF analysis of obsidian artifacts carried out by James et al. (1996:112–114). They present source identifications for artifacts from several other sites in the Fraser Valley and the Fraser Canyon. I will briefly mention the results from two of these sites, Milliken (DjRi 3) and Esilao (DjRi 5), located very close to each other, 70 km upriver from Scowlitz in the Fraser Canyon near Yale (see Mitchell 1990). James and his colleagues studied 54 artifacts from these two sites and found the following pattern, reminiscent of the distribution at Scowlitz: ten from Yukon, five from British Columbia, one from Washington, 18 from Oregon, 14 from Northern California, and six from Wyoming. These artifacts come from a total of 16 different sources.

Carlson (1994:318) presents data for 16 sites some 150–250 km upstream from Scowlitz, in the Middle Fraser River region, most of which span a period overlapping with the occupation and use of the Scowlitz site. All of the obsidian from these sites comes from the Anahim and neighboring sources n = 93—these sources are located about 500 km to the north of the Fraser River Valley).

It is particularly striking that very little obsidian from the northern sources (e.g., Anahim, Mackenzie, Edziza, and Yukon) is found in sites from the Lower Fraser River, the Gulf Islands, southern Vancouver Island, the Puget Sound, and the Lower and Middle Columbia River regions. Likewise, little obsidian from Garibaldi, Vancouver Island, or the Oregon, Idaho, Wyoming, and California sources is found in the interior Plateau sites along the Middle Fraser River.

In contrast to the above pattern, the enormous range of obsidian sources represented at Scowlitz and Milliken/Esilao suggests that people there had an extensive network of trade relations that allowed access to obsidian from both northern British Columbia and Yukon (perhaps via the Middle Fraser River Valley) and the northwestern United States (perhaps via the Lower Columbia, Puget Sound, and Fraser Delta). This certainly gives the impression that sites such as Scowlitz in the Fraser Valley and, to an even greater extent, Milliken/Esilao in the Lower Fraser Canyon sat astride a major thoroughfare that saw, with respect to obsidian, the flow of goods from hundreds of kilometers to the north and south.

Nephrite

The most common objects made of nephrite in the Coast Salish region were celts used in woodworking. Mackie (1992) provides an excellent summary of the ethnographic information about celts and woodworking tools and analyzes almost 1,500 examples from archaeological collections in the Coast Salish area. The role of celts in exchange is touched on briefly in his analysis. Mackie cites an entry from the journal of 1829 from Fort Langley

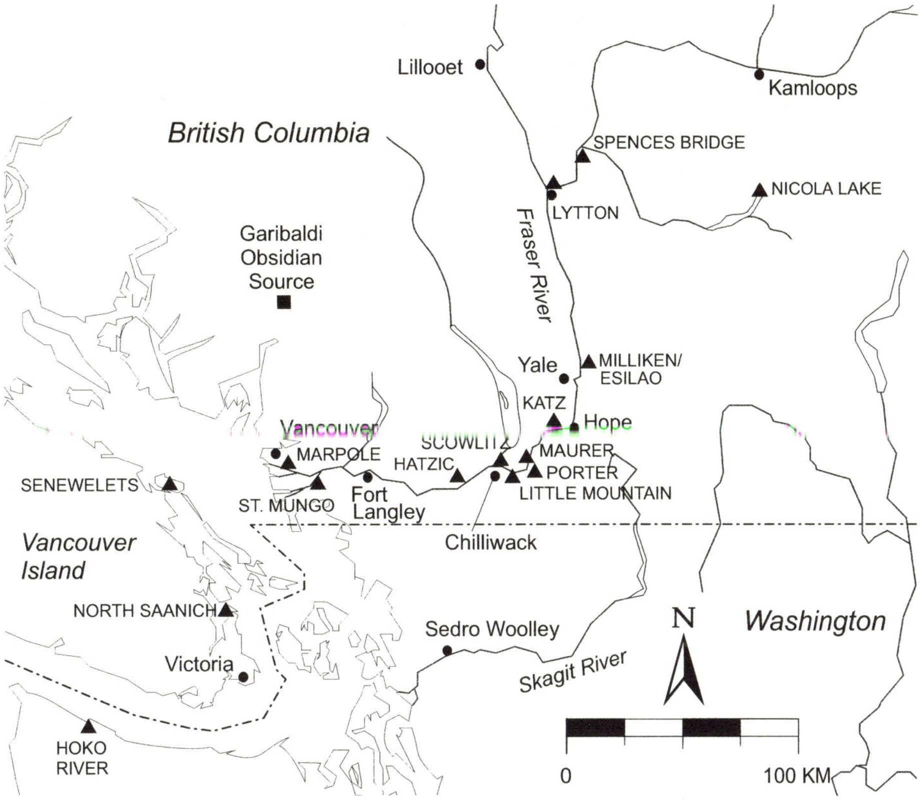

Figure 7.3. Map of southwestern British Columbia and northwestern Washington showing sites mentioned in the text.

(located in Stó:lō territory, 40 km downstream from Scowlitz), in which it was observed by one of the members of the Hudson's Bay Company that downriver people "traded several thousand salmon for 640 small chisels of low quality." There is also a list entry for 18 August 1829 showing 640 salmon for ten small chisels (but these may be iron) (McDonald 1998:124). This shows that chisels were important trade items and even suggests that the primary direction of trade in nephrite was from north to south. The people who acquired them in exchange for salmon would trade them ever farther afield as they moved back to their own winter villages on Vancouver Island.

The primary sources of nephrite are almost all located in the Fraser Canyon, between Yale and Lillooet (Darwent 1997; see Figure 7.1). As mentioned by Mackie, there were also significant quantities of nephrite available along the river downstream from Yale toward Hope. This general region falls mainly in the traditional territory of the interior Salish groups, including Lillooet and Nxla: capma and upriver Stó:lō peoples. Mackie argues that because there are almost no sources of nephrite outside this area, all of the coastal communities that needed it must have traded with these groups. This means that the communities along the Lower Fraser River that had access to nephrite through trade with their neighbors in the canyon could have become important middlemen in the processing and distribution of this important commodity (Burley 1981:403).

Another source of nephrite was located in the Upper Skagit River region near Sedro Woolley in Washington (Ames and Maschner 1999:171; see Figure 7.1). Some of the Scowlitz nephrite artifacts, discussed below, may have originated from this source; although without a reliable sourcing technique, such as we have for obsidian, it is not yet possible to be certain where the nephrite originated.

Scowlitz has a significant number of celts in its assemblage; approximately 50 whole or partial ones have been recovered in the excavations so far. All of them have been found associated with the household refuse deposits that we have tested. They all appear to be made from nephrite and show a wide range of colors, ranging from very light green-gray to dark green. Some also appear to have been heat treated.

However, unlike the case at the Porter site, located just to the south of Scowlitz on the opposite side of the Fraser River, there is no evidence of celt manufacturing. The Scowlitz collection appears to be heavily used and worn, so people were clearly importing celts to carry out their woodworking activities (Figure 7.4). The Scowlitz site inhabitants were probably not involved directly in manufacturing celts using their own imported raw materials. At the Porter site, which has been surface collected, amateur collectors and archaeologists have recovered

Figure 7.4. Examples of nephrite celts and celt fragments from 1992 excavations at Scowlitz. From upper left to lower right: DhRl 269, 393, 385, 739, 786, 323, 399, 356, 261, 358, 273, 392, 401, 357.

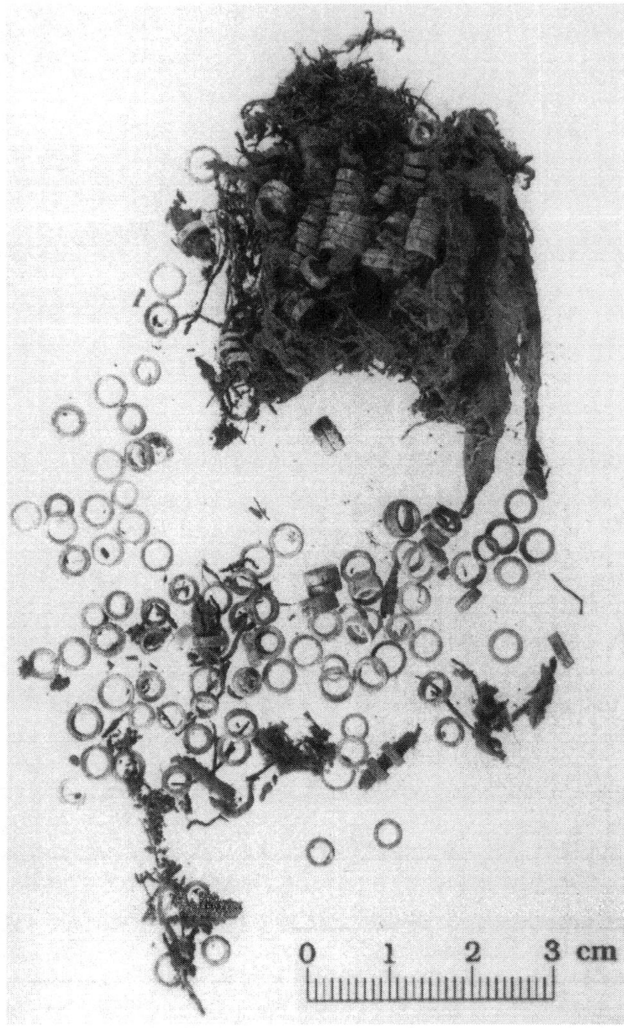

Figure 7.5. Examples of dentalium shell beads (group artifact number DhRl 701), some still in articulated strands, from 1992 excavations in Mound 1 at Scowlitz.

hundreds of examples of nephrite tools and manufacturing debris. It is fair to say that the Porter site shows the greatest range of manufacturing debris types found at any site in the Coast Salish region, although there are several sites near Hope that also have considerable evidence of all stages of the manufacturing process (Archer 1980; Hanson 1973; Mackie 1992; Von Krogh 1980). Remains include cut-nephrite boulders, adze fragments in various stages of manufacture, nephrite flakes, preforms, and unfinished sawn pieces.

Dentalium

There are many sources of dentalium *Dentalium pretiosum* and other species) or tusk shell along the Pacific coast of British Columbia, but the largest number and most prolific of sources in the historic period occurred on the west coast of Vancouver Island (Barton 1994:99; see Figure 7.1). In his exhaustive study, Barton has argued that there may have been important sources other than Vancouver Island and that the precontact exchange patterns may not have been the same as those developed by European traders in the 1800s. Even so, he (1994:134) concludes that the most intensive harvesting and trading of dentalium shells was probably carried out by both the Nuu-chah-nulth and the Kwakwaka'wakw peoples of the west coast, as well as the Haida people of Haida Gwaii (see also Andrews 1989).

From the perspective of the inhabitants of the Scowlitz site, dentalium shell beads must have been procured through coastal trade connections, and their presence at the site indicates clear linkages. Dentalium shell beads are found in only one context at Scowlitz—in strands of necklaces accompanying the person buried in Mound 1. The dentalium beads were cut into thin sections from single long shells, one shell probably producing many individual beads (Figure 7.5). There are approximately 7,000 beads in the necklaces in Mound 1, one of the largest single finds of dentalium shell beads so far recorded in the Pacific Northwest. This burial dates to circa 1400 B.P. (Blake et al. 1993; Lepofsky et al. 2000).

There are only a few other examples of this kind of bead jewelry reported in the archaeological literature for British Columbia. One almost identical example comes from a burial excavated in 1899 on the shore of Nicola Lake, 55 km south of Kamloops, in the interior Plateau region. The collection by Harlan Smith is described as "a necklace of four strands of shell beads of cylindrical form about an eighth of an inch in diameter, and about a thirty-second of an inch in thickness, with a bore of about a thirty-second of an inch. These are strung on a cord made of vegetable fibre twisted to the left.... Suspended from the middle of the front was a perforated copper pendant, a fragment of which remains" (1900: 425). Although he does not identify the shell beads, they are clearly dentalium and were strung just as the beads found at Scowlitz were (Figure 7.6). Furthermore, they were found with the same type of copper pendant as those recovered in Mound 1 (see below).

There are many other examples of dentalium shell beads, though mostly whole ones, from sites in the interior as well as the coast (Andrews1989; Barton 1994), but there are few examples from the Fraser Valley region. This is likely because of the highly acidic soil, which makes long-term preservation of bone and shell almost impossible. More common is the case of the Senewélets site (False Narrows) on Gabriola Island in the Gulf of Georgia. There, many thousands of shell beads were recovered in burials, but by far the most common were perforated discs made of clam and mussel shells (Burley 1989:128). The second most common beads at the site were made from dentalium shells, but none of the 3,815 specimens was of the sawn or sectioned variety found at Scowlitz and Nicola Lake. Schulting (1995, citing Clark 1963) says that cut-dentalium shell beads were, at least in early historic times, considered to be less valuable than whole beads. It is not clear what the equivalency would be, but I would suspect that because of the much greater labor involved in cutting and abrading the beads, a necklace of the same length in cut beads would be much more valuable than one of whole or uncut beads. Even so, a recent experimental study by Holthuysen (2002) has shown that the labor involved in cutting the shells into thin beads is much less than we had previously assumed.

Abalone

Three complete abalone shell pendants were discovered in the Mound 1 burial at Scowlitz (Figure 7.7). In addition, there is a much smaller and thinner fourth abalone shell fragment that may also have been a pendant. One of the large abalone shell pendants rested in close proximity to a copper pendant, causing green staining on the dorsal surface of the shell.

The three complete Scowlitz pendants are made from a large species of California abalone and have tentatively been identified as black abalone *(Haliotis cracherodii)*.[1]

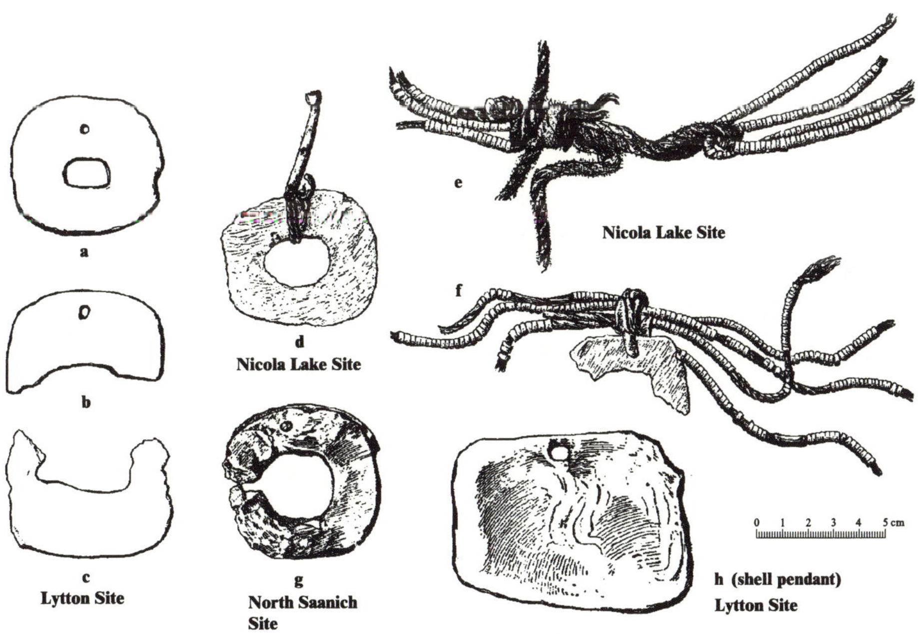

Figure 7.6. Examples of dentalium shell beads, abalone shell pendant, and copper pendants from Harlan Smith and Gerard Fowke's excavations in the 1890s. Items a–c: copper pendants from a single grave at the Lytton site (Smith 1899:151); d–f: copper pendants suspended with twine and strung with dentalium shell beads from grave 5 at the Nicola Lake site (Smith 1900:425); g: copper pendant found in cairn 17 at the North Saanich site on Vancouver Island (Smith and Fowke 1901:65); h: abalone shell pendant from the Lytton site (Smith 1899:152).

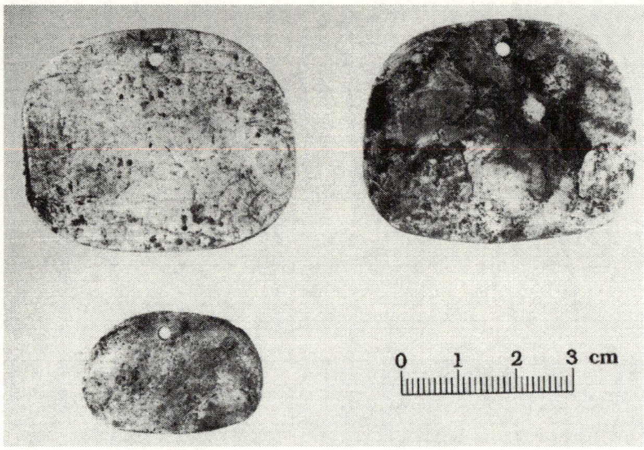

Figure 7.7. Black abalone pendants from 1992 excavations in Mound 1 at Scowlitz. From upper left to lower right: DhRl 16 697, 698, 699.

As with most of the species along the Pacific coast of North America, black abalone occurs primarily south of the San Francisco region of Northern California, although specimens have been noted as far north as the Oregon–California border (Geiger and Poppe 2000; see Figure 7.1). Although very fragmentary and not positively identified, the fourth piece of abalone (not illustrated) appears to have been northern abalone *(H. k. kamtschatkana)*, a much smaller and thinner-shelled species than the California abalones. We obtained a ^{14}C date of 1630 ± 60 B.P. from that shell fragment, though it may have been somewhat younger because of the marine carbon reservoir effect.

The two species that were most commonly used in the west coast trade, because of their large size, smoothness, and green-blue iridescence, are green abalone *(H. fulgens)* and black abalone (Geiger and Poppe 2000; Sloan 2003). Its most common use in prehistoric times was for the manufacturing of large flat pendants. Abalone pendants were probably traded inland to central California, Oregon, and Washington and may have made their way into British Columbia following similar trade routes as obsidian (Ames and Maschner 1999). There is not yet any archaeological evidence for abalone shell working in the Fraser Valley or any other part of British Columbia, so it is most likely that these items were imported in finished form.

Abalone shell pendants have been found in some sites in British Columbia but are relatively rare. One of the earliest reported examples comes from Smith's (1899: 151–152) excavations at the confluence of the Thompson and Fraser rivers near Lytton in the Fraser Canyon. He says: "Several pieces of abalone shell with squared edges were found in a grave at the main site. One of these... was perforated. Probably it was used as a pendant. Such shell ornaments are now highly prized by the coast Indians on account of the iridescence of the shell" (1899: 151). Smith illustrates this example with a specimen that is almost identical to three found in the Mound 1 burial at Scowlitz (Figure 7.6). He (1900:426, 434) also notes the discovery of an abalone pendant in a grave at the Spences Bridge site. Although not yet positively identified, the pendants described by Smith appear to be identical to the ones from Scowlitz and are probably black abalone.

Abalone pendants, similar to the ones in Mound 1, continued to be imported to the Fraser Valley and used up to recent times. The Royal British Columbia Museum has a photograph, dated 1903, showing a woman at Ruby Creek in the Fraser Canyon wearing two such pendants (Carlson 2001:57). California abalone was also common on the west coast of British Columbia, and one can see historic period masks with inlaid mosaics of iridescent green abalone shell. Some of the masks in the Museum of Anthropology at the University of British Columbia and the American Museum of Natural History have inlaid abalone sections that show drill holes, suggesting that they were made from larger pendants that were later cut into smaller sections for use as mask decoration. Two examples can be seen in Halpin and Seguin's (1990:277–279) essay on Tsimshian peoples in the *Handbook of North American Indians*.

Copper

Copper has long been thought to have been one of the most important trade items and status markers on the Northwest Coast. This is partly because large ceremonial "coppers" were among the most significant status markers used in prestige and wealth display in the 19th century. There is accumulating archaeological evidence for this link between copper and prestige extending back at least 2,500 years (Carlson 1994:323). One of the most consistent archaeological occurrences of copper is in burial contexts throughout the Northwest Coast and interior Plateau (Ames and Maschner 1999:171; Matson and Coupland 1995:203; Richards and Rousseau 1987; Schulting 1995).

In Mound 1 at Scowlitz we found four perforated copper pendant discs and a large ring (too large for a finger) (Figure 7.8). The pendants were relatively well preserved, and copper salts from their corrosion preserved parts of the leather thongs that were used to suspend them. They may have been associated with the dentalium bead necklaces and abalone shell pendants discussed above. Two of the copper pendants were larger than the others, but all had the same general form.

These kinds of pendants have been described in archaeological contexts since the late 1800s in British Columbia. Smith illustrates three from Lytton, two from the Nicola Lake site, and one from a stone burial cairn at the North Saanich site on Vancouver Island (1899:151, 1900:425;

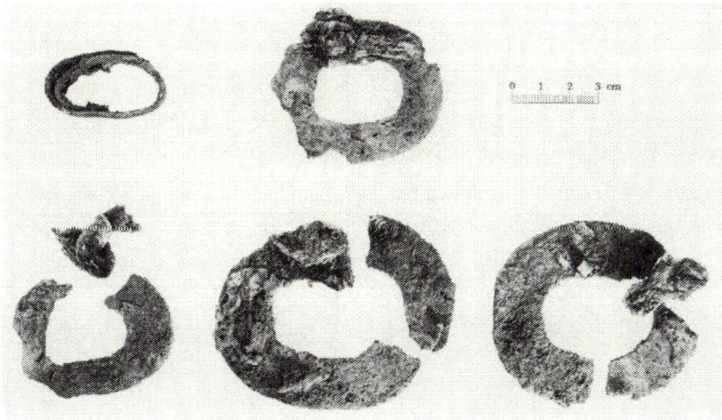

Figure 7.8. Copper artifacts from 1992 excavations in Mound 1 at Scowlitz. From upper left to lower right: DhRl 16 689, 692, 690, 691, 693. Note the leather straps adhering to the four pendants and the occurrence of several articulated dentalium beads. These are almost identical to the example shown in Figure 7.6f from the Nicola Lake site.

Smith and Fowke 1901:65). There is also a similar copper pendant from the Hatzic Burial Mound site located about 30 km downriver from Scowlitz (Hill-Tout 1930).

The source of the copper remains unknown. It was most likely cold-hammered from large nuggets quarried from sources in either Alaska or British Columbia. Much more work needs to be done to locate the sources and to sample artifacts to compare their chemical constituents with known source fingerprints.

DISCUSSION AND CONCLUSIONS

The initial village occupation at the Scowlitz site, between approximately 3000 and 1500 B.P., was one of relative impoverishment compared, impressionistically, with other large village sites along the Fraser River between the Fraser Delta and Hope.[2] The assemblage at the Marpole site, for example, shows a much greater diversity of imported items (other than obsidian) than Scowlitz does (Burley 1980). This might in part be because of the much better physical preservation of the archaeological record at Marpole, for the acidic soils are buffered by the high density of shellfish remains in the midden. However, even at the Little Mountain and Porter sites, only a few kilometers south of Scowlitz, where like Scowlitz there were no shell middens, there is also a greater diversity of artifacts. At both of these sites there are many categories of artifacts that have not been found at Scowlitz, for example, anthropomorphic and zoomorphic stone bowls, high frequencies of nephrite celts, large amounts of nephrite tool-manufacturing debris, and numbers of hand mauls (Doug Brown, personal communication, 2002).

After 1500 B.P. the Scowlitz site and the surrounding region (for perhaps 2 km in all directions) took on a new function as a cemetery, and the village was temporarily abandoned (Lepofsky et al. 2000). More than 200 surface features representing individual graves have been noted by members of our research team since the 1992 season (Nicole Oakes, personal communication, 2003). These include large earthen burial mounds, smaller mounds, and cairns, the smallest of which contain only a few boulders. In addition, there are many other unmarked burials beneath the ground. We excavated the largest burial mound, Mound 1, in 1992 and found a single skeleton, that of an adult male, lying flexed on his right side and contained beneath an elaborate stone cairn. This burial mound dates to about 1400 B.P. and is similar in many respects to other large earthen burial mounds in the Coast Salish region (Thom 1995).

The objects accompanying this individual provide a fascinating glimpse of the link between trade in nonlocal items and social prestige. He had several necklaces of dentalium shell beads, each bead carefully cut and ground. Oftentimes dentalium shells have been found uncut, representing wealth, but involving considerably less labor than that displayed in the collection from Mound 1 at Scowlitz. There are approximately 7,000 beads in the various strands that accompany the burial.

There are also three black abalone shell pendants in the burial—probably traded from California—and one possible northern abalone shell fragment from coastal British Columbia. These are very rare in archaeological assemblages from the period but have occasionally been found in burial contexts in the interior of British Columbia.

Finally, there are four copper pendants, suspended by leather thongs, as well as a large copper ring. The copper pendants are identical in style to those found in other burials both on the coast and in the interior Plateau. These copper objects are from an unknown source, but their closest origin might have been from the copper deposits near Kamloops in the interior of British Columbia.

What is most striking about the objects included in the Mound 1 burial is that they represent one of the most significant expressions of wealth among all the known burial offerings reported from the Coast Salish region. And they are all rare imported objects—likely manufactured at some distant location. That they were associated with a single individual buried in one of the most prominent mortuary features, and thereby taken out of future circulation, further reinforces the link between social prestige and the possession of imported wealth objects.

The dating of this grave (the earliest so far recovered from the site) to approximately 1400 B.P., some 1,000–1,500 years after the initial village occupation, suggests two things. First, members of the 2,500-year-old village were perhaps engaged in very different kinds of trade and expression of social prestige than that represented by the later mortuary population. In other words, the first villagers had access to some imported materials, including obsidian from afar and nephrite tools from nearby sources. But there is little indication of the more complex assemblages of materials and tools found at contemporary sites along the Fraser River. There is also no indication of the investment in high-prestige exchange items such as copper or marine shell ornaments that we see in the later burial and which are known for the Marpole culture in the Straight of Georgia region (Matson and Coupland 1995; Mitchell 1990:352).

Second, it suggests that the conversion of the site into a cemetery for use by people living elsewhere, but presumably nearby, represents a very different prestige system than that which existed earlier. It may be that larger, wealthier communities located nearby replaced the Scowlitz site as the main locations of residence. These people had access to trade items from far away, trade items representing a huge wealth in local terms. They may have been descendants of the original Scowlitz population, many generations removed, but showing their ancestral links to this important river junction and ancient village spot by continuing to use the site as a cemetery.

The burial of prestige exchange items with an important individual expresses two clear dimensions of social and economic connection. It shows that people living in the region between 1500 and 1000 B.P. were connected to the most important place on the landscape—the ancient village where their ancestors had once lived. It also shows that they were connected to a network of social relationships extending from Vancouver Island to the interior Plateau and south to Oregon, California, and Idaho. These connections, both to the ancestors and to the living, were expressed 1,500 years ago by the material record of both ancient village and cemetery. They are still important today to the Stó:lō people who are the inheritors of the place.

NOTES

Acknowledgments. The fieldwork and laboratory research on which this chapter is based were conducted by a creative and hardworking team of archaeologists co-lead by Dana Lepofsky and including Doug Brown, Nicole Oakes, Natasha Lyons, and Sandra Morrison. Our research project is indebted to members of the Scowlitz Band who invited us to work with them and helped with all aspects of the project: Betty Charlie; Clifford Hall; Alan Williams; Jennifer, John, Vi, and Ralph Pennier; Melvin Hall; Johnny Williams Sr. and Johnny Williams Jr.; and Andy and Nancy Phillips. Stó:lō Nation members, employees, and former employees who have encouraged our research from the start and to whom we are grateful include Chief Clarence Pennier, Sonny McHalsie, Dave Schaepe, Keith Carlson, Gordon Mohs, and Brian Thom.

I thank Malcolm James and his colleagues at Simon Fraser University (SFU) for carrying out the obsidian analysis and Scott Fraser and Patricia Murphy, who worked on parts of the obsidian data in undergraduate classes at the University of British Columbia (UBC). Norm Sloan, Anthony Graesch, Daniel Geiger, and Roy Carlson all generously contributed to the identification of the abalone pendants. Joyce Johnson took the artifact photos. My colleagues at UBC contributed greatly with discussions of the materials from Scowlitz: R. G. Matson, David Pokotylo, Brian Chisholm, and Patricia Ormerod. This research was funded by a Social Sciences and Humanities Research Council (SSHRC) Research Grant (410–96–1575), a UBC HSS grant, an SSHRC small grant (31–631359), an SFU President Research Grant, and funds from both the UBC Dean of Arts Office and the SFU Department of Archaeology.

1. These abalone shell pendants, identified in 2002, are probably specimens of black abalone. They were identified with the help of Dr. Norm Sloan, a marine ecologist at Gwaii Haanas National Park Reserve and Haida Heritage Site; Dr. Daniel L. Geiger, a research associate at Santa Barbara Museum of Natural History; and Anthony Graesch, of the Department of Anthropology, University of California, Los Angeles.

2. Doug Brown (personal communication, 2002) has compared the Scowlitz assemblage with those from approximately 25 other contemporary sites in the Fraser Valley and has found that Scowlitz lacks some of the diversity in artifacts recovered at the other sites. Notable is the relative lack of woodworking technology, including hand mauls, at Scowlitz. We also have not yet found any stone bowls at Scowlitz.

III

SOCIAL ORGANIZATION, PLANT RESOURCES, AND THE ABANDONMENT OF PITHOUSE VILLAGES

8

A QUESTION OF INTENSITY

EXPLORING THE ROLE OF PLANT FOODS IN NORTHERN PLATEAU PREHISTORY

Dana Lepofsky and Sandra L. Peacock

Critical food resources play a key role in many models of Plateau pithouse culture. Though most models focus on salmon, several researchers also recognize plant foods and, in particular, root foods as significant in many cultural sequences (Ames and Marshall 1980; Andrefsky et al. 2000, 4: 14.1–14.66; Chatters 1995a, 1998; Galm 1985; Peacock 1998, 2002; Pokotylo and Froese 1983; Pokotylo and Mitchell 1998; Richards and Rousseau 1987; Thoms 1989). Empirical support for the importance of plant foods comes from a limited sample of direct and indirect evidence for ancient plant use, and changes in the nature of this evidence are thought to indicate shifting intensification of plant food use through time.

Before roots or other plant foods can be fully integrated into models of Plateau prehistory, however, fundamental issues about the nature of plant food intensification and about plant foods themselves need to be addressed. The term *intensification* is used in various ways in the literature, yet few researchers in the region have explored the ecological and cultural processes of plant food intensification (but see Ames in press; Peacock 1998). Further, because considerable diversity is encompassed within the general category of "plant foods," or even "root foods," models that incorporate such categories may be of limited utility. Specific attributes of plant species influenced how they were used in the past and how likely we are to recover evidence of their use in the archaeological record.

In this chapter we explore some of these basic issues in the hopes of creating a fuller understanding of the potential role of selected plant resources in the development of Northern Plateau cultures. We focus on the Northern Plateau specifically because our previous research on ancient plant use has concentrated on this region (e.g., Lepofsky 2000a, 2000b; Lepofsky et al. 1996; Peacock 1998, 2002; Peacock and Turner 2000), and thus we are less familiar with the ecology and paleoethnobotany of the Southern Plateau. Of particular note is the fact that our discussions do not include the large camas meadows unique to eastern Washington and western Idaho. Several researchers have already discussed the importance of camas *(Camasia quamash)* harvesting in the development of cultures in that region (Ames and Marshall 1980; Andrefsky et al. 2000, 4:14.1–14.66; Thoms 1989).

Our discussion also focuses on plant foods specifically, rather than plants used for a wider range of purposes (i.e., technological, medicinal, ritual). We do this not because we believe that food plants were absolutely more important than other plants but, rather, because we believe that the availability and abundance of food plants will have a relatively greater influence on the kinds of patterns we can detect archaeologically at a regional level (e.g., settlement patterns, intensification of resource use). Further, because previously proposed models of culture change on the Plateau focus discussions on food plants, our analysis can potentially add to these earlier models.

We begin our chapter by exploring the various pathways by which Plateau peoples could have "intensified" their use of plant foods, identifying several strategies, their effects, and their archaeological correlates. We then turn our attention to the ethnobotanical evidence for plant use, dividing the plant foods into five major groups: root foods, fruits and berries, seeds and nuts, green vegetables, and tree cambium. For select species within each group, we evaluate various attributes that may have influenced their importance to Plateau peoples, including various ecological characteristics, processing requirements, and nutritional values. We then regroup these attributes to assess the accessibility, abundance, palatability, and persistence of each plant and each plant group. Finally, we use these four groups of attributes to arrive at rankings of the potential value of the plants. Based on these assessments, certain species emerge as having the greatest overall potential role in the diet of the Northern Plateau peoples. We then look to the direct and indirect archaeological evidence for plant use on the Northern Plateau in the post-4000 B.P. period and compare this against those plants we expect to have been important in the past. We conclude with a discussion about the potential role of plants in late period communities on the Northern Plateau.

PATHWAYS TO INTENSIFICATION

Though the role of plant food intensification figures prominently in several models of Plateau prehistory, few researchers have addressed the specific processes by which this might have occurred. In this section we examine some of the possible pathways to plant food intensification for Northern Plateau peoples. As we use the term here, *intensification* refers to the process of increasing plant food production (i.e., increased output) via various mechanisms that may or may not involve increased energy costs. As our review illustrates, Plateau peoples may have pursued several different strategies to accomplish this goal.

Models of people–plant interactions (Ford 1985; Harris 1989; Smith 2001) provide the broad theoretical framework that informs our discussion. Expanding on Ford's (1985) model of plant food production, we recognize four possible pathways that Northern Plateau peoples could have taken to intensify plant resources: cognitive, social, technological, and ecological (Table 8.1). Each of these strategies can be expressed in a range of ways, which will in turn result in distinct archaeological signatures. These strategies are not mutually exclusive (for example, technological and ecological solutions may allow for increased harvests), nor are they necessarily hierarchical in the order in which they might be adopted.

Cognitive approaches refer to decisions concerning the kinds and quantities of plant foods utilized. As one strategy, people can choose to extensify (expand diet breadth) by collecting a wider variety of plants. Alternatively—or additionally—people can increase the harvest of resources already being used. Social pathways, such as the expansion of kinship networks and trade relations (cf. Minnis 1985; Suttles 1960), provide another means of increasing access to plant foods. Technological innovations represent a third set of strategies to enhance plant food production. Included in this category are a variety of plant harvesting, processing, and storage technologies (Binford 1980; Minnis 1985; Stahl 1989; Testart 1982). Finally, ecological approaches include various strategies used to maintain and enhance key plant resources, ranging from the maintenance of entire habitats using fire to practices affecting only specific resources (e.g., pruning; see Peacock and Turner 2000).

ATTRIBUTES INFLUENCING INTENSITY OF USE

Decisions about how to intensify production of a particular plant food—and, indeed, whether a plant will be intensified at all—are dependent in large part on the attributes of that species. Of particular importance are where a plant grows, when it can be harvested, how abundant and reliable it is, its nutritional value, how much processing is required before it can be consumed, whether it can be stored, and how it responds to intensive harvesting. In the following discussion, we group these characteristics into four attributes: availability, abundance, palatability, and persistence. In general, we suggest that plants that rank higher in these four attributes are likely to be those that were used most intensively by Northern Plateau peoples.

Availability

The spatial and temporal availability of a plant—where it grows and when it is harvestable—were significant considerations in the scheduling of the seasonal round and likely played a role in determining the overall importance of a plant food in the diet. Some plants are restricted in distribution to specific habitats (e.g., wapato *[Sagittaria latifolia]*, whitebark pine, *[Pinus albicaulis]*) or must be collected over a very short period of time (e.g., cow parsnip *[Heracleum lanatum]*). In contrast, other taxa, including several species of roots and berries, are widely available in different habitats and at different elevations throughout the growing season. The former imposes greater restrictions on scheduling, whereas the latter permits greater flexibility in balancing the need for plant foods with other economic and social demands. In addition, the availability of a plant for consumption once it has been harvested is dependent on whether processing is required before it can be consumed and whether it can be stored for future consumption.

Abundance

We use abundance as a measure of how common a plant is on the landscape. It refers to the number of individuals per unit area and how frequently those areas or habitats are encountered across the landscape. Generally, plants that occur in numerous, dense patches are more profitable to harvest than those scattered throughout the landscape in low numbers. However, species that occur in extremely

TABLE 8.1. Pathways of Plant Food Intensification.

Pathway	Strategy	Effect	Archaeological Evidence
Cognitive	Extensify resource base Increase harvests of particular taxa	Diet breadth increases; foods of lower cultural preference incorporated Larger harvests of particular foods	Remains of more taxa Increase in number of plant remains
Social	Establish/expand trade and kinship networks	Access nonlocal foods through trade or by permission to harvest in neighboring territories	Nonlocal plant remains
Technological	Develop/improve harvesting technology (e.g., digging sticks, bark peelers and scrapers, baskets) Develop/improve processing techniques (e.g., pounding and grinding, pit cooking, boiling, roasting) Develop/improve preservation techniques (e.g., drying, roasting) Storage	Increases harvesting efficiency Increases diet breadth, availability of food energy, palatability, digestibility, storability Increases availability through winter	Artifacts associated with harvesting Mortars, pestles, grinding slabs, earth ovens, hearths, fire-cracked rock, pits Drying racks, mats, hearths, heating elements Storage pits, containers
Ecological	Management of plant foods through pruning, tilling, weeding, prescribed burning	Increases reliability, density, and distribution of plants	Shifts in pollen, charcoal, and sediment sequences

dense aggregations but limited distributions (e.g., bitterroot *[Lewisia rediviva]*) may also be amenable to intensive harvesting.

Palatability

Plant foods contribute carbohydrates, vitamins, and minerals necessary to maintain health and to efficiently metabolize proteins in diets (Kuhnlein and Turner 1991; Speth and Speilmann 1983). Peoples in traditional societies, however, did not select plant foods on the basis of their nutrient content per se, although the health benefits of certain plant foods were clearly recognized. Rather, plant foods were often chosen for palatability (based on the organoleptic properties of taste, texture, and smell) as well as digestibility. To some extent, taste preferences are culturally acquired (as many people who have not grown up eating soapberries will attest). However, the foods people find most palatable are often those that satisfy innate cravings—such as for sweet, salty, or bitter foods—that evolved to assist in satisfying nutritional requirements (e.g., Johns 1990). On the Plateau, some plant foods are inherently palatable and nutritious (e.g., saskatoon berries *[Amelanchier alnifolia]*, thimbleberries *[Rubus parviflorus]*), whereas others, including inulin-rich root foods such as camas *(Camassia quamash)* and balsamroot *(Balsamorhiza sagittata)*, require processing to enhance their taste and nutritional value (Konlande and Robson 1972; Mullin et al. 1997; Peacock 1998).

Persistence

The final attribute we consider is persistence, the ability of a plant population to maintain its numbers under the pressures of intensive harvesting practices, as well as a population's ability to become more productive under management. Plateau peoples practiced a range of management techniques such as selective harvesting, weeding, tilling, tending, transplanting, and landscape burning. These traditional practices, whether applied to a single species (e.g., pruning) or to all species within a particular habitat (e.g., landscape burning), created disturbances that mimicked the natural disturbance regimes required for the perpetuation and continued productivity of plant populations (Peacock 1998; Peacock and Turner 2000; Turner 1999).

ATTRIBUTES OF PLANT FOODS ON THE NORTHERN PLATEAU

Historically, peoples of the Northern Plateau incorporated more than 115 plant taxa into their traditional diets (Turner 1997; Turner et al. 1980; Turner et al. 1990). Though these taxa are often conveniently grouped into five broad categories (root foods, fruits and berries, green vegetables, seeds and nuts, and tree cambium), each plant has its unique anatomical structures, patterns of growth, chemical composition, and seasonal availability, all of which influenced intensity of use.

TABLE 8.2. ATTRIBUTES OF ROOT FOODS USED IN THE NORTHERN PLATEAU.

Species (Common Name)	Part Used	Habitat/ Elevation[a]	Abundance[b]	Productivity[c]	Season Harvested[d]	Processing/ Storage[e]	Persistence[f]
Allium cernuum (nodding onion)	Bulb	Gr, dF, Op/L-M	W, C	H, C	ES, LS	F, P, S	H
Balsamorhiza sagittata (arrow-leaved balsamroot)	Taproot	Gr, Sh, dF, Op/L-H	W, C	H, C	Sp, LS	P, S	H
Calochortus macrocarpus (sagebrush mariposa lily)	Bulb	Gr, dF/L	W, C	H, C	Sp, ES	F, P, S	H
Cirsium undulatum (wild thistle)	Taproot	M, mF, Op/L-H	L, C	H, C	Sp, ES	P	H
Claytonia lanceolata (western spring beauty)	Corm	Gr, Sh, mF, saF, Op/L-H	W, C	H, C	ES	F, P, S	H
Erythronium grandiflorum (yellow glacier lily)	Bulb	saF, aM/M-H	W, C	H, C	ES, LS	P, S	H
Fritillaria lanceolata (chocolate lily)	Bulb	Gr, M, mF/L-H	L, I	H, C	ES	P, S	H
Lewisia rediviva (bitterroot)	Taproot	Gr, Sh, Op/L-M	L, I	H, C	Sp, ES	P, S	H
Lilium columbianum (tiger lily)	Bulb	mF, Op/L-H	W, C	H, C	ES, LS	P, S	H
Lomatium macrocarpum (large-fruited desert parsley)	Taproot	Gr, Sg, Op/L-M	L, C	H, C	Sp	F, P, S	H
Potentilla anserina (silverweed)	Rhizome	Gr, M, Wt/L-M	L, C	H, C	LS, Fa	F, P, S	H
Sagittaria latifolia (wapato)	Tuber	Wt/L-M	L, I	H, C	S, ES	P, S	M
Sium suave (water parsnip)	Rhizome	Wt/L-M	L, C	H, C	Sp, ES	F, P	L

[a]Gr—grassland; Sh—shrubs, thickets; Sg—sagebrush; dF—dry forest; mF—moist forest; M—meadow; saF—subalpine forest; aM—alpine meadows; Wt—wetlands; Op—openings, clearings; L—low elevation; M—moderate elevation; H—high elevation. *Source:* Parish et al. 1996.

[b]W—widespread across landscape, L—localized on landscape, C—common in habitat, I—infrequent in habitat. *Source:* Parish et al. 1996.

[c]H—high productivity per plant, C—constant interannual productivity.

[d]Sp—spring, ES—early summer, LS—late summer, Fa—fall. *Sources:* Turner 1997; Turner et al. 1980; Turner et al. 1990.

[e]F—eaten fresh, P—processed prior to consumption, S—stored. *Sources:* Turner 1997; Turner et al. 1980; Turner et al. 1990.

[f]H—high, harvests are increased dramatically with management, and/or management is required for sustained harvests; M—medium, harvests are increased somewhat with management, and/or minimal management is needed for sustained harvests; L—low, does not respond to management, and/or management is not needed to sustain harvests.

[g]Per 100 g fresh weight. * indicates data taken from related species; — indicates no data available. *Sources:* Kuhnlein and Turner 1991; Loewen 1998 (yellow glacier lily); Peacock 1998 (balsamroot). See Table 8.7 for comparison with Dietary Reference Intakes.

In the following sections, we explore the variation inherent in the Northern Plateau plant foods to more fully understand which of these plants had the greatest overall utility and which may have been intensified in the past. In this section, we first describe the general characteristics of the five broad plant categories and then present details on the ecological and nutritional aspects of 43 plant taxa that were widely used in the historic era (Tables 8.2–8.6). For comparison with the nutritional data, we also present Dietary Reference Intake values for active 35-year-old men and women (Table 8.7). In the next section, we use these data to assess the availability, abundance, palatability, and persistence of these 43 taxa, as well as the plant food groups as a whole.

TABLE 8.2. Attributes of Root Foods Used in the Northern Plateau *(Continued)*.

Species (Common Name)	Nutritional Information[g]						
	Food Energy (kcal)	Protein (g)	Fat (g)	Carbohydrates (g)	Vitamin A (RE)	Vitamin C (mg)	Calcium (mg)
Allium cernuum (nodding onion)	—	2.8*	0.2*	—	—	15.0*	29*
Balsamorhiza sagittata (arrow-leaved balsamroot)	52.5	4.1		11.7	—	—	—
Calochortus macrocarpus (sagebrush mariposa lily)	—	2.1*	0.1*	4.0*	—	—	—
Cirsium undulatum (wild thistle)	—	2.9*	—	—	—	—	—
Claytonia lanceolata (western spring beauty)	—	2.0	0.2	22.2	—	—	—
Erythronium grandiflorum (yellow glacier lily)	118	1.3	0	28.1	—	—	—
Fritillaria lanceolata (chocolate lily)	98*	2.9*	0.3*	21.8*	0*	29.0*	10*
Lewisia rediviva (bitterroot)	94	1.6	0.4	21.6	—	27.0	39
Lilium columbianum (tiger lily)	—	—	—	—	—	—	—
Lomatium macrocarpum (large-fruited desert parsley)	190	2.2	1.0	43.5	—	—	80
Potentilla anserina (silverweed)	132	3.1*	0.6*	29.5*	0.2*	—	37
Sagittaria latifolia (wapato)	103	4.7	0.2	20.0	0	5.0	12
Sium suave (water parsnip)	—	—	—	—	—	—	—

Root Foods

Though "roots" are often referred to as a homogeneous group of plant foods, this category actually comprises a number of different botanical structures including true roots, such as the taproot (e.g., balsamroot); modified stems, such as tubers (e.g., wapato), corms (e.g., Indian potato or spring beauty *[Claytonia lanceolata]*); rhizomes (e.g., silverweed *[Potentilla anserina]*); and modified leaves or bulbs (e.g., nodding onion *[Allium cernuum]*) (Table 8.2). Roots are the major storage organ for plant metabolism, storing carbohydrates and other nutrients for growth and perennation (persistence through the nongrowing season).

Plateau peoples collected approximately 35 species of root foods, beginning in spring and continuing throughout the summer and into the fall, depending on species and elevation. Root foods provided a source of concentrated carbohydrates in the form of starches or fructans (e.g., inulin), as well as lesser amounts of vitamins and minerals (Table 8.2). Most roots were processed via roasting, baking, or steaming—in fact, many required processing to increase palatability and digestibility—and were stored for overwintering (Konlande and Robson 1972; Mullin et al. 1997; Peacock 1998).

As a group, roots tend to be highly productive, though the productivity of many root-gathering grounds was enhanced through various management practices (Table 8.2). These include selective harvesting; weeding, tilling and tending; the incidental or intentional replanting of propagules; the rotation of harvesting locales; and periodic landscape burning (Peacock and Turner 2000).

TABLE 8.3. ATTRIBUTES OF COMMON FRUITS AND BERRIES USED ON THE NORTHERN PLATEAU.

Species (Common Name)	Part Used	Habitat/ Elevation[a]	Abundance[b]	Productivity[c]	Season Harvested[d]	Processing/ Storage[e]	Persistence[f]
Amelanchier alnifolia (Saskatoon)	Berry-like pomes	Gr, dF, mF, Op, Dst/L-M	W, C	H, F	LS	F, P, S	H
Fragaria spp. (wild strawberry)	Berry	dF, mF, Op, Dist/L-H	W, C	L, C	ES, LS	F, P, S	M
Prunus virginiana (chokecherry)	Drupe	Gr, dF, Op/L-M	L, C	H, F	LS	F, P, S	M
Ribes inerme, *R. irrigium* (wild gooseberry)	Berry	Wt, MW, Op, Dst/L-M	L, C	H, C	ES, LS	F	L
Rubus idaeus (red raspberry)	Drupelets	Op, Dist, dF, mF/L-H	L, C	H, C	ES, LS	F	M
Rubus parviflorus (thimbleberry)	Drupelets	F, Op, Dst, Wt/L-H	W, C	L, C	LS	F	M
Sambucus cerulea (blue elderberry)	Berry-like fruits	M, mF, Op, Wt/L-M	L, C	H, C	Fa	F, P, S	L
Shepherdia canadensis (soapberry)	Berry	Op, dF, mF/L-H	W, C	H, F	LS, Fa	F, P, S	H
Vaccinium membranaceum (black huckleberry)	Berry	Op, dF, mF/M-H	W, C	H, F	LS	F, P, S	H
Vaccinium oxycoccos (bog cranberry)	Berry	Wt/L-H	L, C	H, C	LS	F	L
Vaccinium parvifolium (red huckleberry)	Berry	Op, mF/L-M	L, I	H, C	LS	F, P, S	M
Viburnum edule (high bush cranberry)	Berry-like fruits	Wt, M, mF/L-M	W, C	H, C	LS	F	L

[a]Gr—grassland; F—forest; dF—dry forest; mF—moist forest; M—meadow; Wt—wetlands; Op—openings, clearings; Dst—disturbed areas; L—low elevation; M—moderate elevation; H—high elevation. *Source:* Parish et al. 1996.

[b]W—widespread across landscape, L—localized on landscape, C—common in habitat, I—infrequent in habitat. *Source:* Parish et al. 1996.

[c]H—high productivity per plant, L—low productivity per plant, C—constant interannual productivity, F—fluctuating interannual productivity.

[d]ES—early summer, LS—late summer, Fa—fall. *Sources:* Turner 1997; Turner et al. 1980; Turner et al. 1990.

[e]F—eaten fresh, P—processed prior to consumption, S—stored. *Sources:* Turner 1997; Turner et al. 1980; Turner et al. 1990.

[f]H—high, harvests are increased dramatically with management, and/or management is required for sustained harvests; M—medium, harvests are increased somewhat with management, and/or minimal management is needed for sustained harvests; L—low, does not respond to management, and/or management is not needed to sustain harvests.

[g]Per 100 g fresh weight. * indicates data taken from related species; — indicates no data available. *Sources:* Kuhnlein and Turner 1991; Loewen 1998 (yellow glacier lily); Peacock 1998 (balsamroot). See Table 8.7 for comparison with Dietary Reference Intakes.

Fruits and Berries

The term refers to the reproductive structures of herbaceous and woody perennials. In succulent fruits, the seeds are surrounded by a fleshy covering that protects them and ensures the perpetuation of the species. This fleshy covering often is appealing to animals and humans, who ingest the fruit and aid in seed dispersal. This plant food category includes fruits known botanically as berries (e.g., wild gooseberry *[Ribes inerme]*), drupes (e.g., chokecherry *[Prunus virginiana]*), drupelets (e.g., raspberry *[Rubus idaeus]*), and pomes (e.g., saskatoon).

Fruits and berries were major contributors to the traditional diets of Plateau peoples (Table 8.3). Throughout the summer and early fall, depending on species and location, people collected more than 50 species of fruits. Some were eaten fresh, but others were processed and stored for winter, providing an important source of calories and vitamin C, as well as other nutrients such as vitamin A (Table 8.3).

Many species of fruits and berries were abundant on the landscape, though there is considerable variation in the productivity of each species (Table 8.3). The cyclical nature of berry production was well understood by Plateau peoples who managed many species to ensure and increase productivity. Several species (e.g., soapberry *[Shepherdia canadensis]*, black huckleberries *[Vaccinium*

TABLE 8.3. Attributes of Common Fruits and Berries Used on the Northern Plateau *(Continued)*.

Species (Common Name)	Nutritional Information[g] Food Energy (kcal)	Protein (g)	Fat (g)	Carbohydrates (g)	Vitamin A (RE)	Vitamin C (mg)	Calcium (mg)
Amelanchier alnifolia (Saskatoon)	90	0.7	1.2	21.4	86	15.7	69
Fragaria spp. (wild strawberry)	54	0.6	0.9	12.5	—	23.8	64
Prunus virginiana (chokecherry)	—	—	—	—	—	30	—
Ribes inerme, R. irrigium (wild gooseberry)	44*	0.9*	0.6*	10.2*	29*	27.1*	25*
Rubus idaeus (red raspberry)	65	0.6	0.8	15.8	13	22.3	—
Rubus parviflorus (thimbleberry)	105	3.1	1.2	24.7	0	78	129
Sambucus cerulea (blue elderberry)	74	3.4	1.2	14.6	—	33.3	25
Shepherdia canadensis (soapberry)	72	1.8	0.7	6.6	—	—	16
Vaccinium membranaceum (black huckleberry)	54	0.6	0.5	13.1	1	6.6	14
Vaccinium oxycoccos (bog cranberry)	—	—	—	—	—	—	—
Vaccinium parvifolium (red huckleberry)	50	0.8	0.5	12.0	8	15.7	22
Viburnum edule (high bush cranberry)	39	0.1	0.4	9.4	6	13.4	24

membranaceum], chokecherries) were pruned during harvest to encourage growth, and others were enhanced by landscape burning (Peacock and Turner 2000).

Green Vegetables

Green vegetables include the stems (e.g., cow parsnip), leaves (e.g., Indian celery *[Lomatium nudicale]*), shoots (e.g., thimbleberry), and buds of herbaceous and woody perennials (Table 8.4). Approximately 18 species of green vegetables were collected through the spring and summer, depending on species and elevation. Most are palatable only in their young stages and, because of the high moisture content, tended to be eaten fresh in season with little or no processing or storage. A few species, such as cow parsnip, were processed, dried, and eaten during the other seasons (Turner et al. 1990). Greens tend to be low in calories, but some species contain significant amounts of other important nutrients (Table 8.4; see Kuhnlein and Turner 1991).

There is considerable variation in the intensity of management that was applied to greens (Table 8.4). Some were selectively harvested as shoots or leaves according to their age, size, and life-cycle stage. In this way, only the above-ground portions of these perennials were selected, allowing the plant to regenerate afterward. Some species were enhanced by picking, which was essentially a form of pruning or coppicing (Peacock and Turner 2000).

Seeds and Nuts

Seeds and nuts are the dry fruits (as opposed to the fleshy fruits described above) of herbaceous and woody perennials. The term *nut* refers to dry fruits with a single seed enclosed by a woody pericarp that does not open (e.g., acorn *[Quercus* spp.*]*, hazelnut *[Corylus cornuta]*). *Seed* refers to reproductive structures that are many-seeded and open to release those seeds (e.g., balsamroot). Seeds of nonflowering plants, such as the conifers (e.g., *Pinus* spp.), mature in the protection of the cone, which opens for seed dispersal.

Throughout the summer and fall, as many as eight species of seeds and nuts from both herbaceous plants and woody perennials were collected from various eleva-

TABLE 8.4. Attributes of Green Vegetables Used on the Northern Plateau.

Species (Common Name)	Part Used	Habitat/ Elevation[a]	Abundance[b]	Productivity[c]	Season Harvested[d]	Processing/ Storage[e]	Persistence[f]
Balsamorhiza sagittata (balsamroot)	Leaves, stems	Gr, Sh, dF, Op/L-H	W, C	H, C	Sp	F, P	M
Epilobium angustifolium (fireweed)	Stems	Op, Dist, F/L-H	W, C	H, C	Sp, ES	F, P	M
Heracleum lanatum (cow parsnip)	Stalks, leaf stems	Wt, Op, mF/L-H	W, C	H, C	Sp, ES	F, P, S	L
Lomatium nudicale (Indian celery)	Shoots, leaves	Gr, M, dF/L-M	L, C	H, C	Sp, ES	F, P	M
Opuntia fragilis (pricklypear cactus)	Stems	Gr, Sg, dF, Op	W, C	H, C	Sp	P, S	L
Rubus parviflorus (thimbleberry)	Shoots	Op, F, Wt/L-H	W, C	H, C	Sp	F, P	M
Typha latifolia (cattail)	Leaves, shoots	Wt/L-M	L, C	H, C	Sp	F, P	L

[a]Gr—grassland; Sh—shrubs, thickets; Sg—sagebrush; F—forest; dF—dry forest; mF—moist forest; M—meadow; Wt—wetlands; Op—openings, clearings; Dst—disturbed areas; L—low elevation; M—moderate elevation; H—high elevation. *Source:* Parish et al. 1996.

[b]W—widespread across landscape, L—localized on landscape, C—common in habitat. *Source:* Parish et al. 1996.

[c]H—high productivity per plant, C—constant interannual productivity.

[d]Sp—spring, ES—early summer. *Sources:* Turner 1997; Turner et al. 1980; Turner et al. 1990.

[e]F—eaten fresh, P—processed prior to consumption, S—stored. *Sources:* Turner 1997; Turner et al. 1980; Turner et al. 1990.

[f]M—medium, harvests are increased somewhat with management, and/or minimal management is needed for sustained harvests; L—low, does not respond to management, and/or management is not needed to sustain harvests.

[g]Per 100 g fresh weight. — indicates no data available. *Sources:* Kuhnlein and Turner 1991; Loewen 1998 (yellow glacier lily); Peacock 1998 (balsamroot). See Table 8.7 for comparison with Dietary Reference Intakes.

tions (Table 8.5). Although the numbers gathered were small relative to those of other food types, nuts and seeds were valued because they provided alternative sources of calories, protein, and fat in the diet (Table 8.5). Processing techniques varied considerably and included husking (e.g., hazelnut), roasting (e.g., whitebark pine *[Pinus albicaulis]*), grinding, and cooking (e.g., balsamroot seeds). Many were stored after processing for winter.

As with greens, there is considerable variation in the degree to which seeds and nuts were managed. Some species benefited from landscape-burning practices, but management tended to be more incidental than intentional. Hazelnut bushes, however, were burned individually to maintain productivity (Peacock and Turner 2000).

Tree Cambium

Tree cambium, or "inner bark," is a thin layer of actively dividing cells beneath the bark that transports water and nutrients to and from the roots and the leaves. The cambium and adjoining phloem tissue of seven species of deciduous and coniferous trees were collected in early spring when the sap began to flow (Table 8.6).

Trees producing edible cambium are widespread and common on the landscape, though cambium can only be harvested during a narrow time window in the early spring. Generally, cambium was eaten fresh with no further processing. Little is known about the nutrient composition of the taxa we examined, but as a food group, cambium is a good source of carbohydrates and other nutrients (Kuhnlein and Turner 1991).

Of the five plant food categories, tree cambium was managed the least intensively (Table 8.6). Management of trees selected for cambium removal was limited to the selective harvesting of individuals of a suitable size and the removal of only portions of the bark and cambium so as not to girdle the tree (Peacock and Turner 2000).

ASSESSING THE CULTURAL UTILITY OF NORTHERN PLATEAU PLANT FOODS

In this section, we explore in more detail the variation in plant foods used by Northern Plateau peoples to understand which plants may have been preferred under different circumstances (for a different approach to assessing cultural preferences, see Turner 1988). To do this, we tally the ecological and nutritional attributes presented in Tables 8.2–8.6 to evaluate the availability, abundance, palatability, and persistence of each plant food and plant food group (Table 8.8). This, in turn, allows us to make comparisons within and among food groups and to compare food groups as a whole. Finally, we combine attri-

TABLE 8.4. Attributes of Green Vegetables Used on the Northern Plateau *(Continued)*.

Species (Common Name)	Nutritional Information[g] Food Energy (kcal)	Protein (g)	Fat (g)	Carbohydrates (g)	Vitamin A (RE)	Vitamin C (mg)	Calcium (mg)
Balsamorhiza sagittata (balsamroot)	—	1.6	0.3	—	—	13.8	173
Epilobium angustifolium (fireweed)	—	6.5	—	2.9	22	88	175
Heracleum lanatum (cow parsnip)	20	0.4	0.2	3.8	7.5	3.5	28
Lomatium nudicale (Indian celery)	—	—	—	—	—	66	37
Opuntia fragilis (pricklypear cactus)	—	—	—	—	—	—	—
Rubus parviflorus (thimbleberry)	22	0.6	0.4	5.5	41	5.9	24
Typha latifolia (cattail)	68	1.7	0.7	—	—	—	133

butes as proxy measures of the overall utility of taxa and food groups and of the intensification potential of taxa and food groups (Table 8.8).

Assessing Availability

We assess spatial availability by examining the habitats and elevations in which the plant could be harvested, temporal availability by season of harvest, and post-harvest availability by whether a plant could be eaten raw and whether the plant food could be stored for future consumption. Thus, a plant that is found in many habitats and at a range of elevations, does not require processing before it can be eaten, and can also be stored for future use would be a highly available source of food. Based on our assessment of availability, there is little difference among plant groups, though fruits and berries tend to be somewhat more available than the others (Table 8.8). Within these groups, some plants, such as spring beauty *(Claytonia lanceolata)* and strawberries *(Fragaria vesca)*, stand out as being particularly available to Northern Plateau peoples.

Assessing Abundance

We assess abundance by whether a plant is widespread or localized on the landscape, whether within its habitats it is generally common or infrequent, how productive the plants tend to be, and by the consistency of harvests from year to year. A plant that is widespread on the landscape, common in its habitat(s), and regularly produces a large supply of its edible parts is an abundant source of food.

In contrast to our measure of availability, our results demonstrate that there is considerable variation in the abundance of plant foods on the Northern Plateau. At the level of plant food groups, greens and roots are the most abundant, whereas seeds and nuts sit on the other end of the continuum (Table 8.8). Within all food groups, with the exception of cambium, there is considerable variation in the abundance of the different species.

Assessing Palatability

In our analysis we use seven nutritional attributes as proxy measures of the palatability of the different plant foods. Calories, protein, fat, and carbohydrates are included because these are considered essential to healthy diets and the values are widely reported in the literature. We also include values for vitamin A, vitamin C, and calcium, for recent research suggests that First Nations populations may be lacking in these nutrients, in part because of the transition from traditional to modern diets (e.g., Godel et al. 1996; Kuhnlein et al. 1996; Moffat 1995; Receuver et al. 1996). In addition, we use processing requirements as another proxy measure of palatability and digestibility. Thus, a plant that ranks high in the seven nutritional attributes without extensive processing might be considered a more valuable source of food than a plant that after extensive processing has only moderate nutritional value.

Our assessment of palatability is based on fresh, raw foods rather than cooked foods because there is considerably more literature on the nutritional values of raw traditional foods. However, this introduces some bias into

TABLE 8.5. ATTRIBUTES OF SEEDS AND NUTS USED ON THE NORTHERN PLATEAU.

Species (Common Name)	Part Used	Habitat/ Elevation[a]	Abundance[b]	Productivity[c]	Season Harvested[d]	Processing/ Storage[e]	Persistence[f]
Balsamorhiza sagittata (balsamroot)	Seeds	Gr, Sh, dF, Op/L-H	W, C	H, F	ES, LS	F, P, S	M
Corylus cornuta (beaked hazelnut)	Nuts	Op, mF/L-M	L, C	H, F	LS, Fa	F, P, S	H
Pinus albicaulis (whitebark pine)	Nuts	Op, dF/M-H	I, C	H, F	LS, Fa	F, P, S	L
Pinus contorta var. *latifolia* (lodgepole pine)	Seeds	F/L-H	W, C	H, F	Fa	F	L
Pinus ponderosa (ponderosa pine)	Seeds	Gr, dF, Op/L-M	W, C	H, F	Fa	F, P, S	L

[a]Gr—grassland; Sh—shrubs, thickets; F—forest; dF—dry forest; mF—moist forest; Op—openings, clearings; L—low elevation; M—moderate elevation; H—high elevation. *Source:* Parish et al. 1996.

[b]W—widespread across landscape, L—localized on landscape, C—common in habitat, I—infrequent in habitat. *Source:* Parish et al. 1996.

[c]H—high productivity per plant, F—fluctuating inter-annual productivity.

[d]ES—early summer, LS—late summer, Fa—fall. *Sources:* Turner 1997; Turner et al. 1980; Turner et al. 1990.

[e]F—eaten fresh, P—processed prior to consumption, S—stored. *Sources:* Turner 1997; Turner et al. 1980; Turner et al. 1990.

[f]H—high, harvests are increased dramatically with management, and/or management is required for sustained harvests; M—medium, harvests are increased somewhat with management, and/or minimal management is needed for sustained harvests; L—low, does not respond to management, and/or management is not needed to sustain harvests.

[g]Per 100 g fresh weight. * indicates data taken from related species; — indicates no data available. *Sources:* Kuhnlein and Turner 1991; Loewen 1998 (yellow glacier lily); Peacock 1998 (balsamroot). See Table 8.7 for comparison with Dietary Reference Intakes.

our analysis, for the food value of some plants changes significantly after processing. This is particularly true of roots containing inulin (rather than starch), which show a dramatic increase in caloric value after cooking. For instance, pit-cooked balsamroot taproots average 140 kcal/100 g (dry basis), whereas 100 g of the raw taproots average only 40 kcal. This represents an energy increase of approximately 250 percent (Peacock 1998).

Our ability to assess palatability is in large part influenced by the limits of the nutritional database on traditional plant foods. For many species, particularly the cambium, seed, and nut taxa, the data are not available to make comparisons among species. For roots, the evaluation of palatability is limited both by the lack of nutritional information in general and by the fact that our tallies are restricted to raw food values.

Another potential limitation in our analysis of palatability is that we have given equal weight to all the nutritional attributes we examined. We did this because we did not want to bias our analysis in the favor of a specific attribute. However, we are aware that at certain times of the year, some nutritional qualities will be far more important than others. For example, after a winter diet of largely dried foods, access to Indian celery *(Lomatium nudicale)* shoots and leaves, which are rich in vitamin C (Table 8.4), may have been valued highly in the spring months. Likewise, the concentrated source of storable calories that whitebark pine and hazelnuts provided in the fall as preparation for the winter months were likely invaluable.

Of the three plant food groups that we can rank, roots are the most desirable based on our palatability proxies, though there is considerable variation among species (Table 8.8). Of the roots, bitterroot, silverweed, and large-fruited desert parsley *(Lomatium macrocarpum)* are the most desirable. Only saskatoons and thimbleberries in the berries and fruits and fireweed *(Epilobium angustifolium)* in the greens come close to the ranking of these two roots.

Assessing Persistence

Finally, we evaluate the persistence of the plants commonly used by Northern Plateau peoples by assessing how responsive each species is to traditional management practices. We base this assessment on our own ecological knowledge as well as the ethnobotanical literature on how actively plants were managed by Northern Plateau peoples (e.g., Peacock 1998; Peacock and Turner 2000; Turner 1999).

Our ranking demonstrates that the root food group as a whole is by far the highest ranked, with all other groups clustering considerably below this ranking (Table 8.8). Internally, there is high consistency in our persistence ranking for roots. All species, expect wapato and water parsnip *(Sium suave),* for which we have little

TABLE 8.5. Attributes of Seeds and Nuts Used on the Northern Plateau *(Continued)*.

Species (Common Name)	Nutritional Information[g]						
	Food Energy (kcal)	Protein (g)	Fat (g)	Carbohydrates (g)	Vitamin A (RE)	Vitamin C (mg)	Calcium (mg)
Balsamorhiza sagittata (balsamroot)	—	—	—	—	—	—	—
Corylus cornuta (beaked hazelnut)	634*	12.6*	62.4*	16.7*	7*	1.0*	209*
Pinus albicaulis (whitebark pine)	568*	11.6*	61.0*	19.3*	3*	2.0*	8*
Pinus contorta var. *latifolia* (lodgepole pine)	—	—	—	—	—	—	—
Pinus ponderosa (ponderosa pine)	—	—	—	—	—	—	—

ethnographic information, were assigned the highest rank for persistence, that is, they are species that may have increased dramatically with management and even required management to sustain harvest yields. The only other species ranked this high are saskatoons, soapberries, and blue huckleberries in the fruits and berries and balsamroot in the seeds and nuts. As a food group, fruits and berries are highly variable internally in terms of their response to management.

Overall Utility Ranking

To make further comparisons within and among plant groups, we combine our four attributes to arrive at a total rank order for each species (Table 8.8). The highest-ranked species are those that, on average, are the most available, abundant, persistent, and palatable. All things being equal, these are the plants people should choose to use most intensively. Though we recognize that such idealized conditions do not always hold, the ranking does provide a standard against which to compare the different plant foods, as well as a model for which plants were used most intensively in the past.

Of the three groups that we can compare, once again, root foods rank considerably higher than fruits and berries or greens. Within the roots, spring beauty and silverweed rank the highest, with wapato on the other end of the continuum. With the exception of wapato, all roots rank higher than the average ranking for either fruits and berries or greens. This suggests that unless there are overriding circumstances (e.g., a dietary shortage of vitamin A, a desire for diversity in the diet), the harvesting and processing of root foods would have been a priority among Northern Plateau plant food gatherers.

Though as a whole the fruits and berries and greens rank lower than roots, there are some species within these groups that compare with root foods. Of the fruits and berries, saskatoons and soapberries especially are comparable to the root foods, but thimbleberries and blue huckleberries also rank highly. Based on our ranking, in contrast, wild gooseberry was likely a lower-priority food among Northern Plateau peoples. Of the greens, fireweed stands out as a food that was likely sought after. Its availability in early spring undoubtedly increased its desirability.

Intensification Ranking

To evaluate the overall potential of plant foods and food groups to be intensified, we tally some of the data presented in Tables 8.2–8.6. Together, these attributes encompass three of the possible pathways to intensification described earlier (see Table 8.8 notes). Only social mechanisms for plant food intensification (expanding trade and kinship relations) are not included in our tallies.

The remaining three pathways are incorporated into our intensification ranking as follows. Cognitive pathways for increasing harvests can be found by harvesting more from more locations or by harvesting more intensively from a single location. Thus, those plants that occur in more habitats, are abundant in those habitats, are available for multiple seasons, and tend to be highly productive are those that can be intensified more easily through a cognitive pathway.

We assess a plant's ability to be intensified through technological pathways by examining its processing requirements and storage qualities. Technological strategies for intensifying production include improved harvesting technology, processing techniques, and preservation tech-

TABLE 8.6. Attributes of Tree Cambium Used on the Northern Plateau.

Species (Common Name)	Part Used	Habitat/ Elevation[a]	Abundance[b]	Productivity[c]	Season Harvested[d]	Processing/ Storage[e]	Persistence[f]
Abies lasiocarpa (subalpine fir)	Cambium	mF/L-M	W, C	7	Sp	F	M
Picea engelmannii (Engelmann spruce)	Cambium	Wt, mF/L-H	W, C	7	Sp	F	M
Pinus albicaulis (whitebark pine)	Cambium	Op, dF/M-H	I, C	7	Sp	F	M
Pinus contorta var. *latifolia* (lodgepole pine)	Cambium	F/L-H	W, C	7	Sp	F, P S	M
Pinus ponderosa (ponderosa pine)	Cambium	Gr, dF, Op/L-M	W, C	7	Sp	F, P S	M
Populus balsamifera ssp. *trichocarpa* (cottonwood)	Cambium	Wt, mF/L-H	W, C	7	Sp	F	M

[a]Gr—grassland; F—forest; dF—dry forest; mF—moist forest; Wt—wetlands; Op—openings, clearings; L—low elevation; M—moderate elevation; H—high elevation. *Source:* Parish et al. 1996.

[b]W—widespread across landscape, C—common in habitat, I—infrequent in habitat. *Source:* Parish et al. 1996.

[c]H—high productivity per plant, L—low productivity per plant, C—constant interannual productivity, F—fluctuating inter-annual productivity.

[d]Sp—spring. *Sources:* Turner 1997; Turner et al. 1980; Turner et al. 1990.

[e]F—eaten fresh, P—processed prior to consumption, S—stored. *Sources:* Turner 1997; Turner et al. 1980; Turner et al. 1990.

[f]M—medium, harvests are increased somewhat with management, and/or minimal management is needed for sustained harvests.

[g]Per 100 g fresh weight. — indicates no data available. *Sources:* Kuhnlein and Turner 1991; Loewen 1998 (yellow glacier lily); Peacock 1998 (balsamroot). See Table 8.7 for comparison with Dietary Reference Intakes.

niques to enhance storage. Thus, in our analysis, plants that require processing before consumption or are processed to enhance palatability, and are preserved for storage, can be intensified via technological pathways. Finally, the potential for intensification through ecological strategies is incorporated into our measure of persistence.

The results of our analysis demonstrate dramatic differences in the potential for different species and different food groups to be intensified (Table 8.8). As a group, root foods have the greatest potential for intensification via different pathways. Spring beauty and balsamroot are the highest ranked within this group, and water parsnip is the lowest. Following roots, to our surprise, is the green vegetables food group. However, the greens with the greatest potential for intensification are similar in ranking to the lowest ranked of the root foods (i.e., bitterroot).

At the level of the food group, berries and fruits and cambium are similar in their rankings, whereas seeds and nuts rank considerably lower than the other groups. Among the berries and fruits, saskatoons, blue huckleberries, and soapberries are ranked well above the other foods in the group and are roughly equivalent to the median value for the root foods (approximately 2.4). As a whole, all groups except cambium have considerable internal variability in their potential for intensification.

In the end, an interplay of the attributes we examine, in combination with cultural factors that we cannot measure, determined how valuable each plant food was to Plateau peoples. We suggest, however, that the foods that consistently rank higher in more attributes are likely to have been preferred. Further, those that have the greatest potential to be intensified are more likely to have been the focus of resource intensification in the past. Our analyses suggest that, in terms of overall importance and potential to be intensified, most roots, some greens, and saskatoons, soapberries, and blue huckleberries were probably preferred over other plant foods. All things being equal, these preferences should be reflected in the archaeological and archaeobotanical records of the Northern Plateau.

THE ARCHAEOLOGICAL EVIDENCE FOR ANCIENT PLANT FOODS

In the following sections we review the archaeological evidence for plant foods on the Northern Plateau. This will ultimately allow us to compare the archaeological evidence for plant use against our predictions about which plants had the greatest overall cultural utility and which were the focus of resource intensification. First, we review the nature of archaeological evidence for ancient plant use, dividing the discussion into direct and indirect

TABLE 8.6. Attributes of Tree Cambium Used on the Northern Plateau *(Continued)*.

Species (Common Name)	Nutritional Information[g]						
	Food Energy (kcal)	Protein (g)	Fat (g)	Carbohydrates (g)	Vitamin A (RE)	Vitamin C (mg)	Calcium (mg)
Abies lasiocarpa (subalpine fir)	—	—	—	—	—	—	—
Picea engelmannii (Engelmann spruce)	—	—	—	—	—	—	—
Pinus albicaulis (whitebark pine)	—	—	—	—	—	—	—
Pinus contorta var. *latifolia* (lodgepole pine)	—	—	—	—	—	—	—
Pinus ponderosa (ponderosa pine)	—	—	—	—	—	—	—
Populus balsamifera ssp. *trichocarpa* (cottonwood)	230	1.9	—	—	—	—	—

evidence. This is followed by a detailed review of the direct and indirect evidence for ancient plant use on the Northern Plateau. Based on these data, we summarize the archaeological evidence for plant food intensification in the region.

The Nature of the Evidence

In assessing the nature of the evidence for past plant use, we use the term *direct evidence* to refer to the recovery of the archaeobotanical remains of plant food parts that were eaten (e.g., tubers or stems), as well as the inedible parts of the food plant that are discarded during consumption (e.g., choke cherry "pits," hazelnut shells). "Indirect evidence" of ancient plant use refers here to the tools and features that were used to harvest, process, or store food plants. Both direct and indirect kinds of evidence have some limitations; however, when taken together, these data provide a more complete picture of ancient plant use.

In the case of "direct evidence," many taphonomic issues constrain our ability to translate archaeobotanical remains into reconstructions of ancient food use. Of particular importance here are four paleoethnobotanical rules of thumb. These are (1) plant parts that are hard and dense (e.g., balsamroot taproots) are more likely to preserve than those that are fleshy and less dense (e.g., raspberry stems); (2) plant foods that are consumed in their entirety (e.g., blue huckleberries) are less likely to be recovered than those that have inedible parts (e.g., the

TABLE 8.7. Dietary Reference Intake for Men and Women.

Variable	Male	Female
Food Energy	2,897 kcal/day	2,233 kcal/day
Protein	58 g/day	42 g/day
Fat	64 g/day (minimum), 113 g/day (maximum)	50 g/day (minimum), 87 g/day (maximum)
Carbohydrates	130 g/day (recommended dietary allowance)	130 g/day (recommended dietary allowance)
Vitamin A	900 mcg/day	700 mcg/day
Vitamin C	90 mg/day	75 mg/day
Calcium	1,000 mg/day	1,000 mg/day

Numbers presented are for active 35-year-old adults, weighing 72 kg (male) and 52 kg (female). Requirements vary considerably depending on factors such as age, weight, physical activity, and physical condition. *Sources:* Institute of Medicine of the National Academies 1999, 2000, 2001a, 2001b, 2002.

TABLE 8.8. Rank of Plants Used on the Northern Plateau Based on Availability, Abundance, Palatability, and Persistence.

Species (Common Name)	Availability[a]	Abundance[b]	Palatability[c]	Persistence[d]	Total Rank[e]	Total Rank Order	Intensification Rank[f]	Intensification Rank Order
Roots								
Allium cernuum (nodding onion)	0.64	1	0.00	1	2.64	7	2.64	3
Balsamorhiza sagittata (arrow-leaved balsamroot)	0.64	1	0.33	1	2.98	5	2.71	2
Calochortus macrocarpus (sagebrush mariposa lily)	0.50	1	0.00	1	2.5	8	2.50	5
Cirsium undulatum (wild thistle)	0.57	0.75	—	1	—	—	2.39	6
Claytonia lanceolata (western spring beauty)	0.79	1	0.67	1	3.54	1	2.79	1
Erythornium grandiflorum (yellow glacier lily)	0.50	1	0.50	1	3	4	2.57	4
Fritillaria lanceolata (chocolate lily)	0.71	0.5	0.43	1	2.64	7	2.29	8
Lewisia rediviva (bitterroot)	0.57	0.5	0.83	1	2.9	6	2.14	9
Lilium columbianum (tiger lily)	0.57	1	—	1	—	—	2.64	3
Lomatium macrocarpum (large-fruited desert parsley)	0.57	0.75	0.80	1	3.12	3	2.32	7
Potentilla anserine (silverweed)	0.64	0.75	0.83	1	3.23	2	2.39	6
Sagittaria latifolia (wapato)	0.36	0.5	0.57	0.5	1.93	9	1.43	10
Sium suave (water parsnip)	0.43	0.75	—	0	—	—	1.18	11
Average (Range)	0.57	0.81	0.50	0.86	2.84 (3.54–1.93)		2.31 (2.79–1.18)	
Fruits and Berries								
Amelanchier alnifolia (saskatoon)	0.71	0.75	0.71	1	3.18	1	2.46	1
Fragaria vesca (wild strawberry)	0.79	0.50	0.50	0.5	2.29	5	1.79	4
Prunus virginiana (chokecherry)	0.57	0.50	—	0.5	—	—	1.57	5
Ribes inerme, R. irrigium (wild gooseberry)	0.64	0.50	0.14	0	1.29	9	1.07	10
Rubus idaeus (red raspberry)	0.71	0.75	0.29	0.5	2.25	6	2.04	3
Rubus parviflorus (thimbleberry)	0.64	0.50	0.86	0.5	2.50	3	1.57	5
Sambucus cerulea (blue elderberry)	0.64	0.75	0.67	0	2.06	10	1.39	8
Shepherdia canadensis (soapberry)	0.71	0.75	0.40	1	2.86	2	2.46	1
Vaccinium membranaceum (black huckleberry)	0.57	0.75	0.14	1	2.46	4	2.32	2
Vaccinium oxycoccus (bog cranberry)	0.50	0.75	—	0	—	—	1.11	9
Vaccinium parvifolium (red huckleberry)	0.43	0.50	0.00	0.5	1.43	8	1.50	7
Virburnum edule (high bush cranberry)	0.50	1.00	0.00	0	1.50	7	1.43	6
Average (Range)	0.62	0.67	0.37	.046	2.18 (3.18–2.06)		1.73 (2.46–1.07)	

shells of whitebark pine nuts); (3) plant foods that are processed for later use (e.g., saskatoons) are more likely to be recovered archaeobotanically because they will be introduced into a greater number of contexts (i.e., associated with harvesting, processing, storage, and consumption); and (4) because charred plants have a far greater chance of surviving in most archaeological contexts, plant parts that are processed, eaten, or disposed of in or near fire (e.g., hearths, earth ovens) are much more likely to survive than those that are not. In sum, this means that theoretically, though all plant food groups could be recovered in the archaeobotanical record of the Northern

TABLE 8.8. Rank of Plants Used on the Northern Plateau Based on Availability, Abundance, Palatability, and Persistence *(Continued)*.

Species (Common Name)	Availability[a]	Abundance[b]	Palatability[c]	Persistence[d]	Total Rank[e]	Total Rank Order	Intensification Rank[f]	Intensification Rank Order
			Green Vegetables					
Balsamorhiza sagittata (arrow-leaved balsamroot)	0.64	1	0.25	0.5	2.4	2	2.1	1
Epilobium angustifolium (fireweed)	0.64	1	0.80	0.5	2.9	1	2.1	1
Heracleum lanatum (cow parsnip)	0.71	1	0.00	0	1.7	3	1.7	3
Lomatium nudicale (Indian celery)	0.57	0.75	—	0.5	—	—	1.8	2
Opuntia fragilis (pricklypear cactus)	0.50	1	—	0	—	—	1.6	4
Rubus parviflorus (thimbleberry)	0.57	1	0.29	0.5	2.4	2	2.1	1
Typha latifolia (cattail)	0.36	0.75	0.50	0	1.6	4	1.1	5
Average (Range)	0.57	0.93	0.41	0.29	2.2 (2.9–1.6)		1.80 (2.1–1.1)	
			Seeds and Nuts					
Balsamorhiza sagittata (arrow-leaved balsamroot)	0.71	0.75	—	0.5	—	—	1.96	1
Corylus cornuta (hazelnut)	0.50	0.25	—	1	—	—	1.75	2
Pinus albicaulis (whitebark pine)	0.50	0.25	—	0	—	—	0.75	5
Pinus contorta (lodgepole pine)	0.43	0.5	—	0	—	—	0.79	4
Pinus ponderosa (ponderosa pine)	0.57	0.5	—	0	—	—	1.07	3
Average (Range)	0.54	0.45	—	0.30	—		1.26 (1.96–0.75)	
			Tree Cambium					
Abies lasiocarpa (subalpine fir)	0.36	0.75	—	0.5	—	—	1.54	5
Picea engelmannii (Engelmann spruce)	0.50	0.75	—	0.5	—	—	1.68	3
Pinus albicaulis (whitebark pine)	0.43	0.75	—	0.5	—	—	1.61	4
Pinus contorta (lodgepole pine)	0.50	0.75	—	0.5	—	—	1.75	2
Pinus ponderosa (ponderosa pine)	0.57	0.75	—	0.5	—	—	1.82	1
Populus balsamifera (cottonwood)	0.50	0	—	0.5	—	—	1.68	3
Average (Range)	0.48	0.75	—	0.50	—		1.68 (1.82–1.54)	

[a]Availability ranking was calculated in two steps: (1) sum four attributes—number of habitats (1 point each, 5 possible) + number of elevations (1 each, 3 possible) + number of seasons (1 each, 4 possible) + whether available fresh and/or can be stored (1 each, 2 possible); (2) divide sum by the total number of possible points. When all cells are filled, the total possible points is 14. For taxa with data missing from some cells, the total number of possible points is calculated by subtracting from 14 the maximum number of points of those cells.

[b]Abundance ranking was calculated in two steps: (1) sum four attributes—abundance on landscape (widespread = 3.5 points, local = 0) + abundance within habitat (common = 3.5, infrequent = 0) + productivity of individual plants (high = 3.5, low = 0) + interannual productivity (constant = 3.5, fluctuating = 0); (2) divide sum by the total number of possible points. When all cells are filled, the total possible points is 14. For taxa with data missing from some cells, the total number of possible points is calculated by subtracting from 14 the maximum number of points of those cells.

[c]Palatability ranking was calculated in three steps: (1) calculate the average value of each nutritional attribute within a food group; (2) assign a rating for each nutritional attribute, based on this average (above average = 2 points, below average = 0); 3) divide sum by the total number of possible points. When all cells are filled, the total possible points is 14. For taxa with data missing from some cells, the total number of possible points is calculated by subtracting from 14 the maximum number of points of those cells. We include in this rating only those taxa that have nutritional data in three or more cells.

[d]Persistence ranking was calculated in two steps: (1) assign points for how responsive a species is to management (high = 14 points, medium = 7, low = 0); (2) divide sum by the total number of possible points. When all cells are filled, the total possible points is 14. For taxa with data missing from some cells, the total number of possible points is calculated by subtracting from 14 the maximum number of points of those cells.

[e]Availability rank + abundance rank + palatability rank + persistence rank.

[f]Availability rank + abundance rank + persistence rank, except that in this calculation of availability, 1 point is given for whether it was processed prior to consumption instead of whether it was consumed fresh.

TABLE 8.9. Direct and Indirect Archaeological Evidence of Major Categories of Plant Foods on the Northern Plateau.

Plant Food Group	Direct Evidence[a]	Indirect Evidence
Roots	Roots	Earth ovens, drying racks, digging sticks, baskets, grinding and pounding tools, garden plots, upper elevation base camps, storage pits[b]
Fruits and Berries	Seeds, possibly fruit "skins"	Baskets, drying racks, log-trench features, storage pits, pounding tools (e.g., chokecherries)
Green Vegetables	Likely none	Knives/cutting tools
Seeds and Nuts	Exocarps, possibly endocarps	Grinding and pounding tools, storage pits, baskets, roasting pits (e.g., for whitebark pine)
Cambium	Likely none	Bark-stripped trees, bark peelers, bark scrapers, drying racks

[a]Listed are those remains that are likely to be found archaeologically given the taphonomic constraints discussed in the text.

[b]See also Thoms 1989.

Plateau, those most likely to be found are roots, fruits and berries, and seeds and nuts (Table 8.9).

With indirect evidence, the strength of the inferences about ancient plant use depends on the specificity of the tool or feature. Thus, the recovery of a bark scraper, specifically designed to scrape cambium from tree bark, is a relatively strong indication of cambium use. However, a hearth or drying rack that may have been used to process the cambium into storable cakes is considerably weaker evidence. For some plant taxa, indirect evidence may be the only way to infer use (Table 8.9), but the inferences are strongest if used in conjunction with direct, archaeobotanical evidence. Comparisons among various lines of indirect evidence as a measure of relative dietary importance are even more difficult than comparisons with direct remains (e.g., How does one compare 200 bark-stripped lodgepole pine trees to 200 earth ovens?).

Direct Evidence of Plant Use. Direct evidence for plant food taxa on the Plateau is somewhat limited, largely because of the dearth of paleoethnobotanical studies in the region. Of the countless number of archaeological excavations in the region, only 30 or so have included paleoethnobotanical analyses (Lepofsky in press). Of this total, almost two-thirds of the studies are from Southern Plateau sites (Table 8.10). Comparisons between the archaeobotanical records of the Northern and Southern Plateau are hampered by the fact that so few paleoethnobotanical studies have been conducted and the sample sizes of most of those studies are severely limited. However, despite the fact that almost twice as many paleoethnobotanical studies have been conducted on the Southern Plateau, only four more plant food taxa have

TABLE 8.10. Summary of Direct Evidence for Plant Food Taxa Recovered from Archaeological Sites on the Northern and Southern Plateau.

	Number of Taxa Recovered[a]	
Plant Food Group	Northern Plateau	Southern Plateau
Roots	1	5
Fruits and Berries	12	10
Green Vegetables	0	0
Seeds and Nuts	3	5
Cambium	0	0
Total	16	20
Number of Paleoethnobotanical Analyses[b]	11	21

[a]Identifications made to the level of genus or species are included in the tallies.

[b]Approximate numbers as of the year 2001. For specific references, see Lepofsky in press.

been recovered in the Southern Plateau analyses. This suggests that paleoethnobotanical analyses from Northern Plateau sites are likely to be as productive as those from the Southern Plateau are.

To date, over 100 taxa of plant species have been identified on the Northern and Southern Plateau. These come from a variety of site types located in a range of environments and represent foods that were eaten in season and those that were stored for future use (Lepofsky in press). The majority of identified taxa come from the few paleoethnobotanical studies with relatively large samples sizes (Lepofsky 2000a; Stenholm 1985; Wollstonecroft 2000,

TABLE 8.11. Direct and Indirect Plant Food Remains Recovered from Northern Plateau Sites.

Species (Common Name)	Direct Evidence	Indirect Evidence[a]	Sources[b]
Roots		earth ovens	1, 2, 6, 8, 15, 16, 17, 19, 20, 22, 23, 24, 25
		digging sticks	5, 7, 28, 29, 30
		mortar and pestle	26, 27
Lomatium sp. (lomatium)	root tissue	–	14[c]
Liliaceae	root tissue	–	8
Allium sp. (onion)	root tissue	–	8, 14[c], 31, 32
Fruits and Berries		–	
Amelanchier alnifolia (saskatoon)	seeds, fruit "skins"	–	3, 8, 10, 11, 13, 18, 21, 31, 32
Arctostaphylos uva-ursi (kinnikinik)	seeds	–	3, 8, 9, 11, 13
Cornus stolonifera (red-osier dogwood)	seeds?	–	9, 11, 13, 21, 31, 32
Crataegus sp. (hawthorn)	seeds	–	9, 10
Prunus sp. (cherry)	seeds	–	8, 9, 11, 12, 13, 18, 21, 31, 32
Ribes sp. (gooseberry/currant)	seeds	–	9, 11, 13, 31, 32
Rosa sp. (rose)	seeds	–	11, 13
Rubus sp. (thimbleberry/raspberry)	seeds	–	9, 10, 12, 18, 21, 31, 32
Sambucus sp. (elderberry)	seeds	–	3, 8, 9, 10, 11, 13
Smilacina sp. (Solomon's seal)	seeds	–	11, 13
Vaccinium sp. (blueberry/huckleberry)	seeds	–	7, 18, 31, 32
Green Vegetables	–	–	–
Opuntia sp. (pricklypear cactus)	–	seeds	11, 13
Seeds and Nuts			
Corylus cornuta (hazelnut)	"nut shell"	–	31, 32
Pinus albicaulis (whitebark pine)	"nut shell"	–	3, 18
Pinus ponderosa (ponderosa pine)	"nut shell"	–	31, 32
Cambium		bark peeler, bark scraper	6, 29
Pinus contorta (lodgepole pine)	–	bark-stripped trees	28
Pinus ponderosa (ponderosa pine)	–	bark-stripped trees	28

[a]Indirect remains that features that cannot be linked to a plant food group and were used for diverse tasks (e.g., storage pits, baskets, and drying racks) are not included.

[b]1. Alexander et al. 1985; 2. Baker 1974; 3. Cousins 2000; 4. Eldridge 1996; 5. Eldridge and Stryd 1983; 6. Hayden 2000a; 7. Hayden and Schulting 1997; 8. Ketcheson 1979, 9. Lepofsky 1988; 10. Lepofsky 1990; 11. Lepofsky 2000a; 12. Lepofsky et al. 1987; 13. Lepofsky et al. 1996; 14. Lyons 2000; 15. Magne 1984; 16. Magne 1985; 17. Magne and Matson 1984; 18. Mathewes 1980; 19. Matson and Alexander 1980; 20. Matson et al. 1980; 21. Nicholas et al. 1997; 22. Peacock 1998; 23. Peacock 2002; 24. Pokotylo and Froese 1983; 25. Rousseau et al. 1991; 26. Smith 1899; 27. Smith 1900; 28. Stryd 1972; 29. Stryd 1973; 30. Stryd 1983; 31. Wollstonecroft 2000; 32. Wollstonecroft 2002.

[c]Possible identifications based on gross morphology. Scanning electron microscopy not used.

2002). Most of the taxa are represented as charred and uncharred woods, though seeds and tissues are also recovered in abundance. Of the plant food groups, fruits and berries dominate the remains, whereas direct evidence for cambium and green vegetables is entirely lacking (Table 8.11).

Of the plant foods recovered on the Northern Plateau specifically, fruits and berries dominate the archaeobotanical record (Table 8.11). Of these, the remains of saskatoon berries are the most ubiquitous and abundant—a pattern that is paralleled at many Southern Plateau sites. At the pithouse village of Keatley Creek, seeds identified to the Ericaceae (heath) family, which may represent blueberries/huckleberries (cf. Wollstonecroft 2000, 2002), are more common than saskatoon berry seeds. The remaining ten taxa are generally recovered in smaller amounts, though some, such as cherry and *Rubus* spp., are found in small numbers at many sites. The remaining plant food groups are poorly represented in these analyses.

Patterning in the archaeobotanical record of the Northern Plateau reflects a combination of taphonomy, paleoethnobotanical expertise, sample size, and cultural preference. The absence of cambium and green vegetables is at least in part caused by the fact that these plants' parts are unlikely to preserve in the archaeobotanical record. In contrast, many root foods should preserve, yet only two root taxa have been identified. The paucity of root remains likely reflects the fact that root identification often requires special identification techniques not widely used by paleoethnobotanists (e.g., scanning electron microscopy [SEM]; cf. Wollstonecroft 2000, 2002). Until more studies actively seek to identify root tissues, we cannot assess the role of root foods from direct archaeobotanical remains. Finally, seeds and nuts and fruits and berries (represented by their seeds) have a good chance of survival in the archaeobotanical record (Table 8.9) and are relatively easy to identify with simple identification techniques. Thus, the ubiquity of these plants food categories in Northern Plateau sites probably more closely represents cultural preference than findings in the other food categories.

In addition to taphonomic problems, sample sizes severely limit our ability to detect patterning in the use of plant foods. Only the sample of fruits and berries is large enough to *begin* to discern cultural preferences. Within this category, the ubiquity and abundance of saskatoon seeds suggest that the berry was a preferred food (though it may be somewhat overrepresented in the record because it was processed for winter stores). Today, saskatoons are one of the most widely used berries among Northern Plateau First Nations (Parish et al. 1996:55). For all other plant food groups, a considerably larger sample of remains, collected systematically from a range of contexts, is needed before we can sort out cultural preference. Given these limitations, indirect evidence necessarily plays a central role in our reconstructions of ancient plant use on the Northern Plateau.

INDIRECT EVIDENCE. The indirect evidence for plant foods in Northern Plateau sites is weighted toward root foods and to a lesser extent cambium use (Table 8.11). Thus, indirect evidence complements the direct archaeobotanical remains, which tend to be weighted in favor of fruits and berries and seeds and nuts.

Root Foods

Earth ovens used to process a variety of roots (Table 8.2) are the most visible indirect indicators of root use. In fact, on the Northern Plateau, it was the fortuitous discovery of numerous earth ovens in the Upper Hat Creek Valley (Pokotylo and Froese 1983) that prompted Northern Plateau archaeologists to follow Ames and Marshall's (1980) lead and include root foods in models of cultural development. Most recently, Peacock (1998) has synthesized the ecological, ethnobotanical, and archaeological evidence for root processing on the Northern Plateau, developing a model for the intensification of root food production in the region.

Earth ovens have been recorded at a variety of Northern Plateau sites. They are visible on the ground surface as depressions of varying diameter and depth, often with a well-defined rim crest (for descriptions, see Hayden and Cousins, this volume; Peacock 1998; Pokotylo and Froese 1983; Thoms 1989). The larger pithouse villages contain some earth ovens, but their numbers are few relative to the numbers of pithouses (Hayden and Cousins, this volume; Stryd 1973). The majority of earth ovens have been recorded from a series of upland meadows where one or more root foods grow in abundance and where peoples gathered to harvest and process those resources (Baker 1974; Magne 1984, 1985; Matson and Alexander 1980; Peacock 1998, 2002; Pokotylo and Froese 1983; Rousseau and Howe 1987; Rousseau et al. 1991). Although upland root-collecting and -processing activities are relatively well documented in the ethnographic and ethnobotanical literature (Alexander et al. 1985; Dawson 1891; Steedman 1930; Teit 1900; Turner et al. 1990), only a handful of such locales has been investigated archaeologically. These sites are characterized by concentrations of earth ovens used to process the root resources, associated base camps, a variety of lithic tool types, assorted faunal remains, and storage facilities, reflecting lengthy and repeated use of the upland areas for root gathering and other activities. In all, investigations at four locales on the Fraser, Thompson, and Chilcotin Plateau have yielded 178 sites containing 453 earth ovens that vary in age, size, and shape but are generally consistent with the ethnographic record (Table 8.11; see Peacock 1998). Of these, only 33 oven features have been excavated, providing a series of 30 radiocarbon age estimates ranging from cal. 3300 B.P. to the historic period (Figure 8.1). We explore trends in the number and size of earth ovens in the following section.

Although the archaeological remains of these oven features conform well to ethnographic expectations regarding prehistoric patterns of root processing, the definitive identification of earth ovens as root-processing features requires the identification of charred root remains. However, despite the fact that hundreds of earth oven features have been recorded on the Northern Plateau, only three studies have attempted to identify paleoethnobotanical remains from the 33 excavated features themselves (Hayden and Cousins, this volume; Ketcheson 1979; Peacock 2002). None of these studies used SEM to aid in the identification of unknown tissues, and all have limited sample sizes. Given the enormous quantity of charcoal in these features, and the fact that the foods to be cooked were often placed within containers or between wet foliage used for lining the cooking pit, the chances of charring

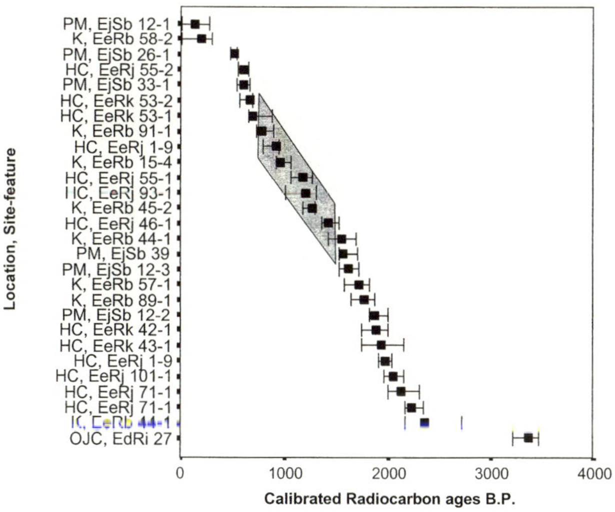

Figure 8.1. Calibrated ages of earth ovens from upland meadows on the Northern Plateau (data from Peacock 1998). The gray area between 1500 and 800 B.P. highlights a reduction in the number of dated ovens relative to before and after this time. Calibrations were done with CALIB Radiocarbon Calibration Program (version 4.3 for MacIntosh; see Stuiver and Reimer 1993; Stuiver et al. 1998). Bars represent minimum and maximum ages at one standard deviation; in cases where there are multiple intercepts, the central intercept is illustrated.

are reduced. Therefore, large sample sizes are required to increase the likelihood of finding charred root remains.

Additional indirect evidence for root harvesting comes from antler handles from digging sticks likely used to harvest roots. A few such handles have been recovered from pithouse sites in the Northern Plateau (Hayden and Schulting 1997; Stryd 1972, 1983). The earliest dated handle comes from a pithouse site dating to 2400 B.P. (Eldridge and Stryd 1983).

Pecked and ground-stone pestles, present on the Northern Plateau in small quantities between 4500 and 2500 B.P., may also be indirect indicators of root food use. On the Southern Plateau, pestles and hopper mortar bases are linked to the pounding and grinding of tough, fibrous roots (Chatters and Pokotylo 1998; Reid 1991a), and these artifacts may have served a similar purpose on the Northern Plateau. As of yet, pestles have not been recovered from later contexts (Richards and Rousseau 1987:89, table 8).

Cambium

Indirect evidence of cambium use on the Northern Plateau is in the form of tools and bark-stripped pine trees (Table 8.11). A bark peeler, used to cut and peel bark from the tree, and one sap scraper, used to scrape cambium from the bark, were recovered from two late prehistoric pithouse villages (Hayden 2000b; Stryd 1973). Other such artifacts may exist in the record of the Northern Plateau, but some researchers may not readily recognize these artifact types.

Far more prevalent evidence for cambium use comes from the bark-stripped pine trees from which cambium has been extracted from one or more strips of bark. Bark-stripped lodgepole pine trees *(Pinus contorta)* are common throughout the Northern Plateau in regions where the tree grows (Stryd 1997). Hundreds of such trees have been observed and recorded by archaeologists in the past decade, though few researchers have tried to compile the data into a meaningful data set (cf. Prince 2001). Stryd (1997) notes that bark-stripped ponderosa pine trees *(Pinus ponderosa)* also occur throughout the region, though they have not been recorded.

Though bark-stripped pines are commonly observed in today's forests, we can make only limited inferences about the dietary importance of cambium in the precontact era. A fundamental limitation is our ability to convert tree scars into the amount of cambium harvested. However, it is more important that, because lodgepole pines rarely live more than 300 years (Parish et al. 1996), very few bark-stripped pines will date to the precontact era. Prince (2001) has demonstrated that mobility patterns of groups north of the Northern Plateau influence the intensity with which cambium is harvested from any single location. However, the relative contribution of cambium in the diet of groups that are mobile versus those that are semisedentary is unknown.

Seeds and Nuts

Indirect evidence for the consumption of seeds and nuts consists of a limited number of grinding and pounding implements (e.g., pestles, grinding slabs; see Richards and Rousseau 1987; Smith 1899, 1900), although, as mentioned, these may represent root-processing tools. The relative paucity of such artifacts on the Northern Plateau, when compared with assemblages on the Southern Plateau (Aikens 1993; Ames and Marshall 1980; Ames et al. 1998; Galm and Matsen 1985; Thoms 1989), may reflect the lower number of seed and nut food species in the north.

ARCHAEOLOGICAL EVIDENCE OF CULTURAL UTILITY AND THE INTENSIFICATION OF PLANT FOODS

Despite our efforts to compile the archaeological evidence of ancient plant use, our ability to evaluate the overall utility and intensification potential of plant foods is restricted by the many limitations of the current archaeobotanical record. In the case of overall cultural utility, the limited archaeobotanical data can be used to suggest only that among the berries, saskatoon, *Rubus* sp., and *Vaccinium* sp. were used most often and, thus, were preferred in many instances. For other plants and plant food groups, however, the data are too sparse to evaluate cultural preferences.

When evaluating intensification potential, we are on slightly firmer ground. Of the four pathways for intensification outlined earlier, there is presently only sufficient evidence to track technological strategies—as represented by root-processing facilities—on the Northern Plateau. Finding evidence of ecological strategies for intensification in the Pacific Northwest is proving extremely difficult (Lepofsky et al. 2003; Lepofsky et al. in press) and, to our knowledge, has not been attempted for the Northern Plateau. Evidence of social strategies is limited to one possible example of traded plant foods (Wollstonecroft 2000)—hardly evidence of intensification. Finally, discerning evidence of a cognitive shift in plant food collecting, particularly an increase in the amount of plant foods harvested or in the kinds of foods that were taken, requires a far more complete record than is currently available. Thus, although indirect evidence allows us to make limited inferences about possible shifts in the utilization of root foods through time, there are no data to allow inferences about changes in the use of the other food groups or about changes in the use of any specific species.

Evidence for the Intensification of Root Foods

As is evident from several chapters here (Hayden and Cousins, this volume; Kuijt and Prentiss, this volume), researchers are increasingly recognizing the importance of "root foods" in Plateau social and economic systems. Many argue that it is not just the consumption of roots but, rather, the "intensification" of root foods that is inextricably linked to other significant social and economic changes in Plateau prehistory. In the following section, we carefully scrutinize the evidence for shifts in the use of root foods through time. To do this, we analyze the variation in upland earth oven size and number through time and across the Northern Plateau. Despite the small number of dated earth ovens from the uplands (approximately 7 percent of recorded ovens), the data reveal trends in root use during the late prehistoric (for a discussion of the limits of this data set, see Peacock 1998). In the following section, we assume that the number of dated earth ovens roughly reflects the number of ovens used, though we recognize that a plethora of taphonomic factors likely influences the number of ovens dated.

The radiocarbon dates from ovens from four upland valleys indicate that root-collecting and -processing activities began sometime before 3,300 years ago and were well under way by 2400 B.P. (Figure 8.1). These data are not likely to represent the oldest ovens but, rather, periods when ovens were built and used regularly enough to leave a patterned record (Thoms 1989). By 2,400 years ago, people of the region began to intensify their use of root foods through technological strategies in a manner consistent with ethnographic practices. By pit cooking roots in earth ovens, Northern Plateau peoples increased their production of root foods by (1) increasing diet breadth through the conversion of raw, inedible species (e.g., balsamroot) into cooked, highly nutritious ones; (2) increasing the nutritional value and palatability of already edible species (e.g., yellow glacier lily); and (3) facilitating preservation for storage. Thus, the initiation of pit cooking represents an intensification of production over noncooked roots or roots processed in other ways.

Although the distribution of dated earth ovens after 2400 B.P. indicates that ovens continued to be used throughout the late prehistoric, use was not constant over this time (Figure 8.1). A close examination of the dates indicates that relatively more ovens were being used from 2400 to 1500 B.P. than from 1500 to 800 B.P. After 800 B.P., the frequency of dated ovens resumes pre-1500 B.P. levels. This shift in numbers of ovens over time is illustrated by the change in "slope" of dated ovens (i.e., a steeper slope indicates more dated ovens; see Figure 8.1). This trend is more clearly illustrated when the difference between the age of each oven is subtracted from the age of the next younger oven. Plotting these differences against time gives a visual representation of the frequency of earth oven use over time (Figure 8.2). Plotted in this way, the data demonstrate that between 1500 and 800 B.P. there are fewer dated features and relatively larger gaps in time between dated features than before or after this period. Taken together, these data suggest that between 1500 and 800 B.P., Northern Plateau peoples were cooking relatively fewer roots in the uplands than at other times in the late prehistoric.

In addition to the number of ovens used, we evaluate changes in intensity of root use by examining changes in oven size through time and across space. Comparing the four upland locations where earth oven diameters have been measured, the mean diameters range from as large as 4.3 m at Upper Hat Creek to as small as 2.11 m at Potato Mountain (Table 8.12; Figures 8.3–8.4). As a group, the mean diameters differ significantly from each other (Analysis of Variance, $p = 0.00$). Between-group comparisons of diameters reveal that the earth ovens from Upper Hat Creek Valley are on average significantly larger than those at Komkanetkwa ($p = 0.00$, Tamhane post hoc test for uneven variances), which in turn are similar in size to those at Oregon Jack Creek ($p = 0.977$). Despite these statistical differences, however, it is impor-

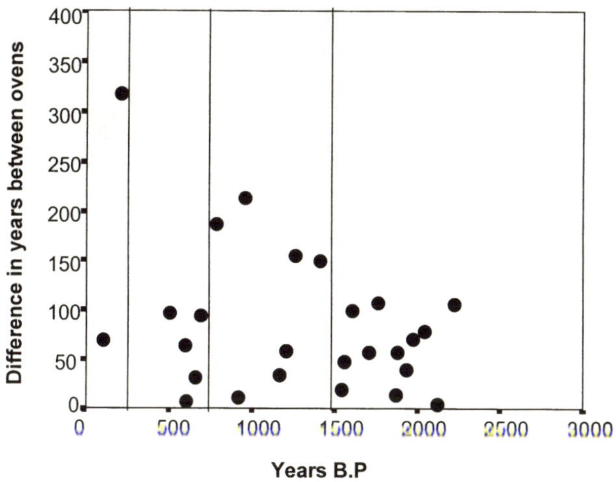

Figure 8.2. The difference (in number of years) between sequentially aged earth ovens plotted against time. Lines dividing the plot distinguish times of relatively more (2500–1500 B.P. and 800 B.P. to the historic period) or fewer (1500–800 B.P.) earth ovens. We have eliminated the outlier data point representing the 1,100-year difference in age between the oldest oven from Oregon Jack Creek (3200 B.P.) and the next younger oven from Komkanetkwa to facilitate interpretations of the data. See text for further explanation.

tant to note that both Komkanetkwa and Oregon Jack Creek also have large earth ovens, and, in fact, the largest recorded ovens occur at Komkanetkwa, not Upper Hat Creek (Figure 8.2). Finally, earth ovens from Potato Mountain are smaller than those from the other three locations ($p = 0.00$ in all three comparisons), though the small sample size limits our ability to make definitive inferences.

Several factors may have influenced these apparent differences in earth oven size across the region. The overall size of the earth oven may reflect the quantities of roots being processed (e.g., Teit 1900), or it may reflect the number of times it was refurbished and reused (Pokotylo and Froese 1983), with the larger features having been reused the most often. Alternatively, the size of the earth oven may be related to the qualities of the roots being processed. Larger ovens may have been used for roots containing inulin (e.g., balsamroot), a complex carbohydrate, which requires longer cooking times—and thus larger heating surfaces—than roots containing starch (e.g., spring beauty). This likely explains the presence of the smaller ovens at Potato Mountain, which, according to the Tsilhqot'in elders, was primarily a spring beauty–harvesting area (Alexander et al. 1985). We cannot yet explain the extreme range of oven sizes at the other three localities, but a combination of the above factors, as well as a myriad of social reasons, likely influenced the form of the ovens.

Examined across time, the existing data also suggest some temporal variation in oven size. Although there is no relationship between oven size and the age of the features when all four localities are considered (regression $r^2 = 0.087$, $p = 0.127$, $n = 28$; see Figure 8.4), when the consistently small Potato Mountain features and the single Oregon Jack Creek feature are removed from the sample, there is a significant positive relationship between size and earth oven age (regression $r^2 = 0.351$, $p = 0.005$, $n = 21$; see Figure 8.5; see also Peacock 1998). However, an examination of the distribution of feature sizes indicates that this relationship is being driven by a few small ovens dating to late in the sequence. Prior to about 800 years ago, there is no correlation between age and size (regression $r^2 = 0.115$, $p = 0.167$, $n = 18$; see Figure 8.5). Thus, for much of the sequence, earth ovens are both large and medium sized (≥ 3.5 m diameter), and after 800 B.P. they are all small (≤ 3.5 m diameter).

Though we have not conducted a comparable analysis of roasting features in lowland village sites, data reported by Hayden and Cousins (this volume) provide some insights into how changes observed in upland root use paralleled changes in lowland villages. Few roasting pits in lowland villages have been dated, and even fewer have been analyzed in detail. However, the existing data indicate that ovens were first associated with large villages dating approximately cal. 1,400 years ago. Ovens found at the Keatley village tend to be large, on par with the large features found in the uplands, though ones from the nearby Fountain site village are described as small (Canadian Archaeological Radiocarbon Database, www.canadianarchaeology.com/radiocarbon/card/card.htm). After this time, the extremely sparse sample from the Keatley site suggests a decline in oven size. These preliminary data suggest that roots begin to be processed at village sites at a time when there were relatively fewer ovens being used in the uplands. It is tempting to speculate that this in turn represents a shift in the way resources were processed and shared. Notably, these changes in root use and processing correspond temporally with the formation of large, aggregated pithouse villages in the region (Kuijt and Prentiss, this volume; Peacock 1998, 2002; Prentiss and Kuijt, this volume).

Putting together the data on the size and number of ovens in the upland meadows and lowland villages, the intensity of root use (as represented by earth ovens) has not been constant through time or across space. The evidence for intensification (and "disintensification") of root resources can be summarized as follows (Figure 8.6):

1. There is an intensification of upland root use beginning 2400 B.P., as represented by an increase in the number of earth ovens.
2. Between 2400 and 1500 B.P., upland root use remained constant. Both large and medium-sized ovens were used, with a tendency toward the use of larger (> 5 m diameter) ovens. This suggests

TABLE 8.12. Summary of Dated Earth Oven Sites from the Northern Plateau.

Locality	Number of Root Processing Sites	Number of Earth Ovens	Median Rim Crest Diameter	Mean ± Standard Deviation Rim Crest Diameter	Number of Excavated Earth Ovens	Number of Dates from Earth Ovens
Komkanetkwa, Thompson Plateau	61	170	3.52 m (n = 150)	3.51 ± 1.20 (n = 150)	11	10
Upper Hat Creek, Fraser/ Thomspon Plateau[a]	44	81	4.23 m (n = 84)	4.3 ± 1.31 (n = 84)	15	13
Oregon Jack Creek, Fraser/Thompson Plateau[b]	38	100	3.00 m (n = 39)	3.35 ± 1.25 (n = 39)	1	1
Potato Mountain, Chilcotin Plateau[c]	35	102	2.00 m (n = 6)	2.11 ± 0.42 (n = 6)	6	6
Total	178	453	279	279	33	30

Source: Peacock 1998.
[a]Pokotylo and Froese 1983.
[b]Rousseau et al. 1991.
[c]Alexander et al. 1985.

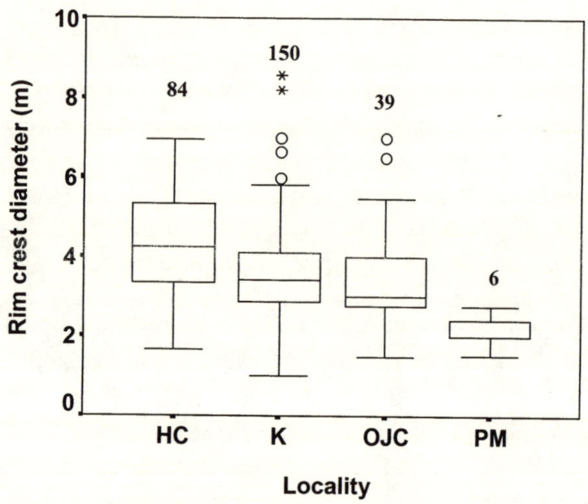

Figure 8.3. Box plots of median rim crest diameter for measured earth ovens from Komkanetkwa (K), Upper Hat Creek (HC), Oregon Jack Creek (OJC), and Potato Mountain (PM). Sample sizes are presented above the box plots (from Peacock 1998).

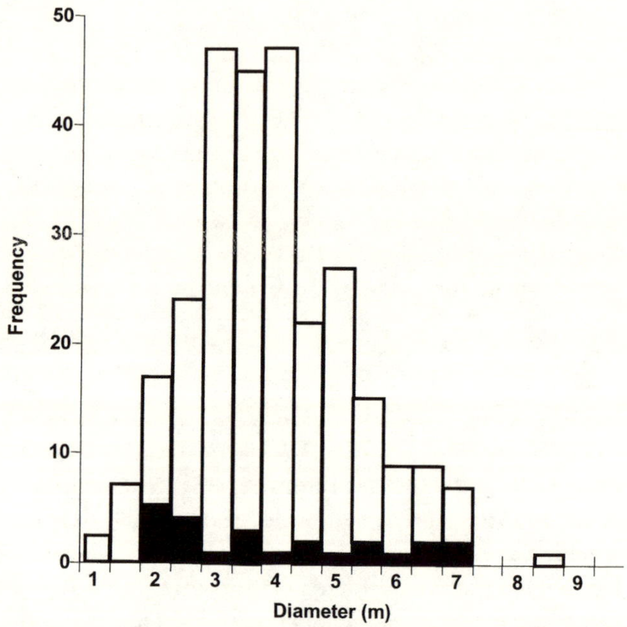

Figure 8.4. Frequency of rim crest diameters from ovens from Komkanetkwa, Upper Hat Creek, Oregon Jack Creek, and Potato Mountain (N= 279; from Peacock 1998). The area filled at the bottom of the bars represents the number of ovens at that size class that have been radiocarbon dated.

that large groups typically came together to process root foods in the upland meadows. There are no data to inform about root use in lowland villages.

3. Between 1500 and 800 B.P., the number of upland ovens declined, but the size of ovens stayed constant (between 3.5 and 7 m diameter). All other factors being equal (e.g., population numbers, species being processed), this suggests a relative decline in upland root use but that large groups continued to come together to process root foods. In the large lowland pithouse villages, there is some indication that ovens tended to be large, at least at the site of Keatley Creek. The decline in the number of ovens in the upland and the beginnings of oven use in large villages are likely linked to other regionwide social and economic shifts.
4. After 800 B.P., oven size decreased dramatically; however, there is some indication that this was coupled with an increase in the *number* of ovens being used relative to the preceding period. Given the small number of dated ovens, we cannot confidently evaluate whether there was an absolute downward shift in the intensity of root use or whether people compensated for the decrease in oven size by build-

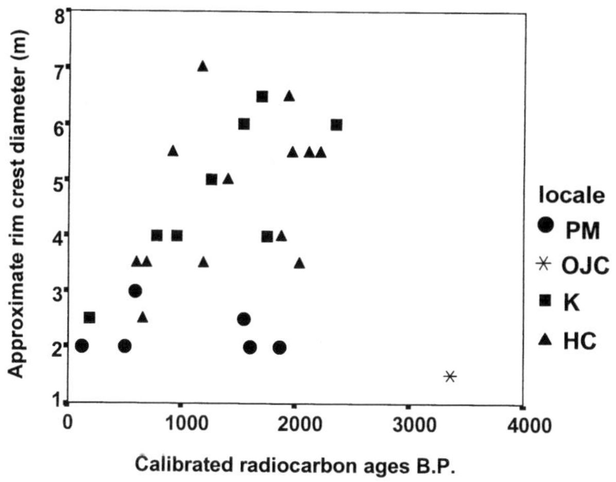

Figure 8.5. Diameters of dated earth ovens from upland meadows on the Northern Plateau (Komkanetkwa [K], Upper Hat Creek [HC], Oregon Jack Creek [OJC], and Potato Mountain [PM]) plotted against time (data from Peacock 1998). Note the presence of large and medium-sized ovens prior to 800 B.P. and the decline in oven size after that time.

ing more ovens. The large number of ovens < 3.5 m in diameter in the uplands (Figure 8.4) lends support to the latter scenario. The shift in oven size and number correlates temporally with the appearance of smaller pithouses and smaller communities in the region. Smaller ovens in the uplands may also suggest the aggregation of smaller social groups.

DISCUSSION

The need and desire to produce more food—whether to compensate for times of stress, to feed increasing populations, or to meet increasing social demands—were likely pervasive among Plateau societies at various times throughout the past. In this chapter we have explored the potential role of plant foods in meeting these needs. We began our essay with a discussion about four pathways to plant food intensification available to Northern Plateau peoples: cognitive, social, technological, and ecological. Encompassed within each of these pathways are different strategies that could have been applied to different plant species at different times in the seasonal and social cycles.

Throughout the chapter we have tried to use language that reflects our understanding that people are active players in human–plant interactions. We recognize that the choices that people made about their use of plant foods were dependent on a range of factors—only some of which we can assess in a general discussion such as this. To better understand these complex choices, and ultimately to evaluate the potential of plants for resource intensification, we have characterized the five plant food groups and a selection of taxa within them according to their availability, abundance, palatability, and persistence. Incorporated into these four categories are ecological and nutritional attributes that likely influenced people's choices about plant food use. Undoubtedly, Plateau peoples constantly reevaluated the relative import of these four categories depending on ever changing social and economic needs.

Our review of 43 roots, fruits and berries, seeds and nuts, greens, and cambium revealed great variability in availability, abundance, palatability, and persistence. In general, we found that among food groups there is little difference in availability but that some plants within these groups, such as spring beauty and strawberries, are considerably more available than other plant foods. If abundance, on the other hand, was a prime concern in resource selection, then greens and roots should have been the most highly sought-after food groups, though not all taxa within these groups would meet these needs. Nuts and seeds, which tend not to be abundant, may not have been as highly valued under these circumstances.

If nutritional needs or responsiveness to management were driving people's decisions about plant foods, then, once again, roots as a whole should have been preferred. However, within this group some foods, such as bitterroot, will meet people's needs better than foods such as onions or wapato. Among the fruits and berries and green vegetables, only saskatoon berries, thimbleberries, and fireweed shoots come close to the overall nutritional value of the most nutritious root foods, while saskatoons, soapberries, and black huckleberries respond well to management.

Finally, when we combine attributes to examine both overall ranking and the potential for intensification via one of the four pathways, we find that, once again, root foods as a group, and many species in particular, should be preferred in many harvesting and processing circumstances. Saskatoon berries, soapberries, thimbleberries, and blue huckleberries compare favorably with roots, as do fireweed shoots. In many circumstances, these species should have been preferentially sought after in the past.

Unfortunately, our ability to compare our predictions about food preferences and intensification potential to the archaeological record is hampered by the limited archaeological evidence for ancient plant use. Certain plant food groups and particular species will always be more evident in the record; some species will be represented by both direct and indirect remains, whereas others, such as greens, are unlikely to be represented at all.

Despite these potential biases, or perhaps because of them, we do see some concordance between our expectations and the archaeological record. The most obvious area of agreement is the evidence for root foods, which we predict should have been preferred in many instances. The archaeological record of earth ovens indicates that

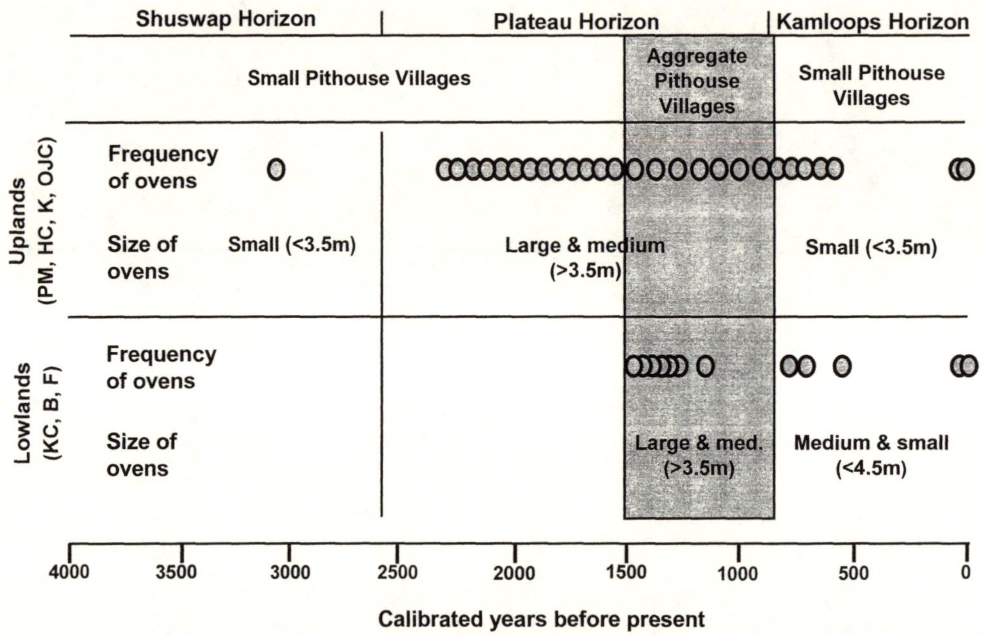

Figure 8.6. Shifts in the intensification of root resources as represented by the number and size of earth ovens located in upland harvesting locales and in lowland village sites. For upland sites, K = Komkanetkwa, HC = Upper Hat Creek, OJC = Oregon Jack Creek, and PM = Potato Mountain. For village sites, KC = Keatley Creek, B = Bell, and F = Fountain. Each dot associated with the frequency of ovens represents the midpoint of one calibrated radiocarbon date from an oven feature. For upland ovens, see Figure 8.1 for radiocarbon dates and Figure 8.5 for oven sizes. Radiocarbon dates and the size of village ovens come from Hayden and Cousins (this volume) and Richards and Rousseau (1987). These were calibrated using CALIB Radiocarbon Calibration Program (version 4.3 for MacIntosh; see Stuiver and Reimer 1993; Stuiver et al. 1998). Note the decline in the number of ovens in the uplands beginning in 1500 B.P. and the corresponding appearance of ovens in the large villages of Keatley, Fountain, and Bell. After 800 B.P, oven size declined, but in the uplands there was an increase in the relative number of ovens.

some root foods began to be processed intensively around 2400 B.P., a practice that continued, with some variation in scale and intensity, until the historic period. Which roots were used most often remains to be determined through careful paleoethnobotanical analyses, though our analyses suggest that spring beauty and balsamroot should be among the most common remains. Determining whether there was a shift in intensification of root use in later prehistory, and how root production relates to other social and economic changes, requires a larger sample of dated earth oven features from more locations throughout the Plateau.

Of our limited evidence for the consumption of berries and fruits, we find some support for a preference for saskatoons, thimbleberries, and black huckleberries. Because thimbleberries and black huckleberries can be identified only to the level of genus (i.e., *Rubus* sp. and *Vaccinium* sp.), we have to infer the presence of these species in the record. Our sample is too small to determine when these species began to be used or if production was intensified through time.

The record is relatively silent with respect to the use of greens and cambium, which is expected given the difficulty of finding evidence of their use. Because greens as a group rank high in intensification potential, we expect that these plant foods held great importance in the past. However, we are unlikely to ever find definitive evidence that these species were eaten, never mind intensified, by Northern Plateau peoples. More concerted efforts to assemble the evidence for bark-stripped trees would in part redress the gap in knowledge about the use of cambium. However, because these trees do not normally live beyond 300 years, we will always be unable to track the process of intensification for this food.

In our previous paleoethnobotanical research, the relative absence of nuts and seeds in the archaeobotanical record surprised us, given the durability and visibility of these remains. However, the comparatively low ranking of this food group may in part account for its small numbers in the record. However, we do expect that, once archaeologists begin to look for nut-collecting sites in appropriate habitats, these remains will be considerably more common (e.g., Eldridge 1996).

In the end, we have been able to assemble some support for previous models that recognize the importance of "the intensification of root foods" on the Northern

Plateau. However, our review also demonstrates that not all roots would have been equally valued and that other plant foods were likely as important. Further, given that the process of intensification can be accomplished in multiple ways, explicit definitions of *intensification* in the context of the Northern Plateau need to be incorporated into these models.

Finally, although it is tempting to end this essay with speculations on the social and economic context for the changes we observe in plant use over time, after completing this review we are most keenly aware of the need to carefully scrutinize the archaeological record for what is really known and what is knowable before we go too far to explain possible patterning. In the case of plant foods, there are considerable gaps in the current data set that prevent us from really understanding the overall utility of plants and specifically their role in resource intensification. To some extent, there will always be an imbalance in the kinds of data that we can retrieve, with some kinds of plant food being better represented than others. However, as more Plateau archaeologists actively incorporate paleoethnobotanical analyses into their research, these gaps in our knowledge about ancient plant use will be narrowed.

Acknowledgments. Many thanks go to Noreen Willows for help compiling the nutritional information presented in the tables and to Ken Lertzman for sharing his creative approach to data analysis. We also extend our thanks to Bill Prentiss and Ian Kuijt for the countless, engaging e-mail discussions about our chapter. Their enthusiasm for this dialogue prompted us to explore our data in new ways and to refine considerably our thinking about the role of plants in the prehistory of the Plateau.

9

THE SOCIAL DIMENSIONS OF ROASTING PITS IN A WINTER VILLAGE SITE

Brian Hayden and Sara Mossop Cousins

With only a few key exceptions, roasting pits have remained largely unexplored in archaeological research on the Northwest Plateau. At the time of our field research (1997–1999) there was a strong focus in British Columbian archaeology on the examination of pithouses. Since that time, Peacock (1998, 2002) has completed studies on prehistoric root harvesting, root processing, and the role of carbohydrates in the Plateau diet. Kuijt and Prentiss (this volume) have also examined these topics. Up until the last few years, roasting pits, if they were identified at all, were generally considered of little value to archaeological research. The pioneering work of Pokotylo and Froese (1983), Alexander et al. (1985), and Thoms (1989) does show, however, that considerable insights into prehistoric socioeconomies may be derived from the study of plant-cooking pits located near upland gathering sites. In 1997, with this early work in mind, we began to examine roasting pits at Keatley Creek, a large winter village site near Lillooet, British Columbia. We wondered if people cooked large amounts of root foods in the lowland winter village sites and if so, why. In particular, Brian Hayden (1995, 2001) had been developing a number of theories on feasting and was curious to know what Keatley Creek might be able to reveal about feasting in the Northwest interior given the apparent cultural complexity of the Keatley Creek community.

Once we were able to identify roasting pits within the village site, it soon became clear that they could provide considerable insights into broad aspects of socioeconomic organization. We examined a number of factors in order to develop and test our theory that at Keatley Creek, the roasting pits demonstrate a pattern of changing social groups and access to resources over time, including a period of large-scale food collection and processing by large corporate groups. We specifically considered the possibility that the large-scale processing might be associated with feasting or other special events in the village. We posed the following questions: When were roasting pits used? What were their size and frequency through time? What species of plants and animals were cooked? How much of a heating element was apparently required? What was the volume of plant foods involved? What structures (domestic or specialized) or resource areas (containing root species, fuel, water, and rocks) were they associated with? What evidence is available from other interior Plateau village sites for similar patterns of resource processing?

As the ethnographic descriptions of roasting pits have been discussed in other publications, we will not include them here. In brief, pits were dug in the ground and heated with fires and large rocks in order to steam cook geophytes (roots) and other foods. This was a fairly common practice among Plateau peoples in the historic period.

TO USE OR NOT TO USE

An important question to consider is why people used roasting pits. Food, including most root foods (geophytes), can be cooked in a number of different ways, including using cooking containers or simply roasting them in the embers of a campfire. Although pit cooking is a common cooking method throughout the world, root-roasting pits do not occur throughout the prehistoric sequence on the Plateau, or even elsewhere in the Americas, as far as we know. Roasting pits, especially those associated with geophyte processing, are conspicuously lacking in the earlier prehistoric horizons. In fact, the earliest root-roasting pit that we are aware of on the Canadian (Northern) Plateau only dates to 2360 B.P. (Peacock 1998, 2002), while the evidence for human history in this area stretches back 7,000 years or more.

(Rousseau et al. [1991:113–121] report a date of 3,130 B.P. for a roasting pit at the Parker site; however, the lack of fire-cracked rock (FCR) and the presence of bifaces with faunal remains make it clear that this was a meat roasting pit.) In 1989, Alston Thoms also documented two small roasting pits on the Columbia (Southern) Plateau, which date to 4150 and 5340 B.P.; however, these may have been meat-roasting pits as well. There is a question, then, as to why root-roasting pits started to be used and why they increased in size and frequency during particular time periods in some areas and then decreased again.

Although we do not have enough data to delve into this topic in any definitive fashion, we would like to suggest that plant-roasting pits only make practical sense if one needs to process large amounts of plant materials. Digging out a pit and collecting the large rocks to heat it would be a great deal of work to cook a few roots unless people had special cooking requirements in order to render them edible, as has been argued by Peacock (1998) for balsamroot *(Balsamorhiza sagittata)* (see also Dawson 1892; Teit 1900; Thoms 1989). Most generalized hunter-gatherers collect only enough food for one or two days and cook these foods as needed over, or in, an open fire for daily meals.

There is no evidence for the use of geophyte-roasting pits among most generalized hunter-gatherers. Some generalized hunter-gatherers dig small pits (which are not lined with rocks) to cook medium-sized game such as kangaroo (Gould 1969:16) or dog (Teit 1909); however, these meat-roasting pits are quite distinct from geophyte-roasting pits. Meat-roasting pits usually contain substantial numbers of animal bones and little or no FCR and are about 100 × 40 × 30 cm in size (Figures 9.1–9.3). According to ethnographic information, nut-roasting pits were used in the Marble Range area of British Columbia, in the general vicinity of Hat Creek and Keatley Creek (Grinder 2001). Comparisons of these pits to plant- and meat-roasting pits would be of interest.

It seems unrealistic to assume that early occupants of the Plateau were ignorant of geophyte resources or that the climate precluded geophyte occurrence, given the dense fields of subalpine lilies *(Erythronium grandiflorum)* and mountain potatoes *(Claytonia lanceolata)* known in the area historically. The environmental information derived from pollen cores (Mathewes and Pellatt 2000) indicates that there has been little climatic change over the past 3,200 years. Therefore, we suggest that geophytes were cooked over, or in the ashes of, open fires until such a time as larger-scale processing was required, which is when we find plant-roasting pits. Cooking in open fires would not normally leave any distinctive archaeological or paleobotanical remains.

If we can assume that larger amounts of geophytes were being processed in roasting pits than were required for daily consumption, then it is reasonable to infer that the extra plants were being roasted either (1) for storage (Turner 1997), (2) in order to reduce water content and weight for transport (Pokotylo and Froese 1983), or

Figure 9.1. The excavation of a meat-roasting pit used by the Pintubi for roasting a medium-sized kangaroo.

Figure 9.2. The singeing of a kangaroo on top of the fire built over the Pintubi meat-roasting pit.

Figure 9.3. Burying the kangaroo in the Pintubi meat-roasting pit after the hot coals were scooped out and used to cover the kangaroo (the legs are protruding out of the pit at an angle).

(3) for feeding large numbers of people at one time. Such motives do not fit what we know of generalized hunter-gatherers, especially given the very substantial time and energy costs of digging roasting pits, acquiring the rocks, transporting plants used for the insulation or protection of the geophytes, and amassing the fuel necessary for their use (Alexander et al. 1985; Thoms 1989). Using roasting pits, especially the larger varieties, does, however, make a great deal of sense for complex hunter-gatherers characterized by collector strategies and semisedentary home bases (Binford 1980; Hayden 1992; Peacock 1998, 2002). All three of the above motives could explain the use of roasting pits. Among complex hunter-gatherers, ethnographic evidence suggests, in fact, that in the Fraser Plateau area pit-cooked root foods were a critical stored resource in winter during the historic period (Teit 1900; Turner 1997), although this focus may have been made possible by the use of horses for transporting bulk items. In contrast to the central role that Kuijt and Prentiss (this volume) propose for geophytes in the prehistoric diets of the region, transporting large amounts of geophytes from upland mountain areas to winter villages would have been more difficult prior to the introduction of the horse but perhaps not impossible. Moreover, access to any stores in the mountains would have been precluded in the winter. Nevertheless, it is apparent that the mere existence of geophyte-roasting pits, particularly the large ones, can be an important element in our understanding of the basic nature of prehistoric economies and sociopolitical organization. This is because of the fact that roasting pit use implies an exploitation of large amounts of root resources and a need or desire to process them cooperatively in the case of the larger roasting pits. Before examining the roasting pits at Keatley Creek, we will discuss some of the more important variables to be examined.

Variability in Size

Within the context of our theoretical framework, size is one of the most important variables to examine. Alexander et al. (1985:97–102) make several important observations about roasting pit size on the basis of their ethnoarchaeological work in the Potato Mountain region of British Columbia. To begin with, they note that plant-roasting pits smaller than about 90 cm in diameter were simply a waste of time to make and use, in part because not enough rocks would be present in order to prevent rapid cooling. They note that the factors affecting increases from this minimum size include the following:

1. the amount of rocks needed to cook specific plant types. This is largely a function of the required cooking time of different types of plants. For instance, mountain potatoes and wild onions require only a few hours and, therefore, a thin layer of rocks (and presumably only a shallow pit). This is in contrast to balsamroot, the tough taproots of which require one–two days of cooking and, consequently, a much larger mass of rocks and a larger, deeper pit to maintain the necessary heat.
2. the number of plants being cooked. This, in turn, may be the result of several factors, such as the amount of food required for winter storage and subsistence; the transport capabilities between resource areas and consumption/storage areas; the size of the cooperating socioeconomic group (corporate group) involved in the acquisition, processing, storage, and consumption of the geophytes; and the number of people participating in special consumption events such as feasts.
3. the effort required to construct the pit. It is clear that there was a lot of work involved in the creation and use of the largest pits. It is difficult to imagine, for example, that the boulders used in some of the larger roasting pits at Keatley Creek could have been transported or manipulated by single individuals over any distance (Figure 9.4).

Alexander et al. (1985) also point out that small increases in pit diameter result in large increases in pit volume. For example, a roasting pit with a diameter of 90 cm has a volume of 0.38 m^3 (380 l), while a roasting pit with a 240 cm diameter has a volume of 1.4 m^3 (1,400 l). For purposes of comparing volumes and estimating the amount of food processed, we used a number of assumptions. Pokotylo and Froese (1983) developed (and performed initial tests on) a formula to calculate an estimate for the diameter of the rock-lined basin of roasting pits from the rim crest diameters. They found that the excavated basin is generally 65 percent of the rim crest diameter. If we use that proportion, the diameter of the rock-lined basin in EHPE 33, for example, is estimated at approximately 4.88 m (65 percent of the rim crest diameter). This would allow for approximately 2.8 m^3 of root material to be roasted at one time (assuming a 15 cm thickness of roots with another 50 cm required for heating rocks, insulating soil, and matting or other material used to protect the roots). We then used the formula of $\Pi(0.65r)^2 \times$ food depth to calculate the volume of food processed.

Given these factors, several spatial and temporal patterns have been noted by Alexander et al. (1985), Pokotylo and Froese (1983), and Peacock (1998, 2002). First, there are substantial differences in the range and mean diameters of roasting pits according to locality (Figure 9.5). These can probably best be interpreted as being caused by different species being processed. At

Figure 9.4. The test excavation of Extra Housepit Excavation 34 showing the boulder size of some of the heating elements in this roasting pit.

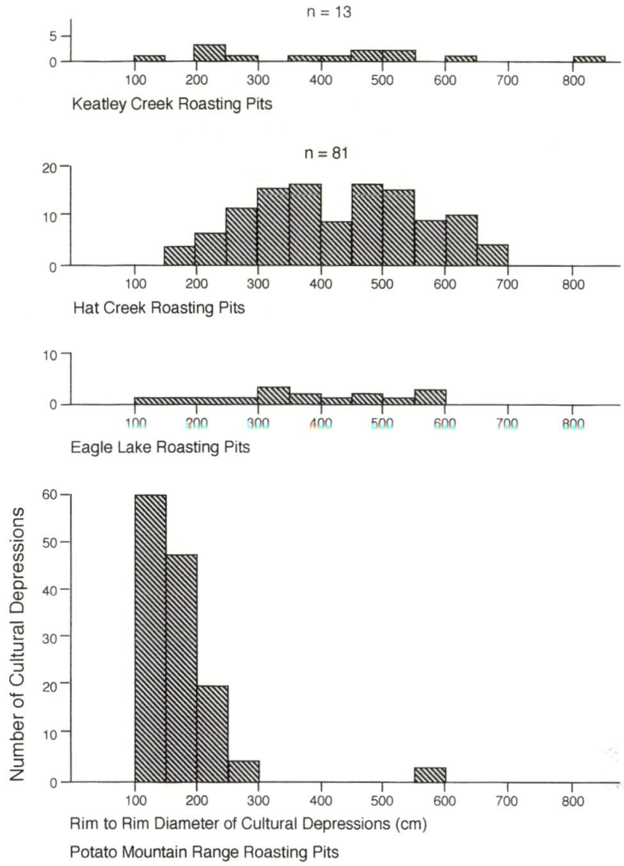

Figure 9.5. A histogram of the relative sizes of roasting pits at Keatley Creek, Hat Creek (a neighboring upland valley), Eagle Lake, and Potato Mountain (both in the Chilcotin). Size differences reflect different plant species being processed as well as socioeconomic factors.

Potato Mountain, where mountain potatoes were the dominant species being processed, roasting pits tended to be small (always less than 2.7 m in diameter). At Eagle Lake (in the Chilcotin) and Hat Creek (near Keatley Creek), where other species such as balsamroot or *Lomatium* were probably being processed, the range of pit diameters is much larger, and the mean diameters at these locations are 3.88 and 4.28 m, respectively.

Previous studies have also suggested that the prehistoric corporate group sizes were larger in the Hat Creek locality than in the Eagle Creek locality and that this, too, is reflected in the larger average size of pits at Hat Creek (Pokotylo and Froese 1983). Similarly, previous studies suggest that both community size and housepit (or corporate group) size have varied substantially in the Lillooet region over time, reaching impressive peaks from about 2500–1000 B.P., after which the large housepits and large villages seem to have been abandoned (Hayden and Ryder 1991). The Keatley Creek site was one of the major villages occupied during this period, with over 100 housepits, several of which approach 20 m in diameter (Figure 9.6). The very large roasting pits recorded in the Hat Creek area (which was probably part of the exploitation range of the prehistoric inhabitants of Keatley Creek) seem to coincide with the peak period of occupation, and corporate group size, at the Keatley Creek site. As we shall see, there are a number of roasting pits located within the Keatley Creek village site as well, the largest of which also date from this period.

Frequency of Occurrence

If an increase in occurrence indicates an increase in resource utilization, as has been suggested, then we might expect variations in occurrence over time. These variations might be caused by climatic, population, or social factors. As far as we know, the climate did not change appreciably from 3,200 B.P. to the present in the Keatley Creek area (Mathewes and Pellatt 2000). The occurrence of roasting pits does vary over time on the Northern Plateau and at Keatley Creek. Twenty-one of the 36 roasting pits (58 percent) tested in the Northern Plateau studies considered in this chapter date to the previously identified peak period of 2500–1000 B.P. (Alexander et al. 1985; Peacock 1998; Pokotylo and Froese 1983; Rousseau et al. 1991; Simonsen 1994; Stryd 1973, 1980). If one considers the cultural occupation of the Northern Plateau to span 7,000 years, then 58 percent of the roasting pits tested to date were used in 21 percent of the time period. When the Keatley Creek results are included and compared with those from local village sites, this apparent peak in use becomes more pronounced, as is discussed below.

Species Roasted

Some species require longer cooking periods, therefore requiring larger pits. A pit might be large for a number of reasons. Without completing a botanical analysis, it is difficult to determine which of these factors was impor-

Figure 9.6. The core of the Keatley Creek site showing the extremely high density of housepit depressions.

tant in specific cases. Identifiable botanical remains can be recovered from roasting pits, including charred root materials (Pokotylo and Froese 1983), making botanical analysis an important part of any study of roasting pits. In addition, some species were cooked for immediate consumption, while others were processed for storage and later use (Turner 1997). Nodding onions *(Allium cernuum)* and balsamroots were prepared for storage this way (Turner 1997). Yellow avalanche lilies *(Erythronium grandiflorum)* were pit cooked to soften them *after* they had been dried and stored (Turner 1997). *Lomatium* species (fresh) might be added to other species being pit cooked in order to add flavor (Turner 1997). If feasting occurred, then we would expect to find species that are known to have been pit cooked for immediate consumption whether dried first or not.

Associated Features or Structures

In the upland mountain sites, roasting pits are associated with known root-harvesting locations, campsites, lithic scatters, and cache pits (Alexander et al. 1985; Peacock 1998; Pokotylo and Froese 1983). People were evidently roasting their roots, eating some, packing some for storage, and moving on. In contrast, roasting pits in village sites can be associated with pithouses, cache pits, specialized structures or features, or lithic scatters. The roots might be carried some distance from collection areas in order to process them in villages, but once cooked they would not have far to go for storage or consumption. In a village, dried stored roots might be pit cooked (again) as mentioned above. If roasting pits located within village sites represent special feasting events, then they might be located near special structures. For example, they might be associated with a particular structure or a local congregating area. Such a structure could be expected to exhibit unusual characteristics, such as special features or unique artifacts different from those associated with daily cooking and other activities.

Important root-gathering areas were sometimes owned by chiefs or families, indicating that a high emic value was attributed to geophyte resources (Turner 1997). A close source of a particular root food species might have been of great value in the village if root foods were a special-purpose food or a highly valued type of food (as argued by Kuijt and Prentiss, this volume). The potential for trade (of dried roots) might also have been an important consideration in a village such as Keatley Creek, where large amounts of salmon or other resources probably provided a surplus of protein-rich food that could be exchanged for carbohydrates. If so, root foods may have constituted luxury foods during the winter and may have been primarily used for special occasions or by persons of high status.

THE ROASTING PITS OF KEATLEY CREEK

The Keatley Creek site is situated on one of the terraces of the Fraser River that abuts the Clear Range Mountains, about 25 km upstream from the town of Lillooet, British Columbia (Figure 9.7). The site was intensively occupied from about 2500 to 1000 B.P. However, there is also some evidence of use from 7,000 years ago to the present. The Keatley Creek site is unique in the area for the amount of analysis that has occurred there and perhaps also for some of its architectural features.

As we have noted above, the climate does not appear to have changed significantly over the last 3,200 years; however, the terraces have been intensively grazed by cattle and horses over the last 100 years, which has probably had a significant impact on root foods (Turner 1997). Today, only limited number of edible geophytes occur on the terraces around the site and at the base of the mountains.[1] These include

- wild onions (*Allium* spp.), in some abundance at the base of the mountains (maximum density greater than ten plants/m^2);
- mariposa lilies *(Calochortus macrocarpus)*, on the village terraces in limited numbers (maximum density approximately one plant/m^2); and
- desert parsley or wild carrot *(Lomatium macrocarpum)*, on the village terraces, also in limited numbers (maximum density one–three plants/m^2).

Balsamroot is also available in the area today but in limited quantities (one–three plants/m^2) on specific hillsides 5–20 km from the village. However, as Turner (1992) points out, despite the lack of major climatic change, plant succession could have occurred and species composition may have changed over time. A major fire occurred on the Keatley site in 1992, for example, but

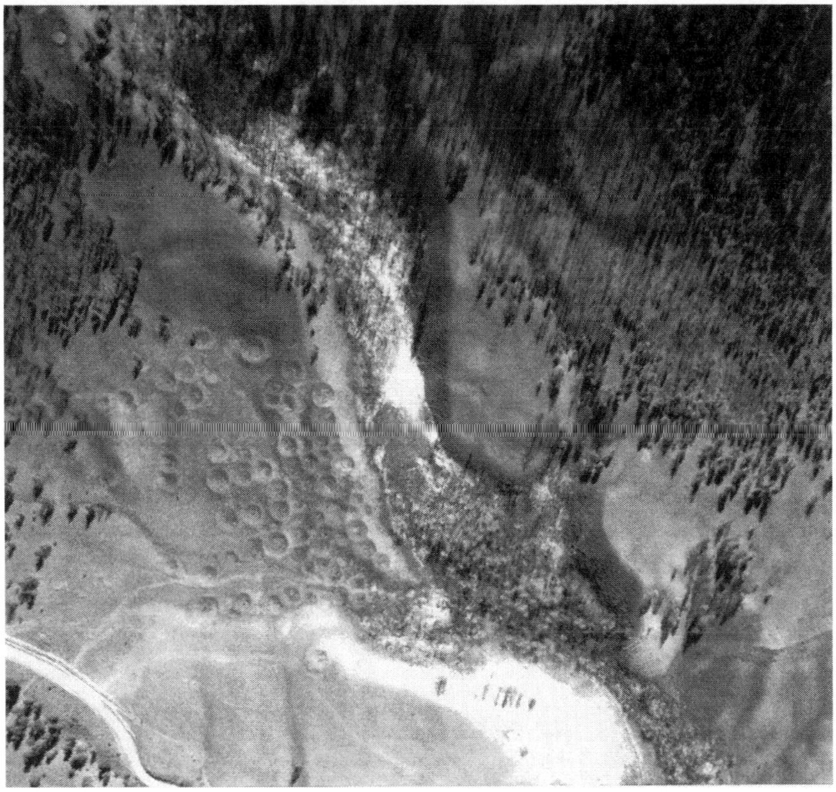

Figure 9.7. Aerial photograph of Keatley Creek showing the dense core and the outlying terraces on which most roasting pits and proposed ritual structures are located. The eastern terraces are in the upper left (Terrace 2 and Structure 105 are visible in the very upper left corner); and the southern terraces are situated to the right of the core across the creek bed that runs vertically down the center of the photograph. Photo courtesy of Arthur Roberts.

this should not have affected balsamroot availability, according to information from the American Fire Effects Information Service (www.fs.fed.us/database/feis, 1998). Arrow-leaved balsamroot is not normally killed by fire, as it will regenerate from regrowth of its thick caudex. In fact, arrow-leaved balsamroot increases in frequency and density after fire following the regrowth of surviving plants and new plants produced through seed production.

Mariposa lilies were once a widespread species on the Southern Plateau, but they are vulnerable to grazing and are now considerably less common (Parish et al. 1996). Sagebrush mariposa lilies, and other bulb plants, are particularly vulnerable to grazing by horses. Horses may pull the bulbs out of the ground when they graze the tops, rather than just clipping the tops as cows will do; horses are also more of a threat through trampling than animals with cloven hooves, such as cows (Wendy Hayes, 100 Mile House Forest District Range Officer, personal communication, 1998). Nodding onion is also known to be eaten by sheep and cattle, which has decreased its presence on the landscape on the Southern Plateau, according to ethnographic research (Palmer 1975). Nodding onion patches near Lytton were traditionally burned to enhance their growth (Turner 1991).

It is difficult to predict what the plant availability would have been at the Keatley Creek 1,500 years ago. The site is currently used for grazing horses, and there was a fire in 1992, as noted above. Ethnographically, all of the species found near the site today were pit cooked if large enough quantities were gathered, and then they might have been eaten immediately or put away for storage (Pokotylo and Froese 1983; Turner 1997). Other edible root plants that might have grown near the village site in the past on dry, open slopes and in wooded areas include yellowbells *(Fritillaria pudica)*, chocolate tips *(Lomatium dissectum)*, bitterroot *(Lewisia rediviva)*, and wild thistle *(Cirsium edule)* (Pokotylo and Froese 1983).

The socioeconomic organization of the unusual size and number of housepits at Keatley Creek has been the focus of the research at the site since 1985 (Hayden 1997, 2000a). One of the other unusual features at Keatley Creek is a series of roasting pits found on the periphery of the site (Figure 9.8), some of which are surprisingly large considering the fairly meager geophyte resources present at the site today. The presence of roasting pits associated with a low-elevation residential site appears to be unusual (or at least largely undocumented). Peacock (1998), Pokotylo and Froese (1983), and early

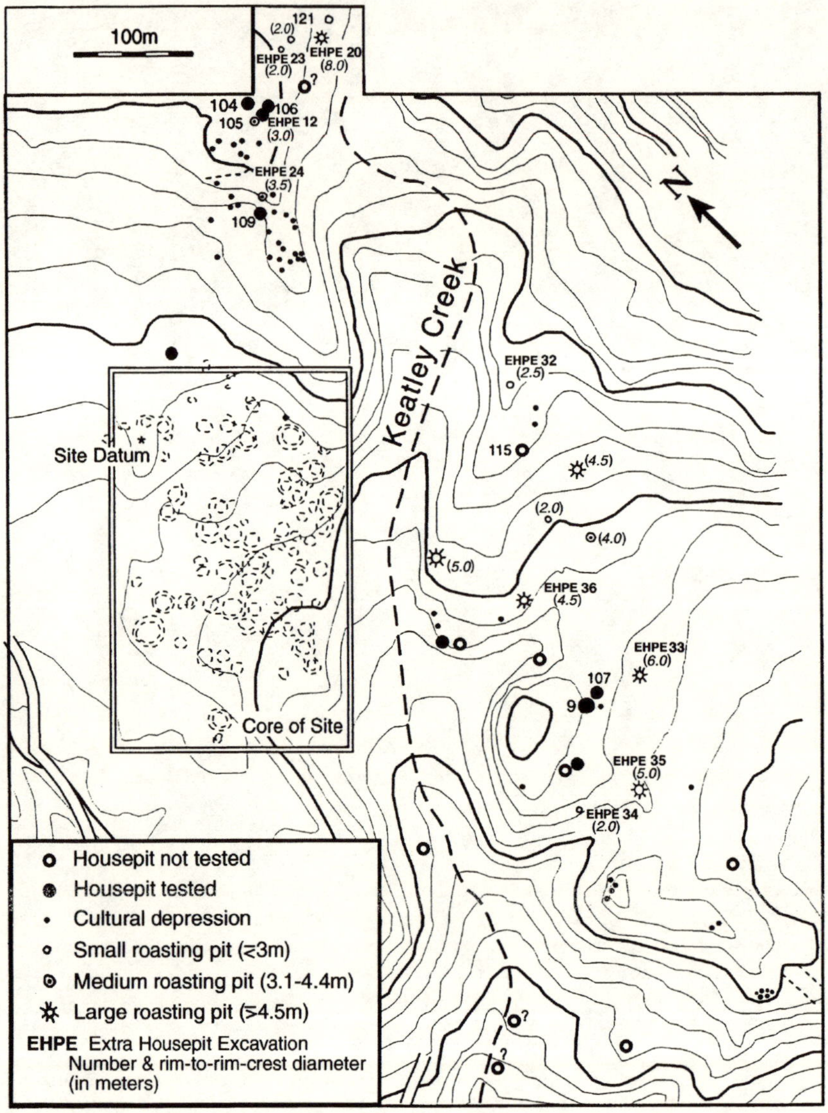

Figure 9.8. Map of Keatley Creek showing the locations of features identified as root-roasting pits (plus EHPE 12, which was a meat-roasting pit).

ethnographic accounts (Dawson 1892:9, 19–20, cited in Peacock 1998, 2002) emphasize that roasting pits are generally located at higher mountainous elevations and that they are associated with the most abundant geophyte resource areas. These authors have also found that small to medium-sized roasting pits occur periodically in isolation across the landscape, usually associated with patches of lower-elevation root species such as balsamroot or bitterroot. Since 1999, Cousins has observed small to medium-sized plant-roasting pits at several Plateau village sites, including Big Bar Lake (EhRk4). These have also been located on terraces at the site periphery. Thus, prior research in the interior has focused on roasting pit complexes that were located in upland gathering areas, well away from village sites. Therefore, it was interesting to find a number of roasting pits of various sizes within the prehistoric village of Keatley Creek. One of the questions we wished to address is the role that these roasting pits played in the socioeconomy of the inhabitants of Keatley Creek. There were clearly not enough roasting pits for each household to have used one. Only a few roasting pits existed at the village for 1,500 years of occupation by 1,000 people or more at a time. This suggests cooperative or special-purpose use.

Intensive exploration of the site core and surrounding small terraces led to the location of 13 geophyte-roasting pits. Their associations with structures at the site are discussed below. Three small additional roasting pits were excavated and found to be meat-roasting pits, and one additional poorly defined roasting area was associated with a large housepit in the core of the site (HP 7). The geophyte-roasting pits we located, and in some cases excavated, varied significantly in size, age, density of FCR, heating element size, and botanical remains. We

TABLE 9.1. Keatley Creek Roasting Pits (Tested).

Roasting Pit	Location and Association	Diameter[a]	Age B.P.[b]	Fire-Cracked Rock Density[c]	Heating Element	Botanical Remains[d]
EHPE 20	Adjacent to the creek bed, NE of Terrace 2	8.0 m	1580 ± 60 (Beta 125900); earlier pit below?	5–40%	10 cm of large cobbles	2 *Chenopodiaceae* sp. (seeds); conifer needles woody charcoal
EHPE 23	Terrace, N of HP 109	4.0 m	30 ± 50 (Beta 125901)			1 *Lomatium* sp. (skin) *(L. dissectum?)*; 1 *Allium* sp. (bulb) *(A. geyeri?)*; woody charcoal; conifer needles and parts
EHPE 24	Terrace 1, adjacent to HP 109	3.0 m	490 ± 40 (Beta 125902)			No root materials; small amount of charred material
EHPE 32	Terrace, above HP 115 (historic)	3.0 m	90 ± 60 (Beta 125904); 120 ± 60 (Beta 125903); evidence for reuse, two layers	5–90%	10 cm of large cobbles	2 unidentified bulbs; 6 unidentified seeds (1 *Ericaceae* sp.?); conifer needles; woody charcoal (including *Arctostaphylos uva-ursi?*)
EHPE 33	Terrace, 60 m SE of HP 9, 107	7.5 m	1540 ± 80 (Beta 125905)	10–60%	20 cm of large cobbles and boulders	4 unidentified tissues; 6 seeds (5 *Ericaceae* sp.; 1 *Smilacina racemosa*?); conifer needles; woody charcoal
EHPE 34	Terrace Slope, 45 m S of HP 108	1.25 m	120 ± 40 (Beta 150794)	2–30%	7 cm of large cobbles and small boulders	No root materials; woody charcoal
EHPE 35	Terrace, 55 m SE of HP 108	4.5 m	1460 ± 70 (Beta 150796); 1530 ± 70 (Beta 150795)	3–75%	20 cm of large cobbles	No root materials; woody charcoal
EHPE 36	Terrace, 60 m N of HP 9, 107	4.5 m	770 ± 60 (Beta 150797); 870 ± 60 (Beta 150798); earlier pit below?	14–60%	5 cm of large cobbles; second layer?	4 root skin fragments (*Lomatium* sp.?)

[a]Measured rim crest to rim crest.
[b]All samples were charred wood from within the heating element matrices; all dates are conventional radiocarbon runs.
[c]Calculated as a percentage of the matrix.
[d]Natasha Lyons provided assistance with the identification of botanical remains.

summarize these variations in geophyte-roasting pit characteristics below and in Table 9.1.

SUMMARY OF EXCAVATION AND ANALYSIS

Fifteen small cultural depressions suspected of being roasting pits, including several within the village core, were tested at Keatley Creek between 1997 and 1999. Of these, eight exhibit the typical characteristics of geophyte-roasting pits (Dawson 1892; Peacock 1998; Pokotylo and Froese 1983; Teit 1900, 1909; Thoms 1989). These characteristics are listed below, along with additional details specific to the Keatley Creek pits:

1. a roughly circular, basin-shaped, shallow depression 1–8 m in diameter (from rim crest to rim crest), 15–40 cm deep at the surface, with or without a clearly defined rim, generally located on a terrace, within a short distance (< 200 m) to a water source;
2. rim deposits of ash and FCR forming a hump, often on one side of the pit, and spread across the surrounding area;
3. sloping inner sides toward the center within the pit, which is generally 30–70 cm in total depth at its maximum;
4. a high concentration of ash, charcoal, blackened soil, and FCR within the pit;

5. few or no lithic flakes, usually found within the pit;
6. few or no faunal remains;
7. at least one group of large, often fire-cracked, cobbles in association toward the bottom of the pit and appearing to have formed a surface at one time;
8. plant materials, including large amounts of conifer needles and charred wood and a few pieces of charred root material that may or may not be identifiable to species.

Table 9.1 lists some roasting pit characteristics, including observations from test excavations and botanical analyses. Five additional plant-roasting pits have been located but not tested; these are found on the northeastern periphery of the site and range from 2 to 5 m in diameter.

Test trenches were placed in eight roasting pits, generally running from the rim to the center, although one test unit was placed in the outer rim or "debris flow" (EHPE 33). Because of the large amounts of fire-cracked rock that were encountered, FCR was recorded by the percentage of the soil matrix that it formed rather than being counted or weighed. Botanical samples were taken from each unit and level. Large amounts of charred geophytes were not anticipated given the fact that food was protected by basketry and matting during cooking (Dawson 1892; Teit 1900; Turner 1997). In hindsight, more testing should have been undertaken in the "debris flow," where Pokotylo and Froese note that better botanical preservation is found.

The botanical samples were floated using the "garbage can method" (Watson 1976) and were sorted and identified with a dissecting microscope (6–40×) and a light microscope (up to 400×). Most wood charcoal was not identified, except to confirm that it was not from geophyte species. Reference collections were consulted. Some samples were not identifiable to species because of their fragmentary nature or the charring process, which may cause significant shrinkage and distortion (Lyons 2000).

Location and Association

Teit and other early ethnographers do not mention roasting pits in village sites. According to Dawson, they are "generally situated at some height above the principal valleys, on the plateau or mountains, where camps are formed during the season of harvest" (1892:9, 19–20). As noted above, most research on roasting pits has focused on these upland types of sites. For example, the Upper Hat Creek Valley study (Pokotylo and Froese 1983) focused on a highland valley with large processing camps returned to year after year. Similarly, most roasting pits in the Oregon Jack Creek drainage occur at higher altitudes (Rousseau et al. 1991:153ff), as is true at Botanie Valley near Lytton. Where significant numbers of roasting pits occur at lower elevations, they may have been used for processing balsamroot or bitterroot, which appears to have been the case at Scheidam Flats near Kamloops (Peacock 1998, 2002; Rousseau and Howe 1987).

The Keatley Creek site is associated with the Hat Creek area because of its geographic proximity and its contemporaneous period of peak occupation (both localities were primarily occupied from 2500 to 1000 B.P.). In fact, the Hat Creek Valley was probably used by the inhabitants of Keatley Creek for hunting and gathering roots. During this period, hunter-gatherers stored food and exhibited increased cultural complexity and sedentism. Pokotylo and Froese (1983) suggest, like Kuijt and Prentiss (this volume), that an increased utilization of root resources, instead of, or as well as, an increased use of salmon, may have led to this complexity.

In our research, which has not been extensive as yet, we found few other examples of roasting pits being located within village sites. The Bell site, a large winter village that is located approximately 6 km down the Fraser River from Keatley Creek, includes at least one roasting pit feature. In a 1980 article for *The Midden,* Arnoud Stryd describes a "rock-filled pit" (1980), and in a 1999 visit to Keatley Creek he suggested to us that it was similar to the ones we were excavating. In addition, Stryd (1973) identified two "cooking ovens" at the Fountain site. The Fountain site is also located on the Fraser River, approximately 8 km to the southwest of Keatley Creek. The site is located in a cultivated field and does not include any intact surface features. The dates of these pits associate them with those at Keatley Creek, as is discussed below. Carlson (1980:95–122) has reported a roasting pit at the Curr site apparently dug into the depression of an earlier housepit and apparently not contemporaneous with the main occupation of the site. Roasting pits have also been tentatively identified in Plateau Period winter village sites in the Dog Creek area, which is located in a similar environment on a Fraser River terrace approximately 50 km north of Keatley Creek (Scott Cousins, National Resource Coordinator for the Stwecemic/Xatlitem First Nation, personal communication, 2001), as well as at a small village site at Big Bar Lake (as previously noted). Other examples include several sites in the Eagle Lake region, including one site with over 50 housepits and ten roasting pits; several sites with only one housepit but several roasting pits (Magne and Matson 1984:140); and a site near Adams Lake (Botecelli Creek) with only a single roasting pit (Bailey et al. 1993). Unfortunately, there is no indication in the early reports as to whether these are meat-roasting pits or root-roasting pits or whether any major geophyte patches occur near the sites.

At Keatley Creek, all the roasting pits are located on terraces or adjacent to the creek along the eastern and northeastern periphery of the site. The tested pithouses located in these areas include Structures 9, 104, 105, 106, 107, 108, 109, and 115. Most, and perhaps all, of these structures may have been used for rituals or specialized activities (Hayden and Adams, this volume). Structure 9 is the most fully excavated. It was occupied in two periods: first during the Plateau Horizon (2400–1200 B.P.) and later during the early Kamloops Horizon (1200–200 B.P.). It appears to have been used by people with special status and access to wealth. Many unique artifacts were found in this structure that suggest unusual activities, including loon bones (associated with shamans ethnographically), pipe fragments, and prestige items such as nephrite and dentalium shells (Hayden 2000a). The only digging stick handle from the site was also found in HP 9, which may be especially significant, as discussed below. Salmon remains were unusually abundant on the floors. The recovered botanical remains from Structure 9 may also suggest unusual access to plant resources (Cousins 2000). Two, and perhaps three, of the roasting pits on the south terrace appear to be associated with this housepit. Roasting pits EHPE 33 and 35 date to approximately 1500 B.P. Roasting pit EPHE 36 dates to approximately 800 B.P. This would place them within the time frame of Structure 9, and they are located nearby on the same terrace (EHPE 33 and 35) or on an adjacent terrace segment (EHPE 36).

If the residents of Structure 9 were involved in special activities involving salmon and plant foods, as it appears, then we might speculate that they were also processing and utilizing root foods in an unusual way. The recovery of the digging stick handle is very unusual, for these items were valuable and normally curated, as evidenced by their rare occurrence in the archaeological record and by their inclusion in burials (Hayden and Schulting 1997; Palmer 1975; Pokotylo and Froese 1983). Perhaps this digging stick handle reflects the special status of root foods in this structure.

Structures 107 and 108 are located approximately 10 and 50 m, respectively, from Structure 9. A distinctive assemblage of lithics was recovered from Structure 107, which includes a brief occupation during the Plateau Horizon and may be ritual in nature (see Hayden and Adams, this volume). Little is known about Structures 108 and 115, other than the evacuation of Structure 115's Plateau deposits by subsequent historic occupants. EHPE 32 dates to approximately 100 B.P. and is located just above Structure 115 on a little subterrace.

Three roasting pits (including EHPE 20 and 23) are located in the Keatley Creek bed just before it leaves the Clear Range Mountains. These roasting pits are located closest to Structures 104, 105, and 106 and may well be contemporaneous with them judging from the unweathered appearance of their contents and rims. EHPE 20 and Structure 105 both date to the Plateau Horizon. The Plateau component of Structure 105 consisted of a storage pit that contained very unique artifacts, notably 72 bone buttons, the largest collection from the Plateau and probably components of a button blanket or garment. Thus, again, we find an unusual housepit with an apparently contemporaneous roasting pit located nearby. EHPE 23 (a small roasting pit) was used very recently, whereas occupations in Structure 104, Structure 106, and the last floor of Structure 105 were from the Protohistoric Period. The third roasting pit in the creek bed has not been tested but appears similar to EHPE 23 and probably is of similar age.

Only a few of the Keatley Creek roasting pits are not located near structures with corresponding dates. For example, EHPE 24 (490 B.P.) is located adjacent to HP 109, which includes Protohistoric and late Shuswap (2400–3500 B.P.) occupations. Three untested plant-roasting pits are located on the southern series of terraced areas, and one is located in the upper creek bed; but without dates they cannot be clearly associated with any of the structures or each other.

We conducted a thorough search for likely roasting pits in the core of the site and tested the most promising depressions associated with each of the large pithouses in the village core. In all cases they proved to be cache pits. It is interesting that none of the depressions in the village core has the surface characteristics of geophyte-roasting pits. Thus, it appears that at Keatley Creek, roasting pits were only used on the periphery of the village. The only other evidence for roasting facilities that we encountered consisted of three meat-roasting pits associated with Structures 104, 105, and 106 on Terrace 2 and a general platform or surficial roasting feature associated with a large housepit in the site core (Structure 7). All four of these roasting pits are clearly different in nature from the geophyte-roasting pits. The platform roasting feature associated with Structure 7 may have been a food-preparation area for feasts held in Structure 7, whereas the meat- and geophyte-roasting pits closest to Structures 9, 104, 105, and 109 may have been used for preparing feasting foods for special secret society or other ritual events held in these structures, as suggested by Hayden and Adams (this volume). It is important to emphasize that there were no meat- or geophyte-roasting pits associated with any structures in the core of the site. The only place where roasting pits occur is in general proximity to structures that we suspect as being ritual or feasting structures based on other criteria such as distinctive assemblages of fauna, lithics, or prestige items, as well as unusual features such as collared central hearths and unusually large interior storage pits. In addition to the spatial association with these suspected ritual structures, the size and frequency of use of the prehistoric roasting pits at Keatley Creek seem to indicate that they were used for feasting or other unusual events, as discussed next.

Size and Reuse

The roasting pits at Keatley Creek range from 1.25 to 8 m in diameter, from rim crest to rim crest, and from 30 to 70 cm in total excavated depth. This suggests a wide range of volumes and cooking capacities. The smaller pits may have been used less repeatedly and for smaller amounts of plants that required shorter cooking times. The largest pits (EHPE 20 and 33; see Figure 9.9) could have cooked up to 2.8–3.3 m^3 (2,800–3,300 l) of root material at a time. Roasting pits the size of EHPE 35 probably processed about 1.0 m^3 (or 1,000 l) of roots. These are very large quantities by any measure. Most pits appear to have been used multiple times. According to Turner (1991, 1997), historic families might have harvested over 50 l of root plants in a season and required 100 kg of stored roots for the winter. The largest roasting pit, EHPE 20, then, could have provided the annual roasting needs for 65 nuclear family households at a time.

At Hat Creek the pits range in size from 1 to 7 m (rim crest to rim crest), with an exterior diameter for the debris cone up to 13 m, and from 7 to 52 cm in surface depth. The larger ones are larger than roasting pits reported from ethnography (Pokotylo and Froese 1983). According to Dawson (1892), for example, the "flow cone" of a roasting pit might spread from 15 to 20 ft after several years of use. The Komkanetkwa pits are as large as 8.6 m in diameter (rim crest to rim crest), with debris cones extending another 2 m on either side.

Pokotylo and Froese (1983) also measured the rim crest diameter versus the exterior edge and found that the roasting pits that had been reused exhibit a larger exterior edge because of a larger accumulation of ash and debris. They calculated a mean of 2.2 m difference for rim crest diameters versus exterior edges in the single-use pits, compared with a 6.43 m difference for the reused pits. Three of the roasting pits at Keatley Creek exhibit clear stratigraphic evidence of reuse, as suggested by the occurrence of superimposed heating features. These include EHPE 20, 33, and 36. In addition, the debris spread on several roasting pits indicates multiple use. EHPE 33, for example, measures 7.5 m from rim crest to rim crest and 12 m from exterior edge to exterior edge, for a difference of 4.5 m. EHPE 36 has a rim crest diameter of 4.5 m and an exterior edge diameter of 7.5 m, for a difference of 3.0 m. If this difference does represent the amount of reuse, then the Keatley Creek pits may have been reused less than those at Hat Creek, though some reuse is suggested. At both sites, the reused pits are of medium to large size and date to 770 B.P. or earlier. It might be suggested that the debris spread of these pits

Figure 9.9. The largest roasting pit at Keatley Creek (EHPE 20) is 8 m in diameter and is shown here to the right of the pine tree with a very substantial debris cone on its right side.

may not represent more than a half dozen repeated uses of these features. Exceptionally, EHPE 20 at Keatley Creek seems to be composed of several small roasting pit events, indicating perhaps that it was only occasionally used to its full capacity and more frequently was used on a smaller scale.

The excavated depth of the Keatley pits fits the pattern noted at Hat Creek and Komkanetkwa, with a range of 25–70 cm. This matches the ethnographic record: "A circular hole is dug in the ground to a depth of two feet and a half" (Teit 1900:236); "they dug a hole knee to waist deep" (Turner 1997:28). It was found at each site that the bottoms of some of the pits reached glacial till.

The size distribution and frequency of the prehistoric roasting pits at Keatley Creek are interesting. If we assume that these roasting pits were used to process locally available roots, then one would expect to see a size and frequency distribution that reflects yearly variations in productivity, that is, a normal bell-shaped curve such as characterizes the roasting pits at Hat Creek and Potato Mountain (Figure 9.5). At the extreme limits, in poor years, one would expect roasting pits to be smaller and fewer in number, while in very productive years, one would expect roasting pits to be larger. Average years with average-sized roasting pits should normally dominate these distributions. One also expects a continuous series of dates for the use of roasting pits associated with productive root patches.

Although we only have data on a limited number of roasting pits, the situation at Keatley Creek appears to be very different from the model just presented. Although the essentially modern roasting pits are small (indicating very limited root resources or that only a small amount of root roasting was undertaken at a time), the prehistoric roasting pits are almost all large (greater than 5 m in diameter), and there are not enough of them to indicate regular use or use by individual families or households or even large individual corporate households (Figure 9.5). The large size of the prehistoric roasting pits would ordinarily indicate an abundant resource patch. However, there is no indication of any regular use of such a hypothetical patch; there are no smaller roasting pits used on a regular basis; and there is no bell-shaped curve of size distributions. Instead, moderate and large pits containing large quantities of roots (1–3 m^3) appear to have been used episodically with long periods of little or no use. This pattern is more consistent with periodic large feasts or other special events rather than the annual exploitation of local resource patches.

We estimated that about 75 houses (including many corporate group residences comprising multiple nuclear families) were occupied by some 1,200–1,500 inhabitants at the peak period of the site (Hayden 1997). Three roasting pits tested at the site, all of which are relatively large, have been dated to that period. As we note above, each one could service 50–100 households' root storage needs, but they were not used across time, and the species used and the spatial association of the roasting pits with special structures suggest nondomestic use. Two medium-sized pits date to the Kamloops Horizon, and the three remaining small to medium pits fall within the historic period. Four more roasting pits could be expected to belong to the Kamloops or Plateau Horizons if size is indeed an indicator, as Pokotylo and Froese (1983) suggest and as our research supports.

Thus, during the peak years of the Keatley Creek occupation, there may have been as many as seven roasting pits used but apparently at infrequent intervals. Whether they were used by residents of corporate groups or for feasts by some type of sodalities cannot be determined in any definitive fashion. But the episodic use, large size, and locally poor geophyte resources plus the association with special structures seem to argue for feasting functions in which contributions were obtained from trade or from the stores of numerous participating families.

Antiquity

The roasting pits at Keatley date from 30–1580 B.P., with an apparent concentration, including three out of eight, or 38 percent, around 1500 B.P.—in fact, clustering within 50 years of each other. Three pits date to the historic period (one of which may be quite modern), and two date to the Kamloops Horizon (200–1200 B.P.). The cluster of dates around 1500 B.P. fits into the peak period of occupation at the site. The Bell and Fountain site examples also fit into this period, with dates of 1250, 1490, and 1505 B.P. (Stryd 1980; Eldridge and Stryd 1983).

The Hat Creek pits include examples from this era, as well as older examples, with a range of 600–2245 B.P. Nine out of 13 in this case date to the peak period of the Classic Lillooet culture, 2500–1000 B.P. With a single exception, the larger, reused pits at Hat Creek date prior to the Kamloops Horizon (i.e., before 1200 B.P.). The most recent dates are from the smallest pits.

At Komkanetkwa dates range from 70 to 2360 B.P., with six out of 12 falling within 1000–2500 B.P. Again, the largest pits (4–8.6 m) are the oldest (1000 B.P. or earlier). The smallest (1–3 m) were used during the historic period.

Twenty-one of the 36 dated roasting pits reviewed in this chapter, or 58 percent, were used during the peak period of the Classic Lillooet culture (1000–2500 B.P.), with a possible peak at approximately 1500 B.P. (19 percent). Local peaks can also be identified when the Bell, Fountain, Hat Creek, and Keatley Creek sites are considered. Fifteen out of 24 (62 percent) of the roasting pits occur during the peak period of the Classic Lillooet culture, and six out of 24 (25 percent) occur in the 1500s B.P. In other words, over a total occupation span of 70 centuries, 25 percent of the roasting pits were used within one century. At Keatley Creek, three out of eight roasting pits, or 38 percent, were used within 1 percent of the time period. In comparison, at Hat Creek 38 percent (five of 13) cluster around 2000 B.P. Feasting needs would have clearly been greater during the Classic Lillooet culture period because of the higher population levels, greater socioeconomic complexity, and increased needs for political integration, in which feasting may have played a critical part.

Of the five roasting pits that were surveyed but left unexcavated at Keatley Creek, all but one are at least 4 m in diameter, suggesting that they are not likely to be historic. It is possible, given their location, that along with EPHE 33 they are also associated with the early occupation of Structure 115 or 9.

It is notable that after the early Kamloops Horizon peak, there is a distinct hiatus in dated roasting pits for a century or more, which seems to correspond to the cultural collapse and depopulation of the region discussed by Kuijt and Prentiss (this volume). Whether such a hiatus could be caused by the limited climatic change that they propose is highly speculative. As yet, there is no pollen indication that there was very much change during this period, and even the period of increased fire frequency (the Fraser Valley Fire Period) lasted only from 2400 to 1300 B.P. This does not correspond to any collapse events. Moreover, geophytes are generally adapted to resist dry periods by using their large storage organs, and it is unlikely that their abundance would have been adversely affected by such minor climatic fluctuations. If anything, the increased churning of root beds from regular digging should increase the productivity of geophyte resources, just as spading increases productivity in domestic gardens (see Peacock 1998). In addition, it is not clear how the proposed climate changes could have also affected coastal subsistence or, indeed, whether dried salmon in the Lillooet area were really so deficient in lipids that heavy reliance on salmon for a few months without carbohydrate supplements would have created health problems. Thus, there are a number of problematical and unsupported aspects to Kuijt and Prentiss's explanatory model for cultural collapse or decline and the corresponding lack of dated deposits thereafter. Nevertheless, it is one of the possible explanations for these events, including the lack of roasting pits during this time period.

Heating Elements

The rock "pavements" that would have formed the heating elements in the Keatley Creek pits included one or more layers of cobbles/boulders from 5 to 20 cm thick. The amount of rocks required for each pit would have depended on the amount of root foods being cooked and the length of time the pit needed to remain hot, as discussed above. It appears that in some cases large amounts of food required cooking for a long period. EHPE 33, for example, contained the largest heating element (Figure 9.10), which included a number of boulders, one of which was approximately 40 × 20 × 20 cm in size. EHPE 35 also contained a 20 cm thickness of rock used for heating. These are two of the three oldest (and largest) roasting pits at the site. The third, EHPE 20, contained 10 cm of cobbles but also very large quantities of broken FCR. In comparison, the smallest pits at the site (EHPE 34 and 36) contained only 5–7 cm of rock for heating.

Figure 9.10. Another very large roasting pit (EHPE 33) is seen here in a test trench section from the rim to the center of the roasting pit. Note again the very large boulder heating elements in the walls.

Botanical Remains

A small sample of floral remains was recovered from the Keatley Creek roasting pits. As anticipated, large amounts of wood charcoal and conifer needles (from matting) were recovered. A fragment of kinnikinnick *(Arctostaphylos uva-ursi)* was identified from the charred wood. *Chenopodium capitatum* and Ericaceae seeds were also found. Geophyte species recovered include examples from the Umbelliferae family, including *Lomatium* sp. *(L. dissectum),* and the Liliaceae family, including *Allium* sp. *(A. geyeri).* Unidentified bulbs and tissues were also recovered.

Kinnikinnick may have been used for matting, given its dense greenery. Many species of Ericaceae are used by Plateau people, including numerous types of blueberries and huckleberries. Berries are known to have been used in roasting pits to flavor bland-tasting roots (Pokotylo and Froese 1983); this could explain their presence in the assemblage. The geophyte species fit with the ethnographic pattern and with the species available at the site today; however, the considerable abundance of these species implied by the size of the prehistoric roasting pits seems inconsistent with the densities of geophytes in the vicinity of Keatley Creek today. Moreover, the size of the roasting pits is also inconsistent with what is known about the processing of most geophytes around the site such as onions and lilies, neither of which require prolonged or intensive heating. This suggests that it was the amount of food being cooked, not the type, that was a factor in the large roasting pits at Keatley Creek.

EHPE 24 is enigmatic because of the minimal amount of charred material recovered from it, although it conforms to the identity of a small root-roasting pit in all other characteristics. It may have been used only once and then cleaned out, given the very small amount of charred material recovered from it. The other roasting pits tested to date include large amounts of charred wood. This fits with the ethnographic accounts of large amounts of wood being burned down to heat the rocks and then swept out of the middle to make room for the plants (Peacock 1998).

The Hat Creek assemblage includes "abundant" floral remains, including vegetable matting (coniferous needles and branches), kinnikinnick, and food remains (*Allium* sp., Compositae, and Liliaceae). Meat and fish remains were also recovered. Most plant remains were recovered from the rim areas.

Komkanetkwa floral remains include wood charcoal, *Chenopodium capitatum* seeds, and unidentified plant tissues. Peacock suggests that the *Chenopodium* seed may not have been incidental, although there is no mention of *Chenopodium* use in roasting pits ethnographically. They are known to have been used for red dye and for face paint (Turner et al. 1990), but there is no mention of their use as food. Other species of chenopods were used for food sources in other areas of North America (Steadman, in Turner et al. 1990), and their frequent occurrence in botanical assemblages on the Plateau (Cousins 2000; Lepofsky 1990; Lepofsky et al. 1996) may suggest that they were used as a food source. The seeds are edible right off the plant, and they could have been used as a cereal. This does not explain their presence in roasting pits, however.

Other Remains

No faunal remains were recovered, which was somewhat surprising given the ethnographic accounts of plants and animals being roasted together (Teit 1900). According to Desmond Peters Sr. (Stl'atl'imx tradition bearer and past chief), salmon was sometimes cooked in roasting pits with the vegetables that required a reasonably short cooking time. In his experience, meat was cooked separately, however, and usually deboned (Peters, personal communication, 1999).

Small lithic scatters were found on the surfaces of or adjacent to several roasting pits. However, most of the Keatley Creek site is littered in this way, and the surface has been much disturbed. Several trachydacite flakes were found in each pit. Several cores were also found. One pisolite flake was recovered. These may all have been incidental, given the heavy use of the site and the refilling of the pits. Similar types of assemblages have also been recovered from Hat Creek and Komkanetkwa roasting pits. A possible hammer stone was recovered from EPHE 32. This was the only smooth stone found in any of the roasting pits. It was hand sized and pitted at one end. It may have been used for the removal of tough root skins, or it also might be incidental.

DISCUSSION AND CONCLUSIONS

The roasting pits at Keatley Creek do not appear to fit into the regular pattern of resource use as identified at harvesting sites. There are 13 pits, not hundreds, and it is not apparent that large amounts of root foods were located in their immediate vicinity (other than wild onions, perhaps, which do not require long cooking periods and large heating elements). Trade might have provided significant amounts of root resources. Along with our study, initial evidence from several other winter village sites indicates that an alternative pattern to the upland harvesting model existed. This alternative pattern consists of large roasting pits located in peripheral areas of large winter village sites occupied during the Classic Lillooet period. They also may appear periodically at other times. More testing should be completed to confirm the existence of this pattern and its potential association with shamanic or feasting activities or other special events. The indications that the large root-roasting pits in villages may have been used for feasting consist of the following:

1. Increased use during time periods of greatest socioeconomic complexity (i.e., the Classic Lillooet period)
2. Temporal and spatial association with suspected feasting/ritual structures, with no apparent associations with normal residences in the core area of the site
3. Spatial association with meat-roasting pits in some cases containing ritual-like biface offerings. As with root-roasting pits, none of the meat-roasting pits was associated with residential structures in the core of the site, but all were associated with arguably ritual/feasting structures on the periphery of the site (see Hayden and Adams, this volume).
4. Size and frequency distributions that indicate episodic, large-scale use rather than continued yearly exploitation of local geophyte patches (further testing in rim accumulations is required to confirm this)
5. Recovered species and pit sizes that do not indicate that the pits were being used to process root foods for storage
6. The limited number of roasting pits at Keatley Creek—clearly not enough for each household to have used one, which indicates a sharing of facilities, limited access to the resource (either plants or cooking pits), or perhaps specialization. Diane Alexander (personal communication, 2001) has suggested that each family that participated in certain ritual feasts may have brought a quantity of roots to be heated and consumed at the feast. This is certainly a consistent pattern for many traditional transegalitarian feasts. We estimate that more than 70 pithouses may have been simultaneously occupied during the height of the site occupation.
7. A scale of use inconsistent with existing geophyte resources and inconsistent with the processing requirements of the most abundant geophytes (onions and lilies) in the vicinity of Keatley Creek

Although more of the prehistoric roasting events at Keatley Creek appear to be associated with the Classic Lillooet occupation of the site, focused around 1500 B.P., it should be noted, of course, that the site was largely abandoned following 1000 B.P., so few roasting events would be expected following this date. It is apparent that the historic and protohistoric occupants were also using roasting pit cooking methods, although on a much smaller scale.

These later roasting pits may represent feasting that occurred in the village or at ritual structures during the winter months. This would mainly have involved stored foods, such as root vegetables, and perhaps fresh or dried meat or dried fish. If the *Chenopodium* seeds were incidental, they likely suggest a late summer use, which would fit with ethnographic patterns of summer gatherings (Alexander, personal communication, 2001; Cousins, personal communication, 2001).

It is perhaps not yet certain that feasting occurred in Classic Lillooet times or the Protohistoric Period, but the observations that we have assembled seem to point in this direction. It is certainly clear that large amounts of food were cooked or preserved on the terraces of Keatley Creek during limited time periods in the occupation. This was probably not for processing, which is what is attested to in the Hat Creek locality, unless there were large amounts of other edible geophytes growing near the Keatley Creek site prehistorically that have not left archaeological remains.

The implications of the large roasting pits at Keatley Creek go beyond the existence of complex, logistically organized hunter-gatherers and feasting, whether part of secret societies or other aggrandizing strategies. Where the more complex socioeconomic structure of these hunter-gatherers existed for some time (as at Keatley Creek), further changes might have ensued. It has been suggested, for example, that the increasing demands for surpluses put on resource production by most complex hunter-gatherers because of competitive pressures associated with feasting likely account for the intensification of resource exploitation, initial steps toward resource manipulation, and the eventual ownership of resource locations (Blanton and Taylor 1995; Hayden 1990, 1992; Modjeska 1982; Tremaine 1997). In the Northwest, Peacock (1998) and Turner (1992) suggest that the encouragement of plants may have occurred to increase yields through controlled burning, tilling, selective harvesting, or even cultivation. In contrast to the idea of feasting and the sociopolitical pressures created by ambitious residents, some researchers have suggested that intensification was caused by resource shortfalls created by variable climates (Peacock 1998). Whatever the eventual resolution of this explanatory conflict concerning the causes of intensification, it is clear that the existence and use of geophyte-roasting pits in villages can be an important element in our understanding of the basic nature of prehistoric economies, sociopolitical organization, and cultural change.

NOTES

Acknowledgments. Funding for this research was provided by the Canadian Social Sciences and Humanities Research Council and by the Xaxli'p First Nation. Special thanks go to Chief Arthur Adolph for his keen interest in this and other heritage research. Natasha Lyons was also extremely helpful in analyzing the flotation samples and helping to refine our botanical analyses. Dana Lepofsky generously provided advice and facilities for which we are grateful. Sandra Peacock and Bob Muir provided comments on earlier drafts. Arthur Roberts generously provided aerial images of the site.

1. A complete plant survey of the immediate village area might be of use, but the usefulness of this would also depend on the fire effect on the geophyte resources. This research should be undertaken.

10

VILLAGES ON THE EDGE

PITHOUSES, CULTURAL CHANGE, AND THE ABANDONMENT OF AGGREGATE VILLAGES

Ian Kuijt and William C. Prentiss

> Possible temporal and spatial variations in reliance upon root and plant foods is essential to an understanding of the past demographic patterns of the plateau.
>
> —Ames and Marshall 1981:41

Recent research has directed new attention to the potential links between social process, economic development, and environmental change and the evolution and eventual abandonment of large pithouse villages of the Fraser and Thompson river regions of central British Columbia, Canada. As outlined elsewhere (Fladmark 1982; Hayden 1997; Pokotylo and Mitchell 1998; Prentiss and Chatters 2003a; Prentiss and Kuijt, this volume; Richards and Rousseau 1987; Rousseau, this volume; Stryd and Rousseau 1996), at some point after approximately 3,500 B.P., Native American groups living in the Lillooet area started to construct and live in large semisubterranean dwellings, generally referred to as pithouses. Up to approximately 1,600 years ago these pithouses were of medium or small diameter and were spatially clustered in small groups (ca. three–eight pithouses). Recent archaeological research illustrates that around 1600–1800 B.P. First Nations groups living in the Fraser River region started to build much larger and deeper pithouses, in greater numbers, and spatially organized their villages with a relatively dense clustering of structures. Current data indicate that the largest of these pithouse villages existed for a relatively short period of time, approximately from 1600 to 1000 B.P. (Kuijt 2001; Lenert 2001; Prentiss et al. 2003a, 2003b; Stryd 1973). These villages, including the Keatley Creek, Bell, and Bridge River sites, are characterized by a high frequency of extremely large (> 15 m diameter) and deep pithouses that are spatially clustered in larger groups (ca. 8–25 pithouses) (for more detail, see Fladmark 1982; Hayden 1997; Pokotylo and Mitchell 1998; Richards and Rousseau 1987). Drawing on the physical clustering of these pithouses, it is widely assumed that these settlements would have existed as winter villages, characterized by social differentiation and powerful families (e.g., Chatters and Pokotylo 1998; Hayden 1997; Hayden et al. 1985). Characteristic of this is the village of Keatley Creek. Although only limited numbers of structures have been radiocarbon dated at Keatley Creek, Hayden (personal communication, 2003) argues that this community would have been composed of around 75 structures occupied contemporaneously and with between 1,200 and 1,500 people living in the village (see also Hayden and Adams, this volume; Hayden and Cousins, this volume). This estimate, however, assumes that the majority of structures were occupied contemporaneously—something that has yet to be demonstrated. Although the exact scale of habitation of Keatley Creek in particular, and these villages in general, remains unclear, there is no question that these aggregate pithouse villages were significantly different from those identified in earlier and later periods of prehistory (Figure 10.1).

ABANDONMENT OF AGGREGATE VILLAGES AS A REGIONAL PHENOMENON

Although there is general agreement that social and cultural practices changed in significant ways with the abandonment of pithouse villages, debate continues as to why these villages were originally established and later abandoned and if this was related to social, economic, or environmental variables (see Chatters, this volume; Rousseau, this volume). Focusing on the issue of abandonment, Hayden and Ryder (1991, 2003) provide what is probably

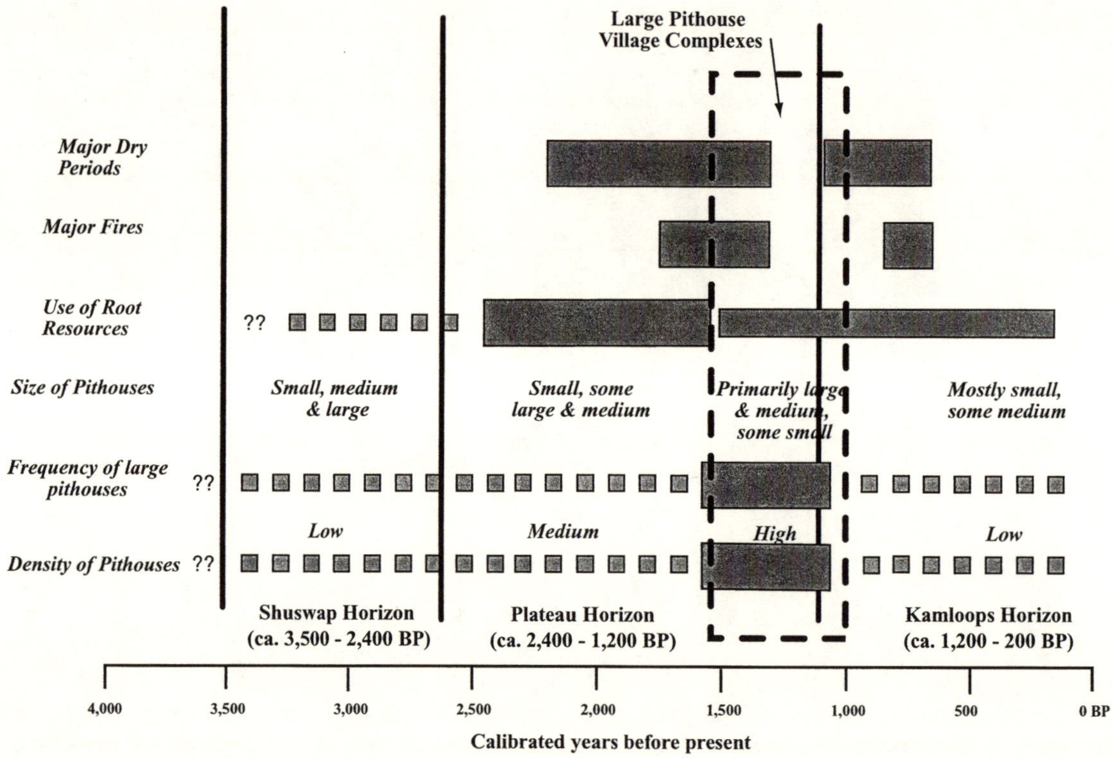

Figure 10.1. Shifting dimensions of the organization of pithouse villages, plant food harvesting and production, and major fire and dry periods through time along the Fraser and Thompson river drainages. Note the changes in the use of root resources with the appearance of large pithouse village complexes and the abandonment of these village complexes (based on Hallett et al. 2003; Hallett et al. in press; Lenert 2001; Peacock 1998; Richards and Rousseau 1987).

the most detailed local environmental-driven model. They argue that the abandonment of pithouse villages in the Lillooet area of the Fraser Valley illustrates a local "cultural collapse," occurring around 800 years ago, caused by a single event, or perhaps multiple landslides, that blocked the Fraser River and resulted in the destruction of salmon resources. Critical review of these arguments and the archaeological data supporting these claims has raised serious questions about this theory (Kuijt 2001; Lenert 2001). It is clear, for example, that First Nations groups continued to occupy the Lillooet region after 800 years ago and that there are substantial archaeological and geological data that contradict arguments for the Texas Creek landslide destroying salmon resources. Having noted the general evidence for occupational continuity within the Lillooet region, recent research (Prentiss et al. 2003b) has questioned whether all areas of the Mid-Fraser Canyon were continuously occupied. Regardless of how one views the issue of regional occupational continuity, there is no question that the majority of pithouse villages in this area do not appear to have been occupied as extensively (that is to say, the frequency and physical spacing of pithouses within a village) and did not have the large pithouses (> 15 m) after circa 800 B.P. compared with the case during the preceding 200–400 years.

Although Hayden and Ryder (1991, 2003) are correct in identifying the timing of this settlement shift along the Fraser River, it is clear that the abandonment of these villages was not a local event as they argue. Rather, the observed abandonment of the Lillooet region is part of a broader regional settlement transition that occurred in interior and coastal areas (Chatters, this volume; Goodale et al., this volume; Kuijt 2001; Prentiss et al. 2003a; Magne 1985; Pokotylo and Mitchell 1998; Rousseau, this volume). Specifically, the local cultural changes along the Lillooet area of the Fraser River at about 1,000 years ago were similar to simultaneous shifts in lifeways occurring in other areas of the Fraser River drainage, other major drainages (such as the Thompson), and even the Gulf of Georgia region of the Pacific Northwest Coast. One aspect to this is the regional development of large, and in some way more complex, aggregate villages before approximately 800 years ago, with a reduction in regional occupational intensity, if not population levels, after this point. Fladmark, for example, observes that there appears to have been a "marked peak of cultural deposition about 1000–1500 B.P. perhaps indicating some kind of climax in the number and size of pit-house settlements at this time" (1982:131). Other more detailed considerations of interregional cultural practices in the interior of British Columbia before and after 800 B.P. (e.g., Pokotylo and Mitchell 1998; Richards and Rousseau 1987) illustrate that in general the periods after 800 B.P. were characterized by reduction in the size of housepits and the abandonment of many, if not most, large pithouse villages. Magne (1985) notes that the large pithouse villages (ca. 100 pithouses) in the Taseko Lakes region date to the Lillooet phase (ca. 2,500–800 B.P.) and that this pattern of large aggregate villages was no longer practiced after circa 800 B.P. Similarly, archaeological research along the Thompson River and Shuswap Lake area illustrates a contemporary appearance of larger pithouse villages from circa 2,500–800 B.P. (Mohs 1981; Wilson 1980). Although pithouse villages were also founded and inhabited after about 1,200–800 B.P., these were considerably smaller in scale than those from the preceding period. Mohs (1981: table 4.1), for example, illustrates that as of 1980 all of the excavated or recorded large pithouse villages (EeRb-3, EdRa-9, EdQx-5) along the South Thompson River Valley date to the period of 2,400–1,200 B.P. Of the remaining dated pithouse villages, four were occupied before 800 B.P., three were occupied before and after 800 B.P., and only three were occupied after this point. Lenert and Goodale (2001) also demonstrate that there is a slight increase in the frequency of dated house floors in Chilcotin and the South Thompson/Western Shuswap Lakes region between 1200 and 800 B.P. This pattern, also in the more general Mid-Fraser region, illustrates short-lived increases in the frequency of housepit construction and occupation at key resource collection places (i.e., fishing sites) not present elsewhere on the Northern Plateau.

Beyond the interior areas, it should be noted that was a remarkably similar simultaneous transition occurred along the Pacific Northwest Coast (Ames and Maschner 1999; Fladmark 1982:111, figure 7; Matson and Coupland 1995). As noted by several researchers, if the Marpole phase represents a form of "cultural florescence" or "culture climax" (e.g., Ames and Maschner 1999:104; Burley 1980; R. Carlson 1996), then, in comparison, the later "Developed Coast" phase can be characterized as "spartan" (to use Fladmark's [1982:115] term). Thus, the pattern on the Gulf of Georgia as well as the evolutionary labels characterizing these perceived cultural florescences are both contemporaneous and strikingly similar to the model seen in multiple areas of the interior of British Columbia and the overall downsizing of communities and material culture after 1200–1000 B.P. A number of researchers (Ames 1991; Chatters 1995a, this volume; Fladmark 1982; Maschner 1991) illustrate that there is a sharp reduction in the number of radiocarbon samples over the last 800–1,000 years. Though there are many possible interpretations for such patterning, one clear possibility is that this reflects a significant population decline along the southern and central Northwest Coast, as well as the Northern Plateau. From this perspective we believe that the significant cultural shifts seen in the Lillooet area of the Fraser River should not be treated as an isolated event. Rather, it is clear that the period of 1000–800 B.P. was one of significant *regional* change in the interior and along the Northwest Coast, and thus researchers need to focus renewed attention to the question of why we see similar shifts from large, aggregate pithouse villages to smaller pithouse occupations after 800 B.P. in many areas of the Northern Plateau and elsewhere.

WHY WERE THE AGGREGATE VILLAGES OF THE NORTHERN PLATEAU ABANDONED?

There are, of course, several important questions related to the regional pattern of the establishment and abandonment of aggregate villages. For instance, why did large aggregate pithouse villages first emerge, how were they maintained as a social and economic unit for this period of time, and finally, why did First Nations groups shift to smaller-scale communities around 800 years ago (for discussion of the first of these topics, see Ames and Marshall 1981; Chatters, this volume; Pokotylo and Froese 1983; Prentiss and Chatters 2003a; Stryd 1973)? In this chapter we want to address three possible dimensions of the shift away from the large aggregate pithouse villages existing from 1600 to 1000 B.P. to smaller communities after this point in time. Specifically, we explore how regional shifts and the abandonment of the large aggregate village system might have been linked to paleoenvironmental shifts at this time, look at how such paleoenvironmental changes may have brought about shifts in the availability and importance of plant foods as a carbohydrate source, and consider how these changes might have been connected to the scale of communities living in winter villages along the Fraser River. In contrast to Hayden and Ryder (1991, 2003), we suggest that the abandonment of large aggregate winter pithouse villages in this area was not brought about by a lack of salmon; rather, it may have been linked to broader cultural and environmental transitions, including paleoenvironmental changes; resource competition; the decreased availability of plant resources in upland areas at this point in time; the nutritional limitations of a diet based on high-protein, low-fat fish; and how these factors might have impacted the time required for community members in large pithouse villages to recover from late spring episodes of food stress. Though this is only a preliminary treatment of these questions, which clearly require further consideration, we believe that an improved understanding of these factors and the complex interrelationship among them is likely to provide new insights into the cultural transition among First Nations groups living along the Thompson and Fraser river drainages around 800 years ago.

We believe that there were a number of interrelated factors involved in the shift from large aggregate villages, with a high density of large pithouses in a single location, to more dispersed communities of a limited number of people living in smaller pithouses. These include an increased (perhaps over?) reliance on salmon within large aggregate villages of circa 1600–800 B.P., an intensification in the use of mammalian resources during the same time frame, an increase in the scale of these villages, and a reduction in the availability and predictability of plant food resources. Members of these communities were highly focused on salmon resources, probably at a level beyond that of earlier periods. Recent evidence (Prentiss et al. 2003a; see also Rousseau, this volume) also suggests an expansion of the role of lean meat from mammals (i.e., deer) in the diets of inhabitants of Mid-Fraser communities. A few key factors include the following:

1. Paleoclimatic changes. In contrast to Hayden and Cousins (this volume), we believe that there is clear evidence of changing paleoclimatic conditions over the last 2,500 years. Specifically, current evidence illustrates that during the Little Climatic Optimum, there may have been considerable variation in the frequency and predictability of various key plant food resources.
2. Spring resource scheduling. In many ways late spring represents the major period of subsistence transition from stored winter foods to subsistence resources for immediate consumption. As is outlined elsewhere (see Lepofsky and Peacock, this volume, Tables 8.2–8.6), plant food resources serve as one of the critical winter recovery foods.
3. Scale of communities. Chatters (1995a) notes that the scale of communities is an important factor in Plateau subsistence and settlement systems. Simply put, more people require collection of food from a greater geographical area, which results, in his terms, in a form of "tethered" collecting. We suspect that with the reduced availability of plant resources between 1500 and 100 B.P. communities became hard-pressed to meet their winter recovery subsistence needs and that this eventually contributed to the dispersal of people into smaller communities: it appears that communities were no longer able to sustain high levels of nucleation.

SUBSISTENCE RESOURCES, NUTRITION, AND DIET BREADTH

One of the critical aspects of the evolution of complex forager/fisher societies centers on the interrelationships between demographic and cultural change during periods of food stress, be it long- or short-term in duration. In focusing on this broader anthropological question, researchers have paid considerable attention to the nature and availability of subsistence resources during the lean seasons of the year in the evolution of complex forager/fisher societies. Archaeological, historical, and ethnographic research has illustrated that human communities relying on hunting-gathering or fishing subsistence practices focused on high-protein, low-fat meat generally approached the problem of surviving such periods of stress in two ways: by incorporating greater quantities of fat-rich food resources into their diets or by complementing this diet with fresh or stored carbohydrate plant food resources (see Bettinger 1991; Kelly 1995; Malainey et al. 2001; Speth 1992; Speth and Spielmann 1983). There is considerable disagreement among researchers, however, as to the relative importance of carbohydrate plant food resources and the degree to which these might have been linked to economic developments. As highlighted by the epigraph at the start of this essay, and echoing the more recent detailed research by Peacock (1998) and Lepofsky and Peacock (this volume), we argue that an improved understanding of the role and use of carbohydrate food plants is critical to developing a more detailed reconstruction of the evolution of complex forager/fisher societies in select areas of North America. Our intent is not to resolve these debates in the context of this chapter but, rather, to suggest that in select cases social patterns associated with population aggregation, growth, and dispersal within complex forager/fisher societies are linked to subtle, yet significant, changes in the balancing of animal and plant food resources.

Previous archaeological and ethnographic research has highlighted the fundamental importance of storable subsistence resources as an economic foundation for the evolution of complex forager/fishing societies in many areas of the world (Arnold 1993, 1996; Chatters, this volume; Hayden 1981; Testart 1982). In the context of the Northern Plateau, the central, storable, meat protein resource was salmon. As is articulated by many researchers (e.g., Hayden 1981; Pianka 1970), fish resources are characterized by high rates of reproduction, rapid development, and the potential to be harvested in large numbers and stored for the winter. These characteristics make salmon suitable for long-term, large-scale exploitation and for supporting the high population levels typical of complex hunter-gatherers. In light of the characteristics of salmon resources, it should come as no surprise that ethnographically observed groups and First Nations members living in these areas today, as well as archaeologists, emphasize the primacy of salmon as the economic and subsistence foundation of past people living in the Lillooet region. Observations made in the historic period by ethnographers and interviews with First Nations members highlight the social and economic importance of salmon for survival at all times of the year. Similarly, archaeological data illustrate that during the period of circa 1600–800 B.P. prehistoric groups relied on salmon more heavily than at any other period. Recognizing this pattern, many, if not most, archaeological and anthropological reconstructions of the past emphasize salmon, at times in combination with terrestrial mammals, over all other food sources. From this has emerged the assumption, often implicitly held, that a continued expansion of salmon harvesting in the past permitted increases in stored food, population growth within a community, and by extension, developments of cultural complexity, a labor surplus, and the development of social inequality.

As an alternative to models prioritizing salmon, a number of studies explore the cultural and economic role of plant food resources in the diet of First Nations groups living in the past (e.g., Alexander 1992; Ames and Marshall 1981; Chatters, this volume; Lepofsky and Peacock, this volume; Peacock 1998; Pokotylo and Froese 1983; Turner 1992). Echoing the works of a number of other authors (e.g., Ames and Marshall 1981; Lepofsky and Peacock, this volume; Lepofsky et al. 1996; Peacock 1998; Pokotylo and Froese 1983), we argue that in combination with salmon, plant resources (specifically those with high carbohydrate sources) were critical to prehistoric lifeways in pithouse villages. As is forcefully argued in the epigraph cited at the start of this essay, Ames and Marshall (1981) illustrate that the initial founding of First Nations settlement and subsistence systems focusing on pithouses was fundamentally rooted on the intensification of plant exploitation in the past. This argument has been furthered by the pivotal research by Pokotylo and Froese, who argue: "It is plausible that the additional stored subsistence resources required by the larger pithouse villages were obtained not from furthering the intensification of the salmon fishery, but by intensified collecting and processing of root crops in upland locations" (1983:152). We would expand this argument and suggest that a more detailed understanding of the relationship between paleoclimatic change and the nature of plant and animal subsistence resources and human demography may shed new light into the social, economic, and environmental factors behind the abandonment of large aggregate pithouse villages circa 800 years ago. When addressing the shift from large pithouse villages of several hundred people to smaller communities, composed of medium to small pithouses and reduced numbers of inhabited residences, it is important to consider the possible interconnections and links among diet breadth, the availability of carbohydrate food resources, resource competition, and the limitations that communities of different sizes faced in adapting to social and environmental changes during the existence of prehistoric Lillooet communities.

Moby Salmon: Potential Problems with High-Protein, Low-Fat Winter Diet

Several important studies have started to model the subtle, yet important, balancing of food sources within the prehistoric diet on the Northern Plateau (e.g., Mullin et al. 1997; Peacock 1998; Plew 1992). These studies represent a welcome departure from many previous approaches, in that they either directly or indirectly illustrate the sophisticated balancing of different food sources among prehistoric peoples and increase our collective awareness of the dietary and cultural complexities of prehistoric subsistence systems. Drawing on these studies, we see two major weaknesses in the traditional modeling of salmon, either intentionally or unintentionally, as a caloric and cultural monocrop. First, it fails to consider the very real nutritional problems that can be associated with high-protein, low-fat diets; and second, it fails to recognize that despite the abundance of salmon, other food sources can serve as critical limiting factors in how much salmon can be utilized.

One potential illustration of these points is seen in the nutritional overreliance on protein. There is, of course, a cascade of negative physiological processes that is triggered if protein consumption exceeds the rate at which the liver can metabolize amino acids and the body synthesizes and excretes urea (see Speth 1992; Speth and Spielmann 1983). Protein should not regularly form more than 50 percent of the total calories of the diet and must be kept below 25–30 percent in the diet of pregnant women. At select times of the year hunter-gatherer/fishing groups clearly existed at this level or even higher (Lazenby and McCormack 1985; Speth 1992; Speth and Spielmann 1983). For example, Lazenby and McCormack (1985) illustrate that at select times of the year diets that are tightly focused on salmon can result in Hypervitaminosis D among children and, in extreme cases, adults. Hypervitaminosis D results when a population acquires more vitamin D than is physiologically required. Fresh and prepared salmon dishes are a rich source of vitamin D, with salmon oil, as well as cod liver oil, having twice as much vitamin D as other sources. It is, in fact, potentially toxic, especially for children. When salmon are the major source of food, especially if combined with calcium sources, vitamin D levels can build up, resulting in short- and long-term symptoms of hypervitaminosis D or even death. In the case of children, for example, this can result from as little as ten times the recommended daily allowance for vitamin D.

Overreliance on high-protein, low-fat sources can quickly bring about some important biochemical changes in the human body—changes that can increase the caloric needs of individuals and potentially influence decision making (Table 10.1). One of the frequently observed by-products of hypervitaminosis D is a sharp reduction in appetite in humans. As a second by-product, and as noted by a number of researchers (e.g., Lazenby and McCormack 1985; Speth and Spielmann 1983), high-protein diets often result in an increased metabolic rate (between 20 and 25 percent), which would in turn require a substantial increase in the daily caloric needs of individuals. These changes are most likely to occur in late winter (Table 10.1). In the context of prehistoric Lillooet pithouse communities, late winter was when fresh plants and animals were unavailable, and stored plant resources were either seriously depleted or totally exhausted. As pointed out by Lazenby and McCormack (1985: table 2), the effect of hypervitaminosis D includes a wide range of dramatic physiological conditions and can be relieved in a relatively short period of time if it is recognized and if alternative food sources are available. Though clearly in need of further study, this is one potential example of some of the critical, yet subtle, paleodietary issues that may have impacted people living in the Northern Plateau in the past.

Plant Resources as a Carbohydrate Source

When considering the role of plant resources in the diet of First Nations groups, it is also important to consider the potential limitations to a salmon-rich diet when access to multiple carbohydrate sources declines or becomes less predictable over time. Several studies, including works by Speth (1992) and Speth and Spielmann (1983), outline that in many cases the long-term success of hunter-gatherer/forager/fisher groups utilizing high levels of a meat source is directly linked to the availability and integration of carbohydrate systems into their diets. The general assumption that increased meat, such as salmon, leads to increased carrying capacity for a community, and by extension a stored resource and the political advancement of individuals, fails to understand that a salmon-based diet is at least partially linked to access to predictable carbohydrate plant resources.

Both of these issues are founded on the assumption that food resources, either fresh or stored, vary in abundance and quality on a seasonal basis and that it is in the winter months that human communities face their most significant challenge in survival. Archaeological, historical, and ethnographic research has illustrated that human communities relying on hunter-gathering or fishing subsistence practices generally approached the problem of surviving the winter in two ways: by incorporating fat-rich food resources or consuming high-protein, low-fat meat with stored carbohydrates (see Malainey et al. 2001; Speth 1992; Speth and Spielmann 1983). In the case of the Northern Plateau, there is considerable evidence to suggest that it was the second of these two approaches that was practiced by First Nations groups. From this perspective, and following other researchers (e.g., Ames and Marshall 1981; Peacock 1998; Pokotylo and Froese 1983; Turner 1992), we argue that the subsistence ceiling, or carrying capacity, among prehistoric groups living in the Lillooet region was limited by not only how much salmon a family or community caught and processed each fall but also, alternatively, how successful they were in locating, maintaining, processing, and storing plant carbohydrate food sources over the summer months.

From an ethnographic and archaeological perspective it is clear that plant resources served a wide range of economic and social functions in the diet of First Nations communities in the past (for more extensive consideration of these topics, see Lepofsky and Peacock, this volume; Peacock 1998; Turner 1992). In this discussion we want to briefly focus on what we see as two of the major roles. First, major geophyte staples—spring beauty and avalanche lily—provided abundant food for people in the spring and, by extension, were the first significant carbohydrate food sources available after the winter (Turner 1992). Second, berries were dried and stored as possibly *the* major plant food source stored for the winter. The timing and richness of spring plant resources were critical for people in the successful transition from the long winter months to the spring (Figure 10.2).

Similar to salmon, plant resources are seasonally available, limited to specific geographic areas, and subject to variation between seasons. As noted by Lepofsky and Peacock (this volume, Tables 8.2–8.6) and Turner (1992, 1997), there were at least three major periods of resource availability for plant species. These include spring (lodgepole pine inner bark, edible green shoots such as cow parsnip and fireweed, and early spring beauty and other root resources), midsummer (black huckleberry, spring beauty, and avalanche lily corms), and fall (whitebark pine seeds). Some of these were very specific in their required harvesting time, whereas others, such as edible roots and black tree lichen, were available over a wider period of time. Turner (1992:411) argues that saskatoon berries were undoubtedly the most important plant staple in traditional Lillooet society. Though careful not to iden-

Table 10.1. Seasonal Aspects of High-Protein, Low-Fat Diet among Prehistoric Lillooet Communities.

	Fall (September)	Midwinter (January)	Early Spring (March–April)	Midsummer (July)
Available Foods	Preserved and fresh plants, salmon, and meat	Preserved plants and salmon, rare fresh meat	Preserved plants and salmon, rare fresh meat	Fresh plants and animals
Relative Abundance of Available Foods	Extremely high, maximum available	Low, depleted	Lowest possible, severely depleted	Medium–high, increasing
Relative Appetite of Individuals	Normal	Normal	Depressed to sharply depressed	Normal
Relative Metabolic Rate	Normal	Normal	Significantly elevated (20–25%)	Normal
Relative Importance of Fresh or Stored Carbohydrates in Utilizing Dietary Protein	Normal	Important	Critical	Normal
Relative Caloric Needs	Normal	Normal	High	Normal
Status of Relative Caloric Needs	Stable	Increasing	Significantly elevated (ca. 20–25%)	Stable

tify a percentage of the overall caloric intake in the past diet of First Nations groups, she suggests that this alone must have been well over 5 percent of all calories, including those from meat and fish. She also notes a wide range of other important plant foods, each of which may well have constituted at least 10 percent of the total vegetable food for early Plateau peoples. These include choke cherries, blackcaps, black huckleberries, spring beauty corms, nodding onions, balsamroot (roots and bud stems), and cow parsnip. These resources were often eaten fresh or were dried and stored as a winter food resource. Thus, plants served as a critical source of carbohydrates. As noted by Lepofsky and Peacock (this volume, Tables 8.2–8.6) and Peacock (1998), seeds, nuts, roots, fruits, berries, and greens provided high levels of carbohydrates and other critical nutrients that balance high-protein, low-fat salmon resources. From a nutritional perspective, all of these plant staples would have been critical in facilitating the intensive use of salmon.

Paleoclimatic Changes: Possible Shifts in the Availability of Plant Resources

Given the importance of plant resources as carbohydrates, it is important to address how broader climatic changes over the last 2,000 years have altered the availability, location, and abundance of key plant resources. As articulated later, we believe that high-carbohydrate food sources were critical to the successful recovery of people living in pithouses in the late spring. Moreover, we believe that changes in vegetation, brought on by regional and global climatic changes starting around just before 2000 B.P. and gradually changing through to 800 years ago, may have led to subtle yet significant decreases in the availability and spatial distribution of critical upland plant food resources. Research on global temperature changes indicates that relatively high-elevation ecotones, such as in the Upper Hat Creek area, may well have undergone significant changes in mean temperature, precipitation, and habitat. Research by Hallett et al. (2003a) and Chatters and Leavell (1995) illustrates that there were two major dry periods: the first at circa 2200–1300 B.P., and the second at circa 1100–750 B.P. On the whole, dry conditions are advantageous for root plants, in that this establishes open area for geophytes. Conversely, wet conditions increase forest cover, closing off meadows that contain geophytes. Late Holocene climatic change, and specifically the development of warm, dry summers, may have altered the natural habitat for many of the plant species utilized. The habitat conditions for plant food vary considerably in terms of necessary temperature, moisture, and sunlight, and as such, it is possible that the growing conditions for plants such as balsamroot, nodding onion, and other members of the lily family may have been altered depending on regional paleoenvironmental patterns. As noted by Chatters and Pokotylo (1998:79) and Hallett et al. (2003a; Hallett et al. 2003b), increased temperatures and reduced precipitation at this period of time would have led to increased forest openings, droughts, and flooding, quite possibly increasing the available habitat for some key economic plant resources in the intermediate grassland and parkland area.

Researchers have noted that many of the root-roasting pits were associated with seasonal camps situated in intermediate grassland and parkland areas, such as the

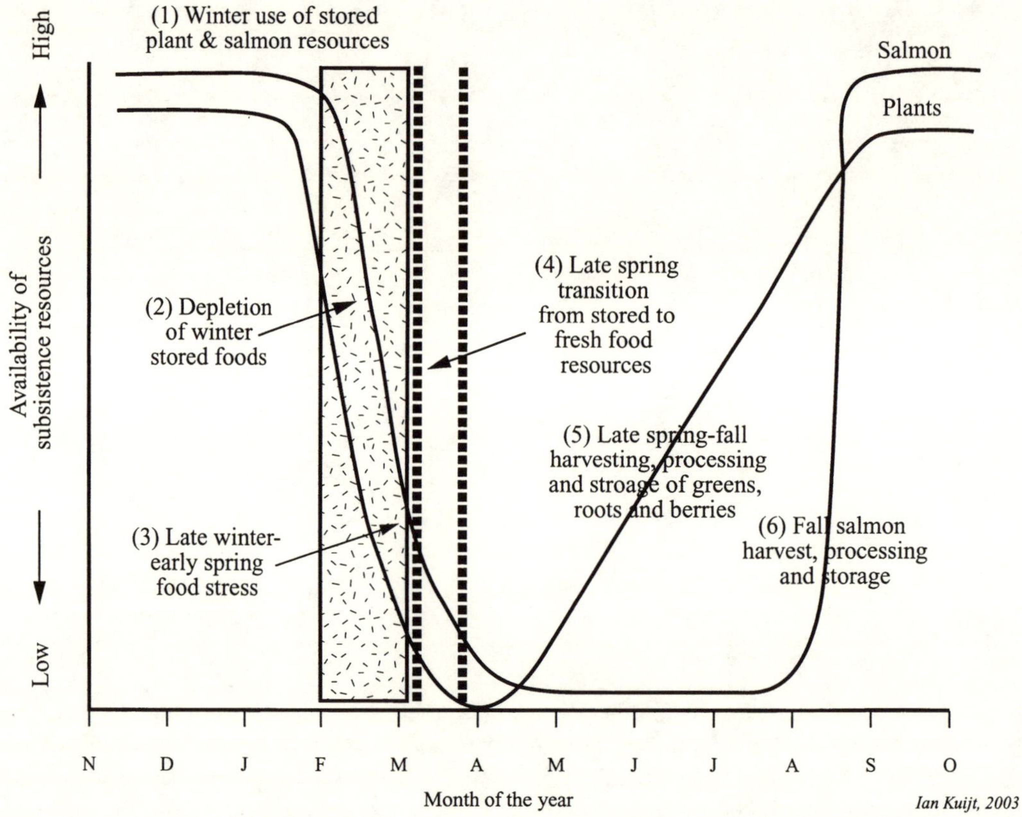

Figure 10.2. Subsistence resources and seasonal cycles among First Nations groups living in the Fraser and Thompson river regions, circa 1600–500 B.P., based on ethnographic sources. Note the late winter/early spring food stress and the gradual and increasing availability of greens, roots, and berries from spring to fall.

Upper Hat Creek Valley area between Lillooet and Cache Creek in late spring to early summer (for detailed consideration of the ethnobotany and archaeological evidence for the plant resource use of First Nations groups, see Lepofsky and Peacock, this volume; Peacock 1998; Pokotylo and Froese 1983; Turner 1992). These pits were often reused. Among others, research by Pokotylo and Froese (1983) has recovered the carbonized remains of fuel (mostly coniferous species), vegetable matting to facilitate cooking (including conifer boughs and needles and kinnikinnick), and plant foods (including onions and other members of the lily family and probably balsamroot). There is some archaeological evidence to suggest that the roasting of root plants was practiced more intensively before 800 B.P. than after this point (Figure 10.1). Although they can be interpreted from multiple perspectives, current data illustrate a peak in root roasting from about 2600 to 1600 B.P. (see Lepofsky and Peacock, this volume; Peacock 1998). In the upland areas of Hat Creek there is extensive archaeological evidence for the intensive utilization of root resources for the period of circa 2,400 to 800 B.P., with the use of circular to oval cultural depressions representing cooking pits (Peacock 1998; Pokotylo and Froese 1983; Pokotylo and Mitchell 1998; Rousseau et al. 1991). Pokotylo and Froese argue, "Given the time and energy invested in the construction and maintenance of such large facilities, as well as the anticipated scale of root collecting necessary to fill the pits, we hypothesize that the period from ca. 300 to ca. 800 B.P. represents a time of more intensive root resource gathering, relative to the Kamloops Phase and the ethnohistoric period" (1983:152). As articulated by Lepofsky and Peacock (this volume), other archaeological evidence, including the reversion to the smaller root-roasting pits of the Kamloops Horizon (ca. 800–200 B.P.), may illustrate a reduction in the scale of root roasting (assuming that feature size is linked to the number of people participating at any one time) but a continuation in frequency with the abandonment of the large aggregate pithouse villages.

It is interesting to note that there may be a temporal correlation between the research findings by Hallett et al. (2003a) and the frequency of root-processing activities (Figure 10.1). In general, the highest frequency and largest size of root-roasting features occurred between circa 2500 and 1500 B.P. (Lepofsky and Peacock, this volume), which is roughly correlated with a relatively dry period. Although based on nonrandom sampling from different regions of the Northern Plateau and in need of detailed analysis, this patterning correlates in a general way with the record of Mid-Fraser village occupations, which show the most intense periods at about 1700–1200 and 800–900 B.P. (Prentiss et al. 2003a). It is also interesting to note that the Hat Creek cooking pits dating prior to circa 800 B.P. are substantially larger than those reported for later periods (Lepofsky and Peacock, this volume; Pokotylo and Mitchell 1998). Moreover, as illustrated by Lepofsky and Peacock (this volume), although the size of roasting features decreased after this point, the frequency remained constant. This pattern indicates that after 800 B.P., either First Nations groups relied less on these plant resources, they shifted to other plant resources, populations declined, or the relative amount of these targeted plant resources was reduced. In brief, we suspect that when it gradually got wetter after circa 800 B.P., the frequency and predictability of plant food sources were reduced while fishing may have actually improved. Although it is possible that this finding is caused by archaeological sampling, these data support the interpretation that the use of upland areas and the harvesting of specific plant resources were reduced after 800 B.P. If so, it is possible that this was at least partially linked to paleoclimatic changes.

SEASONS OF FOOD STRESS, DEMOGRAPHY, AND THE ABANDONMENT OF AGGREGATE VILLAGES

To what extent, then, was the abandonment of Lillooet pithouse villages linked to paleoclimatic change, resource competition, a reduction in the availability of plant carbohydrate resources, and diet breadth? This is, of course, both a very complicated question and one that has only recently drawn the attention of researchers. Although this is only a preliminary consideration of this important question, we believe that there are several issues that are critical to understanding possible interrelationships, including environmental change at this period of time, how the abandonment of these villages might have been linked to the availability and abundance of plant resource–based systems, and how this might be linked to changes in the scale of individual human communities on the Northern Plateau. Understanding the potential links among changing climatic conditions, plant availability, and the abandonment of settlements requires us to examine the economic and subsistence context of winter village life. In particular, we want to draw attention to two critical dimensions of the yearly subsistence schedule: the importance of harvesting and storing sufficient foods to last the winter and the ability of people to locate and harvest plants for immediate consumption in the spring.

Winter Survival: Balancing Different Stored Foods

In prehistoric Plateau communities winter survival was directly linked to success in locating, harvesting, and storing plant and animal resources. Turner (1992, 1997), Alexander (1992), and Lepofsky and Peacock (this volume) provide important syntheses of the seasonal scheduling and use of plant resources. They note that there is considerable year-to-year variation in the availability of certain foods. While all vary to some extent, there is no question that plant carbohydrate sources, such as saskatoons, choke cherries, and soapberries, are particularly susceptible to yearly fluctuations in fruit production. This is, needless to say, very important with foods to be stored over the winter. For example, Turner notes: "An 'off' year for saskatoons or for salmon could be a serious matter and might cause severe hardship, especially in winter and early spring" (1992:420). Indeed, many early ethnographic accounts of contact period Lillooet groups indicate that by late winter/early spring salmon provided the only available food resource. In discussing the winter diet among Lillooet First Nations groups, Elder Sam Mitchell reflected that by late winter a typical meal consisted of dried salmon and a handful of dried berries (Hayden 1992c). Ethnographic accounts have also noted that stored plant resources were usually exhausted before salmon was, sometimes well before fresh plant resources were available (Alexander 1992). Thus, through the winter, the diet of people living in pithouse villages would have become increasingly focused on dried salmon.

There are, however, considerable differences in the fat content among different salmon species. So which of several species did First Nations groups opt to process and dry? Surprisingly, it appears that in many situations First Nations groups opted to process and store lean rather than high-fat salmon. Ethnographic research by Romanoff (1992b) illustrates that groups storing salmon adopted one of two strategies for the selection of salmon depending on their long-term goals and the season of the year: they either selected high-fat salmon for immediate consumption or systematically selected lean salmon to preserve for the winter. Both of these strategies entail trade-offs in terms of caloric value versus preparation time and period of storage. The strongest argument for the selection of low-fat salmon is that lean salmon species can be dried in less time, preserve better for the winter, and are less likely to go rancid in the late winter (for extensive discussion of this, see Romanoff 1992b:259–262). If one were willing to accept that the constraints of salmon storage and preparation are similar for the past and the present, then this suggests that prehistoric First Nations groups would have deliberately targeted lean salmon as a winter resource. This would have ensured stored salmon for the winter, and a high level of protein, but reduced the level of fat compared with intake during other times of the year.

From a nutritional perspective there is one major drawback to this strategy: successful salmon preservation and storage are at least partially linked to fat minimization over the winter months. This was probably not a problem over the majority of the winter. In years of low salmon harvest or those with long winters, however, the limited availability of fat may well have become a major concern. The late winter is, as noted earlier, the time when stored plant/carbohydrate sources become exhausted and the relative appetite of individuals is likely to become depressed; and even short-term reliance on a high-protein, low-fat diet can lower metabolic rates and result in an increased caloric need. Simultaneously individual and community needs for stored plant resources with high carbohydrates are at the lowest level of the year. In addition, it is clear that at certain times of the year, such as late winter, life in these aggregate villages must have been quite difficult environments for adults and, more importantly, children. Collectively, this provides us with a nutritional picture complementary to ethnographic accounts, which highlight the urgent, if not potentially dangerous, nature of the subsistence transition from the early to late spring in prehistoric pithouse communities.

Spring Recovery: Immediate Consumption and the Scale of Communities

In many ways the early spring can be characterized as a potential period of food crisis within prehistoric pithouse communities (Table 10.1, Figure 10.1). A reduction in the predictability and levels of high-carbohydrate plant resources would have impacted aggregate pithouse communities in several ways. First, it would have increased the amount of time necessary for community members to successfully transition from stored to fresh resources in the late spring/early summer. Second, this would have resulted in increased transportation costs for moving select food resources (e.g., fresh or prepared root resources from upland areas) from procurement area to residential location. Ames and Marshall (1981) note that changes in the scale of communities, subsistence resources, and community organization are often interrelated. In the context of the Northern Plateau, it is possible that reduced availability—and perhaps, more importantly, reduced predictability—of plant resources would have increased the amount of time required for larger communities to recover from the winter, in that this would have increased foraging costs and time (Figures 10.3–10.4). Depending on the nature of subsistence resource concentrations (such as density, seasonality, and visibility), increases in the number of people living in communities would have required people to forage farther for food or to harvest existing plants more extensively. Depending on where these resources were located vis-à-vis the settlement, this might represent several more days of time to travel to a likely regional location, set up a temporary camp, and identify individual patches of plants.

Foraging time, of course, could have been mitigated by harvesting previously identified plant resources located in close proximity to the winter pithouse village. While this is an attractive short-term solution, it creates the potential for the overexploitation of plant resources situated in an ecologically fragile environment. Turner (1992) notes that little is known about the prolonged and continuous harvesting of populations of wild food plants. With Hayden (1992c), she argues that picking berries and harvesting wild greens might not be expected to have a major impact on healthy plant populations. She does, however, believe that the intensive harvesting of edible roots and underground parts, such as spring beauty and yellow avalanche lily, could have resulted in significant depletion of the plants. To deal with this potential problem, groups must have been attentive to overexploitation and must have practiced some limited means of selecting for specific plants, such as tilling and perhaps the intentional scattering of seeds. From a long-term perspective this has the potential to exhaust patches located close to the settlement and, in light of the potential reduction of plant resources because of environmental change, irreversibly reduce the extent to which plant food resources could contribute to the overall diet. In light of our understanding of the importance of plants in combination with salmon and other lean protein sources, any reduction in the availability and quantity of plant resources for winter storage would have also reduced the number of weeks during the winter that First Nations communities would have had stored plant carbohydrate food sources available and, by extension, how many people could be supported in these communities.

Differences in the scale of communities influence the number of options available to deal with short- and long-term resource stress. In general, it would take more time for larger communities to make the transition to spring/summer resources, and as such, smaller communities would be better suited to adjust to gradually reduced or less predictable carbohydrate sources (Figure 10.3). As outlined by Kelly (1998), the length of time people can remain at an individual settlement and the number living within this settlement depend on the density, abundance, and spatial distribution of food resources relative to com-

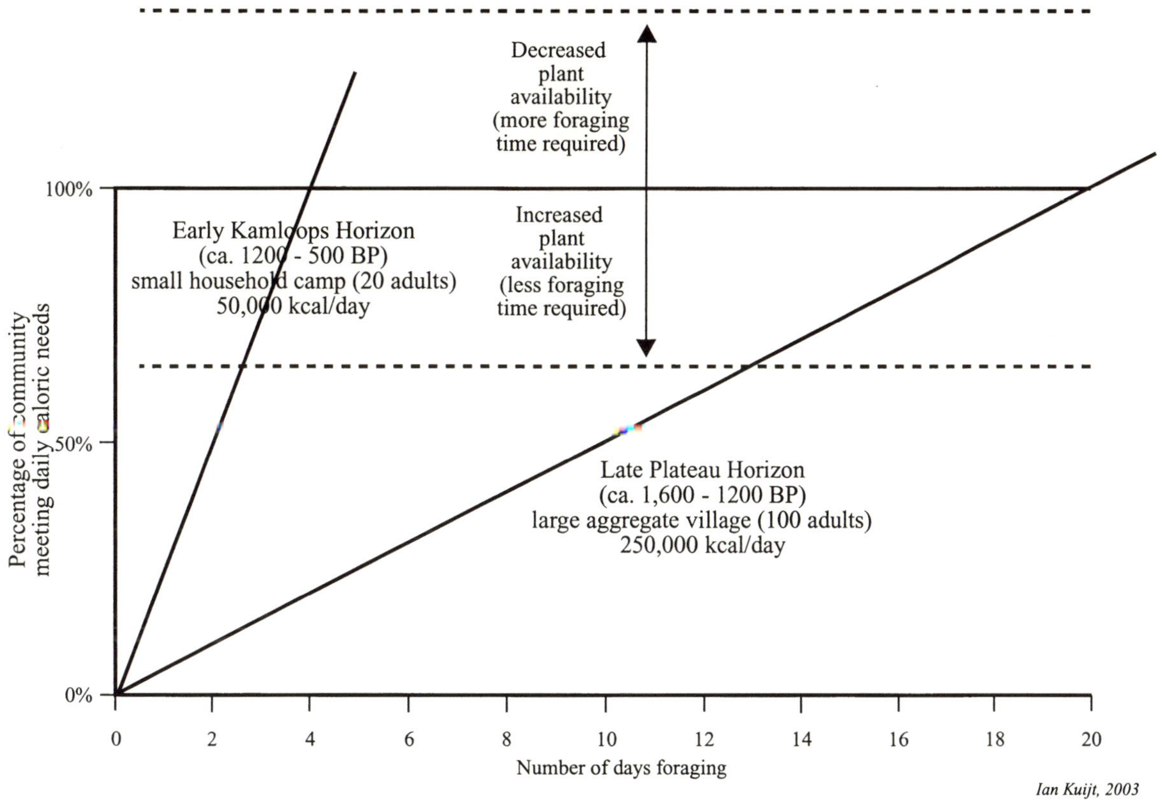

Figure 10.3. Model of the relationship between community size and the estimated time necessary to procure plant food resources (mostly greens and roots) in the late spring, assuming an expanded subsistence catchment radius of 5 km for five individuals/day. Foraging time ranges from four days for the early Kamloops Horizon to 20 days for the late Plateau Horizon. Note the high potential impact of the reduced or delayed availability of plant subsistence resources (e.g., long winter, poor summer growing conditions) on large versus small communities. This would have increased the amount of time necessary for communities to recover from the period of late winter food stress.

munity size. In the case of the Northern Plateau, we argue that the availability, location, and density of plant resources were critical in determining how much time it took for communities of different sizes to recover from winter food stress and ensure that all members of the community would have their daily caloric needs matched.

DISCUSSION AND CONCLUSION

If one accepts the argument that there was a cultural florescence, for lack of a better term, in the development of large aggregate pithouse villages between 1,600 and 800 years ago, then it is important to understand why this distinctive regional village system originally appeared and why it was abandoned. Despite the importance of understanding this process, relatively little archaeological research has directly addressed the social, economic context of aggregation and the abandonment of pithouse villages. In modeling the process of aggregation and later abandonment it is important to recognize that the cultural and environmental processes that originally brought people together in these villages may not be the same processes that led First Nations groups to shift lifeways and abandon this system of aggregate villages.

Collectively, this discussion of current archaeological, ethnographic, and biophysical data provides an interesting perspective on the interrelationships of cultural and environmental change, in general, and plant gathering and the emergence and abandonment of large, complex aggregate pithouse settlements in the Northern Plateau, in particular. Following Lepofsky and Peacock (this volume), we argue that current data suggest that the most extensive use of root intensification predates the emergence of aggregate pithouse villages in the Mid-Fraser area between circa 1600 and 800 B.P. Lepofsky and Peacock's work clearly demonstrates that there were fewer root-roasting facilities in upland areas between 1500 and 800 B.P. and a greater frequency of facilities associated with lowland pithouse villages at the same time. They also note that after 800 B.P. root-roasting practices changed once again. This time there was a decrease in the size of root-roasting ovens and an increase in their frequency. Thus, there is an overall temporal link among the shifts in the size of pithouses, the abandonment of pithouse

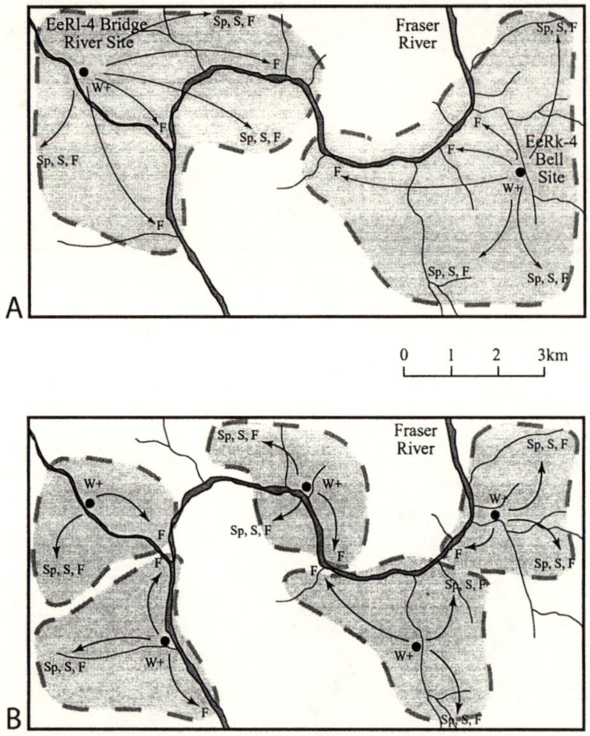

Figure 10.4. Model of the shift in immediate catchment areas from (A) large aggregate villages and seasonal camps of the late Plateau Horizon (ca. 1600–1200 B.P.) to (B) small household winter camp settlements and seasonal camps of the early Kamloops Horizon (ca. 1200–500 B.P.). For seasonal designation, W+ = winter and other seasons, Sp = spring, S = summer, and F = fall. Note the greater subsistence catchment of large versus small communities and how population nucleation would have increased the foraging costs and time necessary for communities to recover from the period of late winter food stress. Note also that with the exception of EeRl-4 and EeRk-4, site location is hypothesized. Estimated catchment areas are immediate and local (within a day's walk) for illustrative purposes. Actual settlement practices would have been much more extensive, with both local and nonlocal landscapes (such as upland meadows for plant resources) being utilized by groups.

villages, and the transition in root roasting in this area. We also argue that these cultural and demographic transitions were linked to paleoclimatic changes. In general, dry conditions favor aggregation in big aggregate villages, with payoffs coming from control of salmon access as long as root and berry resources were plentiful. When it got wetter, salmon resources remained plentiful everywhere, but resources for roots and berries declined. Therefore, the payoff for large village nucleation probably declined after circa 800 B.P., and people dispersed to smaller settlements after this point. Simply put, increased residential mobility was required again to access plants and mammals, even while salmon were relatively ubiquitous. This contrasts with the settlement system seen during the period of prolonged summer droughts and dry, hot climate between 2400 and 800 B.P. (Bennett et al. 2001; Hallett and Walker 2000; Hallett et al. 2003b), with generally dry conditions through 800 B.P., and as seen with a big peak in fire frequency in interior forests of the eastern Plateau at circa 800–900 B.P. These lines of evidence illustrate the temporal linkage among changing paleoclimatic conditions, various subsistence systems, and the abandonment of aggregate pithouse villages.

Although largely beyond the scope of this chapter, it is interesting to reflect on some of the other possible interconnections between population aggregation/the abandonment of large pithouse villages and cultural developments at this period. Chatters (this volume) argues that conflict was an important factor in the formation of villages. As noted by Rousseau (this volume) and Chatters (this volume), for example, the bow and arrow made their appearance by at least 1500 B.P., possibly earlier, and data from Keatley Creek indicate the intensification of hunting midsized mammals (Prentiss et al. 2003b). Chatters (this volume) suggests that the bow and arrow may also have increased the lethality of warfare, thus offering a greater payoff for population aggregation as protection from attack.

Another possibility is that the original appearance of these large pithouse villages was related to social competition for control of salmon and plant resources. Warm and dry conditions likely hastened the beginnings of a desertification process, leading to increased sediment in rivers and concomitant impacts on salmon populations (Chatters and Leavell 1995). To exacerbate the situation, there is some evidence to suggest that the North Pacific was warming, reducing the intensity of the Aleutian Low pressure index, further affecting salmon populations (Mann et al. 1998). Select portions of the Fraser, Thompson, and Columbia river systems (Lillooet, South Thompson, Chilcotin, Slocan, and The Dalles) may have offered significantly elevated returns on salmon compared with the levels in other areas. With increasing competition for control of these places after 1600–800 B.P., there was a strong payoff for aggregation in big villages along major rivers. This payoff was probably linked to the control and maintenance of positions in trade networks and protection from other competing groups. The need for control of these locations may have necessitated reduced mobility, led to the consolidation of large pithouse village complexes, and resulted in intensive local resource use (such as outlined by Lepofsky and Peacock, this volume) and eventually local resource depression in nonfish resources—perhaps including roots. From our perspective, changes in the frequency and size of root-roasting features, including at Keatley Creek, are likely to be related to both the relative availability and the predictability of select plant resources, as well as the social context of household and village organization. As specific resources became scarce, large villages split up along household lines, and people may have ceased public preparation of this food, thus perhaps avoiding obligations to share and enhancing household reserves (Flannery 2002).

The shift away from large pithouse villages back to smaller household-oriented pithouse communities may have been linked to the peak Little Climatic Optimum; changes in the availability, spatial distribution, and density of plant food resources; and the nutritional limitations of a high-protein, low-fat diet based on fish. We suspect that when the stress of warm, dry conditions peaked, so did the process of salmon and root intensification along the rapids of the Mid-Fraser River. As cooler and wetter conditions returned, the villages broke up and people returned to the pre-1600–800 B.P. foraging strategy. Early investment in aggregate communities paid off with rising populations, eventual wealth, and the reduced threat of violence. As local resources became exhausted, or as the characteristics of critical foods (such as plants) were altered, the populations struggled to maintain aggregate villages and former status. Prior to the abandonment of the Lillooet area, the largest households of villages like Keatley Creek increasingly sought control of a wider range of resources and foraging landscapes. But this last act of desperation was probably not enough to salvage a regional system on the edge. We may never know the exact proximate cause of the breakup, but it likely lies in the relationship between a population pushed to its economic and physical limit and the impact of changing resource conditions.

In this essay we have explored how regional population change along the Fraser River some 800 years ago might be linked to subsistence systems, settlement practices, the scale of communities, and paleoenvironmental change and seasonal food stresses. In this chapter we have tried to expand the discussion of the abandonment of pithouse communities to a more holistic interpretation looking at paleoclimatic changes, resource availability, and the scale of communities. Drawing on other studies (e.g., Lepofsky and Peacock, this volume; Peacock 1998; Turner 1997), we have tried to explore some of the potential roles of plant food resources in the diet to understand how changes in the availability of these resources might be interlinked to storage systems for salmon. Expanding on this, we argue that the high-protein salmon and deer diet of First Nations communities living in aggregate pithouse villages between 1600 and 1000 B.P. would have been facilitated by plant food resources—and would have been affected as the predictability and availability of these changed during this period. People in these communities were increasingly susceptible to seasonal food shortages and may well have been subjected to nutritional problems related to their high-protein, low-fat diet in the winter months. Additionally, it is clear that it would have taken longer for members of the large communities of this period to transition to fresh resources in the spring.

We suggest that with changes in the nature of plant food availability, scheduling, and predictability, it became increasingly difficult to maintain nucleation in villages. As highlighted by Chatters (this volume), nucleation requires complex social and economic relationships, and people are constantly faced with the option of segmenting larger communities back into small household settlements. We should note, however, that in many ways the details of this model and interpretive scheme are in need of further development. Research by plant ecologists, for example, is clearly required to better understand how the habitats of individual plant species might be affected by regional climatic changes. Such research is clearly necessary to develop a comprehensive understanding of how climatic conditions change microenvironments; which economic plant resources would have been impacted by these changes; and how this would have altered the availability, abundance, and seasonality of these plant resources. Although we recognize the need for additional future research, there is no question that there is strong archaeological evidence for changes in plant food processing in these areas at the same time as we see regional changes in settlement systems, and we believe that it is entirely plausible that this might be interrelated with broader cultural and paleoenvironmental changes. From this standpoint, then, we move toward an improved understanding of prehistoric change along the Fraser River some 1,000 years ago, one that recognizes some of the complexities and interrelationships of humans and their environments.

Acknowledgments. This chapter draws on conversations with many researchers over the years and has been supported directly and indirectly by several funding sources. Financial support for this research has been provided by the University of Lethbridge, the Institute for Scholarship in the Liberal Arts, the Department of Anthropology of the University of Notre Dame, and the Department of Anthropology of the University of Montana, Missoula. We have benefited enormously from dialogue with numerous friends and colleagues over the years on issues related to this topic. They include Walter Aufrecht, Doug Hallett, Mike Rousseau, Brian Hayden, Michael Lenert, James Chatters, Nathan Goodale, Kenneth Ames, Dana Lepofsky, Sandra Peacock, and Jeanne E. Arnold. Special thanks are given to Meredith S. Chesson, who has read more versions of this chapter than any normal human being should be required to. We would especially like to acknowledge the detailed comments of Mike Rousseau, Dana Lepofsky, and Sandra Peacock. We have benefited enormously from frank and wide-ranging personal discussions with these individuals and tried to address their comments and suggestions in a manner that recognizes their significant research contributions to the field and understanding of specific data. We are especially thankful for their comprehensive observations as we have explored the possible long-term evolutionary implications of their research and the possible links of this work to regional cultural and paleoenvironmental changes. Finally, we would like to thank Herb Maschner and one anonymous reviewer who provided us with the opportunity to revise and clarify our ideas, organization, and presentation in this chapter. While not agreeing with some of the arguments developed in this study, these individuals contributed comments and suggestions that have been critical to the development of the arguments presented in this chapter, and we thank them for them.

IV

DISCUSSION AND IMPLICATIONS

11

A TRANSCONTINENTAL PERSPECTIVE ON THE EVOLUTION OF HUNTER-GATHERER LIFEWAYS ON THE PLATEAU

DISCUSSION AND REFLECTION

Jeanne E. Arnold

Many hunter-gatherers of the North American Plateau lived at least seasonally in quite substantial pithouse communities. Some of these communities were constituted by large structures housing many people of various social ranks (including in some cases slaves) who were interacting in complex but not broadly understood ways. One of the main anthropological issues that is now being addressed for the region is where these groups fit in wider discussions of generalized, affluent, and complex hunter-gatherers in North America (Arnold 2001:4). An important subtext of this issue is whether later Plateau cultural configurations evolved in place or people moved in (or brought significant influences) from the neighboring Northwest Coast. Productive research programs and innovative analyses across the Plateau during the past decade are bringing researchers much closer to answering these questions. To the degree that we can now more closely examine salient dimensions of the resource base, explore the organization of labor, and begin to reconstruct the fundamentals of the nature of leadership, we can advance by leaps and bounds in tracing the emergence and cycling of economic and political integration in this important region.

Most hunter-gatherers around the world lived in small communities, maintained fairly fluid and mobile lifeways, had a strong sharing ethic and intricate risk-reduction strategies, and possessed a largely egalitarian ethos (Kelly 1995; Lee 1982). These groups are typically labeled simple or "generalized" hunter-gatherers. As individuals and as groups, they typically neither settled in permanently anywhere on the landscape nor specialized in any particular kinds of resource extraction or production. Politically, they were not complex, and their resource bases were adequate to support small to modest rather than dense populations.

The hunter-gatherers I term "affluent," on the other hand, had much more raw material with which to work (Arnold 2001). Typically, available resources and water supplies were more formidable and could support larger and denser populations. Semisedentism (or sedentism) was possible. Kin group property ownership lessened the ubiquity of sharing or changed the way more distantly related people shared with one another, and interfamily inequality and the accrual of prized valuables were more pronounced. Such groups frequently lived in riverine and coastal settings where resource hotspots allowed fairly good-sized aggregations of people to settle in (Renouf 1991), or they were situated to exploit vast herds of terrestrial animals or other concentrations of resources (well-known examples include certain European Upper Paleolithic and Mesolithic groups and North American Archaic cultures). These affluent hunter-gatherers were fairly populous and socially and economically quite complex but did not exhibit any signs of political centralization, institutionalized formal leadership, or sustained control of labor of non-kin (Arnold 1996a, 1996b, 2000; Hayden 1994). People who took on leadership tasks, such as elders or orators, did so situationally, and their authority did not extend to matters in other realms. Leadership and power were "heterarchically" distributed. Social, ritual, and technological elaborations abounded—but in the absence of formal political elaboration.

"Affluent" hunter-gatherers are similar in certain respects to our third type, the "complex" hunter-gatherers, but differ in important ways. Foremost among these, complex hunter-gatherers had distinct forms of labor organization and qualitatively different relations between leaders and supporters. Leadership and elite status (and commoner status) were ascribed; individuals with chiefly power, titles, and rights existed; and these chiefs had sustained, renewable control over the labor of non-kin in their communities or regions (or large multifamily "Houses" on the Northwest Coast; see Ames 1995; Arnold 1996a, 2000, 2001; Hayden 1994, 1995, 1996b; Marquardt 2001; Roscoe 2000). Labor relationships may have included elite control over slaves (as among the Calusa of Florida and many peoples of the Northwest Coast), elite control over the labor and products of skilled free specialists who were non-kin (e.g., the Calusa and the Chumash of California), or other forms of sustained labor manipulation. These groups also had unusually rich but variable resource bases, typically situated along productive coasts with diverse arrays of plant foods and marine mammals, fish, and shellfish or along rivers with major runs of anadromous fish. Their environments were not characterized by unmitigated bounty but, rather, presented significant, periodic challenges that had to be met by new strategies.

Complex hunter-gatherers were generally marked by large populations clustered into moderate to large communities. The people in these communities had differential access to prestige items, pronounced resource ownership, and elaborated physical (or social) storage systems, often accompanied by sophisticated resource-procurement technologies. They practiced semisedentary to sedentary lifeways. This set of characteristics helps to highlight many of the *conditions* that facilitated and accompanied complexity, but our focus should remain on the structure of complexity, which centers on labor organization (control of non-kin labor by leaders) and ascribed/inherited leadership. These are the two basic *organizational* features that separate human societies based largely on family/domestic principles from those with formal political economies. The emergence of formal political relationships based on labor control was a pivotal change in the basic way of conducting society.

For the Plateau, then, we want to know about how members of society strategized to mobilize labor for gathering, processing, and storing resources during both ordinary and climatically unfavorable times. It is important also to establish the community size and organization that predominated in various periods. Last, researchers should attempt to evaluate what kinds of control leaders had (if any) over the labor of slaves or unrelated free people and whether social status was achieved or ascribed. New data in these domains will allow scholars to trace cycles or trajectories of affluence and complexity, but these features are, of course, not easily detected in the archaeological record.

Contributors to this volume have identified several creative ways to begin to tackle these thorny problems. These include detailed analyses of the characteristics and contents of special plant-roasting features and unusual ritual structures in one of the region's large pithouse villages, both of which may signal community-integrating events. Researchers also are closely examining changing tactics in conflict and defense and the development of long-distance exchange systems through the last three millennia or so, which may herald rapidly evolving forms of interaction on a regional scale. Much is being derived as well from new reconstructions of internal community organization, long-term changes in the uses of crucial resources such as root foods through periods of demographic and environmental change, and the evolution of artifact styles panregionally through time.

PITHOUSE VILLAGES

Keatley Creek along the Middle Fraser Canyon is the first large pithouse village that I visited on the Canadian Plateau, and it is a site that makes quite an impression. Anyone accustomed to "typical" hunter-gatherer sites is struck by the site's tightly clustered, very large, and numerous housepits (about 120) distributed across several thousand square meters. Such sites have few equivalents outside the Plateau in western North America. *The emergence of large pithouse villages on the Plateau stands in remarkable contrast to earlier hunter-gatherer lifeways* there and elsewhere. Clearly, not all houses at Keatley were contemporaneous, but if just half were inhabited at some peak in the site's history, the village had quite a substantial population. Sheer individual pithouse size (averaging about 12 m and ranging up to 22 m in diameter) prompts us to ponder the size and composition of the social groups that occupied these structures. Many hunter-gatherer groups on a roughly equal plane of sociopolitical complexity lived in houses with far smaller capacities for people and storage and in communities with far smaller numbers of houses—particularly the groups that occupied much of California. Presumably, these differences in the architectural mode and size of the basic social units of society are meaningful and deserving of our attention.

One conclusion to be drawn from a Plateau–California comparison is that absolute house size is not a simple indicator of a society's overarching sociopolitical complexity. Among California's most complex hunter-gatherers, in some of the more favorably provisioned coastal and riverine areas (e.g., the territory of the Island Chumash of Southern California), small nuclear or extended families occupied relatively small (averaging 6–8 m in diameter) and simple basic residential structures, but these social units were linked into regionally oriented and overtly hierarchical polities (where intensive intervillage trade was also characteristic). There was evidently a more corporate or multifamily mien of residential organization on the Plateau, possibly overseen by local leadership within the larger communities. This is not unlike the pattern in parts of the Northwest Coast, where large, cedar-plank houses were occupied by strong local kin groups, with power invested in titleholders who held sway over household activities and perhaps intracommunity activities but who seemingly had no intercommunity power. Was this cross-cultural variability in residential building style and the size of the household social unit driven by politics or more fundamentally a practical solution to climatic and resource issues?

Clearly, there was a payoff to be found on the Plateau in securing a fairly sizable number of family members and perhaps others (and their labor) in a 10–20 m diameter pithouse to provision the group during harsh and lengthy winters. Each household presumably needed people across a range of ages and genders to accomplish food acquisition, food processing, gear maintenance, ritual tasks, spiritual tasks, child rearing, tool and clothing manufacturing, coalition maintenance, and other tasks each season. Household recruitment to ensure adequate labor to ride out the winter—and perhaps occasionally secure a modest surplus—may have led to large households (and large communities, especially if defense was a prime consideration) but not particularly pronounced vertical leadership within and among the communities. No doubt there is a more nuanced explanation for variability in architectural style among regions (and certainly there are many additional variables that affect political evolution), but house form/size may well have its roots in this practical, climate-driven strategy. Mike K. Rousseau argues that increasingly harsh winter weather played a crucial stimulating role in the emergence and then widespread adoption of pithouses on the Canadian Plateau by circa 4400 B.P. He suggests that the placement of pithouses in clusters in sheltered valley bottoms near varied resources was critical for survival as the region's climate deteriorated. Populations from the Northwest Coast and Lower Fraser River, rather than local populations, may have spurred the earliest use of pithouses on the Plateau at about 5000–4400 B.P.

Very large pithouses and smaller pithouses may signal important organizational differences. The large pithouses of the Mid-Fraser Canyon or of the eastern Plateau (e.g., Slocan Narrows; see Goodale et al., this volume) provided various problems and opportunities for occupants. Most importantly, from a political and economic standpoint, large pithouses brought a potentially very large labor force under one roof, creating strong social bonds and clear economic obligations among house leaders, kin, non-kin family units, and perhaps slaves. This labor force could be used for food harvests and storage, fuel collection, manufacturing, and other forms of wealth production. If a household experienced highly favorable conditions, then the *overproduction* of foods or goods could generate surpluses for feasts and ceremonies within the community and for exchange with similarly flush trade partners beyond. But huge pithouses were also relatively costly to build, requiring more and longer timbers to support the roof, and they were apparently relatively difficult to keep warm. Moreover, there seems to be little doubt that they were more complex (socially) to manage. Both successes and failures—in developing social standing and perhaps nascent leadership—likely occurred on a grander scale in these houses than in smaller households.

Families in small pithouses, on the other hand, united much smaller labor forces, were easier to direct and organize, and were probably at somewhat lower risk for total economic failure, assuming that they maintained sharing or trade relationships with kin and neighbors in other households. But at the same time they could not marshal the labor to regularly build wealth, host feasts, and the like. Less was ventured, less was gained, and these were not the movers and shakers of Plateau society. The dynamics of corporate group size and how household leaders chose to direct corporate labor may in part explain the different kinds of sociopolitical activity associated with the big pithouse villages as opposed to small villages with only small houses on the Plateau, but we must not forget that certain other hunter-gatherer societies operating out of small households (e.g., the Chumash) found different ways to build power and complexity. So it is not house size and the size of the house-based labor unit alone that shape the course of political evolution.

Attention has been drawn recently to the archaeological indicators of what Feinman et al. (2000) label *corporate* and *network social strategies* in intermediate societies (see also McGuire and Saitta 1996). Feinman et al. (2000: 453) suggest that house form, size, and composition may be important independent markers of the emergence of corporate versus network modes in some cases. Using data drawn from the early pithouse villages of the Southwest, they note a tendency for more variable house size or house quality, which may reflect status differences among household units in a village, to correlate with the presence of a network social strategy. In contrast, large houses and more uniform house size overall within a village correlate with corporate organization. By tracking emergent hierarchical organization alongside this corporate network dimension, we may begin to understand the evolution of pithouse communities on the Plateau. During early phases after the emergence of pithouses, current evidence suggests that Plateau social organization was nonhierarchical, and mostly small and similarly sized pithouses were common. In later periods, the scale and organization of households were increasingly more corporate in character, *and* Plateau society became more hierarchical, according to Hayden (1997) and others. Some enormous pithouses appeared, accompanied by a more pronounced dichotomy in house size within much larger communities (Hayden 1997:49). Still later, in a postflorescent (and perhaps politically simpler) phase, smaller structures and villages again prevailed. Comparisons with the Southwest may be instructive: certain late period southwestern pueblos also became both corporate and hierarchical, although not necessarily at the same time (Feinman et al. 2000:464–465). The point is that in regions undergoing sociopolitical change, associated changes in house form can be profound, as we see in parts of the Plateau, but in some cases no concurrent, visible architectural change may occur. Among the Chumash, houses were rather simple and small and carried little symbolic weight both early and late, even as they transitioned from a nonhierarchical mode to a network/hierarchical mode. Clearly, signals derived from house form alone may be telling, but they are not sufficient to gauge political evolution.

My final observation here about Plateau pithouse villages centers on the fact that substantial Plateau houses—representing significant construction labor investments—were occupied *seasonally* (during long winters), although populations returned annually and also spent parts of other seasons at them. This seasonal use is initially surprising to archaeologists who deal with much smaller, simpler, and lower-investment houses that were occupied year-round (exemplified, again, by parts of coastal California). But this should serve to remind us that sedentism is enabled by important conditions such as resource distribution, scheduling strategies, and storage technologies. Sedentism is not an absolute indicator of complexity, and sedentism does not arise in lockstep with the emergence of complexity. There is, moreover, no simple cross-cultural relationship between sedentism and the degree of labor investment in houses or the size of houses (Arnold 1996a: 101–105). Plateau archaeologists and, of course, Northwest Coast archaeologists have long known this, but scholars elsewhere have been slow to catch on and recognize variability in these relationships.

RESOURCE BASES AND FEASTING

The dynamics of Plateau social relations almost certainly involved ritually and sociopolitically charged uses of foods at various scales as well as more ordinary food processing and consumption. Recent investigations at Keatley Creek have focused on the social implications of large plant-roasting pits and on sets of ritual structures at the site's margins. Brian Hayden and Sara Mossop Cousins's chapter in this volume suggests that root-roasting pits at Keatley Creek indicate large-scale food processing by either corporate groups or special ritual parties in association with feasting events, perhaps competitive feasts. Given the effort involved in making and using roasting pits, when roots *can* be cooked in other ways and *would* be cooked in smaller numbers for ordinary single-household consumption, the pits almost certainly represent the activity of some larger social unit(s). There are ways to prepare such foods other than in massive pits 3–8 m in diameter, and thus this particular processing configuration is likely mapped onto important social demands. Large roasting pits in the Plateau lowlands (such as at Keatley Creek) seem to be positively correlated with local peaks in social complexity, on-site storage capacity, and large-scale processing.

Hayden and Cousins contend that the position of roasting pits at the periphery of the site points to the consumption of these plant foods in feasting rather than in ordinary subsistence. The presence of just a dozen or so such pits at the site means also that there were not enough pits for each household. These were not, in other words, a family resource, nor were they reused regularly. Close analysis suggests that they were subject to episodic rather than annual use. Furthermore, their concentration in two zones of the site near structures that do not appear to be ordinary residences (with atypical hearths, atypical storage configurations, and so on) means that use of the pits could well have been associated with ritual. These are intriguing explorations of the data, but unambiguous confirmation of the ritual connection will require the establishment of close temporal ties among the pits, possible ritual structures, and other ritual activities. Others (Ian Kuijt, personal communication, 2002) suggest that large roasting pits may be rare at Keatley Creek because root foods were uncommon (and likely overexploited) in the vicinity. Or perhaps the number of roasting pits at the site periphery is low because villagers during the final phase of the florescence of Keatley Creek conducted most root roasting inside their pithouses, sharing fewer of these foods (William C. Prentiss, personal communication, 2002).

We should keep in mind that the labor to construct a roasting pit was not beyond the means of any generalized hunter-gatherer group, and such features seem to turn up in many western North American sites, from a large and well-preserved 2500 B.P. bulb-roasting pit at a site on the central coast of California (Glassow 1996:72–74) to camas-roasting pits on the San Juan Islands of Washington. Moreover, although there seems to be little doubt that large-scale roasting of cherished root foods might have been a major focal point for various gatherings such as feasts at Keatley, noncompetitive forms of sharing could instead (or also) be implicated. Certainly, the northern mainland Coastal Chumash at 2500 B.P. (Glassow 1996) were rather generalized hunter-gatherers, and there is no evidence to suggest that they were engaged in major political tussles involving competitive feasting. But those people, and the Keatley Creek residents during certain periods, did choose to invest in robust roasting pit construction and use, and this investment presumably paid off in *some* form of valuable social or ritual capital. This should only serve to underline the labors involved in acquiring of the foods to be roasted, collecting the fuel to be burned, and processing the food itself, all of which were considerable. Moreover, the contexts of consumption were likely significant and socially charged. Our goal is to sort out various contexts of use and payoffs in various regions and develop some understanding of the interactions that produced them. Discerning the nature of food-based social relationships often proves quite crucial in reconstructing processes of cultural evolution.

However it may have emerged, the pattern of seemingly intensified manipulations of plant foods when the population and political complexity at Keatley initially peaked is interesting and has some parallels elsewhere. Throughout California, groups late in prehistory and at contact were known to stimulate the growth and yields of many wild plants by burning, selective pruning, coppicing, and other practices (Anderson 1993). Coastal Southern Californians regularly burned huge areas of grassland and chaparral to stimulate seed output and acorn yields and to attract deer and elk to expanses of emerging greens. Acorn and seed use clearly intensified in later prehistory, and mainland Chumash people apparently routinely harvested surpluses of nuts and seeds, processed them, and traded them to densely populated places with more depauperate local plant resources such as the Channel Islands (Arnold 2001).

Whereas the exploration of root roasting at a large lowland Plateau community provides fine-grained insights into diet and social integration, a comprehensive assessment of all plant foods across the Northern Plateau by Dana Lepofsky and Sandra L. Peacock (this volume) provides important new regional-scale insights. Their thorough analysis is fundamental to the successful exploration of social evolution in the region. They provide a useful measure of the *food value* of dozens of plants, which is an overall ranking based on each species's availability, abundance, palatability, and persistence under intensive harvesting. They also examine the intensification potential of these plants. The clear importance of root foods emerges in their analysis, but also some greens and berries were of obvious and exceptional value to Plateau peoples.

Direct archaeological evidence for ancient uses of plant foods on the Plateau is rather limited. Relatively little paleobotanical work has been conducted, and limited preservation restricts interpretations of the results. However, indirect evidence can be recovered in the form of selected tools, processing features, and storage features. Lepofsky and Peacock suggest that large earth ovens for roasting roots indicate intensification of this food source on the Canadian Plateau uplands at about 2400 B.P. Populations from the lowland winter villages converged seasonally around the most productive upland meadows. From 2400 to 1500 B.P., the processing and use of root foods remained steady in the uplands. Importantly, there is no indication of *progressive* intensification after 2400 B.P.; indeed, there is a decline in root roasting ovens in the uplands of the Plateau between 1500 and 800 B.P. (and a peak in root roasting at large lowland villages such as Keatley Creek at ca. 1500 B.P.). The trend reverses after 800 B.P., with a new phase of intensification in the uplands, albeit using smaller earth ovens. Lepofsky and Peacock note that this last set of changes corresponds to the smaller pithouses and villages of the Plateau lowlands after 800 B.P.; smaller social units were converging to process roots in the uplands. Remarkably, then, the frequency and morphological characteristics of root-roasting ovens in the mountains may capture important shifts in household size and community size in lowland winter villages over the course of a two-millennia period. Obviously, plant foods were critical to survival on the Plateau, and several scholars have suggested that plant foods exceeded even salmon in importance in the region's basic economy. Clearly, there has been, until recently, insufficient emphasis placed on the crucial role of plants in Plateau cultural evolution.

RITUAL ACTIVITIES

Brian Hayden and Ron Adams (this volume) propose that several sets of pit structures on the margin of the Keatley Creek site may have been secret society ritual structures, something they suggest we should expect to find (and do find, from New Guinea, to the U.S. Southwest, to the Neolithic Near East) at the sites of complex hunter-gatherers and prestate farming societies. Assemblages associated with such structures should include little or no domestic refuse (except, perhaps, from a live-in custodian) and some or all of the following: storage features, evidence of feasting, rare ritual objects (cult property), manufacturing waste from prestige items such as nephrite tools, central hearths, formal benches and flooring, and possibly intentional post-use destruction. Hayden and Adams note that at large Plateau villages like Keatley, many private rituals probably took place within pithouse structures (which I would surmise might have been audible to neighbors) but that *secret society* rituals needed to transpire in remote locations.

Keatley Creek has at least two pairs of atypical small structures located more than 200 m from the main habitation area of the site. One of each pair is a structure with prestige items or unusual faunal items, and the second is almost devoid of cultural remains. The latter,

Hayden and Adams suggest, could have served as a meeting place for more public feasting after secret rituals were conducted nearby. These structures are secluded, odd in their contents, and paired, and the scenario of secret society structures seems plausible. At least one of the structure pairs corresponds, as we might expect, to the era of greatest social complexity at the site, the Plateau Horizon. Hayden and Adams indicate that Keatley Creek may have been politically heterarchical, even in that period. Perhaps ritual leadership played a notable (and shared) role in village leadership dynamics. The suggestion of heterarchy seems to depart from Hayden's (e.g., 1997; Hayden and Schulting 1997) earlier discussions of hierarchy and elite leadership at Keatley, but I think that this may be a judicious interpretation given the presently limited *regional-scale* data that can be used to examine labor control, status ascription, the manufacturing and control of valuables, and the local political economy. Such an interpretation in no way closes the door on "complexity" at these large Middle Fraser Canyon communities, but it does suggest that there is much more work to be done on several scales, including more household excavation and interhousehold comparison at a wider array of villages, to shed additional light on community organization and status variability across the region.

Among many California groups, the most important and routinely identified ritual structure is the sweat lodge, which was often fairly centrally situated or on the coastal edge of a village, close to houses rather than in a remote position. These were heavily used by adult men on a daily basis, however, and thus are not the same kind of ritual structure that Hayden and Adams discuss. The activities carried out by more specialized ritual Chumash subgroups were probably either at partially screened or fenced dance floors within main habitation areas or at very distant (several kilometers away) ridge-top rock shrines or rock shelter sites where elaborate rock art was created. Given the small size of villages and outdoors orientation of activities permitted by the mild California climate, there would have been few opportunities for highly secretive, clandestine ritual activity anywhere *within* Chumash villages. Nothing quite like the Keatley Creek structures was made or used by the Chumash, it appears.

CULTURAL EVOLUTION: PALEOCLIMATE, MIGRATION, AND POPULATION PRESSURE

William C. Prentiss and Ian Kuijt's "evolution of collector systems" essay (this volume) brings welcome rigor to the study of broad cultural history by challenging assumptions and more effectively tracing continuity and change in a regional sequence than work by prehistorians typically attempts. Every region in North America would benefit from such comprehensive analysis. They test two contrasting models of the origins of collectors (as opposed to foragers, sensu Binford 1980) on the Canadian Plateau—on the one hand, that such systems arose gradually in place and, on the other, that the collector way of life originated on the Northwest Coast and emerged in the Plateau after the Neoglacial abandonment.

Their first test uses interassemblage variability in lithic artifacts across time and space to identify collectors. The key idea linking population mobility and lithic assemblages, which is discussed in a rather extensive recent literature, is that in a given landscape more formal stone tools tend to be associated with forager adaptations (because such tools are highly reliable, maintainable, and transportable) and more expedient tools (such as flake tools) tend to be associated with collectors and their increasingly sedentary lifeways. Second, Prentiss and Kuijt assess manufacturing style diachronically to study processes of cultural inheritance (as discussed elsewhere by Michael O'Brien and R. Lee Lyman [2000]). Third, they use radiocarbon dates to search for gaps and relationships. Employing principal components analysis, Prentiss and Kuijt assess more than 20 lithic assemblages from various Plateau sites. They find a recurring combination of flake tools and ground-stone tools at a subset of components attributed to collector lifeways, and they are able to infer the presence of semisedentism and delayed-return economies where those sets of artifacts also co-occur with storage features.

This analysis makes a great deal of sense, and I believe that their conclusions are robust, but *some* fully sedentary fishing-gathering-hunting collectors would grade out as "foragers" using the first of their test methods (the one focused on lithic technology). The Chumash are among the great specialized microblade-producing societies in world prehistory, manufacturing them by the millions and using them to drill large quantities of shell beads and ornaments (Arnold 1987, 2001). Technological systems of this type, dominated by formal tool types such as microblades and microdrills and combined with a near absence of expedient flake tools, would match a forager rather than a collector profile. But, of course, the Chumash were prototypical sedentary collectors (Arnold 1996a, 2001). Microblade cores, microblades, and associated debitage account for perhaps 90 percent of the Channel Islands Chumash lithic assemblages in later prehistory (Arnold 1987). The Chumash further confound the model by having had moderate numbers of formal bifaces and also having had storage structures (above-ground granaries for acorns and seeds) that were perishable and thus not archaeologically detectible. Despite these problems that would emerge from applying the test in California, I endorse the Prentiss/Kuijt analysis, and it appears that the test works well for the Plateau.

Prentiss and Kuijt then use point shape, haft, and stem characteristics to trace patterns of cultural transmission, or inheritance, although for data reasons they could not apply a rigorous frequency seriation technique. They find several distinct stylistic traditions that lend credibility to their provisional conclusions about wholesale cultural replacement on the Canadian Plateau by populations from the Northwest Coast, likely about 4000 B.P. The radiocarbon analysis, too, illuminates a period of abandonment coincident with dramatic environmental change, the economic collapse of mobile foraging traditions (termed Lochnore), and a replacement by collectors of the Shuswap Horizon who could survive in new, colder conditions. These are important new conclusions about major developments on the Plateau, now backed at least provisionally by a diverse array of data. Still, it is not entirely clear that there is firm accord among contributors about the impact of Northwest Coast peoples on the Plateau; nor, significantly, does there seem to be evidence for a comparable cultural replacement (or melding of populations) in the Southern (Columbia) Plateau. Rousseau suggests that an influx of population to the Canadian Plateau from Coast Salish territories of the coast and Lower Fraser River took place at about 5000–4400 B.P., as much as a millennia earlier than proposed by Prentiss and Kuijt. So regional researchers appear to have more chronological work to do to achieve consensus on the timing of this incursion from the coast. It will be of great interest to many scholars if Plateau archaeologists can augment these new interpretations and further address these migration-related issues during the next few years.

Several contributors describe a period of notable cultural florescence on the western Canadian Plateau from roughly 2400 to 1000 B.P. (Prentiss and Kuijt, this volume; Rousseau, this volume) and on the Columbia Plateau after circa 2000 B.P. (Andrefsky, this volume; Chatters, this volume). Whereas pithouses first appeared at 5000 B.P. and small villages became established by 3500 B.P., much larger villages with larger and more variable structure types as well as more storage facilities appeared at 2000 B.P. on the Columbia Plateau. These developments were accompanied by early use of the bow and arrow and greater conflict throughout the region, as discussed below (Chatters, this volume). The Plateau Horizon on the Canadian Plateau (2400–1000 B.P.), according to Rousseau and others, was a warmer, drier period that witnessed the region's greatest population density. Large villages were occupied (seasonally) for centuries; people had excellent access to roots, berries, and salmon and developed substantial storage capacity; and they seasonally used special camps at high elevations. Many pithouses of this phase were smaller than their counterparts in the preceding phase (and seemingly represented a shift to nuclear-family households, according to Rousseau), except in the Middle Fraser Canyon (e.g., Keatley Creek), where some very large houses—up to 22 m in diameter—appeared.

It strikes me that such a divergence in architectural practices within the Canadian Plateau indicates that very different cultural trajectories were unfolding at large Middle Fraser Canyon communities compared with the case at villages elsewhere on the Plateau. In the one case, households grew larger, more complex, and more divergent within the community, possibly indicating new forms of status differentiation and almost certainly indicating new forms of labor organization; whereas in many other places on the Plateau, smaller houses may have been an adaptive response to pressure on limited resources, leading to more social interdependence and risk reduction.

This brings us to one of the region's most salient controversies. Hayden and Ryder (1991; Hayden 1997) argue that the Keatley Creek village collapsed roughly a millennia ago, immediately after this florescence in house size and community size, because of a massive rockslide that temporarily dammed the powerful Fraser River and dramatically affected the river's salmon resources for decades. In the wake of this devastating event, the immediate region's society crumbled. However, new and more comprehensive evidence, some summarized for the first time in here (see Kuijt and Prentiss, this volume), suggests that around 1000 B.P. there was actually a *widespread* population decline throughout the Plateau and a rather universal reversion to smaller villages. Rousseau describes this as a phase of relentless overpredation and harvesting stress on the region's terrestrial flora and fauna throughout the Plateau. In this view (see also Kuijt 2001), rather than a singular calamitous event on the Fraser River at the start of this phase, there were more general processes at work.

Kuijt and Prentiss outline these processes, building the case that a large expanse of the Northern Plateau experienced decline stemming from long-term, chronic population/resource imbalances. They argue that the larger villages of the western Plateau were perched precariously "on the edge" of survival for many years. Their discussion focuses on the fragile salmon/plant balance in the traditional diet of the Plateau in late winter, a season when people were dependent on the last reserves of their stored foods. The decline of the very large pithouse villages at roughly 1000 B.P. can be linked, they suggest, to habitually inadequate supplies of stored roots and berries at the end of winter, combined with a winter season overdependence on lean salmon. These problems were exacerbated by climatic disturbances associated with the Little Climatic Optimum (the Medieval Climatic Anomaly) of circa 800–1,000 years ago. This hypothesis is of interest to many archaeologists in the North American West, considering that major environmental and cultural changes occurred also at that juncture in places such as the Colorado Plateau and the Channel Islands of California. Extended droughts played a role in settlement shifts, the intensification of exchange systems involving plant foods and other goods, and labor reorganization and political centralization in these other western regions (Arnold 2001; Jones et al. 1999). On the Plateau, the demise of the large pithouse villages may have been spurred by the systematic overexploitation of crucial plant foods, a climatically induced drop in available carbohydrates, and increasing dependence on proteins in the diet that could have led to serious nutritional problems each early spring season.

If Kuijt and Prentiss are correct, the region's flora clearly could not have supported large communities through long winters. Populations in smaller villages required fewer stored roots and other plant foods, and they were better situated to ride out the winter and to rapidly gather enough early spring plants to avoid health-damaging subsistence imbalances. The huge villages occupied between 2000 and 1000 B.P. may have thrived for a short time into this drier period by means of their continued control of optimal salmon-fishing sites and surplus production of salmon, but ultimately, Kuijt and Prentiss argue, the root resources were too seriously depleted for them to continue. How long did it take for severe nutritional stresses to emerge and villages to collapse? Maladaptive subsistence regimes cannot endure for long; perhaps some desperately needed plant foods were traded in through regional networks from less populous areas for a time before populations dispersed. Researchers might test these ideas by looking for accelerated local trade or signs of chronic nutritional stress in skeletal remains.

The newly developed sequence for the Upper Columbia River drainage (eastern Plateau), entailing an analysis of a new radiocarbon series and an examination of the settlement system, reveals a series of cultural changes that echo those elsewhere on the Plateau (although somewhat offset chronologically). These changes include a hiatus in settlement that may indicate abandonment of the eastern Plateau at around 4200–3800 B.P. (Goodale et al., this volume). There were two periods of greater pithouse use and intensification of root foods (and associated storage), each followed by population dispersal or decline and lowered pressure on plant food resources. The second of these peaks in pithouse living was the Collector II, which corresponds to 1200–600 B.P. and thus significantly postdates the collapse in the Middle Fraser Canyon and elsewhere. The effects felt so widely on the Plateau at circa 1000 B.P. may not have impacted the Upper Columbia. At about A.D. 1400 (corresponding to the Little Ice Age), the construction of earthworks may mark more defensive poses and at least modest population declines in the eastern Plateau.

One site dating to the contact era in the Upper Columbia has yielded exceptional burials, including an infant and fetus together with large numbers of glass beads, copper tube beads, dentalium beads, and elk-tooth pendants. Goodale et al. infer "complex" social organization on the basis of these burials, but I would caution that even with very large arrays of mortuary data (that is, excavations of nearly complete cemeteries), it may be perilous to interpret status ascription and political organization *from grave goods alone* (see Arnold and Green 2002). Even after the excavation and analysis of thousands of burials in the Coastal Chumash region, investigators are greatly challenged to identify the timing of regional political centralization based solely on the mortuary realm, in large measure because practices of inheritance and destructive mourning ceremonies precluded or distorted the interment of many markers of wealth and occupation. As well, rich child burials are notoriously ambiguous and do not unequivocally indicate status ascription (Arnold and Green 2002; see also Hayden 1997:115). We find the Chumash *residential* data to be more abundant, straightforward, and reliable indicators of status and economic organization (Arnold 2001; Arnold and Green 2002), and I encourage Plateau archaeologists to also focus largely on the vast reservoirs of household data awaiting excavation for their interpretations of status differentiation, labor organization, and the political economy. The potential is clearly there for communities such as Slocan Narrows to have been characterized by complex organization, but the recovery of further evidence from the Upper Columbia area is needed before settling on the term *complex* or *affluent* to best describe these collectors. Ideally, we would want more data on politics, labor organization (including slavery), social units, community organization, and achieved/ascribed status.

INTERACTION

Situated between the Vancouver coast and the Canadian Plateau, the Scowlitz site on the banks of the Lower Fraser River just west of the Plateau was well positioned to broker local and long-distance trade. Data from the site are used by Michael Blake (this volume) to examine the role of a large community in interregional exchange relationships and expressions of social prestige. One individual in the large, mound-dominated cemetery at Scowlitz was buried with an exceptional number and quality of wealth items, including copper and elaborate shell ornaments imported from great distances. Earlier residents obtained obsidian and nephrite from afar, but later people seem to have had better access to a greater array of valued items. The site represents long-term investment in and identification with this important location by people who could readily tie into vast interaction networks using water-based trade. Rousseau calls the more interior-oriented expression of this system the "Plateau Interaction Sphere" and cites Hayden and Schulting's (1997) discussion of Plateau–Northwest Coast interactions. Rousseau accounts for the rise of these interaction systems in functional, risk-buffering terms, whereas Blake and especially Hayden (1997) are more inclined to see them as originating out of manipulations of the economy by entrepreneurial, ambitious, and well-situated individuals in these communities.

In any case, it is clear that some circulations of prestige goods occurred both within the region and between these two neighboring regions (and beyond). Villages that produced surpluses of transportable foods (e.g., dried salmon, roots) or manufactured prized goods made of rare materials (such as nephrite adzes, whose source areas may have been primarily in the Middle Fraser Canyon [Darwent 1998]) could have been major players in these exchange spheres. Oddly, there is not yet a substantial corpus of *production* evidence to unambiguously support suggestions about intensive regional interaction in the Lower and Middle Fraser River areas, although some sites have produced grave goods or limited tool-production data on which we can build. If specialization and intensive or extensive trade in prized goods had been of supreme importance in wealth and status building for the elites in these communities, then one might have expected far more archaeological data to have come to light on nephrite production, surplus food production, and so forth from various Middle Fraser and Lower Fraser sites.

In a collaborative field project in the Lower Fraser Valley (for which I am co-investigator with Dana Lepofsky, Mike Blake, and others), we have as a goal to further our understanding of Stó:lō (Coast Salish of the Fraser Valley) regional social and economic relationships through the last 2,000–3,000 years and into the early contact period. We will investigate several possibilities, including whether we have not always looked in the right places for indicators of regional interaction spheres, whether these kinds of exchange ties were less significant in the Lower Fraser than previously thought, and whether specialized production and exchange were primarily in perishables. Clearly, Lower Fraser River (coastal) and Middle Fraser Canyon (Plateau) populations have quite ancient as well as quite recent cultural ties. As noted above, several authors in this volume argue that the post-4000 B.P. or even post-5000 B.P. developments on the Plateau can be linked to an influx of population from this area of the coast. Indeed, it has been suggested that the idea for the pithouse as an architectural form may have originated with Coast Salish peoples.

Issues of conflict and defense are also important in tracing interaction, accounting for the locations of sites on the landscape, and tracking the emergence of large pithouse communities. Both the positioning of sites on certain kinds of landforms and the aggregations of substantial populations into large communities have been advanced as evidence that people on the Columbia Plateau sought to defend against attacks. James C. Chatters (this volume) notes that the largest pithouse village sites on the Columbia Plateau were located on islands and in other difficult-to-access localities. These sites originated at the same time that bow and arrow technology was incorporated into local tool assemblages, or about 2400 B.P., which marked the earliest appearance of the bow and arrow complex in temperate North America. Coalescence into large winter villages was sometimes also accompanied by fortifications and high storage capacity, suggesting that people gathered into defensive, nucleated groups with sufficient stored foods to reduce the number of times they would have to venture away from protection. There is also skeletal evidence for lethal violence on a large scale.

The costs and benefits of living in large villages are several, including the costs associated with escalating personal clashes, overtaxed local resources, and more disease. At the same time, large communities enhance residents' access to marriage partners, persons with special skills or abilities, and pooled labor, but Chatters largely dismisses the potential impacts of these benefits here. He finds cohesion and safety (strength in numbers against neighbors with the bow and arrow) to be the overriding explanation for the rise of large villages on the Columbia Plateau. Despite Chatters's substantial and persuasive evidence regarding ancient ambushes of families and other violence, Rousseau argues that the bow and arrow had even more significant impacts when people began using them extensively for new subsistence strategies at about 1500 B.P. Indeed, a reorganization in subsistence may have ensued; Rousseau suggests that deer (and other land animals best procured with arrows) became important constituents in the diet, reducing a narrow dependence on salmon and high-elevation plant foods and releasing labor and time for social elaboration and ceremonialism.

DISCUSSION

From the perspective of a broad interest in affluent and complex hunter-gatherers throughout the Americas, it is clear that in the Plateau there is the potential to make great gains in our understanding of several anthropologically significant phenomena. I highlight four of these. First, detailed and fascinating data are coming to light about the *economic foundations of settled life in large villages,* including the underlying resource conditions that were needed to sustain sizable populations, the season-by-season nutritional requirements and potential health-related stresses in aggregated populations, and the economic strategies people had to employ to accumulate surplus. It will be productive for archaeologists to focus on the nature of labor investments (time allocation for tasks) during the distinct seasons and on the manufacture of locally critical tools and valuables (woodworking tools, nephrite, and the like). We should also gather more household data to gauge intra- and interhousehold variability in diet and crafts, internal household social organization, and the role of storage in sustaining social units of different sizes.

Second, recent and meticulous attention to the *paleoenvironment* by various scholars highlights the often fragile balance between human groups and the suites of resources on which they depend. These relationships remind us how profoundly peoples' ability to survive in a region could be altered by climatic or ecosystemic change. People may disperse or coalesce, abandon an area entirely, develop new technologies, develop new trading networks, intensify subsistence labor, and so on. Chumash Islanders about 900 years ago developed creative new labor, production, and exchange strategies to address climatic problems (Arnold 2001), and data are emerging regarding a variety of interesting responses to extreme climatic flux on the Plateau.

Third, a wealth of information about *intercommunity relations* is waiting to be mined. The political relationships among villages and the direction, frequency, and content of middle- and long-distance exchange all have ramifications for understanding provisioning, territoriality, hierarchy, and conflict in the Plateau region. Moreover, potential or probable migration episodes into or around the Plateau deserve further exploration and analysis. Direct immigration from the Northwest Coast, if it occurred, clearly had profound implications for the unfolding of Northern Plateau prehistory.

Fourth, *complexity* most fundamentally is about political organization or the presence or absence of hereditary leadership and leaders' ability to control non-kin labor on a sustained basis. In its interesting parallels and contrasts with parts of the American Southwest, Northwest Coast, Florida coast, and California, the Plateau continues to have great potential for expanding our studies of labor and politics among the more complex hunter-gatherers. Outside of Hayden and his colleagues' work on the Lillooet-area sites, there is not much focus on political complexity, per se, right now in the Plateau, but the region holds great promise in this regard, with its tremendous wealth of still untapped household, community, and regional data.

There are some fundamental differences among North America's affluent and complex hunter-gatherers. In the Plateau, there was quite complex community organization—with notable surplus food production and storage during certain phases—but there are few signs of systematic or specialized large-scale craft production for exchange with other villages or regions (and this is true as well for much of the Northwest Coast). We can see the material manifestations of interaction spheres in the modest numbers of finished products from exotic regions that occur at many sites (see Hayden and Schulting 1997), but few craft-manufacturing loci have been identified or excavated on the Plateau. Finding these (or establishing that such activities did *not* exist on a large scale and were solely small scale and house based) should be a research priority.

At the region's larger communities, there were medium to large cooperating and cohabiting social groups, but the nature of village political organization is not clear. The food surpluses that may have marked the florescent periods and enabled certain kinds of labor manipulations and status differentiations to thrive evaporated later when the region's plant (and possibly other) resources may have become chronically overexploited or were seriously diminished by climatic changes.

The Plateau also had very pronounced seasonality, and essential resources such as salmon (in the great river systems) and roots (primarily in the high meadows) were widely separated topographically. Such a distribution of resources precluded year-round settlement in one locality. In contrast, among the Calusa of Florida and the Chumash of California there was no strong seasonality in the resource base; nor were key resources at great distances from communities or one another. Cohabiting groups (households) were smaller, although some villages were quite large; sedentism was the predominant settlement strategy; and, very importantly, hierarchical relations and forms of labor control extended across multiple communities (Arnold 2001). Boat ownership, control of trade, and heavy dependence on craft specialists were salient features of elite wealth and status building. All of these groups shared features such as extensive interaction spheres, relatively rich resource bases, and fluctuating climates that created new challenges and opportunities through time.

It seems that if we deconstruct the strategies and aspirations of Plateau dwellers at places like large winter villages along major rivers, the path to family success was marked by a warm, spacious, well-stocked house, perhaps with lower-status residents to carry out menial tasks. Firewood and ample reserves of dried salmon and roots were essential. Large houses and nephrite adzes were likely key symbols of elevated rank. Leading families held ownership of the best fishing platforms and good resource-collection territories in the uplands and controlled enough labor to produce surpluses during the fall salmon runs. Those surpluses were used in turn to acquire prestige goods. Possibly the surplus production of roots was more important than the salmon in supporting sedentism and stimulating affluence or complexity. Presently available data may not yet point clearly to that. But if collecting or processing root resources could have been controllable in some way or if large labor investments over a short term were required, I believe that these might have met the preconditions for playing a central role in political change. Whether roots, or salmon, or some combination of resources was most crucial to surviving on the Plateau, the region is remarkable for its unique configuration of large households occupying expansive winter villages during prosperous periods, preceded and followed by long periods during which people made a living in smaller communities. Plateau hunter-gatherers clearly deserve much wider attention in current and future discussions of sociopolitical evolution in North America.

Acknowledgments. I thank Bill Prentiss and Ian Kuijt for inviting me to be part of a stimulating Society for American Archaeology session and to contribute to this volume. Mike Lenert has been a valuable source of firsthand information about recent, unpublished excavations at Keatley Creek. Several comments and clarifications by Ian and Bill have assisted me in the final production of this chapter. I acknowledge the University of California, Los Angeles, Academic Senate Committee on Research for funding field travel in British Columbia that served to galvanize my interest in the Plateau.

REFERENCES

Aikens, C. Melvin

1978 Archaeology of the Great Basin. *Annual Review of Anthropology* 7:71–87.

1993 *Archaeology of Oregon.* U.S. Department of Interior, Bureau of Land Management, Portland.

Aikens, C. Melvin, David L. Cole, and Robert Stuckenrath

1977 Excavations at Dirty Shame Rockshelter, Southeastern Oregon. Tebiwa: Miscellaneous Papers of the Idaho State University Museum of Natural History, 4. Idaho State University, Pocatello.

Aikens, C. Melvin, and Dennis L. Jenkins (editors)

1994 *Archaeological Researches in the Northern Great Basin: Fort Rock Archaeology since Cressman.* Anthropological Papers, 50. University of Oregon, Eugene.

Alexander, Diane

1992 A Reconstruction of Prehistoric Land Use in the Mid-Fraser River Area Based on Ethnographic Data. In *A Complex Culture of the British Columbia Plateau: Traditional Stl'átl'imx Resource Use,* edited by Brian Hayden, pp. 99–176. University of British Columbia Press, Vancouver.

2000 Pithouses on the Interior Plateau of British Columbia: Ethnographic Evidence and Interpretation of the Keatley Creek Site. In *The Ancient Past of Keatley Creek: vol. 2: Socioeconomy,* edited by Brian Hayden, pp. 29–56. Archaeology Press, Burnaby, B.C.

In press Report on the 1992 Excavations of Housepit 9 at the Keatley Creek Site. In *The Ancient Past of Keatley Creek, vol. 3: Excavation Reports* (CD), edited by Brian Hayden. Archaeology Press, Burnaby, B.C.

Alexander, Diane, R. Tyhurst, R. G. Matson, and L. Burnard

1985 A Preliminary Ethnoarchaeological Investigation of the Potato Mountain Range and the Eagle Lake Area. On file, Archaeology Branch of the B.C. Government, Victoria.

Ames, Kenneth M.

1985 Hierarchies, Stress, and Logistical Strategies among Hunter-Gatherers in Northwestern North America. In *Prehistoric Hunter-Gatherers: The Emergence of Cultural Complexity,* edited by T. Douglas Price and J. A. Brown, pp. 155–180. Academic Press, Orlando.

1991a The Archaeology of the *Longue Duree:* Temporal and Spatial Scale in the Evolution of Social Complexity on the Southern Northwest Coast. *Antiquity* 65:935–945.

1991b Sedentism: A Temporal Shift or a Transitional Change in Hunter-Gatherer Mobility Patterns. In *Between Bands and States,* edited by Susan A. Gregg, pp. 108–134. Center for Archaeological Investigations Occasional Paper, 9. Southern Illinois University, Carbondale.

1995 Chiefly Power and Household Production on the Northwest Coast. In *Foundations of Social Inequality,* edited by T. Douglas Price and Gary M. Feinman, pp. 155–187. Plenum, New York.

In press Intensification of Food Production on the Northwest Coast and Elsewhere. In *Keeping It Living: Traditions of Plant Use and Cultivation on the Northwest Coast,* edited by D. E. Deur and Nancy J. Turner. University of Washington Press, Seattle.

Ames, Kenneth M., Don E. Dumond, Jerry R. Galm, and Rick Minor

1998 Prehistory of the Southern Plateau. In *Handbook of North American Indians, vol. 12: Plateau,* edited by Deward E. Walker Jr., pp. 103–119. Smithsonian Institution Press, Washington, D.C.

Ames, Kenneth M., James P. Green, and Margaret Pfoertner

1981 *Hatwai (10NP143): Interim Report.* Archaeological Reports, 9. Boise State University, Boise.

Ames, Kenneth M., and Alan G. Marshall

1980 Villages, Demography, and Subsistence Intensification on the Southern Columbia Plateau. *North American Archaeologist* 2:25–52.

Ames, Kenneth M., and Herbert D. G. Maschner

1999 *Peoples of the Northwest Coast: Their Archaeology and Prehistory.* Thames and Hudson, London.

Anastasio, A.

1985 The Southern Plateau: An Ecological Analysis of Intergroup Relations. *Northwest Anthropological Research Notes* 7:109–229.

Anderson, Kat

1993 Native Californians as Ancient and Contemporary Cultivators. In *Before the Wilderness: Environmental Management by Native Californians,* edited by Thomas C. Blackburn and Kat Anderson, pp. 151–174. Ballena Press, Menlo Park, California.

Andrefsky, William, Jr.

1994 Raw-Material Availability and the Organization of Technology. *American Antiquity* 59(1):21–34.

1995 Cascade Phase Lithic Technology: An Example from the Lower Snake River. *North American Archaeologist* 16:95–115.

2000 Project Summary. In *The Calispell Valley Archaeology Project Final Report: Volumes 1–5,* edited by William Andrefsky Jr., Greg C. Burtchard, Kira M. Presler, Stephen R. Samuels, Paul H. Sanders, and Alston V. Thoms, pp. 19.1–19.11. Center for Northwest

Anthropology Project Report, 16. Washington State University, Pullman.
In press Revisiting the Type Concept in Archaeology: A Cobble Artifact Example. In *Tools or Cores: The Identification and Study of Alternative Core Technology in Lithic Assemblages,* edited by S. B. McPherron. University of Pennsylvania Press, Philadelphia.

Andrefsky, William, Jr., Greg C. Burtchard, Kira M. Presler, Stephen R. Samuels, Paul H. Sanders, and Alston V. Thoms (editors)
2000 *The Calispell Valley Archaeology Project Final Report,* vols. 1–5. Center for Northwest Anthropology Project Report, 16. Washington State University, Pullman.

Andrefsky, William, Jr., Laurie Hale, and David A. Harder (editors)
1996 *Archaeological Survey on the Hanford Reach.* Center for Northwest Anthropology Project Report, 29. Washington State University, Pullman.

Andrefsky, William, Jr., and Alissa Nauman
2003 *A Preliminary Report on the Birch Creek Site (35ML181): Five Seasons of WSU Archaeological Field School Study 1998–2002.* Center for Northwest Anthropology, Contributions in Cultural Resource Management, 68. Washington State University, Pullman.

Andrefsky, William, Jr., Erica Schmeller, David Harder, and Matthew Van Pelt
1999 *Northeast Oregon Cultural Resource Survey Report.* Center for Northwest Anthropology, Contributions in Cultural Resource Management, 65. Washington State University, Pullman.

Andrews, Rebecca W.
1989 Hiaqua: Use of Dentalium Shells by the Native Peoples of the Pacific Northwest. Unpublished M.A. thesis, Department of Anthropology, University of Washington, Seattle.

Antevs, Ernst
1955 Geologic-Climatic Dating in the West. *American Antiquity* 20:317–335.

Antiquus Archaeological Consultants Ltd.
1999 Archaeological Investigations Conducted for the 1998 Botanie Lake Dam Upgrading Project at Site EcRj 15, near Lytton, Southwestern B.C. On file, Department of Archaeological Planning and Assessment, Victoria.

ARCAS Consulting Archaeologists, Ltd.
1985 Excavations at the Rattlesnake Hill Site (EeRh61), Ashcroft, B.C. On file, B.C. Ministry of Small Business, Culture and Tourism, Archaeology Branch, Victoria.
1986 Archaeological Excavations at the Valley Mine, Highland Valley, B.C. On file, B.C. Ministry of Small Business, Culture and Tourism, Archaeology Branch, Victoria.

Archer, David J. W.
1980 Analysis of Spatial Patterns at a Prehistoric Settlement in the Lower Fraser Canyon, B.C. Unpublished M.A. thesis, Department of Anthropology, University of Victoria.

Arima, Eugene Y., and John Dewhirst
1990 Nootkans of Vancouver Island. In *Handbook of North American Indians, vol. 7: Northwest Coast,* edited by Wayne Suttles, pp. 391–411. Smithsonian Institution Press, Washington, D.C.

Arnold, Jeanne E.
1987 *Craft Specialization in the Prehistoric Channel Islands, California.* University of California Press, Berkeley.
1991 Transformation of a Regional Economy: Sociopolitical Evolution and the Production of Valuables in Southern California. *Antiquity* 65:953–962.
1993 Labor and the Rise of Complex Hunter-Gatherers. *Journal of Anthropological Archaeology* 12:75–119.
1996a The Archaeology of Complex Hunter-Gatherers. *Journal of Archaeological Method and Theory* 3:77–126.
1996b Organizational Transformations: Power and Labor among Complex Hunter-Gatherers and Other Intermediate Societies. In *Emergent Complexity: The Evolution of Intermediate Societies,* edited by Jeanne E. Arnold, pp. 59–73. International Monographs in Prehistory, Ann Arbor.
1996c Understanding the Evolution of Intermediate Societies. In *Emergent Complexity: The Evolution of Intermediate Societies,* edited by Jeanne E. Arnold, pp. 1–33. Archaeological Series, 9. International Monographs in Prehistory, Ann Arbor.
2000 Revisiting Power, Labor Rights, and Kinship: Archaeology and Social Theory. In *Social Theory in Archaeology,* edited by Michael B. Schiffer, pp. 14–30. University of Utah Press, Salt Lake City.
2001a The Chumash in World and Regional Perspectives. In *The Origins of a Pacific Coast Chiefdom: The Chumash of the Channel Islands,* edited by Jeanne E. Arnold, pp. 1–19. University of Utah Press, Salt Lake City.

Arnold, Jeanne E. (editor)
2001b *The Origins of a Pacific Coast Chiefdom: The Chumash of the Channel Islands.* University of Utah Press, Salt Lake City.

Arnold, Jeanne E., and Terisa M. Green
2002 Mortuary Ambiguity: The Ventureño Chumash Case. *American Antiquity* 67:760–771.

Bailey, J., I. Franck, P. Merchant, Mike K. Rousseau, K. Russell, S. Woods, and Rick J. Schulting
1993 The 1992 Archaeological Investigations at the Botticelli Creek Site, Adams Lake, South-Central B.C. Archaeology Branch Permit 1992–79. On file, Archaeology Branch of the B.C. Government, Victoria.

Baker, J.
1974 Report on the Archaeological Research Done in the Lytton Region, May to August 1974. Permit 1974–27. On file, Archaeology Branch, Victoria.

Bamforth, Douglas B.
1986 Technological Efficiency and Tool Curation. *American Antiquity* 51(1):38–50.
1993 Indigenous People, Indigenous Violence: Precontact Warfare on the North American Great Plains. *Man* 29:95–115.
1997 Adaptive Change on the Great Plains at the Paleoindian/Archaic Transition. In *Changing Perspectives of the Archaic on the Northwestern Plains and Rocky Mountains,* edited by M. L. Larson and J. E. Francis, pp. 14–55. University of South Dakota Press, Vermillion.

Barnard, A., and J. Woodburn
1988 Property, Power and Ideology in Hunting and Gathering Societies: An Introduction. In *Hunter-Gatherers:*

Property, Power and Ideology, edited by T. Ingold, D. Riches, and J. Woodburn, pp. 4–31. Berg, New York.

Bartholomew, M. J.
1982 Pollen and Sediment Analysis of Clear Lake, Whitman County, Washington, the Last 600 Years. Unpublished M.A. thesis, Department of Anthropology, Washington State University, Pullman.

Barton, Andrew J.
1994 Fishing for Ivory Worms: A Review of Ethnographic and Historical Recorded Dentalium Source Locations. Unpublished M.A. thesis, Department of Archaeology, Simon Fraser University, Burnaby, B.C.

Bar-Yosef, O., and R. H. Meadow
1995 The Origins of Agriculture in the Near East. In *Last Hunters First Farmers,* edited by T. Douglas Price and A. B. Gebauer, pp. 39–94. School of American Research Press, Santa Fe.

Bar-Yosef, O., and T. Schick
1989 Early Neolithic Organic Remains from Nahal Hemar Cave. *National Geographic Research* 5(2):176–190.

Baugh, T. G., and J. E. Ericson (editors)
1994 *Prehistoric Exchange Systems in North America.* Plenum Press, New York.

Bedwell, Stephen F.
1970 Prehistory and Environment of the Pluvial Fort Rock Late Area of Southcentral Oregon. Unpublished Ph.D. dissertation, University of Oregon, Eugene.
1973 *Fort Rock Basin: Prehistory and Environment.* University of Oregon Books, Eugene.

Bedwell, Stephen F., and Luther S. Cressman
1971 Fort Rock Report: Prehistory and Environment of the Pluvial Fort Rock Lake Area of South-Central Oregon. In *Great Basin Anthropological Conference 1970: Selected Papers,* pp. 1–25. Anthropological Papers, 1. University of Oregon, Eugene.

Bégouën, R., J. Clottes, J.-P. Giraud, and F. Rouzàud
1993 Os plantés et peintures ruputres dons la caverne d'Enlène. *118th Congrès National des Sociétés Historiques et Scientifiques, Paris:*283–306.

Bennett, J. R., B. F. Cumming, P. R. Leavitt, M. Chiu, J. P. Smot, and J. Szeicz
2001 Diatom, Pollen and Chemical Evidence of Postglacial Change at Big Lake, South-Central British Columbia, Canada. *Quaternary Research* 55:332–343.

Bense, Judith A.
1972 The Cascade Phase: A Study in the Effect of the Altithermal on a Cultural System. Ph.D. dissertation, Washington State University, Pullman. University Microfilms, Ann Arbor.

Benson, J. R.
1986a Site 45OK382. In *The Wells Reservoir Archaeological Project, Washington, vol. 2: Site Reports,* edited by James C. Chatters. Central Washington Archaeological Survey, Archaeological Reports, 86–6. Central Washington University, Ellensburg.
1986b Site 45OK383. In *The Wells Reservoir Archaeological Project, Washington, vol. 2: Site Reports,* edited by James C. Chatters. Central Washington Archaeological Survey, Archaeological Reports, 86–6. Central Washington University, Ellensburg.

Berreman, G. D.
1978 Scale and Social Relations. *Current Anthropology* 19:225–247.

Berry, K.
2000 Prehistoric Salmon Utilization at the Keatley Creek Site. In *The Ancient Past of Keatley Creek, vol. 2: Socioeconomy,* edited by Brian Hayden, pp. 135–142. Archaeology Press, Burnaby, B.C.

Bettinger, Robert L.
1991 *Hunter-Gatherers: Archaeological and Evolutionary Theory.* Plenum Press, New York.

Bettinger, Robert L., and M. A. Baumhoff
1982 The Numic Spread: Great Basin Cultures in Competition. *American Antiquity* 47:485–503.

Bettinger, Robert L., R. Boyd, and P. J. Richerson
1996 Style, Function, and Cultural Evolutionary Process. In *Darwinian Archaeologies,* edited by Herbert D. G. Maschner, pp. 133–164. Plenum Press, New York.

Bettinger, Robert L., and Jelmer Eerkens
1999 Point Typologies, Cultural Transmission, and the Spread of Bow-and-Arrow Technology in the Prehistoric Great Basin. *American Antiquity* 64(2):231–242.

Bicchieri, B.
1975 Units of Culture and Units of Time: Periodization and Its Use in Syntheses of Plateau Prehistory. *Northwest Anthropological Research Notes* 9:246–266.

Bilderback, David E., and J. H. Stone
1987 Persistence of Mount St. Helens Ash on Conifer Foliage. In *Mount St. Helens 1980: Botanical Consequences of the Explosive Eruption,* edited by David E. Bilderback, pp. 282–301. University of California Press, Berkeley.

Binford, Lewis R.
1965 Archaeological Systematics and the Study of Culture Process. *American Antiquity* 31(2):203–210.
1968a Post-Pleistocene Adaptations. In *New Perspectives in Archaeology,* edited by S. R. Binford and Lewis R. Binford, pp. 313–341. Aldine, Chicago.
1968b Some Comments on Historical versus Processual Archaeology. *Southwestern Journal of Anthropology* 24:267–275.
1977 General Introduction. In *For Theory Building in Archaeology,* edited by L. R. Binford, pp. 1–10. Academic Press, New York.
1978 *Nunamiut Ethnoarchaeology.* Academic Press, New York.
1979 Organization and Formation Processes: Looking at Curated Technologies. *Journal of Anthropological Research* 3:255–273.
1980 Willow Smoke and Dogs' Tails: Hunter-Gatherer Settlement Systems and Archaeological Site Formation. *American Antiquity* 45(1):4–20.
1981 *Bones: Ancient Men and Modern Myths.* Academic Press, Orlando.
2001 *Constructing Frames of Reference: An Analytical Method for Archaeological Theory Building Using Ethnographic and Environmental Data Sets.* University of California Press, Berkeley.

Blackburn, T.
1976 Ceremonial Integration and Aboriginal Interaction in Aboriginal California. In *Native Californians:*

A Theoretical Perspective, edited by L. Bean and T. Blackburn, pp. 225–244. Ballena Press, Ramona, California.

Blake, Michael, Gary Coupland, and Brian D. Thom

1993 Dating the Scowlitz Site. *The Midden* 25(1):7–9.

Blanton, Richard E., and Jody Taylor

1995 Patterns of Exchange and the Social Production of Pigs in Highland New Guinea. *Journal of Archaeological Research* 3:113–145.

Bleed, Peter

1986 The Optimal Design of Hunting Weapons: Maintainability or Reliability? *American Antiquity* 51(4): 737–747.

Blinman, Eric, Peter J. Mehringer Jr., and John C. Sheppard

1979 Pollen Influx and the Deposition of Mazama and Glacier Peak Tephra. In *Volcanic Activity and Human Ecology,* edited by P. D. Sheets and D. K. Grayson, pp. 393–425. Academic Press, New York.

Blitz, J. H.

1988 Adoption of the Bow in Prehistoric North America. *North American Archaeologist* 9:123–145.

Blong, R. J.

1984 *Volcanic Hazards: A Source Book of the Effects of Eruptions.* Academic Press, Orlando.

Boas, Franz

1890 The Shuswap. *Report of the British Association for the Advancement of Science,* 1886–1889:632–647.

1895 The Tinneh Tribe of the Nicola Valley. *Fifth Report of the Indians of British Columbia, British Association for the Advancement of Science, Annual Report:*30–34.

1966 *Kwakiutl Ethnography.* Edited by Helen Codere. University of Chicago Press, Chicago.

[1930] 1969 *The Religion of the Kwakiutl Indians,* 2 pts. Columbia University Contributions to Anthropology, 10. Reprint. AMS Press, New York.

Bogan, A.

1983 Evidence for Faunal Resource Partitioning in Eastern North American Chiefdoms. In *Animals and Archaeology,* edited by J. Clutton-Brock and C. Grigson, pp. 305–325. BAR International Series, 163. British Archaeological Reports, Oxford.

Bolt, B. A., W. L. Horn, G. A. MacDonald, and R. F. Scott

1977 *Geological Hazards.* Springer-Verlag, New York.

Bonnichsen, R., M. T. Beatty, M. D. Turner, and M. Stoneking

1996 What Can Be Learned from Hair? A Hair Record from the Mammoth Meadow Locus, Southwestern Montana. In *Prehistoric Mongoloid Dispersals,* edited by T. Akazawa and E. J. E. Szathmary, pp. 201–213. Oxford University Press, New York.

Borden, Charles E.

1968 The Prehistory of the Lower Mainland. In *Lower Fraser Valley: The Evolution of a Cultural Landscape,* edited by A. Siemans, pp. 9–26. Geographical Series 9. University of British Columbia, Vancouver.

Bostwick, T. W., and C. E. Downum

1994 Site Structure and Ceremony at Pueblo Grande. In *Archaeology of the Pueblo Grande Platform Mound and Surrounding Features, vol. 2: Features in the Central Precinct of the Pueblo Grande Community,* edited by T. W. Bostwick and C. E. Downum, pp. 297–386. Anthropological Papers, 1. Pueblo Grande Museum, Phoenix.

Boyd, R., and P. Richerson

1985 *Culture and the Evolutionary Process.* University of Chicago Press, Chicago.

Brauner, David R.

1975 *Archaeological Salvage of the Scorpion Knoll Site, 45AS41, Southeastern Washington.* Archaeological Research Center Project Report, 23. Washington State University, Pullman.

1976 Alpowai: The Cultural History of the Alpowa Locality, 2 vols. Unpublished Ph.D. dissertation, Department of Anthropology, Washington State University, Pullman.

1985 *Early Human Occupation in the Uplands of the Southern Plateau: Archaeological Investigations at the Pilcher Creek Site (35UN147), Union County, Oregon.* On file, Department of Anthropology, Oregon State University, Corvallis.

Brauner, David R., R. Lee Lyman, Howard Gard, Stephan Matz, and Rebecca McClelland

1990 *Archaeological Data Recovery at Hatiuhpuh, 45WT134, Whitman County, Washington.* Department of Anthropology Report. Oregon State University, Corvallis.

Breschini, G. S.

1979 The Marmes Burial Casts. *Northwest Anthropological Research Notes* 3(2):111–158.

Broughton, J. M.

1994 Late Holocene Resource Intensification in the Sacramento Valley, California: The Vertebrate Evidence. *Journal of Archaeological Science* 21:501–514.

Browman, David L., and David A. Munsell

1969 Columbia Plateau Prehistory: Cultural Development and Impinging Influences. *American Antiquity* 34: 249–264.

Brown, J. A.

1985 Long-Term Trends to Sedentism and the Emergence of Complexity in the American Midwest. In *Prehistoric Hunter-Gatherers: The Emergence of Cultural Complexity,* edited by T. Douglas Price and J. A. Brown, pp. 435–442. Academic Press, San Diego.

Brunton, B. B.

1998 Kootenai. In *Handbook of North American Indians, vol. 12: Plateau,* edited by Deward E. Walker Jr., pp. 223–237. Smithsonian Institution Press, Washington, D.C.

Bryan, Alan L.

1980 The Stemmed Point Tradition: An Early Technological Tradition in Western North America. In *Anthropological Papers in Memory of Earl H. Swanson, Jr.,* edited by L. B. Harten, Claude N. Warren, and Donald R. Tuohy, pp. 77–107. Museum of Natural History Special Publication. Idaho State University, Pocatello.

Bryan, Alan L., and Donald R. Tuohy

1960 A Basalt Quarry in Northeastern Oregon. *Proceedings of the American Philosophical Society* 104: 485–510.

1999 Prehistory of the Great Basin/Snake River Plain to About 8500 Years Ago. In *Ice Age Peoples of North America,* edited by R. Bonnichsen, pp. 249–263. Oregon State University Press, Corvallis.

Burch, E. S., Jr.

1981 *The Traditional Eskimo Hunters of Point Hope, Alaska: 1800–1875.* North Slope Borough, Barrow, Alaska.

Burch, Ernest S., Jr., and Linda J. Ellanna (editors)

1994 *Key Issues in Hunter-Gatherer Research.* Berg, Oxford.

Burchard, Greg C.

1998 *Environment, Prehistory, and Archaeology of the John Day Fossil Beds National Monument, Blue Mountain Region, North-Central Oregon.* National Park Service, Seattle.

Burley, David V.

1980 *Marpole: Anthropological Reconstructions of a Prehistoric Northwest Coast Culture Type.* Department of Archaeology Publication, 8. Simon Fraser University, Burnaby, B.C.

1981 Inter-Regional Exchange in the Gulf of Georgia during the Marpole Phase, 490 B.C. to A.D. 500. In *Networks of the Past: Regional Interaction in Archaeology,* edited by P. D. Francis, F. J. Kense, and P. G. Duke, pp. 397–410. Archaeological Association of the University of Calgary, Calgary.

1989 *Senewélets: Culture History of the Nanaimo Coast Salish and the False Narrows Midden.* Memoir, 2. Royal British Columbia Museum, Victoria.

Butler, B. Robert

1959 Lower Columbia Valley Archaeology: A Survey and Appraisal of Some Major Archaeological Resources. *Tebiwa* 2:6–24.

1961 *The Old Cordilleran Culture in the Pacific Northwest.* Occasional Papers of the Idaho State College Museum, 5. Idaho State College, Pocatello.

1963a An Early Man Site at Big Camas Prairie, Southern-Central Idaho. *Tebiwa* 6:22–33.

1963b Further Notes on the Burials and the Physical Stratigraphy at the Congdon Site, a Multi-Component Middle Period Site at the Dales on the Lower Columbia River. *Tebiwa* 6(2):16–32.

1965 Perspectives on the Prehistory of the Lower Columbia Valley. *Tebiwa* 8:1–16.

1978 Bison Hunting in the Desert West before 1800: The Paleoecological Potential and the Archaeological Reality. *Plains Anthropologist* 23:106–112.

1986 Prehistory of the Snake and Salmon River Area. In *Handbook of North American Indians, vol. 11: Great Basin,* edited by Warren L. D'Azevedo, pp. 127–134. Smithsonian Institution Press, Washington, D.C.

Butler, B. Robert, and J. R. Fitzwater

1965 A Further Note on the Clovis Site at Big Camas Prairie, South-Central Idaho. *Tebiwa* 8:38–40.

Butler, Virginia L.

1993 Natural versus Cultural Salmonid Remains: The Origin of The Dalles Roadcut Bones, Columbia River, Oregon, USA. *Journal of Archaeological Science* 20:1–24.

Butler, Virginia L., and James C. Chatters

1994 The Role of Bone Density in Structuring Prehistoric Salmon Bone Assemblages. *Journal of Archaeological Science* 21:413–424.

Butler, Virginia L., and Randall F. Schalk

1986 Holocene Salmonid Resources of the Upper Columbia. In *The Wells Reservoir Archaeological Project,* vol. 1, edited by James C. Chatters, pp. 232–252. Archaeological Survey Report, 86-6. Central Washington University, Ellensburg.

Byrd, Brian F.

1994 Public and Private, Domestic and Corporate: The Emergence of the Southwest Asian Village. *American Antiquity* 59(4):639–666.

Caldwell, W., and O. L. Mallory

1967 *Hells Canyon Archaeology.* River Basin Surveys Publications in Salvage Archaeology, 6. Smithsonian Institution Press, Washington, D.C.

Campbell, Sarah K. (editor)

1985 *Summary of Results, Chief Joseph Dam Cultural Resources Project, Washington.* Office of Public Archaeology, Institute for Environmental Studies, University of Washington, Seattle.

Cannell, Kevin G.

2001 Site 45GA26 and Its Place in the Snake River Period. Unpublished M.A. thesis, Washington State University, Pullman.

Cannon, A.

1992 Conflict and Salmon on the Interior Plateau of British Columbia. In *A Complex Culture of the British Columbia Plateau: Traditional Stl'átl'imx Resource Use,* edited by Brian Hayden, pp. 506–524. University of British Columbia Press, Vancouver.

Carlson, Catherine

1980 Excavations at the Curr Site. In *The Archaeology of Kamloops,* edited by Robert L. Wilson and Catherine Carlson, pp. 87–125. Department of Archaeology, Simon Fraser University, Burnaby, B.C.

Carlson, Keith Thor

1996 Stó:lō Exchange Dynamics. *Native Studies Review* 11(1):5–48.

Carlson, Keith Thor (editor)

2001 *A Stó:lō–Coast Salish Historical Atlas.* Douglas & McIntyre, Vancouver; University of Washington Press, Seattle; and Stó:lō Heritage Trust, Chilliwack.

Carlson, Roy L.

1983a The Far West. In *Early Man in the New World,* edited by Richard Shutler, pp. 73–96. Sage Publishing, Beverly Hills.

1983b Prehistory of the Northwest Coast. In *Indian Art Traditions of the Northwest Coast,* edited by Roy L. Carlson, pp. 13–32. Archaeology Press, Burnaby, B.C.

1994 Trade and Exchange in Prehistoric British Columbia. In *Prehistoric Exchange Systems in North America,* edited by T. G. Baugh and J. E. Ericson, pp. 307–361. Plenum Press, New York.

1996 The Later Prehistory of British Columbia. In *Early Human Occupation in British Columbia,* edited by Roy L. Carlson and Luke Dalla Bona, pp. 215–226. University of British Columbia Press, Vancouver.

Chance, D. H., and J. V. Chance

1977 *Kettle Falls: 1976.* Anthropological Research Manuscript Series, 39. Department of Sociology/Anthropology, University of Idaho, Moscow.

1979 *Kettle Falls 1977: Salvage Archaeology in Lake Roosevelt.* Research Manuscript Series, 53. Laboratory of Anthropology, University of Idaho, Moscow.

1982 *Kettle Falls, 1971 and 1974: Salvage Archaeology in Lake Roosevelt.* Anthropological Research Manuscript Series, 69. Laboratory of Anthropology, University of Idaho, Moscow.

1985 *Kettle Falls 1978: Further Archaeological Excavations in Lake Roosevelt.* Anthropology Reports, 84. Alfred W. Bowers Laboratory on Anthropology, University of Idaho, Moscow.

Chang, K. C.

1981 The Affluent Foragers in the Coastal Areas of China: Extrapolation from Evidence on the Transition to Agriculture. *Senri Ethnological Studies* 9:179–186.

Chatters, James C.

1982 Evolutionary Human Paleoecology: Culture Change and Human Adaptation in the Pahsimeroi Valley, Idaho, 2500 B.P. to the Present. Unpublished Ph.D. dissertation, Department of Anthropology, University of Washington, Seattle.

1984 *Human Adaptation along the Columbia River 4700–1600 B.P.: A Report of Test Excavations at River Mile 590, North Central Washington.* Occasional Paper, 1; Research Report, 84–1. Central Washington University, Ellensburg.

1986a *The Ellisford Cremations: Internecine Hostilities in the 5th Century A.D.* Central Washington Archaeological Survey Archaeological Report, 86–1. Central Washington University, Ellensburg.

1986b *The Wells Reservoir Archaeological Project, vol. 1: Summary of Findings.* Occasional Paper, 1; Research Report, 86–6. Central Washington University, Ellensburg.

1987 Hunter-Gatherer Adaptations and Assemblage Structure. *Journal of Anthropological Archaeology* 6: 336–375.

1989a The Antiquity of Economic Differentiation in the Puget Sound Region, Northwest Coast. In *Households and Communities,* edited by S. MacEachern, D. Archer, and R. Gavin, pp. 168–178. University of Calgary Archaeological Association, Calgary.

1989b Pacifism and the Organization of Conflict on the Plateau of Northwestern America. In *Cultures in Conflict: Current Archaeological Perspectives,* edited by D. C. Tkaczuk and B. C. Vivian, pp. 241–252. University of Calgary Archaeological Association, Calgary.

1989c Resource Intensification and Sedentism on the Southern Plateau. *Archaeology in Washington* 1:3–19.

1993 Bison, Salmon Productivity, and the Development of Southern Plateau Settlement Systems. Paper presented at the 58th Annual Meeting of the Society for American Archaeology, St. Louis, Missouri.

1995a Population Growth, Climatic Cooling, and the Development of Collector Strategies on the Southern Plateau, Western North America. *Journal of World Prehistory* 9(3):341–400.

1995b Resource Intensification and Demography on the Plateau of Western North America. Paper presented at the 60th Annual Meeting of the Society for American Archaeology, Minneapolis.

1998 Environment. In *Handbook of North American Indians, vol. 12: Plateau,* edited by Deward E. Walker Jr., pp. 29–48. Smithsonian Institution Press, Washington, D.C.

2000 The Discovery and Initial Analysis of the Skeleton Known as Kennewick Man. *American Antiquity* 65:261–316.

2002 Osteoarchaeology and Mortuary Practices of the Sinkaietk. Report prepared for the Douglas County PUD by Applied Paleoscience. Bothell, Washington.

2003 *Osteology and Mortuary Practices of the Sinkaietk: Analysis and Repatriation of Human Remains and Associated Objects from the Wells Project, Okanogan County, Washington.* Report prepared for Douglas County PUD, East Wenatchee, Washington. Applied Paleoscience, Bothell, Washington.

Chatters, James C., Virginia L. Butler, M. J. Scott, D. M. Anderson, and D. A. Neitzel

1995a A Paleoscience Approach to Estimating the Effects of Climatic Warming on the Salmonid Fisheries of the Columbia River Basin. In *Climate Change and Northern Fish Populations,* edited by R. J. Beamish, pp. 489–496. Canadian Special Publication in Fisheries and Aquatic Sciences, 121. Ottawa.

Chatters, James C., Sarah K. Campbell, G. D. Smith, and P. E. Minthorn

1995b Bison Procurement in the Far West: A 2,100-Year-Old Kill Site on the Columbia Plateau. *American Antiquity* 60:751–763.

Chatters, James C., S. Hackenberger, A. J. Busacca, L. S. Cummings, R. L. Jantz, T. W. Stafford Jr., and E. R. Taylor

2000 A Second Early Holocene Skull from Eastern Washington, USA? *Current Research in the Pleistocene* 17:93–94.

Chatters, James C., and J. L. Langdon

2002 Patterning in the Cultural Landscape. In *Archaeological Survey of Hells Canyon: Hells Canyon Dam to the Mouth of the Salmon River,* edited by James C. Chatters and M. J. Root, pp. 43–68. Idaho Power Co., Boise.

Chatters, James C., and D. Leavell

1995 Harding Lake: A Study of Fire, Succession, and Sedimentation since 350 AD in the Subalpine Fir Forests of the Yaak River, Northwestern Montana. APS Research Report P-4. On file, Kootenai National Forest, Libby, Montana.

Chatters, James C., and C. R. Pasternak

1992 A Possible Case of Prehistoric Brucellosis from Northwestern America. *American Journal of Physical Anthropology,* supp. 14:59.

Chatters, James C., and David L. Pokotylo

1998 Prehistory: Introduction. In *Handbook of North American Indians, vol. 12: Plateau,* edited by Deward E. Walker Jr., pp. 73–80. Smithsonian Institution Press, Washington, D.C.

Chatters, James C., and M. J. Root (editors)

2002 *The Archeological Survey of Hells Canyon from Hells Canyon Dam to the Mouth of the Salmon River.* Idaho Power Co., Boise.

Chatters, James C., and M. W. Zweifel

1987 *The Cemetery at Sntlxwenewixwtn.* Central Washington Archaeological Survey Archaeological Report, 87–1. Central Washington University, Ellensburg.

Chisholm, Brian S.
1986 Reconstruction of Prehistoric Diet in British Columbia Using Stable-Carbon Isotopic Analysis. Unpublished Ph.D. dissertation, Department of Archaeology, Simon Fraser University, Burnaby, B.C.
Chisholm, Brian S., and D. E. Nelson
1983 An Early Human Skeleton from South-Central British Columbia: Dietary Inference from Carbon Isotopic Evidence. *Canadian Journal of Archaeology* 7:85–86.
Choquette, Wayne
1981 The Role of Lithic Raw Material Studies in Kootenay Archaeology. "Fragments of the Past: British Columbia Archaeology in the 1970s," edited by Knut R. Fladmark. *B.C. Studies* 48:21–36.
Christenson, Andrew L.
1986 Projectile Point Size and Projectile Aerodynamics: An Exploratory Study. *Plains Anthropologist* 31:109–128.
Clark, R. B.
1963 The Economics of Dentalium. *Veliger* 6(1):9–19.
Cleland, C.
1965 Appendix 2: Analysis of the Faunal Remains of the Fatherland Site. In *Archaeology of the Fatherland Site*, edited by Robert Neitzel, pp. 96–101. Anthropology Papers of the American Museum of Natural History, 51(1). American Museum of Natural History, New York.
Cohen, M. N.
1977 *The Food Crisis in Prehistory: Overpopulation and the Origins of Agriculture.* Yale University Press, New Haven.
1985 Prehistoric Hunter-Gatherers: The Meaning of Social Complexity. In *Prehistoric Hunter-Gatherers: The Emergence of Cultural Complexity*, edited by T. Douglas Price and J. A. Brown, pp. 99–119. Academic Press, New York.
Cole, David L.
1968 *Archaeological Excavations in Area 6 of Site 35GM9, the Wildcat Canyon Site.* Museum of Natural History Report. University of Oregon, Eugene.
Cole, David L., and Luther S. Cressman
1961 *Interim Report 1960–1961, John Day Reservoir Project, Columbia River.* Museum of Natural History Report. University of Oregon, Eugene.
Condrashoff, Nancy
1980 The Pithouse. On file, Royal British Columbia Museum, Victoria.
Connolly, Thomas J.
1999 *Newberry Crater: A Ten-Thousand-Year Record of Human Occupation and Environmental Change in the Basin–Plateau Borderlands.* University of Utah Anthropological Papers, 121. University of Utah Press, Salt Lake City.
Cousins, Sara Mossop
2000 A Paleoethnobotanical Comparison of Four "Small" Housepits. In *The Ancient Past of Keatley Creek, vol. 2: Socioeconomy*, edited by Brian Hayden, pp. 87–102. Archaeology Press, Burnaby, B.C.
Craven, Sloan
2003 Lithic Variation in Hafted Bifaces at the Lind Coulee Site (45GR97), Washington. Unpublished M.A. thesis, Department of Anthropology, Washington State University, Pullman.
Crellin, David
1994 Is There a Dog in the House? The Cultural Significance of Prehistoric Domesticated Dogs in the Mid-Fraser River Region of British Columbia. Unpublished M.A. thesis, Department of Archaeology, Simon Fraser University, Burnaby, B.C.
Crellin, David, and Ty Heffner
2000 The Dogs of Keatley Creek. In *The Ancient Past of Keatley Creek, vol. 2: Socioeconomy*, edited by Brian Hayden, pp. 151–166. Archaeology Press, Burnaby, B.C.
Cressman, Luther S., David L. Cole, Wilbur A. Davis, Thomas M. Newman, and Daniel J. Scheans
1960 Cultural Sequences at The Dalles, Oregon: A Contribution to Pacific Northwest Prehistory. *Transactions of the American Philosophical Society* (n.s.) 50(10).
Crockford, Susan J., and Cameron J. Pye
1997 Forensic Reconstruction of Prehistoric Dogs from the Northwest Coast. *Canadian Journal of Archaeology* 21(2):149–153.
Croes, Dale R.
1977 Basketry from the Ozette Village Archaeological Site. Unpublished Ph.D. dissertation, Washington State University, Pullman.
1996 *The Hoko River Archaeological Site Complex: The Wet/Dry Site (45CA213), 3,000–1,700 B.P.* Washington State University Press, Pullman.
Cybulski, J. S.
1992 *A Greenville Burial Ground.* Mercury Series, Archaeological Survey of Canada Paper, 146. Canadian Museum of Civilization, Ottawa.
Dalquest, Walter W.
1948 *Mammals of Washington.* Museum of Natural History, Publication 2. University of Kansas, Lawrence.
Darwent, John
1998 *The Prehistoric Use of Nephrite on the British Columbia Plateau.* Publication, 25. Archaeology Press, Burnaby, B.C.
Daubenmire, Rexford F.
1969 Ecological Plant Geography of the Pacific Northwest. *Madrono: A West American Journal of Botany* 20:111–128.
1970 *Steppe Vegetation of Washington.* Cooperative Extension Bulletin, 62. Washington State University, Pullman.
1985 The Western Limits of the Range of American Bison. *Ecology* 66:622–624.
Daugherty, Richard D.
1956 Archaeology of the Lind Coulee Site, Washington. *Proceedings of the American Philosophical Society* 100:223–278.
1962 The Intermontaine Western Tradition. *American Antiquity* 28:144–150.
Davis, Loren G.
2001 Lower Salmon River Cultural Chronology: A Revised and Expanded Model. *Northwest Anthropological Research Notes* 35:229–247.
Dawson, George M.
1892 Notes on the Shuswap People of British Columbia.

Proceedings and Transactions of the Royal Society of Canada (1st series) 9(2):3–44.

Dean, Emily
1994 Faunal Remains from Structure 3 at the Big M Site, Fort Rock Basin, Oregon. In *Archaeological Researches in the Northern Great Basin: Fort Rock Archaeology since Cressman,* edited by C. Melvin Aikens and Dennis L. Jenkins, pp. 505–530. Anthropological Papers, 50. University of Oregon, Eugene.

DeBoer, W. R.
1988 Subterranean Storage and the Organization of Surplus: The View from Eastern North America. *Southeastern Archaeology* 7:1–20.

de Laguna, Frederica
1972 *Under Mt. St. Elias: The History and Culture of the Yakutat Tlingit.* Smithsonian Contributions to Anthropology, 7. Smithsonian Institution Press, Washington, D.C.

Diamond, Jared
1992 The Arrow of Disease. *Discover* 13(10).
1997 *Guns, Germs, and Steel: The Fates of Human Societies.* W. W. Norton and Co., New York.

DiScipio, Aimee M.
1997 Archaeological Investigations at the Ferry Canyon Site (35WS261): A Pithouse Village on the Lower Deschutes River, Oregon. Unpublished M.A. thesis, Washington State University, Pullman.

Dixon, E. James
1999 *Bones, Boats, and Bison: Archaeology and the First Colonization of Western North America.* University of New Mexico Press, Albuquerque.

Donald, L., and D. Mitchell
1975 Some Correlates of Local Group Rank among the Southern Kwakiutl. *Ethnology* 14:325–346.

Draper, John A.
1986a Final Site Report: 45DO387 (the Plew Site). In *Wells Reservoir Archaeological Project, vol. 2: Site Reports,* edited by James C. Chatters. Central Washington Archaeological Survey Archaeological Report, 86–6. Central Washington University, Ellensburg.
1986b Site Report: 45OK422. In *Wells Reservoir Archaeological Project, vol. 2: Site Reports,* edited by James C. Chatters. Central Washington Archaeological Survey Archaeological Report, 86–6. Central Washington University, Ellensburg.
1991 Artifact Descriptions for the Upper Landing Site (10IH1017). In *Prehistory and Paleoenvironments at Pittsburg Landing: Data Recovery and Test Excavations at Six Sites in Hells Canyon National Recreation Area, West Central Idaho,* edited by Kenneth C. Reid, pp. 649–754. Center for Northwest Anthropology Project Report, 15. Washington State University, Pullman.
1993 *An Intensive Cultural Resources Inventory Survey of the Dworshak Reservoir Drawdown Zone, North Fork Clearwater River, West-Central Idaho.* Center for Northwest Anthropology Project Report, 11. Washington State University, Pullman.

Draper, John A., and David R. Brauner
1989 *Archaeological Survey and Reevaluation of Prehistoric Sites within the Palouse Canyon Archaeological District.* Department of Anthropology Report. Oregon State University, Corvallis.

Draper, John A., and Maury Morgenstein
1993 *Archaeological Testing in the Palouse Canyon Archaeological District: 1992 Field Season.* BOAS, Inc., Seattle.

Driver, Harold E., and William C. Massey
1957 Comparative Studies of North American Indians. *Transactions of the American Philosophical Society* (n.s.) 47(2).

Du Bois, Cora A.
1935 *Wintu Ethnography.* Publications in American Archaeology and Ethnology, 36(1). University of California, Berkeley.

Dumond, Don E., and Rick Minor
1983 *Archaeology in the John Day Reservoir: The Wildcat Canyon Site, 35-GM-9.* Anthropological Papers, 30. University of Oregon, Eugene.

Dunnell, R. C.
1970 Seriation Method and Its Evaluation. *American Antiquity* 35:305–319.
1973 Fire, Air, Earth and Water: A Rational Classification. *Mankind* 9:127–131.
1978 Style and Function: A Fundamental Dichotomy. *American Antiquity* 43:192–202.
1980 Evolutionary Theory and Archaeology. In *Advances in Archaeological Method and Theory,* vol. 3, edited by Michael B. Schiffer, pp. 35–99. Academic Press, New York.
1986 Methodological Issues in Americanist Artifact Classification. In *Advances in Archaeological Method and Theory,* vol. 9, edited by Michael B. Schiffer, pp. 149–207. Academic Press, New York.

Eldridge, Morley
1974 *Recent Archaeological Investigations near Chase, B.C.* Cariboo College Papers in Archaeology, 2. Kamloops, B.C.
1984 Vallican Archaeological Site (DjQi 1): A Synthesis and Management Report. On file, B.C. Heritage Conservation Branch, Victoria.
1996 Archaeological Impact Assessment of Paradise Creek Area Cutblocks in the Lillooet Forest District. On file, Archaeology Branch, Victoria.

Eldridge, Morley, and Arnoud H. Stryd
1983 CN Rail Rail-Yard Expansion Project: Heritage Mitigation Study, Kamloops Junction, B.C. Report prepared by ARCAS Associates. On file, Heritage Resource Center; Ministry of Small Business, Tourism, and Culture; Archaeology Branch, Victoria.

Ellis, Florence (Hawley)
1945–1953 Ethnographic Fieldnotes including Kinship, Social, and Religious Organization, Ceremonies, Crafts, Witchcraft, Death in Isleta Pueblo, New Mexico. MS in Ellis's possession.

Ellis, Florence Hawley
1979 Isleta Pueblo. In *Handbook of North American Indians, vol. 9: Southwest,* edited by Alfonso Ortiz, pp. 351–365. Smithsonian Institution Press, Washington, D.C.

Elmendorf, W. W.
1965 Linguistic and Geographic Relations in the Northern

Plateau Area. *Southwestern Journal of Anthropology* 21:63–78.
Endacott, Neal A.
1992 The Archaeology of Squirt Cave: Seasonality, Storage, and Semi-Sedentism. Unpublished M.A. thesis, Department of Anthropology, Washington State University, Pullman.
Endzweig, Pamela E.
1994a Housepits on the John Day and Deschutes Rivers: A Summary of the Evidence. In *Contributions to the Archaeology of Oregon 1990–1994*, edited by P. W. Baxter, pp. 45–63. Occasional Papers, 5. Association of Oregon Archaeologists.
1994b Late Archaic Variability and Change on the Southern Columbia Plateau: Archaeological Investigations in the Pine Creek Drainage of the Middle John Day River, Wheeler County, Oregon. Unpublished Ph.D. dissertation, University of Oregon, Eugene.
Erickson, Kevin
1983 Marine Shell Utilization in the Plateau Culture Area. Unpublished M.A. thesis, University of Idaho, Moscow.
Fagan, John L.
1988 Clovis and Western Pluvial Lakes Tradition Lithic Technologies at the Dietz Site in South-Central Oregon. In *Early Human Occupation in Far Western North America: The Clovis–Archaic Interface*, edited by Judith A. Willig, C. Melvin Aikens, and John L. Fagan, pp. 389–416. Anthropological Papers, 21. Nevada State Museum, Carson City.
Feinman, Gary M.
1998 Corporate/Network: A New Perspective on Leadership in the American Southwest. In *Hierarchies in Action: Who Benefits?* edited by M. A. Diehl, pp. 152–180. Center for Archaeological Investigations, Southern Illinois University, Carbondale.
Feinman, Gary M., Kent G. Lightfoot, and Steadman Upham
2000 Political Hierarchies and Organizational Strategies in the Puebloan Southwest. *American Antiquity* 65: 449–470.
Fewkes, Walter F.
1899 The Winter Solstice Altars at Hano Pueblo. *American Anthropologist* 1(2):251–276.
Fitzhugh, William
1978 Maritime Archaic Cultures of the Central and Northern Labrador Coast. *Arctic Anthropology* 15:61–95.
Fladmark, Knut R.
1982 An Introduction to the Prehistory of British Columbia. *Canadian Journal of Archaeology* 6:95–156.
Flanagan, J. C.
1989 Hierarchy in Simple "Egalitarian" Societies. *Annual Review of Anthropology* 18:245–266.
Flanagan, J. C., and S. Rayner
1988 *Rules, Decisions, and Inequality in Egalitarian Societies.* Gower, London.
Flannery, Kent V.
1976 Interregional Religious Networks. In *The Early Mesoamerican Village*, edited by Kent Flannery, pp. 329–368. Academic Press, New York.
2002 The Origins of the Village Revisited: From Nuclear to Extended Households. *American Antiquity* 67:417–434.
Foit, Franklin F., Jr., Peter J. Mehringer Jr., and John C. Sheppard
1992 Age, Distribution, and Stratigraphy of Glacier Peak Tephra in Eastern Washington and Western Montana, United States. *Canadian Journal of Earth Science* 30:535–552.
Ford, R. I.
1985 The Processes of Plant Food Production in Prehistoric North America. In *Prehistoric Food Production in North America*, edited by R. I. Ford, pp. 1–18. Museum of Anthropology Anthropological Papers, 75. University of Michigan, Ann Arbor.
Franklin, Jerry F., and C. T. Dyrness
1973 *Natural Vegetation of Oregon and Washington.* Technical Report, PNW 8. USDA Forest Service, Portland.
Fraser, Scott
1994 XRF Analysis of the Scowlitz Obsidian: A Preliminary Report. On file, Laboratory of Archaeology, University of British Columbia, Vancouver.
Freeman, L., and J. Gonzalez Edhegaray
1981 El Juyu: A 14,000-Year-Old Sanctuary from Northern Spain. *History of Religions* 21:1–19.
French, D. H., and K. S. French
1998 Wasco, Wishram and Cascades. In *Handbook of North American Indians, vol. 12: Plateau*, edited by Deward E. Walker Jr., pp. 360–377. Smithsonian Institution Press, Washington, D.C.
Freidel, David A., and Linda Schele
1989 Dead Kings and Living Temples: Dedication and Termination Rituals among the Ancient Maya. In *Word and Image in Maya Culture: Explorations in Language, Writing, and Representation*, edited by W. F. Hanks and D. S. Rice, pp. 233–243. University of Utah Press, Salt Lake City.
Galm, Jerry R.
1985 The Avey's Orchard Site in Regional Perspective. In *Avey's Orchard: Archaeological Investigations of a Late Prehistoric Columbia River Community*, edited by Jerry R. Galm and Ruth A. Masten, pp. 321–334. Archaeological and Historical Services, Reports in Archaeology and History, 100–42. Eastern Washington University, Cheney.
1994 Prehistoric Trade and Exchange in the Interior Plateau of Northwestern North America. In *Prehistoric Exchange Systems in North America*, edited by T. Baugh and J. E. Ericson, pp. 279–305. Plenum, New York.
Galm, Jerry R., and Stan Gough
2000 Site 45KT1362, ac. 10,000 Yr B.P. Occupation in Central Washington. *Current Research in the Pleistocene* 17:29–31.
Galm, Jerry R., Glenn D. Hartman, Ruth A. Masten, and Garry O. Stephenson
1981 *A Cultural Resources Overview of Bonneville Power Administration's Mid-Columbia Project, Central Washington.* Reports in Archaeology and History, 100–16. Eastern Washington University, Cheney.
Galm, Jerry R., and Ruth A. Masten (editors)
1985 *Avey's Orchard: Archaeological Investigations of a Late Prehistoric Columbia River Community.* Archaeological and Historical Services, Reports in Archaeology

and History, 100–42. Eastern Washington University, Cheney.

Garber, J. F.

1986 The Artifacts. In *Archaeology at Cerros, Belize, Central America,* vol. 1, edited by R. A. Robertson and David A. Freidel, pp. 117–126. Southern Methodist University Press, Dallas.

1989 *The Artifacts: Archaeology at Cerros, Belize, Central America,* vol. 2. Southern Methodist University Press, Dallas.

Garrard, Andrew, D. Baird, S. Colledge, L. Martin, and K. Wright

1994 Prehistoric Environment and Settlement in the Azraz Basin: An Interim Report on the 1987 and 1988 Excavation Seasons. *Levant* 26:73–109.

Gehr, K. D.

1976 The Archaeology of the Hihium Lake Locality, British Columbia. On file, Archaeological Assessment and Planning, Victoria.

Geiger, Daniel L., and Guido T. Poppe

2000 *A Conchological Iconography: The Family Haliotidae.* Conchbooks, Hackenheim, Germany.

Gerlach, C., and O. K. Mason

1992 Calibrated Radiocarbon Dates and Cultural Interaction in the Western Arctic. *Arctic Anthropology* 29:54–81.

Gilbow, D. W.

1978 *Archaeological Testing Program for the Walla Walla District Corps of Engineers, 1977 Mission.* Laboratory of Anthropology Project Report, 62. Washington State University, Pullman.

Glassow, Michael A.

1996 *Purisimeño Chumash Prehistory: Maritime Adaptations along the Southern California Coast.* Harcourt Brace, Forth Worth.

Godel, J. C., T. K. Basu, H. F. Pabst, R. S. Hodges, P. E. Hodges, and M. L. Ng

1996 Perinatal Vitamin A (Retinal) Status of Northern Canadian Mothers and Their Infants. *Biology of the Neonate* 69:133–139.

Goodale, Nathan B.

2001 Evolution of Hunter-Gatherer Socioeconomic Systems during the Middle to Late Holocene in the Upper Columbia and Interior Northwest. Unpublished M.A. thesis, Department of Anthropology, University of Montana, Missoula.

Gough, Stan

1990 *A Cultural Resources Overview, Sampling Survey, and Management Plan, Colville Indian Reservation, Okanogan and Ferry Counties, Washington.* Reports in Archaeology and History, 100–74. Eastern Washington University, Cheney.

Gould, Richard

1969 *Yiwara.* Scribners, New York.

Grabert, Garland

1974 Okanagan Archaeology: 1966–1967. *Syesis* 7 (supp. 2):1–82.

Gramly, Richard M.

1996 The East Wenachee Clovis Site (Richey-Roberts Site): Summary of Findings and Current Status. *Current Research in the Pleistocene* 13:19–20.

Grater, Barbara A.

1966 The Archaeology of the Votaw Site: Lower Snake River, Washington. Unpublished M.A. thesis, San Francisco State University.

Green, Thomas

1993 Aboriginal Residential Structures in Southern Idaho. *Journal of California and Great Basin Anthropology* 15:58–72.

Greengo, Robert

1982 *Studies in Prehistory: Priest Rapids and Wanapum Reservoir Areas, Columbia River Washington.* Final Report to the U.S. Department of Interior. Department of Anthropology, University of Washington, Seattle.

Greenspan, Ruth

1985 Fish and Fishing in Northern Great Basin Prehistory. Unpublished Ph.D. dissertation, University of Oregon, Eugene.

1994 Archaeological Fish Remains in the Fort Rock Basin. In *Archaeological Researches in the Northern Great Basin: Fort Rock Archaeology since Cressman,* edited by C. Melvin Aikens and Dennis L. Jenkins, pp. 485–504. Anthropological Papers, 50. University of Oregon, Eugene.

Grinder, Philip

2001 Marble Range Provincial Park Strawberry Lake Archaeological Assessments Permit Report. Heritage Inspection Permit 2000–273. Arcas Consulting Archaeologists.

Grove, J. M.

1988 *The Little Ice Age.* Methuen, London.

Gustafson, Carl E.

1972 Faunal Remains from the Marmes Rockshelter and Related Archaeological Sites in the Columbia Basin. Unpublished Ph.D. dissertation, Washington State University, Pullman.

Hackenberger, S.

1990 Knight Creek (35WA767). On file, Wallowa Whitman National Forest, Baker City, Oregon.

Haley, Shawn

1996 The Pasika Complex Revisited. In *Early Human Occupation in British Columbia,* edited by Roy L. Carlson and Luke Dalla Bona, pp. 51–64. Univeristy of British Columbia Press, Vancouver.

Hall, Eugene R.

1981 *Mammals of North America.* John Wiley, New York.

Hallett, Doug J., Dana Lepofsky, R. Mathews, and Kenneth P. Lertzman

2003a 11,000 Years of Fire History and Climate in the Mountain Hemlock Rainforest of Southwest British Columbia Based on Sedimentary Charcoal. *Canadian Journal of Forest Research* 33:292–312.

Hallett, Doug J., Rolf W. Mathewes, and R. C. Walker

2003b A 1000-Year Record of Forest Fire Drought and Lake Level Change in Southeastern British Columbia. *The Holocene* 13:751–761.

Hallett, Doug J., and R. C. Walker

2000 Paleoecology and Its Application to Fire and Vegetation Management in Kootenay National Park, British Columbia. *Journal of Paleolimnology* 24:401–414.

Halpin, Marjorie M., and Margaret Seguin

1990 Tsimshian Peoples: Southern Tsimshian, Coast Tsimshian, Nishga, and Gitksan. In *Handbook of North American Indians, vol. 7: Northwest Coast,* edited by W. Suttles, pp. 267–284. Smithsonian Institution Press, Washington, D.C.

Hampton, O. W. "Bud"

1999 *Culture of Stone: Sacred and Profane Uses of Stone among the Dani.* Texas A&M University Press, College Station.

Hanes, Richard C.

1988 Early Cultural Traditions of the Owyhee Uplands as Seen from Dirty Shame Rockshelter. In *Early Human Occupation in Far Western North America: The Clovis–Archaic Interface,* edited by Judith A. Willig, C. Melvin Aikens, and John L. Fagan, pp. 361–372. Anthropological Papers, [illegible] Nevada State Museum, Carson City.

Hansel, Victoria J.

2003 The Dalles Roadcut (Fivemile Rapids) Avifauna: Evidence for a Cultural Origin. Unpublished M.A. thesis, Washington State University, Pullman.

Hanson, Gordon W.

1973 The Katz Site: A Prehistoric Pithouse Settlement in the Lower Fraser Valley, British Columbia. Unpublished M.A. thesis, Department of Anthropology and Sociology, University of British Columbia, Vancouver.

Harder, David A.

1998 A Synthetic Overview of the Tucannon Phase in the Lower Snake River Region of Washington and Idaho. Unpublished M.A. thesis, Department of Anthropology, Washington State University, Pullman.

Harkins, S. K.

1980 The Prehistoric Occurrence and Aboriginal Utilization of *Bison* sp. in the Central Columbia Basin. Unpublished M.A. thesis, Department of Anthropology, Washington State University, Pullman.

Harris, D. R.

1989 An Evolutionary Continuum of People–Plant Interactions. In *Foraging and Farming: The Evolution of Plant Exploitation,* edited by D. R. Harris and G. C. Hillman, pp. 11–26. Unwin Hyman, London.

Harris, Stephen L.

1988 *Fire Mountains of the West: The Cascade and Mono Lake Volcanoes.* Mountain Press Publishing Co., Missoula.

Hartman, Glenn D.

1975 *The Archaeology of Cox's Pond Site, 45DO172.* Washington Archaeological Research Center Report. Washington State University, Pullman.

Hauptmann, Harold

1999 The Urfa Region. In *Neolithic in Turkey,* edited by A. Ozdogan, pp. 65–86. Arkeoloji ve Samat Yayimlari, Istanbul.

Haviland, W. A.

1981 Dower Houses and Minor Centers at Tikal, Guatemala: An Investigation into the Identification of Valid Units in Settlement Hierarchies. In *Lowland Maya Settlement Patterns,* edited by Wendy Ashmore, pp. 89–117. University of New Mexico Press, Albuquerque.

1988 Musical Hammock at Tikal: Problems with Reconstructing Household Composition. In *Household and Community in the Mesoamerican Past,* edited by R. R. Wilk and Wendy Ashmore, pp. 121–134. University of New Mexico Press, Albuquerque.

Hawkes, K.

1993 Why Hunter-Gatherers Work: An Ancient Version of the Problem of Public Goods. *Current Anthropology* 34:341–361.

Hawkes, K., J. F. O'Connell, and N. G. Blurton Jones

2001 Hunting and Nuclear Familes: Some Lessons from the Hadza about Men's Work. *Current Anthropology* 42: 681–709.

Hayden, Brian

1979 *Paleolithic Reflections: Lithic Technology and Ethnographic Excavations among Australian Aborigines.* Australian Institute of Aboriginal Studies, Canberra.

1981 Research and Development in the Stone Age: Technological Transitions among Hunter-Gatherers. *Current Anthropology* 22:519–548.

1989 From Chopper to Celt: The Evolution of Resharpening Techniques. In *Time, Energy, and Stone Tools,* edited by R. Torrence, pp. 7–16. Cambridge University Press, Cambridge.

1990 Nimrods, Piscators, Pluckers, and Planters: The Emergence of Food Production. *Journal of Anthropological Archaeology* 9:31–69.

1992a Ecology and Complex Hunter/Gatherers. In *A Complex Culture of the British Columbia Plateau: Traditional Stl'átl'imx Resource Use,* edited by Brian Hayden, pp. 525–563. University of British Columbia Press, Vancouver.

1992b Introduction: Ecology and Culture. In *A Complex Culture of the British Columbia Plateau: Traditional Stl'átl'imx Resource Use,* edited by Brian Hayden, pp. 3–46. University of British Columbia Press, Vancouver.

1994 Competition, Labor, and Complex Hunter-Gatherers. In *Key Issues in Hunter-Gatherer Research,* edited by Ernest S. Burch Jr. and Linda J. Ellanna, pp. 223–239. Berg, Oxford.

1995 Pathways to Power: Principles for Creating Socioeconomic Inequalities. In *Foundations of Social Inequality,* edited by T. Douglas Price and Gary M. Feinman, pp. 15–86. Plenum Press, New York.

1996a Feasting in Prehistoric and Traditional Societies. In *Food and the Status Quest: An Interdisciplinary Perspective,* edited by Polly Wiessner and Wulf Schiefenhoevel, pp. 127–146. Berghahn Books, Oxford.

1996b Thresholds of Power in Emergent Complex Societies. In *Emergent Complexity: The Evolution of Intermediate Societies,* edited by Jeanne E. Arnold, pp. 50–58. International Monographs in Prehistory, Ann Arbor.

1997 *The Pithouses of Keatley Creek: Complex Hunter-Gatherers of the Northern Plateau.* Case Studies in Archaeology Series, edited by Jeffrey Quilter. Harcourt Brace College Publishers, Fort Worth.

1998 Practical and Prestige Technologies: The Evolution of Material Systems. *Journal of Archaeological Method and Theory* 5:1–55.

2000a The Opening of Keatley Creek: Research Problems and Background. In *The Ancient Past of Keatley Creek, vol. 1: Taphonomy,* edited by Brian Hayden, pp. 1–34. Archaeology Press, Burnaby, B.C.

2000b Prestige Artifacts at Keatley Creek. In *The Ancient Past of Keatley Creek, vol. 2: Socioeconomy,* edited by Brian Hayden, pp. 189–202. Archaeology Press, Burnaby, B.C.

2000c Socioeconomic Factors Influencing Housepit Assemblages at Keatley Creek. In *The Ancient Past of Keatley Creek, vol. 2: Socioeconomy,* edited by Brian Hayden, pp. 3–28. Archaeology Press, Burnaby, B.C.

2001 Fabulous Feasts: A Prolegomenon to the Importance of Feasting. In *Feasts: Archaeological and Ethnographic Perspectives on Food, Politics, and Power,* edited by Michael Dietler and Brian Hayden, pp. 23–64. Smithsonian Instituion Press, Washington, D.C.

2003a *The Ancient Past of Keatley Creek,* vol. 3. Archaeology Press, Burnaby, B.C.

2003b *Shamans, Sorcerers, and Saints: The Prehistory of Religion.* Smithsonian Institution Press, Washington, D.C.

Hayden, Brian (editor)

1992c *A Complex Culture of the British Columbia Plateau: Traditional Stl'átl'imx Resource Use.* University of British Columbia Press, Vancouver.

2000a *The Ancient Past of Keatley Creek, vol. 1: Taphonomy.* Archaeology Press, Burnaby, B.C.

2000b *The Ancient Past of Keatley Creek, vol. 2: Socioeconomy.* Archaeology Press, Burnaby, B.C.

Hayden, Brian, Edward Bakewell, and Rob Gargett

1996a The World's Longest-Lived Corporate Group: Lithic Analysis Reveals Prehistoric Social Organization near Lillooet, British Columbia. *American Antiquity* 61: 341–356.

Hayden, Brian, Morley Eldridge, Anne Eldridge, and Aubrey Cannon

1985 Complex Hunter-Gatherers in Interior British Columbia. In *Prehistoric Hunter-Gatherers: The Emergence of Cultural Complexity,* edited by T. Douglas Price and J. A. Brown, pp. 181–199. Academic Press, New York.

Hayden, Brian, N. Franco, and J. Spafford

1996b Evaluating Lithic Strategies and Design Criteria. In *Stone Tools: Theoretical Insights into Human Prehistory,* edited by George H. Odell, pp. 9–50. Plenum Press, New York.

Hayden, Brian, Gregory A. Reinhardt, Richard McDonald, Dan Holmberg, and David Crellin

1996c Space Per Capita and the Optimal Size of Housepits. In *People Who Lived in Big Houses: Archaeological Perspectives on Large Domestic Structures,* edited by G. Coupland and E. Banning, pp. 151–164. Prehistory Press, Madison, Wisconsin.

Hayden, Brian, and June M. Ryder

1991 Prehistoric Cultural Collapse in the Lillooet Area. *American Antiquity* 56(1):50–65.

2003 Cultural Collapses in the Northwest: A Reply to Ian Kuijt. *American Antiquity* 68(1):157–160.

Hayden, Brian, and Rick J. Schulting

1997 The Plateau Interaction Sphere and Late Prehistoric Cultural Complexity. *American Antiquity* 62(1):51–85.

Hebda, Richard J.

1982 Postglacial History of Grasslands of Southern British Columbia and Adjacent Regions. In *Grassland Ecology and Classification, Symposium Proceedings, June 1982,* edited by A. C. Nicholson, A. McLean, and T. E. Baker, pp. 157–194. B.C. Ministry of Forests Publication, Victoria.

1995 British Columbia Vegetation and Climate History with Focus on 6 KA BP. *Geographie physique et Quaternaire* 49(1):55–79.

Heffner, Ty

2000 The Lithic Assemblages of Two Small Housepits. In *The Ancient Past of Keatley Creek, vol. 2: Socioeconomy,* edited by Brian Hayden, pp. 179–188. Archaeology Press, Burnaby, B.C.

Hibben, Frank C.

1937 *Excavation of the Riana Ruin and Chama Valley Survey.* Anthropological Series, 2(1). University of New Mexico, Albuquerque.

Hicks, Brent A., and Maurice E. Morganstein

1994 *Archaeological Studies in the Palouse Canyon Archaeological District.* BOAS Research Report, 9212.2. BOAS, Inc., Seattle.

Higham, C.

1995 The Transition to Rice Cultivation in Southeast Asia. In *Last Hunters First Farmers,* edited by T. Douglas Price and A. B. Gebauer, pp. 127–156. School of American Research Press, Santa Fe.

Hill, K., and A. M. Hurtado

1996 *Ache Life History: The Ecology and Demography of a Foraging People.* Aldine de Gruyter, Hawthorne, England.

Hill-Tout, Charles

1930 Prehistoric Burial Mounds of British Columbia. *Museum and Art Notes* 5(4):120–126.

Holthuysen, Jaime

2002 Clues to the Past: The Manufacturing of Dentalium Shell Beads. Daniel Weetaluktuk Award, Canadian Archaeological Association. On file, Laboratory of Archaeology, University of British Columbia, Vancouver.

Huelsbeck, D. R.

1989 Food Consumption, Resource Exploitation, and Relationships within and between Households at Ozette. In *Households and Communities,* edited by S. MacEachern, D. Archer, and R. Gavin, pp. 157–167. University of Calgary Archaeological Association, Calgary.

Hunn, Eugene S.

1990a *Nch'i-Wana "The Big River."* University of Washington Press, Seattle.

1990b The Plateau Culture Area. In *Native North American Indians: An Ethnohistorical Approach,* edited by D. L. Boxberger, pp. 361–385. Kendall/Hunt Publishing, Dubuque.

Hunn, Eugene S., and D. H. French

1998 Western Columbia River Sahaptians. In *Handbook of North American Indians, vol. 12: Plateau,* edited by Deward E. Walker Jr., pp. 378–394. Smithsonian Institution Press, Washington, D.C.

Imamura, K.
1996 *Prehistoric Japan.* University of Hawai'i Press, Honolulu.

Institute of Medicine of the National Academies
1999 *Dietary Reference Intakes for Calcium, Phosphorous, Magnesium, Vitamin D, and Fluoride.* Standing Committee on the Scientific Evaluation of Dietary Reference Intakes. National Academic Press, Washington, D.C.
2000 *Dietary Reference Intakes for Vitamin C, Vitamine E, Selenium, and Carotenoids.* Report of the Panel on Dietary Antioxidants and Related Compounds et al. National Academic Press, Washington, D.C.
2001a *Dietary Reference Intakes (DRIs): Recommended Intakes for Individuals, Elements.* National Academic Press, Washington, D.C.
2001b *Dietary Reference Intakes for Vitamin A, Vitamin K, Arsenic, Boron, Chromium, Copper, Iodine, Iron, Manganese, Molybdenum, Nickel, Silicon, Vanadium, and Zinc.* Report of the Panel on Macronutrients et al., Standing Committee on the Scientific Evaluation of Dietary Reference Intakes. National Academic Press, Washington, D.C.
2002 *Dietary Reference Intakes for Energy, Carbohydrate, Fiber, Fat, Fatty Acids, Cholesterol, Protein, and Amino Acids (Macronutrients).* Report of the Panel on Macronutrients et al., Standing Committee on the Scientific Evaluation of Dietary Reference Intakes. National Academic Press, Washington, D.C.

Irwin, Ann M., and Ula L. Moody
1978 *The Lind Coulee Site (45GR97).* Washington Archaeological Research Center Project Report, 56. Washington State University, Pullman.

Jackson, H., and S. Scott
1995 The Faunal Record of the Southeastern Elite. *Southeastern Archaeology* 14:103–119.

Jaehnig, Manfred E. W.
1983 *Archaeological Investigations at Site 45OK258, Chief Joseph Dam Project.* Office of Public Archaeology, University of Washington, Seattle.
1984 *Archaeological Investigations at Site 45OK258, Chief Joseph Dam Project, Washington.* Office of Public Archaeology, University of Washington, Seattle.

James, Malcolm A.
1995 X-Ray Fluorescence Sourcing Analysis of Artifacts from Site DhRl 16, British Columbia. On file, Laboratory of Archaeology, University of British Columbia, Vancouver.
2003 Preliminary Summary of the XRF Analysis of 29 Artifacts from Site DhRl 16. On file, Laboratory of Archaeology, University of British Columbia, Vancouver.

James, Malcolm A., Jeff Bailey, and John M. D'Auria
1996 A Volcanic Glass Library for the Pacific Northwest: Problems and Prospects. *Canadian Journal of Archaeology* 20:93–122.

Janetski, J. C.
1997 Fremont Hunting and Resource Intensification in the Eastern Great Basin. *Journal of Archaeological Science* 24:1075–1088.

Jenkins, Dennis L., and Thomas J. Connolly
1994 *Archaeological Excavations at the Paquet Gulch Bridge Site: A Pithouse Village in the Deschutes River Basin, Southwestern Columbia Plateau, Oregon.* Anthropological Papers, 49. University of Oregon, Eugene.
1996 *Mid-Holocene Occupations at the Heath Cliffs Site, Warm Springs Reservation, Oregon.* Anthropological Papers, 53. University of Oregon, Eugene.

Johns, T.
1990 *With Bitter Herbs They Shall Eat It: Chemical Ecology and the Origins of Human Diet and Medicine.* University of Arizona Press, Tucson.

Jones, Terry L., G. M. Brown, L. Mark Raab, J. L. McVickar, W. G. Spaulding, Douglas J. Kennett, Andrew York, and Phillip L. Walker
1999 Environmental Imperatives Reconsidered: Demographic Crises in Western North America during the Medieval Climatic Anomaly. *Current Anthropology* 40:137–170.

Junker, Laura, Karen Mudar, and Marla Schwaller
1994 Social Stratification, Household Wealth, and Competitive Feasting in 15th/16th-Century Philippine Chiefdoms. *Research in Economic Anthropology* 15:307–358.

Kaestle, F.
1997 Molecular Analysis of Ancient DNA from Western Nevada. *Nevada Historical Quarterly* 40:85–96.

Keeler, Robert W.
1973 *An Upland Hunting Camp on the North Fork of the Clearwater River, North-Central Idaho.* Occasional Papers of the Idaho State University Museum, 30. Idaho State University, Pocatello.

Keene, A. S.
1991 Cohesion and Contradiction in the Communal Mode of Production: The Lessons of the Kibbutz. In *Between Bands and States,* edited by Susan A. Gregg, pp. 376–394. Center for Archaeological Investigations Occasional Paper, 9. Southern Illinois University, Carbondale.

Kelly, Robert L.
1983 Hunter-Gatherer Mobility Strategies. *Journal of Anthropological Research* 39:277–306.
1988 The Three Sides of a Biface. *American Antiquity* 53:717–734.
1995 *The Foraging Spectrum: Diversity in Hunter-Gatherer Lifeways.* Smithsonian Institution Press, Washington, D.C.
1998 Foraging and Sedentism. In *Seasonality and Sedentism: Archaeological Perspectives from Old and New World Sites,* edited by T. R. Rocek and O. Bar-Yosef, pp. 9–23. Peabody Museum Bulletin, 6. Harvard University, Cambridge.

Kenaston, Monte Ray
1966 *The Archaeology of the Harder Site, Franklin County, Washington.* Laboratory of Anthropology Report of Investigations, 35. Washington State University, Pullman.

Kennedy, Dorothy I. D., and Randall T. Bouchard
1978 Fraser River Lillooet: An Ethnographic Summary. In *Reports of the Lillooet Archaeological Project, no. 1: Introduction and Setting,* edited by Arnoud H. Stryd and Stephen Lawhead, pp. 22–55. Mercury Series,

Archaeological Survey Paper 73. National Museum of Man, Ottawa.
1992 Stl'átl'imx (Fraser River Lillooet) Fishing. In *A Complex Culture of the British Columbia Plateau: Traditional Stl'átl'imx Resource Use,* edited by Brian Hayden, pp. 266–354. University of British Columbia Press, Vancouver.
1998 Northern Okanagan, Lakes, and Colville. In *Handbook of North American Indians, vol. 12: Plateau,* edited by Deward E. Walker Jr., pp. 238–252. Smithsonian Institution Press, Washington, D.C.

Kent, S.
1980 Pacifism—A Myth of the Plateau. *Northwest Anthropological Research Notes* 14:125–134.

Ketcheson, M. V.
1979 Floral Analysis of Archaeological Sites in the Hat Creek Valley. On file, Department of Anthropology and Sociology, University of British Columbia, Vancouver.

Kew, J. E. Michael
1990 History of Coastal British Columbia since 1846. In *Handbook of North American Indians, vol. 7: Northwest Coast,* edited by W. Suttles, pp. 159–168. Smithsonian Institution Press, Washington, D.C.
1992 Salmon Availability, Technology, and Cultural Adaptation in the Fraser River Watershed. In *A Complex Culture of the British Columbia Plateau: Traditional Stl'átl'imx Resource Use,* edited by Brian Hayden, pp. 177–221. University of British Columbia Press, Vancouver.

Kim, Jae-On, and Charles W. Mueller
1978 *Introduction to Factor Analysis.* Sage University Paper 13. Sage Publications, Beverly Hills.

Kimberling, A. Jon, and Philip L. Jackson (editors)
1985 *Atlas of the Pacific Northwest.* Oregon State University Press, Corvallis.

Konlande, J. E., and J. R. K. Robson
1972 The Nutritive Value of Cooked Camas as Consumed by Flathead Indians. *Ecology of Food and Nutrition* 2:193–195.

Koyama, S., and D. H. Thomas (editors)
1981 Affluent Foragers. *Senri Ethnological Studies* 9.

Krantz, G. S.
1979 The Earliest Skeletons from the Marmes Site. *Northwest Anthropological Research Notes* 13:159–173.

Kroeber, Alfred L.
1939 Cultural and Natural Areas of Native North America. *University of California Publications in American Archaeology and Ethnology* 38:1–242.

Kuhn, Steven L.
1994 A Formal Approach to the Design and Assembly of Mobile Toolkits. *American Antiquity* 59(3):426–442.

Kuhnlein, H. K., R. Soueida, and O. Receveur
1996 Dietary Nutrient Profiles of Canadian Baffin Island Inuit Differ by Food Source, Season, and Age. *Journal of the American Dietetic Association* 96:155–162.

Kuhnlein, H. K., and Nancy J. Turner
1991 Traditional Food Plants of Canadian Indigenous Peoples: Nutrition, Botany, and Use. In *Food and Nutrition in History and Anthropology,* vol. 8, edited by S. Katz, pp. 364–421. Gordon and Breach Science Publishers, Philadelphia.

Kuijt, Ian
1989 Subsistence Resource Variability and Culture Change during the Middle–Late Prehistoric Cultural Transition on the Canadian Plateau. *Canadian Journal of Archaeology* 13:97–118.
2001 Reconstructing the "Cause" of Cultural Collapse in the Lillooet Area of British Columbia, Canada: A Geoarchaeological Perspective. *American Antiquity* 66(4): 692–703.

Kuijt, Ian, and N. Goring-Morris
2002 Foraging, Farming and Social Complexity in the Pre-Pottery Neolithic of the Southern Levant: A Review and Synthesis. *Journal of World Prehistory* 16(4): 361–440.

Kusmer, Karla D.
2000a Animal Resource Utilization and Assemblage Formation Processes at Keatley Creek. In *The Ancient Past of Keatley Creek, vol. 1: Taphonomy,* edited by Brian Hayden, pp. 135–164. Archaeology Press, Burnaby, B.C.
2000b Zooarchaeological Analysis at Keatley Creek: Socioeconomy. In *The Ancient Past of Keatley Creek, vol. 2: Socioeconomy,* edited by Brian Hayden, pp. 119–134. Archaeology Press, Burnaby, B.C.

Kutzbach, J. E., P. J. Behling, and R. Selin
1993 Simulated Climatic Changes: Results of the COHMAP Climatic-Model Experiments. In *Global Climates since the Last Glacial Maximum,* edited by H. E. Wright, J. E. Kutzbach, W. F. Ruddimann, F. A. Street-Perrot, and T. Webb, pp. 24–93. University of Minnesota Press, Minneapolis.

Lambert, P., and D. Walker
1991 Physical Anthropological Evidence for the Evolution of Social Complexity in Southern California. *Antiquity* 65:962–973.

Lane, R. B.
1953 Cultural Relations of the Chilcotin Indians of West-Central British Columbia. Unpublished Ph.D. dissertation, University of Washington, Seattle.

Langemann, E. Gwyn
1998 A Description and Evaluation of Eight Housepit Sites in Banff National Park, Alberta. Paper presented at the 31st Annual Meeting of the Canadian Archaeological Association, Victoria.
2002 Zooarchaeological Research in Support of a Reintroduction of Bison to Banff National Park. Paper presented at the 9th Conference of the International Council of Archaeozoology, University of Durham, Durham, England, August.

Langemann, E. Gwyn, and William Perry
2002 Banff National Park of Canada, Archaeological Resource Description and Analysis. On file, Parks Canada, Cultural Resource Services, Western Canada Service Centre, Calagary.

Lawhead, Stephen, and Arnoud H. Stryd (Arcas Associates)
1985 Excavations at the Rattlesnake Hill Site (EeRh 61), Ashcroft, B.C. On file, Department of Archaeological Planning and Assessment, Victoria.

Lawhead, Stephen, Arnoud H. Stryd, and Joanne Curtin (Arcas Associates)

1986 Archaeological Excavations at Valley Mine, Highland Valley, B.C. On file, Department of Archaeological Planning and Assessment, Victoria.

Lazenby, R. A., and P. McCormack

1985 Salmon and Malnutrition on the Northwest Coast. *Current Archaeology* 26(3):379–383.

Leaming, S.

1971 *Rock and Mineral Collecting in British Columbia.* Geological Survey of Canada Paper, 72–53. Geological Survey of Canada, Ottawa.

LeBlanc, S. A.

1997 Modeling Warfare in Southwestern Prehistory. *North American Archaeologist* 18:235–278.

Lee, Richard

1982 Politics, Sexual and Non-Sexual, in an Egalitarian Society. In *Politics and History in Band Societies,* edited by Eleanor Leacock and Richard Lee, pp. 23–35. Cambridge University Press, Cambridge.

Lenert, Michael

2001 Calibrated Radiocarbon Dates and Culture Change: Implications for Socio-Complexity in the Mid-Fraser Region, British Columbia. *Northwest Anthropological Research Notes* 35(2):211–228.

Lenert, Michael, and Nathan B. Goodale

2001 Calibrated Radiocarbon Dates and Cultural Change on the Canadian Plateau. Paper presented at the 66th Annual Meeting of the Society for American Archaeology, New Orleans.

Leonhardy, Frank C.

1970 Artifact Assemblages and Archaeological Units at Granite Point Locality 1 (45WT41), Southeastern Washington. Unpublished Ph.D. dissertation, Department of Anthropology, Washington State University, Pullman.

Leonhardy, Frank C., and David G. Rice

1970 A Proposed Culture Typology for the Snake River Region of Southeastern Washington. *Northwest Anthropological Research Notes* 4(1):1–29.

Lepofsky, Dana

1988 Floral Remains from EeQw 30. In *Archaeological Excavations at the Sahhaltkum Bridge Site (EeQw 30), Chase, B.C.* Report prepared by Arcas Associates. On file, Archaeology Branch, Victoria, B.C.

1990 *Appendix III—Floral Remains from Archaeological Sites EfQv 121, 123, and 133, Squilax, B.C., Archaeological Excavations at Sites EfQv 121, EfQv 123, and EfQv 133 near Squilax, B.C.*, vol. 2. Report prepared by ARCAS Consulting Archaeologists, Ltd. On file, Archaeology Branch, Victoria, B.C.

2000a Site Formation Processes at Keatley Creek: The Paleoethnobotanical Evidence. In *The Ancient Past of Keatley Creek, vol. 1: Taphonomy,* edited by Brian Hayden, pp. 105–134. Archaeology Press, Burnaby, B.C.

2000b Socioeconomy at Keatley Creek: The Botanical Evidence. In *The Ancient Past of Keatley Creek, vol. 2: Socioeconomy,* edited by Brian Hayden, pp. 75–86. Archaeology Press, Burnaby, B.C.

In press The Northwest. In *People and Plants in Ancient North America,* edited by P. Minnis. Smithsonian Institution Press, Washington, D.C.

Lepofsky, Dana, Michael Blake, D. Brown, S. Morrison, N. Oakes, and N. Lyons

2000 The Archaeology of the Scowlitz Site, Southwestern British Columbia. *Journal of Field Archaeology* 27(4):391–416.

Lepofsky, Dana, D. Hallett, Kenneth P. Lertzman, K. Washbrook, S. McHalsie, and Rolf W. Mathewes

In press Documenting Precontact Plant Management on the Northwest Coast: An Example of Prescribed Burning in the Central and Upper Fraser Valley, British Columbia. In *Keeping It Living: Traditional Plant Tending and Cultivation on the Northwest Coast,* edited by D. E. Deur and Nancy J. Turner. University of Washington Press, Seattle.

Lepofsky, Dana, Emily K. Heyerdahl, Kenneth P. Lertzman, David M. Schaepe, and Bob Mierendorf

2003 Historical Meadow Dynamics in Southwest British Columbia: A Multidisciplinary Analysis. *Conservation Ecology* 7(3):5, available at www.consecol.org/vol7/iss3/art5.

Lepofsky, Dana, Karla D. Kusmer, Brian Hayden, and Kenneth P. Lertzman

1996 Reconstructing Prehistoric Socioeconomies from Paleoethnobotanical and Zooarchaeological Data: An Example from the British Columbia Plateau. *Journal of Ethnobiology* 16(1):31–62.

Lepofsky, Dana, Stephen Lawhead, Arnoud H. Stryd, and Karla D. Kusmer

1987 Archaeological Investigations of Site EeRl 12, Lillooet, B.C. On file, Archaeology Branch, Victoria, B.C.

Lewis, M.

1961 *The Lewis and Clark Expedition.* J. B. Lippincott, New York.

Loewen, D. C.

1998 Ecological, Ethnobotanical and Nutritional Aspects of Yellow Glacier Lily, *Erythronium grandiflorum* Pursh (Likiaceae), in Western Canada. Unpublished M.S. thesis, Department of Biology, University of Victoria.

Lohse, Ernest S.

1984 *Archaeological Investigations at Site 45OK11, Chief Joseph Dam Project, Washington.* Office of Public Archaeology, University of Washington, Seattle.

Lohse, Ernest S., and Dorothy Sammons-Lohse

1986 Sedentism on the Columbia Plateau: A Matter of Degree Related to the Easy and Efficient Procurement of Resources. *Northwest Anthropological Research Notes* 20(2):115–136.

Lourandos, H.

1988 Palaeopolitics: Resource Intensification in Aboriginal Australia and Papua New Guinea. In *Hunters and Gatherers, vol. 1: History, Evolution and Social Change,* editd by T. Ingold, D. Riches, and J. Woodburn, pp. 148–160. Berg, New York.

Lucas, Robert E.

1986 Recovery of Game Fish Populations Impacted by the May 18, 1980 Eruption of Mount St. Helens: Winter-Run Steelhead in the Toutle River Watershed. In

Mount St. Helens: Five Years Later, edited by S. A. C. Keller. Eastern Washington University Press, Cheney.

Ludowicz, D.

1983 Assemblage Variation Associated with Southwestern Interior Plateau Microblade Technology. Unpublished M.A. thesis, Department of Anthropology and Sociology, University of British Columbia, Vancouver.

Luebben, Ralph A.

1953 Leaf Water Site. In *Salvage Archaeology in the Chama Valley, New Mexico,* complied by Fred Wendorf, pp. 9–33. Monographs of the School of American Research, 17. School of American Research, Santa Fe.

Lyman, R. Lee

1980 Freshwater Bivalve Molluscs and Southern Plateau Prehistory: A Discussion and Description of Three Genera. *Northwest Science* 54:121–136.

1984 A Model of Freshwater Clam Exploitation in the Prehistoric Southern Columbia Plateau Culture Area. *Northwest Anthropological Research Notes* 18:97–107.

1985a Cultural Resource Management and Archaeological Research in the Interior Northwest: A Note to NARN Readers on the Translucency of Northwest Archaeology. *Northwest Anthropological Research Notes* 19: 161–168.

1985b The Paleozoology of the Avey's Orchard Site. In *Avey's Orchard: Archaeological Investigation of a Late Prehistoric Columbia River Community,* edited by Jerry R. Galm and Ruth A. Masten, pp. 243–320. Reports in Archaeology and History, 100–42. Eastern Washington University, Cheney.

Lyman, R. Lee, and Stephanie D. Livingston

1983 Late Quaternary Mammalian Zoogeography of Eastern Washington. *Quaternary Research* 20:360–373.

Lyman, R. Lee, and M. J. O'Brien

1998 The Goals of Evolutionary Archaeology: History and Explanation. *Current Anthropology* 39:615–652.

Lynch, A. J.

1978 Analysis of Human Skeletal Remains from Umatilla, Oregon. In *Archaeological Burial Relocation at Old Umatilla, Oregon,* edited by D. Rice, pp. 72–91. Laboratory of Anthropology, University of Idaho, Moscow.

Lynn, Chris

1993 Navan Fort. *Current Archaeology* 134(2):44–55.

Lyons, Natasha

2000 An Analysis of Archaeobotanical Tissues from Roasting Pit Features at Keatley Creek. On file in author's possession, Paleoethnobotanical Laboratory, Department of Archaeology, Simon Fraser University, Burnaby, B.C.

MacDonald, Richard

2000 Structureal Strategies for Pithouses at the Keatley Creek Site. In *The Ancient Past of Keatley Creek, vol. 2: Socioeconomy,* edited by Brian Hayden, pp. 221–239. Archaeology Press, Burnaby, B.C.

Mack, Richard N.

1987 Effects of Mount St. Helens Ashfall in Steppe Communities of Eastern Washington: One Year Later. In *Mount St. Helens 1980: Botanical Consequences of the Explosive Eruption,* edited by David E. Bilderback, pp. 262–281. University of California Press, Berkeley.

Mackie, Quentin

1992 Classification and Use-Life Cycle of Ground Stone Celts from Coast Salishan British Columbia. Unpublished M.A. thesis, Department of Anthropology, University of Victoria.

Magne, M. P. R.

1984 Taseko Lakes Prehistory Project: Report on a Preliminary Survey. On file, Archaeology Branch, Victoria.

1985a *Lithics and Livelihood: Stone Tool Technologies of Central and Southern Interior British Columbia.* Mercury Series, Archaeological Survey of Canada Paper 133. National Museum of Man, Ottawa.

1985b Taseko Lakes Prehistory Project: A Preliminary Report. *The Midden* 17(3):10–12.

1985c Taseko Lakes Prehistory Project, Phase II: Preliminary Excavations. On file, Archaeology Branch, Victoria.

1996 Comparative Analysis of Microblade Cores from Haida Gwaii. In *Early Human Occupation in British Columbia,* edited by Roy L. Carlson and Luke Dalla Bona, pp. 151–158. University of British Columbia Press, Vancouver.

Magne, Martin, and R. G. Matson

1984 Athapaskan and Earlier Archaeology at Big Eagle Lake, British Columbia. University of British Columbia report to the Social Sciences and Humanities Research Council of Canada. Permit No. 1983–7b. On file, Archaeology Branch, Victoria, B.C.

Malainey, M. E., R. Przybylski, and B. L. Sherriff

2001 One Person's Food: How and Why Fish Avoidance May Affect the Settlement and Subsistence Patterns of Hunter-Gatherers. *American Antiquity* 66(1):141–161.

Mallory, O. L.

1966 A Comparative Cultural Analysis of Textiles from McGregor Cave, Washington. Unpublished M.A. thesis, Department of Anthropology, Washington State University, Pullman.

Malouf, C.

1998 Flathead and Pend d'Oreille. In *Handbook of North American Indians, vol. 12: Plateau,* edited by Deward E. Walker Jr., pp. 297–312. Smithsonian Institution Press, Washington, D.C.

Mann, D. H., A. L. Crowell, T. D. Hamilton, and B. P. Finney

1998 Holocene Geologic and Climatic History around the Gulf of Alaska. *Arctic Anthropology* 35:112–131.

Marquardt, William H.

2001 The Emergence and Demise of the Calusa. In *Societies in Eclipse: Archaeology of the Eastern Woodlands Indians, AD 1400–1700,* edited by David S. Brose, C. Wesley Cowan, and R. C. Mainfort Jr., pp. 157–171. Smithsonian Institution Press, Washington, D.C.

Maschner, Herbert D. G

1991 The Emergence of Cultural Complexity on the Northern Northwest Coast. *Antiquity* 65(6):924–934.

Maschner, Herbert D. G., and K. L. Reedy-Maschner

1998 Raid, Retreat, Defend (Repeat): The Archaeology and Ethnohistory of Warfare on the North Pacific Rim. *Journal of Anthropological Archaeology* 17:19–51.

Mason, O. K.

1998 The Contest between the Ipiutak, Old Bering Sea, and Birnirk Polities and the Origin of Whaling during the

First Millenium A.D. along Bering Strait. *Journal of Anthropological Archaeology* 17:240–325.

Mathewes, Rolf W.

1980 Plant Remains from the Lillooet Archaeological Project, B.C. Abstract of paper presented at Botany 80. Botanical Society of America, Misc. Ser. No. 158.

1985 Paleobotanical Evidence for Climatic Change in Southern British Columbia during Late-Glacial and Holocene Time. *Climatic Change in Canada 5*, edited by C. R. Harington. *Syllogeus* 55:397–422.

1993 Evidence for Younger Dryas-Age Cooling on the North Pacific Coast of America. *Quaternary Science Reviews* 12:321–331.

Mathewes, Rolf W., and Miriam King

1989 Holocene Vegetation, Climate, and Lake Level Changes in the Interior Douglas-fir Biogeoclimatic Zone, British Columbia. *Canadian Journal of Earth Sciences* 26: 1811–1825.

Mathewes, Rolf W., and Marlow G. Pellatt

2000 Holocene Climate in the South Central Interior of British Columbia. In *The Ancient Past of Keatley Creek, vol. 1: Taphonomy,* edited by Brian Hayden, pp. 59–64. Archaeology Press, Burnaby, B.C.

Matson, R. G.

1976 *The Glenrose Cannery Site.* Mercury Series, Archaeological Survey of Canada, 52. National Museum of Man, Ottawa.

Matson, R. G., and Diane Alexander

1980 Potato Mountain: The Archaeology of Alpine Root Procurement. Paper presented at the Canadian Archaeological Association, Whitehorse, Yukon.

Matson, R. G., and Gary Coupland

1995 *The Prehistory of the Northwest Coast.* Academic Press, New York.

Matson, R. G., Martin Magne, D. Ludowics, and David L. Pokotylo

1980 The Eagle Lake Archaeological Project: Report on the 1979 Season. On file, Archaeology Laboratory, University of British Columbia, Vancouver.

Maxwell, David

2000 Using Faunal Remains to Recognize and Interpret Prehistoric Ceremonial Deposits: An Example from San Nicolas Island, California. Paper presented at the Canadian Archaeological Association Annual Meeting, Ottawa, May. On file, Statistical Research, Inc., Burnaby, B.C.

Maxwell, Moreau S.

1985 *Prehistory of the Eastern Arctic.* Academic Press, Orlando.

McAnany, P. A.

1995 *Living with the Ancestors: Kinship and Kingship in Ancient Maya Society.* University of Texas Press, Austin.

McDonald, Archibald

1998 Journal Kept by Archibald McDonald, 1829–30. In *The Fort Langley Journals 1827–30,* edited by Morag MacLaclan, pp. 98–140. University of British Columbia Press, Vancouver.

McGhee, R.

1996 *Ancient People of the Arctic.* University of British Columbia Press, Vancouver.

McGuire, Randy H., and Dean J. Saitta

1996 Although They Have Petty Captains, They Obey Them Badly: The Dialectics of Prehispanic Western Pueblo Social Organization. *American Antiquity* 61:197–216.

McPherson, Penny J., David M. Hall, Vincent J. McGlone, and Nancy J. Nachtwey

1981 Site Specific Analysis and Intersite Comparisons. In *Archaeological Excavation in the Blue Mountains: Mitigation of Sites 35UN52, 35UN74, and 35UN95 in the Vicinity of Ladd Canyon, Union County, Oregon,* vol. 2. Western Cultural Resource Management, Inc., Boulder, Colorado.

Mehringer, Peter J., Jr., Eric Blinman, and Kenneth L. Petersen

1977 Pollen Influx and Volcanic Ash. *Science* 198:257–261.

Mehringer, Peter J., Jr., and Franklin F. Foit Jr.

1990 Volcanic Ash Dating of the Clovis Cache at East Wenatchee, Washington. *National Geographic Research* 6:495–504.

Middleton, William

2000 Chemical Identification of Activity Areas in the Keatley Creek Housepits. In *The Ancient Past of Keatley Creek, vol. 2: Socioeconomy,* edited by Brian Hayden, pp. 103–117. Archaeology Press, Burnaby, B.C.

Miller, J.

1998 Middle Columbia River Salishans. In *Handbook of North American Indians, vol. 12: Plateau,* edited by Deward E. Walker Jr., pp. 253–270. Smithsonian Institution Press, Washington, D.C.

Mindeleff, Victor

1891 A Study of Pueblo Architecture in Tusayan and Cibola. In *8th Annual Report of the Bureau of American Ethnology for the Years 1886–1887,* pp. 3–228. Smithsonian Institution, Washington, D.C.

Minnis, P.

1985 *Social Adaptations to Food Stress: A Prehistoric Southwestern Example.* University of Chicago Press, Chicago.

Minor, Rick, S. D. Beckham, Kathryn A. Toepel, and Ruth L. Greenspan

1987 *Prehistory and History of the Ochoco National Forest, Central Oregon, part 1: Overview.* Cultural Resource Report, 3. Heritage Research Associates, Eugene.

Minor, Rick, and Kathryn A. Toepel

1986 *Archaeological Assessment of the Bob's Point Site (45KL219), Klickitat County, Washington.* Report 42. Heritage Research Associates, Eugene.

Mitchell, Donald H.

1971 Archaeology of the Gulf of Georgia, a Natural Region and Its Cultural Types. *Syesis* 4(1).

1990 Prehistory of the Coasts of Southern British Columbia and Northern Washington. In *Handbook of North American Indians, vol. 7: Northwest Coast,* edited by W. Suttles, pp. 340–358. Smithsonian Institution Press, Washington, D.C.

Modjeska, Nicholas

1982 Production and Inequality: Perspectives from Central New Guinea. In *Inequality in New Guinea Highland Societies,* edited by Andrew Strathern, pp. 50–108. Cambridge University Press, Cambridge.

Moffat, M. E. K.
1995 Current Status of Nutritional Deficiencies in Canadian Aboriginal People. *Canadian Journal of Physiology and Pharmacology* 73:754–758.
Mohs, G.
1981 *An Assessment and Evaluation of Heritage Resources in the South Thompson River Valley of British Columbia.* Occasional Paper, 8. Heritage Conservation Branch, Victoria.
1982 Vallican Archaeological Project, Heritage Site DjQj 1. On file, B.C. Heritage Conservation Branch, Victoria.
Montgomery, Susan
1990 Ecological Consequences of the Mt. Mazama Ash-Fall and Human Response in the Archaeological Record. Paper presented at the 43d Annual Northwest Anthropological Conference, Oregon State University, Eugene, May 1990.
Morice, Adrian G.
1893 Notes Archaeological, Industrial, and Sociological on the Western Denes. *Transactions of the Canadian Institute, Session 1892–1893* 4:1–222.
Moura, G.
1986 Excavations at 45DO372. In *The Wells Reservoir Archaeological Project, Washington, vol. 2: Site Reports,* edited by James C. Chatters, pp. 45DO372 1–80. Central Washington Archaeological Survey Archaeological Report, 86–6. Central Washington University, Ellensburg.
Muir, Robert
1999 Zooarchaeology of Sand Canyon Pueblo, Colorado. Unpublished Ph.D. dissertation, Department of Archaeology, Simon Fraser University, Burnaby, B.C.
Mullin, J., Sandra L. Peacock, D. C. Loewen, and Nancy J. Turner
1997 Macronutrient Content of Balsamroot and Yellow Glacier Lily: Crops Used by Precontact Indigenous Peoples of North America. *Food Science and Technology (Lebensmittel-Wissenschaft und-Technologie)* 30(10): 769–775.
Munsell, David A.
1968 The Ryegrass Coulee Site. Unpublished M.A. thesis, University of Washington, Seattle.
Murdock, George P.
1941 *Ethnographic Bibliography of North America.* Yale Anthropological Studies, 1. Yale University, New Haven.
Muto, Guy R.
1976 The Cascade Technique: An Examination of a Levallois-Like Reduction System in Early Snake River Prehistory. Unpublished Ph.D. dissertation, Washington State University, Pullman.
Myers, A.
1989 Reliable and Maintainable Technological Strategies in the Mesolithic of Mainland Britain. In *Time, Energy and Stone Tools,* edited by Robin Torrence, pp. 78–91. University of Cambridge Press, Cambridge.
Nakonechny, Lyle D.
1998 Archaeological Analysis of Area A, Wexpusnime Site (45GA61). Unpublished M.A. thesis, Washington State University, Pullman.
Nelson, Charles M.
1969 *The Sunset Creek Site (45KT28) and Its Place in Plateau Prehistory.* Laboratory of Anthropology Report of Investigations, 47. Washington State University, Pullman.
1973 Prehistoric Culture Change in the Intermontane Plateau of Western North America. In *The Explanation of Culture Change: Models in Prehistory,* edited by C. Renfrew, pp. 371–390. Duckworth, London.
Nicholas, G. P., M. Wollstonecroft, and G. Baptiste
1997 *Long-Term Secwepemc Plant-Use: Initial Results of Archaeobotanical Investigations in the Interior Plateau.* Archaeological Research Reports 2. Archaeology Department, Secwepemc Cultural Education Society-Simon Fraser University Program, Burnaby, B.C.
Oberg, Kalervo
1973a *The Social Economy of the Tlingit Indians.* Monographs, 55. American Ethnological Society, Washington, D.C.
1973b *The Social Organization of the Tlingit Indians.* University of Washington Press, Seattle.
O'Brien, M. J., and R. Lee Lyman
2000 *Applying Evolutionary Archaeology.* Kluwer Academic/Plenum Publishers, New York.
Oetting, Albert C.
1994 Chronology and Time Markers in the Northern Great Basin: The Chewaucan Basin Cultural Chronology. In *Archaeological Researches in the Northern Great Basin: Fort Rock Archaeology since Cressman,* edited by C. Melvin Aikens and Dennis L. Jenkins, pp. 41–62. Anthropological Papers, 50. University of Oregon, Eugene.
Ormerod, Patricia L.
2002 Reading the Earth: Multivariate Analysis of Feature Functions at Xa:ytem (the Hatzic Rock Site, DgRn 23), British Columbia. Unpublished M.A. thesis, Department of Anthropology and Sociology, University of British Columbia, Vancouver.
Osborne, D.
1957 *Excavations in the McNary Reservoir Basin near Umatilla Oregon.* River Basin Surveys Papers, 8; Bureau of American Ethnology Bulletin, 166. Smithsonian Institution Press, Washington, D.C.
Osborne, D., and D. Crabtree
1961 Two Sites in the McNary Reservoir. *Tebiwa* 14(2): 19–36.
Overstreet, D. F.
1993 *Chesrow: A Paleoindian Complex in the Southern Lake Michigan Basin.* Great Lakes Archaeological Press, Milwaukee.
Owens, D'Ann, and Brian Hayden
1997 Prehistoric Rites of Passage: A Comparative Study of Transegalitarian Hunter-Gatherers. *Journal of Anthropological Archaeology* 16:121–161.
Özdogan, Asli
1999 Çayönü. In *Neolithic in Turkey,* edited by Asli Özdogan, pp. 35–65. Arkeoloji ve Samat Yayinlari, Istanbul.
Palmer, Gary B.
1975a Cultural Ecology in the Canadian Plateau: Pre-Contact to the Early Contact Period in the Territory of the

Southern Shuswap Indians of British Columbia. *Northwest Anthropological Research Notes* 9:199–245.
1975b Shuswap Indian Ethnobotany. *Syesis* 8:29–81.

Parish, Roberta, Ray Coupé, and Dennis Lloyd
1996 *Plants of the Southern Interior of British Columbia.* B.C. Ministry of Forests and Lone Pine Press, Vancouver.

Park, Robert W.
1993 The Dorset–Thule Succession in Arctic North America: Assessing Claims for Culture Contact. *American Antiquity* 58:203–234.

Parr, R. L., S. W. Carlisle, and D. H. O'Rourke
1996 Ancient DNA Analysis of Fremont Amerindians of the Great Salt Lake Wetlands. *American Journal of Physical Anthropology* 99:507–518.

Parry, W. J., and Robert L. Kelly
1987 Expedient Core Technology and Sedentism. In *The Organization of Core Technology,* edited by J. K. Johnson and C. A. Morrow, pp. 285–304. Westview, Denver.

Parsons, Elsie (Clews)
1940 Relations between Ethnology and Archaeology in the Southwest. *American Antiquity* 5:214–220.
1962 Introduction. In *Isleta Paintings,* edited by Esther S. Goldfrank, pp. 1–12. Bureau of American Ethnology Bulletin, 181. Smithsonian Institution, Washington, D.C.

Pauketat, Timothy, Lucretia S. Kelly, Gayle J. Fritz, Neal H. Lopinot, Scott Elias, and Eve Hargrave
2003 The Residues of Feasting and Public Ritual at Early Cahokia. *American Antiquity* 67:257–279.

Pavesic, Max G.
1971 Archaeology of Hells Canyon Creek Rockshelter. Unpublished Ph.D. dissertation, Department of Anthropology, University of Colorado, Denver.

Peacock, Sandra L.
1998 Putting Down Roots: The Emergence of Wild Plant Food Production on the Canadian Plateau. Unpublished Ph.D. dissertation, School of Environmental Studies, University of Victoria.
2002 Perusing the Pits: The Evidence for Prehistoric Geophyte Processing on the Canadian Plateau. In *Hunter-Gatherer Archaeobotany: Perspectives from the Northern Temperate Zone,* edited by S. L. R. Mason and J. G. Hather, pp. 44–61. Institute of Archaeology Occasional Publication. Archetype Publications, University College London, London.

Peacock, Sandra L., and Nancy J. Turner
2000 "Just Like a Garden": Traditional Resource Management and Biodiversity Conservation on the Interior Plateau of British Columbia. In *Biodiversity and Native America,* edited by P. Minnis and W. Elisens, pp. 133–179. University of Oklahoma Press, Norman.

Pearson, G. W., and M. Stuiver
1986 High-Precision Calibration of the Radiocarbon Time Scale, 500–2500 BC. *Radiocarbon* 28:839–862.

Peckham, Stewart
1974 The Palisade Ruin LA 3505: Archaeological Salvage Excavations near the Abiquiu Dam, Rio Arriba County, New Mexico. On file, Museum of New Mexico, Laboratory of Anthropology, Santa Fe.

Pianka, E.
1970 *Evolutionary Ecology.* Harper and Row, New York.

Pielou, E. C.
1991 The Measurement of Diversity in Different Biological Collections. *Journal of Theoretical Ecology* 13:131–144.

Plew, Mark G.
1992 Nutritional Analysis of Camas *(Carnassia quamash)* from Southern Idaho. *Northwest Anthropological Research Notes* 26(2):217–223.
2000 *The Archaeology of the Snake River Plain.* Boise State University Press, Boise.

Pokotylo, David L., Marian E. Binkley, and A. Joanne Curtin
1987 *The Cache Creek Burial Site (EeRh 1), British Columbia.* Contributions to Human History, 1. British Columbia Provincial Museum, Victoria.

Pokotylo, David L., and Patricia D. Froese
1983 Archaeological Evidence for Prehistoric Root Gathering on the Southern Interior Plateau of British Columbia: A Case Study from the Upper Hat Creek Valley. *Canadian Journal of Archaeology* 7(2):127–157.

Pokotylo, David L., and D. Mitchell
1998 Prehistory of the Northern (Canadian) Plateau. In *Handbook of North American Indians, vol. 12: Plateau,* edited by Deward E. Walker Jr., pp. 81–102. Smithsonian Institution Press, Washington, D.C.

Prentiss, William C.
1993 Hunter-Gatherer Economics and the Formation of a Housepit Floor Lithic Assemblage. Unpublished Ph.D. dissertation, Department of Archaeology, Simon Fraser University, Burnaby, B.C.
2000 The Formation of Lithic Debitage and Flake Tool Assemblages in a Canadian Plateau Winter Housepit Village: Ethnographic and Archaeological Perspectives. In *The Ancient Past of Keatley Creek, vol. 1: Taphonomy,* edited by Brian Hayden, pp. 213–230. Archaeology Press, Burnaby, B.C.
2001 Reliability and Validity of a Distinctive Assemblage Typology: Integrating Flake Size and Completeness. In *Lithic Debitage: Context, Form and Meaning,* edited by William Andrefsky Jr., pp. 147–172. University of Utah Press, Salt Lake City.

Prentiss, William C., and James C. Chatters
2003a Cultural Diversification and Decimation in the Prehistoric Record. *Current Anthropology* 44(1):33–58.
2003b The Evolution of Collector Systems on the Pacific Coast of Northwest North America. *Senri Ethnological Studies* 63:49–82.

Prentiss, William C., James C. Chatters, and Melisse P. Burns
2003a The Late Prehistoric Evolution of Social Inequality on the Western Plateau of British Columbia. Paper prepared for the Annual Meeting of the Society for American Archaeology, Milwaukee.

Prentiss, William C., Ian Kuijt, Nathan B. Goodale, and Melisse P. Burns
2001 Report on the 2000 Excavations at the Slocan Narrows Village (DkQi 1 and DkQi 2). On file, B.C. Heritage Conservation Branch, Victoria.

Prentiss, William C., Michael Lenert, Nathan B. Goodale, and Trinity Schlegel
2003b Calibrated Radiocarbon Dating at Keatley Creek:

The Chronology of Occupation at a Complex Hunter-Gatherer Community. *American Antiquity* 68(4): 719–736.

Prentiss, William C., Michael Lenert, and Holly Stelton
2000 Report of the 1999 University of Montana Investigations at the Keatley Creek Site (EeRl7). On file, Archaeology Branch, Provincial Government of British Columbia, Victoria.

Presler, Kira M.
2000 The Numipu Phase: Contact and Culture Change in the Lower Snake River Region, Southeastern Washington. Unpublished M.A. thesis, Washington State University, Pullman.

Price, T. Douglas
1985 Affluent Foragers of Mesolithic Southern Scandinavia. In *Prehistoric Hunter-Gatherers: The Emergence of Cultural Complexity*, edited by T. Douglas Price and J. A. Brown, pp. 341–363. Academic Press, New York.

Price, T. Douglas, and J. A. Brown (editors)
1985 *Prehistoric Hunter-Gatherers: The Emergence of Cultural Complexity.* Academic Press, New York.

Prince, P.
2001 Dating and Interpreting Pine Cambium Collection Scars from Two Parts of the Nechako River Drainage, British Columbia. *Journal of Archaeological Science* 28:253–263.

Randolf, Joseph, and Max Dahlstrom
1977 *Archaeological Test Excavations at Bernard Creek Rockshelter.* Laboratory of Anthropology, Anthropological Research Manuscript Series, 42. University of Idaho, Moscow.

Ray, Verne F.
1932 The Sanpoil and Nespelem. *University of Washington Publications in Anthropology* 5:1–235.
1936 Native Villages and Groupings of the Columbia Plateau. *Pacific Northwest Quarterly* 27:99–152.
1939 *Cultural Relations on the Plateau of Northwestern America.* Publications of the Frederick Webb Hodge Anniversary Publications Fund, 3. Southwest Museum, Los Angeles.

Receveur, O., M. Boulay, and H. V. Kuhnlein
1996 Decreasing Traditional Food Use Affects Diet Quality for Adult Dene/Metis in 16 Communities of the Canadian Northwest Territories. *Journal of Nutrition* 127: 2179–2186.

Reeves, B. O. K.
1969 The Southern Alberta Paleo-Cultural Paleo-Environmental Sequence. In *Post Pleistocene Man and His Environment on the Northern Plains,* edited by R. G. Forbis, C. B. Davis, O. A. Christensen, and G. Fedirchuk, pp. 6–46. University of Calgary Archaeological Association, Calgary.
1983 *Culture Change in the Northern Plains: 1000 B.C.–A.D. 1000.* Occasional Paper, 20. Archaeological Survey of Alberta, Edmonton.

Reid, Kenneth C.
1991a Late Holocene Cultural and Environmental Change along the Lower Snake River. In *Prehistory and Paleoenvironments at Pittsburg Landing: Data Recovery and Test Excavations at Six Sites in the Hells Canyon National Recreation Area, West Central Idaho,* edited by Kenneth C. Reid, pp. 12–53. Center for Northwest Anthropology Project Report, 15. Washington State University, Pullman.
1991b The Lower Snake Basin: Hells Canyon to the Columbia. In *An Overview of Cultural Resources in the Snake River Basin: Prehistory and Paleoenvironments,* edited by Kenneth C. Reid, pp. 17–159. Center for Northwest Anthropology Project Report, 13. Washington State University, Pullman.

Reid, Kenneth C., and James D. Gallison
1992 *Site Testing and Data Recovery Plan, Crane Flats Site (FS8–35.5–1), North Fork John Day District, Umatilla National Forest, Grant County, Oregon.* Rainshadow Research Project Report, 2. Pullman.
1993 *Test Excavations at Cache Creek (FS6N47E-23–07), Oregon and Kirkwood Bar (10IH699), Idaho, Hells Canyon National Recreation Area, Wallowa-Whitman National Forest.* Rainshadow Research Project Report, 15. Pullman.

Reimer, Rudy
2000 The Garibaldi Obsidian Industry at the Marpole Site (DgRs 1). *The Midden* 32(1):7–10.

Renfrew, C., and S. Shennan (editors)
1982 *Ranking, Resource and Exchange.* Cambridge University Press, Cambridge.

Renouf, M. A. P.
1991 Sedentary Hunter-Gatherers: A Case for Northern Coasts. In *Between Bands and States,* edited by Susan A. Gregg, pp. 89–107. Center for Archaeological Investigations Occasional Paper, 9. Southern Illinois University, Carbondale.

Rice, D. G.
1969 *Preliminary Report, Marmes Rockshelter Archaeological Site, Southern Columbia Plateau.* Report to the National Park Service, San Francisco. Laboratory of Anthropology, Washington State University, Pullman.
1972 *The Windust Phase in Lower Snake River Region Prehistory.* Laboratory of Anthropology, Reports of Investigations, 50. Washington State University, Pullman.
1978 An Archaeological Burial Relocation at Old Umatilla, Oregon. On file, U.S. Army Corps of Engineers, Portland District.

Rice, Harvey S.
1965 The Cultural Sequence at Windust Caves. Unpublished M.A. thesis, Washington State University, Pullman.

Richards, Thomas H.
1978 Excavation at EeRl171. On file, Department of Archaeological Planning and Assessment, Victoria.
1988 *Microwear Patterns on Experimental Basalt Tools.* BAR International Series, 460. British Archaeological Reports, Oxford.

Richards, Thomas H., and Mike K. Rousseau
1982 Archaeological Investigations on the Kamloops Indian Reserve, no. 1: Kamloops, British Columbia. On file, Kamloops Indian Band, Kamloops, and Department of Archaeological Planning and Assessment, Victoria.
1987 *Late Prehistoric Cultural Horizons on the Canadian Plateau.* Department of Archaeology Publication, 16. Simon Fraser University, Burnaby, B.C.

Rick, J. W.
1987 Dates as Data: An Examination of the Peruvian Preceramic Radiocarbon Record. *American Antiquity* 52:55–73.

Roll, T. E., and S. Hackenburger
1998 Prehistory of the Eastern Plateau. In *Handbook of North American Indians, vol. 12: Plateau,* edited by Deward E. Walker Jr., pp. 120–137. Smithsonian Institution Press, Washington, D.C.

Rollefson, G. O.
1983 Ritual and Ceremony at Neolithic 'Ain Ghazal (Jordan). *Paléorient* 9(2):29–38.
1986 Neolithic 'Ain Ghazal (Jordan): Ritual and Ceremony, II. *Paléorient* 12(1):45–52.

Romanoff, S.
1985 Fraser Lillooet Salmon Fishing. *Northwest Anthropological Research Notes* 19:119–160.
1992a The Cultural Ecology of Hunting and Potlatches among the Lillooet Indians. In *A Complex Culture of the British Columbia Plateau: Traditional Stl'átl'imx Resource Use,* edited by Brian Hayden, pp. 470–505. University of British Columbia Press, Vancouver.
1992b Fraser Lillooet Salmon Fishing. In *A Complex Culture of the British Columbia Plateau: Traditional Stl'átl'imx Resource Use,* edited by Brian Hayden, pp. 222–265. University of British Columbia Press, Vancouver.

Roscoe, Paul
2000 Costs, Benefits, Typologies, and Power: The Evolution of Political Hierarchy. In *Hierarchies in Action: Cui Bono?* edited by Michael Diehl, pp. 113–133. Center for Archaeological Investigations Occasional Paper, 27. Southern Illinois University, Carbondale.

Rosenberg, Michael
1994 Pattern, Process, and Hierarchy in the Evolution of Culture. *Journal of Anthropological Archaeology* 13:307–340.

Rosenberg, Michael, and Richard W. Redding
2000 Hallan Çemi and Early Village Organization in Eastern Anatolia. In *Life in Neolithic Farming Communities: Social Organization, Identity, and Differentiation,* edited by Ian Kuijt, pp. 39–61. Kluwer Academic/Plenum Publishers, New York.

Ross, A.
1956 *Fur Hunters of the Far West.* University of Oklahoma Press, Norman.

Rousseau, Mike K.
1982 An Interpretive and Descriptive Analysis of Lithic Artifacts from Site DjQj1, Vallican, Slocan Valley, British Columbia. On file, B.C. Heritage Conservation Branch, Victoria.
1991 Landels: An 8500 Year-Old Deer Hunting Camp. *The Midden* 23(4):6–9.
1992 *Integrated Lithic Analysis: The Significance and Function of Key-Shaped Formed Unifaces on the Interior Plateau of Northwestern North America.* Department of Archaeology Publication, 20. Simon Fraser University, Burnaby, B.C.
1993 Early Prehistoric Occupation of South-Central British Columbia: A Review of the Evidence and Recommendations for Future Research. *B.C. Studies* 99:140–183.
2000 Results of the Keatley Creek Archaeological Project Lithic Source Study. In *The Ancient Past of Keatley Creek, vol. 1: Taphonomy,* edited by Brian Hayden, pp. 165–184. Archaeology Press, Burnaby, B.C.

Rousseau, Mike K., and D. Geordie Howe
1987 Scheidam Flats: A Prehistoric Root Roasting Area near Kamloops. *The Midden* 14(2):7–10.

Rousseau, Mike K., R. Muir, Diane Alexander, J. Breffitt, S. Woods, K. Berry, and T. van Gaalen
1991 Results of the 1989 Archaeological Investigations Conducted in the Oregon Jack Creek Locality, Thompson River Region, South-Central British Columbia. Permit 1989–76. On file, Ministry Library, Ministry of Tourism and Ministry Responsible for Culture, B.C. Archaeology Branch, Victoria.

Rousseau, Mike K., and Thomas H. Richards
1985 A Culture-Historical Sequence for the South Thompson River–Western Shuswap Lakes Region of British Columbia: The Last 4000 Years. *Northwest Anthropological Research Notes* 19(1):1–31.
1988 The Oregon Jack Creek Site (EdRi-6): A Lehman Phase Site in the Thompson River Valley, British Columbia. *Canadian Journal of Archaeology* 12:39–63.

Rowly-Conwy, P.
1983 Sedentary Hunters: The Ertebölle Example. In *Hunter-Gatherer Economy in Prehistory: A European Perspective,* edited by G. N. Bailey, pp. 111–126. Cambridge University Press, Cambridge.

Rummel, R. J.
1970 *Applied Factor Analysis.* Northwestern University Press, Evanston, Illinois.

Ryder, June M., M. J. Bovis, and M. Church
1990 Rock Avalanches at Texas Creek, British Columbia. *Canadian Journal of Earth Sciences* 27:1316–1329.

Salo, L. V.
1985 Large Scale Analytic Units: Chronological Periods and Types. In *Summary of Results, Chief Joseph Dam Cultural Resources Project, Washington,* edited by Sarah K. Campbell, pp. 183–122. Office of Public Archaeology, Institute for Environmental Studies, University of Washington, Seattle.

Sanders, Paul H.
1982 A Lithic Analysis of the Windust Phase Component, Hatwai Site (10NP143) Nez Perce County, Idaho. Unpublished M.A. thesis, University of Wyoming, Laramie.

Sanger, David
1967 Prehistory of the Pacific Northwest as Seen from the Interior of British Columbia. *American Antiquity* 32(2):186–197.
1968a The Chase Burial Site in British Columbia. *National Museum of Canada Bulletin* 224:86–185.
1968b Prepared Core and Blade Traditions in the Pacific Northwest. *Arctic Anthropology* 5(1):92–120.
1968c *The Texas Creek Burial Site Assemblage, British Columbia.* Anthropology Paper, 17. National Museum of Canada, Ottawa.
1969 Cultural Traditions in the Interior of British Columbia. *Syesis* 2:189–200.
1970 The Archaeology of the Lochnore–Nesikep Locality, British Columbia. *Syesis* 3 (supp. 1):1–129.

Sappington, Robert L.

1985 *Ten Corps of Engineers Sites.* Alfred W. Bowers Laboratory of Anthropology Letter Report, 88–8. University of Idaho, Moscow.

1994 *The Prehistory of the Clearwater River Region, North Central Idaho.* Anthropological Reports, 95. University of Idaho, Moscow.

Schaepe, David M.

1998 Recycling Archaeology: Analysis of Material from the 1973 Excavation of an Ancient House at the Maurer Site. Unpublished M.A. thesis, Department of Archaeology, Simon Fraser University, Burnaby, B.C.

Schalk, Randall F.

1977 The Structure of an Anadromous Fish Resource. In *For Theory Building in Archaeology,* edited by Lewis R. Binford, pp. 207–249. Academic Press, New York.

1981a *Cultural Resource Investigations for the Second Powerhouse Project at McNary Dam near Umatilla, Oregon.* Laboratory of Archaeology and History Project Report, 1. Washington State University, Pullman.

1981b Land Use and Organizational Complexity among Foragers of Northwestern North America. In *Affluent Foragers,* edited by S. Koyama and D. H. Thomas, pp. 53–76. Senri Ethnological Studies, 9. National Museum of Ethnology, Osaka.

Schalk, Randall F. (editor)

1983a *The 1978 and 1979 Excavations at Strawberry Island in the McNary Reservoir.* Laboratory of Archaeology and History Project Report, 19. Washington State University, Pullman.

1983b *Cultural Resource Investigations at the Lyons Ferry Fish Hatchery Project, near Lyons Ferry, Washington.* Laboratory of Archaeology and History Project Report, 8. Washington State University, Pullman.

Schalk, Randall F., and G. C. Cleveland

1983 A Chronological Perspective on Hunter-Gatherer Land Use Strategies in the Columbia Plateau. In *Cultural Resource Investigations at the Lyons Ferry Fish Hatchery Project, near Lyons Ferry, Washington,* edited by Randall F. Schalk, pp. 11–56. Laboratory of Archaeology and History Project Report, 8. Washington State University, Pullman.

Schalk, Randall F., and D. Olson

1983 The Faunal Assemblages. In *The 1978 and 1979 Excavations at Strawberry Island in the McNary Reservoir,* edited by R. F. Schalk, pp. 75–107. Laboratory of Archaeology and History, Project Report 1. Washington State University, Pullman.

Schele, Linda, and David A. Freidel

1990 *A Forest of Kings: The Untold Story of the Ancient Maya.* Morrow, New York.

Schmeller, Erica L.

1999 Lithic Artifact Scatter Variability among Six Sites in the Vicinity of the Lower Powder River, Oregon. Unpublished M.A. thesis, Washington State University, Pullman.

Schmidt, K.

2001 Göbekli Tepe, Southeastern Turkey: A Preliminary Report on the 1995–1999 Excavations. *Paléorient* 26(1):45–54.

Schroedl, Gerald L.

1973 *The Archaeological Occurrence of Bison in the Southern Plateau.* Laboratory of Anthropology Reports of Investigations, 51. Washington State University, Pullman.

Schulting, Rick J.

1995 *Mortuary Variability and Status Differentiation on the Columbia–Fraser Plateau.* Archaeology Press, Burnaby, B.C.

Schwartz, Marion

1998 *A History of Dogs in the Early Americas.* Yale University Press, New Haven.

Seymour, Deni

1994 Peripheral Considerations: Defining the Spatial and Physical Correlates of Storage Behavior in Hohokam Structures. *Kiva* 59:377–394.

Sheppard, John C., Peter E. Wigand, Carl E. Gustafson, and Meyer Rubin

1987 A Reevaluation of the Marmes Rockshelter Radiocarbon Chronology. *American Antiquity* 52:118–125.

Shiner, Joel L.

1961 *The McNary Reservoir: A Study in Plateau Archaeology.* River Basin Surveys Paper, 23; Bureau of American Ethnology Bulletin, 179. Smithsonian Institution Press, Washington, D.C.

Shott, Michael J.

1992 Radiocarbon Dating as a Probabalistic Technique: The Childers Site and Late Woodland Occupation in the Ohio Valley. *American Antiquity* 57:202–230.

1997 Stones and Shafts Redux: The Metric Discrimination of Chipped-Stone Dart and Arrow Points. *American Antiquity* 62:86–101.

Simonsen, Bjorn

1994 Report on the Results of Archaeological Investigations in the Scheidam Flats Locale near Kamloops, B.C. Report prepared by the Bastion Group Heritage Consultants for Mandell Pinder, Barristers and Solicitors, Vancouver.

Skinner, Mark F.

1994 Osseous Treponemal Disease: Limits on Our Understanding. In *The Origin of Syphilis in Europe: Before or After 1493?* In *Actes de Colloque International de Tulons 25–28 Nov 1993,* edited by O. Dutour, G. Palfi, J. Berato, and J-P. Bruhm, pp. 191–201. Centre Archaeologuque du Var edition, Errance.

Skinner, Mark F., and Stanley S. Copp

1986 The Nicoamen River Burial Site (EbRj 7), near Lytton, British Columbia. On file, Department of Archaeological Planning and Assessment, Victoria.

Sloan, Norman A.

2003 Evidence of California-Area Abalone Shell in Haida Trade and Culture. *Canadian Journal of Archaeology* 27:273–286.

Smith, Alan H.

2000 Kalispel Ethnography and Ethnohistory. In *The Calispell Valley Archaeology Project Final Report: Volumes 1–5,* edited by William Andrefsky Jr., Greg C. Burtchard, Kira M. Presler, Stephen R. Samuels, Paul H. Sanders, and Alston V. Thoms, pp. 7.1–7.151. Center for Northwest Anthropology Project Report, 16. Washington State University, Pullman.

Smith, B. D.
1995 Seed Plant Domestication in Eastern North America. In *Last Hunters First Farmers,* edited by T. Douglas Price and A. B. Gebauer, pp. 193–214. School of American Research Press, Santa Fe.
2001 Low-Level Food Production. *Journal of Archaeological Research* 9(1):1–43.
Smith, Harlan I.
1899 *Archaeology of Lytton, British Columbia.* Memoirs of the American Museum of Natural History, 1(3). American Museum of Natural History, New York.
1900 *Archaeology of the Thompson River Region, British Columbia.* Memoirs of the American Museum of Natural History, 2(6). American Museum of Natural History, New York.
Smith, Harlan I., and Gerard Fowke
1901 *Cairns of British Columbia and Washington.* Memoirs of the American Museum of Natural History, 3(2). American Museum of Natural History, New York.
Smith, W. C.
1977 *Archaeological Explorations in the Columbia Basin: A Report on the Mesa Project, 1973–1975.* Department of Anthropology, Central Washington Archaeological Survey. Central Washington University, Ellensburg.
Sneed, P.
1971 Of Salmon and Men: An Investigation of Ecological Determinants and Aboriginal Man in the Canadian Plateau. In *Aboriginal Man and Environments on the Plateau of Northwestern America,* edited by Arnoud H. Stryd and R. A. Smith, pp. 229–242. Student's Press, University of Alberta, Calgary.
Spafford, Jim
2000a An Analysis of the Distributions of Lithic Artifacts in the Roofs of Three Housepits at Keatley Creek. In *The Ancient Past of Keatley Creek, vol. 2: Socioeconomy,* edited by Brian Hayden, pp. 231–250. Archaeology Press, Burnaby, B.C.
2000b Socioeconomic Inferences from Floor Distributions of Lithics at Keatley Creek. In *The Ancient Past of Keatley Creek, vol. 2: Socioeconomy,* edited by Brian Hayden, pp. 167–178. Archaeology Press, Burnaby, B.C.
Speiser, Felix
[1923] 1996 *Ethnology of Vanuatu.* University of Hawai'i Press, Honolulu.
Speth, J. D.
1983 *Bison Kills and Bone Counts: Decision Making by Ancient Hunters.* University of Chicago Press, Chicago.
1990 Seasonality, Resource Stress, and Food Sharing in So-Called "Egalitarian" Foraging Societies. *Journal of Anthropological Archaeology* 9:148–188.
1992 Protein Selection and Avoidance Strategies of Contemporary and Ancestral Foragers: Unresolved Issues. In *Foraging Strategies and Nature of Diet of Monkeys, Apes and Humans,* edited by A. Whiten and E. M. Widdowson, pp. 105–110. Clarendon Press, Oxford.
Speth, J. D., and K. A. Spielmann
1983 Energy Source, Protein Metabolism, and Hunter-Gatherer Subsistence Strategies. *Journal of Anthropological Archaeology* 2(1):1–31.
Spier, L., and E. Sapir
1930 Wishram Ethnography. *University of Washington Publications in Anthropology* 3:151–300.
Spinden, H. J.
1908 *The Nez Perce Indians.* Memoirs of the American Anthropological Association, 2(3). American Anthropological Association, Washington, D.C.
Stahl, A. B.
1989 Plant-Food Processing: Implications for Dietary Quality. In *Foraging and Farming: The Evolution of Plant Exploitation,* edited by D. R. Harris and G. C. Hillman, pp. 171–194. Unwin Hyman, London.
Statham, Dawn S.
1975 A Biogeographic Model of Camas and Its Role in the Aboriginal Economy of the Northern Shoshone in Idaho. *Tebiwa* 18:59–80.
Steedman, E. V. (editor)
1930 The Ethnobotany of the Thompson Indians of British Columbia. Based on Field Notes of James A. Teit. *Bureau of American Ethnology, 30th Annual Report,* 1908–1909:22–102.
Stehnolm, N. A.
1985 Botanical Assemblage. In *Summary of Results, Chief Joseph Dam Cultural Resources Project, Washington,* edited by Sarah K. Campbell, pp. 421–453. Office of Public Archaeology, Institute for Environmental Studies, University of Washington, Seattle.
Stephen, Alexander M.
1936 *Hopi Journal of Alexander M. Stephen.* Edited by Elsie C. Parsons. Contributions to Anthropology, 23. Columbia University, New York.
Stó:lō Nation and Antiquus Archaeological Consultants Ltd.
1999 Preliminary Archaeological Excavation of DgRk 10: A Ts'elweyeqw Pithouse Village Settlement in the Chilliwack River Valley. On file, Stó:lō Nation Archives, Chilliwack, and Department of Archaeological Planning and Assessment, Victoria.
Stordeur, D., M. Brenet, G. Der Aprahamian, and J.-C. Roux
2001 Les Bâtiments Communautaires de Jerf el Ahmar et Mureybet Horizon PPNA (Syrie). *Paléorient* 26(1): 29–44.
Stryd, Arnoud H.
1972 Housepit Archaeology at Lillooet, British Columbia: The 1970 Field Season. *B.C. Studies* 14:17–46.
1973 The Later Prehistory of the Lillooet Area, British Columbia. Unpublished Ph.D. dissertation, Department of Archaeology, University of Calgary.
1980 A Review of the Recent Activities Undertaken by the Lillooet Archaeological Project. *The Midden* 122:5–20.
1983 Prehistoric Mobile Art from the Mid-Fraser and Thompson River Areas. In *Indian Art Traditions of the Northwest Coast,* edited by Roy L. Carlson, pp. 167–182. Archaeology Press, Burnaby, B.C.
1997 *Culturally Modified Trees of British Columbia.* British Columbia Ministry of Forests, Nanaimo.
Stryd, Arnoud H., and Mike K. Rousseau
1996 The Early Prehistory of the Mid-Fraser–Thompson River Area. In *Early Human Occupation in British Columbia,* edited by Roy L. Carlson and Luke Dalla

Bona, pp. 177–204. University of British Columbia Press, Vancouver.
Stuiver, M., and P. J. Reimer
1993 Extended ^{14}C Database and Revised CALIB Radiocarbon Calibration Program. *Radiocarbon* 35:215–230.
Stuiver, M., P. J. Reimer, E. Bard, J. W. Speck, G. S. Burr, K. A. Hughen, B. Kromer, F. G. McCormac, J. van der Plicht, and M. Spark
1998 IntCAL 98 Radiocarbon Age Calibration, 24,000–0 Cal B.P. *Radiocarbon* 40:1041–1083.
Stuiver, M., P. J. Reimer, and T. F. Braziunas
1998 High Precision Radiocarbon Age Calibration for Terrestrial and Marine Samples. *Radiocarbon* 40: 1127–1151.
Suttles, W.
1960 Affinal Ties, Subsistence and Prestige among the Coast Salish. *American Anthropologist* 62:296–305.
Svensson, Mac
2002 Palisade Enclosures. In *Behind Wooden Walls: Neolithic Palisaded Enclosures in Europe,* edited by A. Gibson, pp. 28–58. BAR International Series, 1013. Archaeopress, Oxford.
Swanson, Earl H., Jr.
1962a Early Cultures in Northwestern North America. *American Antiquity* 28:151–158.
1962b *The Emergence of Plateau Culture.* Occasional Papers of the Idaho State Museum, 8. Idaho State Museum, Pocatello.
1972 *Birch Creek: Human Ecology in the Cool Desert of the Northern Rocky Mountains 9000 B.C.–A.D. 1850.* Idaho State University Press, Pocatello.
Swanton, J. R.
[1909] 1975 *Contributions to the Ethnology of the Haida.* American Museum of Natural History Memoirs, 5(1). E. J. Brill, Leiden, the Netherlands.
Teit, James A.
1900 *The Thompson Indians of British Columbia.* Memoirs of the American Museum of Natural History 2(4). American Museum of Natural History, New York.
1906 *The Lillooet Indians.* Memoirs of the American Museum of Natural History 4(5). American Museum of Natural History, New York.
1909 *The Shuswap.* Memoirs of the American Museum of Natural History 4(7). American Museum of Natural History, New York.
1912 *Mythology of the Thompson Indians.* Memoirs of the American Museum of Natural History 12. American Museum of Natural History, New York.
1928 *The Middle Columbia Salish.* Publications in Anthropology, 2(4). Univeristy of Washington, Seattle.
1930 The Salishan Tribes of the Western Plateaus. *45th Annual Report of the Bureau of American Ethnology for 1927–1928* 45:295–396.
Testart, A.
1982 The Significance of Food Storage among Hunter-Gatherers: Residence Patterns, Population Densities, and Social Inequalities. *Current Anthropology* 23(5): 523–537.
Thom, Brian D.
1995 The Dead and the Living: Burial Mounds and Cairns and the Development of Social Classes in the Gulf of Georgia Region. Unpublished M.A. thesis, Department of Anthropology and Sociology, University of British Columbia, Vancouver.
Thomas, C. H.
1978 Arrowheads and Atlatl Darts: How the Stones Got the Shaft. *American Antiquity* 43:461–472.
Thompson, R. S.
1984 Late Pleistocene and Holocene Environments of the Great Basin. Unpublished Ph.D. dissertation, University of Arizona, Tucson.
Thoms, Alston V.
1989 The Northern Roots of Hunter-Gatherer Intensification: Camas and the Pacific Northwest. Unpublished Ph.D. dissertation, Department of Anthropology, Washington State University, Pullman.
Titiev, Mischa
1944 *Old Oraibi: A Study of the Hopi Indians of Third Mesa.* Paper of the Peabody Museum of American Archaeology and Ethnology, 22(1). Harvard University, Cambridge.
Toepel, Kathryn A., W. F. Willigham, and Rick Minor
1980 *Cultural Resource Overview of BLM Lands in North-Central Oregon: Archaeology, Ethnography, History.* Edited by C. Melvin Aikens. Anthropological Papers, 17. University of Oregon, Eugene.
Toom, D. L.
1992 Early Village Formation in the Middle Missouri Subarea of the Plains. In *Research in Economic Anthropology, supp. 6: Long Term Subsistence Change in Prehistoric North America,* edited by D. R. Croes, R. A. Hawkins, and B. L. Isaac, pp. 131–191. JAI Press, Greenwich, Connecticut.
Torrence, Robin
1983 Time Budgeting and Hunter-Gatherer Technology. In *Hunter-Gatherer Economy in Prehistory: A European Perspective,* edited by G. Bailey, pp. 11–22. Cambridge University Press, Cambridge.
1989a Re-Tooling: Towards a Behavioral Theory of Stone Tools. In *Time, Energy and Stone Tools,* edited by Robin Torrence, pp. 57–66. University of Cambridge Press, Cambridge.
Torrence, Robin (editor)
1989b *Time, Energy and Stone Tools.* Cambridge University Press, Cambridge.
Toups, P. A.
1967 Arrow Beach Site Report. On file, Idaho State University Museum, Pocatello.
Tremaine, Kim
1997 Social Incentives: Explaining Subsistence Intensification in Prehistoric and Central California. Unpublished Ph.D. dissertation proposal, Anthropology Department, University of California, Davis.
Turnbull, C.
1977 Archaeology and Ethnohistory in the Arrow Lakes, Southeastern British Columbia. Mercury Series, Archaeological Survey of Canada Paper, 65. National Museum of Man, Ottawa.
Turner, Nancy J.
1988 "The Importance of a Rose": Evaluating the Cultural

Significance of Plants in Thompson and Lillooet Interior Salish. *American Anthropologist* 90:272–291.
1991 Burning Mountain Sides for Better Crops: Aboriginal Landscape Burning in British Columbia. *Archaeology in Montana* 32(2):57–73.
1992 Plant Resources of the Stl'átl'imx (Fraser River Lillooet) People: A Window into the Past. In *A Complex Culture of the British Columbia Plateau: Traditional Stl'átl'imx Resource Use*, edited by Brian Hayden, pp. 405–469. University of British Columbia Press, Vancouver.
1997 *Food Plants of Interior First Peoples*. Royal British Columbia Museum Handbook. University of British Columbia Press, Vancouver.
1998 *Plant Technology of First Peoples in British Columbia*. University of British Columbia Press, Vancouver.
1999 "Time to Burn": Traditional Use of Fire to Enhance Resource Production by Aboriginal Peoples in British Columbia. In *Indians, Fire and the Land*, edited by R. Boyd, pp. 185–218. Oregon State University Press, Corvallis.

Turner, Nancy J., Randall T. Bouchard, and Dorothy I. D. Kennedy
1980 *Ethnobotany of the Okanagan-Colville Indians of British Columbia and Washington*. Occasional Paper, 21. British Columbia Provincial Museum, Victoria.

Turner, Nancy J., Laurence C. Thompson, M. Terry Thompson, and Annie Z. York
1990 *Thompson Ethnobotany: Knowledge and Usage of Plants by the Thompson Indians of British Columbia*. Memoir, 3. Royal British Columbia Museum, Victoria.

Tyhurst, R.
1992 Traditional and Contemporary Land and Resource Use by Ts'kw'aylaxw and Xaxli'p Bands. In *A Complex Culture of the British Columbia Plateau: Traditional Stl'átl'imx Resource Use*, edited by Brian Hayden, pp. 470–507. University of British Columbia Press, Vancouver.

Van Vuren, Dirk
1987 Bison West of the Rocky Mountains: An Alternative Explanation. *Northwest Science* 61:65–69.

Vickers, Roderick
1986 *Alberta Plains Prehistory: A Review*. Occasional Paper, 27. Archaeological Survey of Alberta, Edmonton.

Vivian, Gordon
1965 *The Three-C Site: An Early Pueblo II Ruin in Chaco Canyon, New Mexico*. University of New Mexico Press, Albuquerque.

Von Krogh, Henning
1980 *Archaeological Investigations at the Flood and Pipeline Sites, near Hope, B.C.* Occasional Papers of the Heritage Conservation Branch, 4. Government Printer, Victoria.

Walker, Deward E., Jr.
1973 *American Indians of Idaho*. Anthropological Monographs of the University of Idaho, 2. University of Idaho, Moscow.

Walker, P.
1989 Cranial Injuries as Evidence of Violence in Prehistoric Southern California. *American Journal of Physical Anthropology* 80:313–323.

Walker, William H.
1995 Ceremonial Trash? In *Expanding Archaeology*, edited by M. Skibo, William H. Walker, and A. Neilson, pp. 67–79. University of Utah Press, Salt Lake City.

Walker, William H., and Lisa J. Lucero
2000 The Depositional History of Ritual and Power. In *Agency in Archaeology*, edited by Marcia-Anne Dobres and John E. Robb, pp. 130–147. Routledge, London.

Warren, Claude N.
1968 *The View from Wanas: A Study in Plateau Prehistory*. Idaho State University Museum Occasional Papers, 24. Idaho State University, Pocatello.

Warren, Claude N., Steven Sims, and Max G. Pavesic
1968 Cultural Chronology in Hells Canyon. *Tebiwa* 11(2):1–37.

Washington, Nate W.
1973 Mesa Top Cliff Dwellers of Eastern Washington. Unpublished MS, Ephrata, Washington.

Wason, Paul
1994 *The Archaeology of Rank*. Cambridge University Press, Cambridge.

Watson, P. J.
1976 In Pursuit of Prehistoric Subsistence: A Comparative Account of Some Contemporary Flotation Techniques. *Mid-Continental Journal of Anthropology* 1:77–100.

Welch, Paul D., and C. Margaret Scarry
1995 Status-Related Variation in Foodways in the Moundville Chiefdom. *American Antiquity* 60(3):397–419.

Wenatchee Daily World
1962 Doctor Discovers Arrow Lodged in Indian Relic. *Wenatchee Daily World*, 21 March 1962: 14.

Wiessner, Polly
1982 Beyond Willow Smoke and Dog's Tails: A Commentary on Binford's Analysis of Hunter-Gatherer Settlement Systems. *American Antiquity* 47(1):171–178.
2001 Of Feasting and Value: Enga Feasts in a Historical Perspective (Papua New Guinea). In *Feasts: Archaeological and Ethnographic Perspectives on Food, Politics, and Power*, edited by Michael Dietler and Brian Hayden, pp. 115–143. Smithsonian Institution Press, Washington, D.C.

Wigand, Peter E.
1987 Diamond Pond, Harney County, Oregon: Vegetation History and Water Table in the Eastern Oregon Desert. *Great Basin Naturalist* 47:427–458.

Wilcox, D. R., T. R. McGuire, and C. Sternberg
1981 *Snaketown Revisited*. Arizona State Museum of Anthropology Series, 155. University of Arizona, Tucson.

Wilfong, C.
1990 *Following the Nez Perce Trail: A Guide to the Nee-Mee-Poo National Historical Trail with Eyewitness Accounts*. Oregon State University Press, Corvallis.

Willey, G. R., W. R. Bullard, J. B. Glass, and J. C. Gifford
1965 *Prehistoric Maya Settlements in the Belize Valley*. Peabody Museum of Archaeology and Ethnology Papers, 54. Harvard University, Cambridge.

Willey, G. R., and P. Phillips
1958 *Method and Theory in American Archaeology*. University of Chicago Press, Chicago.

Willig, Judith A.
1988 Paleo-Archaic Adaptations and Lakeside Settlement Pattern in the Dietz Sub-Basin of Alkali Lake, Oregon. In *Early Human Occupation in Far Western North America: The Clovis–Archaic Interface,* edited by Judith A. Willig, C. Melvin Aikens, and John L. Fagan, pp. 417–482. Anthropological Papers, 21. Nevada State Museum, Carson City.

Wilshusen, Richard H.
1986 The Relationship between Abandonment Mode and Ritual Use in Pueblo I Anasazi Protokivas. *Journal of Field Archaeology* 13:245–264.

Wilson, Douglas, and William Rathje
2001 Garbage and the Modern American Feast. In *Feasts: Archaeological and Ethnographic Perspectives on Food, Politics, and Power,* edited by Michael Dietler and Brian Hayden, pp. 404–422. Smithsonian Institution Press, Washington, D.C.

Wilson, Ian R.
1991 Excavations at EdQx 41 and 42, and Site Evaluation at EdQx 43 Monte Creek, B.C. I. R. Wilson Consultants Ltd. Permit 1990–140. On file, Department of Archaeological Planning and Assessment, Victoria.
1992 Excavations at the Baker Site EdQx 43, Monte Creek Permit 97–107. On file, Department of Archaeological Planning and Assessment, Archaeology Branch, Victoria.

Wilson, Ian R., B. Smart, N. Heap, J. Warner, T. Ryals, S. Woods, and S. MacNab
1992 Excavations at the Baker Site, EdQx 43, Monte Creek. Permit 1991–107. On file, Department of Archaeological Planning and Assessment, Victoria.

Wilson, Norman L.
1957–1963 Nisenan Fieldnotes. MS in Wilson's possession.

Wilson, Norman L., and Arlean H. Towne
1978 Nisenan. In *Handbook of North American Indians, vol. 8: California,* edited by Robert F. Heizer, pp. 387–397. Smithsonian Institution Press, Washington, D.C.

Wilson, Robert L.
1980 Archaeological Investigations near Kamloops. In *The Archaeology of Kamloops,* edited by Robert L. Wilson and Catherine Carlson, pp. 1–83. Department of Archaeology Publication, 7. Simon Fraser University, Burnaby, B.C.

Winham, R. P., and F. A. Calabrese
1998 The Middle Missouri Tradition. In *Archaeology on the Great Plains,* edited by W. R. Wood, pp. 269–307. University Press of Kansas, Lawrence.

Wisner, Gary
1998 Cooper's Ferry Spear Cache, One of NW's Oldest Sites. *Mammoth Trumpet* 14:3–6.

Wollstonecroft, M. M.
2000 The Fruit of Their Labour: A Paleoethnobotanical Study of Site EeRb 140, a Multi-Component Open-Air Archaeological Site on the British Columbia Plateau. Unpublished M.A. thesis, Department of Archaeology, Simon Fraser University, Burnaby, B.C.
2002 The Fruit of Their Labour: Plants and Plant Processing at EeRb 140 (860 ± 60 Uncal to 160 ± 50 Uncal B.P.), a Late Prehistoric Hunter-Gatherer Site on the Southern Interior Plateau, British Columbia, Canada. *Vegetation History and Archaeobotany* 11:61–70.

Womack, Bruce R.
1977 An Archaeological Investigation and Technological Analysis of the Stockhoff Basalt Quarry, Northeastern Region. Unpublished M.A. thesis, Department of Anthropology, Washington State University, Pullman.

Woodburn, J.
1980 Hunters and Gatherers Today and Reconstruction of the Past. In *Soviet and Western Anthropology,* edited by E. Gellner, pp. 95–117. Duckworth, London.

Woodman, P. C.
1985 Mobility in the Early Mesolithic of Northwestern Europe: An Alternative Explanation. In *Hunters and Gatherers, vol. 1: History, Evolution and Social Change,* edited by T. Ingold, D. Riches, and J. Woodburn, pp. 325–339. Berg, New York.

Wyatt, David J.
1972 The Indian History of the Nicola Valley, British Columbia. Unpublished Ph.D. dissertation, Department of Anthropology, Brown University.

CONTRIBUTORS

RON ADAMS
Department of Archaeology
Simon Fraser University
Burnaby, British Columbia, Canada V5A 1S6

WILLIAM ANDREFSKY JR.
Department of Anthropology
Washington State University
Pullman, Washington, USA 99164–4910

JEANNE E. ARNOLD
Department of Anthropology
University of California, Los Angeles
Los Angeles, California, USA 90095–1553

MICHAEL BLAKE
Department of Anthropology and Sociology
University of British Columbia
Vancouver, British Columbia, Canada V6T1Z1

JAMES C. CHATTERS
Tetra-Tech FW, Inc.
Bothell, Washington, USA 98011

SARA MOSSOP COUSINS
Williams Lake, British Columbia, Canada

NATHAN B. GOODALE
Department of Anthropology
Washington State University
Pullman, Washington, USA 99164–4910

BRIAN HAYDEN
Department of Archaeology
Simon Fraser University
Burnaby, British Columbia, Canada V5A 1S6

IAN KUIJT
Department of Anthropology
Notre Dame University
Notre Dame, Indiana, USA 46556–5639

DANA LEPOFSKY
Department of Archaeology
Simon Fraser University
Burnaby, British Columbia, Canada V5A 1S6

SANDRA L. PEACOCK
Department of Anthropology
Okanagan University College
Kelowna, British Columbia, Canada V1V 1V7

WILLIAM C. PRENTISS
Department of Anthropology
University of Montana
Missoula, Montana, USA 59812

MIKE K. ROUSSEAU
Antiquus Archaeological Consultants Ltd.
Maple Ridge, British Columbia, Canada V4R 2T3

INDEX